WEB PROGRAMMING

TECHNIQUES FOR INTEGRATING PYTHON, LINUX, APACHE, AND MYSQL

ISBN 0-13-041065-9

9 780130 410658

90000

WEB PROGRAMMING

TECHNIQUES FOR INTEGRATING PYTHON, LINUX, APACHE, AND MYSQL

George K. Thiruvathukal, Ph.D.
LOYOLA UNIVERSITY AND NORTHWESTERN UNIVERSITY

John P. Shafaee
HOSTWAY CORPORATION

Thomas W. Christopher, Ph.D.
TOOLS OF COMPUTING LLC

PRENTICE HALL PTR
UPPER SADDLE RIVER, NJ 07458
WWW.PHPTR.COM

Library of Congress Cataloging-in-Publication Available

Acquisition Editor: *Mary Franz*
Editorial Assistant: *Noreen Regina*
Editorial/Production Supervision: *Rose Kernan*
Composition: *Eileen Clark, Maureen Brigham*
Marketing Manager: *Dan DePasquale*
Manufacturing Manager: *Alexis Heydt-Long*
Manufacturing Buyer: *Maura Zaldivar*
Cover Design: *Anthony Gemmellaro*
Cover Design Director: *Jerry Votta*
Series Design: *Gail Cocker-Bogusz*

© 2002 Prentice Hall PTR
Prentice-Hall, Inc.
Upper Saddle River, NJ 07458

The publisher offers discounts on this book when ordered in bulk quantities. For more information, contact Corporate Sales Department, Prentice Hall PTR, One Lake Street, Upper Saddle River, NJ 07458. Phone: 800-382-3419; FAX: 201-236-714; E-mail: corpsales@prenhall.com

Product names mentioned herein are the trademarks or registered trademarks of their respective owners.

Printed in the United States of America

10 9 8 7 6 5 4 3 2 1

ISBN 0-13-041065-9

Pearson Education Ltd., *London*
Pearson Education Australia Pty., Limited, *Sydney*
Pearson Education Singapore, Pte. Ltd.
Pearson Education North Asia Ltd., *Hong Kong*
Pearson Education Canada, Ltd., *Toronto*
Pearson Education de Mexico, S.A., de C.V.
Pearson Education–Japan, *Tokyo*
Pearson Education Malaysia, Pte. Ltd.
Pearson Education, *Upper Saddle River, New Jersey*

We collectively dedicate this book to the loving memory of great programming languages that have come and gone.

—GKT, JPS, TWC

Contents

Chapter 7
CGI Programming in Python   *313*

Chapter 8
Database Essentials Featuring MySQL   *361*

Part 2
WPL MODULES *431*

Chapter 9
Template Processing with the WriteProcessor *433*

Chapter 12
Miscellaneous Utility Modules and Classes *565*

Part 3
APPLICATIONS *597*

Chapter 13
The Slither Application Development Framework *599*

Acknowledgments

I wish to extend thanks and love to my wife, Nina, who has been a constant source of support throughout this project. It is a joy and a privilege to have a home environment that is conducive to being a writer. You're the best, Bumks!

Happiness is working on a great project with two great friends! This project presented a great challenge to all of us as we faced many changes during the past year. Thanks to both John and Thomas for their patience and efforts on this project. Let's get some beer before we forget that we've written this book.

I wish to extend a special thank you to Konstantin Laufer of Loyola University for helping me to find my way back to the computer science faculty at Loyola and Alok Choudhary for his support as an adjunct professor and visiting scholar at Northwestern University. It is an honor to have colleagues like both of you, and this book is very much made possible by your support.

Finally, I wish to extend a special thanks to Mary Franz at Prentice Hall for her enduring faith in us and our work. I would also like to extend my appreciation to our entire production staff, including but not limited to Rose Kernan, Eileen Clark, and Maureen Brigham. It is truly a pleasure to work with them (again). I think of them as the last leg in a track and field relay event.

I wish to dedicate this book to my father, who still goes around showing the previous book to his friends and other family members, and to the memory of my dog Fuzzy.

Go Cubs! Better luck next year.

—George K. Thiruvathukal, Chicago, Illinois, August 19, 2001

I would like to thank all of the people at Hostway for their insightful ideas and comments. Specifically I would like to thank Jason K. Duffy for the countless hours spent exploring and improving on the concepts and applications discussed in the text. He has provided great insight on the Slither architecture and several of the underlying components. I would also like to thank Jason M. Abate and Joe Eaton for introducing me to new Python Web technologies and working with several of the early, unstable versions of the wpl libraries. Finally, I would like to give many thanks to Lucas Roh for his support and guidance throughout this project as well as at Hostway. I could not have finished this book and explored the listed technologies if it was not for his encouragement and backing.

We truly enjoyed working on the book at the Zirve! lab. I would also like to thank Joseph Brunzelle and Marie Perez for helping proofread chapters and using the tools and applications presented here before they were fully developed. I would also like to thank Robert Luzynczyk for his patience and support.

Finally, I would like to dedicate this book to my family (Iraj, Shahla, and Pantra). I could not have done this without your love and support.

–John P. Shafaee, Chicago, Illinois, June 17, 2001

I would like to thank my wife Patricia Guilbeault and my son Nick Guilbeault for providing my life with a sense of meaning and belonging that has allowed me to devote my attention to writing this book. My appreciation also goes to the Department of Computer Science at Illinois Institute of Technology in Chicago where I was a professor for 20 years.

–Thomas Christopher, Evanston, Illinois, June 15, 2001

Part 1

FOUNDATIONS

This part of the book covers the foundations. Without foundations, no discipline can be respectable (for long) or repeatable. The discussion begins with a general overview of Python, which introduces the language in a self-contained and structured discussion. Chapters 2 and 3 cover the details of functions and classes, which are the building blocks of modules, used extensively in the WPL and Slither programming libraries presented in Part III. After introducing the Python language, we present an overview of Linux (Chapter 4), computer networking (Chapter 5), Apache Web Server and network configuration (Chapter 6), CGI programming (Chapter 7), and MySQL Database Essentials (Chapter 8).

We will rely upon all of this material later in the book. We encourage you to follow the discussion by trying our examples on your own computer. Everything shown here can be done on a computer running a modern version of Unix. We have been able to get everything shown in the book to run on the Windows platform as well, with the exception of the material presented in the GNU/Linux chapter.

1

Introduction

The Web is (still) a great place to be. At the time of this writing, there are millions of Web sites, and the number is anticipated to keep growing for decades to come. While industrialized nations comprise most of the Internet as we know it today, this is destined to change. Web technologies appear destined for true internationalization, and we believe the Web is well on its way to becoming an international phenomenon.

So why have we written a book about the Web? Why Python? Why Linux? Why Apache? And why a book that covers these and other open-source technologies (including our own) all in one text? We undertook the writing of this book when we noticed that one of the dominant platforms for hosting Web sites has a scarce number of quality books that address how actually to implement working commerce sites using the technology. This is not much of a surprise, since each technology that supports a Web strategy typically requires an entire book (or several) just to cover the technology adequately.

This book aims to be unlike any you've ever read about the Web. It is both a general reference book (the first half) and a collection of patterns and techniques for developing real Web applications/application servers. Each chapter covers a specific aspect of creating such applications and is organized toward building a real Web site, all in the comfort and safety of your own Linux box. Yes, you will not even require a Net connection should you wish to develop a Web site on a confined personal computer. Before we get to that point, however, a few words are in order about Linux, Python, and the Apache Web Server.

Linux

Inertia is the word du jour. Linux has established itself as major player due primarily to inertia. Hillary Clinton has said that "It takes a village to raise a child." While one might be inclined to dismiss this as rhetoric spoken by a politician, there is something to be said for it. Linux has every reason to be taken seriously because it has a very large, committed community that is determined to nurture it and ensure its success. For many of its followers, success for Linux has little to do with economic success. Success is defined by its continued advancement as a serious computing platform. And this success can only come about when developers join the effort to help in areas where help is needed. Because there is plenty of community from which talent and expertise can be drawn, Linux does continue to improve.[1]

Why does the community care so much about Linux? This question is more than rhetorical. These authors have all struggled with this seemingly eternal question after repeated reboots of their personal computers running a particular operating system whose name begins with letter "W" that descends from an operating system beginning with the letter "D." The creator of Linux, Linus Torvalds, created the first version of Linux to make it possible for him to use an OS for which he would not have to pay a licensing fee. His primary need was to have a great cost-effective platform for developing systems software, including the operating system itself. We thank him for aspiring to this noble goal; otherwise, there probably would not be any serious alternatives, since most of the alternatives are proprietary and those that are nonproprietary (such as BSD) were not designed expressly to run on PC hardware (a somewhat daunting task) and were positioned at the higher end inhabited by servers and supercomputers.

Almost as soon as Linux was stabilized it became apparent that it was going to have to become something better than an OS for developing operating systems software. We three authors each have a geek coefficient near 1.0 and really enjoy hacking on systems (like Linus); however, such people are in the distinct minority of those who use computers. And thus Linux began the long, evolutionary process toward presenting a serious alternative to "W" on the desktop. To that seemingly insurmountable goal, the community has rallied to produce

---

1. As we were writing this, the 2.4 kernel was released. It has been reported that with this release, Linux has finally emerged as a serious enterprise-class operating system. Our application codes running on this platform with Python and MySQL confirm that excellent performance and responsiveness are being achieved.

replacements for just about every single thing found on other operating systems. Most notably, great progress has been made on the desktop. There are excellent window managers, desktop applications (editors, word processors, spreadsheets, presentation graphics, HTML editors), development tools (Java, C, C++, Python), clustering software, server software, and much more available for Linux. Not long ago, when software was developed on the Unix platform, it was usually developed on Sun's operating systems, including Solaris. The landscape is completely different today—almost all applications are developed first on Linux and then ported to the other Unix variants.

Speaking of other Unices, Linux is probably not the best Unix implementation. One of the authors (GKT) has worked extensively with many different versions of Unix. Each has its strengths. Sun Solaris is a very nicely done operating system that has even been ported to Intel hardware, long before Linux was a robust OS with serious applications. It has always been a great server-class operating system, with an excellent threads model for exploiting multiprocessing capability. The development tools have always been among the best. IBM AIX is also a pretty decent operating system. Again, it is an OS positioned for the server side, with excellent support for multiprocessing (both SMP and multicomputing), high-performance file systems (e.g., the Journaling File System, JFS), and excellent power management on the IBM workstations. Even SGI and HP have ultimately been able to produce decent Unix implementations with advanced features, although both have a history of somewhat unstable releases. BSD has always been a good Unix implementation, again positioned more for server class machines.

None of this might seem important, except for one detail: Linux was not initially positioned as a server operating system; the others were. It started with a desktop focus but in fact has not been perfected for either focus. The desktop is somewhat clunky compared to the "W" or "A" environments, while the server aspects are still somewhat lacking, especially to exploit the power of bigger iron machines, such as symmetric multiprocessors. Nonetheless, the picture is changing. There is nearly continuous activity to make Linux a serious "clustering" option (ongoing at the time of writing), and thread support is improving.

It might seem like a misstep to write a book on a topic and, at the onset, send a mixed message. We think an informed user is a power user. Linux has a great deal going for it. It runs practically nonstop and appears to be getting better. In 1998–99, two authors (GKT and JPS) had Linux up and running for almost 150 days in their university laboratory before it was brought down. The cause: a power outage. This is a very strong point in its favor. Not that the other mentioned Unices cannot boast a similar record, but they should! After all, Linux is free.

A second advantage is the ability to experiment. Linux can be used to do some pretty crazy things. Usually, the people doing the crazy things are willing to share. For example, at home the authors all have their Linux boxes configured as *routers*. Each has a LAN connected to a DSL or cable modem. Linux can be configured to allow all of the computers (Linux and non-Linux) to share the connection, using something called *ipchains*. This will be covered briefly in one of the chapters, since it proves indispensible for developing and testing your Web site. This capability might not seem like a big deal but it really *is* a big deal. You would have to spend mucho dinero to purchase a router or software to perform the equivalent task on Windows. Worse, you would not be able to customize the sharing nearly as well. The *ipchains* software can even be used to forward incoming requests to another computer. Linux gives us unprecedented power to do cool things, and at zero cost. It is hard to envision more of a killer app than routers, which made the Internet what it really is today (and companies like Cisco very rich!)

Python

So the next question is, "Why Python?"

Every so many years we all find ourselves asking that question. The whole idea of creating any language in the first place is to communicate.[2] Whether this communication is taking place with another human or a computer is not the question. In the computing field we are just learning to communicate intelligently. The new millenium brings many challenges in software engineering that are going to require higher performance design, development, and maintenance techniques. Python might well be the first in a series of languages dedicated to bringing about a needed change in how software is developed.

Let's take a look at why Python is so great.

Interpreted Environment

We believe that the most attractive feature of Python is that it is an interpreted language. This means that you can experiment with the Python languages and libraries without even writing a complete program—a

---

2. Sadly, when you look at most programming languages, they really are not that attractive in terms of expressiveness at a human level, filled with arcane rules and mired in complexity.

technique called rapid prototyping–which is extremely helpful from a learning standpoint. This is reminiscent of the early BASIC and Lisp programming languages, which also provided this capability.

Interpreted languages are ideal for Web application development. The reason boils down to this: Web application development is still very experimental. Unlike development of graphical applications on the Mac or Windows, the concepts of reuse and patterns are just beginning to take form. The ability to "see whether something will work" requires the ability to experiment. It requires the ability to do something interactively and see whether the desired result is achieved. And it requires the ability to do it quickly. Interpreted environments have always had the advantage of shortening the life cycle of software development, since the compilation step is eliminated. Performance is typically slower than that of a compiled language, depending on what you are doing. The fundamental performance differences (as we discussed for Java) are in handling of scalar data, which often run 10 to 100 times slower than native code. However, in handling higher level structures such as arrays, lists, tables, and strings, the performance differences begin to fade. In Python, the performance of these higher level structures is very good, especially when considered in the context of the overall environment. Scalar performance is not that great. However, as the Web is largely a story about working with text, computational performance is a secondary consideration.

Rapid Prototyping

Python may well be the first language really to deliver on the promise of rapid prototyping. With Python one is provided a language with very high-level syntax and semantics. This is perhaps best illustrated by example. Let us consider the Java versus Python solutions for building a list of values[3]:

```
myList = [ 1, 2, 3.0 ];
```

---

3. At first this might seem like a really unfair comparison. Before rushing to judgment, keep in mind that this is not intended as an attack on Java. The Java Collections do provide a very powerful and customizable framework for container classes, but at the expense of code size. For large-scale applications, you'll probably see better performance in a Java collection. The comparison would be even more unfair in C or C++ (although C++ has STL, so the code would be almost as short as the Python equivalent).

In Java this is done as follows:

```
Vector myList = new Vector();
myList.addElement(new Integer(1));
myList.addElement(new Integer(2));
myList.addElement(new Double(3.0));
```

This example highlights a key deficiency of Java: code bloat. The bloating factor is much greater when you consider that the Python code (as shown) can immediately be executed as a full Python program, whereas the Java code must be augmented with a class definition and main method, both of which are legislated by the Java language specification.

Rapid prototyping refers to the ability to go from conception (the idea) to realization (working software with tolerable performance) in the shortest possible time. The ideas of Python are not entirely new. Lisp, other functional programming languages, and Icon all are roots in the language tree leading to Python. The remainder of the points, however, illustrate just how different Python is from these languages.

Object–Oriented Optional

Python more closely follows the object model found originally in the Smalltalk environment. Thus it is possible to use Python as a pure object–oriented programming environment; however, unlike Java, the use of objects is not legislated. In other words, the first thing a programmer does not need to learn is the notion of classes and objects. This enables an entire class of applications that don't need objects to be developed (usually called scripts).

Although the use of classes is optional, in a sense this is a white lie. When you write Python code, you will be making use of built-in data types and high-level data structures. All of these types, in fact, are objects. The earlier example of list constructor syntax (1, 2, 3.0) builds a list object in Python; however, the key difference between Python and Java is its impact on users. In Python, users are shielded from the innards of objects until there's an actual need to define a general class of objects; Java forces you to think about very low-level considerations from the get-go, which comes as a surprise to most programmers, who have heard that Java is a simplification of C++. It may be simpler for compiler writers to implement the language, but the language in many respects is harder to program in.[4]

Dignified Access to Legacy Code

Python's single greatest contribution may not be any of the aforementioned topics. It may well be the elaborate extensions framework that is provided that allows you to access legacy code, say, that was written in C, C++, and even FORTRAN.

The approach taken by Java is that most code virtually needs to be rewritten in Java. Although Java provides the JNI (Java Native Interface), the framework performs relatively poorly when compared to Python. The integration of native code with Java requires you to have innate knowledge of the peculiarities of Java's garbage collector. Python and its libraries are usually written in the C language (with some C++). Like Java, Python prohibits the direct manipulation of pointers in native code; however, unlike Java, Python makes it very easy to integrate codes. At the time of writing, tools exist to extract the interfaces from a C or C++ code and generate the Python wrapper. Similar tools are under development for Java but require extensive manual intervention.

This book will not discuss the issue of extension modules in depth, opting for a pragmatic approach; however, the extension modules have enabled Python to surpass Java in many respects, since many useful C and C++ libraries can be directly leveraged in a safe and platform-independent way. Furthermore, excellent performance is achieved.

True Portability and Write-Once Run Everywhere

This should not come as much of a surprise.

Python is the truly portable language that delivers on the write-once run everywhere principle. At the time of this writing, Java's portability has been achieved on two platforms with the Java 2 Enterprise Edition: Windows and Solaris. This does not mean that Java fails to work at all on other platforms—it often doesn't work as well. The personal and embedded Java products are very stripped-down versions of the core Java language. Microsoft and HP have developed their own versions of Java that are incompatible with Sun's Java.

---

4. I'm not going to belabor the point; however, the absence of templates from the current Java language and operator overloading make many applications much harder to program in Java than their equivalent in C++.

Python is not owned by a company and thus has a community that is committed to its ubiquity and evolution, in much the same fashion as Linux. What may come as a surprise is that Python has already achieved much more portability than Java. In fact, there is a version of Python that is implemented in Java (JPython), which in practical terms means that you can embed Python (the core language and runtime) in a Java program (something you might want to do if you're developing Web applications in Java proper) to take advantage of its scripting facilities, say, in a Servlet (we will show how this can be done). Python runs on dozens of tested platforms, including all flavors of Unix (not an easy feat), all versions of Windows 3.2 (there is even a graphical development environment called PythonWin), Macintosh, and many others (BeOS, QNX).

Of course, write-once run everywhere is best for situations where you actually want it. The truth of the matter is that Unix and Windows programmers alike are virtually united on this issue: They don't want it most of the time. It is often the case that you need platform-specific functionality. This is especially true in embedded computing, where you may have specific devices, and in systems programming, where you may need to make specific system calls, etc. Python allows you to step outside of the write-once run everywhere box when needed, and it will not punish you for it, unless you blatantly violate the rules.

Ready for the Enterprise

Python is 100 percent enterprise-ready. Before we even got a chance to breathe, Python had already evolved sophisticated database support (modules for MySQL, Oracle, and Postgres are alive and well). XML is available with full support for the DOM and SAX parsers. CORBA (a distributed object computing framework) and XML/RPC (a remote procedure calling system) are both available for Python. One is hard-pressed to find a language that is more ready than Python. From our early experiments, we have yet to encounter bugs.

Why Apache?

The Apache Web Server is a free Web server that runs on most versions of Unix and, recently, Windows NT and 2000. It is a commercial-grade server that was derived from the NCSA httpd implementation. Apache is a very popular server, especially with Web hosting companies, particularly due to its rich feature set. At this writing, it is used by approximately 60 percent of the Web sites out there.

Despite Apache's popularity, configuring it and taking advantage of its special features is not completely trivial. The documentation can and will get you to the answers but is really written by and for system administrators. There are other books on Apache proper; this book does not strive to be the quintessential Apache reference manual. Instead, we focus on a number of useful *activities* to get you to the point where you can host (or have someone else host) a fully functional Web site and take advantage of Linux and Python as well.

Apache is a great Web server, particularly from a developer's point of view. There are a number of features we plan to employ in this book:

- Logging
- CGI scripts
- Plug-in scripts
- Virtual hosts
- Running multiple instances

Of course, features themselves are relatively meaningless unless they support a development process. As an example, consider the notion of a virtual hosting environment. Support for virtual hosts is addressed by the Apache Web Server using the VirtualHost configuration section. Virtual hosts are extensively used in Web hosting companies to make your domain (http://www.domain.com) look like it's running on its own machine. There are different ways to support the notion, but in real hosting environments, hundreds (if not thousands) of domains may actually be hosted on a handful of machines.

There is another opportunity for virtual hosting, and that is to support the notion of a *development sandbox*. It is fairly straightforward to create a development sandbox, even on a machine that isn't connected to the Internet. The concept is used in most software development organizations at one stage or another in the development process. For Web programming, it is indispensible. This example, among others, will show how the Apache discussion is structured. Even if you already know it, you might benefit from reading about how we use it.

What About MySQL?

MySQL is a great database. We chose MySQL primarily because of its excellent overall balance between ease-of-use and power. MySQL is a full relational database. One of its particular attractions is that it does not pretend to be an enterprise database server (Oracle, Informix). There is nothing wrong with these databases, but they are not freely available and are not particularly easy to manage. We are not trying to discourage you from using these enterprise servers; however, unless you have hard-core data management needs, it is unlikely that you will benefit from them.

We wish to point out that we have considered the use of PostgreSQL. In fact, our data access and record set processing classes have all been tested with PostgreSQL. PostgreSQL is probably better than MySQL. In fact, we are pretty convinced from a technical point of view that PostgreSQL can give Oracle a run for its money; however, we are not crazy about it from an administrative or lightweightedness perspective. Nevertheless, there are things you get from PostgreSQL and enterprise databases that are not available in MySQL: referential integrity, triggers, object/relational support, etc. We are not convinced that these features are must-haves. Although argued to be relevant for years, they are seldom used in practice. One of the authors has actually worked in two environments where Informix and Oracle were used in significant, large-scale database applications. In these applications, features such as referential integrity, object/relational support, and others (such as parallel query execution) were seldom, if ever, used. And, ironically, the result is one that can best be summarized as a disadvantage. A big server solution is being used for managing a few tables. A sledgehammer is being used to hang up a picture on your wall. Any questions?

MySQL has been reported to scale up to tables having millions of records. So has PostgreSQL. Both are freely available. Unless you foresee having more than a million records in your tables, you are unlikely even to flex the muscles of MySQL or PostgreSQL.

If you don't want to take our word for it, consider many of the major sites that are still in business: Freshmeat, Slashdot, and Source-Forge. NASA has even recently switched many of its servers to run MySQL from Oracle. If it is good enough for NASA, which has gone to the moon and the rest of the solar system, it is good for the world (and other worlds!).

Book Contents

This book aims to be a self-contained reference on building Web applications entirely from free software: Linux, the Apache Web Server, and

Python. It is organized in two parts: Foundations and Applications. The intention is to spend equal time on each part.

Part I: Foundations

Without foundations, there is no discipline. The Web today is built around a number of interesting (cool) technologies with few documented patterns and development techniques.[5] Patterns and techniques are essential building blocks of a software development process. In this section, the focus is entirely dedicated to developing principles, patterns, and techniques from the ground up to support the next part (applications). We will discuss each of the major topics (chapters) to be included and their purpose.

Chapter 2: Introduction to Python • This book assumes you are a practicing programmer who probably has some experience with Perl or Java. As we have chosen Python as the teaching (or learning) language for this book, we have divided the discussion into two chapters. This is the first of the two chapters, which is a self-contained reference and basic guide to the language. Python itself has a number of books devoted to it, and a number of good tutorial documents available on the Web. This chapter will provide everything you need to get bootstrapped with Python quickly.

Chapter 3: More Advanced Python • Python has foundations in a variety of language paradigms, including functional, object, procedural, and very high-level programming. It is not just a scripting language. The language also features a sophisticated extensions framework that allows you to grow the language. In this chapter, the functional and object-oriented aspects of Python are presented in detail. We also present the concepts of namespaces and metaprogramming, which represent two of Python's core language features (features that are not commonly found in other programming languages to the degree that they're supported in Python). In many of the WPL programming modules, we will make use of these advanced features. This chapter will be useful as a reference to the features as they are used in actual code.

Chapter 4: Introduction to GNU/Linux • Linux is a Unix-like operating system. Although it is well beyond the scope of this book to cover

---

5. There are pockets of excellence, especially in the Java and Python communities, where strong use of patterns can be found.

Linux in detail, we cover it at two different levels. First, we provide a more or less self-contained introduction to the basic principles behind Linux (and Unix, for that matter), and the essentials of using and managing it. We have chosen to limit this discussion to the command-line environment, as this is more representative of the kind of environment in which you will encounter Linux, especially if you choose a Web hosting provider to develop your site.

Chapter 5: Introduction to Internetworking and HTTP • This chapter provides a brief overview of networking and the essential principles needed to do serious Web development. This chapter will be useful to those who are new to but somewhat familiar with networking principles, and as a comprehensive overview. Networking protocols, addressing, routing, and basic TCP/IP services are covered. You will want to read this chapter to get a perspective on the HTTP protocol without having to pore over complex jargon and code examples. The CGI chapter will assume complete familiarity and detailed understanding of the HTTP protocol discussion.

Chapter 6: Network Setup and Apache Configuration • The Apache Web Server comes preconfigured with most of the major Linux distributions out there. However, as with most preconfigured software, somebody thought they knew what was best for you. Worse yet, something you wanted wasn't installed and you ended up having to do everything over again. Such is the nature of working with today's Linux distributions. This chapter will cover the basic installation and configuration of Apache and make you aware of its more advanced options, with the ultimate goal of getting a basic working setup established that allows you to view a collection of pages and to run Python CGI scripts. We will also talk about typical setups that will work for (1) home networks connected by DSL or cable modem, (2) a dedicated or co-located host, and (3) a shared hosting provider that allows you to run your own scripts.

Chapter 7: CGI Programming in Python • Python contains innate support for Common Gateway Interface (CGI) programming. This chapter provides an overview of the CGI module and how you can use it directly to write Web applications. As will be shown later in the book, we provide a layer of abstraction above this module, which allows you to develop applications in a more modular fashion. Nonetheless, an understanding of CGI is essential to developing for the Web as it is today and is likely to be for years to come. (This is true even if you program in so-called application frameworks like Servlets, which are based on the same programming model as CGI that deals with explicit HTTP requests and responses.) This understanding will also help you to see the value in more project-oriented frameworks such as Slither, covered in the last part of this book.

Chapter 8: Database Essentials Featuring MySQL • Database support is freely available for Linux, freeing you from the licensing fees typically associated with other commercial RDBMS. This chapter will introduce the basics of working with MySQL (one of the freely available databases) and address the issues of basic table definition, inserts, updates, deletes, table joins, and transactions. We will show how the ability to interpret Python on the fly can be used to evolve a stored procedure framework that, remarkably, makes a strong case for Python as a database extension language.

Database access is beginning to be standardized in much the same fashion as ODBC and JDBC in the Microsoft and JavaSoft worlds, respectively. With Python 2.0, a new database specification has appeared. While these specifications are on the right track, actual applications require the ability to operate at a higher level. We introduce the DatabaseFactory, a library designed to support our development with MySQL and Postgres in Python. We also introduce the Record class, which is used to support result sets.

Part II: Modules

Chapter 9: Template Processing with the Write Processor • XML looks like a technology that will radically change the world of Web and enterprise application development, and we use it in this book for some aspects of developing Web applications. However, HTML is here to stay. Web interfaces are typically envisioned by a concept team that dreams what the application could look like (without necessarily being functional). The development team puts "skins" onto the actual code. This is very much a template-driven approach and requires the ability to easily hook the interface (often consisting of a number of chunks of HTML) into the application code. In this chapter we present a sophisticated template processing framework (the so-called Write Processor) that allows substitutions to be performed, including simple one-time variable substitutions, include processing, and looping substitutions, which are pattern-oriented so that a collection of variables on one or more lines of template text can be substituted repeatedly using an implicit iteration on an underlying Python data structure. We show the beginnings of a general-purpose (yet customizable) approach for generating just about everything HTML and XML from basic building blocks, which is expanded further in the second half of the book.

Chapter 10: Form Processing with WebForm • WebForm is a much friendlier interface to the CGI module that automatically dispatches Python objects and binds them to a set of form variables. This abstraction will be a key building block for the PyCart portal library, which can be used to build virtually any Web commerce application.

Chapter 11: Debugging and Logging Techniques and Tools • Web programming, more so than other kinds of programming (e.g., stand-alone programs), suffers from a woefully inadequate environment for debugging or, more important, finding bugs. Increasingly, there is a perception–addressed by a recent article: Log4J (a Java-based logging framework) http://jakarta.apache.org–that debuggers are the wrong thing for Web applications and that logs tend to provide more useful information to aid in problem resolution. We have worked out a framework for logging and debugging CGI programs. Applications can log events (easily) using the wpl.logging module. Unlike typical logging, wpl.logger supports the notion of event contexts, attributes, and details, all of which can be used to direct searches for success (or failure) events of interest.

Chapter 12: Miscellaneous Utility Modules and Classes • This chapter describes a number of useful classes and modules that we developed that simply did not fit in any chapter but nevertheless are used extensively in our Slither foundation class library and the applications developed toward the end of the book. Some of these modules are used to encapsulate useful utility functions.

The **Path** module is used to automate the construction of the Python path by allowing it to be constructed from a configuration file. As those who program in Java and Python already know, object-oriented programming has introduced one unpleasantry into programming: setting environment variables. Our aim here is to automate this as much as possible using the Path class.

The **Trace** module is used to provide very detailed traceback information, not only when issuing error messages, but when logging failure events.

The **Directory** class is a general-purpose, scoped data structure that is used in a number of different situations but most notably to keep persistent state information for different functions in a Web application with proper namespace management. It is the same concept as the Unix or Windows file system: You can store objects in the directory and create pathnames to refer to different subdirectories and entries within directories. The only wrinkle is that it is an entirely memory-resident concept. Every operation found in the file system is supported in the Directory class with the exception of permissions.

Finally, the **KeyGen** module is used for generating unique keys (identifiers). This is used for creating unique session names to index the persistent state information from disk. You'll hear a lot about this in the Slither chapter (and Slither applications) when we discuss something called the *user profile*.

Part III: Applications

Chapter 13: The Slither Application Development Framework • The Slither foundation classes are an implementation of an application development framework for Python Web programming. This class library allows you to write an application without being mired in the excruciating details typically associated with CGI programming. This class library makes extensive use of the Python language (in particular, its metaprogramming features for discovering things about your code), and both Python and our own class libraries as presented in the book. The key to our approach is lightweight design and flexibility and the ability to easily integrate HTML interface code in your application without ever directly mixing the two. We will strive to convince you (but have already witnessed how) this approach improves productivity when it comes to designing, implementing, and maintaining application code, especially over the long haul. Our approach is compared and contrasted with other frameworks available in the marketplace today toward the end of the chapter.

Chapter 14: Slither Applications • This chapter presents a "starter" application and two significant (i.e., nontrivial) applications written entirely using the Slither foundation classes and other core classes, such as the WriteProcessor. The two applications are very representative of the kinds of applications gaining attention on the Internet after the **dotcom** crash. The first, SlyWiki, is a collaborative text authoring system.

We used Slither here to enhance the functionality of an existing tool called MoinMoin and enable other useful extensions. SlyWiki features a database to store all user, page, and access control information, page-related operations (creating, viewing, and editing), indexing, searching, file upload/download, and many other features.

SlitherShopping is a do-it-yourself shopping portal that allows a business to create its own online presence. It features both a customer and an administrative interface and, similar to SlyWiki, features an access control framework. Both of these applications are completely functional and can even be deployed securely. While companies have already burned through millions of dollars in venture capital trying to get people to use their proprietary versions of the same software, you can download these applications and extend them for your own needs.

2

Introduction to Python

In this chapter, we will examine the basic facilities of the Python programming language, and go on to the more advanced features in the next.

Characteristics of Python

Here is a high-level look at the features of Python, for those with a background in programming languages.

Scripting • Python is a scripting language. This loosely means that you do not have to compile Python programs; Python can execute them directly. In fact, you can type lines directly into the Python interpreter and have it execute them interactively. Python does compile programs into code it interprets, but it will handle the compilation itself, without troubling you.

Nondeclarative • Python programs consist of executable statements. They don't have declarations. In most languages, you declare a function; in Python, you execute a statement that creates a function object and assigns it to a variable. In other languages, you call a function by giving its name and an argument list. The Python call looks exactly the same, but instead of the name of the function, you specify the name of the variable containing the function as its value.

Typeless • Python is a *typeless* or *dynamically typed* language. That means that variables do not have types; values have types. Variables are not declared. A value of any type may be assigned to any variable.

High-Level • Python is a high-level language. It has high-level data structures built into the language, such as dictionaries that allow you to associate values with objects. As of Python2, Python has had a garbage collector. You allocate objects whenever you need them, but you don't have to delete them. When there is no way left for the program to access the object, when there are no pointers left that point to it, Python automatically frees its storage. Older versions of Python also deallocate objects automatically with a reference count scheme, which will not reclaim storage of circularly linked, inaccessible structures.

Modular • Python programs are organized as collections of modules kept in libraries. Each module is kept in a separate file, and the libraries in directories. A good programming practice, when writing larger programs, is to use as many preexisting modules as possible and to divide the code you do write into general-purpose modules. These modules can be debugged individually and can be reused in other programs.

Object-Oriented • Python has facilities that allow object-oriented programming. It has classes and inheritance, as any proper object-oriented programming language should. But Python is not perfectly object oriented. Python does not provide private or otherwise restricted scopes for names. The information-hiding aspects of object-oriented programming are on the honor system.

With Operator Declarations • Python allows you to create functions for the built-in operators, to be used when the operators are applied to instances of certain classes. This allows you to implement abstract data types, new types of objects with their own set of operators. The operators include subscripting operators, so you can implement new types of objects that behave like arrays.

With Metaprogramming Facilities • What Python calls metaprogramming, other languages refer to as introspection or reflection. The program itself can examine and modify its interpreter's own state and components while it is running. This is useful for debugging and for changing the running program under program control.

Executing Programs

Interactive Use

You can execute Python from the command line in a command window. It will come up with a greeting and a command prompt (>>>):

```
[tc@tclinux tc]python
Python 1.5.2 (#0, Apr 13 1999, 10:51:12) [MSC 32 bit (Intel)] on win32
Copyright 1991-1995 Stichting Mathematisch Centrum, Amsterdam
>>>
```

You type Python statements at the command prompt, and Python executes them immediately. If you type an expression, Python will evaluate it and type out the value.

```
>>> 12+14+20
46
```

We will use the command interpreter to try out Python features to show how they work.

Python statements can extend beyond the end of a line, in which case the interpreter will give a different prompt (. . .) for the continuation:

```
>>> (1+2
... )*3
9
```

Python can't always figure out that you wish to continue a statement to another line. The way you force it to continue to the next line is to put a backslash, \, as the last character on a line. This is customary in Unix-like systems. It incorporates the following character, the newline, into the current line as white space.

Scripts in Files

You can also place programs in files and execute them from there. For example, you can edit a file SayHi in the current directory, containing:

```
#!/usr/bin/env python
print 'Hello'
```

Then set SayHi's execute permissions and execute it:

```
chmod a+x SayHi
./SayHi
Hello
```

The `#!/usr/bin/python` is a comment to the shell, the command interpreter on Linux. It tells the shell that the way to execute this file is to execute the program in file `/usr/bin/python`, and pass it the rest of the file as its input. The print statement tells Python to write out the string Hello on the standard output, which will write it to you. The `print` is required when Python is executing a script in a file. When you are typing directly to it, Python knows to write out the values of expressions, but when it is executing scripts, it assumes you do not want the value of every expression you execute cluttering up your output, so it will not write out the values of expressions.

Arithmetic Expressions

Arithmetic Types

Python has four built-in arithmetic data types:

1. *Integer*–fixed sized (at least 32-bit) signed integers
2. *Long integer*–variably sized, unbounded precision signed integers
3. *Float*–floating point approximations to real numbers
4. *Complex*–complex numbers (with real and imaginary parts) for engineering calculations. We will not consider complex numbers further, since they are not typically relevant to Web enterprise applications.

Integer literals can be written in decimal, octal, or hexadecimal (base 16) format using the same syntax as in C or C++:

- Octal integers begin with 0 and contain only octal digits (0–7). Strangely, that means zero is written in octal.
- Decimal integers begin with a decimal digit other than zero and contain only decimal digits.

- Hexadecimal integers begin with 0x or 0X. The prefix is followed by a string of hexadecimal digits, 0–9, a–f, A–F. The letters A, B, . . . F, of course, represent the values, 10, 11, . . . 15.

```
>>> 20
20
>>> 020
16
>>> 0x20
32
```

Long integers are written as an integer followed with an L (in upper- or lowercase, but lowercase is too hard to distinguish from the digit one). The difference between integer and long integer is that integers are fixed sized. Integer arithmetic will overflow if the results get too large. Long integers occupy as much storage as they need. Long integer arithmetic does not overflow. For example, 2^{32} cannot be represented in 32 bits. So here is what happens when we try to take two to the 32nd power, written 2**32 in Python:

```
>>> 2**32
Traceback (innermost last):
  File "<stdin>", line 1, in ?
OverflowError: integer pow()
>>> 2L**32
4294967296L
```

(This example also shows Python's response to an error.)

Since integers occupy single machine words, computers perform integer arithmetic very fast. Long integer arithmetic typically requires much more time.

Floating point numbers are written with a decimal point or an exponent, or both. For example: .2, 2.0, 20., 2000e-1, 2E3.

Python allows mixed-mode arithmetic, as we saw above with 2L**32. If the two operands of an arithmetic operator have different types, Python will convert them to a common type. Python converts the operand whose type has the smaller range of values to the type of the operand with the wider range of values. (This is called a *widening coercion*: The "narrower" operand is forced to be the type of the wider.) So, if they are mixed in expressions, integers will be converted to long integers or floats, and long integers will be converted to floats. The conversions to float may lose some low-order digits.

Operators

Table 2–1 is a complete list of Python operators and their precedence levels. Some of the operators won't be discussed until later sections; we'll refer to the table then. The operators with higher precedence levels are performed before those with lower precedence.

The arithmetic operators in Python are much the same as those in C or C++. They are at precedence levels 9 through 12. The bit-wise operators (ANDs, ORs, shifts) are mostly at levels 5 through 8. Since they are not used much in Web enterprise applications, we won't discuss them further.

We will discuss the logical and comparison operators later when we discuss `while` loops.

Table 2–1
Operators and Precedence Levels

Precedence	Operators	Comments
1	x or y	This is the logical OR operation. It will return true if either x or y is true, i.e. non-zero. Like the || operator in C, it is *short-circuited*: It will not evaluate y if x determines the value of the expression. It first evaluates x and returns the value of x if x is not zero. If x is zero, it evaluates and returns the value of y. By "x is zero" we mean that it would be considered zero in an `if` or `while` expression. Other values than a number zero also count as zero.
2	x and y	This is the logical AND operation. It will return true if both x and y are true, i.e. non-zero. Like the && operator in C, it is short-circuited: It will not evaluate y if x determines the value of the expression. It first evaluates x and returns x if x is zero. If x is not zero, it evaluates and returns the value of y. By "x is zero" we mean that it would be considered zero in an `if` or `while` expression. Other values than a number zero also count as zero.

Table 2–1
Operators and Precedence Levels (Continued)

Precedence	Operators	Comments
3	`not x`	This is the logical NOT operator. It returns 1 if `x` is zero; it returns 0 if `x` is anything else.

4	`x < y`
	`x <= y`
	`x > y`
	`x >= y`
	`x == y`
	`x != y    x <> y`
	`x is y`
	`x is not y`
	`x in y`
	`x not in y`
		The relational operators are much like they are in other languages. Operators `!=` and `<>` both mean *not equal.*
		Testing for equality, `==` and `!=`, can be applied to structured objects, as we will discuss later. They attempt to find out if the structured objects have equal components. Operators `x is y` and `x is not y` test whether two names reference the same object, so they will be much faster than `==` and `!=` for structured objects, but they don't perform the same test.
		We will discuss `x in y` and `x not in y` later, when we discuss sequence types.

5	`x | y`	This is the bitwise OR operation, ORing the corresponding bits in two integers.
6	`x ^ y`	This is the bitwise EXCLUSIVE-OR (XOR) operation, XORing the corresponding bits in two integers.
7	`x & y`	This is the bitwise AND operation, ANDing the corresponding bits in two integers.
8	`x << y` `x >> y`	These are the shift operators. They apply to integers or long integers. The bits in `x` are shifted left (`<<`) or right (`>>`) the number of positions indicated by `y`. The right shifts are *arithmetic:* The sign bit will be shifted in at the top, preserving the sign of the `x` operand.
9	`x + y` `x - y`	Addition and subtraction. Operator `+` also performs concatenation on sequences, as we will see later.

Table 2–1
Operators and Precedence Levels (Continued)

Precedence	Operators	Comments

10	`x * y`
	`x / y`
	`x % y`
		Multiplication, division, and modulus (or remainder). Operator `%` will also work with floating point numbers. Operator `*` also applies to sequence types, and operator `%` has a special function for strings. We will look at these other uses later.

11	`- y`
	`~ y`
	`+ y`
		Negation, bitwise complement, and unary plus (no operation for numbers).

12	`x ** y`	Exponentiation, x^y.

13	`f(...)`
	`x.attr`
	`x[i]`
	`x[i:j]`
		Function call, attribute access, subscription, and slicing. We will discuss these later.

14	`(...)`
	`[...]`
	`{...}`
	`` `...` ``
		These are used to construct built-in structured objects: tuples, lists, directories, and strings. We will discuss them later.

Built-In Arithmetic Functions

Python has a number of built-in functions you can call. Arithmetic functions include those shown in Table 2–2. Other mathematical functions can be found in module `math`. Complex arithmetic functions are in module `cmath`.

Table 2–2
Built-In Arithmetic Functions

Function call	Explanation
`v=abs(x)`	Assigns v the absolute value of x
`v=cmp(x,y)`	Compares x and y and assigns v a negative value if x<y, zero if x==y, and positive if x>y

Table 2–2
Built-In Arithmetic Functions (Continued)

Function call	Explanation
`u,v=coerce(x,y)`	Determines the common type for x and y required for arithmetic operators then assigns x converted to that type to u and y converted to that type to v
`u,v=divmod (x, y)`	If x and y are integers or long integers, it assigns u=x/y and v=x%y. If x and y are floating point numbers, it assigns $u = \lfloor x/y \rfloor$, the largest integer less than or equal to x/y, and $v = x - (\lfloor x/y \rfloor \cdot y)$.
`v=float(x)`	Assigns v the value of x converted to a floating point value
`v=int (x)`	Assigns v the value of x converted to an integer value
`v=long (x)`	Assigns v the value of x converted to a long integer value
`v=complex(x)` `v=complex(x,y)`	Converts x to a complex number, or x to the real part and y to the imaginary part of a complex number
`v=max(x1, x2, ...)`	Assigns v the x with the largest value
`v=min(x1, x2, ...)`	Assigns v the x with the smallest value
`v=pow(x,y)`	Assigns v the value of x raised to the y power, x**y
`v=pow(x,y,z)`	Assigns v the value of x raised to the y power modulus z, i.e., x**y%z
`v=round(x,y)`	Assigns v the floating point number x rounded to have n digits after the decimal point. If you omit y, it defaults to zero.

Assignments and Variables

Variables are not declared. You create a variable simply by assigning a value to it. The simplest form of an assignment is:

```
variable = expression
```

For example

```
>>> a=10
>>> a
10
>>> b=a+2
>>> b
12
```

Variable names and other identifiers in Python are composed of letters, digits, and underscore characters. The first character of the identifier must not be a digit. The letters are the ISO-Latin characters A–Z and a–z; Python has not yet been fully internationalized.[1] Any of these is okay: _1, a, a_, pi3_14159.

You can also do several assignments on the same line; for example let's swap the values of a and b:

```
>>> a,b
(10, 12)
>>> a,b=b,a
>>> a,b
(12, 10)
```

We will look at this again later. Note also that we can list more than one expression on a line in interactive mode and Python will write out all their values. Both the multiple assignments and the multiple values on a line use tuples, a kind of sequence which we will discuss in "Tuples" on page 48.

---

1. Although Python2 does have Unicode strings.

Creating Functions

You may create a function and assign it to a variable with the `def` statement, for example:

```
>>> def diff(x,y):
...       return abs(x-y)
...
>>> diff(-10,5)
15
```

creates a function `diff` that returns the absolute difference between values x and y. There are several things to note about this function creation:

1. The `def` line introduces the code for the function. It gives the name we will call the function, `diff`, and the argument list. The function will be called with two arguments, x and y. The `def` line is terminated with a colon.
2. The name, `diff`, is not exactly the name of the function. It is a variable that is assigned the function as a value. It is an assignment as much as assigning `diff=value` would be, and indeed, `diff` can be reassigned.
3. The body of the function is indented. All statements in the same group of statements must be indented the same amount. Soon we'll look at `while` statements, whose bodies must be indented beneath the `while`.
4. The function returns a value with a `return` statement.
5. If there is no `return` statement, the function does not return a value, and the call of the function should be used only as a statement, not within an expression.
6. A function is called by the form `f(args)` where f is a variable containing the function and `args` are the arguments being passed in.

When you use a variable name in a function, Python will look in three places to try to find what it means:

1. The function's local variables. The arguments are already placed there; other variables assigned values in the function are also placed there.

2. The module variables. These are the variables assigned values in the interactive session or in the file that Python is executing.

3. The built-in names in the Python system. For example, the function abs() is a built-in name in Python.

The scopes are pictured in Figure 2–1. The search for a name starts in the innermost scope and proceeds outward until the name is found or until there are no more scopes. To find the name referenced in a function, at most three scopes will be searched. When a variable is assigned a value in a function, its name will be placed in the local scope if it is not already there. For example, in Figure 2–1, if the function looks up the value of x, it will get 1, the value of variable x in the function itself. The variable x with a value 2 is in the global scope and is hidden by the local x. If the function tries to look up y, it won't find it in the local scope, but will find it in the module scope with a value 3.

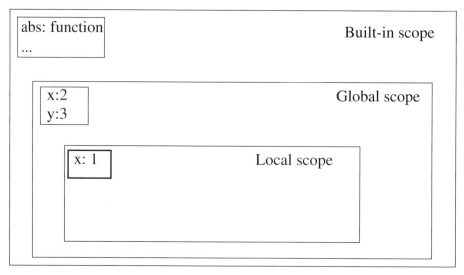

Figure 2–1
Scopes for Names Known in a Function

Modules

As we discussed in "Scripts in Files" on page 21, you can put Python programs in files and execute them. However, the primary reason to put Python programs in files is to allow other Python programs to import and use the functions. A Python program that is used by other Python programs is called a *module.*

The way you access a module is by the `import` statement:

```
import moduleName
```

The `import` statement sees if the module has already been imported. If it hasn't been imported yet, Python finds the file that contains the module. It will have the name *moduleName.py*, and will be found in one directory in a list of directories (path). Python's built-in library of modules is on the path, so you can use all the modules in Python's library without difficulty.

Whether or not the module gets loaded, the `import` statement assigns a module object to a variable in the local scope that has the same name as the module, i.e., it behaves the same way as an assignment statement. So

```
import moduleName
```

behaves like

```
moduleName = moduleObject
```

When Python loads a module, Python reads in the module's file executing the commands. The commands assign values to variables within the module's namespace that it puts the names in. These are available in the module object, so you can access the names defined in the module by the expression

```
moduleName.variable
```

For example, the module `string` has a built-in function `atof()` to convert strings to floating point numbers. It also has a string variable `hexdigits` that contains all the hexadecimal digits. So,

```
>>> import string
>>> string.atof
<built-in function atof>
>>> string.atof("314e-2")
3.14
>>> string.hexdigits
'0123456789abcdefABCDEF'
```

If you wanted to refer to the function by its own name directly, rather than prefixed by the module name, you could assign it to a local variable with the same name

```
>>> atof=string.atof
>>> atof("314e-2")
3.14
```

or you could just import the names you want from the module:

```
>>> from string import atof, hexdigits
>>> hexdigits
'0123456789abcdefABCDEF'
```

If you are using an interactive session to debug modules, you will have to reload the module after every change. You reload a module using the built-in `reload()` function:

```
reload(moduleObject)
```

This will look up, load, and initialize the module. The new definitions of variables within the module will override the previous definitions. The module object will be changed in place, so all parts of the program that have variables pointing to that module (i.e., all that have imported it) will see the new definitions when referencing its attributes through the module name, `moduleName . variable`.

However, there are problems that may force you to start a new interactive session. If you use the `from-import` statement,

```
from moduleName import name
```

then the assignment to `name` will have been done when the `from-import` statement was executed and `name` will have the value of `moduleName.name` at that time. It won't automatically be updated. After reloading `moduleName`, you will have to execute the `from-import` again to have the new value of the attribute assigned to `name`. If names from module A are imported into module B and you change module A, you will need to reload module A to get the new definitions and then reload module B to assign the new definitions to local names. This can quickly get confusing.

Python2 provides the ability to import modules and assign them to variables with different names (i.e., not the name of the module), or import functions, classes, and variables from modules assigning them to local variables with different names. The syntax is

```
import module as name
from module import name1 as name2
```

Files

As with all programming languages, Python allows you to read and write files. Python uses file objects for the operations. You create a file object by calling the built-in function open()

```
f=open(name, mode)
```

where the name string gives a path to the file and the mode string indicates whether the file is to be read from or to be written. The mode is a string. Here's a list of the modes:

- 'r' Open for reading. This is the default.
- 'w' Open for writing. This will replace a current file with the same name.
- 'a' Open for appending. Data will be added to the end of a currently existing file.
- 'r+' Open for both reading and writing.

You may omit the mode parameter if you are opening the file for reading.

File objects have *methods* for reading and writing and other operations. A method is a function attached to the object. The method has a syntax that differs a bit from regular functions. The object the method operates on precedes the function call, separated by a dot:

```
object.function(args)
```

This syntax has a couple of virtues:

- It makes clear which object the method is operating on. Otherwise, the object would have to be one of the arguments, and you couldn't be sure which.
- It allows different kinds of objects to have methods with the same name; the system can find the correct one for the object. Many objects have similar operations. It would be a pain to have to invent different names for those operations, or to have

to keep changing a single function to test what kind of object it has been given and execute some specific code for it.

There are three methods you especially need to know for files:

1. `f.readline()`—Reads the next line from a text file and returns it in a string. The string ends with the line termination character or characters, on Linux the newline character `'\n'`. Empty lines thus consist of a single newline character. On end of file, `readline()` returns an empty string, `''`.

2. `f.write(string)`—Writes a string to the file. The `string` is not made into a line, i.e., the newline character is not appended. If you want it, you will have to write it yourself.

3. `f.close()`—Finishes processing the file, either reading or writing it. All system resources the file was using are freed up. No further methods can be called for the file.

We will present a complete list of the file operations in "Text Files in `bash`" on page 151 of Chapter 4.

`print` Statement

The `print` statement writes to the standard output. You can find the standard output file object in the `sys` module, `sys.stdout`. The form of the print statement is

```
print e1, e2, ...
print e1, e2, ... ,
```

The expressions are evaluated and converted into strings and written out with a blank between each pair. If the print statement does not end with a comma, the output line is terminated after the last expression is written (a newline character is written). If it does end in a comma, the line is not terminated, so the next print will continue to fill in the line.

The expressions are optional. You use a print with no expressions to write out a newline.

Python 2 allows you to specify a different file to write on. It begins `print >> file`, thus:

```
print >> file, e1, ....
```

while **Loops**

while

The form of a while loop is

```
while expression :
        indented body
```

The *expression* is evaluated to get a truth value. Python considers zero to be false and any non-zero value to be true. It considers empty strings (and other sequences) to be false, nonempty ones, true. If the expression evaluates to true, the body of the loop is executed once and the loop is restarted. As soon as the expression evaluates false, Python stops evaluating the loop and goes on to the statement following it.

The statements in the body of the loop must be indented a uniform amount of space beneath the while statement proper. Of course, if any of the contained statements are while statements, their bodies must be indented further.

Example: listfile

Here is an example of the use of a while statement in listing a text file. If you want to follow along, you will need the Python interpreter to be executing in the same directory as your code files. You can get Python to your directory by

```
>>> import os
>>> os.chdir("directory")
```

The function chdir() in module os changes the current working directory. Now, suppose the following code is in a file listfile.py:

```
def listfile(name):
        f=open(name)
        L=f.readline()
        while L :
                print L,
                L=f.readline()
        f.close()
```

We can import it and use it to list itself:

```
>>> from listfile import listfile
>>> listfile("listfile.py")
def listfile(name):
        f=open(name)
        L=f.readline()
        while L :
                print L,
                L=f.readline()
        f.close()
```

The code should be pretty obvious except for two points.

1. `while L :` Python considers an empty string to be false and a nonempty string to be true. That makes this loop easy, since end-of-file results in `readline()` returning an empty string. In general, structured objects can sometimes be considered equivalent to zero for logical tests. We'll try to point out these cases as we discuss them. Here, while we are discussing logical operators, we will just say zero and non-zero, or false and true, and not keep repeating that some things other than the number zero are also considered to be false.

2. `print L,` The final comma prevents Python from inserting a newline following the string that has been written. Since the lines returned by `readline()` all are terminated by newlines anyway, they come out single-spaced. If the comma weren't there, the lines would come out double-spaced.

Relational Expressions

The expressions in `while` statements most commonly use relational operators to compare operands. Since there is no logical or Boolean data type in Python, and Python is like C in using zero for false and non-zero for true, relational operators return numeric values 0 and 1. For example,

```
>>> 1<2
1
>>> 1>2
0
```

Unlike most other languages, Python allows relational operators to be cascaded:

```
>>> -2 < -1 < 0
1
>>> (-2 < -1) < 0
0
```

The first of the two expressions is equivalent to -2 < -1 and -1 < 0. Python duplicates the value between the two operators and does both comparisons separately. In the second expression, (-2 < -1) yields 1, then 1<0 yields 0.

Logical Expressions

Python provides the usual three logical operators, or, and, and not, at the low precedence levels, 1, 2, and 3. See Table 2–1.

1. x or y—The lowest precedence Python operator is or. The expression x or y is *short-circuited*: It will not evaluate y if x determines the value of the expression. It first evaluates x and returns the value of x if x is not considered false. If x counts as false,[2] it evaluates and returns the value of y. So the true value it may return is either the value of x or the value of y.

2. x and y—The and operator, like or, is *short-circuited*: It will not evaluate y if x determines the value of the expression. It first evaluates x and returns x if x counts as false. If x is true, it evaluates and returns the value of y. That has the effect of returning zero if either x or y is zero. If neither x nor y is zero, it returns the value of y to represent true.

3. not x—The not operator, at precedence level 3, although a unary operator, has a much lower precedence than the other unary operators at precedence 12. In fact, it is a lot more useful at a low precedence level. If it had a high precedence level, we would usually have to put parentheses around its operand. It returns 1 if x is zero; it returns 0 if x is anything else.

---

2. We say "x is considered false" and "x counts as false," because various values, like zero, None, and empty sequences, are treated as being false by and and or operators and while and if statements.

Lists

Lists in Python are like arrays in other languages. Actually, they are *flex arrays*, arrays whose size can change during program execution.

Lists can be created with a *display*. Just list the values between opening and closing brackets:

```
[e₀, e₁, ..., eₙ₋₁]
```

A list of length n is created. The expressions e_0, e_1, etc., are evaluated and their values placed in the list.

In addition, Python 2 has a more sophisticated form of display, the *list comprehension*. We will discuss it later, after we've discussed the `for-` and `if-` statements it is based on.

Like arrays, lists can be subscripted by following the list's name with the index of the item in brackets, thus

```
>>> L=["a","b","c"]
>>> L[1]
'b'
>>> L[0]
'a'
>>> L[2]
'c'
>>> L[3]
Traceback (innermost last):
  File "<stdin>", line 1, in ?
IndexError: list index out of range
```

The positions in the list are numbered from zero, left to right. You can also assign to positions in a list

```
>>> L[1]=1
>>> L
['a', 1, 'c']
```

Notice that the items in a list do not need to be of the same data type. Python lists, like variables, are typeless. Also notice that Python is able to write out an entire list when you ask for it, certainly more convenient than the arrays in some languages that you have to write out in a loop.

You can check the length of a list with the `len()` function:

```
>>> len(L)
3
```

Often you will need a list with successive integers in it. Python has a built-in function, range(), to give that to you.

```
>>> range(10)
[0, 1, 2, 3, 4, 5, 6, 7, 8, 9]
>>> range(-10,0)
[-10, -9, -8, -7, -6, -5, -4, -3, -2, -1]
```

Call range(i,j) gives you a list of the j-i integers from i up to, but not including, j. Call range(n) is the same as range(0,n). Why "up to, but not including"? It is compatible with the indexing of lists, where a list of length *n* has indices 0 through *n−1*.

You can also create a list of values some step size apart, not just sequential, by specifying the step size as the third argument to range():

```
>>> range(0,10,2)
[0, 2, 4, 6, 8]
```

If you are using lists as arrays, you obviously have to be able to create a list of some length. The length you need may be computed as the program runs, so you obviously can't always use a list display. How do you create a list of length *n*?

You use the replication operator, *. Of course, this is the same as the multiplication operator. If one operand of the * operator is a list, L, and the other is a number, *n*, then L*n concatenates n copies of L together.

```
>>> L
['a', 1, 'c']
>>> L*3
['a', 1, 'c', 'a', 1, 'c', 'a', 1, 'c']
>>> 2*L
['a', 1, 'c', 'a', 1, 'c']
```

A way to allocate an array of length 10 is

```
>>> ary=[0]*10
>>> ary
[0, 0, 0, 0, 0, 0, 0, 0, 0, 0]
```

You can concatenate two lists by using the + operator:

```
>>> L+["d","e"]
['a', 1, 'c', 'd', 'e']
```

You can compare two lists for identity or for equality. The `is` operator compares two objects to see if they are identical, i.e., really the same object. The `==` operator compares objects for equality. Two lists are considered equal if their contents are equal. The equality test can be a lot slower than the identity test.

```
>>> [1,2] is [1,2]
0
```

These two displays create separate lists, so `is` returns false, but the two lists are equal:

```
>>> [1,2] == [1,2]
1
```

Warning: The `==` test in Python1 uses a simple recursive search to test for equality. If you have a circularly linked structure, e.g. a list embedded within itself, the `==` operator may crash your program. Python2 uses a more sophisticated algorithm, so it shouldn't be a problem.

Other relational operators work on lists as well. They operate *lexicographically*. The comparison works left to right through the lists, comparing the elements at the same positions, until it finds elements that are unequal, whereupon it uses the relationship of those elements as the relationship of the lists, for example

```
>>> [1,2,3]<[1,4,3]
1
>>> [1,2,3]<[1,0,3]
0
```

There are two special operators to test for list membership: `x in y` reports true if `x` is in the list `y` and false otherwise; `x not in y` reports just the opposite.

```
>>> 2 in [1,2,3]
1
>>> 2 not in [1,2,3]
0
```

You can get a copy of a part of a list using slicing. Slicing is like subscripting, but it specifies a range of indices.

```
>>> r=range(10)
>>> r
[0, 1, 2, 3, 4, 5, 6, 7, 8, 9]
>>> r[3]
3
>>> r[3:4]
[3]
>>> r[3:6]
[3, 4, 5]
>>> r[3:1]
[]
```

Notice a few things:
- Subscripting, r[3], returns the object that is at that position.
- Slicing, e.g., r[3:4], returns a list.
- The slice extends from the starting index up to, *but not including*, the ending index.
- If the ending index of a slice is less than or equal to the starting index, slicing returns the empty list.

You can use negative indices to indicate positions from the end of the list:

```
>>> r=range(10)
>>> r[-1]
9
>>> r[-10]
0
>>> r[-3:-1]
[7, 8]
```

If you leave out the start or the end positions when specifying a slice, they default to the beginning or the end of the list:

```
>>> r=range(10)
>>> r[:5]
[0, 1, 2, 3, 4]
>>> r[5:]
[5, 6, 7, 8, 9]
>>> r[:]
[0, 1, 2, 3, 4, 5, 6, 7, 8, 9]
```

The form `r[:]` may seem pointless, but it is a way to make a copy of a list.

You can assign to a slice of a list by specifying the slice on the left-hand side of an assignment and a list on the right-hand side.

```
>>> L
['a', 'c']
>>> L[1:1]=['b']
>>> L
['a', 'b', 'c']
>>> L[0:2]=L[1:3]
>>> L
['b', 'c', 'c']
```

Assigning to a slice gives you a way of deleting elements:

```
>>> r=range(10)
>>> r[3:5]=[]
>>> r
[0, 1, 2, 5, 6, 7, 8, 9]
```

You can also delete an item from a list using the `del` statement:

```
>>> r=range(10)
>>> del r[3]
>>> r
[0, 1, 2, 4, 5, 6, 7, 8, 9]
>>> r=range(10)
>>> del r[3:5]
>>> r
[0, 1, 2, 5, 6, 7, 8, 9]
```

List objects have a number of methods you can call, as shown in Table 2–3. They fall into several groups. Two of the methods add ele-

Table 2–3
List Methods

Method	Description
L.append(x)	Places x at the end of the list L, increasing the length of L by one.
L.extend(x)	Places the list of elements x at the end of the list L, increasing the length of L by the length of x. L.extend(x) is equivalent to L[len(L):]=x.

Table 2–3
List Methods (Continued)

Method	Description
`L.insert(i, x)`	Inserts item x at position i in list L. All items in L at positions i and above are moved to the right, i.e., their indices increase by one. `L.insert(len(L),x)` is equivalent to `L.append(x)`.
`L.pop()` `L.pop(i)`	Removes and returns an item from the list. If an index, i, is provided, `pop()` removes and returns the item at that position. If no index is provided, it removes and returns the last item–the index defaults to -1.
`L.remove(x)`	Removes the first item in L that is equal to x. It is an error if x doesn't occur in L.
`L.count(x)`	Counts the number of items in L that are equal to x.
`L.index(x)`	Returns the index of the first item in L that is equal to x. It is an error if x doesn't occur in L.
`L.reverse()`	Reverses the order of the elements of the list L in place.
`L.sort()` `L.sort(cmpfn)`	Sorts the elements of the list L in place into non-decreasing order. Function `cmpfn(x,y)` is called to compare x and y and return a negative integer if x precedes y in the desired ordering, 0 if they are to be considered equal, and a positive integer if x follows y. To sort into descending order, you could use: `def cmpfn(x, y): return -cmp(x,y)`

ments to the list. Method call `L.append(x)` adds an element x to the end of the list L (the new highest position). Method call `L.insert(i,x)` inserts an element x at any position i in the list L. All elements previously at that position or beyond are moved up one position. The index i can be at the end of the list, whereupon `insert()` behaves like `append()`.

Method call `L.remove(x)` finds the first (lowest indexed) occurrence of x in list L and removes it. All elements with higher indices are moved down one. If you know the position, i, of the element you wish to remove, use `del L[i]`. If you want to examine the item at a particular position and remove it, use `L.pop(i)`. If you want to examine the last item and remove it, use `L.pop()`.

To use L as a stack, use `L.append(x)` to push x on the stack, and `x=L.pop()` to pop it off. To use L as a queue, use `L.append(x)` to enqueue x and `x=L.pop(0)` to dequeue it.

Two methods examine the list for elements equal to a particular value. Call `L.count(x)` returns a count of the number of occurrences of value x in list L. Call `L.index(x)` returns the position of the first occurrence of x in L. Remember, the expressions `x in L` and `x not in L` test to see if the list L contains element x.

Two methods permute the order of the elements of the list, in place. `L.reverse()` reverses the order of the elements of the list L. `L.sort()` sorts the elements of L into nondecreasing order.

Example: Self–Organizing List • In a self-organizing list, you move items that are accessed to the front so you can find them more quickly in subsequent searches. Here's how you could implement self-organizing lists using list methods:

```
>>> def reorder(L,x):
...        L.remove(x)
...        L.insert(0,x)
...
>>> r=range(10)
>>> r
[0, 1, 2, 3, 4, 5, 6, 7, 8, 9]
>>> reorder(r,5)
>>> r
[5, 0, 1, 2, 3, 4, 6, 7, 8, 9]
```

Example: Median Value of a List of Numbers • The median number in a list is the middle number in the sorted list, if there is an odd number of items. If there is an even number, the median is the average of the two middle numbers. Here is a function to compute the median:

```
>>> def median(L):
...        s=L[:]
...        s.sort()
...        n=len(s)
...        return (s[n/2]+s[(n-1)/2])/2.0
...
>>> median(range(5))
2.0
>>> median(range(6))
2.5
```

There are a couple of things to note about this code:

- Rather than modify the array, L, we make a copy before sorting it.
- Whether the number, n, of elements is even or odd, we compute the median by averaging the elements at positions n/2 and (n-1)/2. This gives the correct answer in either case.

for **loops**

In Python, for loops exist to allow an index variable to take on each element in a list, or other sequence object. (We'll discuss other sequences below.) The form of a for loop is:

```
for var in sequence :
    indented body of loop
```

Probably the most common form of for loop is

```
>>> for i in range(len(L)):
...         ...
```

where i takes on the index of each item in the list, L. If you only need to examine the items in the list but do not need to know their positions, you can use the loop

```
>>> for x in L:
...         ...
```

continue

If you decide that you are finished with the current iteration of a loop, you can execute the continue statement. It consists of the single word

```
continue
```

It will immediately end the current iteration and jump back to the top of the loop and start the next iteration. If there are no more iterations to do, of course, it falls out of the loop.

One major use for the `continue` statement is to filter the items in the loop. Suppose we wish to print only those strings in a list that are at least five letters long; we might do it as follows:

```
>>> x=["book","placid","right","table","mother","gone"]
>>> for s in x:
...         if len(s)<=5:
...                 continue
...         print s,
...
placid mother
```

break **and** else **in Loops**

Often you will use a loop to search for something. Once you've found it, you want to escape from the loop. If you don't find it, you often need to take some default action. Python makes it easy to do both of these.

If in the midst of a loop you wish to stop iterating, you can execute the `break` statement. It consists of the keyword `break`:

```
break
```

If you want to execute some code if the loop terminated normally, i.e., if it didn't exit by a `break`, you can attach an `else` clause on the end of the loop. Loops with `else` clauses have the form:

```
while expr :
    indented loop body containing break
else :
    indented code to execute
    if the loop exits normally
```

or

```
for var in sequence:
    indented loop body containing break
else :
    indented code to execute
    if the loop exits normally
```

Of course, the keyword `else` is usually used in `if` statements. It is in Python too. It is perhaps not the best word to express the concept of "on normal termination," but it is what Python uses.

`if` **Statements**

`if else`

An `if` statement will execute code based on whether an expression is true. The form of an `if` statement is

```
if expr:
    indented code to be executed if expr is true
```

If you want to execute other code if the expression is false, use the `else` clause:

```
if expr:
    indented code to be executed if expr is true
else:
    indented code to be executed if expr is false
```

`elif`

Of course, you often want to test a sequence of conditions and execute code for the first one that's true. Because of indentation, it would be annoying if you had to put another `if` within the `else` and indent further. Python avoids this problem with the `elif` clause, equaling an `else` plus an `if`. The general syntax of an `if` statement is:

```
if expr1:
    indented code to be executed if expr1 is true
elif expr2:
    indented code to be executed if expr1 is false
        and expr2 is true
...
else:
    indented code to be executed if all exprs are false
```

Here would be an appropriate place to mention that Python does not have a switch statement. Switch statements choose one out of several blocks of statements to execute based on the value of a single expression. You will probably use an `if` statement with a sequence of `elif` clauses for that purpose. (What else could you use? Well, you could put functions into a list, index into the list, and execute one of them, but that's a lot of trouble.)

pass and One-Line Code Blocks

The expressions in the `if` and `elif` clauses are executed in order until one evaluates true; the block of code associated with that expression is executed and then control passes to the statement following the `if` statement. This means that the earlier expressions must test for more specific cases; if you test for the more general case first, you will never get to the code for the subcase.

But what if the desired behavior for the more specific case is to do nothing? You need a statement that doesn't do anything. In Python this is the `pass` statement, which consists wholly of the keyword `pass`:

```
pass
```

The `pass` statement is only useful as a complete code block, and it is short. Giving it an entire indented line to itself makes programs longer. That may force related code to extend beyond a page or a computer screen. So Python allows one statement block of code to be placed on the same line as the statement that selects it. Just write the statement following the colon of the `if`, `elif`, `else`, `while`, `for`, `def` (or of any other statement that ends in a colon introducing a block of code).

Indeed, you can put several simple statements following a colon just by placing semicolons between them.

Tuples

A tuple is an immutable list: It is just like a list except that you can't change the contents. You create a tuple by a display consisting of expressions in parentheses separated by commas, for example:

```
>>> (1,2)
(1, 2)
```

Notice that Python writes out a tuple in the parenthesized notation.

The one place where parentheses become ambiguous is in constructing a tuple of length one. In that case, if you want a tuple of length one, put a comma following the expression, just before the final parenthesis. If you only intend a parenthesized expression, do not put in a comma.

```
>>> (1,)
(1,)
>>> (1)
1
```

You can have tuples with no components. Just use parentheses without anything between them:

```
>>> ()
()
```

You can subscript and slice tuples just like lists, pulling out elements or creating a copy of a section of a tuple. You cannot, however, assign to an element or a slice of a tuple; you can't use the subscript or the slice operator on the left–hand side of an assignment. You can't use the delete statement on a part of a tuple.

```
>>> q=(1,2)
>>> q
(1, 2)
>>> del q[0]
Traceback (innermost last):
  File "<stdin>", line 1, in ?
TypeError: object doesn't support item deletion
>>> del q[0:1]
Traceback (innermost last):
  File "<stdin>", line 1, in ?
TypeError: object doesn't support slice deletion
>>> q[1]=3
Traceback (innermost last):
  File "<stdin>", line 1, in ?
TypeError: object doesn't support item assignment
>>> q[0:1]=()
Traceback (innermost last):
  File "<stdin>", line 1, in ?
TypeError: object doesn't support slice assignment
```

You can concatenate tuples and replicate them, just like lists, using the + and * operators. These operators produce new tuples; they don't modify an already existing tuple.

```
>>> (1,2)+(3,4)
(1, 2, 3, 4)
>>> (1,2)*2
(1, 2, 1, 2)
```

You can convert a tuple to a list using the `list()` built-in function and a list to a tuple using the `tuple()` built-in function:

```
>>> list( (1,2,3) )
[1, 2, 3]
>>> tuple(range(3))
(0, 1, 2)
```

If you are constructing a tuple of at least one element on the right–hand side of an assignment statement, you don't have to surround the expressions in parentheses. If it is to be of length one, you do have to be sure to put in a trailing comma:

```
>>> x=1,2,3
>>> x
(1, 2, 3)
>>> x=1,
>>> x
(1,)
```

The same applies to `return` statements. You can return a tuple from a function, and you can construct the tuple in the `return` statement without enclosing it in parentheses, unless of course it is length zero.

You can compare two tuples for identity or for equality. The `is` operator compares two objects to see if they are identical. The `==` operator compares objects for equality. Two tuples are considered equal if their contents are equal.

```
>>> (1,2) is (1,2)
0
>>> (1,2) == (1,2)
1
```

These two displays create separate tuples, so `is` returns false, but they have the same contents, so `==` returns true.

Warning: The `==` test in Python1 uses a simple recursive search to test for equality. If you have a circularly linked structure, e.g., a tuple containing a list that is embedded within itself, the `==` operator may crash your program. You cannot, however, embed a tuple within itself directly, since it cannot be modified once it is created. It would already have to exist before it is created to be made a component of itself.

The relational operators that compare lists compare tuples the same way:

```
>>> (1,2,3) < (1,0,3)
0
>>> (1,2,3) < (1,4,3)
1
>>> 2 not in (1,2,3)
0
>>> 2 in (1,2,3)
1
```

List Comprehensions

A list comprehension, present in Python2 but not Python1, has the form

```
[expression for index in range optional-for-and-if-clauses]
```

For example,

```
[(x,y,x+y) for x in range(5) if x%2!=0 for y in range(5) if
y!=x]
```

yields

```
[(1, 0, 1), (1, 2, 3), (1, 3, 4), (1, 4, 5), (3, 0, 3), (3,
1, 4), (3, 2, 5), (3, 4, 7)]
```

The behavior is as if you initialized an empty list and then appended the expression to it in nested `for` and `if` statements. For example:

```
[ (x,y,x*y) for x in range(10) if x%2!=0 for y in range(10)
if y!=x]
```

is equivalent to

```
L=[]
for x in range(10):
    for y in range(10):
      if x%2!=0 and y!=x:
        L.append((x,y,x*y))
```

where `L` is now the list to use.

If you use a tuple as the expression in the list comprehension, you must put parentheses around it.

None

Lists and tuples, because they can contain references to other objects, allow you to build linked list data structures. For example, some languages (starting with Lisp) have built lists out of "cons cells" containing two references to other objects. These two references are sometimes called the head and tail of the list: The head is the first item, the tail is the rest of the list. (In Lisp they're called the CAR and the CDR.)

You could have much the same effect by using two element tuples with the head being at index zero and the tail being at index one. The problem, though, is that you need some way to indicate the end of a list. Lisp uses NIL. In C it's usually called NULL; in Java, null. Python provides the value None. You might create a linked list (1 2 3) as follows:

```
>>> x=(1,(2,(3,None)))
>>> x
(1, (2, (3, None)))
```

Another use for None is as a placeholder. If you assign a variable the value None, the variable will exist, but the value None can indicate that it hasn't had its value computed yet. The program can test to see if it has a value without having to test first whether it exists. Trying to access it if it doesn't exist causes a runtime error, as shown here:

```
>>> x=None
>>> x==None
1
>>> del x
>>> x
Traceback (innermost last):
  File "<stdin>", line 1, in ?
NameError: x
```

None is considered to be false in logical expressions.

More on Assignment

Now we will consider assignment statements more closely. There are five things that need to be considered:

1. Multiple assignments of the same value

2. Unpacking sequences, assigning components of sequences to different variables at the same time
3. Operate-and-becomes assignments in Python2, e.g. +=
4. The order of evaluation in assignment statements
5. Where variables are bound

We will consider these in order.

Multiple Assignments

First, you can include several assignments in the same statement. The form is

```
targets = targets = ... = expressions
```

This will assign the variables in the targets the value(s) of the expressions. For example:

```
i=j=0
```

would assign both i and j zero.

Unpacking Sequences

Second, as we have already seen, more than one value may be assigned at the same time by separating the values with commas, for example:

```
j,m=0,1
```

This can be used to swap values

```
a,b=b,a
```

And multiple assignment and unpacking sequences can be used together, albeit somewhat confusingly:

```
>>> i,m=j,n=0,1
>>> i,j,m,n
(0, 0, 1, 1)
```

You can assign from any sequence type, as long as the length of the variable list is the same as the length of the sequence. Lists, tuples, and strings are sequences, so

```
>>> i,j=(3,4)
>>> i,j
(3, 4)
>>> i,j=[5,6]
>>> i,j
(5, 6)
>>> i,j="ab"
>>> i,j
('a', 'b')
```

Moreover, you can include subsequences on the left–hand side of the assignment, enclosing the list of variables in parentheses or brackets, thus:

```
>>> i,(j,[m,n])=x=[1,[2,(3,4)]]
>>> i,j,m,n,x
(1, 2, 3, 4, [1, [2, (3, 4)]])
```

Notice that if there are several assignments in the statement, each one is matched separately to the value of the right–hand side. The different targets don't have to look alike. Notice also that the parentheses and brackets on the left–hand side of the assignments do not have to correspond to tuples and lists respectively on the right–hand side.

As with tuples, a parenthesized variable is treated as a simple variable, but including a comma after it causes it to be matched to the contents of a single element sequence, as shown in the following:

```
>>> (x)=[9]
>>> x
[9]
>>> (x,)=[9]
>>> x
9
```

Operate and Becomes

Python2 allows certain binary operators to be combined with the assignment operator. The general rule is that x op= y is equivalent to x = x op y.

So,

```
x+=1
```

increments x.

The operators that you can combine with an assignment are:

- The arithmetic operators: +, -, *, /, %, **
- The bitwise operators: &, |, ^
- The shift operators: <<, >>

Evaluation Order

The evaluation of an assignment statement evaluates the expression(s) on the right–hand side first, then assigns the resulting value to each of the targets from *left* to *right*. Within the targets, it also goes left to right making assignments. This can produce some confusion. Consider the following code:

```
>>> r=range(10)
>>> r.reverse()
>>> r
[9, 8, 7, 6, 5, 4, 3, 2, 1, 0]
>>> i=2
>>> i,r[i]=r[i],i
>>> r
[9, 8, 7, 6, 5, 4, 3, 2, 1, 0]
```

Since i has an initial value of two, you would expect that the assignment

```
>>> ...,r[i]=...,i
```

would assign 2 to r[2], replacing 7 with 2 in the sequence. But before that happens, we assign

```
>>> i,...=r[i],...
```

which is to say, we assign i=r[2], or seven. Then we assign r[7] the value 2, which was already there.

Assignment to Local Scope

When Python performs an assignment, it assigns to the variable in the innermost scope. If it is executing a function (within a `def`), the variable will only be seen by code in that function and will exist only as long as the function is executing. If the assignment is at the top level of a module, i.e., in a file but not inside a `def` or `class` statement (we'll talk about classes later), then the variable will be known in the module and will exist as long as the program is running–unless you explicitly delete it.

`global` **Statement**

So what if you want to assign a value to a module-scope variable in a function? You can't just assign a value to the variable name; that would create a local variable with the same name. What you can do is use the only declaration in the Python language, the `global` statement. The global statement has the form

```
global id1, id2,...
```

It declares that the variable names `id1`, `id2`, etc. are variables of the surrounding module and are to be fetched and assigned there. The `global` statement must appear before the variables are used.

Deleting Variables

You create a variable in a scope just by assigning to it. You can delete it from the scope using the `del` statement.

```
>>> x=9
>>> x
9
>>> del x
>>> x
Traceback (innermost last):
  File "<stdin>", line 1, in ?
NameError: x
```

Dictionaries

A dictionary is a mutable, associative structure. Considering these characteristics one at a time:

- *Mutable*–You can add key-value pairs to a dictionary and remove them.
- *Associative*–Dictionaries map keys into values. Given a key, you can look up its value. It looks like indexing a list or tuple, but unlike lists and tuples, the keys can be almost any immutable data type, not just integers. (It is peferrable that keys be immutable because if you put the key in the table and then changed its contents, you might not be able to look it up again.)

Dictionaries are like small, in-memory databases. Table 2–4 shows the operators, functions, and methods available for dictionaries.

Table 2–4
Operations on Dictionaries

Operator, Function, Method	Explanation
`{k:v,...}`	Creates a dictionary with the given key-value pairs.
`d[k]`	Returns the value associated with key k in dictionary d. It is an error if the key is not present in the dictionary. See methods `has_key()` and `get()`.
`d[k]=v`	Associates value v with key k in dictionary d. The key must be "hashable," that is, it should *not* be mutable. Python won't accept lists as keys.
`del d[k]`	Deletes key k and its associated value from dictionary d. It is an error if the key doesn't exist.
`d.clear()`	Removes all key-value pairs from dictionary d.
`d.copy()`	Creates a copy of dictionary d. This is a *shallow* copy: The dictionary itself is copied, but none of the key or value objects it contains are copied.
`d.get(k)`	Returns the value associated with key k in dictionary d. If k isn't present in the dictionary, it returns None.
`d.get(k,v)`	Returns the value associated with key k in dictionary d. If k isn't present in the dictionary, it returns v.

Table 2–4
Operations on Dictionaries (Continued)

Operator, Function, Method	Explanation
d.has_key(k)	Returns true (1) if dictionary d contains key k and false (0) otherwise.
d.items()	Returns [(k,v),...], a list of all the key-value pairs currently in the dictionary d. The key-value pairs are tuples of two elements (key,value).
d.keys()	Returns a list of all the keys currently in dictionary d.
d.update(m)	Adds all the key-value pairs from dictionary m to dictionary d. Any key in d that is the same as a key in m has its value reassigned.
d.values()	Returns a list of all the values currently in dictionary d.

d.setdefault(k)
 d.setdefault(k,x)
	Python2. Combining get() with initialization. As if defined
	 ```def setdefault(self,k,x=None):```
	 ``` if self.has_key(k):```
	 ``` return self[k]```
	 ``` else:```
	 ``` self[k]=x```
	 ``` return self[k]```

You can create an empty dictionary by writing an open-close-brace pair:

```
>>> d={}
>>> d
{}
```

You can create a dictionary with initial contents by placing one or more associations in the braces:

```
>>> d={"a":1,1:(2,3),(2,3):"a"}
>>> d
{(2, 3): 'a', 1: (2, 3), 'a': 1}
```

In this example, we associate the string key "a" with the value 1; key 1 with the value tuple (2,3); and the key tuple (2,3) with the string value "a." (They don't have to form a cycle like this.)

You can look up the value for a key by subscripting the dictionary with the value of the key.

```
>>> d[1]
(2, 3)
>>> d[(2,3)]
'a'
```

Since Python uses the equality operator, ==, to test the keys, equal numbers are considered to be the same key:

```
>>> d[1.0]
(2, 3)
```

Be careful, though, with floating point numbers. They are not exact, and they may differ by a few bits in the low order positions even if they look equal.

It is a runtime error to look up a nonexistent key in a dictionary.

```
>>> d[10]
Traceback (innermost last):
  File "<stdin>", line 1, in ?
KeyError: 10
```

If you don't want to worry about an error when looking up a value, you can use the get() method. The call d.get(k) will yield the value for key k in dictionary d, if it exists, or return the value None if it doesn't. The call d.get(k,v) is the same, except that it returns the value v if the key isn't present.

```
>>> d
{(2, 3): 'a', 1: (2, 3), 'a': 1}
>>> d.get(10)
>>> d.get(10)==None
1
>>> d.get(10,"absent")
'absent'
```

Notice that the Python interpreter doesn't write out the value None in interactive mode.

Alternatively, you can ask whether the dictionary contains the key before subscripting with it. Method call d.has_key(k) will return true or false (1 or 0) depending on whether the dictionary d contains the key k or not. (Operator in does *not* apply to dictionaries.)

```
>>> d.has_key(1)
1
>>> d.has_key(10)
0
```

You can insert a new key-value pair into the dictionary by sub-scripting a dictionary on the left–hand side of an assignment operator with the key and assigning it the value. You can assign a new value to a key the same way:

```
>>> d[10]=10
>>> d
{(2, 3): 'a', 10: 10, 1: (2, 3), 'a': 1}
>>> d[10]="a"
>>> d
{(2, 3): 'a', 10: 'a', 1: (2, 3), 'a': 1}
```

The len() function will tell you the number of associations the dictionary contains:

```
>>> d
{(2, 3): 'a', 10: 'a', 1: (2, 3), 'a': 1}
>>> len(d)
4
```

You can use the del statement, del *dictionary[key]*, to remove associations from the dictionary.

```
>>> del d[10]
>>> len(d)
3
>>> d
{(2, 3): 'a', 1: (2, 3), 'a': 1}
```

There are three methods to examine the contents of a dictionary without knowing the keys:

1. Call d.keys() to get a list of all the keys currently in the dictionary.
2. Call d.values() to get a list of all the values.
3. Call d.items() to get a list of all the key-value pairs in d.

The key-value pairs are in (*key,value*) tuples.

```
>>> d
{(2, 3): 'a', 1: (2, 3), 'a': 1}
>>> d.keys()
[(2, 3), 1, 'a']
>>> d.values()
['a', (2, 3), 1]
>>> d.items()
[((2, 3), 'a'), (1, (2, 3)), ('a', 1)]
```

To create a copy of a dictionary, you could create an empty dictionary and then update it from the one you want to copy, for example:

```
>>> e={}
>>> e.update(d)
>>> e
{(2, 3): 'a', 1: (2, 3), 'a': 1}
```

Method call e.update(d) behaves the same as:

```
>>> for k in d.keys(): e[k]=d[k]
```

But it is easier to use the copy() method:

```
e=d.copy()
```

When you copy a dictionary, you get a shallow copy. The dictionary object is copied, but none of the keys or values it contains are. Consider the following example:

```
>>> x={"a":[0]}
>>> y=x.copy()
>>> x is y
0
>>> y["a"][0]=1
>>> x
{'a': [1]}
```

The value associated with key "a" in dictionary x is a list containing a single value, zero. When we copy x, we get a new, different dictionary, y. Dictionaries x and y are not the same, but the lists they contain are, so when we change the list associated with key "a" in dictionary y, that is the same list we see associated with "a" in dictionary x.

Relational operators work on dictionaries the same way as sequences: They do a lexicographical compare. They compare the components in sorted order by key. Expect this to be slow.

```
>>> D1={"x":1,"y":2,"z":3}
>>> D2={"x":1,"y":4,"z":3}
>>> D1==D2
0
>>> D1<D2
1
```

Strings

Strings are a kind of immutable sequence, like tuples. Once the string has been created, you can't change its contents. Unlike tuples, where the elements of the sequence may be of any data type, the elements of a string are characters. You can subscript a string, but you don't get an individual character. Python has no character data type. You get a string of length one containing the character.

The original strings in Python contained byte-sized, Latin character set/ASCII characters. Python2 also provides Unicode character strings. We will assume the original character set in our discussion except where we explicitly discuss Unicode.

String Literals

There are several ways to write string literals. If you are going to write the string on a single line, you can enclose it in single quotes (´), or double quotes (″). This easily allows you to enclose a string containing one kind of quote inside the other kind of quotes, for example:

```
>>> 'He said, "Hi."'
'He said, "Hi."'
```

If you need both kind of quotes, you can write more than one string in a row and let Python concatenate them for you. Here we use three strings in a row:

```
>>> 'He said, "She said,' "'Hi.'" '"'
'He said, "She said,\'Hi.\'"'
```

The output here shows Python's incorporation character, the backslash. The backslash tells Python that the following character is to have a special interpretation within the string. Python's incorporation sequences are shown in Table 2–5.

Table 2–5
Incorporation Character Sequences in String Literals

Sequence	Meaning
\ *end-of-line*	Continues the string literal to the next line, without including a newline character
\\	Includes a backslash character
\'	Includes a single quote
\"	Includes a double quote
\a	Includes an attention signal (beep) character
\b	Includes a backspace character
\e	Includes an escape character
\f	Includes a form feed character
\n	Includes a line feed (newline) character
\t	Includes a tab character
\r	Includes a carriage return character
\v	Includes a vertical tab character
\0	Includes a null character. (Unlike C, Python allows null characters in strings.)
\ooo	Includes the character whose octal code is *oo*.
\xhh	Includes the character whose hexadecimal code is *hh*.
\uhhhh	Only in Unicode strings, incorporates the character whose hexadecimal number in the Unicode character set is *hhhh*.

Suppose you need a string to extend beyond the end of a line. There several ways to do it. You can get Python to continue the statement on the next line and put quoted parts of the string on the separate lines. Since Python understands that unbalanced parentheses require continuing the statement to another line, this will work:

```
>>> ("a"
... "B")
'aB'
```

Python will also continue a statement if the last character on the line is a backslash.

```
>>> "a"\
... "B"
'aB'
```

For that matter, a backslash also works within strings:

```
>>> "a\
... B"
'aB'
```

Python also allows strings to be enclosed in triple quotes, either """ or '''. These strings may extend beyond the end of a line without special handling. However, they include a newline character (octal number 012) for each line boundary they cross:

```
>>> '''a
... B'''
'a\012B'
```

If you do not want a newline character included for the end of a line, put a backslash character at the end of the line:

```
>>> '''a\
... B'''
'aB'
```

Python also allows you to specify raw strings. In a raw string, you get the characters exactly as written. The incorporation character has no special meaning. This is more useful to people using Windows, since backslash is used to separate directories and files on paths, and it would be annoying to have to incorporate each one of them:

```
>>> r"D:\Tests\SayHi.py"
'D:\\Tests\\SayHi.py'
```

One warning: A backslash may not be the last character of a raw string. Python tries to gobble up the following character as part of the string.

You write Unicode string literals by preceding the string with u, e.g., u'ab\u12adyz'. If you concatenate two string literals, one of which is Unicode, the Python compiler merges them into a single Unicode string.

String Operators

The string operators are the same as those that apply to tuples, with one extra operator for string formatting. The operators are shown in Table 2–6.

Table 2–6
String Operators

Operator	Meaning
s+u	Produces a new string which is the concatenation of strings s and u. An ordinary string concatenated with a Unicode string gives a Unicode string result.
n*s s*n	Creates a new string composed of n copies of string s, where n is an integer.
s % t	String formatting–Creates a new string by formatting values in tuple t and inserting them into specified places in string s. We discuss this later in the text.
s % d	String formatting–Creates a new string by formatting values in dictionary d and inserting them into specified places in string s. We discuss this later in the text.
s[i]	Yields a one-character string composed of the character at position i in string s.

Table 2–6
String Operators (Continued)

Operator	Meaning
s[i:j]	Yields a string composed of the characters from position i up to but not including position j in string s.
` e `	Converts the value of expression e into a string. Note: These are back-quotes. Regular quotes are used for string literals.
x_0, x_1, x_2, ..., x_{n-1}=s	Assigns the n one-character substrings of string s from left to right to variables x_0, x_1, x_2,...x_{n-1}.This is just a multiple assignment statement.

String Displays • The equivalent of [...] for lists and (...) for tuples is `...` for strings. The form `x` evaluates expression x and converts its value to a string, for example:

```
>>> a=1;b=2
>>> 'a+b'
'3'
>>> '(a,b)'
'(1, 2)'
```

Sequence Operators • Strings are a kind of sequence, so the sequence operators apply to strings. Expression u+v will concatenate strings u and v. Expression s*n will concatenate n copies of string s.

Slicing will deliver a substring. Expression s[i:j] yields a string composed of the characters from position i up to but not including position j in string s.

Unlike lists and tuples, subscripting, s[i], cannot deliver an individual character. Python does not have characters. Instead, it returns a string consisting of the one character at position i. Expression s[i] is equivalent to s[i:i+1].

String Formatting • String formatting behaves like the formatting strings used in the printf() function in C. String formatting is specified by the s%t operator in Python. The string s to the left of the % is the format. The tuple or dictionary to the right of the % supplies the values to be formatted. Generally, characters in the format string are just copied as is into the result string, but certain special character sequences are replaced with values from the tuple or dictionary. Since tuples and dictionaries behave differently, we will discuss the tuples first and then explain the differences with dictionaries.

Tuples   The formatting sequences are matched left to right with the values in the tuple. Each formatting sequence specifies how to convert the value to a string. The converted value is then inserted into the resulting string, replacing its formatting sequence. For example, the following produces a string with the number 65 translated into octal, decimal, and hexadecimal, the translations separated by colons:

```
>>> "%o:%d:%x" % (65,65,65)
'101:65:41'
```

If there is only one value to be formatted, you needn't include it in a tuple, for example:

```
>>> "|%d|" % 5
'|5|'
```

The formatting sequences have the form:

```
% m f
```

The modifiers, m, are optional. The formatting character, f, tells Python (internally, the C library) what conversion to perform. The formatting characters are

- d—Decimal integer. The corresponding element of the tuple is converted to an integer and the integer is converted to a string in decimal format.
- i—Decimal integer. The same as %d.
- u—Unsigned integer. The same as %d, but the integer is interpreted as unsigned. The sign bit is interpreted as adding a large positive amount to the number, rather than a large negative amount.
- o—Octal integer. The corresponding element of the tuple is converted to an integer and the integer is converted to a string in octal format.
- x—Hexadecimal integer. The corresponding element of the tuple is converted to an integer and the integer is converted to a

string in hexadecimal format. Lowercase x uses lowercase letters for the digits 10 through 15.

```
>>> "%x" % (-2)
'fffffffe'
```

- X—Hexadecimal integer. The corresponding element of the tuple is converted to an integer and the integer is converted to a string in hexadecimal format. Uppercase X uses uppercase letters for the digits 10 through 15.

```
>>> "%X" % (-2)
'FFFFFFFE'
```

- f—Floating point format, with decimal point but without an exponent.

```
>>> "%f" % (0.5e-100)
'0.000000'
```

- e—Floating point format, with decimal point and an exponent (with a lowercase e).

```
>>> "%e" % (0.5e-100)
'5.000000e-101'
```

- E—Floating point format, with decimal point and an exponent (with an uppercase E).

```
>>> "%E" % (0.5e-100)
'5.000000E-101'
```

- g—Choose either f or e, depending on the size of the exponent.
- G—Choose either f or E, depending on the size of the exponent.
- s—String, or any object being converted to a string.

```
>>> "%s" % ([1,2])
'[1, 2]'
```

- r—Like s, but uses `repr()` rather than `str()` to convert the argument (in Python2).
- c—A single character. The value to be converted can either be an integer that is the internal code for a character or a string of length one.

```
>>> "%c" % (88)
'X'
>>> "%c" % ("Y")
'Y'
```

- %—This does not match an element from the tuple. It is the way to incorporate a percent sign into the string.
  The modifiers, if present, have the form

```
a w .p
```

each of which is optional. These parts are as follows:
- a—The alignment; can be a plus sign, a minus sign, or 0, or some combination of them. They mean the following:
  - -: Align the characters at the left in the field
  - +: Include a sign for numeric values, even if positive. (Normally only a negative sign would be included.)
  - 0: Zero-fill the number in the field.
- w—The width; specifies the minimum field width the formatted value is to occupy. This allows nicely aligned output, at least with fixed-width fonts, if the values fit within the field width specified. If they don't fit, they will use all the character positions required.

```
>>> "|%4d|" % 5
'|   5|'
>>> "|%4d|" % 500000
'|500000|'
```

- .p—The precision; follows a decimal point. It has one of three meanings:

1. For strings, the precision specifies the maximum number of characters that may be printed from the string.

```
>>> "|%.3s|" % ("abcdef")
'|abc|'
```

2. For floating point numbers, it specifies the maximum number of digits following the decimal point.

```
>>> "|%.4f|" % (1.0/3.0)
'|0.3333|'
```

3. For integers, the precision specifies the minimum number of digits to represent.

```
>>> "|%4.2d|" % 5
'|  05|'
```

If you want to compute the width or precision, you can use stars, *s, in width or precision fields. The star tells Python to use the next item in the tuple, which must be an integer, as the value in the field, for example:

```
>>> "|%*.*d|" % (4,2,5)
'|  05|'
```

Dictionaries   You can use a dictionary instead of a tuple. You instruct Python what value to format by putting the key string in parentheses just after the opening %, inside the formatting sequence:

```
>>> "|%(x)4.2d|" % {"x":5}
'|  05|'
```

However, this doesn't work for the formatting fields:

```
>>> "|%(x)4.(p)d|" % {"p":2,"x":5}
Traceback (innermost last):
  File "<stdin>", line 1, in ?
ValueError: unsupported format character '(' (0x28)
```

The String Module and String Methods

The string module provides a number of useful functions and constants. In Python2, functions from the string module were made into methods of string objects. Table 2–7 shows the most useful of these functions and methods.

Table 2–7

Most Important String Functions and Methods

String Module	Method (Python2)	Explanation

`find(s,sub)`
`find(s,sub,start)`
`find(s,sub,start,end)`
	`s.find(sub)`
	`s.find(sub,start)`
	`s.find(sub,start,end)`
		Find the index of the first occurrence of `sub` in string `s`. If they are provided, find the first occurrence at or beyond `start` and not extending beyond `end`. Returns minus 1 if it is not found.

`index(s,sub)`
`index(s,sub,start)`
`index(s,sub,start,end)`
	`s.index(,sub)`
	`s.index(sub,start)`
	`s.index(sub,start,end)`
		Find the index of the first occurrence of `sub` in string `s`. If they are provided, find the first occurrence at or beyond `start` and not extending beyond `end`. Raise a `ValueError` exception if it is not found.

`rfind(s,sub)`
`rfind(s,sub,start)`
`rfind(s,sub,start,end)`
	`s.rfind(sub)`
	`s.rfind(sub,start)`
	`s.rfind(sub,start,end)`
		Find the index of the last occurrence of `sub` in string `s`. If they are provided, find the rightmost occurrence lying totally within the range beginning at `start` and not extending beyond `end`. Returns minus 1 if it is not found.

Table 2–7
Most Important String Functions and Methods (Continued)

String Module	Method (Python2)	Explanation

`rindex(s,sub)`
`rindex(s,sub,start)`
`rindex(s,sub,start,end)`
	`s.rindex(,sub)`
	`s.rindex(sub,start)`
	`s.rindex(sub,start,end)`
		Find the index of the last occurrence of `sub` in string `s`. If they are provided, find the rightmost occurrence lying totally within the range beginning at `start` and not extending beyond `end`. Raise a `ValueError` exception if it is not found.

`split(s)`
`split(s,sep)`
`split(s,sep,maxtimes)`
	`s.split()`
	`s.split(sep)`
	`s.split(sep,maxtimes)`
		Return a list of the substrings of `s` separated by string `sep`. If `sep` is `None`, or omitted, return the substrings separated by white space. If `maxtimes` is present, return no more than `maxtimes` substrings followed by the remainder of `s`, if any.

`join(seq)` `join(seq,sep)`	`sep.join(seq)`	Concatenate the strings in list or tuple `seq`. Put `sep` between each pair. Use a single blank if `sep` is omitted.
`lower(s)` `upper(s)`	`s.lower()` `s.upper()`	Return a copy of `s` with all letters converted to lower or uppercase.

`strip(s)`
`lstrip(s)`
`rstrip(s)`
	`s.strip()`
	`s.lstrip()`
	`s.rstrip()`
		Return a copy of `s` with all white space removed from both ends, from the left, or from the right.

Table 2–7
Most Important String Functions and Methods (Continued)

String Module	Method (Python2)	Explanation
ljust(s,w) rjust(s,w) center(s,w)	s.ljust(w) s.rjust(w) s.center(w)	Return a copy of s padded with blanks, left justified, right justified, or centered in a field of width w. Return s itself if it is as long as or longer than w.
expandtabs(s) expandtabs(s,w)	s.expandtabs() s.expandtabs(w)	Return a copy of s with tabs expanded into blanks. The tab stops occur each w characters, eight characters if w is omitted.
	s.endswith(suffix) s.startswith(prefix) s.startswith(prefix,pos)	True if s ends with the suffix, begins with the prefix, or contains prefix starting at position pos.

Built-In String Functions

- chr(i)—Returns the character (in a one-character string), whose ASCII code is integer i. This is equivalent to ("%c" % i).
- eval(s)—Evaluates the string s as if it were a Python expression.

```
>>> eval("[1,2]")
[1, 2]
```

You can also give eval() dictionaries to look up variables in: eval(s,globals) or eval(s, globals, locals):

```
>>> eval("x+y",{"x":1,"y":2},{"x":3})
5
```

- hex(i) —Returns a string representation of integer i converted to hexadecimal representation.

```
>>> hex(65)
'0x41'
```

It is not equivalent to ("%x" % i), which does not put "0x" on the front.

- intern(s) —Returns string s or a copy of the string s. Each call to intern() with an equal string will return the identical string. You use this to speed up compares and to save storage.

Equal strings may be different objects, i.e., both have the same characters, but they were created at different times. It is faster to compare strings for identity (x is y) than for equality (x == y), since Python only has to compare the memory addresses for identity, but must compare the characters in them for equality. Therefore, if you are going to have a set of strings that you are comparing for equality frequently, you can speed up your program by interning them and just comparing their interned values.

```
>>> "ab"=="a"+"b"
1
>>> "ab" is "a"+"b"
0
>>> intern("ab") is intern("a"+"b")
1
```

Moreover, by interning strings that are used throughout your data structures, all instances of the string will occupy the same block of storage, rather than many blocks. This may save considerable storage.

- int(s) —Converts a string to an integer. (It will also convert long integers and floating point numbers to integers.)
- oct(i) —Converts integer i to a string representation of it as an unsigned octal integer.

```
>>> oct(65)
'0101'
>>> oct(-1)
'037777777777'
```

- `ord(c)`—Returns the integer representing the single character in string `c`.
- `repr(x)`—Returns a string representation of object `x`. It is the same as `‘x‘`.
- `str(s)`—Returns a string representation of object `x`. Unlike `repr()`, `str()` does not attempt to be the inverse of `eval()`. It attempts to make the translated string legible.

Summary

In this chapter we looked at elementary Python programming. We examined expressions and simple control statements like `while`, `for`, and `if`. We looked at arithmetic data types, lists, tuples, strings, and dictionaries. We learned a little bit about modules and functions. And we used the interpreter to try out code to see what it would do.

Problems

2.1   Write a function `fib(n)` that will write out the first *n* Fibonacci numbers. Fibonacci numbers form a sequence 1, 1, 2, 3, 5, 8, ... where each number after the first two is the sum of the two numbers preceding it. Use a loop. Use a single assignment statement in the loop. Make sure `fib(100)` works.

2.2   Put your solution to Problem 2.1 into a script. Have the script take the value of *n* from its command line and write out that many Fibonacci numbers. The command line parameters are in variable `argv` in module `sys`. The name of the program being executed is in `argv[0]`. The first parameter is in `argv[1]`.

2.3   Write a script that takes a string as its first command line parameter and file names as the subsequent parameters. Have it write out the names of the files that contain the string. See Problem 2.2 for how to find the command line parameters.

2.4   Write a script that, given a file name, will count the number of words in the file and write out the total. For our purposes, a word is any sequence of non-white-space characters at the beginning of a line, at the end of a line, or surrounded by white space. See Problem 2.2 for how to find the command line parameters.

2.5 Write a script that, given a file name, will count the number of occurrences of each word in the file and write out a sorted list of words with the number of occurrences. For our purposes, a word is any sequence of non-white-space characters at the beginning of a line, at the end of a line, or surrounded by white space. See Problem 2.2 for how to find the command line parameters.

3

More Advanced
Python

Now we will now examine Python's facilities for developing larger programs and systems.

Functions

In Chapter 2, we looked at creating functions using the `def` statement. Actually, we only discussed a simplified version of function definition and call. Python allows you more flexibility than we saw there. Python allows you to define functions with variable-length argument lists and to call functions with keyword parameters. Python also allows you to define default values for parameters that are not included in the call.

In addition, Python provides facilities for functional programming, a style of programming whereby you use a collection of functions to transform the input into the output. The functions take all their inputs from their parameter lists and produce all their output in the values they return, rather than executing statements that make incremental changes in global variables. In a later section, we will look at how to use some of Python's functional programming techniques for simple database-like operations.

Parameters • Recall that the form of a function definition is

```
def fn(parameters):
    body
```

and a call is

```
fn(args)
```

In Chapter 2, we considered only what are called *positional parameters*. There are several other possibilities:

- Defaulted parameters
- Variable-length parameter lists
- Keyword arguments

Defaulted parameters are types of positional parameters, but we will treat them as a separate type. Defaulted parameters have a default value that is specified when the function is created, with the form `parameterName=defaultValue`. They occur at the end of the parameter list. You have to pass arguments for them in the call if the default is fine.

Python allows you to use keyword arguments in a call. You give the name of the parameter and the value you are assigning to it, again using an equal sign: `parameterName=actualValue`. You can supply values to any of the positional and defaulted parameters by name.

Python allows variable-length parameter lists, whereby you can supply any number of additional arguments and additional keyword arguments that don't correspond to named parameters.

Here is a more precise definition of the `def` statement:

```
def fn(positionals,defaulteds,
    *extra_positionals,**extra_keywords):
    body
```

where each of these parameter sections is optional. And here is a more precise form of the function call:

```
fn(positional_args,keyword_args)
```

The main function of these different kinds of parameters and arguments is to make it easier to program around Python's lack of function overloading. Overloading, available in some other programming languages, allows you to declare several functions with the same name. The compiler decides which one to call based on the number and types of parameters. Because Python does not have declared types, overloading could use only the number of parameters, which is not useful enough. These varying kinds of parameters and arguments allow you to write a single function you can call in multiple ways and have the function decide which kind of call you mean.

Since it is difficult to find a practical example that exercises all these features, we will use this contrived example before discussing the actual use of these kinds of parameters and arguments:

```
>>> def fun(w,x=1,*y,**z):
...         print w,x,y,z
...
>>> fun(5,6)
5 6 () {}
>>> fun(5)
5 1 () {}
>>> fun(x=10,w=9)
9 10 () {}
>>> fun(5,p=9,q=10)
5 1 () {'p': 9, 'q': 10}
>>> fun(5,6,7,8,p=9,q=10)
5 6 (7, 8) {'p': 9, 'q': 10}
```

The positional parameters are just names. They must be assigned values by the call. The example has only one strictly positional parameter, w. The defaulted parameters have the form name=expression. The defaulted parameters need not be given values in the call. If they are, they get that value. If they are not, they get the value specified when the function was created. In the example, the call fun(5,6) supplies values to the parameters w and x. The call fun(5) supplies only a value for w; x gets the default value. Default parameters allow you to simplify function calls to supply only the most relevant parameters.

You can assign a value to a parameter by name when you call the function. Just say name=expression. These are called keyword arguments. The call fun(x=10,w=9) assigns w and x values. Notice that you don't have to list them in order.

If you have specified **name at the end of your parameter list, you can call the function with extra keyword arguments. The name is assigned a dictionary containing the extra names and values from the argument list. The call fun(5,p=9,q=10) passes 5 to positional parameter w, defaults x to 1, and creates a dictionary containing p and q for parameter z.

The call fun(5,6,7,8,p=9,q=10) shows both the extra positional and the extra keyword arguments. A parameter of the form *name specifies that the name is to be assigned a tuple containing any positional arguments supplied in the call beyond the number of positional and defaulted parameters declared in the def. In this call, w and x get 5 and 6. Parameter y gets a tuple containing (7,8), and z, as before, gets a dictionary containing the additional keyword arguments.

An extra positional parameter, *name, or an extra keyword parameter, **name, should be the last parameter in the parameter list. If both are present, they must be in order with the * parameter next to last and the ** parameter last.

You use the extra positional parameters for those cases, like the sum function shown in Figure 3–1, where you need to process a sequence of a variable length.[1] The sum() function takes a single, extra-positionals parameter. The call is supposed to be the same as for the built–in functions max() and min(). You can pass either a variable number of numeric parameters which will be summed up, or a single sequence whose elements are to be summed. The built-in function isinstance(x,y) asks whether x is an instance of type y. Here we ask if a single parameter is a list or tuple. If so, we replace L with it so its elements will be summed. Otherwise, we assume that the single parameter is numeric and doesn't require special treatment.

You can use defaulted and extra keyword parameters in the declaration and keyword arguments in the calls when:

- There are too many parameters for a positional parameter list. You wouldn't be able to remember the significance of all the positions.
- A large number of combinations of options is possible. You don't want the user to have to provide meaningless positional arguments that don't apply to the options being used.

```
import types
def sum(*L):
    if len(L)==1 and \
       ( isinstance(L[0],types.ListType) or \
         isinstance(L[0], types.TupleType) ) :
       L=L[0]
    s=0
    for k in L:
       s=s+k
    return s
```

Figure 3–1
Function sum(): Extrapositional Parameters

---

1. An example from the C programming language is the printf() function.

- You have some special cases that should not be exposed to the user of the function. For example, the users of a module may have one interface to a function, whereas other functions in the module can have a different interface. Instead of having separate functions for the internal and external uses, you can have special parameters for internal use.

One thing that may seem strange is that the equals sign has a different precedence in a parameter or argument list than in an assignment statement. In the assignment statement,

```
a,b=c
```

both a and b are being assigned values from c; the comma groups a and b together and the equals sign assigns to the entire group, so equals has lower precedence than comma. In a parameter or argument list,

```
def funct(a,b=c):
```

c assigns only to b; the comma separates the a and the b=c parts; the comma has lower precedence than equals.

When you use defaulted parameters, the default value is computed when the def statement is evaluated, not when the function is called. Consider the following code:

```
>>> y=1
>>> def g(x=y):return x
...
>>> y=2
>>> g()
1
```

When we call g(), we get the default value of x, which was defined to be y. But we get the value of y when the def statement was executed creating the function g, not the value of y when g was called.

Another strange facility in Python is the ability to decompose sequences in a call, the same as in an assignment. Consider the following:

```
>>> def h((u,(v,w)),x):print u,v,w,x
...
>>> h([1,(2,3)],4)
1 2 3 4
>>> h([1,"yz"],4)
1 y z 4
```

If we group a bunch of parameters within parentheses, a single argument must be passed in their position. The argument must be a sequence, i.e., a list, tuple, or string, that could be assigned to the parenthesized group in an assignment statement.

Namespaces • *Namespace* is a metaphor for the set of variables that code can access by name. When functions are executing, there are three namespaces, or places where the function can find the variables it is referring to. These were discussed in Chapter 2 and shown in Figure 2–1. There is the local namespace, a table that was created when the function started running and that will be deleted when the function terminates. There is the global namespace, the namespace of the module in which the function is defined. It exists from when the module is loaded until the program terminates. Then there is the built-in namespace, where Python's built-in functions and variables are defined. It exists for the duration of the program execution. Each namespace has a dictionary of the names defined in it.

We envision these namespaces as being nested. The built-in namespace is the outermost, the module namespace within it, and the function namespace within the module's.

When we're executing code within the function, we are executing within the function's namespace. When the code needs the value of a variable, Python searches the namespaces for it, from the innermost to the outermost, in order. First it looks up the variable's name in the dictionary of the function. If it finds it there, it uses the value it finds. If it doesn't find the name in the function's dictionary, it then looks it up in the module's, and then, if necessary, in the built-in namespace.

When the function assigns a value to a variable, it stores the value with the name in the innermost directory, the function's dictionary.

But what if you need to assign to a shared variable in the module rather than a private one in the function? Recall from Chapter 2 that Python's global statement lets you declare that a name you are using in a function is really a module scope name. The global statement has the form

```
global name1, name2, ...
```

You put the global statement in your function, and Python will not create the names in its list in the local function's dictionary, but rather in the module's dictionary

Documentation Comment • You can include a special comment with a function explaining how it works. This documentation comment is simply a string. You put the string immediately after the def statement as the first thing in the body of the function. For example,

```
>>> def f():
...         "f() returns None, does nothing"
...
```

defines a function that consists solely of a comment. The way to see the comment is to look at the func_doc attribute of the function object:

```
>>> f.func_doc
'f() returns None, does nothing'
```

There is another attribute of the function object that contains the same documentation string, __doc__:

```
>>> f.__doc__
'f() returns None, does nothing'
```

Attribute __doc__ is more general than func_doc because it works for many other kinds of objects as well.

You can examine the documentation of built-in functions from the command line if you want help on using them, for example:

```
>>> print min.__doc__
min(sequence) -> value
min(a, b, c, ...) -> value

With a single sequence argument, return its smallest item.
With two or more arguments, return the smallest argument.
```

You can also get the name of a function with either the __name__ or the func_name attribute.

```
>>> f.__name__
'f'
>>> f.func_name
'f'
```

Note that only a string on the first line of a function is a comment

```
>>> def g():
...      "g() documentation"
...      "g() expression statement"
...
>>> g.__doc__
'g() documentation'
```

Normal program comments begin with # and continue to the end of the line. They aren't statements. They are ignored by Python. For example, in:

```
>>> def g():
... #showing regular comments aren't statements
...      "g() documentation" #documentation comment
...      "g() expression statement" #just an expression
...
>>> g.__doc__
'g() documentation'
```

The comment line following the def statement doesn't become the documentation comment and it doesn't prevent the string in the following statement from becoming the documentation. Similarly the comments on the lines following the strings are ignored.

Assert Statement • The assert statement is a kind of executable comment. It has the form

```
assert expression
```

or

```
assert expression, data
```

The assert statement says that the expression is supposed to be true at this place in the program. The expression is evaluated, and if it is false, it will stop executing the code at that point. It will "raise an exception." We will discuss exceptions later. Unless you make provision for handling the error, your program's execution will terminate with a message. The optional data field can be used to provide extra information for debugging, for example:

```
>>> x=1
>>> assert x==2
Traceback (innermost last):
  File "<stdin>", line 1, in ?
AssertionError
>>> assert x==2, "x is really "+str(x)
Traceback (innermost last):
  File "<stdin>", line 1, in ?
AssertionError: x is really 1
```

Once your code is debugged, you can turn off the `assert` statement tests. The easiest way is to use the `-O` command line option when running Python.

Database-Like Operations Using Functions

Python provides several functions that make it easy to process lists of data in a functional programming style. This style is often a lot easier to write and understand than a bunch of loops.

Python provides a collection of functions that can be used to treat lists (or any sequence) as a kind of small, in-memory database. Given a list, they allow you to construct a new list from it by applying a function to each element, or by selecting out those elements for which a function returns true. They allow you to accumulate a value by applying an operation over all the elements of a list.

We will use two examples. In accompanying figures, we will show how functions may be used to process lists of files. For our in-line examples, we will use a little database composed of name-value pairs kept in a list, `[(name,value),...]`. Here it is:

```
>>> data
[('Weiser', 20000), ('Adams', 1000), ('Walker', 4000),
('Beam', 5000)]
```

We will be using the file `listdb`, shown in Figure 3–2. We import the module with

```
import listdb
```

```
"""Data-base-like list operations"""
def write(x):print x
def sort(x,f=cmp):
    y=x[:]
    y.sort(f)
    return y
def select(i):
    return lambda y,j=i:y[j]
```

Figure 3–2
Listdb.py, Database-Like List Operations

Notice that the module begins with a documentation string, the way a function can.

```
>>> listdb.__doc__
'Data-base-like list operations'
```

Map • Python provides a built-in function, map(), that builds a list of the results of applying a function to every element of a sequence. The form is

```
map(function, sequence)
```

or

```
map(function, sequence0, sequence1, ...)
```

The function write() in listdb just prints out its argument, so we can use it to try out map():

```
>>> map(listdb.write,data)
('Weiser', 20000)
('Adams', 1000)
('Walker', 4000)
('Beam', 5000)
[None, None, None, None]
```

The final list, [None, None, None, None], is the list that the call to map() returns. Function write() returns None, so map() creates a list with one None for every element.

When you provide more than one sequence, Python constructs the ith element of the result list by applying the function to a tuple constructed of the ith elements of all the sequences. Shorter sequences are extended to the length of the longest with None values.

If you use None for a function, map gives you a list of tuples with the ith tuple being composed of the ith elements from the input sequences:

```
>>> map(None, (1,2),(3,4))
[(1, 3), (2, 4)]
```

In our examples of applying these functions to a list of files, we will use the files in the directory shown in Figure 3–3. Here we assign to variable fs a list of files in the current directory. The listdir(d) function in module os gives a list of the names of files in the directory d. We will be looking at module os in much more detail in Chapter 4.

Figure 3–4 shows the results of mapping the function os.stat() on the list of file names. Function stat returns a tuple of information for each file. We will wait until Chapter 4 to explain all the fields.

Lambda • Since map() requires a function to apply to each element of the list, it could be awfully inconvenient to use if you had to write a def statement for every function. So Python makes it easier to put small functions in line. If the body of the function returns only the value of a simple expression, you can use the lambda expression.

The form of the lambda expression is

```
lambda parameterList : expression
```

It behaves somewhat as if it were defined

```
def uniqueName(parameterList):return expression
```

and then uniqueName were used in place of the lambda expression.

```
>>> import os,listdb,stat,operator
>>> fs=os.listdir('.')
>>> fs
['.emacs', '.bash_logout', '.bash_profile', '.bashrc',
'.screenrc', '.xauth', '.bash_history', 'SayHi.py',
'listdb.py', 'listfile.py', 'maxprioque.py', 'myarray.py',
'prioque.py', 'test.py', 'tst.txt', 'listdb.pyc', '.gnome',
'.gnome_private']
```

Figure 3–3
Filename List Returned by os.listdir()

```
>>> stats=map(os.stat,fs)
>>> map(listdb.write,stats)
(33261, 357685, 2053, 1, 504, 504, 333, 972226320, 972226320, 972226320)
(33188, 357697, 2053, 1, 504, 504, 24, 972617808, 972226320, 972226320)
(33188, 357698, 2053, 1, 504, 504, 230, 973614653, 972226320, 972226320)
(33188, 357699, 2053, 1, 504, 504, 124, 973614653, 972226320, 972226320)
(33188, 357700, 2053, 1, 504, 504, 3394, 972226320, 972226320, 972226320)
(16832, 357701, 2053, 2, 504, 500, 4096, 973591322, 972228217, 972228217)
(33152, 357705, 2053, 1, 504, 504, 1525, 973614653, 973200618, 973200618)
(33200, 357666, 2053, 1, 504, 504, 32, 972405736, 972404539, 972578683)
(33204, 357667, 2053, 1, 504, 504, 185, 973614926, 973614239, 973614665)
(33200, 357668, 2053, 1, 504, 504, 107, 972859549, 972312263, 972578683)
(33200, 357669, 2053, 1, 504, 504, 435, 972405736, 972312263, 972578683)
(33200, 357670, 2053, 1, 504, 504, 203, 972405736, 972312263, 972578683)
(33200, 357671, 2053, 1, 504, 504, 550, 972405736, 972312263, 972578683)
(33200, 357672, 2053, 1, 504, 504, 8, 972405736, 972312263, 972578683)
(33200, 357673, 2053, 1, 504, 504, 4, 972517613, 972312263, 972578683)
(33200, 357665, 2053, 1, 504, 504, 647, 973615257, 973614926, 973614926)
(16832, 634048, 2053, 3, 504, 504, 4096, 973591322, 972529250, 972529250)
(16832, 634049, 2053, 2, 504, 504, 4096, 973591322, 972529250, 972529250)
[None, None, None, None, None, None, None, None, None, None, None, None,
None, None, None, None, None, None]
```

Figure 3–4
Mapping os.stat on a List of Files

Selection • Lambda expressions can be used in map() calls to create new lists of selected fields of records. This is called selection. For example, if we wanted a list of the names in the database, we could write:

```
>>> map(lambda x:x[0],data)
['Weiser', 'Adams', 'Walker', 'Beam']
```

Or we could get a list of the values with:

```
>>> map(lambda x:x[1],data)
[20000, 1000, 4000, 5000]
```

The function select() in the listdb module handles this kind of selection without requiring a lambda expression in line. Call select(k) and it will give you a function that extracts the kth component of its argument, for example:

```
>>> map(listdb.select(1),data)
[20000, 1000, 4000, 5000]
```

The code uses tricks that you will often need in writing `lambda` expressions. Consider its code:

```
def select(i):
    return lambda y,j=i:y[j]
```

The first trick is having a function that returns a function: `select()` itself returns a function, the `lambda` expression created in the return statement. When you call `listdb.select(k)`, it is supposed to give you a function that will give you the kth component of any sequence it is applied to.

The second trick is the way the returned function remembers which element it is to return. When you call `select(i)`, you want it to give you a function of one argument, `y`, that gives you the ith element of the sequence, `y`. The way we have written `select()`, it returns a function that takes two arguments. Why couldn't we just have `select()` return `lambda y:y[i]`? The problem is that Python only has three levels of scope. Within the `lambda` expression, if the expression tried to fetch the value of variable `i`, it wouldn't find it. It's not a variable in the `lambda` expression, not a variable in the module, and not a built-in variable. So what we do is use variable `i` in `select()` to initialize the default value for the second parameter, `j`, in the `lambda` expression. When we apply the `lambda` function to a single argument, it can use the default value of `j` to choose which component of its argument to return. (By the way, `lambda  y,i=i:y[i]` would have worked too.)

Because Python is typeless, you can use the same function to extract a value from a table, for example:

```
>>> listdb.select("x")({"x":1,"y":2})
1
```

The module `stat` gives us named indices into the tuple returned by the `os.stat()` function, such as the size, the owner, and the time of last modification. In Figure 3–5, we use the index of the size field to select the sizes of the files.

```
>>> szs=map(listdb.select(stat.ST_SIZE),stats)
>>> szs
[333, 24, 230, 124, 3394, 4096, 1525, 32, 185, 107, 435,
203, 550, 8, 4, 647, 4096, 4096]
```

Figure 3–5
Selecting the File Sizes Out of the Stats.

Python lists have a method to sort the elements of a list. Since it sorts the list in place, changing its contents, it is not in the spirit of functional programming. For functional programming, it should leave the argument list alone and return a new list. We provide a sort() function in the listdb module that does just that. As shown in Figure 3–2, it first assigns variable y a copy of the list, then sorts y in place, and returns y. Will this work if the components of the list are tuples?

```
>>> listdb.sort(data)
[('Adams', 1000), ('Beam', 5000), ('Walker', 4000),
('Weiser', 20000)]
```

Yes, the sort() method compares the tuples by comparing their components, left to right.

What if we want to compare them based on some other field, or some other criterion? We have the function call, sort(sequence,function), that sorts the elements of the sequence according to the ordering of values that function returns when applied to its elements. If we don't specify the comparison function, it defaults to the built-in function cmp().

```
>>> listdb.sort(data,lambda x,y: cmp(x[1],y[1]) )
[('Adams', 1000), ('Walker', 4000), ('Beam', 5000),
('Weiser', 20000)]
```

```
>>> listdb.sort(data,lambda x,y: -cmp(x[1],y[1]) )
[('Weiser', 20000), ('Beam', 5000), ('Walker', 4000),
('Adams', 1000)]
```

Reduce • What if we want to sum up the numbers in a list? Python provides a built-in function that allows us to do it, the reduce() function, which is called in one of two ways: reduce(f,s) or reduce(f,s,init), which return either f(...f(s[0],s[1]), ...s[n-1]) or f(...f(f(init,s[0]), s[1]),...s[n-1]), respectively, where len(s)==n.

To add up a list of numbers, s, you could use reduce(lambda x,y:x+y,s). But rather than writing a lambda expression each time you want an arithmetic operator, you can use function from the operator module. The operator module has a function for each built-in operator. For example, to sum up the numbers in our little database, you could write:

```
>>> reduce(operator.add,szs)
20089
```

Figure 3–6
Using reduce() to Add Up File Sizes

```
>>> import operator
>>> reduce(operator.add,map(listdb.select(1),data))
30000
```

Figure 3–6 adds up the sizes of the files.

Filter • Another thing we often want to do is select a subset of records that meet a certain criterion. The built-in function filter(f,s) creates a new list out of those elements of sequence s for which function f returns true, for example:

```
>>> filter(lambda x: x[1]>2000, data)
[('Weiser', 20000), ('Walker', 4000), ('Beam', 5000)]
```

If you specify None as the function, you get a list of those elements of the sequence that can be considered true, i.e. nonzero:

```
>>> filter(None,(1,0,2,[],[3],'','a'))
(1, 2, [3], 'a')
```

In Linux, files whose names begin with a dot are considered *hidden* files. They are not usually included in file listings. However, os.listdir() does include those files. Figure 3–7 shows the use of filter() to remove the hidden files from the list.

```
>>> vis=filter(lambda x:x[0]!='.',fs)
>>> vis
['SayHi.py', 'listdb.py', 'listfile.py', 'maxprioque.py',
'myarray.py', 'prioque.py', 'test.py', 'tst.txt',
'listdb.pyc']
>>> sortedVis=listdb.sort(vis)
>>> sortedVis
['SayHi.py', 'listdb.py', 'listdb.pyc', 'listfile.py',
'maxprioque.py', 'myarray.py', 'prioque.py', 'test.py',
'tst.txt']
```

Figure 3–7
Filtering and Sorting

Callable • The built-in function `callable()` will return false for any object that cannot be used as a function in a function call, and true for any object that can at least sometimes be used that way. If `callable(f)` is false, `f(...)` will always result in an error. If `callable(f)` is true, `f(...)` may still fail, for example, if the arguments don't match the parameters.

Objects other than functions can be callable. Classes (to be discussed next) are callable: Calling them constructs instances of the class. Instance objects are callable if their class defines (or inherits) the `__call__()` method, as we will see in sections "Special Methods: Operator Declarations" on page 98 and "Object–Oriented Programming" on page 107.

Apply • When you are working with functions, sometimes you have to build a list of function arguments and need to pass them to a function. You can't do this directly, as in

```
args=L+[y,z]
f(args)
```

because that would pass a single argument of type `list` to `f`. Suppose `L` is `[x]`, and we want to call `f(x,y,z)`. The call `f(args)`, alas, gives us `f([x,y,z])`.

Python provides a way to do what we want. The built-in function `apply()` allows us to apply a function to an argument list. The form of a call to `apply()` is:

```
apply(fn, posargs, kwargs)
```

where `fn`, of course, is the function to apply, `posargs` is a sequence of the positional arguments, and `kwargs` is a dictionary containing the keyword arguments. The `kwargs` argument is optional; omit it if there aren't any.

Because the `posargs` can be any sequence, you can use a tuple, a list, or even a string.

In Python2, there is a special form of call to accomplish the same thing as `apply`:

```
fn(*posargs, **kwargs)
```

Classes

Having the right data types makes your programs a lot shorter, easier to write, easier to understand, easier to debug, and easier to extend. Python's class declaration gives you a way to create the new data types you need. Be sure to use classes in your programs.

In Python, you can create objects that have named attributes in which you can store data. You can create your own kinds of such objects. In C these types are called `structs`. In Python, they are called classes. You create the kinds of such objects with the `class` statement. For example, consider the following empty class declaration:

```
>>> class Point:pass
...
```

It creates a `class` object with the name `"Point"` and assigns it to the variable `Point`, just like a `def` statement creates a function object that it assigns to a variable with the same name. We can ask the name of a class by referring to its __name__ attribute:

```
>>> Point.__name__
'Point'
```

The whole purpose of classes is to create objects that are instances of the classes. The class object can be used as a function that generates instances:

```
>>> p=Point()
```

You can test to see if an object is an instance of a class with the `isinstance()` built-in function:

```
>>> isinstance(p,Point)
1
```

The purpose of most instance objects is to contain data in named attributes. However, the class statement doesn't actually declare what attributes the instances have. You have to assign to them explicitly, for example as follows:

```
>>> dir(p)
[]
>>> p.x=1
```

```
>>> p.y=2
>>> dir(p)
['x', 'y']
>>> p.x,p.y
(1, 2)
```

The `dir()` (directory) built-in function can be used to get a list of the attributes of an object. Initially p's list is empty because no attributes have been assigned. We refer to an attribute with the form `object.attribute`. Here we assign to the x and y attributes of the point p. Function `dir()` now tells us that p has the attributes, and we fetch the values.

It would be inconvenient to have to assign values explicitly to every attribute when you create the instance. Fortunately, there's a way around that. You can define a constructor for the class. The constructor is has the name `__init__`. It is a function created by a `def` statement inside the class statement. Here we create a class, `Point3d`, with a constructor that will initialize three instance attributes, x, y, and z.

```
>>> class Point3d:
...     def __init__(self,*pos):
...             if len(pos)!=3 :
...                     self.x=self.y=self.z=0
...             else:
...                     self.x,self.y,self.z=pos
...
```

When `Point3d()` is called, it calls the constructor. The constructor `__init__()` is given the instance that has just been created as its first parameter and the parameters that were passed to `Point3d()` as the rest of its parameters. Here, if we call `Point3d` with no parameters, `__init__()` gets only one parameter, called `self`. The variable parameter list parameter, `pos`, gets a list of length zero.

```
>>> q=Point3d()
>>> q.x,q.y,q.z
(0, 0, 0)
```

But if we pass three parameters to `Point3d`, `self` still gets the instance object and `pos` now gets the three parameters in a list:

```
>>> q=Point3d(1,2,3)
>>> q.x,q.y,q.z
(1, 2, 3)
```

Notice that the only way to access the attributes of an instance is through a reference to the instance, `object.attribute`, so `__init__()` had to use `self.x`, etc. Unlike some other languages with classes, the constructor doesn't get to refer to the attributes of the instance directly by name, but has to use its first parameter.

You can also have attributes in your class object just by assigning to attribute names within the class statement. This creates an attribute that is shared by all instances of the class, but it is not within any of the instances. Consider:

```
>>> class X: y=1
...
>>> X.y
1
>>> p=X()
>>> p.y
1
>>> p.y=2
>>> p.y
2
>>> X.y
1
```

Here we create a class `X` that has a class attribute `y`. We can see `y` when we look in the class object, `X.y`. We can also see it if we look in an instance, `p.y`. But if we assign a new value to `p.y`, `p.y=2`, we create an attribute in the instance, `y`, that hides the attribute with the same name in the class, `X`, but it doesn't change the class attribute, `X.y`.

Methods

You can create methods for a class using `def` statements in the `class` declaration. These have the form:

```
def methodName(self,parameters):body
```

They are called with the form:

```
instance.methodName(arguments)
```

Parameter `self` will be given the reference to the *instance*. The `arguments`, if any, are passed to the `parameters`, if any. Using the parameter name `self` is just a convention. If you are a Java or C++

programmer, you might want call it this. Using its first parameter, the body of the method can use and set the attributes of the instance, call other methods of the instance, and pass the instance to other functions.

Example: Priority Queue • One big use for methods is to create abstract data types, new kinds of objects that have certain operations they can perform. Consider the definition of a priority queue data type contained in Figure 3–8. We will discuss the first three def statements here and the rest along with other special methods in the next section.

What we want is to be able to create instances of a priority queue, insert items into the queue with an associated priority, and get the highest priority item from the queue.

The constructor method, __init__(), creates an attribute, q, that contains a sorted list of the items and their priority. Each item and

```
"""Priority queue
linear list implementation"""
class prioque:
    def __init__(self):
      self.q=[]
    def put(self,prio,item):
      i=0
      while i<len(self.q):
        if self.q[i][0]>prio:
          self.q.insert(i,(prio,item))
          break
        i=i+1
      else:
        self.q.append((prio,item))
    def get(self):
      if len(self.q)>0:
        item=self.q[0]
        del self.q[0]
      else:
        item=(None,None)
      return item
    def __len__(self):
      return len(self.q)
    def __getitem__(self,i):
      return self.q[i]
    def __nonzero__(self):
      return not not self.q
```

Figure 3–8
Priority Queue Module, prioque

its priority will be contained in a tuple, (*priority*, *item*). In this priority queue implementation, the priority will be a number, with the lower number representing the higher priority.

The method call r.put(p,x) will put item x into priority queue r with priority p. Method put() looks through the list q, finds the appropriate place, and inserts the pair (p,x) there.

Method r.get() simply removes and returns the first (*priority*, *item*) pair in r. If the queue is empty, get() returns the pair (None,None).

Calling Methods As Functions • You don't have to use the object.methodName(parameters) form for calling methods. You can call them like functions. Suppose you have the class statement

```
>>> class C:
...        def __init__(self):self.z=0
...        def M(self,x,y):
...                self.z=self.z+x*y
...                print x,y,self.z
...
```

and you have created an instance

```
>>> d=C()
```

Then you can call M either by d.M(s,t) or by C.M(d,s,t). That is, if you use the class name you get the full function, requiring that all its parameters, including self, be passed in the call.

```
>>> d.M(2,2)
2 2 4
>>> C.M(d,1,1)
1 1 5
```

You can assign a method to a variable where it can be used as a function. You can get a function of two parameters for M by writing f=d.M. This will give M with its self parameter already bound to d. This function need only be called for the remaining part of its parameter list. For example:

```
>>> f=d.M
>>> f(3,3)
3 3 14
```

And as you'd expect, f=C.M gives f a function of three parameters, which expects an instance of class C as its first parameter.

Special Methods: Operator Declarations

The best thing about creating your own data type in Python is that you can specify what it should do when used in expressions with the built-in operators, e.g., what it should do when you try to add something to it, or when you try to subscript it. An intuitive collection of operators makes your code shorter and simpler.

"Special methods" allow you to define operators, that is, define how Python's operators will work when applied to instances of classes. Special methods have names that begin and end with two underscores. We have already seen the __init__() method that gets called when an instance of a class is being constructed.

Most operators in Python have one or more special methods associated with them. When an operator is applied to an instance of a class, Python looks up the corresponding special method in the class. You will need to provide special methods for the operators you wish to apply to instances of your class.

Operators in `prioque` • Consider the special methods we provided for our priority queue in Figure 3–8, __len__(), __getitem__(), and __nonzero__(). The first of them, __len__(), is called by built-in function len() when it is applied to an instance of a class. Since our priority queue has a certain number of items in it at any time, length is meaningful, so we define __len__(). It just asks the contained list, q, how long it is.

```
>>> import prioque
>>> r=prioque.prioque()
>>> len(r)
0
>>> r.put(3,"z")
>>> r.put(1,"x")
>>> r.put(2,"y")
>>> len(r)
3
```

Method __getitem__(self,i) corresponds to subscripting. The r[i] operator calls __getitem__(r,i), for example:

```
>>> r[1]
(2, 'y')
```

There is a different special method, __setitem__(), that is called when you are trying to assign a value to the ith position.

The for statement uses __getitem__() when it is asked to iterate over the contents of an instance of a class. It calls __getitem__() with indices 0, 1, 2,..., until it is done. So implementing __getitem__() also gives us the ability to use our priority queues in a for statement, as follows:

```
>>> for s,t in r: print "item %s has priority %d" % (t,s)
...
item x has priority 1
item y has priority 2
item z has priority 3
```

The __nonzero__() method is used by if and while statements to see if an instance of a class should count as true (nonzero) or false (zero). So, for example, we can loop removing item from the priority queue while it is not empty:

```
>>> while r:
...        print r.get()
...
(1, 'x')
(2, 'y')
(3, 'z')
>>> r.get()
(None, None)
```

Table 3–1 lists the special methods that you may define for classes. The methods are called by Python in various contexts. Most of them correspond to operators. There are several groups of these methods.

Some methods potentially apply to all objects. The __init__() method is called when the object is being created. It initializes the attributes of the object. The __del__() method is called by Python's garbage collector when it is about to destroy the object. You can use it to free up system resources, such as closing files, but it is better to release resources explicitly if you know when to. The __del__() method might not be called for a while, not until all references to the object have been overwritten or deleted, and that will tie up resources. Indeed, it may not be called at all, if your program terminates before the garbage collector reclaims it, so don't count on it opening a file and writing its object's contents to disk.

Additionally, it may be difficult to figure out. Consider this example:

```
class SayBye:
    def __init__(self,say,times):
        self.times=times
        self.say=say
    def __del__(self):
        global byeptr
        if self.times>0:
            self.times=self.times-1
            print self.say
            byeptr=self
```

An object is collected when its reference count goes to zero, when there are no more variables referencing it. The SayBye class writes out a message when it is about to be collected, but in addition, it saves a pointer to itself in a global variable so that it no longer should be garbage collected. It restricts the number of times it will do this, to avoid the possibility of an infinite loop. So we test this by creating two SayBye objects, pointing the same variable to each:

```
byeptr = SayBye("A",4)
byeptr = SayBye("B",4)
```

You would expect, if you think about it for a while, that when the "B" object is assigned to byeptr, it will cause the "A" object to almost be collected, executing its __del__() method, but then the "A" object will assign itself to byeptr, causing the __del__() method of "B" to be called, which will assign a reference to "B" to byeptr, causing "A".... So anyway, what does this code write out? This:

```
A
B
A
A
A
```

Can you figure out why? Neither can we.

Method __cmp__() compares an object to another. If you don't provide it, Python compares objects for identity, i.e., do they have the same address?

Python uses method __hash__() when it looks up objects in dictionaries. If two objects are equal, Python should be able to find one of them in the dictionary if it looks up the other one. This means that if they compare equal with __cmp__(), they should have the same hash value computed by __hash__(). Method __hash__() tells Python where to start looking in the dictionary, and if Python doesn't start looking in the same place for both, it may not discover the equal object already present.

Method __nonzero__(), as we have already seen for our priority queues, tells whether an object would be considered true or not. It is used in if and while statements.

Python has two ways to convert objects to strings. One way is supposed to give a Python expression that would evaluate to the object; the other way gives a string for casual use. These are implemented by the __repr__() and __str__() methods, respectively.

A number of the special methods are used to allow objects to mimic sequences or other containers. The method __len__() returns the number of items the container has in it. Methods __getitem__(), __setitem__(), and __delitem__() tell the container to look up, replace, or delete objects they contain. Methods __getslice__(), __setslice__(), and __delslice__() do the same for slices. Strangely, when you use a negative index, __getitem__(self,i), __setitem__(self,i,x), and __delitem__(self,i) will be given the negative index, i, as is, whereas __getslice__(), __setslice__(), and __delslice__(self,i,j) will be given len(self)+i or len(self)+j if i or j is negative.

Methods are available to allow you to override attribute access. Method __getattr__() allows you to compute the value of an attribute. It is only called if Python doesn't find the attribute by the usual means. Method __setattr__() allows you to write something that looks like an attribute assignment but really performs computations. Unfortunately, it overrides the usual way of assigning to attributes, so you have to implement all the real attribute assignments in it using a dictionary operation. Within the __setattr__() method, you cannot write self.name=value for any "normal" attribute name. It would cause infinite recursion. You will have to write self.__dict__[name] = value. However, elsewhere you can write self.name=value and let __setattr__() do the actual assignment for you.

You can get objects to behave like functions by providing a __call__() method. This is quite an important facility. You often want to implement some general behavior that you can parameterize with policies and strategies. These policies and strategies can be provided by functions to call when decisions must be made. For the priority queue, you might want to specify whether the smallest value has the highest priority, or the largest, and whether equal priorities are to be processed FIFO or LIFO. These could all be handled by giving a priority queue object a single function to use to compare the objects it is inserting with ones already there.

The largest class of special methods is associated with the arithmetic operators. There are two special methods for each operator, used depending on whether the object is the left or the right operand. Suppose Python encounters the expression x-y where x and y are both instance objects. Python will call x.__sub__(y) if x has a __sub__() method. If x does not have a __sub__() method, Python will call y.__rsub__(x)—as in reverse sub–if y has such a method. There is a __coerce__() method to handle "mixed mode" expressions. It has subtle interactions with the operator and reverse operator methods. You should probably play it safe and avoid using it.

Table 3–1
Special Methods

Method	Called by/to: Explanation
All Objects	
__init__(self, args)	Object creation, ClassName(args)
__del__(self)	The garbage collection about to destroy the instance, not necessarily when a del statement is applied to the instance
__repr__(self)	repr(x) and `x` convert the object into a string. The string should either be a Python expression that will recreate the object if executed, or a descriptive string such as "<description>" if such an expression is not possible.
__str__(self)	str(x) and print statements: an informal string representation of the object
__cmp__(self,x)	Compare self to object x, self<x yields negative, self==x: 0, self>x: positive

Table 3–1
Special Methods (Continued)

Method	Called by/to: Explanation
__hash__(self)	Compute a hash value when the object is being placed in a dictionary. It is required that if x.__cmp__(y) == 0, then x.__hash__() == y.__hash__(). The hash value tells the dictionary where to start looking for the object. To find an equal object, the dictionary must start looking for the two equal objects in the same place.
__nonzero__(self)	Test whether the object counts as true (nonzero) when used in if and while statements
Container Operations	
__len__(self)	len(): returns the number of objects in a container
__getitem__(self,key)	self[index]: returns the contained item associated with the key
__setitem__(self,key, value)	self[key]=value: assigns a value to the key in the container
__delitem__(self,key)	del self[key]: deletes the item associated with the key from the container
__getslice__(self,i,j)	self[i:j]. Requires __len__(self): negative indices have the length added before being passed in
__setslice__(self,i,j,seq)	self[i:j]=seq. Requires __len__(self): negative indices have the length added before being passed in
__delslice__(self,i,j)	del self[i:j]

Table 3–1
Special Methods (Continued)

Method	Called by/to: Explanation
Attribute Operations	
__getattr__(self,name)	self.name: Called if the name attribute is not found by normal lookup. This allows some attributes to be computed.
__setattr__(self,name, value)	self.name=value. Python calls this if present, rather than doing the normal assignment. If you have this method, you can't use self.name=value to directly assign values to attributes, even within this method. You must use self.__dict__[name]=value.
__delattr__(self,name)	del self.name. It has similar restrictions to __setattr__().
Function Call	
__call__(self, args)	self(args). Built-in function callable() will return true for an instance object if its class has this method.
Arithmetic	
__add__(x,y) __radd__(y,x)	x+y
__sub__(x,y) __rsub(y,x)	x-y
__mul__(x,y) __rmul(y,x)	x*y
__div__(x,y) __rdiv(y,x)	x/y
__mod__(x,y) __rmod(y,x)	x%y
__divmod__(x,y) __rdivmod__(y,x)	divmod(x,y)

Table 3–1
Special Methods (Continued)

Method	Called by/to: Explanation
`__pow__(x,y)` `__rpow(y,x)`	`x**y`, `pow(x,y)`
`__lshift__(x,y)` `__rlshift(y,x)`	`x<<y`
`__rshift__(x,y)` `__rrshift(y,x)`	`x>>y`
`__and__(x,y)` `__rand(y,x)`	`x&y`
`__or__(x,y)` `__ror(y,x)`	`x|y`
`__xor__(x,y)` `__rxor(y,x)`	`x^y`
`__contains__(x,y)`	`y in x`, Python2
`__neg__(self)`	`-self`
`__pos__(self)`	`+self`
`__abs__(self)`	`abs(self)`
`__invert__(self)`	`~ self`
`__int__(self)`, `__long__(self)`, `__float__(self)`, `__complex__(self)`	`int(self)`, `long(self)`, `float(self)`, or in a mixed-mode context, converts to the specified numeric type
`__oct__(self)`, `__hex__(self)`	`oct(self)`, `hex(self)`: to convert to an octal or hexadecimal string representation
`__coerce__(x,y)`	Binary arithmetic operation: Returns a tuple of x and y converted to a common type, or None if the coercions are not possible

Python2 allows certain binary operators to be combined with assignment, so

```
x+=y
```

means

```
x = x + y
```

When the value of x is an instance of a class, Python is willing to look up its __add__() method, do the addition, and store its result back into x. But what if you want to do the update in place? One of the advantages of operate-and-becomes forms is that they allow you to specify changes to objects: x+y properly means "create a new object," whereas x+=y means "change x."

So when the left–hand side of the operate-and-becomes assignment is an instance of a class, Python will first look in the class for a special method to handle precisely that kind of assignment. These methods are shown in Table 3–2. Only if it doesn't find the special operate-and-becomes method will it use the binary operator method. The special method has the same name as the binary operator with an i in front: The += operator translates into a call of the __iadd__() method. The method returns an instance of the same class, which will be assigned back to the variable on the left–hand side. If you are implementing a mutable object, you can just modify its contents and return self. If you are implementing pure values (like strings and numbers, so that you can't change the contents), you can just let it use the binary operator.

Table 3–2
Python2's Combined Operate and Assign

Function	Operator	Function	Operator
__iadd__(x,y)	x+=y	__ipow__(x,y)	x**=y
__isub__(x,y)	x-=y	__ilshift__(x,y)	x<<=y
__imul__(x,y)	x*=y	__irshift__(x,y)	x>>=y
__idiv__(x,y)	x/=y	__iand__(x,y)	x&=y
__imod__(x,y)	x%=y	__ior__(x,y)	x|=y

Object–Oriented Programming

All Python data values are objects, entities with certain operations that can be performed on them. We can declare our own, new classes of objects with `class` statements. This is enough to allow object-based programming.

For object-oriented programming, we need to be able to declare hierarchies of classes related by inheritance. In Python, the syntax of a class declaration with inheritance is:

```
class name(superclass,...):body
```

Consider the class statement:

```
class A(B,C):...
```

This declares class A to be related to classes B and C. A is a subclass of each of B and C. B and C are superclasses of A. It means that A is a kind of a B and a kind of a C, that what we know about B and C will also apply to A, that we will be able to use an A wherever we could use either a B or a C. In the jargon, A inherits from both B and C.

Consider a real-world example: A mallard is a kind of a duck, which is a kind of aquatic bird, which is a kind of bird. What we know about ducks, aquatic birds, and birds should apply to mallards, e.g., feathers, bills, egg-laying....

For objects in a program, two things are important: behavior (what operations they can perform) and state (the data they contain).

Python allows us to define the operations that objects of classes can perform by the `def` statements in the class statement. The data is more implicit: It is set by assignment to the attributes of the instance.

Suppose we create an instance x of the class A defined above,

```
x=A()
```

and we try to perform an operation `op()` on it:

```
x.op()
```

Python will search for the definition of `op()` by first checking if x has an attribute `op` that is a function. If so, this is not really an operation on x, just a call of the function that x contains in its `op` attribute. If x does not have such an attribute, Python checks to see if class A has a method op() defined in it. If not, Python looks to see if class B knows how to do op(). If not, Python looks to see if class C can do op(). Checking classes B and C to see if they can do the operation constitutes inheritance. Class A inherits the operations that B and C have. But by checking first to see if A has a definition of op(), Python allows A to *override* the operations in B and C.

There are a number of ways to use inheritance in your program:

- You can use it to group various classes of interchangeable things; for example, circles, squares, triangles, and other shapes can be treated the same by many operations.
- You can share code among a bunch of classes by inheriting the common code from a superclass.
- You can take working classes and derive modified versions of them, overriding some of the behavior with modified versions of the methods.

Example maxprioque • As an example of creating a subclass definition to get modified behavior, consider maxprioque, whose definition is given in Figure 3–9. The class prioque gave us priority queues such that the lower the numeric value of the priority, the higher its priority was considered to be. This fits with usages such as "first priority," "secondary priority," and such. But what if we want to have a priority queue whereby the higher the numeric value, the higher the priority? Class maxprioque modifies prioque to give us such a priority queue.

```
"""Max Priority queue
(largest priority value is highest priority)
linear list implementation"""
import prioque
class maxprioque(prioque.prioque):
    def __init__(self):
      prioque.prioque.__init__(self)
    def put(self,prio,item):
      prioque.prioque.put(self,-prio,item)
    def get(self):
      p,x=prioque.prioque.get(self)
      return -p,x
    def __getitem__(self,i):
      p,x=prioque.prioque.__getitem__(self,i)
      return -p,x
```

Figure 3–9

maxprioque, Priority Queue with Largest Priority Being Highest

Let's test out `maxprioque`:

```
>>> import maxprioque
>>> r=maxprioque.maxprioque()

>>> r.put(3,"z")
>>> r.put(1,"x")
>>> r.put(2,"y")
>>> len(r)
3
>>> for s,t in r: print "item %s has priority %d" % (t,s)
...
item z has priority 3
item y has priority 2
item x has priority 1
>>> while r:
...        print r.get()
...
(3, 'z')
(2, 'y')
(1, 'x')
>>> len(r)
0
```

As you can see, `maxprioque` behaves the same way as `prioque`, except that the items with the larger priority number are queued in front of those with smaller numbers.

Since `maxprioque` inherits from `prioque`, we expect it to have all the operations of `prioque`, and it does. It has `put()`, `get()`, and `__getitem__()`. These are defined in the `maxprioque`'s code. It has `__len__()` and `__nonzero__()`. These are inherited from `prioque`.

The trick with `maxprioque` is that it simply allows `prioque` to perform all the operations. Class `maxprioque` simply catches some of the operations, those that use the priority, and negates the priority before passing it on to `prioque`, or passing it back from `prioque` to the caller. By negating the priority, the higher *numeric* priority, that `maxprioque` considers to be higher priority, will become the lower *numeric* priority, that `prioque` considers to be higher priority.

Consider the code. Since `maxprioque` is a separate module, it imports `prioque`. To get at the class `prioque` in module `prioque`, it uses the qualified name `prioque.prioque` throughout. (This would be a good place to use `from-import`.)

The initialization code

```
def __init__(self):
    prioque.prioque.__init__(self)
```

passes the job of initialization to `prioque`'s initialization. Why didn't
we say `self.__init__()`? Because that would call our own initialization code again recursively and the program would crash. We looked
up the `__init__()` method of our superclass and told it to initialize
our object. Remember that when we look up a method in the class
object, we get a function that requires all the arguments, including the
object itself (the `self` argument).

The `put()` method simply passes the `put` operation on to the
superclass with the priority negated. The `get()` and `__getitem__()`
methods pass the operation on to the superclass and then pass the result
back to the caller with the priority negated. These also have to find the
method to call in the superclass's class object. Calling a method in a
superclass is called an *up call*.

Methods `__len__()` and `__nonzero__()` are not defined here.
They are inherited from `prioque`. When they are called in a
`maxprioque` object, the methods with those names will be called
directly in `prioque`.

Here are some questions that may have occurred to you:

Why do we provide `__init__()` that just calls `prioque`'s
`__init__()`? Why not just inherit it the way we did with
`__len__()`?

We could have just inherited it. It would work the same in this
case. We wanted to emphasize here that unlike some other object-oriented languages, initialization code is not automatically called by the
constructor for all the classes and superclasses. Only one `__init__()`
method will be called. With multiple inheritance especially, you should
be sure to catch an `__init__()` call and pass it on to all of your superclasses, otherwise some vital initialization may not get done at all.

Why did we pass all operations on to the superclass? For example,
wouldn't it have been more efficient to assign `q=[]` in `__init__()`?
And the same question applies to `__getitem__()`. Why not just do
the operation in line?

Yes, it might be more efficient to put the code directly in
`maxprioque`, but it would have been bad programming practice. It
would mean that we couldn't change our implementation of `prioque`

without having to change our implementation of `maxprioque`, which isn't even in the same module. It would mean that a change of code in one place would break code somewhere else. And would we change the code? If you have studied data structures, you have probably already thought that using a heap in `prioque` would make it a lot more efficient.

Why did we inherit from `prioque` rather than just having an attribute in `maxprioque` that points to a `prioque`? We could pass on the operations the same way we are doing now.

That is a viable solution. It is called delegation, rather than inheritance. It would mean that we would have had to write code for `__len__()` and `__nonzero__()` to pass those operations on as well, but that is not a major problem. An argument against using delegation here is that it loses the documentation that a `maxprioque` is a kind of `prioque`, that it has the same operations and same general kind of behavior and can be used in the same places as a `prioque`.

Scopes of Qualified Names in Instances • To understand how Python finds the meanings of names in class instances, consider the example in Figure 3–10. Here there are five classes: A, B, C, D, and E. A inherits from B and C. B inherits from D. C inherits from D and E. If you

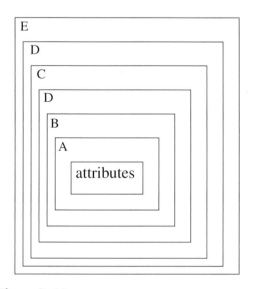

```
class D:...
class E:...
class B(D):...
class C(D,E):...
class A(B,C):...
```

Class declarations.

Class hierarchy.

Figure 3–10
Scopes of Qualified Names

have an instance x of A, e.g., you executed x=A() and you refer to x.n, Python goes looking for the meaning of n as follows:

1. Python looks in the attributes of the object x.
2. Python looks in the directory of class A, the class of object x.
3. Python then looks in the superclasses of A, depth first, left to right. The left-to-right refers to the order in which the superclasses are listed in the declaration. This means:

> a. Python will look in class B, since A listed B before C.
> b. Python will then look in D, because B listed D as a superclass, and Python is searching depth first.
> c. Python will then look in C.
> d. Python will look in D, because C listed D as a superclass first.
> e. Python will look in E, because C listed E second.

The order of search is shown by the nesting of scopes. Python finds the occurrence of name n in the innermost scope. Python will not search all these classes; it will stop as soon as it finds name n in any of the places it is looking.

Notice several things:

- The rules say Python searches D more than once. Any subsequent searches are unnecessary, since if the name is present in D, it will be found the first time Python looks. We're just including D a second time to show what the rule says.
- There is only one scope for the attributes of the object. You may be familiar with object-oriented languages in which the fields (a.k.a. members) of each class are kept individually in the object. There may be several fields with the same name, although the code in a method will be able to see one at most. Python isn't like that. If several classes use the same name for an attribute, they get the identical attribute. This is the same as making all members *virtual* in C++.
- If more than one of the superclasses declares the same method, Python will find only one of them: the first one it comes to in the left-to-right, depth-first search. This allows a method defined in a superclass to override a method defined in a subclass. Suppose a method, n, was defined in both D and C. The search from A would find n in D first, during the depth-first search through B, and it wouldn't even look in C. This is contrary to expectations, at least if you know other object-oriented languages.

Name Mangling • Because all attributes of an instance are in the same table, Python has two problems:

1. *Name collisions*–Several classes may be using the same name for attributes that keep part of their own state. Since they don't agree on what the names mean, methods in one will clobber the data that methods in another class have stored in the attributes.

2. *No private data*–One of the important concepts of object-oriented programming is information hiding, keeping the user of an object from knowing how it is implemented. Information hiding should allow you to make changes in one part of your system without breaking the code in another part. But since all attributes are visible, Python makes it easy for the users of a class instance to examine its state. This invites the user to write code that is dependent on its state.

Python provides a facility to ameliorate these problems, if not quite eliminate them. If you use an identifier beginning with two underscores within a class, Python replaces it with a new identifier including the class name. For example, consider the code:

```
>>> class className:
...     def __init__(self):
...             self.__x=1
...
>>> dir(p)
['_className__x']
>>> p._className__x
1
```

Notice that the new name consists of one underscore, the class name, and the identifier with its two underscores. There are some additional rules, such as Python stripping the initial underscores of the class name, if any; so if you try exotic things with name mangling, you may encounter some difficulties.

Testing Class Membership • Suppose you have some object and you need to find out what kind of object it is. There are several approaches.

Let's suppose we have the classes shown in Figure 3–10, and we create an instance x of class A.

```
>>> x=A()
```

If we ask for the type of x with the built-in function `type()`, we get an indication that it is an instance type.

```
>>> type(x)
<type 'instance'>
```

If we need to process this information internally, rather than just writing it out, we need to import the module `types`. It has an object for each Python type that we can compare to.

```
>>> import types
>>> type(x)==types.InstanceType
1
```

All this does is tell us that we have an instance of some class; it doesn't tell us which one. However, once we know we have an instance, we can access its __class__ attribute that gives us a pointer to its class object. We can compare that to class objects to see which one it is.

```
>>> x.__class__==A
1
```

An exact match for `class` is not always what we want. By the principles of object-oriented programming, subclasses have an *is-a* relationship to superclasses. An instance of a subclass should also be counted as an instance of any of its superclasses. Python provides a built-in function, `isinstance()`, to test this.

```
>>> isinstance(x,A)
1
>>> isinstance(x,D)
1
```

Python says that x is an instance both of A and of D, a superclass of A. Note that D is not a direct superclass of the class of x. It is an ancestor in the class hierarchy. If we create an instance of B, however, Python does not agree that it is a C:

```
>>> y=B()
>>> isinstance(y,C)
0
```

Python also allows you to test the relationships of classes directly. The issubclass() built-in function will test two class objects. The call issubclass(C1, C2) will return true if C1 is the same class as C2 or if C1 is a subclass of C2. It does not require C1 be a direct subclass of C2, merely that C2 be C1 or an ancestor of C1 in the class hierarchy. Testing this:

```
>>> issubclass(A,A)
1
>>> issubclass(A,E)
1
>>> issubclass(E,A)
0
>>> issubclass(B,C)
0
```

Example RestrictedList • To show the uses of inheritance and type testing, consider the problem of designing a kind of *list* that only allows objects of a particular type to be placed in it.

We show our solution to the problem in Figure 3–11. In fact, we have overdesigned our solution to provide both a TypeRestrictedList, a list that may only contain elements of a specified type, and a RestrictedList, a list that allows only the values that pass a test to be inserted. The classes are:

- TypeRestrictedList(*type, optionalinitialvalues*)
  —When you create a TypeRestrictedList, you must provide a type object. All values added to the list are tested to see if they are instances of the type. If they are, they are put in the list. If not, the attempt to add them raises an exception (we will discuss exceptions later). Basically, when you raise an exception, your program jumps out of the code that raised the exception and back to some code to handle the problem. After the type, you can optionally pass in a sequence of values to initialize the list. These values are also tested against the type.
- RestrictedList(*testfn, optionalinitialvalues*) — A RestrictedList is more general than a TypeRestrictedList. When you create a RestrictedList, you give it a function, testfn. RestrictedList calls the testfn for every value you try to put in the list. If testfn returns true, it allows the value in the list. If testfn returns false, it throws an exception.

```
import UserList
class TypeTest:
    def __init__(self,type):
      self.type=type
    def __call__(self,arg):
      if isinstance(arg,self.type):
        return 1
      else: return 0

class RestrictionError(Exception): pass

class RestrictedList(UserList.UserList):
    def __init__(self,testfn,init=[]):
      self.testfn=testfn
      self.testall(init)
      UserList.UserList.__init__(self,init)
    def test(self,x):
      if not self.testfn(x):
        raise RestrictionError(repr(x))
    def testall(self,L):
      for x in L: self.test(x)
      return
    def append(self,x):
      self.test(x)
      UserList.UserList.append(self,x)
    def extend(self,L):
      self.testall(L)
      UserList.UserList.extend(self,L)
    def insert(self,i,x):
      self.test(x)
      UserList.UserList.insert(self,i,x)
    def __setitem__(self,i,x):
      self.test(x)
      UserList.UserList.__setitem__(self,i,x)
    def __setslice__(self,i,j,L):
      self.testall(L)
      UserList.UserList.__setslice__(self,i,j,L)
class TypeRestrictedList(RestrictedList):
    def __init__(self,type,init=[]):
      RestrictedList.__init__( \
        self,TypeTest(type),init)
```

Figure 3–11
RestrictedList

- TypeTest(type)—The TypeTest class creates a function. If you create the function f=TypeTest(T), then f(x) will return true if x is an instance of type T, and false otherwise.

Since this uses the built-in function isinstance(), it will also return true if x is an instance of class T, or some subclass of it.

- RestrictionError(message)–A RestrictionError is the kind of exception raised if the value to be added to a list doesn't pass the test. The message is a string explaining the problem further.

The inheritance hierarchy is this: TypeRestrictedList inherits from RestrictedList, which inherits from UserList. UserList is in the Python library. A built-in list doesn't allow creating subclasses, so UserList was invented to provide that facility. When you create an instance of UserList, it contains a field, data, pointing to a real list. UserList has been written to pass on all list operations to the real list. For our purposes, we wish to override all operations that insert values into the list. Our version will test the value before inserting it.

So RestrictedList contains two methods, test(x) and testall(L), that it uses to see whether x passes the test, or whether all elements in list L pass the test. If a value doesn't pass the test, the test() method raises an exception. The function with which to test the values is saved in the testfn attribute.

RestrictedList overrides all UserList methods that add values to the list: append(), extend(), insert(), __setitem__() and __setslice__(). The form of these methods can be seen in the append() method:

```
def append(self,x):
  self.test(x)
  UserList.UserList.append(self,x)
```

On the attempt to append x to the list, first we check to see if x passes the test. Method call self.test(x) will raise an exception if self.testfn(x) returns false. Assuming x passes the test, we call the append() method in our superclass UserList, to actually perform the operation. Notice the way we call it: We have to specify the class to get the right append() method, and calling it in this way, we are required to pass self explicitly. Here we could have called self.data.append(x). Whether that is preferable is open to debate: It's more efficient, but in principle, we ought not to know how our superclass implements an operation, so we ought to just give it the chance to do its thing its own way.

TypeRestrictedList inherits from RestrictedList. Its only contribution is its initialization code:

```
def __init__(self,type,init=[]):
    RestrictedList.__init__( \
        self,TypeTest(type),init)
```

It creates a TypeTest object to test the type of values being added to the list and calls the initialization code of its superclass, RestrictedList, to install that test. Again, we have to give the superclass's name to get the right initialization code.

The TypeTest class gives us instances that are used as functions. Its work is done by the __call__() method, which is invoked when the instance is called as a function.

Metaprogramming: Analyzing Scopes

What compilers keep in their symbol tables must be available at run-time in interactive languages like Python. Python allows you to get at that information, to examine the state of your program while it is running. This is called *metaprogramming* in Python. Other languages call it *reflection* or *introspection.*

We will show a bit of metaprogramming by way of writing a module, scopes.py, to analyze scopes, particularly the qualified names in instances and classes. It gives a good example of the use of functions type() and isinstance() as well.

First, let's see it in action. When asked to analyze the module abcde.py in Figure 3–12, (based on the example in Figure 3–10), scopes writes out the report in Figure 3–13. When asked to report on class A, it writes out Figure 3–14.

The report on abcde.py shows it is a module and that it has attributes D, E, B, C, and A, and that each of these attributes is a class defined within the module. There are no functions defined by the module.

When asked to report on class A in module abcde, scopes reports on the entire class hierarchy. For A, it shows that has an attribute x with the value 10 and a function (a.k.a. method) m(). Indented beneath A are A's superclasses, B and C. B has nothing in it, but indented beneath it is B's superclass, D. D contains function n(). Class C has two methods, m() and n(). Both of these are overridden by other functions. Function m() is overridden in class A, a subclass, which is proper. Function n(), however, is overridden in class D, which is not a subclass, but which is encountered first in the depth-first search order. The scopes module gives a warning in

```
class E:
    def m():pass
class D:
    def n():pass
class C(D,E):
    def m():pass
    def n():pass
class B(D): pass
class A(B,C):
    def m():pass
    x=10
```

Figure 3–12
Multiple Inheritance Example, abcde.py

this case. Finally, C's superclasses are listed. D has already been encountered. E has one method, which is overridden in A.

The code for scopes is shown in the next several figures. Figure 3–15 shows the entry to the scopes module. Function analyze is called to analyze some object. It checks the object's type. It dispatches to other functions for class instances, modules, and classes. If the object is none of these, analyze() writes out its value and type.

In general, throughout this code, parameter c is the object being analyzed, cs a table of the classes encountered so far, ms a table of the methods encountered so far, and d an integer indicating the depth of nesting, used for indenting. The table cs is used to avoid analyzing a class more than once. Table ms is used to report whether a method is overloaded. Function analyzeFunction is a special case. Parameter m (as in "method") is the function being analyzed. Parameter c is the class it is defined in.

```
Module abcde
  attributes:
    D : class abcde.D
    E : class abcde.E
    B : class abcde.B
    C : class abcde.C
    A : class abcde.A
  functions:
      no functions
```

Figure 3–13
Report on Module abcde

```
Module abcde
 attributes:
   D : class abcde.D
   E : class abcde.E
   B : class abcde.B
   C : class abcde.C
   A : class abcde.A
 functions:
     no functions
class abcde.A
 attributes of class:
 x : 10
 functions:
   m()
  class abcde.B
   attributes of class:
      no class attributes
   functions:
     no functions
    class abcde.D
     attributes of class:
        no class attributes
     functions:
       n()
  class abcde.C
   attributes of class:
      no class attributes
   functions:
     n() overridden in abcde.D , NOT A SUBCLASS
     m() overridden in abcde.A
    class abcde.D  -- already encountered
    class abcde.E
     attributes of class:
        no class attributes
     functions:
       m() overridden in abcde.A
```

Figure 3–14
Report on Module abcde's Class A

Function analyzeInstance, shown in Figure 3–16, analyzes class instances. Given an instance c, it writes out information about c itself and c's class. An instance has a reference to its class in a special, built-in attribute, __class__. First, analyzeInstance writes out the module c's class as defined in, c.__class__.__module__, and the name of the class, c.__class__.__name__. Then it writes out the attributes using another special, built-in attribute, c.__dict__, a

```
#!/usr/bin/python
"""scopes.analyze(x)
where x is module, instance, or class
or execute the command line
   ./scopes module [class1, class2,...]"""
import types,os,string
def analyze(c,cs=None,ms=None,d=0):
    #c - a class or an instance
    #cs - table of classes encountered so far
    #ms - table of methods encountered so far
    #d - how many recursive calls, indentation
    if cs==None: cs={}
    if ms==None: ms={}
    if type(c)==types.InstanceType:
      analyzeInstance(c,cs,ms,d)
      return
    if type(c)==types.ModuleType:
      analyzeModule(c,cs,ms,d)
      return
    if type(c)==types.ClassType:
      analyzeClass(c,cs,ms,d)
      return
    print c,type(c)
    return
```

Figure 3–15
Module Scopes: Main Entry to Analyze Instances, Classes, and Modules

dictionary containing all the normal attributes of the instance. Finally, it goes on to analyze the class.

Function analyzeModule, in Figure 3–17, writes out the information about a module. It simply writes out the documentation com-

```
def analyzeInstance(c,cs,ms,d):
    print "instance of %s.%s" % ( \
      c.__class__.__module__, \
      c.__class__.__name__)
    print " attributes:"
    for a in c.__dict__.items():
      if type(a[1])==types.ClassType:
        print "  ",a[0],": class",a[1]
      else:
        print "  ",a[0],":",a[1]
    analyzeClass(c.__class__,cs,ms,d+1)
    return
```

Figure 3–16
Module Scopes: Analyzing Class Instances

ment of the module followed by the attributes in the dictionary for the module, except those special attributes beginning with "__". Function showdoc() is responsible for writing out the documentation comments of an object. The documentation comment, if any, is kept in the special attribute __doc__ of the module, class, or function.

The function analyzeClass() is shown in Figure 3–18. It writes out the class's module and name. If we have already encountered the class, indicated by the class being in dictionary cs, it will just report that it has already been encountered. Otherwise, it writes the class's documentation comment, attributes, functions, and superclasses. The dictionary c.__dict__ contains all the names defined in the class. For attributes, we are only interested in those that are not functions. So analyzeClass() iterates over c.__dict__, skipping those attributes whose names begin with "__" and those that are functions. You might think that the functions declared in classes should be called methods and should have the type types.MethodType, which is defined inside the types module. But it is only when you use the form instance.function that you get a method object. Inside the class object, the methods are represented by function objects.

For all the attributes other than functions or those beginning with "__", analyzeClass() writes the name and value. To handle the functions, it calls analyzeFunctions().

All the class objects for the superclasses are kept in a tuple stored in the __bases__ attribute. Function analyzeClass() calls itself recursively for each of these.

```
def analyzeModule(c,cs,ms,d):
    print "Module",c.__name__
    showdoc(c,d)
    print " attributes:"
    for a in c.__dict__.items():
      if a[0][0:2]=="__" :
        continue
      if type(a[1])==types.ClassType:
        print "   ",a[0],": class",a[1]
      elif type(a[1])!=types.FunctionType:
        print "   ",a[0],":",a[1]
    print " functions:"
    analyzeFunctions(c,{},d+1)
    return
```

Figure 3–17
Module Scopes: Analyzing Modules

```
def analyzeClass(c,cs,ms,d):
    print "%sclass %s.%s" % (
      "  "*d,c.__module__,
      c.__name__),
    if cs.get(c): #already encountered
      print " -- already encountered"
    else:
      print
      showdoc(c,d)
      cs[c]=c
      print "  "*d,"attributes of class:"
      count=0
      for a in c.__dict__.items():
        if a[0][0:2]=="__" :
          continue
        if type(a[1])==types.FunctionType:
          continue
        count=count+1
        print "  "*d,a[0],":",a[1]
      if count==0:
        print "  "*d,"    no class attributes"
      print "  "*d,"functions:"
      analyzeFunctions(c,ms,d)
      for s in c.__bases__:
        analyzeClass(s,cs,ms,d+1)
    return
```

Figure 3–18
Module Scopes: Analyzing Classes

Function analyzeFunctions(), shown in Figure 3–19, takes a module or class object, c. It iterates over the dictionary looking for the functions. For each function, it calls analyzeFunction() (same figure) to write out a description of the function.

Function analyzeFunction() takes the function to be analyzed in parameter m (mnemonic "method") and the class it is defined in, in parameter c. The function stringargs() produces a parameter list for the function. We ignore whether the function takes an extra positional parameters argument (*L) or an extra keywords argument (**D).

If the function has been overridden, analyzeFunction() reports that. Table ms maps function names into the class in which they are first encountered in a depth-first search through the scopes, i.e., the class whose function definition will be used. If the name is already present, we know that definition overrides the current definition. We also check whether the class where the function is defined is a subclass of the current class. If it isn't, the overriding is not what would be con-

```
def analyzeFunction(m,c,ms,d):
    n=m.__name__
    print "%s    %s(%s)" % (
      "  "*d,n,
      stringargs(m.func_code,m.func_defaults)),
    if ms.get(n):
        print "overridden in %s.%s" % (
          ms[n].__module__,
          ms[n].__name__),
        if not issubclass(ms[n],c):
            print ", NOT A SUBCLASS",
    else:
        ms[n]=c
    print
    showdoc(m,d)
def analyzeFunctions(c,ms,d):
    count=0
    for m in c.__dict__.values() :
        if type(m)!=types.FunctionType:
            continue
        count=count+1
        analyzeFunction(m,c,ms,d)
    if count==0:
        print "  "*d," no functions"
```

Figure 3–19
Module Scopes: Analyzing Functions

sidered proper in many object-oriented languages, so we report the fact. If we haven't encountered the function before, then we remember the current class in ms as the class where the function was first encountered. After the heading for the function, we show the function's documentation string, if it has one.

Figure 3–20 shows three things:

1. The function showdoc() that writes out documentation strings
2. The function stringargs() that produces an argument string for a function
3. Code that will be executed when scopes is called as a script

Function showdoc() takes the object containing the documentation and an indentation depth. It pulls the documentation string out of the object. If it does not exist, i.e., is None, showdoc() just returns. Otherwise, it splits the string up into a list of lines. Function split() in the strings module will split a string into a series of substrings sepa-

```
def showdoc(o,d):
    if not o.__doc__: return
    L=string.split(o.__doc__,os.linesep)
    for s in L:
        print "   "*d,"     ",s

def stringargs(code,defaults):
    if not defaults: defaults=()
    s=""
    nargs=code.co_argcount
    ndflts=len(defaults)
    firstdflt=nargs-ndflts
    for i in range(nargs):
        s=s+ code.co_varnames[i]
        if i>=nargs-ndflts:
            s=s+"="+repr(defaults[i-firstdflt])
        if i<code.co_argcount-1:
            s=s+","
    return s

if __name__=='__main__':
    import sys
    exec 'import '+sys.argv[1]
    exec 'analyze('+sys.argv[1]+')'
    for n in sys.argv[2:]:
        exec 'analyze('+sys.argv[1]+'.'+n+')'
```

Figure 3–20
Module Scopes: Utility Functions and Script

rated by a delimiter. The delimiter we use is the line separator string contained in os.linesep, '\n' for Linux.

The stringargs() function uses a large number of built-in types. To begin with, it is called

```
stringargs(m.func_code,m.func_defaults)
```

where m is a function object. A function object has a special, built-in attribute func_code that points to a code object, containing among other things the compiled, interpretive code for the function. The function object also has a special, built-in attribute func_defaults that contains a tuple of the default values for any defaulted arguments. If there are none, func_defaults contains the value None. We replace None with an empty tuple for later programming convenience.

So stringargs() gets the reference to the function's code object in parameter code, and a reference to the tuple of default values in parameter `defaults`. The code object has two relevant attributes. Attribute `co_argcount` contains the number of positional and defaulted parameters the function takes. Attribute `co_varnames` contains a tuple of the variable names known in the function in the order they were encountered. The parameters are listed first in `co_varnames`, so `code.covarnames[:code.co_argcount]` is a list of the positional and defaulted parameters. Since the defaulted parameters follow the positional parameters, the last `len(defaults)` of the parameter list will have default values. The central loop of `stringargs()` concatenates the parameter names onto a string. As soon as we have gotten to the position of the first defaulted argument, we also put in an `"="` *default value*. We put commas after each parameter other than the last.

We could see if there were more variables in the function and suggest what the extra positional and extra keyword parameters would be if they existed, but we thought that would clutter up the display.

The code for the script will be discussed in the next section, since it uses the `exec` statement.

`eval` **and** `exec`

Python is a scripting language, which means it does not distinguish strongly between a compile time and runtime. Some scripting languages don't have a compile time at all; they interpret the text of their programs while they are running without translating it into any intermediate executable form. Python does compile the textual form of a program into an internal form and then interprets that, but Python is quite happy to do the translation while a program is running, not in a separate compilation before executing begins.

Python allows you to execute string representations of expressions and statements whenever you want to. In this section, we'll look at the ways you can do that.

import Statement • We have already used the `import` statement a lot. The first time it is executed for a particular module, it causes the module it names to be loaded into the Python interpreter and executed. The form, remember, is:

```
import name
```

In the `import` statement, the name cannot be a string. This can cause a problem if you are trying to write some code to help you debug modules, perhaps writing reports on what functions and classes they contain. You want to have your report writer run as a script, taking the name of the module it is supposed to report on in the command line and loading it, but you can't give the string to the import statement.

exec Statement • The `exec` statement allows you to execute Python statements contained in strings. The form of the `exec` statement is

```
exec code
```

where `code` may be a string. The `exec` statement executes the code in the current environment, with access to the current local and global namespaces. Warning: *Never* take a string from the user and just `exec` or `eval` it. It is a security hole. The user, for example, could type in: `os.system('rm -R /')` and delete all your files.

The `exec` statement allows us to get around the problem expressed immediately above. Suppose we want to load and report on a module whose name is in variable m. We could write:

```
exec "import"+m
report(locals()[m])
```

The `exec` statement concatenates two strings to get an `import` statement and then executes it in the current environment. The `import` statement defines the module name as a variable in the local environment. Built-in function `locals()` gives a copy of the local environment as a dictionary. We look up the module's name in that environment and pass it to our routine `report()`, presumably to do the report we want.

We use this trick in the code to execute scopes as a script, shown in Figure 3–20. The code to run scopes as a script uses the built-in variable __name__. When a file is being run as a script, __name__ has the value "__main__". When it's imported as a module, __name__ contains the name of the module. In either case, the code in the file is executed. All the `def`'s create function objects and assign them to their names. The code for the script comes at the end. Protected by an `if` statement, it will be executed only if the file is running as a script.

When run as a script, scopes will take its first command line parameter as the name of a module to analyze and any subsequent names as attributes of the module, e.g., contained classes, that we want analyzed. The argument list of a script is kept in variable `argv` in module `sys`. (The name should be familiar to you if you're a C programmer.) Each element is a string. The first element, `sys.argv[0]`, is the name of the program being executed (a path to the script). The subsequent elements are the command line parameters passed in. We will have a fuller discussion of this when we look at Linux fundamentals in Chapter 4.

Since the import statement takes the module name, not a string containing the module name, we have to construct a string representation of the import statement and execute that:

```
exec 'import '+sys.argv[1]
```

Similarly, our analyze function takes an object, not a string naming an object, so we have to construct a call and execute that:

```
exec 'analyze('+sys.argv[1]+')'
```

Similarly, when we want to look up an attribute of the module to analyze, we again construct and execute the line because we have the module name as a string:

```
exec 'analyze('+sys.argv[1]+'.'+n+')'
```

although we could have looked up the module in a scope directory after importing it, as described above, with either of these:

```
analyze(locals()[sys.argv[1]].__dict__[n])
analyze(globals()[sys.argv[1]].__dict__[n])
```

We can execute more than a single statement at a time by separating them with newline characters in the string:

```
>>> exec "a=1\nb=2"
>>> a,b
(1, 2)
```

You can also execute the contents of a file. Open the file and pass it to the `exec` statement, thus:

```
>>> f=open("SayHi.py")
>>> exec f
Hello
>>> f.close()
```

Recall our SayHi.py example from the last chapter is:

```
#!/usr/bin/python
print 'Hello'
```

execfile() • The built-in function execfile() executes a file. You give it the file name in a string, and it handles opening and closing it. For example,

```
>>> execfile("SayHi.py")
Hello
```

Again, it evaluates the file in the current scopes, as the following shows:

```
>>> f=open("test.py","w")
>>> f.write("a=5\nb=6")
>>> f.close()
>>> a=b=0
>>> a,b
(0, 0)
>>> execfile("test.py")
>>> a,b
(5, 6)
```

eval() • Built-in function eval() evaluates the code for a Python expression and returns its value, for example:

```
>>> eval("3*3+4*4")
25
```

Explicit Scopes • Recall that Python code is always executing in at most three nested scopes. The outermost, built-in scope is fixed. The global scope corresponds to the module the code is running in. For a script or an interactive session, there is a special module named "__main__". Finally, there is an innermost scope. If the code is executing in a function, the local scope contains the parameters and local variables of the function. If the code is executing at the outermost level of a module, the local and global scopes are the same.

You can get dictionaries for the global and local scopes using built-in functions `globals()` and `locals()`, respectively.

When you execute the `exec` statement or call `execfile()` or `eval()`, you can supply environments to use for the global and local scopes. The full forms of these constructs are shown in Table 3–3. The parameters `globals` and `locals` are dictionaries. Variables are looked up in these dictionaries. Any variables assigned values will be placed in the local dictionary.

Table 3–3
Specifying Environments for Code Execution

Current Environment	Explicit, `global` and `local` Identical	Explicit `global` and `local`
`exec code`	`exec code in globals`	`exec code in globals, locals`
`execfile(name)`	`execfile(name,globals)`	`execfile(name,globals, locals)`
`eval(code)`	`eval(code,globals)`	`eval(code,global,locals)`

`compile()` • If you are going to execute the same string or file many times, it is more efficient to compile it first and then use the compiled version. Python allows you to do this. You can call the `compile()` built-in function with the code you are going to use. It will handle all the translation and give you a code object. The code object can then be passed to an `exec` statement or the `eval()` function. Compile has the form:

```
compile(string, whereFrom, kind)
```

where

`string` is the string to compile.

`wherefrom` is a string identifying the source of the string for printing in error trace-backs. You can use `"<string>"`.

`kind` is a string indicating the use of the compiled code:

- `"exec"` says it is going to be used in `exec` statements; therefore, Python should expect to find a sequence of statements.

- "eval" says it is going to be passed to the eval() function; therefore, Python should expect to find an expression.
- "single" says it should be treated as a single statement. If it is an expression, the value it returns will be written out.

The difference between "exec" and "single" kinds of compilation can be seen in the following:

```
>>> exec compile("2*3","<string>","exec")
>>> exec compile("2*3","<string>","single")
6
```

The "exec" form doesn't write out the result. The "single" form does.

Exceptions

When something goes wrong while your program is executing, you need to stop what you're doing, since it doesn't make sense to continue. But rather than having your program crash, it might be preferable to try to recover from the error and do something else.

Python facilitates the handling of runtime errors with its exception mechanism. There are two kinds of exceptions, the old kind with strings representing the exception types and the new kind with classes. We will discuss the new kind first. The old way may eventually be eliminated from the language; you need it only for understanding old programs.

Raising Exceptions • Suppose you have discovered something is wrong while you are executing, e.g., a file you need isn't there. You can "raise an exception" by using the raise statement:

```
raise FileNotPresent
```

where FileNotPresent is an exception class you have declared for this purpose.

When you execute the raise statement, Python immediately jumps to some code that might be able to handle the problem. You create this code with the try statement:

```
try:
    protected code
except FileNotPresent:
    code to handle the problem
```

If you raise the `FileNotPresent` exception while executing the *protected code*, Python will immediately stop executing it and run the *code to handle the problem*. If the protected code executes to completion without raising an exception, then Python skips that code.

The `raise FileNotPresent` statement does not have to be written between the `try` and the `except` statements. It only has to be executed while the protected code is executing. It could be in some function or method called by that code.

There are several variants of the `raise` statement. All are variants of

```
raise className, instance
```

where `instance` is an instance of the named class. That is, if you are passing back a value, it should be an instance of the class you are specifying in the `raise` statement. Another option is simply to specify the instance in the `raise` and let Python figure out its class. Thus

```
raise instance
```

is equivalent to

```
raise instance.__class__, instance
```

You can also provide data that isn't an instance. In this case, Python will construct an instance of the class, passing the data to the class's constructor:

```
raise className, stuff
```

or

```
raise className, (stuff, ...)
```

is translated into

```
raise className, className(stuff,...)
```

Similarly, you can leave out the `stuff` and use the class alone. Python will create the instance, so

```
raise className
```

is equivalent to

```
raise className, className()
```

Example: Restricted Lists • Figure 3–11 gives the code for restricted lists, discussed previously. When a value being placed in the list fails to pass the restriction test, `RestrictedList` and its subclass `TypeRestrictedList` will throw a `RestrictionError`, which is declared as follows:

```
class RestrictionError(Exception): pass
```

It is a subclass of `Exception`, the base type of all the exception and error classes provided by Python. Although it is not currently enforced, Python programmers are encouraged to make their exception classes be subclasses of `Exception`.

There is no code in class `RestrictionError`. It will use the constructor for `Exception`, which takes any number of arguments to be the explanation of the error. It saves them all in the exception object as attribute `args`. You can use them any way you wish in exception handling.

The code uses the `raise instance` form of the raise statement:

```
raise RestrictionError(repr(x))
```

It would have been fine to use either of these forms as well:

```
raise RestrictionError,repr(x)
raise RestrictionError,x
```

Example: CircularQueue • Figure 3–21 and Figure 3–22 show the code for a circular queue. Items are put into the queue with the `put()` method and removed from the queue with the `get()` method. The queue is first-in/first-out. The queue, like a list, can grow and shrink in size, but it has a maximum size that it may not exceed.

The queue is not a list. It lacks most list methods: no `append()`, no `insert()`, and so on. It is called a circular queue because the head and tail positions move cyclically around a list, going from the last position to the first. If you just implement a queue as a list, appending at the end and removing from the beginning, removal

```
""" CircularQueue - fixed size queue """
import sys
class QueueEmptyError(LookupError):pass
class QueueFullError(Exception):pass
class CircularQueue:
    """CircularQueue(n) to create a queue
    holding up to n elements"""
    def __init__(self,size):
      if size<=0: raise ValueError,size
      self.rep=[None]*size
      self.hd=0
      self.size=0
    def put(self,x):
      "Put at end of a CircularQueue: q.put(x)"
      if self.size==len(self.rep):
        raise QueueFullError
      self.rep[(self.hd+self.size)%len(self.rep)]=x
      self.size=self.size+1
    def get(self):
      "Get item from front of a CircularQueue: q.get()"
      if self.size==0:
        raise QueueEmptyError
      x=self.rep[self.hd]
      self.rep[self.hd]=None
      self.hd=(self.hd+1)%len(self.rep)
      self.size=self.size-1
      return x
    def copy(self):
      "Copy of a CircularQueue: q.copy()"
      x=CircularQueue(1)
      x.rep=self.rep[:]
      x.hd=self.hd
      x.size=self.size
      return x
```

Figure 3–21
CircularQueue, Part 1 of 2

from the queue takes time proportional to the number of items in the queue. With a CircularQueue, both insertion and removal are handled in constant time.

The queue has methods __getitem__() and __getslice__(), so you can examine elements with q[i] and q[i:j] and you can iterate over the items with for x in q:. However, you cannot assign to elements or slices.

An attempt to get an item from an empty queue raises the QueueEmptyError, a subclass of the built-in exception

```
      def __getitem__(self,j):
        "Look at i-th item: q[i]"
        i=j
        if i<0: i=i+self.size
        if i<0 or i>=self.size:
          raise IndexError, repr(j)
        return self.rep[(self.hd+i)%len(self.rep)]
      def __getslice__(self,i,j):
        "get elements in range: q[i:j]"
        if j==sys.maxint: j=self.size
        if not (0<=i<=self.size and 0<=j<=self.size):
          raise IndexError,"circularQueue["+\
            str(i)+":"+str(j)+"]"
        if i==j: return []
        L=len(self.rep)
        h=(self.hd+i)%L
        t=(self.hd+j)%L
        print h,t
        if t<=h:
          return self.rep[h:]+self.rep[:t]
        else:
          return self.rep[h:t]
      def __len__(self):
        return self.size
      def __nonzero__(self):
        return self.size!=0
      def __repr__(self):
        j=self.hd+self.size
        if j<=len(self.rep):
          s=self.rep[self.hd:j]
        else:
          s=self.rep[self.hd:]+  \
            self.rep[:j%len(self.rep)]
        return "CircularQueue("+repr(s)+")"
      __str__ = __repr__
```

Figure 3–22
CircularQueue, Part 2 of 2

LookupError, itself a subclass of StandardError, a subclass in turn
of Exception. Why? QueueEmptyError seemed to be the same
kind of error as subscripting out of bounds. An out-of-bounds subscript
raises an IndexError, a built-in subclass of LookupError. It is open
to debate whether it is appropriate to raise the same kinds of errors as
the Python system itself. In favor: It's that kind of error, so it probably
should be handled as the same kind of exception. Opposed: It may be

confusing to throw an error that is a kind of `StandardError`. It might give the false impression that the Python system generated the error.

An attempt to put an item in a full queue will raise a `QueueFullError`. `QueueFullError` is a subclass of `Exception`. None of the more precise built-in exception classes seem to cover the case.

Methods `__getitem__()` and `__getslice__()` raise `IndexError` if they are given an index that is out of range. Again, `IndexError` is built in, and it could be argued that code we write should not be throwing standard errors, that that should be reserved for the Python interpreter; but `IndexError` is precisely the error Python raises for out-of-bounds indices.

In method `__getitem__(self,i)`, if index `i` is negative, we add size (the length of the queue) to it to handle negative indices the same way that lists do. After adding the size, we check to see if the index is out of bounds. In the method `__getslice__(self,i,j)`, negative values of indices `i` and `j` have already had the length of the queue added to them before they are passed in. We do not add it ourselves. If they are negative on arrival, they are out of bounds.

In `RestrictedList`, we inherited from class `UserList`, which provided code for the usual list operations. Why didn't we do that here? Mainly because we are using a different representation. Our queues don't begin at the start of the list. Therefore, the `UserList` operations would not work and we would not be able to reuse any of its code. In fact, we would be forced to implement our own versions of all its operations, just to override the versions that don't work, and we don't need those operations for queues.

`try` Statements • The general form of the `try` statement is

```
try:
    protected code
except clauses
else clause
```

The `try` statement is followed by code that may raise an exception. The `except` clauses begin with `except` statements and contain blocks of statements to be executed if the exception they specify is raised in the protected code. There must be one or more of the `except` clauses. The `else` statement, as usual, has the form:

```
else:
    block
```

The block of statements contained in the `else` will be executed only if control leaves the protected code normally, not by an exception being raised. The `else` clause is optional.

The `except` clauses specify one or more exceptions. They can have any of the forms shown in Table 3–4. As the explanation shows, the except clauses can be thought of as a sequence of `if` statements. Just translate them into the code indicated, with proper indentation, and you should have a representation of what is going on.

There are three basic options for the `except` statement:

1. The `except` with nothing following it but a colon matches all exceptions.

Table 3–4
Forms of except Clauses

except **Statement**	**Loosely Equivalent to**

`except name:`
`    block`
	`if isinstance(exception, name):`
	`    block`
	`else:`

`except name,var:`
`    block`
	`if isinstance(exception, name):`
	`    var=exception`
	`    block`
	`else:`

`except (name1,...):`
`    block`
	`if isinstance(exception,name1) or \`
	`    isinstance(exception,name2) or \`
	`        ...:`
	`    block`
	`else:`

`except (name1,...),var:`
`    block`
	`if isinstance(exception, name1) or\`
	`    isinstance(exception, name2)   or\`
	`        ...:`
	`    var=exception`
	`    block`
	`else:`

`except:`
`    block`
	`if 1 :`
	`    block`
	`else:`

`#end of excepts`	`raise #pass exception back`

2. Otherwise the `except` may list one class or more than one class. If it lists more than one, they must be in parentheses. The `except` will match any of the classes named in its list. Moreover, a class name will match an exception of its own class or of any descendant class.

3. The `except` statement may optionally specify a variable. If it does, the variable will be assigned the instance of the exception class that was specified in the `raise` statement.

Since Python examines the `except` clauses in order from top to bottom, if you specify the same class more than once, Python will select the first occurrence; so there's no point in listing the same class more than once. Nor should you list a subclass after its superclass. The super-class will match everything the subclass will. If you use an `except` without any names in its list, naturally you should put it last. It will match all exceptions, so there is no possibility of matching any subsequent `except` clause.

Python has a number of built-in exception *classes*. For example, Python has an exception class `ArithmeticError`, which is a superclass of `OverflowError`, `ZeroDivisionError`, and `FloatingPointError`.

If you want to test for a particular type of arithmetic error, you can; but if you want to catch any of them, you can write:

```
except ArithmeticError: ...
```

What happens if none of the `except` clauses match the exception? It passes right on through the `try` statement and tries to find another surrounding `try` to handle it. Python keeps a stack of active `try` statements. It pushes a `try` statement on the stack when it enters the `try` and pops it off the stack when it leaves the `try` statement. When an exception is raised, Python first pops the top `try` statement off the stack and tries to match the exception to any of its `except` clauses. If none match, Python pops the second `try` statement off the stack and tries to match it, and so on until an `except` clause matches or the stack is empty. If the stack is empty, then Python prints out an error message of the kind we have been seeing in these chapters.

If you do catch an exception in an `except` statement and then decide you want to pass it on to a surrounding `try`, you have a couple of options:

```
except name,v:
    raise name,v
```

or

```
except name,v:
    raise
```

The first is obvious: Just raise it anew. However, it is possible to get a traceback to where an exception was raised (Python prints this out for uncaught exceptions). By raising a new exception, the next handler no longer has that information.

The second form just re-raises the exception, preserving its traceback and letting it propagate to the next `try` statement.

The code in Table 3–4 specifies that the end of the except clauses corresponds to `else: raise`. This says that an uncaught exception propagates through.

Example: UnboundedQueue • As an example of how you can catch exceptions and recover from errors, consider the UnboundedQueue class shown in Figure 3–23. A problem with the CircularQueue class (Figure 3–21 and Figure 3–22) is that it has a fixed maximum capacity. If you exceed the capacity, it raises a QueueFullError. What if we don't know how many items we are going to have in the queue? We could allocate a huge circular queue, much larger than the maximum number of items we would ever expect to have in it. Problem: This wastes space and it still could fail.

A solution is a queue that grows as needed. The UnboundedQueue does this. It contains an attribute q, a CircularQueue, that does the actual work of enqueueing items. UnboundedQueue provides all the methods that CircularQueue does. Almost all of these are just passed on to q. The relevant exception is put(). The put() method calls self.q.put(x), which will raise an exception if the CircularQueue, q, is full. So UnboundedQueue protects the self.q.put(x) call in a try statement. If it fails, UnboundedQueue allocates another CircularQueue twice as large, copies the contents of q into it, puts the value x at the end, and replaces attribute q with the new queue.

```
""" UnboundedQueue - unlimited size queue """
import CircularQueue,string
class UnboundedQueue:
    """UnboundedQueue(n) to create a queue
    holding up to n elements"""
    def __init__(self,size):
      self.q=CircularQueue.CircularQueue(size)
    def put(self,x):
      "Put at end of a UnboundedQueue: q.put(x)"
      try:
        self.q.put(x)
      except CircularQueue.QueueFullError:
        p=CircularQueue.CircularQueue(2*len(self.q))
        for y in self.q:
          p.put(y)
        p.put(x)
        self.q=p
    def get(self):
      "Get item from front of a UnboundedQueue: q.get()"
      return self.q.get()
    def copy(self):
      "Copy of a UnboundedQueue: q.copy()"
      y=self.q.copy()
      x=UnboundedQueue(1)
      x.q=y
      return x
    def __getitem__(self,i):
      "Look at i-th item: q[i]"
      return self.q.__getitem__(i)
    def __getslice__(self,i,j):
      "get elements in range: q[i:j]"
      return self.q.__getslice__(i,j)
    def __len__(self):
      return len(self.q)
    def __nonzero__(self):
      return self.q.__nonzero__()
    def __repr__(self):
      s=repr(self.q)
      s=s[string.find(s,'('):]
      return "UnboundedQueue"+s
    __str__ = __repr__
```

Figure 3–23
Unbounded Queue

String Exception Types • The older version of exceptions used strings rather than classes to represent the exception types. For example, you might write:

```
raise FileNotPresent
```

where you have previously assigned

```
FileNotPresent = "File not present"
```

The forms of the raise statement are the same:

```
raise name
```

and

```
raise name, value
```

In both cases the `name` is a variable whose value is used to select which `except` clause to execute. The `value`, if present, allows you to provide more information about what causes the exception.

The exception types in the `except` clauses are variables with string values, not classes. The test for a matching value is by the `is` operator, not by `==`. Only the identical string object will match. Even strings with the identical characters will probably not be the identical string. That is why names are used, rather than literal values or expressions, in `raise` and `except` statements. You should use the same variable to be sure it has the same value. Most likely the variable will be a qualified name, `module.name`. You will use a single variable in a single module to represent a single type of exception.

try-finally • There is another form of the `try` statement that doesn't catch exceptions. It is used for releasing resources when control leaves a section of code. It has the form:

```
try:
    code
finally:
    finally-block
```

The `code` will be executed. No matter how it terminates, when control leaves the code, the `finally-block` of `code` will be executed. A common example of where this is used is:

```
f=open("filename")
try:
    use file f
finally:
    f.close()
```

The `finally` clause guarantees that the file will be properly closed, no matter how control leaves the `try` statement.

Summary

In this chapter we have discussed some of the more complex features of Python, in particular, classes, operator definitions, object-oriented programming, and exceptions.

Problems

3.1 There is a class, `UserDict`, that is to dictionaries as `UserList` is to lists. Use `UserDict` to provide `RestrictedDict` and `TypeRestrictedDict` classes. You will have to design them yourself. Make them able to restrict the keys or the values (or both) that can be placed in the dictionary.

3.2 Implement an improved version of `prioque`:
   a. Use the `bisect` module to help with insertion.
   b. Raise an exception on attempts to remove an item from an empty queue.
   c. Provide a `head()` method to allow you to look at the first item without removing it.
   d. [If you're using Python2] Make "+=" a synonym for `put()`.

3.3 Using the functional programming operations, write code to produce a list of all files in the immediate subdirectories of the current directory. (See "Database-Like Operations Using Functions" on page 85.) Function `os.path.isdir(filenamepath)` returns true if the file indicated by the string `filenamepath` is a directory.

3.4 Write a function `which(c,n)` that will tell you the name and module's name of the class, x, that defines the name n that class c inherits.

3.5 Design and implement a new container data type, `SinglesList`, with the property that no two items in the list may be equal. Attempts to insert a new item equal to an item already in the list will not insert the new item, but you need to do something reasonable. For example, perhaps an attempt to insert a duplicate item at a particular position should move the item already in the list to that position. And then, what should __setitem__() do?

4

Introduction to GNU/Linux

We will now examine the facilities provided by the Linux operating system. Since Linux behaves like Unix, this introduction is generally applicable to both. We assume:

- You are getting in via a terminal session, typing commands to a shell program. This is the normal way to administer remote systems. If you are using a graphical desktop, the advice here is for what to type into xterm windows.
- You are using the `bash` shell ("Bourne-Again SHell"). The shell is the program that you type commands to. We will show `bash` commands and how to set and use environment variables in it.
- Python is installed on the Linux machine, of course. For the Linux (Unix) operating system commands, we will show both the `bash` and the Python versions.

There are a lot of commands available in the shell, and these have a lot of options. We will neither mention all the commands available nor all the options of the commands we discuss. If you need information about a command, type to your shell program:

```
man commandName
```

If you don't know which commands are relevant to what you want to do, type

```
man -k keyword | more
```

and type space and enter to move down the document and q to quit.

Linux Basics

Linux provides four major things:

1. Concurrent use by multiple users
2. A file system
3. Processes, programs that can execute concurrently, overlapped in time
4. Protection of the users from each other combined with an ability to share files and work together

The Linux system comes with a number of programs that you can use. These run mostly as processes. Among the most useful are text editors, shells (programs that obey your typed commands to run other programs), and utility programs that give you access to the underlying system. We will discuss several of these in this chapter, describing the facilities provided by Linux and showing how to access these facilities through the bash shell and Python.

We will give a bit of an overview before going into details.

File System • The Linux file system is generally tree-structured. There are two major kinds of files: ordinary files and directories. The ordinary files contain text, data, and executable programs. The directories map file names into files.

There is a single root directory in the file system. Unlike MS Windows, different disks do not have their own separate roots. They are all included in a single overall tree. When they are "mounted," they are placed in directories in the file system.

You specify a *path* to a file, which can go through a number of intermediate directories. For example, the path /home/wpl/SayHi.py says to start at the root directory (the initial "/" says that), look up the directory "home," look up the directory "wpl" in it, and look up the file "SayHi.py" in that. A path that begins with "/" is called an *absolute* path. The bash shell also handles a special form of path, beginning with a "~userid." When it sees such a path, it replaces the ~username with the absolute path to the home directory of the user with that login name. This form only works when you are running the shell. It will not work from Python.

Every process that is executing has a current directory associated with it. When you are typing commands to Linux, you are actually typing them to a shell process, so you are using the shell's current working directory. You can use a *relative* path, which starts at the current working directory. Simply leave off the initial "/". Suppose we log in as user wpl and wpl's home directory is /home/wpl. Unless and until we change our working directory, our relative paths will begin from directory /home/wpl. So if we specify the file name `SayHi.py`, we are really specifying the same thing as the absolute path `/home/wpl/SayHi.py`.

These paths are summarized in Table 4–1.

As we said, the file system is *generally* tree-structured; there are a few exceptions. It is possible to have an ordinary file in more than one directory. Since ordinary files are the leaves of the tree, this means the leaves can be shared. But a directory cannot itself be in more than one directory. There are no directed cycles in the file system. If, for example, you want to list all the files in a directory and its subdirectories, and theirs, etc., you can safely write a recursive function to do it. You won't get into an infinite loop, since the directories are tree-structured. It is also important to Linux. Linux keeps track of the number of directories that link to a file. When a file is removed from its last directory, the count goes to zero and the file is removed from the system. Cycles of directories would keep the link counts from going to zero and prevent the cycle from being collected when it becomes inaccessible.

Table 4–1
Forms of Paths

Form of Path	Meaning
`/dir/.../basefilename`	Absolute path from root of the file system. Handled by Linux.
`dir/.../basefilename`	Relative path, from the current directory of this process. Handled by Linux.
`~username/dir/.../basefilename`	Path from the login directory of the account with login name `username`; bash **only**; *not handled by Linux itself.*
`...${id}...`	Include the string value of the environment variable at this point in the path (see "Environment variables in bash" on page 212); bash **only**; *not handled by Linux itself.*

There are a few other file types. For example, there are special files that correspond to things like I/O devices, and there are symbolic links. The symbolic links allow the semblance of cycles in the directory graph. Specially marked symbolic link files contain an absolute path to another file or directory. When the system is searching a path, it can follow a symbolic link by extracting the absolute path it contains, following that path, and continuing from there. A symbolic link can be broken (invalidated) if files are removed or renamed along the absolute path.

Symbolic links give you all the advantages and disadvantages of cycles in the file system without disrupting Linux's reference count garbage collection of files.

Processes • A process is an executing program. When you log into Linux, a process is created that runs a shell program. The customary shell used by Linux is bash, which stands for Bourne-Again SHell, a derivative of an earlier Bourne shell developed for Unix. Other shells are available as well, but we will stick to describing bash.

How does Linux know which shell to use? Actually, there is a process running that listens for logins. When you log in, it looks you up in the password file. The password file contains information about you including, among other things, a path to the shell to use and a path to your home directory. Linux uses the information in the password file to initialize your shell process.

The way one process creates another in Linux is by *forking*. The fork system call tells Linux to create a copy of the process that executes it. The process that executes the fork becomes the parent, and the copy becomes the child process. Linux copies everything about the parent, with a few tiny exceptions. Linux copies the contents of the parent's memory. Linux copies its list of open files (so now they are open in both the parent and the child). Linux copies information about the identity of the user that the process is running for. The differences? For example, for every process Linux keeps track of its *process id*, a positive integer, and its parent's process id. These are, of course, different in the child.

System commands return values, like function calls. The fork command is weird. One process calls it, but it returns in two processes. In the parent, it returns the process id of the child. In the child, it returns zero. This is how your program will know whether it is the parent or the child.

So after the fork, you have two processes running the same program. To have the child execute a different program, you have it issue some version of the Linux exec command. The exec commands replace the currently running program with a new program loaded from disk. All data memory is also replaced except for a few parameters and environment variables that are being passed.

In `bash`, you create and run a child process by giving a path to its program file and some command line parameters. The customary form is:

```
command options arguments
```

where `command` is a path to the program file and the command line parameters are divided into options (typically, letters or identifiers preceded by hyphens) and arguments (typically, paths to other files). The only essential part is the command. It is up to the program itself to make sense of the options and arguments.

Generally, the shell runs the commands as subroutines. After creating the child process, it waits for the child to terminate before continuing to read and execute commands. There are ways to run the subprocesses concurrently, which we will discuss later.

As a convenience, the shell doesn't force you to specify the entire path to the program file to run. The shell keeps a search path, a list of paths to directories. When you specify a file name as a command, the shell will look in each of the directories in its search path until it finds the file with that name. So, you should be able to run Python interactively just by typing

```
python
```

or run a Python program SayHi.py in your directory by typing:

```
python SayHi.py
```

Suppose the program SayHi.py is the following:

```
#!/usr/bin/python
print 'Hello'
```

Suppose further that file SayHi.py has "execute permission" (which we'll discuss later), and the Python interpreter is in directory `/usr/bin`. Then we can run the program from `bash` by typing

```
./SayHi.py
```

Here the "`./`" tells `bash` to look for the file "SayHi.py" in the current directory. Since SayHi.py does not have the format of a directly executable program file, bash considers whether it might be a script. The first line is a kind of script comment (it begins with a "#"). The comment #!/usr/bin/python tells bash to execute the program that path /usr/bin/python leads to and pass it the rest of the file as its input.

You can also put shell commands in a file, set its execute permissions, and execute it like a program. If the file contains shell commands, you do not have to put in the #!path initial comment. The bash shell will assume the file contains bash commands unless told otherwise.

Protection • The Linux system allows many user accounts. Some of these belong to human users of the system. Others exist for system or networking processes. There is precisely one user, the *superuser*, to whom all things are permitted. All other users are restricted in what operations they may perform and which files they may access.

Externally, users are identified by name. Inside the system, they are identified by integers. Linux users belong to groups, with each user potentially belonging to several groups. The groups are also identified by integers internally.

The system keeps a collection of attributes for a process that can only be changed by system calls. These identify processes and the users they belong to. The attributes are used to determine if a process has the right to access some file or execute certain system commands.

When a user logs in, he or she is given a shell process whose attributes identify the user and the primary group the user belongs to.

A file identifies who owns it and what group of users it is associated with. Files have three fields of protection codes:

1. *Owner,* that gives permission for the file's owner
2. *Group,* that gives permissions for the other members of the group the file is associated with
3. *Other,* that gives permissions for everyone else

When a process tries to access a file, the process's user and group are compared to those of the file. The permissions are determined by the first of the following rules that apply:

- If the user of the process is the superuser, it can do whatever it wishes to the file.
- If the user attribute of the process is the same as the user attribute of the file, the file's *user* permissions determine if the access is permitted.

- If the group attribute of the process matches the group attribute of the file, the *group* permissions determine if the access is permitted.
- Otherwise, the *other* permissions are used.

The permission fields specify permission to read, permission to write, and permission to execute the file. Read and write permissions are obvious. Execute permission gives the right to execute a program. For directories, execute permission gives the right to include the directory on a search path.

Communicating with Processes • Processes communicate with each other and the world mostly through open files. Among the attributes of a process is an array of *file descriptors*. When a process opens a file, it allocates a file descriptor. When it closes the file, the file descriptor again becomes available.

Processes are typically run with three file descriptors already allocated to the standard input, standard output, and standard error files.

When you fork off a child process, you can arrange to provide it with its standard input from a file you have written. You can arrange to have it write its output to a file you will read. You can supply its input or read its output while you both are running by using pipes or FIFOs (both are buffers that allow one process to write bytes in and another to read bytes out concurrently). You can have it read, write, or modify some particular named files.

There are a few other communication mechanisms as well. When a process terminates, it provides a status code (one byte) to its parent. By convention, a status of zero means the child process was successful, and nonzero means an error occurred. The status can be used in any way you wish.

There are also signals, interrupts that can be sent from one process to another, or from the kernel to a process. Normally they kill the process, although you can try to catch them or turn them off. It's best not to try to use them.

File System

The file system keeps information about files in *inodes*. A disk contains an array of inodes. Internally, a file is identified by the index of its inode.

If you want to examine the information that the system keeps in inodes, you can use the `stat` command. Here we show the results of `stat` on a text file, `listdb.py`, in Figure 4–1.

```
[wpl@tclinux wpl]$ stat listdb.py
  File: "listdb.py"
  Size: 283          Filetype: Regular File
  Mode: (0664/-rw-rw-r--)   Uid: (  504/ wpl)  Gid: (  504/ books)
Device:  8,5   Inode: 357667     Links: 1
Access: Mon Oct 23 14:17:28 2000(00000.20:59:50)
Modify: Mon Oct 23 09:44:23 2000(00001.01:32:55)
Change: Mon Oct 23 09:44:23 2000(00001.01:32:55)
```

Figure 4–1
Output of a stat Command

The stat program just executes the stat system call and formats its results for us. Stat tells us that the file is a regular file, as opposed, for example, to a directory. Its size is 283 bytes. The mode tells us the file's permissions, both as an octal number, 0664, and written out. The "-rw-rw-r--" form is broken into the four fields -, rw-, rw-, and r--, which correspond to the file type, the user (owner) permissions, group permissions, and other–everybody else's–permissions.

- The rightmost three bits, octal digit 4, "r--", say that others have the right to read the file, but not write to or execute it.
- The middle three bits give permission to other members of the group to read or write to the file: 6 or "rw-".
- The third octal digit from the right gives permission to the owner to read or write.

You will sometimes have to put permission bits together, for example, when examining or setting permission bits in Python. Table 4–2 lists the octal values of the permission bits. You can just add or *OR* together those you want. (If you have difficulty *OR*ing together octal numbers, just pretend they're decimal and add.)

The owner is shown in the Uid field and the group in Gid. These fields show both the numbers (contained in the inode) and the text versions.

Table 4–2
Permission Bits

	Read	Write	Execute
User	0400	0200	0100
Group	0040	0020	0010
Other	0004	0002	0001

You don't need to worry about the device in this book, or the inode number. The number of links indicates how many directories link to the file. The times have these meanings:

- Access: The last time the file was read
- Modify: The last time the contents of the file were modified, i.e., written
- Change: The last time the file's status changed, almost anything except the file being read

Although the stat command lists the file name along with information from its inode, the inode itself doesn't contain the file's name. Naming of files is totally the responsibility of directories, and the same text file can be in several directories, even several times in the same directory, under different names.

The following shows how the stat command handles a directory. The "." refers to the current directory:

```
[wpl@tclinux wpl]$ stat .
  File: "."
  Size: 4096           Filetype: Directory
  Mode: (0700/drwx------)    Uid: (  504/ wpl)  Gid:(  504/  books)
Device:  8,5    Inode: 357684    Links: 3
Access: Wed Oct 25 18:47:32 2000(00000.00:00:35)
Modify: Wed Oct 25 18:47:46 2000(00000.00:00:21)
Change: Wed Oct 25 18:47:46 2000(00000.00:00:21)
```

Notice that the initial letter of the mode is "d" for a directory.

Text Files in bash

Linux includes a lot of programs you can call from the shell to handle text files. We'll look at some of them here.

wc • The word count command will tell you the number of lines, words, and characters in one or more text files, for example:

```
[wpl@tclinux wpl]$ wc *
      1       3        32 SayHi.py
     14      25       283 listdb.py
      5      31      1031 listdb.pyc
      7      11       107 listfile.py
     15      32       435 maxprioque.py
     17      23       203 myarray.py
     27      47       550 prioque.py
      1       2         8 test.py
      0       1         4 tst.txt
     87     175      2653 total
```

The * is a file name pattern. When you use a file name pattern in a shell command, the shell replaces it with all the file names that match the pattern. A * in a pattern will match any number of characters, so the single star is replaced with all file names from the current directory that refer to files that aren't "hidden."

trick • If you have a process that is supposed to write a file, you can run it in the background—we'll discuss how later—and watch its progress by running the `wc` program on the file every so often. If the counts don't increase for a while, you may suspect something has gone wrong.

echo • The `echo` command simply writes out its line, all its options and arguments. However, it is executed after the shell does file name expansion, so we can use it to see what a file name pattern expands into.

```
[wpl@tclinux wpl]$ echo *
SayHi.py listdb.py listdb.pyc listfile.py maxprioque.py
myarray.py prioque.py test.py tst.txt
```

File Name Patterns • The bash shell (and the other shells) allows you to use patterns to specify sets of files. This is called globbing. In a file name pattern, most characters match themselves: A character in the pattern must match the same character in a file name. Special characters or character sequences have special meanings, as shown in Table 4–3. These special pattern elements are called wildcards, after those cards in card games that can be used as equivalent to other cards.

Table 4–3
Example File Name Pattern Elements in `bash`

Wildcard	Matches
*	Any sequence of zero or more characters in the file name.
?	Any single character.
[01234567]	Matches any octal digit. A sequence of characters within brackets matches any one of the characters listed.

Table 4–3
Example File Name Pattern Elements in bash (Continued)

Wildcard	Matches
[a-zA-Z0-9]	Matches any letter or digit. Within the brackets, a hyphen between two characters is interpreted as all the characters in the character set between them.
[!0123456789]	Matches any character other than a digit. If the open bracket is followed by an exclamation point, it matches any single character other than those listed between the exclamation point and the close bracket.

```
[wpl@tclinux wpl]$ ls
SayHi.py    listdb.pyc    maxprioque.py    prioque.py    tst.txt
listdb.py   listfile.py   myarray.py       test.py
[wpl@tclinux wpl]$ echo li*
listdb.py listdb.pyc listfile.py
[wpl@tclinux wpl]$ echo li*py
listdb.py listfile.py
[wpl@tclinux wpl]$ echo [lm]*
listdb.py listdb.pyc listfile.py maxprioque.py myarray.py
[wpl@tclinux wpl]$ echo [!lm]*
SayHi.py prioque.py test.py tst.txt
[wpl@tclinux wpl]$ echo [!lm]*[yc]
SayHi.py prioque.py test.py
[wpl@tclinux wpl]$ echo [!lm]*[!yc]
tst.txt
[wpl@tclinux wpl]$ echo [lm]?x*
maxprioque.py
```

In bash *scripts*   When you are writing bash scripts, you can use these file name patterns to select the code to run in a case statement. The form of a case statement in bash is:

```
case value in
pattern1) commands1 ;;
pattern2) commands2 ;;
...
esac
```

You have to spread this out on multiple lines. The value is matched against each pattern. Upon a successful match, the following commands are executed. The commands may extend across multiple lines.

It is probably best to have "*)" as the final pattern to handle the default case of no other match.

In Python   If you need to do this sort of pattern matching in Python, there are several modules available to help. The module `fnmatch` has a function, `fnmatch(filename,pattern)` that will test whether the file name matches the pattern.

The module `glob` has a function `glob(pathpattern)` that will return a list of names of all files that match the pattern. The pattern may include a path to the relevant directories as well as shell wildcards.

However, in your programs, you may prefer to use regular expressions instead of the limited pattern-matching capabilities of Unix/Linux wildcards. The module `re` gives you regular expression matching. (See Table 4–4 later in this section.)

cat • The `cat` command concatenates all the files whose names are passed as arguments and writes them to its standard output.

When you log in, your shell takes its standard input from the terminal and writes its standard output to the terminal. When you run a command like `cat` from your shell, it will write its output to the terminal, too. Thus, we can view a short file such as `SayHi.py` using `cat`.

```
[wpl@tclinux wpl]$ cat SayHi.py
#!/usr/bin/python
print 'Hello'
```

If you use a hyphen as a file name, `cat` will read its standard input as that file. This allows you to sandwich the standard input between other files. In Figure 4–2, we concatenate `SayHi.py` on both sides of the input. The first `abcdef` is what we typed in. The second was echoed by `cat`.

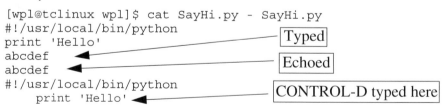

Figure 4–2
Example of `cat`

If the file is too long to fit in your window and you are not able to scroll your window back to see the parts you want, use one of the following:

```
cat filename | more
cat filename | less
more filename
```

The vertical bar sends the output of the `cat` to the program on its right. We'll discuss these commands in their own sections.

more and less • The command `more` will show you a file a screenful at a time. It is invoked as:

```
more filename
```

When you wish to see `more`, type space to see a full screenful or enter to see another line. When you are finished looking, type q to quit.

If you don't give it a file name, `more` displays its standard input. This is used for piping the output of one command into `more` so you can see it before it scrolls off the screen, for example:

```
cat filename | more
```

Program `less` is based on `more`,[1] but in addition, it allows you to move backward and forward in the file by using the up and down cursor arrows.

I/O Redirection • When you run a program from the shell, it is given three open files: its standard input, its standard output, and its standard error output files. Normally, the input will come from your terminal, and the output and error output will go to your terminal. Often you want the input to come from a file, or the output or errors to go to a file, or the output of one program to be the input of another.

There are a number of ways to redirect the input and output of a command you run from a shell. The simplest form is

```
command opts args <inputfile >outputfile
```

---

1. Less is more. Get it?

which executes the command with its options and arguments, but the command takes its standard input from `inputfile` and writes its standard output to `outputfile`.

A full collection of the I/O redirection operations is described in Table 4–4.

Table 4–4
I/O Redirection in `bash`

Form	Means
`< file`	Read the standard input from `file`.
`> file`	Write the standard output to `file`, replacing the current contents.
`>> fileS`	Append the standard output to `file`.
`&> file`	Write both the standard output and the standard error output to `file`. However, `&>>` doesn't work.
`2> file`	Write the standard error output to `file`.
`2>> file`	Append the standard error output to `file`.
`> /dev/null`	Throw away the standard output.
`2> /dev/null`	Throw away the error output.
`command1 | command2`	Run `command1` and `command2` at the same time, piping the standard output of `command1` into the standard input of `command2`.

The I/O redirection operations (other than `|`) do not have to come after the arguments of the command. They can be anywhere following the command name.

head • If you want to glance at the content of a file, the `cat` command is not the best. It will spew the entire contents past you too fast to read. There are other commands that get around this problem. If you just want to read the initial few lines of a file, looking at an initial comment to remind yourself if it is the file you are interested in, you can run the `head` command. For example:

```
[wpl@tclinux wpl]$ head -3 prioque.py
"""Priority queue
```

```
linear list implementation"""
class prioque:
```

The option -*n* where *n* is an integer will restrict the output to at most *n* lines. If you don't specify this option, the number defaults to 10.

tail • Sometimes you will want to look at the end of a file. Naturally, the command for that is tail.

```
[wpl@tclinux wpl]$ tail -3 prioque.py
      return self.q[i]
   def __nonzero__(self):
      return not not self.q
```

As with head, the option -*n* restricts tail to writing out at most *n* lines.

tail has an option that has special importance when running independent processes. As an example, if you write a CGI (Common Gateway Interface) program, it will be run by a Web server. You won't be able to completely try it out from your shell, which makes it a problem to debug. What you can do is have the CGI program write out errors to a log file. You can perform tail on that file to watch for new errors. But it would be a nuisance to have to enter the tail operation over and over, so you use the -f option, as follows:

```
tail -f logfile
```

With the -f option, tail does not return once it has written the final lines in the file. It keeps running, writing new lines to its output as some other process writes them into the file. So you set up one window with tail -f running in it, and watch the errors appear.

grep • The grep command allows you to find the files, and the lines in files, containing a pattern. (You may also find versions under the names egrep and fgrep.) The invocation is:

```
grep pattern filesopt
grep optionsandpattern filesopt
```

where the *pattern* is a regular expression (which can be as simple as a string) and *filesopt* is a list of zero or more files or directories to search through. If the files are omitted, grep reads the standard input. You will usually need to put quotes around the pattern to prevent bash from trying to expand it as a file name pattern. Patterns elements are shown in Table 4–5. The differences from the file name patterns (see Table 4–3) are that file name pattern "*" becomes regular expression ".*" and "?" becomes ".".

The normal output is *filename:line*, the name of the file containing the pattern and the contents of the line that contains the pattern. If grep is reading from its standard input, it only writes the matching line.

The options include -r, which makes grep recursively search files in subdirectories. If you use this, you should probably redirect the error output with 2>/dev/null to avoid messages about inaccessible directories cluttering the desired output.

The -l option will list (on separate lines) the paths to the files that contain the pattern.

The -c command will list the names of all the files and give the number of matching lines in each file (including zero).

When you list the lines containing the pattern, you are able to specify how many lines of context you want. A *-number* option will write out *number* lines before and after the line containing the pattern.

Table 4–5
Regular Expression Elements

Element	Matches
Ordinary character, i.e., none of the special characters	Itself
.	Any character other than newline
\c	c
[*list*]	Any character in list. Ranges of characters can be indicated by forms such as a-z, A-Z, and 0-9.
[^*list*]	Any character *not* in list. Ranges of characters can be indicated by forms such as a-z, A-Z, and 0-9.
^	The empty string at the beginning of the line
$	The empty string at the end of the line

Table 4–5
Regular Expression Elements (Continued)

Element	Matches
(e)	The strings matched by expression *e*. The matched string can be referred to later to match the same string; see *n*.
e?	Zero or one occurrences of expression *e*
e*	Zero or more occurrences of expression *e*
e+	One or more occurrences of expression *e*
e f	An occurrence of expression *e* followed by an occurrence of expression *f*
e | f	An occurrence of expression *e* or an occurrence of expression *f*
e{n} e{n,m} e{n,}	Exactly *n* occurrences of expression *e*, or between *n* and *m* occurrences of expression *e*, or *n* or more occurrences of expression *e*
n	The string previously matched by the *n*th parenthesized expression, where *n* is a digit

Text Files in Python

The way you create a regular file in Linux is by writing it.

File access in Python was briefly discussed in Chapter 2 (see "Files" on page 33.) There we did not go into detail about the methods available to manipulate file objects. Here we will discuss the file methods in more detail and the underlying Linux operations they use. We will also discuss related functions in some Python library modules.

Methods of File Objects • The methods that file objects support are shown in Table 4–6.

The Linux system keeps a current file position for each open file. Reads and writes take bytes from or put bytes in the file at the current position. At the end of the operation, the current position will be left just following the bytes read or written. If you are writing the file, the current position will normally be the end of the file, but you can set it to other values with the seek() method to achieve random access. There is a danger, or opportunity, you should be aware of. When you create a

Table 4–6
File Object Methods

Method Call	Meaning

f=open(path)
f=open(path,
  mode)
f=open(path,
  mode, bufsize)
	The open() built-in function opens a file and returns a file object. The path gives the path to the file. The modes are:
	'r' Open for reading. This is the default.
	'w' Open for writing. This will replace a current file with the same name.
	'a' Open for appending: Data will be added to the end of a currently existing file.
	'r+' Open for both reading and writing.
	'w+' Open for both reading and writing. The file is truncated to empty.
	'rb', 'wb', 'ab', 'r+b', 'w+b' Open it as a binary file.
	The bufsize integer tells the system how large a buffer to allocate. It is probably better to let Python use the default buffer size.

f.read()	Reads in the entire file and returns it as a string.
f.read(n)	Reads in at most n bytes of the file and returns them as a string. It returns fewer, of course, if the file has fewer than n bytes left.
f.readline()	Reads the next line of the file and returns it as a string. The line-terminating character, "\n", is at the end of the string. It returns an empty string, "", on end of file. An empty string counts as false to while and if statements.
f.readlines()	Reads all the remaining lines and returns them in a list.
f.write(s)	Writes the characters in string s to the file.
f.writelines(L)	Writes all the strings in list L into the file. L must be a list, not a tuple. The strings in L must contain their own line-termination characters to be lines in the file: The characters are written as is without any additional characters being added.
f.close()	Closes the file. Further I/O operations on the file are not permitted.

Table 4–6
File Object Methods (Continued)

Method Call	Meaning
f.flush()	Forces the buffered bytes to be written out.
f.truncate()	Resets the file length to zero.
f.truncate(n)	Sets the file size to be no more than n bytes. If n is shorter than the current length of the file, the bytes beyond position n are chopped off. The value of n should not be larger than the length of the file.
f.seek(offset, from)	Sets the current file position. This is the position from which bytes will be read or to which bytes will be written. If from is 0, the current position is set to offset. If from is 1, this current position is set to the current position plus offset. If from is 2, the position is set to the length of the file plus the offset; a negative offset leaves the file position somewhere within the file, whereas a positive position extends the file with zeros to the position requested. To extend the file, it needs to be opened with r+' or 'w+' mode (or 'r+b' or 'w+b').
f.tell()	Returns the current file position.
f.isatty()	Returns true if the file is an interactive terminal.
f.fileno()	Returns the file descriptor number for the file, an integer.

subprocess, it will share your open files, so both you and it can be making changes to the same file, including changes to the current position.

To see how the file methods work, we will consider several functions for copying a file. First consider Figure 4–3. The source and destination names are actually paths, either absolute or relative. The code:

- Opens both files.
- Reads the entire file in at once and assigns it to s.
- Writes out the entire file.
- Closes both files.

The problem with reading and writing the entire file at once is that a huge file would put a serious strain on main memory. Therefore, it may be better to use the copy program shown in Figure 4–4 that reads

```
def cp(srcname,dstname):
    src=open(srcname,'r')
    dst=open(dstname,'w')
    s=src.read()
    dst.write(s)
    src.close()
    dst.close()
```

Figure 4–3
Python Version of cp *file file* Reading and Writing the Entire File

and writes blocks of up to 4096 bytes at a time. The block size is probably large enough to get good performance out of the file system and the disk hardware. We use string variable s to hold the blocks of bytes. On end of file, read() will return an empty string. Since Python considers an empty string to be equivalent to zero or false, the "while   s:" means "while not end-of-file."

Both cp and cpblocks work for binary and text files. Function cptext, Figure 4–5, copies only text files. It is set up to replace the line-termination characters of the source file, whether they be for Unix/Linux or Windows/DOS, with the line-termination character, \n, of the Linux machine cptext is running on. The readline() method reads a text line including the line-termination characters. On Linux and Unix, lines are terminated by a single newline character \n, while for Windows, lines are terminated by the two-character return-newline sequence, \r\n. In either case, Linux will terminate the line when it sees the newline. Also in either case, the line-termination character or characters will be at the end of the line read in. Function cptext will strip the two or one characters off the line.

```
def cpblocks(srcname,dstname):
    bsz=4096
    src=open(srcname,'r')
    dst=open(dstname,'w')
    s=src.read(bsz)
    while s:
        dst.write(s)
        s=src.read(bsz)
    src.close()
    dst.close()
```

Figure 4–4
Python Version of cp *file file* Reading and Writing Blocks

```
def cptext(srcname,dstname):
    src=open(srcname,'r')
    dst=open(dstname,'w')
    s=src.readline()
    while s:
      if s[-2:]=="\r\n": #MS
        dst.write(s[:-2])
        dst.write(os.linesep)
      elif s[-1]=='\n' or s[-1]=='\r':
        # Unix, Linux, Mac
        dst.write(s[:-1])
        dst.write(os.linesep)
      else: #unterminated trailing line
        dst.write(s)
        break
      s=src.readline()
    src.close()
    dst.close()
```

Figure 4–5
Copying Text Files, Fixing Termination Characters

After it writes out the line, cptext writes out the line-termination character or characters in os.linesep, which will be \n on a Linux system. If you are running under Windows, you get \r\n. So whichever system you are running on, you can read text files created under either system and write them out with correct line termination for your own.

Creating Temporary Files • Often you need to create temporary files. Linux has default temporary directories, /tmp and /var/tmp, where you can create files that you don't need to keep. The assumption is that any files in this directory can be deleted every so often with no loss.

You have to come up with unique names for your temporary files. One common way to do this is to include your process id in the file name. All processes executing at any one time have unique ids. (We will be discussing processes later in this chapter.)

If you don't want to go through the trouble of constructing temporary file names yourself, the python tempfile module can help. The mktemp() function constructs a path to a unique temporary file and returns it as a string. You will have to open it yourself. Its two forms are:

```
name=tempfile.mktemp()
name=tempfile.mktemp(suffix)
```

The optional suffix parameter is concatenated on the right end of the file name. Usually that will be an extension giving its type, e.g., `.py`, if you are generating Python source code.

```
>>> import tempfile
>>> tempfile.mktemp()
'/var/tmp/@2774.1'
>>> tempfile.mktemp(".py")
'/var/tmp/@2774.2.py'
```

To create and open a temporary file, you can use one of these calls:

```
file=tempfile.TemporaryFile()
file=tempfile.TemporaryFile(mode)
file=tempfile.TemporaryFile(mode,bufsize)
file=tempfile.TemporaryFile(mode,bufsize,suffix)
```

If you don't specify any parameters, the mode defaults to `'w+b'`. Actually, there doesn't seem to be any reason to use a mode other than `'w+'` or `'w+b'`. The `'w'` is appropriate because the file shouldn't exist before you open it, so you want it to start at zero length anyway. You want the `'+'` because there is little reason to create a file unless you are going to both write and read it. If you wish to write a file first and then open it again later to read, you need to generate the name with `mktemp()`. The files created with `TemporaryFile()` won't exist after they are closed.

Creating FIFOs in Python • As we'll see when we discuss processes, you often want to have processes communicate through a stream of characters. You could have one process write a file and the other read it, but the writer would have to complete before the reader runs. If they run at the same time, the reader could try to read characters before the writer has written them and would get an end-of-file indication that it wouldn't be able to distinguish from the real end of the writer's output. Besides, writing to a file wastes disk space. You don't need to keep the characters the reader has already read.

To facilitate this kind of communication, Linux provides FIFOs, first-in-first-out queues of bytes. FIFOs are in the file system. They have names in directories. You can create a FIFO in Python using the `mkfifo()` function in the `os` module.

```
os.mkfifo(path,permission)
```

creates a FIFO with the name given by the path and with the permissions given by the integer `permission`. (See Table 4–2.)

Directories and File Access

A directory is very much like a normal file. It just contains an alternating sequence of file names and inode numbers.

In the following sections we will be using examples based on the home directory for a user with id wp1. It contains the visible files:

```
SayHi.py    listdb.pyc   maxprioque.py   prioque.py   tst.txt
listdb.py   listfile.py  myarray.py      test.py
```

Linux won't let you write a directory yourself. You have to ask the system to do it for you. That's the only way to be sure the number of links to an inode is correct and there are no cycles among directories and in general that the directory structure doesn't get garbled.

Here we will examine a number of operations that work on directories.

Listing Directories: ls • The Linux command to list a directory is *ls* (as in "LiSt", not the *dir* as in "DIRectory" Windows use). If you don't provide a directory name, ls will use its (the shell's) current directory. Table 4–7 gives the most useful ls options. In the following examples, we are logged on as wp1, and we start in wp1's login directory.

```
[wp1@tclinux wp1]$ ls
SayHi.py    listdb.pyc   maxprioque.py   prioque.py   tst.txt
listdb.py   listfile.py  myarray.py      test.py
```

Table 4–7
Some Options for ls

Option	Effect
-l	Show the long format.
-a	Show all the files, including the "hidden."
-A	Show all the files, including the "hidden," but omit "." and ".".
-d	List a directory itself, not its contents.

The `ls` command listed the files in the login directory of user `wpl` that weren't hidden. By convention, any file whose name begins with a dot is a hidden file, which basically means that `ls` isn't supposed to mention it. If you want to see the hidden files as well, use the `-a` option on the `ls` command:

```
[wpl@tclinux wpl]$ ls -a
.                 .bash_logout    .emacs        SayHi.py
listfile.py       prioque.py
..                .bash_profile   .screenrc     listdb.py
maxprioque.py     test.py
.bash_history     .bashrc         .xauth        listdb.pyc
myarray.py        tst.txt
```

Most of these hidden files are where programs store information about the user running them. For example, the `bash` shell is using four of them. Two of these files merit special mention:

1. "**.**" (dot): Refers to the current directory.
2. "**..**" (dot dot): Refers to the parent directory, the directory that contains a link to this directory. Since the directories are tree-structured, the parent directory is unique.

We can get a long directory listing, containing extra information about the files. For example:

```
[wpl@tclinux wpl]$ ls -l
total 36
-rw-rw-r--    1 wpl        books          32 Oct 23 09:44 SayHi.py
-rw-rw-r--    1 wpl        books         283 Oct 23 09:44 listdb.py
-rw-rw-r--    1 wpl        books        1031 Oct 23 14:17 listdb.pyc
-rw-rw-r--    1 wpl        books         107 Oct 23 09:44 listfile.py
-rw-rw-r--    1 wpl        books         435 Oct 23 09:44 maxprioque.py
-rw-rw-r--    1 wpl        books         203 Oct 23 09:44 myarray.py
-rw-rw-r--    1 wpl        books         550 Oct 23 09:44 prioque.py
-rw-rw-r--    1 wpl        books           8 Oct 23 09:44 test.py
-rw-rw-r--    1 wpl        books           4 Oct 23 09:44 tst.txt
```

The `total 36` tells the number of blocks of disk storage occupied by the files. For each of the files, the fields on its line give, from left to right:

- The file's type and permissions
- The number of links to the file
- The file's owner
- The file's group

- The number of bytes in the file
- The file's time of last modification
- The file's name

There is one more option on the `ls` command that needs mentioning. Normally if you specify a directory, `ls` lists the contents of the directory. If you want to see just the directory itself, you use the `-d` option, which can be combined with other options as the following shows:

```
[wpl@tclinux wpl]$ ls -ld .
drwx------    5 wpl        books        4096 Oct 25 22:03 .
```

Listing Directories in Python: `os.listdir()` • Inside a Python program, you get at most of the facilities we'll be talking about in the `os` module. The function that provides directory listings is `listdir(dir)`. The directory, `dir`, is specified by a string giving a path to it. Function `listdir()` will return a list of the names of all the files contained in the directory, including the hidden files, but not "`.`" or "`..`", so `os.listdir(x)` is the equivalent of `ls -A x` in the shell. For example:

```
>>> import os
>>> os.listdir(".")
['.emacs', '.bash_logout', '.bash_profile', '.bashrc',
'.screenrc', '.xauth', '.bash_history', 'SayHi.py',
'listdb.py', 'listfile.py', 'maxprioque.py', 'myarray.py',
'prioque.py', 'test.py', 'tst.txt', 'listdb.pyc',
'SayHi.py~']
```

Stat in Python: `os.stat()` • The Python function to get the status of a file is `os.stat(fn)`, where `fn` is a path to the file. The function returns a tuple of the information gathered from the file's inode. For example, compare the following to the results of the `stat` command shown in Figure 4–1:

```
>>> os.stat("listdb.py")
(33204, 357667, 2053, 1, 504, 504, 283, 972404447,
972312263, 972312263)
```

Python module `stat` has the constants and functions shown in Table 4–8 to make analyzing the tuple a little easier. For example, `os.stat(fn)[stat.ST_MODE]` gives the mode field. You can ana-

Table 4–8
Contents of `os.stat()` Results

Index	Stat Attribute Name	Functions in Modules `os.path` **and** `os`	Meaning
0	`stat.ST_MODE`	`os.path.isfile(fn)` `os.path.isdir(fn)` `os.access(fn,mode)`	File's mode, which includes permissions and file type information. The low-order nine bits are the permissions, so `os.stat(fn)[stat.ST_MODE] & 0777` gives the permissions. Function `os.path.isfile(fn)` returns true if `fn` is the path to a normal file; `os.path.isdir(fn)` returns true for a directory. Function `os.access()` tests whether this process can access the file in a certain way. The mode in `os.access()` consists of a sum or OR of `os.R_OK`, `os.W_OK`, `os.X_OK`, to test whether this process can access the file to read, write, or execute. Mode `os.F_OK` will simply test for the file's existence. For other functions, consult the documentation.
1	`stat.ST_INO`		File's inode number
2	`stat.ST_DEV`		FIle's device field
3	`stat.ST_NLINK`		Number of links pointing to the file
4	`stat.ST_UID`		User id of the file's owner
5	`stat.ST_GID`		Group id of the file's group
6	`stat.ST_SIZE`	`os.path.getsize(fn)`	The size of the file in bytes

Table 4–8
Contents of `os.stat()` Results (Continued)

Index	Stat Attribute Name	Functions in Modules `os.path` **and** `os`	Meaning
7	`stat.ST_ATIME`	`os.path.getatime(fn)`	The time of last access to the file. See the `time` module for how to convert the number into human-readable form.
8	`stat.ST_MTIME`	`os.path.getmtime(fn)`	The time of last modification of the file's contents. See the `time` module for how to convert the number into human-readable form.
9	`stat.ST_CTIME`		The time of the last change of the file's status, i.e., the inode (except for the access time field) or the file's contents. See the `time` module for how to convert the number into human-readable form.

lyze the mode field directly with functions provided by the `stat` module, for example:

- `stat.S_ISDIR(os.stat(fn)[stat.ST_MODE])` returns true if the file with name `fn` is a directory.
- `stat.S_ISREG(os.stat(fn)[stat.ST_MODE])` returns true if the file with name `fn` is a regular file.

But if you just want to do these tests, you don't need to get the file status. Functions `os.path.isdir(path)` and `os.path.isfile(path)` do the same tests, given the path to a file.

accessibility of a file: `os.access()` • You could figure out in Python whether a file is accessible directly from the file's permission bits, owner, and group and the current process's user and group, but that would be a pain. Instead, you use the access function in the `os` module.

```
if os.access(fn,mode): ...
```

will execute the conditional statements if the current process is permitted to access the file in the way specified. The mode consists of one or more of the following fields ORed or added together:

- os.W_OK–Is it okay to write?
- os.R_OK–Is it okay to read?
- os.X_OK–Is it okay to execute?
- os.F_OK–Does the file exist?

As you would expect, the values of W_OK, R_OK, and X_OK are 4, 2, and 1, but you might want to use their symbolic forms for documentation and portability. They all test for the file's existence as well. If you are only interested in whether the file exists, use F_OK, value 0.

When you OR them together, they test for all of the conditions you specify being simultaneously satisfied: The bits are ORed, but the tests are ANDed.

Current Working Directory: `pwd`, `os.getcwd()` • Every process in Linux has a current working directory associated with it. Since you change this directory from time to time, you sometimes need to be reminded where you are. In bash, you use the pwd command:

```
[wpl@tclinux wpl]$ pwd
/home/wpl
```

In Python, you call the getcwd() function in the os module:

```
>>> os.getcwd()
'/home/wpl'
```

Creating a Directory: `mkdir` • You create a new directory in the shell with the mkdir command.

You give mkdir a path to the desired directory:

```
mkdir dir1/dir2/.../dirN/newdir
```

Each directory, *dir1*, *dir2*,..., *dirN*, on the path must already exist. The new directory will be created and put into *dirN* with the *newdir* name. You must have write permission in *dirN*, of course.

```
[wpl@tclinux wpl]$ mkdir code
[wpl@tclinux wpl]$ ls
SayHi.py   listdb.py    listfile.py     myarray.py    test.py
code       listdb.pyc   maxprioque.py   prioque.py    tst.txt
```

Changing the Current Directory: cd • You change the current working directory of your shell process with the cd command.

```
cd path
```

will make the current working directory of your shell process the directory indicated by path. If you omit the path,

```
cd
```

your current working directory will be set to your login directory. There are numerous examples of cd in the following sections.

Copying Files: cp • The cp command copies files. It has the forms

```
cp srcfile dstfile
cp srcfiles dstDirectory
cp -l srcfiles dstDirectory
cp -l srcfile dstfile
```

The options are:

- You can copy a file from the path given by srcfile creating the file dstfile. This allows you to change the base name of the file as you copy it.
- You can copy a list of files into a destination directory. In this case, the files will have the same base names.
- You can specify, by the -l flag, that the files are not to be copied, but rather that the destination will contain a link to the files' inodes, that is that the files will be shared. This makes cp the equivalent of the ln (link) command discussed below.

The difference between copying and linking is:

1. If the file is copied, you will duplicate the bytes on the disk, doubling the space requirements.
2. If you link the files rather than copying them, when you change the contents of one, you are changing the contents of the other as well, since they are the identical file.

In the following example, we go down into directory code and list its contents. Since it is empty, the ls has no output. Then we copy all Python source files from the parent directory (/home/wp1) to the current directory (/home/wp1/code) and list them.

```
[wpl@tclinux wpl]$ cd code
[wpl@tclinux code]$ pwd
/home/wpl/code
[wpl@tclinux code]$ ls
[wpl@tclinux code]$ cp ../*.py .
[wpl@tclinux code]$ ls
SayHi.py    listfile.py     myarray.py   test.py
listdb.py  maxprioque.py  prioque.py
```

Removing Files: rm • You remove files with the rm command (not "del"). Remove is a better mnemonic than delete because rm removes a file from a directory, but it doesn't necessarily delete the file. The file can have links to it from several directories. Only when the last link to a file is removed is the file deleted. The form of an rm command is

```
rm files
```

where files is a list of one or more paths to files. Command rm will remove all the files in the list that it can.

For example:

```
[wpl@tclinux code]$ ls
SayHi.py    listfile.py     myarray.py   test.py
listdb.py  maxprioque.py  prioque.py
[wpl@tclinux code]$ rm test.py
[wpl@tclinux code]$ ls
SayHi.py listdb.py  listfile.py  maxprioque.py  myarray.py
prioque.py
```

Removing Directories: rmdir and rm -r • You can remove a directory with rmdir. The directory must be empty for you to do so. If you want to remove all the files in a directory and all its subdirectories and then remove the directories themselves, you can use the **-r** (recursive) flag on the rm command, "rm -r". The form of the rmdir command is:

```
rmdir directory
```

The form of the rm -r command is

```
rm -r directory
```

As an example, here we show that we cannot remove the directory code with either rm or rmdir alone:

```
[wpl@tclinux wpl]$ ls
SayHi.py  listdb.py   listfile.py    myarray.py  test.py
code      listdb.pyc  maxprioque.py  prioque.py  tst.txt
[wpl@tclinux wpl]$ rm code
rm: code: is a directory
[wpl@tclinux wpl]$ rmdir code
rmdir: code: Directory not empty
```

But if we use rm -r, we can remove code and whatever is in it all at once.

```
[wpl@tclinux wpl]$ rm -r code
[wpl@tclinux wpl]$ ls
SayHi.py    listdb.pyc   maxprioque.py  prioque.py  tst.txt
listdb.py   listfile.py  myarray.py     test.py
```

We could have removed the code directory by removing all the files in it and then using rmdir, thus:

```
[wpl@tclinux wpl]$ rm code/*
[wpl@tclinux wpl]$ rmdir code
[wpl@tclinux wpl]$ ls
SayHi.py    listdb.pyc   maxprioque.py  prioque.py  tst.txt
listdb.py   listfile.py  myarray.py     test.py
```

The pattern code/* will be replaced with a list of paths to all the files in the code directory.

Linking to a File: ln • The ln (link) command inserts a link to an existing file into a directory. This differs from copying a file. Both directory entries will refer to the same inode; they will share the same file. If you modify the file, you will be able to see the changes through both directory entries. This is equivalent to using the cp -l command.

The forms of ln are

```
ln srcfile dstfile
```

where *srcfile* is the source file and *dstfile* is the new filename, which can include a path to the directory it is to be placed in, or

```
ln srcfiles dstdirectory
```

where *srcfiles* is a sequence of one or more source files and *dstdirectory* is the directory the links are to be placed in. The files will have the same base names in the destination directory.

In this example, we create a subdirectory, code, and list its contents. Since it is empty, ls writes nothing out, not even a blank line. Then we put links to all the files in the current directory whose names end in .py into the directory code.

```
[wpl@tclinux wpl]$ mkdir code
[wpl@tclinux wpl]$ ls code
[wpl@tclinux wpl]$ ln *.py code
[wpl@tclinux wpl]$ ls code
SayHi.py    listfile.py     myarray.py    test.py
listdb.py   maxprioque.py   prioque.py
```

Moving and Renaming Files: mv • Use the mv (MoVe) command either to move a file from one directory to another, or to rename a file. It has the form

```
mv srcfile dstfile
mv srcfiles dstdir
```

where *srcfile* has a path to the file to be moved, and *dstdir* is a path to the directory it is to be placed in with the same name or *dstfile* is the new location and name of the file. Similarly, you can move one or more files in a list to a destination directory.

In this example, we move some files around. We:

1. Create a subdirectory, code.
2. List the files in our current directory.
3. Move all the files with the .py extension to the code directory.
4. List the current directory to show they are gone.
5. List the subdirectory to show they are there.
6. Move them back up to the current directory.
7. Get rid of the code directory.

```
[wpl@tclinux wpl]$ mkdir code
[wpl@tclinux wpl]$ ls
SayHi.py  listdb.py    listfile.py     myarray.py    test.py
code      listdb.pyc   maxprioque.py   prioque.py    tst.txt
[wpl@tclinux wpl]$ mv *.py code
[wpl@tclinux wpl]$ ls
```

```
code   listdb.pyc   tst.txt
[wpl@tclinux wpl]$ ls code
SayHi.py    listfile.py    myarray.py   test.py
listdb.py   maxprioque.py  prioque.py
[wpl@tclinux wpl]$ mv code/* .
[wpl@tclinux wpl]$ ls
SayHi.py  listdb.py    listfile.py    myarray.py   test.py
code      listdb.pyc   maxprioque.py  prioque.py   tst.txt
[wpl@tclinux wpl]$ ls code
[wpl@tclinux wpl]$ rmdir code
```

Creating a Directory in Python: `os.mkdir()` • You create a directory in Python using the `os.mkdir()` function in the `os` module. You call it as:

```
os.mkdir(path_to_new_directory)
```

For example, here we create a subdirectory in the `wpl` directory:

```
>>> os.mkdir('code')
>>> os.listdir(".")
['.emacs', '.bash_logout', '.bash_profile', '.bashrc',
'.screenrc', '.xauth', '.bash_history', 'SayHi.py',
'listdb.py', 'listfile.py', 'maxprioque.py', 'myarray.py',
'prioque.py', 'test.py', 'tst.txt', 'listdb.pyc', 'code']
```

Changing the Current Directory in Python: `os.chdir()` • You change the current working directory of your process in Python with the `os.chdir()` function:

```
os.chdir(path_to_new_current_directory)
```

Continuing the example from the previous section, we dive into the subdirectory `code` and list the files in it:

```
>>> os.chdir('code')
>>> os.listdir(".")
[]
```

Linking to a File in Python: `os.link()` • You can create links to files using the `os.link()` function. It has the form

```
os.link(srcfile,dst)
```

where the source, `srcfile`, is not a directory; the destination, `dst`, names a file to be created. The file `dst` is created as a "hard" link to `srcfile`, not a "symbolic link." It throws an exception if `dst` already exists.

Here, continuing the example from the last section, we create links in the `code` directory to all the Python source files in its parent directory:

```
>>> L=os.listdir("..")
>>> for f in L:
...     if f[-3:]=='.py':
...             os.link('../'+f,f)
...
>>> os.listdir(".")
['SayHi.py', 'listdb.py', 'listfile.py', 'maxprioque.py',
'myarray.py', 'prioque.py', 'test.py']
>>> os.remove('test.py')
>>> os.listdir(".")
['SayHi.py', 'listdb.py', 'listfile.py', 'maxprioque.py',
'myarray.py', 'prioque.py']
```

Creating Symbolic Links in Python • If you wish to create a symbolic link rather than a hard link, use `os.symlink()`. It has the same general form as `link()`:

```
os.symlink(srcfile,dst)
```

You can create symbolic links to directories as well as to ordinary files. Remember that a symbolic link contains the absolute path to its destination. The link can be broken if directories or files are renamed, moved, or deleted.

Copying Files in Python • To copy files, you can use one of the programs given in Figure 4–3 or Figure 4–4, or you can use a copy function from the `shutil` module.

```
shutil.copyfile(src,dst)
shutil.copy(src,dst)
```

Both copy the file indicated by the path `src` to the destination file, `dst`. They differ in how they treat permissions. Function `copyfile()` will replace the contents of `dst` if it exists, preserving the permissions it already has. Function `copyfile()` will create a new file if `dst` does

not exist, giving it the default permissions for a new file. Function
copy() will copy the permissions as well, giving dst the permissions
of src.

Moving Files in Python • To move a file or directory, use

os.rename(src,dst)

which moves the file indicated by the path src to dst. In bash, you
use mv even when you mean "rename"; in Python's os module, you use
rename() even when you mean "move."

Removing Files and Directories in Python • You remove a file
from a directory with either the os.remove() or the os.unlink()
function. They are the same. They have the forms:

os.remove(path)
os.unlink(path)

where path leads to the file that is to be removed from the directory
that precedes it on the path. If you just give a file name, it is removed
from the current directory.

If you wish to remove a directory, use os.rmdir(). It has the
call:

os.rmdir(path)

where path leads to the directory to remove from the preceding directory on the path, or the current directory if the path is a single name.
You cannot remove a directory unless it is empty.

Here we continue our example. We move back up from the code
subdirectory and then remove the code directory and all its contents.
We show that os.remove() does not work because code is a directory, rather than a normal file. Neither does os.rmdir() work; the
directory is not empty. So we loop through all the files in code, unlink-
ing them. Now code is empty, so rmdir() works.

```
>>> os.chdir('..')
>>> os.remove('code')
Traceback (innermost last):
  File "<stdin>", line 1, in ?
OSError: [Errno 21] Is a directory: 'code'
>>> os.rmdir('code')
```

```
Traceback (innermost last):
  File "<stdin>", line 1, in ?
OSError: [Errno 39] Directory not empty: 'code'
>>> for f in os.listdir('code'):
...      os.unlink('code/'+f)
...
>>> os.listdir("code")
[]
>>> os.rmdir('code')
>>> os.listdir("code")
Traceback (innermost last):
  File "<stdin>", line 1, in ?
OSError: [Errno 2] No such file or directory
```

Python's equivalent to "rm -r path" is in the shutil module.

```
shutil.rmtree(path)
shutil.rmtree(path,ignore_errors)
shutil.rmtree(path,ignore_errors,on_error)
```

These functions will remove the directory indicated by path and all subdirectories and all files all the way down the tree. If ignore_errors is true, errors will be ignored. If on_error is present, it is a function that will be called when an error is encountered. Look it up in the documentation if you need it.

Changing a File's or Directory's Permissions • You can change the permission bits in a file or directory you own to give more or fewer rights to you, the owner, members of a group, or all other users. In bash, you use the chmod command. The forms of the chmod command are:

```
chmod who+rights files
chmod who-rights files
```

The who field indicates who is to have rights added or removed. It is composed of one or more of the following:

- u—User, the file's owner
- g—Group, members of the file's group
- o—Others, all other users
- a—All the above

The rights field indicates the rights that are being added or removed. They are some combination of:

- r—Read
- w—Write
- x—Execute

As you would expect, the plus or minus specifies whether the rights are being added or removed. All the files in the list have their rights modified, at least if you are the owner of the file or are the superuser.

In this example, we look at our home directory, /home/wpl, and, discovering that other members of its group, books, don't have access, give them read, write, and execute access to it.

```
[wpl@tclinux wpl]$ ls -ld .
drwx------    5 wpl       books        4096 Oct 26 11:41 .
[wpl@tclinux wpl]$ chmod g+rwx .
[wpl@tclinux wpl]$ ls -ld .
drwxrwx---    5 wpl       books        4096 Oct 26 11:41 .
```

Then we remove read permission for other users from each of the files in this directory:

```
[wpl@tclinux wpl]$ ls -l
            total 36
-rw-rw-r--    1 wpl       books          32 Oct 23 09:44 SayHi.py
-rw-rw-r--    1 wpl       books         283 Oct 23 09:44 listdb.py
-rw-rw-r--    1 wpl       books        1031 Oct 23 14:17 listdb.pyc
-rw-rw-r--    1 wpl       books         107 Oct 23 09:44 listfile.py
-rw-rw-r--    1 wpl       books         435 Oct 23 09:44 maxprioque.py
-rw-rw-r--    1 wpl       books         203 Oct 23 09:44 myarray.py
-rw-rw-r--    1 wpl       books         550 Oct 23 09:44 prioque.py
-rw-rw-r--    1 wpl       books           8 Oct 23 09:44 test.py
-rw-rw-r--    1 wpl       books           4 Oct 23 09:44 tst.txt
[wpl@tclinux wpl]$ chmod o-r *
[wpl@tclinux wpl]$ ls -l
total 36
-rw-rw----    1 wpl       books          32 Oct 24 11:22 SayHi.py
-rw-rw----    1 wpl       books         283 Oct 23 09:44 listdb.py
-rw-rw----    1 wpl       books        1031 Oct 23 14:17 listdb.pyc
-rw-rw----    1 wpl       books         107 Oct 23 09:44 listfile.py
-rw-rw----    1 wpl       books         435 Oct 23 09:44 maxprioque.py
-rw-rw----    1 wpl       books         203 Oct 23 09:44 myarray.py
-rw-rw----    1 wpl       books         550 Oct 23 09:44 prioque.py
-rw-rw----    1 wpl       books           8 Oct 23 09:44 test.py
-rw-rw----    1 wpl       books           4 Oct 23 09:44 tst.txt
```

Changing a File's Permissions in Python: `os.chmod()` • You change a file's mode in Python with the `os.chmod()` function. Its call has the form:

```
os.chmod(path,permissions)
```

where `path`, a string, leads to the file and `permissions`, an integer, gives the read, write, and execute permissions for the user, group, and others. You have to encode the permission bits as an integer, adding together the octal values, shown in Table 4–2.

Changing the Owner and Group of a File • The `bash` command to change the owner and group of a file is `chown`. It has one of the forms:

```
chown options owner.group files...
chown options owner files...
chown options owner. files...
chown options .group files...
```

For the *owner* and *group*, you can use either the login name and group name or the numeric ids.You can change both the owner and the group of each file in the list to values you specify with the *owner.group* form. If you specify only the *owner* without a dot or dot group, the owner is changed, but the group isn't. If you follow the owner with a dot (without white space), *owner.*, the owner of the files is set to the owner specified and the group to the login group of the new owner. If you omit the owner, only the group is changed.

The most important options are:

- `-c` – Report changes.
- `--dereference` – Follow symbolic links, rather than change the symbolic link itself.
- `-R` – Process subdirectories recursively.
- `-v` – Verbose: Output information on each file processed.

In Python, you change the owner and group of a file using the `os.chown()` function. Its call is:

```
os.chown(path, uid, gid)
```

where `path` leads to the file, `uid` is the integer user id of the new owner, and `gid` is the integer new group id. You can find the current user id and group id from the file's status, as shown in "Stat in Python: `os.stat()`" on page 167. To find the numeric user and group ids for user and group names, see the next section.

Looking Up Users and Groups in Python • If you want to look up the integer group id for a group with a particular name, or conversely, look up the name for an id, you can import the `grp` module. The `getgrnam()` function looks up information given the name of a group. The `getgrgid()` function looks up the information for a numeric group id.

```
grp.getgrnam(name)
grp.getgrgid(id)
```

They each return a tuple:

```
(name,password,gid,members)
```

where `name` is the string name of the group, `gid` is the integer group id, and `members` is a list of the names of the users in that group.

```
>>> import grp
>>> grp.getgrnam("books")
('books', '!', 504, ['tc', 'wpl'])
>>> grp.getgrgid(504)
('books', '!', 504, ['tc', 'wpl'])
```

If you need to look up information on users, import module `pwd`, which allows you to look up information in the password file. Function `getpwuid(uid)` returns the entry corresponding the user with the integer user id, `uid`. Function `getpwnam(name)` looks up the information for the string name of the user. They are called:

```
pwd.getpwnam(name)
pwd.getpwuid(uid)
```

They return a tuple:

```
(name,passwd,uid,gid,gecos,dir,shell)
```

where

- `name` is the user name.
- `passwd` is the user's encrypted password.

- uid is the user's numeric user id.
- gid is the numeric group id of the group the user starts out in. The user can change this during execution.
- gecos contains the user's name, etc. It is named gecos for historical reasons.
- dir is a path to the user's home directory. (The bash shell replaces an initial ~username in a path with this string.)
- shell is a path to the user's shell program

File Examination and File Name Manipulation in Python

Module os.path (bound to the path attribute in module os) contains a number of useful functions for examining and manipulating file paths and examining the status of files the paths lead to. These functions generally are divided into four groups: path manipulation, file examination, tests for file identity, and a recursive walk over the directory structure.

Path Manipulation • The os.path module contains a number of functions to break down a path into its parts, build a path, and edit it.

The call dirname(path) will return the directory part of the path, the part of the path that leads to the directory the file is in. The call basename(path) returns the base name of the file, the name it has in the last directory on the path. To get both together, you can call split(path), which returns the tuple (dirname(path), basename(path)).

```
>>> p='/home/wpl/SayHi.py'
>>> os.path.dirname(p)
'/home/wpl'
>>> os.path.basename(p)
'SayHi.py'
>>> os.path.split(p)
('/home/wpl', 'SayHi.py')
```

Function splitext(path) returns a tuple (path up to extension, extension). The extension is the final dot-identifier of the base file name. You use this to look up the implied type of the file's contents.

```
>>> os.path.splitext(p)
('/home/wpl/SayHi', '.py')
```

Function `isabs(path)` returns true if the path is an absolute path (starting with "/"). Function `abspath(path)` converts path into an absolute path, editing out backtracking sequences "id/..".

```
>>> os.path.abspath('SayHi.py')
'/home/wpl/SayHi.py'
>>> os.path.abspath('../wpl/SayHi.py')
'/home/wpl/SayHi.py'
>>> os.path.isabs('SayHi.py')
0
>>> os.path.isabs(p)
1
```

There are two functions to perform bash-style editing of paths. Function `expanduser(path)` will replace an initial ~user with the absolute path to the user's home directory. Function `expandvars(path)` will replace $envvar and ${envvar} in the path with the value of the environment variable envvar.

```
>>> os.path.expanduser('~wpl/SayHi.py')
'/home/wpl/SayHi.py'
>>> os.environ['X']='~wpl'
>>> os.path.expandvars('$X/SayHi.py')
'~wpl/SayHi.py'
```

Function `join(path1, path2,...)` will concatenate the paths into a single path, inserting "/" separators where necessary.

```
>>> os.path.join('/','home','wpl','SayHi.py')
'/home/wpl/SayHi.py'
```

File Examination • There are several functions to gather information about the files that paths lead to. Function `exists(path)` returns true if the path does lead to a file. You can test whether the file is a directory, a normal file, or a symbolic link with `isdir(path)`, `isfile(path)`, and `islink(path)`.

You can test whether it is a mount point for another disk with `ismount(path)`. Linux puts all disk file systems into a single root directory by allowing you in effect to replace a file in one directory with the entire file system on another disk. That file is the mount point.

You get the size of a file with function `getsize(path)`. You can find the time of last access and last modification of a file with `getatime(path)` and `getmtime(path)`.

```
>>> import os
>>> os.path.isfile('SayHi.py')
1
>>> os.path.isdir('SayHi.py')
0
>>> os.path.isfile('.')
0
>>> os.path.isdir('.')
1
>>> os.path.getatime('SayHi.py')
974914756
>>> os.path.getmtime('SayHi.py')
974572848
>>> os.path.getsize('SayHi.py')
38
```

Tests for File Identity • There are three ways to find out if two files are really the same file. Function samefile(path1,path2) tells whether two paths lead to the same file. Function sameopenfile(fd1, fd2) tells whether two file descriptors are attached to the same file. Function samestat(stat1,stat2) tells whether two file status tuples are for the same file.

```
>>> os.path.join('/','home','wpl','SayHi.py')
'/home/wpl/SayHi.py'
```

Walk the Directory • There is a function to perform a recursive walk over a directory tree-calling a function for each directory. You can use this to search for a file, list files, change the modes on files, and other such useful things. The form of call is:

```
os.path.walk(path, visitorfunction, arg)
```

where path leads to the directory at the root of the directory subtree you wish to walk over, visitorfunction is a function that will be called at each directory, and arg is an argument to be supplied to the function at each call. You can use it to share or accumulate information between calls. The form of the visitorfunction is:

```
def visitorfunction(arg,dirname,basenames):...
```

where arg is the arg object passed into walk, dirname is the path to the directory, and basenames is the list of file names in the directory.

The `visitor` function is called before `walk` recurses into the subdirectories. You can remove subdirectory names from consideration by removing them from the `basenames` list.

Figure 4–6 shows a Python program to find files whose base names contain a given string. It is run as:

```
python findname.py name directory...
```

The function `printname(arg,dn,bns)` is the visitor function. Parameter `arg` is the string of characters the file name is to include. Directory name `dn` is the name of the directory being considered. Parameter `bns` is the list of base names in the directory. Function `printname` first prints out the absolute path to the files (including directories) whose names contain the specified string. Then `printname()` prunes from the list of files those that are directories but are inaccessible (cannot be used on a path because they lack the execute permission). Without this, `findname` would crash upon finding the first inaccessible directory.

```
#!/usr/bin/python
import os,sys,string
def printname(arg,dn,bns):
    for f in bns:
      if string.find(f,arg)>=0:
        absname=os.path.join(dn,f)
        print absname
    i=0
    while i<len(bns):
      absname=os.path.join(dn,bns[i])
      if os.path.isdir(absname):
        if not os.access(absname,os.X_OK):
          del bns[i]
          continue
      i=i+1

p=sys.argv[1]
for d in sys.argv[2:]:
    os.path.walk(d,printname,p)
```

Figure 4–6
Example of `os.path.walk`: `findname.py`

File Examination in `bash`

Scripts in `bash` allow you to examine the status of files and execute commands conditionally based on the status. Let's look at `if` statements first. The `if` statement in `bash` has the form:

```
if command
then
commands
else
commands
fi
```

The `else` part is optional. The command following the `if` is executed. If it is completed successfully, the commands following the `then` are executed. If the command failed, the commands following the `else`, if any, are executed.

What does it mean for a command to complete successfully? The command is run as a process, and when it terminates, a process returns a completion status number to the process that started it. By convention, zero means successful completion. Any other number means unsuccessful.

The command we use in `bash` to examine files also allows us to do string and numeric comparisons. It is the `test` command. It has the form:

```
test expression
```

If the expression evaluates true, the test command terminates successfully with a zero exit status. If false, it terminates with a nonzero status. The expressions allowed in the test command that examine files are shown in Table 4–9. The expressions not related to files are shown in Table 4–10.

Table 4–9
File Expressions Allowed in a Test Command

Expression	Meaning
`-e file`	True if file exists
`-f file`	True if file is a regular file
`-d file`	True if file is a directory

Table 4–9
File Expressions Allowed in a Test Command (Continued)

Expression	Meaning
`-L file`	True if file is a symbolic link
`-p file`	True if file is a FIFO (a named pipe, hence -p)
`-r file`	True if file is readable
`-w file`	True if file is writable
`-x file`	True if file is executable
`-O file`	True if file is owned by the effective user ID of this process
`-G file`	True if file is owned by the effective group ID of this process
`file1 -ef file2`	True if `file1` and `file2` are the same file, i.e., have the same device and inode number
`file1 -nt file2`	True if `file1` is newer than `file2` as indicated by the modification date
`file1 -ot file2`	True if `file1` is older than `file2`
`-s file`	True if file exists and has a size greater than zero

Table 4–10
Other Test Expressions

Expression	Meaning
`-n s`	True if string s has a nonzero length
`-z s`	True if string s has a zero length
`s1 = s2`	True if string s1 is equal to string s2. Note the *single* equal sign.
`s1 != s2`	True if string s1 is not equal to string s2
`i1 -eq i2`	True if integer i1 is equal to integer i2
`i1 -ne i2`	True if integer i1 is not equal to integer i2

Table 4–10
Other Test Expressions (Continued)

Expression	Meaning
i1 -ge i2	True if i1 is greater than or equal to i2
i1 -gt i2	True if i1 is greater than i2
i1 -le i2	True if i1 is less than or equal to i2
i1 -lt i2	True if i1 is less than i2
\(... \)	Enclose a subexpression
e1 -a e2	True if and only if both e1 and e2 are true
e1 -o e2	True if either e1 or e2 or both are true
! e	Not e. True if e is false and false if e is true.

There are some other file examination expressions in addition to the ones listed, but these should be sufficient for most uses.

The other test expressions compare strings and integers and perform logical operations.

The test command is also used frequently in looping commands. The while statement in bash has the form:

```
while command
do
commands
done
```

and the until statement has the form:

```
until command
do
commands
done
```

The while statement repeatedly executes the *commands* as long as the *command* terminates successfully. The until statement executes the *commands* as long as the *command* terminates unsuccessfully.

find Command • The find command is a utility program in Linux to find files and process them. It is an analog of os.path.walk() in Python. It is invoked by:

```
find directories rules
```

The *directories* parameter is a list of one or more directories to search. The rules select files and perform some actions on them. The rules allow a variety of tests including the characters in the file names, the owner or group of the file, the creation and modification times, etc. The default action is to print the file name. The file name can be passed to other commands or listed in a specified format.

Our Python findname.py program (Figure 4–6), executed by:

```
./findname.py .py /home
```

is approximately equivalent to:

```
find /home -name '*.py*'
```

The find command has a multitude of types of rules. Generally, the rule is evaluated left to right for each file in the directories until either it evaluates false or it is complete. There are certain rule elements that control the overall processing, some that test the file, and some that perform operations on the file.

Overall control operations include:

-follow	Follow symbolic links
-maxdepth n	Descend at most *n* levels into directories
-mindepth n	Don't test or process files at less than *n* levels deep. Usually used with n=1 to say, "Don't process the command line arguments themselves."
-depth	Process a directory's contents before the directory itself

In the tests, numeric arguments use plus and minus signs to indicate greater than and less than, so

10 means exactly 10

-10 means less than 10

+10 means more than 10

There are a number of types of tests. The most obviously useful are those that match the name of a file to a pattern.

`-name pat`	The file's base name matches the shell pattern `pat`.
`-path pat`	The file's entire path matches the shell pattern `pat`.

A number of tests examine the file's time of last access, status change, or modification.

`-amin n`	The file was accessed n minutes ago. Remember, a plus or minus sign indicates more than or less than.
`-atime n`	The file was accessed n days ago (more precisely, $n{*}24$ hours ago).
`-cmin n`	The file's status was changed n minutes ago.
`-ctime n`	The file's status was changed $n{*}24$ hours ago.
`-mmin n`	The file was modified n minutes ago.
`-mtime n`	The file was modified $n{*}24$ hours ago.
`-newer otherfile`	The current file is newer than `otherfile`, i.e., was modified more recently.
`-anewer otherfile`	The current file was accessed more recently than `otherfile`.
`-cnewer otherfile`	The current file's status was changed more recently than `otherfile`'s.

There are tests for the file's ownership or group and permissions.

`-user name`	The file belongs to `user name` (numeric user id okay here).
`-group name`	The file belongs to `group name` (numeric group id okay here).
`-nouser`	The file does not belong to any known user.
`-nogroup`	The file does not belong to any known group.
`-perm mode`	The file's permissions are exactly mode (octal or symbolic okay here).

-perm -mode   All permissions bits in mode are set for the file.

-perm +mode   At least one of the permission bits is set for the file.

And there are some miscellaneous tests.

-type c   The file has the type indicated by the letter c. *Inter alii,* f means a regular file; d, a directory; p, a FIFO (named pipe, hence p); and l, a symbolic link.

-empty   The file is a regular file or directory and is empty.

-false   False. Cut off a branch of the testing.

The tests are ANDed as one goes left to right. You can specify matching one test or another with a expr1 -o expr2 rule. You can group tests within \ (and \ ). The incorporation character is needed to keep bash from trying to do something with the parentheses. The rule -not expr (equivalent to ! expr) is true if expr is false and false if expr is true.

The normal action is to print the file name. There are some other options:

-ls   List the file in a format similar to that which ls -dil would use.

-exec command \;   Execute the command on the file. The file can be referenced inside the command as \{ }. The incorporation character, "\", is required to keep bash from trying to process the characters itself.

-prune   Don't process this directory recursively.

Processes

Essentials

A process is a running program. Programming in Linux, you'll use processes a lot. Most shell commands are run in subprocesses: The command name is the base name of a program file. bash finds the file, creates a subprocess, and runs the program in it. CGI programs, i.e., programs that respond to user requests on the Web, are run in separate processes. Server programs run in separate processes. You will usually be running many processes at the same time.

Linux keeps three memory areas for each process:

1. Program section—This contains the instructions for the program that is executing.
2. Data section—This contains the user's data.
3. Process control section—This is kept in the kernel and used for keeping data that the process should not manipulate directly for security reasons.

The process control section contains, among other things,

- The file descriptors that link the process to its open files
- The process id, an integer, unique for each process in existence at any time
- The process id parent process; when one process creates another, the first is the parent and the second is the child
- The current working directory
- A mask used to remove permissions from files the process creates; a mask of zero means everybody can read, write, and execute it
- The number of the process group and session the process is associated with
- The user id (uid) and group id (gid) of the user running the process
- The effective user id (euid) and effective group id (egid) of the process

The effective user and group ids are used to test whether the process has the right to access a file. What's the difference between uid and euid? Mostly they are the same, but remember that only the super-user can perform certain operations. Linux allows you to flag certain programs so that when you execute them, they will take on the identity, owner, and/or group of the file they are in. When you execute them, your process's euid and/or egid will be changed. So the way to execute some operations as superuser is to put them in files belonging to the superuser, set the protections so only the owner can change the contents of the file, and mark the file to set the euid, although anybody can execute it. You have to be running as the superuser to do that, for security reasons. The uid and gid allow the program to know who it is performing the operation for.

File Descriptors • When a process opens a file, it allocates a file descriptor for it. Since there is a limit on the number of file descriptors, that is also the limit on the number of files a process can have open at any one time.[2] The file descriptors are also used for other means of communication: They are used for pipes, connecting the output of one process to the input of another; for FIFOs, which are named pipes; and for sockets, which allow communication across a network.

When you start running, typically three of your file descriptors are already in use:

1. `stdin`—File descriptor zero is your standard input file. Those operations that read the standard input use that file descriptor.
2. `stdout`—`print` statements, for example, write to this file descriptor.
3. `stderr`—This is why `2> filename` is used to redirect the standard error output; the "2" gives the file descriptor number.

As we'll discuss later, when processes create child processes, the child processes will inherit the file descriptors of the parent. We will show how the parent process can open file descriptors and the children can use them to communicate.

In Unix and Linux documentation, the phrase "file descriptor" is used frequently to mean the integer index of the file descriptor element in the array of file descriptors associated with the process.

You get to perform lower-level I/O using file descriptors instead of Python file objects. The operations are in module `os`, if you need them. We will show how to use several of these file descriptor functions later, when we show how to run subprocesses in Python.

Getting Process Information in Python • There are a number of functions in the `os` module that allow you to look up information about your process. Table 4–11 shows several of these functions.

---

2. We ran a test that crashed at 1024 open files. The limited number of file descriptors may not be a practical problem.

Table 4–11
Getting Information about Your Process in Python

Function	Action
`os.geteuid()`	Get the effective user id of your process
`os.getegid()`	Get the effective group id of your process
`os.getuid()`	Get the real user id of your process
`os.getgid()`	Get the real group id of your process
`os.getpid()`	Get the process id of your process. This will be unique among all the processes in existence. Of course, they are recycled when processes terminate.
`os.getppid()`	Get the process id of your parent process.
`os.umask(mask)`	Specify which permission bits are to be *cleared* in files created by this process. Use Table 4–2 to build a mask specifying what permissions you wish the files you create *not* to have.

Creating New Processes in `bash`

When the shell executes a command, it usually executes it in a subprocess. (There are just a few commands that ask the shell about its internal state. The shell has to execute these itself.) There are several ways to have the shell create more than one subprocess at a time. The process you are communicating with in your command window is called the *foreground process*. All processes you have running that you are not communicating with are *background processes*.

Executing commands • Recall the way you specify a command for the shell to execute:

```
command command_line_arguments
```

If the shell doesn't recognize the command as an internal command, it searches for a program to run with that name. We will describe later how the shell decides which directories to search through; they are contained in the environment variable PATH.

If you want to know precisely which file would be executed, use the command:

```
which commandName
```

It will give the absolute path to the file the command would execute.

You can explicitly specify the path to an executable file for the shell to run. For example, if the file is in the current directory, you can use:

```
./programfile command_line_arguments
```

The shell will create a subprocess and the subprocess will load and run the program in the program file, if it is a binary file. If it is a shell script, the subprocess will run a copy of the shell, taking its commands from the file. If the file is a script in some other programming language, it needs to begin with a comment line telling the shell which language processor to run. This first line has the form:

```
#!pathToLanguageProcessor
```

For example:

```
#!/usr/bin/python
print 'Hello'
```

If you don't know where the language processor is, use the `which` command.

Whatever way you run a subprocess, it will be given two things: a list of command line arguments–these arguments are separated by white space in the shell command–and an environment.

We will discuss writing both `bash` and Python scripts in later sections, describing how arguments and environments are passed to subprocesses and how they are accessed.

cmd1 | cmd2 • The shells use the vertical bar to specify a pipe. The commands cmd1 and cmd2 will be run at the same time. The standard output of cmd1 will be fed into the standard input of cmd2. They are connected by a *pipe* object. Of course, they use file descriptors to access the pipe: file descriptor one (standard output) for cmd1, and file descriptor zero for cmd2 (standard input). For example:

```
[wpl@tclinux wpl]$ echo *| cat -
SayHi.py listdb.py listdb.pyc listfile.py maxprioque.py
myarray.py prioque.py test.py tst.txt
```

cmd & • You can create a process to run a command in the background. You get to go on using the shell while it runs. You do this by following the command with the & sign. Note that the & sign must be on the same line as the command. If you try to wait until the next line, the shell will already have started the command and be waiting for it to terminate, so you won't be able to type the &. For that case, see the next section on control-Z and `bg`.

As can be seen in the following example, & writes out the process id of the process it has created and a small integer you can use to refer to it in the shell. When the process terminates, the shell will write out a *Done* message.

If you don't redirect the input and output of the process you run in the background, it will use the same source and destination as the shell, which could produce annoying output while you are trying to do other work.

Example: Using FIFOs Rather Than Pipes • Linux allows you to plug commands together in a pipeline through pipes, but that only works when the processes are created from the same parent. The parent opens the pipe, the children inherit it, and they plug themselves together through it. To allow pipe-like communication among processes created separately, you use FIFOs. FIFOs behave like pipes, but they exist in the file system. They have inodes. They are named in directories.

Here is an example showing the use of a FIFO instead of a pipe:

```
[wpl@tclinux wpl]$ mkfifo f
[wpl@tclinux wpl]$ echo * >f & cat - <f
[1] 5999
SayHi.py f listdb.py listdb.pyc listfile.py maxprioque.py
myarray.py prioque.py test.py tst.txt
[1]+  Done                    echo * >f
```

^Z, `bg`, and `fg` • If a command is already running and you want to put it into the background, you first type CONTROL-Z, which suspends execution of the command and sends control back to your shell. Then you execute the `bg` command, which starts the suspended command running in the background. To let a background command run again in the foreground, use the `fg` command:

```
fg
fg num
```

Consider, for example, Figure 4–7. The `sleep 60` command just suspends execution for 60 seconds. But rather than wait a minute, we

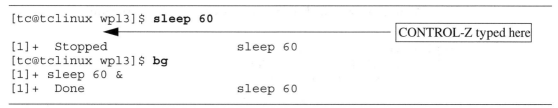

```
[tc@tclinux wpl3]$ sleep 60
                                                                CONTROL-Z typed here
[1]+  Stopped                    sleep 60
[tc@tclinux wpl3]$ bg
[1]+ sleep 60 &
[1]+  Done                       sleep 60
```

Figure 4–7
Putting a Subprocess in the Background

typed CONTROL-Z, which stopped the sleep command and returned control to bash. The [1] gives the number of the stopped process that we could use later to refer to it. The bg command allowed the stopped process to resume running in the background. When it finishes execution, bash writes out a Done message.

Figure 4–8 demonstrates the ps f command (ps is discussed in the next section) and retrieval of subprocesses by number. Here we create two sleep subprocesses and a ps f process, which shows a forest representation of the active processes. The fg 1 brings the first of the background processes back into the foreground.

Seeing What Processes Are Running • As shown in Figure 4–8, you can see what processes you have running with the ps (process status) command:

```
ps options
```

For example,

```
ps f
ps l
ps ax
```

```
[tc@tclinux wpl3]$ sleep 50&sleep 60&ps f
[1] 3050
[2] 3051
  PID TTY STAT   TIME COMMAND
 2817  ?  S      0:00 bash
 3050  ?  S      0:00  \_ sleep 50
 3051  ?  S      0:00  \_ sleep 60
 3052  ?  R      0:00  \_ ps f
[tc@tclinux wpl3]$ fg 1
sleep 50
```

Figure 4–8
Retrieving a Process from the Background

A simple `ps` will show the processes you have running.

```
[wpl@tclinux wpl]$ ps
  PID TTY STAT   TIME COMMAND
13072  ?  S     0:00 -bash
13093  ?  R     0:00 ps
```

The `f` option gives a "forest" representation of the output, showing by indentation and `\_` which processes are subprocesses of other processes.

```
[wpl@tclinux wpl]$ ps f
  PID TTY STAT   TIME COMMAND
13072  ?  S     0:00 -bash
13099  ?  R     0:00 \_ ps f
```

If you would like to see a tree representation of all processes in the system, you can execute:

```
pstree
```

Here are the first several lines of `pstree`'s output:

```
init-+-apmd
     |-atd
     |-crond
     |-enlightenment
     |-gdm-+-X
     |     '-gdm---gnome-session
     |-gen_util_applet
     |-gmc
     |-gnome-help-brow
     |-gnome-name-serv
     |-gnome-smproxy
     |-2*[gnome-terminal-+-bash]
     |                   '-gnome-pty-helpe]
     |-gnome-terminal-+-bash---su---bash---pstree
     |                '-gnome-pty-helpe
     |-gnomepager_appl
 ...
```

The `l` (lowercase L) option provides more information in a long output.

```
[wpl@tclinux wpl]$ ps l
 FLAGS    UID    PID   PPID PRI   NI    SIZE    RSS WCHAN   STA TTY  TIME COMMAND
   100    504  13072  13069  10    0    1704    948 wait4   S    ?   0:00 -bash
100000    504  13097  13072  11    0    1116    400         R    ?   0:00 ps l
```

To debug network servers and CGI programs that have to examine processes that are not part of your session, use the ax option to get information on all processes running. If you want to select out those belonging to a particular user or execution for a particular program, you can pass the list of processes through the grep program. Grep hunts through files, or by default its standard input, for lines containing a regular expression (see "grep" on page 157.) The ps command itself also provides some extra options to select what processes it will show.

```
[wpl@tclinux wpl]$ ps axl | grep 504
   100    504  13072  13069  15    0    1704    948 wait4   S    ?   0:00 -bash
100000    504  13104  13072  12    0    1136    428         R    ?   0:00 ps axl
    40    504  13105  13072  15    0    1704    948         R    ?   0:00 -bash
```

If you wish to see which processes are using most of the processor time, run top, which will fill a window with a list of the running processes that are using most of the processor time, one per line, with information about them. It will refresh this information every so often. You may not recognize a lot of these processes: They are part of the system, or belong to other users (see Figure 4–9).

Terminating Processes • When you start running processes in the background, you are sometimes going to have to force them to terminate. There are several ways.

Terminating a process waiting for input.   Some processes terminate when they reach an end-of-file on their standard input. The shell is one of these. You give an end-of-file by typing CONTROL-D.

Killing a foreground process.   If a process is running in the foreground, you need to get rid of it, and CONTROL-D won't do the job, you can type CONTROL-C. If it is running in the background, you can bring it to the foreground with the fg command and then CONTROL-C it.

Terminating your shell and subprocesses.   If you type CONTROL-D to your shell, it will terminate and your session will end. This will typically terminate all the processes you have created during your session as well. Processes are associated with a session, which typically has a controlling terminal or interactive command window. When the session ends, all the processes in that session are killed.

```
[wpl@tclinux wpl]$ top

  5:38pm   up 5 days, 18:09,   0 users,   load average: 0.02, 0.04, 0.00
72 processes: 69 sleeping, 2 running, 1 zombie, 0 stopped
CPU states:   0.0% user,   0.7% system,   0.0% nice, 99.2% idle
Mem:   257744K av, 204036K used,   53708K free,   78920K shrd,   93084K
buff
Swap: 530104K av,    460K used, 529644K free                    38704K
cached

    PID USER      PRI  NI   SIZE   RSS SHARE STAT   LIB %CPU %MEM   TIME COMMAND
  13106 tc          8   0    496   496   388 R        0  0.5  0.1   0:00 top
  12316 root       12   0  52800   51M  2044 R        0  0.1 20.4   0:58 X
      1 root        0   0    476   476   404 S        0  0.0  0.1   0:11 init
      2 root        0   0      0     0     0 SW       0  0.0  0.0   0:00 kflushd
      3 root        0   0      0     0     0 SW       0  0.0  0.0   0:00 kupdate
      4 root        0   0      0     0     0 SW       0  0.0  0.0   0:00 kpiod
      5 root        0   0      0     0     0 SW       0  0.0  0.0   0:00 kswapd
      6 root      -20 -20      0     0     0 SW<      0  0.0  0.0   0:00 mdrecoveryd
    145 root        0   0    396   376   300 S        0  0.0  0.1   0:00 nscd
    343 root        0   0    704   700   572 S        0  0.0  0.2   0:00 pump
    393 bin         0   0    416   404   324 S        0  0.0  0.1   0:00 portmap
    408 root        0   0      0     0     0 SW       0  0.0  0.0   0:00 lockd
    409 root        0   0      0     0     0 SW       0  0.0  0.0   0:00 rpciod
    418 root        0   0    516   512   428 S        0  0.0  0.1   0:00 rpc.statd
    432 root        0   0    400   388   332 S        0  0.0  0.1   0:00 apmd
    483 root        0   0    504   500   404 S        0  0.0  0.1   0:08 syslogd
    492 root        0   0    668   664   304 S        0  0.0  0.2   0:14 klogd
```

Figure 4–9
Example Output of Top

Preserving processes past "hang up." Sometimes you won't be able to access your processes through the current shell. They may have been started by the Web server as CGI programs, which we'll examine in Chapter 7. Or you may have left them running after you hung up.

You may not want all of your processes killed when you hang up. For example, you may be writing a server, and you're ready to test it out by leaving it up for a few days. Or maybe you're running a test program and you want it to run overnight.

If you do want to start a process and have it continue running after you log off, you can wrap your command in the nohup (no hang up) command:

nohup *yourcommand* &

Be sure to redirect the input and output of your command. It could crash trying to read from a terminal that is no longer available. The nohup command will redirect the output to files for you if you leave the standard output or error output directed to a terminal, but you probably want to specify which files they go to yourself.

For example, we have a little Python program, loop.py, which consists of the single command while 1: pass. Here we set it running so that it will keep on running past when we log off:

```
[tc@tclinux wpl3]$ nohup ./loop.py&
[1] 3102
[tc@tclinux wpl3]$ nohup: appending output to 'nohup.out'
```

The [1] 3102 is in response to the & command that started the command running in the background. It tells us what number we can refer to the background process as in the shell, [1], and the process id of the process, 3102. The message from nohup about where it was placing the output came out after the new command prompt from the shell, but it is logically unconnected to it.

Now we can log off and log back on and find the loop process is still there. But once we have logged on with a new shell, we can't get the loop process into the foreground with an fg 1 command. It wasn't created by this shell. If we want to get rid of it, we need to kill it by process id:

```
kill 3102
```

Killing a process by process id   If you are running a process in the background with the nohup command and in a later session you want to terminate it, you use the kill command to get rid of it.

```
kill pids
```

will kill the processes with process ids *pids*. You can find the process ids of your running processes with the ps command.

The kill command sends a signal to the indicated process. Signals normally kill processes unless the process has made provision to ignore the signal or catch it and handle it itself. The kill command sends a SIGTERM signal, a request for termination. If the process catches it, the process is told to clean up and terminate. If the process doesn't catch it, the process is terminated crudely. What if there is a flaw in handling the SIGTERM and the process doesn't terminate itself? In that case, you can get rid of it by sending a SIGKILL signal to the process. A process cannot handle or turn off the `SIGKILL` signal, so it will be terminated. `SIGKILL` is signal number nine, so the way to send it to a process is:

```
kill -s 9 pids
```

You can specify the signal by either the signal's number or the signal's name. If you want a list of signal names, execute:

```
kill -l
```

If the process you wish to get rid of has itself created subprocesses, you may be able to get rid of them by killing the process itself, but then again, you may have to get rid of all of them individually.

su • You can in effect change your user id by running the `su` (set user) program. You execute one of these:

```
su - newuser
su -l newuser
su newuser
su -
su -l
su
```

In any case, the `su` program is run in a subprocess. It will ask for the password associated with the user whose login name is `newuser`. If you give the password, then the process will set its effective user id to the id of `newuser` and replace itself with a shell program. So once again, you are talking to a shell, although it is in a subprocess of your original shell. When you are done running as that user, you can type CONTROL-D to this subprocess's shell, it will terminate, and you will be talking to your previous shell.

If you specify - or `-l` on the `su` command, you start executing in the home directory of `newuser`. If you don't specify it, the working directory won't change. If you leave off the `newuser`, `su` will try to log you in as the superuser (login name "root").

newgrp • You can change your group in a manner similar to changing your effective user id. Use the command

```
newgrp groupname
```

which will create a subprocess running a shell and with its effective group id changed. You must be a member of the group you are changing to.

Again, this is a subprocess running the shell. When you wish to go back to the previous group, give the subshell a CONTROL-D. It will terminate and you will again be talking to your previous shell.

Creating Processes in Python

fork • The way Linux creates new processes is by the `fork` system call. Figure 4–10 shows the effect of the fork. The parent's code and data segments are copied into new segments allocated for the child. The parent's system data is partially copied into the child's system data, although some parts are replaced. In particular, the file descriptors are copied, so the parent and child have the same open file objects. It's more than simply having the same files open; they share the same position field, so that if one does a seek, the other one will see the new file position. There are, however, some changes. The child process has a new process id. Its parent id is the process id of the parent.

The `fork` operation looks like a subroutine call:

```
id=os.fork()
```

It is strange: One process calls the subroutine; two processes return from it. The two processes that return (the parent and the child) have the same data and the same program. The only difference between them that they can immediately see is this: The fork call in the parent returns the process id of the child. The fork in the child returns zero. This is how the parent and child know which one they are.

An example of using fork is the parallel file copy in Figure 4–11. A Python program would call `cpparallel(src,dst)`. Function `cpparallel` is to copy all readable files in the source directory, `src`, to the destination directory, `dst`. Function `cpparallel` gets a list of the file names in the source directory, filters out those that aren't normal files, as determined by `os.path.isfile()`, and then filters out those that aren't readable. It then calls `cpparlist()` to arrange for the copying.

Function `cpparlist()` calls function `cplist()` to do the actual copying. If there are enough files to justify creating a subprocess,

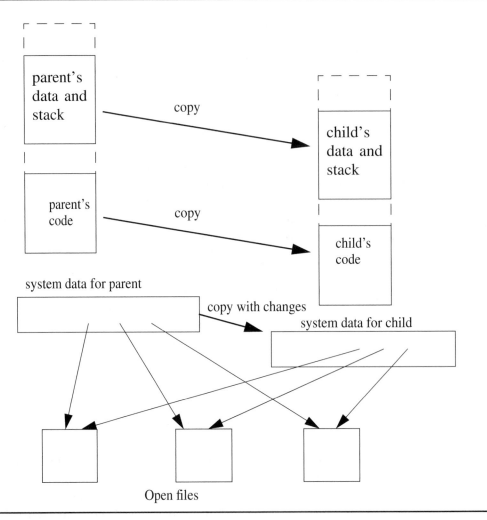

Figure 4–10
Forking a Child Process

cpparlist() forks, using os.fork() to create a child, and then the parent and the child each copy half the list. The significant code is this:

```
id=os.fork()
if id==0:
  cplist(srcdir,dstdir,d[len(d)/2:])
  sys.exit(0)
else:
  cplist(srcdir,dstdir,d[:len(d)/2])
```

```
import os, os.path, sys
splitpoint=2
def cpparallel(srcdir,dstdir):
    d=os.listdir(srcdir)
    d=filter(lambda
f,s=srcdir:os.path.isfile(s+os.sep+f),d)
    d=filter(lambda
f,s=srcdir:os.access(s+os.sep+f,os.R_OK),d)
    cpparlist(srcdir,dstdir,d)
def cpparlist(srcdir,dstdir,d):
    if len(d)>splitpoint:
        id=os.fork()
        if id==0:
            cplist(srcdir,dstdir,d[len(d)/2:])
            sys.exit(0)
        else:
            cplist(srcdir,dstdir,d[:len(d)/2])
            os.wait()
    else:
        cplist(srcdir,dstdir,d)
def cplist(srcdir,dstdir,d):
    for f in d:
        try:
            cpbuffered(srcdir+os.sep+f,   \
                dstdir+os.sep+f)
        except: pass
```

Figure 4–11
Parallel File Copy

```
os.wait()
```

The os.fork() call creates the child process. When fork() returns in the parent, it assigns the process id of the child, a positive integer, to variable id. When fork() returns in the child, it assigns id zero.

Each process immediately tests the value of id. The child takes the true part of the if statement, copies the top part of the list, and then terminates by calling sys.exit(). The parent takes the else part of the if, copies the bottom part of the list, and then calls on os.wait() to wait for the child to terminate.

The exit function,

```
sys.exit(status)
```

terminates the execution of the process and returns its parameter as the exit status of the process. The exit status is a byte. By convention, zero means successful termination.

A call of the `wait()` function has the form:

```
pid,status=os.wait()
```

Calling `wait()` will wait for any child process to terminate. It returns a 16-bit status composed of two bytes. If the bottom byte is zero, the child exited on its own and the high byte contains the exit status. If the lower byte is nonzero, the child was forcibly terminated, e.g., by a kill or by crashing, and the low byte indicates what kind of signal terminated it. For a list of the signal types, look in the module `signal`. If the high-order bit of the low byte is set, then a core file was written to allow post-mortem debugging.

If you want to wait for a specific child process to terminate, you can use `os.waitpid()`:

```
pid,status=os.waitpid(idpat, option)
```

The `idpat` argument specifies what kind of child process to wait for: If `idpat` is `-1`, it will wait for any child process to terminate. If `idpat` is a positive integer, it will wait for the child process with that process id to terminate.[3]

If `option` is zero, this will wait for a child process to terminate and return its process id and status. If `option` is `os.WNOHANG`, it will return immediately. If `waitpid()` did not find a terminated child process, `pid` is assigned zero.

Is this parallel copy program any faster than a single copy? If the computer has more than one processor, they could actually be running in parallel. Even on a uniprocessor, it might be faster: Each of the processes can be executing while the other is waiting for disk I/O. Moreover, an operating system will divide the processor's time among all the runnable processes. If you have more processes working on your job, you are likely to get more of the processor's time.

---

3. There are options to specify any child in a specific process group, but we won't consider them here.

We could have created even more processes by recursively calling `cpparlist()` rather than `cplist()`. That would build a tree of processes copying parts of the list of files. A concern, though, is whether the time required for creating the subprocesses would be more than the savings in time spent copying the files.

Running Shell Commands from Python • If you want to execute a shell command from Python, you can call `os.system()`:

```
os.system(command)
```

This behaves very much as a command typed in to the shell itself. The `command` is run in a subprocess using the same standard input, output, and error files as your Python program. Your Python program waits for the command to complete: `system()` returns after the subprocess terminates. If you don't want the command to write its output to your output, but rather to give it back to you, you should redirect its output to a file.

popen • Often you want to use the output of a shell command in your Python program. For example, you can get lists of processes from the `ps` command, but it would be difficult to get them directly in Python. You could use `os.system()` and redirect the output of the command to a file, then read the command's output from the file, but this, of course, involves creating a name for the temporary file, opening it, closing it, and deleting it, in addition to simply reading the information you want. What you can do instead is use `os.popen()` to run a command in a subprocess that will pass information directly to you through a pipe, thus:

```
f=os.popen(command)
```

The `command` is a string containing the command, as with `os.system()`. Function `popen()` returns a file-like object that lets you read the output of the command as it is being written. The connection is by a *pipe*. A pipe is a bounded buffer, i.e., a buffer with a limit on the number of bytes it can contain. You access a pipe from your program like a file; it even uses a file descriptor. But it isn't really a file. It doesn't have a name in a directory. Because it is not in the file system, a pipe can only be used by a parent process and its children. The parent creates a pipe and the children inherit it.

There are two ways to use `popen()`. You can create a process that will send its output to you through a pipe, the default, or you can create a process that will take its input from you through a pipe. You specify this by a `mode` parameter on `popen()`:

```
f=os.popen(command,mode)
```

where `mode` is `'r'` or `'w'` for read or write. Use `'r'` (or omit the mode) when you want to read from the pipe. The other end of the pipe will be attached to the command's standard output. Use `'w'` when you want to write to the pipe. The other end of the pipe will be attached to the command's standard input. In either case, `popen()` returns a file object open for reading or writing as the mode specifies.

Here is an example. We write the message "hi, there" to a file, `x.txt`, by the circuitous route of creating a "cat" subprocess that will copy its standard input to its standard output. Since we used a `popen()` with the mode `'w'`, it will get its standard input from what we write to it. Its standard output is redirected to the file. After we write our message, we close the pipe, which terminates `cat`, which closes `x.txt`. We then read the contents of `x.txt` in a similar manner, creating a `cat` process that takes its input from the file and writes it to a pipe. We read the entire file and close the pipe.

```
>>> d=os.popen('cat - >x.txt','w')
>>> d.write('hi, there')
>>> d.close()
>>> d=os.popen('cat - <x.txt')
>>> d.read()
'hi, there'
>>> d.close()
```

What if you want to write text to the subprocess and read its output? We recommend you don't try. You can find a module `popen2` that offers the facility, but it comes with a high risk of deadlock. Suppose you are trying to write data to the subprocess but the pipe to its standard input is full. You will block, waiting for it to read something. Now suppose the subprocess is trying to write data to its standard output, but the pipe is full. It will block, waiting for you to read something. Neither of you will execute.

To Kill a Process in Python • The `os.kill()` function behaves the same way as the shell's `kill` command. It sends a signal to a process. You need to specify the process id and the signal you want to send. The signals are given names in the signal module. You should call

```
os.kill(pid,signal.SIGTERM)
```

to send a termination signal to the process. It gives the process a chance to clean up and terminate gracefully. If it ignores the SIGTERM, send it a SIGKILL signal, which it is unable to ignore:

```
os.kill(pid,signal.SIGKILL)
```

Executing New Programs

We have seen how Linux forks off a copy of a process as a subprocess. We have seen how to run commands using os.system() and os.popen(). The question is: How does it get from a copy of a process with the same instructions and data to a process running a different program? For this you use some form of the *exec* system call. The exec calls tell the system to replace your program and data with a program loaded from an executable file and its initialized data area. The only data you can pass from your program to the newly loaded program is a list of command-line parameter strings and an environment composed of names and their string values.

Execute Commands in Python • The versions of the exec command are shown in Table 4–12. The variations are indicated by letters at the end of the name. The name can include a lowercase L or lowercase V. An "l" at the end of the name indicates that all the arguments are in a single parameter list, including the argument strings, *arg0*,..., that are to be passed to the new program. The "v" indicates that the string argument list to the program is included in a tuple or list as a single argument to the exec function.

If the exec function has a trailing e, it means that the environment is being passed to the new program explicitly. The explicit environment is in the dictionary-valued parameter env. If the environment is not passed explicitly, the environment of the calling program is passed. We will discuss environments a bit later (see "Environment variables in bash" on page 212).

If the exec function name includes a p, then Python uses the current PATH variable to help look up the program to execute. The PATH environment variable contains not a single path, but a sequence of paths to directories separated by colons, $d0:d1:\ldots:dn$. Python will try out the `path` parameter directly, and then each directory $d0$, $d1$, ... in the PATH in order, $d0/path$, $d1/path$, ... hunting for the file to execute.

Table 4–12
exec Commands

Command	Explanation
`execv(path,(arg0,...))`	Replaces the current program and data with the program and data loaded from the executable file indicated by `path`. Passes `arg0`, ... as the argument strings. Passes the current environment.
`execve(path,(arg0,...),env)`	Replaces the current program and data with the program and data loaded from the executable file indicated by `path`. Passes `arg0`, ... as the argument strings. Passes directory `env` as the environment.
`execvp(path,(arg0,...))`	Replaces the current program and data with the program and data loaded from the executable file indicated by `path`. Passes `arg0`, ... as the argument strings. Passes the current environment. Uses the PATH environment variable to find the executable file indicated by `path`, i.e., if `path` is not absolute, combines it with each path in the PATH variable until it indicates an executable file.
`execvpe(path,(arg0,...),env)`	Replaces the current program and data with the program and data loaded from the executable file indicated by `path`. Passes `arg0`, ... as the argument strings. Passes directory `env` as the environment. Uses the PATH environment variable to find the executable file indicated by `path`, i.e., if `path` is not absolute, combines it with each path in the PATH variable until it indicates an executable file.
`execl(path,arg0,...)`	`execv(path,(arg0,...))`
`execle(path,arg0,...,env)`	`execve(path,(arg0,...),env)`
`execlp(path,arg0,...)`	`execlp(path,arg0,...)`

Because programs expect to receive their name as their first parameter, you will need to repeat the `path` parameter, or its base file name, as the *arg0*.

```
#!/usr/bin/python
import os
os.execvp('ls',('ls','-l'))
```

Accessing Arguments • We have just examined how to pass arguments to a program. Now let's look at the other side: how to access the arguments.

Accessing arguments in Python. When a Python program is run as a script, the command line parameters are in a tuple in variable `argv` in the `sys` module, `sys.argv`. It is exactly the same if the Python script is run as the result of an `exec` command. The name of the script is in `sys.argv[0]`.

Accessing arguments in `bash`. `Bash` is also a scripting language, so you can put `bash` commands in a file, mark the file executable, and execute it like a program. When the `bash` script is executed, its command line argument list can be accessed in variables `$1`, `$2`, ...`$9`. Variable `$0` is the name of the script running. The number of arguments is in variable `$#`. The entire argument list is in `$*` and `$@`. See Table 4–13.

Table 4–13
Argument List

Variables	Used For
`$1, $2, ...$9`	The first, up to nine, command line parameters.
`$0`	The name of the script running.
`$#`	The number of command line parameters.
`$*, $@`	The entire argument list considered a single word, or as a sequence of words. In many cases, interchangeable.
`$$`	The current process's process id.
`$?`	The exit status of the previous command.

If you need more than nine command line parameters, or any sophisticated programming, consider using Python instead of `bash`. But you can get at parameters beyond nine in `bash` scripts in one of two ways:

1. To shift the parameters down by one, losing the first, you can execute the `shift` command.
2. To iterate over the entire argument list, you can use the `for` statement.

The form of the `for` statement is:

```
for var in list
do
commands
done
```

These do need to be spread out on several lines. The variable `var` is just an identifier. It will be given each value in the list, one at a time, left to right. Within the commands, the value in `var` is referenced as `$var` or `${var}`. The form `${var}` is useful if the value is to be substituted adjacent to letters or digits and `$var` would be ambiguous. As will be seen next, this means that `var` is made an environment variable.

The `for` statement is also used frequently with back-quoted commands. If you include a command within back-quotes, the command is run and its output is used as the value of the back-quoted command. For example:

```
for f in `ls -d *`
do
echo $f
done
```

Environment Variables • Environment variables have string names and string values. They are used to pass information to processes about, well, their execution environment. When you are passing an environment to a program, you get to use any environment variables you want, but some are used by convention in all programs. The most important environment variables are shown in Table 4–14.

Environment variables in `bash`.   In `bash`, you assign values to variables with simple assignment statements.

```
var=value
```

Table 4–14
Customary Environment Variables

Variable	Used For
HOME	Absolute path to the user's home directory
LOGNAME	User's login name
HOSTNAME	This computer's Internet name
PATH	A sequence of paths to directories separated with colons for searching for programs to be run

The variable, `var`, is an identifier. The main function of variables in `bash` is to substitute text into command lines. You replace a variable with its value by one of the forms:

```
$var
${var}
```

The `${var}` form is used if adjacent characters can be part of identifiers.

The environment variables passed to `bash` comprise its initial set of variables. These variables will also be passed to processes `bash` starts. The `bash` script can assign values to other variables, but these are not automatically passed to subprocesses. To pass a new variable to a subprocess, you must declare it for export:

```
export var
```

Environment variables in Python.   You will find a dictionary containing the inherited environment in the `environ` variable in the `os` module, `os.environ`. To get the value of a variable named `k`, just look it up in the dictionary:

```
os.environ[k]
```

or

```
os.environ.get(k)
```

You can also assign new values to environment variables or create new environment variables with a simple subscripted assignment:

```
os.environ[k]=v
```

The new variables and new values will be passed to subprocesses.

PATH   The most important environment variable is PATH. When trying to find a program to run for a command, bash searches the path. So does Python when you call os.execvp, os.execvpe, or os.execlp.

The name, PATH, really ought to be plural. It contains a list of paths to directories separated by separator characters, ":"s on Linux, "d0:d1:....:dn", ("; "s on Windows). When searching for a file to execute for the command, c, both bash and Python will try out c as a file name and then combined with each directory d0, d1, ... in PATH, d0/c, d1/c, ...

In bash, you refer to the PATH as $PATH or ${PATH}. Usually, you refer to PATH to add more directories to it, for example:

```
PATH=${PATH}:/x/y
```

In Python, of course, you look up PATH in the environment, for example:

```
os.environ['PATH']=os.environ['PATH']+ \
    os.pathsep+os.sep+'x'+os.sep+'y'
```

The attribute os.pathsep is the string that separates directory paths in the PATH string, ":" on Linux and Unix and "; " on Windows. Attribute os.sep is the string used to separate directories and files in a path, "/" on Linux and Unix, "\" on Windows. There are also strings os.curdir and os.pardir, which are used to refer to the current and the parent directories, "." and "..". You would use these to make your code more system-independent.

5

Introduction to Internetworking and HTTP

The Internet is at the heart of Web-based enterprise programming. Before developing Web-based applications, it is important to have a strong understanding of how the Web is organized. This will form the foundation for more complicated concepts. A sound understanding of these concepts is necessary for you to understand the limitations of the Web, because it is the limitations that bound your capabilities. As in any programming paradigm, knowing what you can and can't do will drive your design decisions. The topics covered in this chapter are normally spread over several different books. Their presentation here will help the practicing programmer understand the fundamentals of the Web and will provide a review for more advanced readers.

The two fundamental concepts that all Web-based applications are built on are networking and the HTTP protocol. This chapter covers both of these concepts in adequate depth to help you understand topics covered in later chapters. In the first half, we explore the history of the Internet and network computing. The main focus will be on TCP/IP networks and the various organizational strategies and mechanics employed in routing information across a network. Then we shift gears and discuss the HTTP protocol. Emphasis will be placed on topics that directly impact Web-based programming.

In the Beginning

The word *internet* means a network of distributed computers. The construction of the first internet began in 1962 as a U.S. Department of Defense project called ARPANET. The goal of ARPA (Advanced

215

Research Projects Agency) was to explore investments in computing technology. At the time, computers were simple batch-processing circuits designed to perform computations. Dr. J.C.R. Licklider, the appointed chairman of ARPA, had a different vision of computer usage, as a new avenue of communication. Licklider focused ARPA's efforts on creating communities of computers that joined to create an intergalactic communication network. To realize this goal, ARPA organized and funded the research of selected universities and private institutions. ARPA's management had two side effects: the development of advanced network technologies leading to the first internetwork of computers, and new standards for documenting large, complicated, distributed group projects in a collection of documents called RFCs (Requests for Comments).

The process of creating a network of computers was plagued by two problems: utilizing existing telephony relay and switches for the communication of data; and understanding, designing, and implementing network communication rules, known as network protocols. Many academic research groups began investigating solutions to these problems. The outcome of these network research projects led to the creation of the Internet.

The Network Foundation: The Data Communication Model

All networks are based on a data communication model. The model describes the steps involved when communicating data over a network. The best-known data communication model is the Open Systems Interconnect (OSI) Reference Model formulated by the International Standards Organization. OSI's popularity is not in its wide implementation or adoption, but in its international recognition as the ideal data communication model. As with other ideal concepts, there are many complex ideas that exceed software and hardware limitations. However, the OSI model has led to practical solutions. One such solution is TCP/IP networking. It is important to have a high-level understanding of the OSI model, as it is the basis for many other networking models, such as TCP/IP.

The OSI model is organized into seven different layers. Each layer defines a functional piece of the communication protocol, a set of rules that govern communication between systems. Figure 5–1 depicts each of the seven layers. Together, the layers form a protocol stack. The most important aspect of the OSI model is the flow of data through the stack.

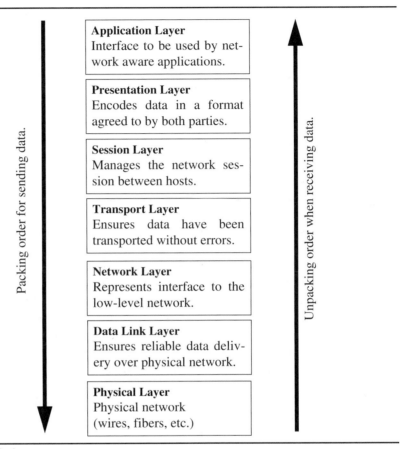

Figure 5–1
OSI Communication Model

When sending, the data flows from the application layer down through the stack to the physical layer. When receiving, data are obtained at the physical layer and flow upward toward the application layer.

The layers are intended to be functionally independent. Working in a peer-oriented model, each layer operates on the message received from a neighboring layer. The operation performed on the message depends on the direction of flow through the stack. When sending a message, each layer adds control information, called a header, onto the message. This process encapsulates the original message in a larger one. As a result, the message grows increasingly longer at each layer, as depicted in Figure 5–2. When data are received, each layer performs the reverse of the encapsulation operation by unpacking the header

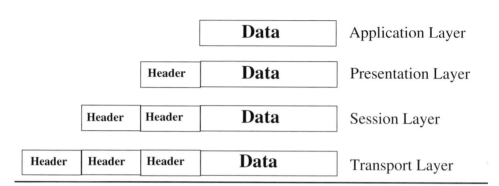

Figure 5–2
Encapsulation of Messages

from the message. The header is used by the layer and the remaining message is passed to a neighboring layer. This operation is performed at each layer until the application layer performs the final unpacking of the message and delivers it to the intended network application.

Each layer plays a small role in transporting application data across the network. Layering effectively simplifies and organizes all considerations and algorithms required to perform this operation. Layers also make the overall framework more flexible, allowing for different combinations of algorithms to be employed based on the type of physical and logical network topology at hand.

From OSI to TCP/IP

TCP/IP is the combination of two communication protocols in a single protocol stack. Figure 5–3 depicts the TCP/IP protocol stack. Unlike the OSI model, there are only four layers to TCP/IP. The top layer is the application layer. As with OSI, the application layer is responsible for bridging the gap between network applications and the protocol stack. The second layer is the transport layer, responsible for proper delivery and receipt of data. This layer implements the Transport Control Protocol, the TCP part of TCP/IP. Below the transport layer is the Internet layer, responsible for the routing of data through the network. The Internet layer implements the Internet Protocol, the IP part of TCP/IP. Finally, there is the network access layer, which implements methods for accessing the physical network.

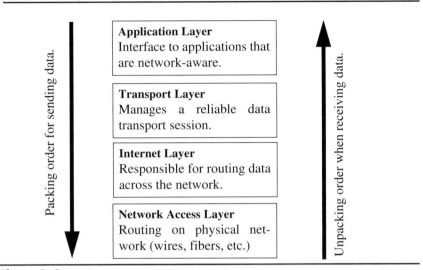

Figure 5–3
TCP/IP Protocol Stack

The key to how TCP/IP works lies within the operations performed at each layer of the protocol stack. Since the application and physical layers cap the protocol stack, their main objective is to initiate and complete flows through the stack. This leaves the bulk of the routing and transmission work to be done by the transport and Internet layers. Without these two layers, the data being communicated would never reach the intended host. The following subsections investigate how these TCP/IP layers work to facilitate communication between hosts on the Internet.

IP Layer

The Internet Protocol layer (IP) is mainly concerned with the routing and delivery of the data. At this layer, the data are referred to as a datagram. The IP layer uses a 32-bit addressing scheme to deliver data across the network. At some point or another, you must have come across an IP number such as: 192.168.0.1. The IP number is organized into four bytes. Since each byte has 8 bits, the largest numerical value of each of the four bytes is 255. There are no negative numbers, making 0 the smallest value contained. Why four bytes? The IP number is used to identify a system uniquely on a network. Since the Internet is such a vast network of computers, a scheme is needed that can locate millions of computers, and the four bytes in the IP number do just that. Each byte compounds the number of unique addresses available by 255. Four bytes is also a convenient grouping, as it fits inside a 32-bit word.[1]

In creating a TCP/IP network, each computer on the network is assigned a unique IP number known as the IP address. The IP layer uses the IP address to route data through the network. Let's examine what events take place when a host, named A, wishes to communicate with another host, named B, on the Internet. Host A's IP layer prepares to transmit data to host B, by including both the senders's IP number (host A's IP number) and the recipient's IP number in the message header along with other control statements. When the message reaches the physical network, it is sent to the local gateway. A gateway is a host computer that has knowledge of more than one network. Gateways typically have multiple network interfaces, each connected to a physically different network. In some cases, the network topology may also vary, such as when a gateway is connected to both an ATM and a TCP/IP network. A variant of the gateway is a dual-homed system. Gateways bridge the gap between networks.

The IP layer of the gateway's TCP/IP protocol stack will unpack the message sent by host A and read the IP address of the intended recipient. Using routing information available for the various networks that the gateway is connected to along with the recipient's IP address, the gateway will make an educated guess as to which network the message should be transmitted to. The message will then reach another gateway that will perform the same operation. This process continues until eventually the message reaches a gateway that knows about host B.

You may be wondering, if each gateway makes a best guess in routing messages, how do data reach their destination in a timely manner? The answer to this lies in the structure of the IP address and the gateway's routing table. As explained earlier, IP numbers are composed of four bytes that identify a particular host on a particular network. Each IP number is organized into two components: network address and host number. To separate the host number from the network address, a netmask is used. The netmask is a special four-byte IP address. Masking is accomplished by applying the logical AND operation between the netmask and the IP address. For example, the logical AND of the netmask 255.255.255.0 and the IP address 64.1.2.23 results in the network number 64.1.2.0 and the host number 23. Notice that the network address ends with 0. The values 0 and 255 can never be used to identify hosts and are reserved for identifying net-

---

1. A *word* is a unit of memory that consists of 4 bytes or 32 bits.

works and broadcast addresses, respectively. Figure 5–4 shows how the logical AND operator is used. As another example, the network mask `255.255.255.252` when applied to the same IP number, `64.1.2.23`, results in the network address `64.1.2.20` and host number `3`. Customized masks, called subnet masks, can be used to create customized networks that have adequate host IP addresses. Subnets are important organizational structures that help deal with IP number shortages.

Now that we know how a netmask is used, we can understand how gateways make routing decisions. Upon receiving a datagram, the gateway applies a netmask to obtain the network address of the receiving host. Using a routing table, the gateway's IP layer will make one of two decisions: The recipient is on the local network and the data are delivered, or the recipient is on a remote network and the data are passed to the local gateway of that network. By design, routing tables list only network addresses associated with available network interfaces. Thus, like using individual city maps for a cross-country journey, routing tables help in selecting networks that may know about a particular host. This system distributes routing information across many gateways on the Internet. It would be nearly impossible to build a table that has all routes to all hosts on the Internet.

You can view your local routing table using the Linux `netstat` command. `Netstat` provides many different pieces of information about your host's network configuration. In order to view the routing

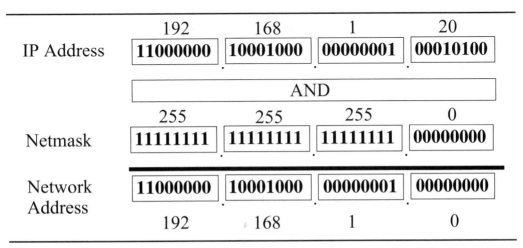

Figure 5–4
Applying a Netmask to an IP Address

```
[pshafae@john pshafae]$ netstat -nr
Kernel IP routing table
Destination      Gateway          Genmask          Flags  MSS Window  irtt Iface
192.168.0.201    0.0.0.0          255.255.255.255  UH       0 0          0 eth0
192.168.0.0      0.0.0.0          255.255.0.0      U        0 0          0 eth0
127.0.0.0        0.0.0.0          255.0.0.0        U        0 0          0 lo
0.0.0.0          192.168.0.1      0.0.0.0          UG       0 0          0 eth0
```

Figure 5–5
A Typical Routing Table

table, you will have to use the -nr option. The -n option instructs netstat to display numerical values or IP numbers, as opposed to resolved domain names. The -r option specifically instructs the printing of the routing table. Figure 5–5 is an example of output generated by netstat. As you can see, the table serves to associate network interfaces to network addresses, and network addresses to authoritative gateways. The destination column lists network addresses, although it can be used to identify a particular host. Besides specific IP numbers, the destination column also contains a default destination, identified by the IP address 0.0.0.0. This is the default route used for messages that do not fit any of the other listed destinations. The default route typically leads to another gateway that has a broader view of the entire network. Next to destination is the gateway column. This column lists the IP address of the authoritative gateway for a particular destination. When routing to a destination, the message is passed to the authoritative gateway of the destined network.

The flags column classifies the route type. There are four different flags that may appear. They are summarized in Table 5–1.

Table 5–1
Routing Table Flags

Code	Description
U	Indicates a network that is functional and accessible.
H	This is a route to a host.
G	Indicates that the route is to a remote gateway. These are remote networks that are controlled by the associated gateway.
D	Identifies a redirect. The details of redirects are beyond the scope of our discussion, but simply put, they define alternative routes to particular networks.

The last column of interest is labeled "Iface," short for network interface. It defines the physical network interface that is used to access a particular network.

The `netstat` command provides a lot more information that is not covered here. You are encouraged to read the manual pages (`man netstat`) to see additional information that may be obtained about your system's network configuration.

Each pass of a message from one gateway to another is referred to as a hop. Using the `traceroute` command in Linux, you can view all of the hops made when sending data from one host to another across the Internet. Figure 5–6 depicts the output of `traceroute` for tracing the hops between the host `brahms.siteprotect.com` to `www.toolsofcomputing.com`. The `traceroute` command not only reports the IP address and domain name of the intermediary gateways, but the time it took to reach the particular gateway. Each hop is traced multiple times to improve the average delay time (the delay time for each attempt is listed after the IP address of the gateway visited). `traceroute` uses the Internet Control Message Protocol (ICMP) to obtain this information. ICMP is beyond the scope of our discussion, but note that it plays a role in obtaining information about a network.

The construction of routing tables is a critical activity. The biggest problem in creating routing tables is the dynamic nature of networks. At any time, individual hosts on a network or entire networks may go off-line. Equally important is the addition of new networks. Newly added gateways need to construct a routing table based on the network information available. An entire set of protocols has been developed to help solve some of

```
brahms:~$ traceroute www.toolsofcomputing.com
traceroute: Warning: Multiple interfaces found; using 209.100.98.20 @ eth0
traceroute to www.toolsofcomputing.com (208.231.15.33), 30 hops max, 40 byte packets
 1  64.26.0.1 (64.26.0.1)  0.333 ms  1.349 ms  0.475 ms
 2  500.Serial2-8.GW2.CHI2.ALTER.NET (157.130.119.49)  1.885 ms  2.937 ms  1.775 ms
 3  so-4/0/0.XL1.CHI2.ALTER.NET (152.63.64.158)  2.119 ms  1.766 ms  2.037 ms
 4  0.so-7-0-0.XR1.CHI2.ALTER.NET (152.63.67.130)  1.964 ms  1.788 ms  2.032 ms
 5  193.ATM3-0.TR1.CHI4.ALTER.NET (152.63.64.218)  2.670 ms  2.913 ms  2.710 ms
 6  106.at-7-0-0.TR2.DCA8.ALTER.NET (146.188.138.178)  26.431 ms  26.514 ms  27.713 ms
 7  0.so-4-3-0.XR1.DCA8.ALTER.NET (152.63.144.50)  28.589 ms  26.655 ms  26.320 ms
 8  189.ATM9-0-0.GW1.BWI1.ALTER.NET (152.63.37.173)  24.164 ms  29.322 ms  28.195 ms
 9  skynetbwi-gw.customer.ALTER.NET (157.130.39.138)  31.798 ms  29.118 ms  29.217 ms
10  c6509rtr2-vlan3.skynetweb.com (208.231.4.4)  24.870 ms  22.286 ms  21.503 ms
11  toolsofcomputing.com (208.231.15.33)  22.807 ms  25.250 ms  22.471 ms
```

Figure 5–6

Output of `traceroute` from brahms.siteprotect.com to www.toolsofcomputing.com

the difficulties encountered with keeping routing tables current. For example, the Border Gateway Protocol (BGP) is used to communicate routing information between gateways that share network borders. This is one protocol used to create routing tables that correctly identify routes to remote networks. The Gateway–Gateway Protocol (GGP) is another example of how routing information is shared. Entire texts have been written on these protocols, so we will not go into any more detail here, but it is important to know that such frameworks do exist and are used to construct and maintain routing tables.

To help visualize the routing of messages, consider the steps involved in mailing a letter to a friend who lives in another country. The letter that you send is composed of the letter itself (data) placed inside an envelope (encapsulation of data in the TCP/IP message) that contains your friend's residential address (IP address and IP layer routing information). The first line of the address identifies your friend's house number (the host number) on a particular street (local network where the host is located). The second and third lines identify the city, state, and country (increasingly large networks). Your local post office (local gateway) uses the address information to begin routing the data. Seeing that it is not local (data belongs to a remote network), the local post office sends the letter to a larger post office (another gateway) that has a broader view of the address system (knows about other larger networks). This is done until the letter reaches your friend's local post office (destination host's local gateway). The letter is then delivered.

Before we wrap up our discussion of the IP layer, it is important to consider several special IP addresses. The first special address is commonly referred to as the loopback address; it is assigned the IP number 127.0.0.1. All addresses that belong to the 127.0.0.0 network are the logical address of the local host. They always define "self" relative to the network. The loopback address never results in data being placed on the physical network; it exists solely to support special functionality required by network-aware applications.

Beside the loopback address, three classes of IP numbers are considered private and non-routeable by public Internet gateways. These classes include all IP numbers that are on the following networks: 10.0.0.0, 172.16.0.0, and 192.168.0.0. Hosts that have these IP numbers cannot receive data from a public network and require a special gateway that implements Network Address Translation. Since the addresses are non-routeable, any number of private networks can be created. Private addresses help deal with depleting IP numbers and provide a simple scheme for private networking.

Finally, a set of reserved addresses exists for identifying all hosts on a network: broadcast and mulitcast addresses. We have already seen that all addresses that end in zeros identify a network. Similarly, all addresses that end with 255s identify a broadcast address or an address that includes all of the computers on the particular network. For example, the broadcast address 64.1.255.255 includes all of the hosts on the 64.1.0.0 network. The broadcast address is used to send a message to all hosts on a particular network, whereas the multicast address applies to specific hosts that belong to a designated group. Broadcast and multicast addresses are used to stream multimedia data on a network.

Domain Names and the DNS

In the view of the World Wide Web, each computer on the network can potentially be running a Web server that serves Web pages. However, to access Web pages, we don't typically use the IP number of the Web server. Instead, we use a domain name such as www.toolsofcomputing.com.

If the IP layer uses IP numbers, how is it that the Web browser can locate the host serving the Web pages of toolsofcomputing.com? IP numbers may be very well suited for computers, but they are not all that meaningful to humans. We tend to associate locations by names. To overcome this convenience issue, each unique IP number is mapped to a domain name. For example, the IP number 208.231.15.33 is mapped to the domain name www.toolsofcomputing.com. This relationship is stored in a dictionary managed by an application called the domain name server (DNS). Every time that you type in a domain name in your Web browser, the browser first contacts a designated DNS and translates the domain name into an IP address. The process of translating the domain name into an IP address is called domain name resolution. The browser then uses the IP address to communicate with the particular host that is serving the Web page. The DNS can also be used to perform a reverse lookup of an IP address to resolve the domain name that it points to.

A hierarchical scheme is used to organize domain names. The complete domain name is composed of subdomains separated by periods. The top-level domain is the root for all other domains. There are a number of top-level domains, including com, org, net, edu, and gov. The domain name john.dev.toolsofcomputing.com has the top-level domain com. The first subdomain name, called the first-level domain name, identifies an organizational network. In our example, the first- level domain name `toolsofcomputing` refers to the Tools of Computing LLC network. From this point on, all subdomain names are numbered relative to the first-level domain. The second-level domain name, `dev`, identifies a particular subnetwork within `toolsofcomputing`. This is not always the case. If dev were the last identifier in the domain name, it would most likely refer to a particular host on the toolsofcomputing network, as opposed to a subnetwork. In our example, john is the identifier of the host, as it is the left-most domain name.

The hierarchical structure of DNS provides a mechanism to describe the hierarchical nature of organizations. A DNS server is used at each level of the hierarchy, allowing organizations to customize their internal network name structure. The top-level DNS knows about all of the hosts under a particular top-level domain. Each of these hosts uses a local DNS to serve the domain name hierarchy of the organization. This pattern can be extended to have many deep and highly organized subnets, as are often found in large institutions such as universities.

The Linux command `nslookup` can be used to consult a DNS server and resolve the IP address of a host. Figure 5–7 depicts the use of `nslookup` in discovering the IP number associated with `www.toolsofcomputing.com`. Much like `nslookup`, your Web browser first translates each domain name to an IP number by contacting a DNS server. Performing this lookup can slow down your browser. You can install a local caching DNS server to help speed this process: A caching DNS caches the IP addresses of domain names that you often visit. It is much faster to query the local DNS for an IP number than a remote one, hence speeding up the process of surfing the Web.

DNS can also be used to perform basic load balancing. For example, using nslookup to resolve the IP address of `www.cnn.com` results in the output listed in Figure 5–8. As you can see, there are 12 different IP addresses associated with `www.cnn.com`. Each time your browser

```
[pshafae@john pshafae]$ nslookup www.toolsofcomputing.com
Server:    santana.hostway.com
Address:   192.168.0.102

Non-authoritative answer:
Name:     www.toolsofcomputing.com
Address:   208.231.15.33
```

Figure 5–7
Output of `nslookup` for www.toolsofcomputing.com

```
[pshafae@john pshafae]$ nslookup www.cnn.com
Server:  santana.hostway.com
Address:  192.168.0.102

Non-authoritative answer:
Name:    cnn.com
Addresses:  207.25.71.20, 207.25.71.22, 207.25.71.23, 207.25.71.24
            207.25.71.25, 207.25.71.26, 207.25.71.27, 207.25.71.28, 207.25.71.29
            207.25.71.30, 207.25.71.5, 207.25.71.6
Aliases:  www.cnn.com
```

Figure 5–8
nslookup Output for www.cnn.com

attempts to resolve the address www.cnn.com, there is a good possibility of getting an inconsistent answer. As a consequence, a different host is contacted for the same information. This balances the load that would otherwise be placed on a single server over a cluster of systems. For proper load balancing, the administrators of www.cnn.com must ensure that each of the listed hosts contains an exact mirror of the main site.

Transport Layer

As we have seen, the IP layer is mainly concerned with the routing of data through the network. The management of data delivery to the destination host is the responsibility of the transport layer. The transport layer implements several different protocols, the two most popular being Transport Control Protocol (TCP) and User Datagram Protocol (UDP). Each protocol has a different set of properties that governs how a connection is made and how communication is conducted between any two hosts. Collectively, the variations can be thought of as transmission policies. The user can choose the best policy for the type of operation being performed.

Transmission protocols are necessary to control communication in a packet-based system. There is no such thing as a real connection on a network, since data are transported in segments; there is only the concept of a logical connection. Logical connections are agreements made between two hosts on the type and length of data to be communicated. The logical connection is used to ensure that data originating from one host correctly reach another. Without transmission protocols, it would be nearly impossible to control the delivery of data across a network.

Each transmission protocol is assigned a unique number. A listing of protocols and their associated numbers can be found in the /etc/protocols file. Figure 5–9 contains a sample /etc/protocols file. The first column identifies the protocol name. The second column contains

```
ip        0     IP          # internet protocol, pseudo protocol number
icmp      1     ICMP        # internet control message protocol
igmp      2     IGMP        # Internet Group Management
ggp       3     GGP         # gateway-gateway protocol
ipencap   4     IP-ENCAP    # IP encapsulated in IP (officially "IP")
st        5     ST          # ST datagram mode
tcp       6     TCP         # transmission control protocol
egp       8     EGP         # exterior gateway protocol
pup       12    PUP         # PARC universal packet protocol
udp       17    UDP         # user datagram protocol
hmp       20    HMP         # host monitoring protocol
xns-idp   22    XNS-IDP     # Xerox NS IDP
rdp       27    RDP         # "reliable datagram" protocol
iso-tp4   29    ISO-TP4     # ISO Transport Protocol class 4
```

Figure 5–9
Sampling of the `/etc/protocols` File

the integer assigned to the protocol. There is a third optional column for the protocol alias. Any comments set off by the pound sign (#) are ignored by the system. It is critical that all systems use the same numbers to identify a protocol. To this end, the numbers are standardized and assigned based on the Assigned Numbers RFC.

TCP. The TCP protocol is synonymous with end-to-end connectivity and reliable transport. This reputation is the result of a strict policy used to initiate, maintain, and terminate a remote connection. Table 5–2 highlights the two main qualities of TCP.

At the transport layer, the data stream is called a packet. As in the IP layer, each packet has a header and a data section. The TCP packet header is quite involved. There are many different control fields that are used to manage a logical connection. Much like a scoreboard, the header fields are used to track all of the events that occur during a dialogue.

The stateful nature of TCP originates from the creation of the logical connection. The mechanism used to create the connection is called a three-way handshake. Just as people shake hands when they meet, hosts perform a logical handshake to acknowledge the creation of a network connection. The handshake is accomplished by using special TCP

Table 5–2
Qualities of TCP

Stateful	Hosts are aware of a logical connection and track each transmission.
Reliable	Receiving host acknowledges receipt of data sent and sending host manages packet loss.

packets, referred to as segments, that act as flags. The segments are used by each host to communicate connection information. As an example, host A starts by sending to remote host B a "Synchronize sequence numbers" (SYN) segment. Upon receipt, host B realizes that host A would like to create a connection and replies with a packet that has both the SYN and Acknowledgment (ACK) flags set. In the reply, the ACK segment acknowledges receipt of host A's sequence number and the SYN segment describes the sequence number that host B would like to use. The sequence numbers play a key role in ensuring proper delivery of packets once a connection is made, but more on this later. To complete the three-way handshake, host A replies with an ACK packet that also contains part of the data that will be transmitted during the connection. Although we have only covered the basics of the three-way handshake, it is important to note that each of the three steps plays an important role in ensuring a proper path of communication.

Once the connection is established, host A begins transmitting data packets to host B. There are two problems that commonly occur during data transmission: Packets may get lost or may become corrupted. The solution to the first problem is based on sequence numbers. The sending host sets the sequence number of the packet being sent. Upon receipt, the receiving host replies with an ACK packet that contains the sequence number of the packet received. If the sending host does not receive acknowledgment on a sent packet, it will consider it lost and retransmit a copy. This algorithm not only ensures proper transmission of the packet, but also allows the receiving host to track the proper ordering of the packets when reassembling the original message.

The problem with corrupted data is resolved by a checksum algorithm. Before transmitting a packet, the sender will apply a numerical algorithm to the data stored in the packet. This results in a numerical value, called a checksum, that acts as a key. Before using the data, the receiving host applies the same algorithm to the data in the packet. It then compares the stored checksum with the numerical value computed. A discrepancy indicates data corruption and host B requests a retransmission of that particular packet.

Once all of the packets have been sent, the sending host initiates a connection teardown by using a FIN segment. Similar to the three-way handshake, care is taken to make sure both parties are aware of the connection termination. In every aspect of the communication, extra precautions are taken to ensure delivery of uncorrupted data. This is a very important concept with respect to network computing. Network-aware applications do not need to be concerned with the low-level details of network communication. Instead, they pass the data to the protocol stack and the transport layer ensures proper delivery to the intended host.

Many programming paradigms require reliable communication of data. For example, without a reliable communication mechanism, data sent by a Web server may come across corrupted or in partial form. Users would not only see inconsistent views of the same HTML pages, but in some cases no views at all. TCP ensures that every byte of data sent by the server reaches the browser without additional overhead on the part of the server or the browser.

UDP.   UDP is the simpler of the two transport protocols. Unlike TCP, UDP has a reputation for being an unreliable and connectionless protocol. In this paradigm, data packets are sent to a remote host without any guarantee of delivery. At the cost of reliability, this protocol provides a fast and efficient means of data delivery.

UDP packets have considerably simpler headers compared to TCP packets. The only fields that are available are the source address, destination address, data length, checksum, and the data stream. There are no fields for transmission control. The connectionless nature of UDP means that no connection is negotiated before transmission takes place. Without a connection, there is no guarantee that the receiving host is alive and ready for networking.

Although there is no guarantee made on the delivery of data, UDP does provide a means for the receiving host to check the integrity of the data. As with TCP, a checksum is calculated based on the data being sent. This is important as there is no other way to check the integrity of the data received.

So what happens when packets do not reach the intended host? Believe it or not, nothing. The protocol is employed in programming paradigms for which speed of service is more important than reliability of delivery. The most popular use of UDP is with streaming media on the Web. For example, a network-based radio station may choose to broadcast its service to a number of hosts. UDP is employed to deliver the sound bytes as fast as possible. Some bytes may get lost en route, but a majority will be delivered. The lost packets will not drastically affect final quality of the broadcast, since each packet makes up a very small piece of the recording. In many cases, the user may not even recognize that some of the information is missing.

There are also network applications that choose to handle the delivery of information at a higher level. UDP gives these types of applications the means to transport the data on the network without the additional overhead of transmission control.

Ports and Sockets

We have seen how the Internet and Transport layers are responsible for the routing and delivery of data on a network. Once received, the data need to be delivered to a particular network application, such as your Web browser.

In almost the same way that IP numbers are used to uniquely identify a host, a combination of port and protocol numbers is used to uniquely identify applications on a particular host. Network applications such as your Web browser or TELNET are typically referred to as network services. A network service must register itself with the operating system before being able to use the available network connection. The registration process results in the network service's obtaining a port number. Port numbers are 16-bit positive integers. This means that the lower and upper bounds for port numbers are 1 and 65,535.

Port numbers are not unique. Each port number may be paired with one or more protocol numbers. As you may recall from our discussion of transmission protocols, protocol numbers are integers assigned to each transport protocol. Usually you will see the same port number paired with both the UDP and TCP protocol. The /etc/services file contains a number of port/protocol combinations for well-known network services. Figure 5–10 contains a sampling of data stored in /etc/services. The first column of the services file identifies the network service. The second column identifies the port/protocol combinations. As you can see, the same port number appears more than once, but the port/protocol number combination is unique. The data in this file are used as a reference table for delivering data to applications based on the protocol used and the port number assigned to the application.

Data packets sent to a particular host contain as their destination address the IP address of the remote host as well as the port number of a network service the packet is intended for. The protocol number is identified by the type of packet sent. When the packet reaches the remote host the port/protocol number combination is used to call a network service. During this time, the network service lies dormant, listening for connections on the specified port. Once the network application receives the data, it can begin processing it. The combination of an IP address and a port number is referred to as a socket. Sockets provide a guaranteed unique identification of a network service on the Internet.

A number of network services are ubiquitous and are assigned standard or well-known port numbers. For example, the TELNET server always listens for connection on port 23, whereas the Web server

```
. . .
netstat          15/tcp
qotd             17/tcp        quote
msp              18/tcp                          # message send protocol
msp              18/udp                          # message send protocol
chargen          19/tcp        ttytst source
chargen          19/udp        ttytst source
ftp-data         20/tcp
ftp              21/tcp
fsp              21/udp        fspd
ssh              22/tcp                          # SSH Remote Login Protocol
ssh              22/udp                          # SSH Remote Login Protocol
telnet           23/tcp
# 24 - private
smtp             25/tcp        mail
. . .
```

Figure 5–10
Sampling of /etc/services

listens for connections on port 80. This does not mean that these services cannot be configured to use different port numbers. Standardized port numbers help speed up network connections by eliminating the need to look up the port number for a well-known service.

One of the fundamental reasons for networking is to share resources. If only one network connection could be made at any time, sharing resources on a multiuser system such as Linux would not be effective or economical. The basic problem in sharing resources on a network is the fact that each network service is defined by a unique number. In order to share a service concurrently on a single system, a network service needs to be identified by more than one socket. The effective solution to this problem is the use of dynamically allocated port numbers.

To understand best how dynamically allocated port numbers are used, we will go through a simple scenario of two users surfing the Web on a single Linux system. As you discovered in the previous section, Web servers listen on the well-known port 80. Each browser used by the two users begins by creating a connection to a remote server. In the destination field, the connection packet contains the remote server's IP address and port 80. However, each browser will choose a dynamically assigned port number in the source address field (the address that the Web server will use to send information back). Since there are considerably more port numbers than network services, the operating system has a pool of available port numbers that can be used for dynamic assignment. The operating system maintains this pool by only assigning available port numbers and replenishing the pool with port numbers that are no longer being used. This ensures that each browser session on the system obtains a different dynamic port number.

Upon connection, the Web server responds using its source address (the server's IP address and port 80) and the destination IP address and port number of the packet received. Since each browser has a different port number, the packets will reach the appropriate browser. If dynamic port numbers were not used, each user would have to wait for the other to complete a connection using the single port number.

This concludes our introduction to networking. The most important aspect of networking is how numerical addresses are used to identify network services uniquely. Without unique addresses, it would be nearly impossible to route information on a network. You should now have a great appreciation for IP, port, and protocol numbers, as they are the key to how the Internet works. It is amazing to realize that a few integers are all that are needed to make a network connection that spans the Atlantic.

HTTP and the World Wide Web

Building the Internet is only half of the story. The Internet provides both the physical connections and network protocols needed to create a massive network of computers that spans the globe. However, when we think of the Internet, we really think in terms of the "services" that are available on the Internet. Internet services are applications that use the Internet as the infrastructure for the sharing of information. Some examples of services include e-mail, news, and the World Wide Web. The rest of this chapter will concentrate on the World Wide Web and the HTTP protocol. If you are confident in your knowledge of these two topics, feel free to skip to the next chapter.

A Walk Down Memory Lane

Until the early 1990s the Internet was a cold and desolate world occupied mainly by academics and scientists. The limited network services available made it possible to share information on a worldwide scale, but at the cost of an intimate knowledge of computers and networks. The average person could not easily contribute or search for information.

The need to simplify the system of sharing information fueled network services research. Gopher and Archie (short for Archive browser) were two of the more popular network services designed for sharing, publishing, and accessing information banks. Gopher used a hierarchical system of information servers, organized as a series of directories and documents. Using Gopher, when you connect to a particular server you are presented with a set of directories that contain various categories of information. Upon selection of a directory, you are presented with the contents of that directory. The contents may include other directories or documents. Much like the Linux file system, you search through the directories until you reach the document that you are looking for. The Archie system used a similar hierarchical scheme to locate anonymous FTP servers. The FTP servers could have many documents pertaining to the topic that you were searching for.

As Gopher and Archie gained popularity, their limitations were quickly realized. With information being added daily, more and more time was needed to refine searches. It was clear that the hierarchical model could not keep up with the rapid growth of information. In 1989, Tim Berners-Lee, a researching faculty member at CERN, the European Organization for Nuclear Research, was investigating ways to share large quantities of multimedia documents gathered at the research institute. His efforts, along with those of his colleague Robert Calliau, resulted in a series of papers describing a new Internet-based service called the World Wide Web. Yes, the World Wide Web (the Web) is *not* the Internet. It is simply a service available on the Internet. Unfortunately, most of us were introduced to the Internet at a time when every academic and commercial establishment pushed to advertise its place on the Web, and we have come to equate the Web with the Internet.

Tim Berners-Lee's solution to the problem of organizing shared information relied on a culmination of old ideas. A system called hypertext, which originated at Apple Computing laboratories, was used to associate related documents. Hypertexts, as you may know, are cross-references that can appear in a text document. By selecting the hypertext, you are taken to the source of the cross-reference. What makes this system more powerful than the hierarchical schemes of Gopher and Archie is its ability to include any number of cross-references on any number of documents. Hypertext captures the relational nature of information.

To facilitate hypertexts in documents, a new language called the Hyper Text Markup Language (HTML) was invented. HTML not only described cross-references between documents, but also captured various aspects of multimedia documents, including word decorations and images. The entire language uses a series of tags to mark up plain text. The details of HTML are beyond the scope of our discussion; however, we recommend that you investigate HTML if it is new to you. We will be using it extensively throughout the text.

The browser was implemented to render the HTML documents, referred to as pages, on a graphical display. The first browser was very limited. In 1994, Marc Anderson, a graduate student at the National Center for Supercomputing Applications, joined the efforts of the young Web community by authoring and freely distributing the first version of the Mosaic HTML browser. This was a more powerful browser, later commercialized under the name Netscape. There are now many free and commercial browsers that support the latest versions of HTML.

HTML resolved the problem of organizing multimedia documents, but there was still the problem of sharing the documents on the Internet. The World Wide Web model was invented to resolve exactly this problem. In this model, the HTML documents live on servers, similar to documents on Gopher and Archie servers. The browser, acting as a client, connects to a server and retrieves documents. Servers are located using a Uniform Resource Identifier (URI), which we will discuss later. Each hypertext on a document could then specify a URI to reference other documents anywhere on the Web. The CERN group developed the Hyper Text Transport Protocol (HTTP) to standardize the sharing of HTML documents between browsers and servers. You should not confuse the role of HTTP with that of TCP/IP. All HTTP requests and responses are transmitted over the Internet using the TCP/IP protocol discussed in the previous section.

Shortly after the release of HTTP, an organization named W3C (short for World Wide Web Community) was formed to oversee standardization and future innovations to the HTTP and related protocols and languages. The W3C manages all of the RFCs related to HTTP.

The HTTP protocol is the foundation for all Web-based enterprise applications. To effectively develop Web-based applications, you need to have a sound understanding of HTTP. In the next few sections we will present the most relevant aspects of HTTP. Although this introduction is meant to be complete, it is by no means definitive. We recommend that you investigate HTTP beyond the text presented here in order to strengthen your understanding of the environment that you will be programming for.

HTTP Basics

As mentioned earlier, HTTP is based on a client/server model. We have all used a Web browser such as Netscape or Microsoft Internet Explorer to view Web pages. Each time that you select a hyperlink or submit a form, your browser performs a series of tasks, starting with locating and connecting to a Web server. Web servers are network applications that listen for connections on the well-known port number 80 (this is the norm, not the rule).

The series of tasks that your browser performs is collectively referred to as an HTTP transaction. Each HTTP transaction is executed in four distinct steps, which are listed in Table 5–3.

There are two consequences as a result of these four steps. First, all transactions must be initiated by the client. The server does not have the ability to begin a transaction. Later, when we discuss server-side programming, you will see the major advantages and disadvantages of programming with this limitation.

Second, there is at most one transaction per connection. Once the connection is closed, the server does not store any information regarding the "state" of the last transaction. This categorizes HTTP as a "stateless" protocol. The burden of state management is placed on the programmer. In the following chapters, we will cover various programming techniques available for maintaining state in Web applications.

All HTTP operations are carried out in plain text. This feature allows you to use TELNET as a client to interact with a Web server. Using TELENT, you will be able to perform manually all of the operations that your browser performs when retrieving Web resources. We will be using this technique in coming examples to show how HTTP works.

Table 5–3
Steps in an HTTP Transaction

1	Client (your browser) creates a connection to the specified Web server.
2	Client makes a request for a resource on the server.
3	Server sends back a response.
4	Server closes the connection.

More Advanced HTTP

The HTTP protocol provides a set of methods that clients can invoke. Invoking a method results in a request, named after the fact that all HTTP transactions begin with a client seeking a resource. The three most-used HTTP methods are HEAD, GET, and POST. Issuing a HEAD request instructs the server to send back only information about a resource and not the resource itself. The other two methods, GET and POST, instruct the server to return the specified resource or receive client data.

All requests are made by assembling and sending a request header that contains all of the information needed to carry out a particular request. The request header is structured as a set of fields. The first field is called the method field; it is used to specify the method and the resource identifier. Each request field is separated from the next by a carriage/return line feed (CRLF) character combination. When all of the fields have been specified, a blank line containing only CRLF is issued. If additional data must be sent to the server (in the case of FORM fields), the data are sent immediately after the CRLF blank line in the body of the request. The blank CRLF line plays the critical role of marking the end of the request header, the start of the request body, and finally the end of the request.

Once the server reads the blank line that terminates the client's request, it begins processing the request. The server assembles and returns a response header. Much like the request header, the response header contains a set of fields, each separated by a CRLF character. Similarly, a blank line containing only the CRLF character is used to distinguish the end of the response header from the response body. If the user requested a document, the data contained in the document is sent after the blank line in the response body. The server completes the transaction by terminating the connection.

We will now use TELNET to demonstrate the mechanics of a basic HTTP transaction. This exercise will help illustrate how a request header is formed and what a response header looks like. Using the TELNET session, we will manually perform all of the steps required to request and obtain an HTML Web page. Let's assume you are viewing an HTML document that has the following hyperlink (we will cover the meanings of the HTML tags later):

```
<A href="http://liszt.toolsofcomputing.com/wpltest/telnet_doc.html">A Simple Doc</a>
```

```
<HTML>
<BODY>
<H1>Welcome!</h1>
You have obtained a simple HTML document.
</BODY>
</HTML>
```

Figure 5–11
Contents of `telnet_doc.html`

Selecting this hyperlink instructs your browser to contact the Web server at `liszt.toolsofcomputing.com` and perform a GET request for the document `/wpltest/telnet_doc.html`. Once the browser obtains the document, it renders the HTML to your screen. Using TELNET, we will manually obtain the same HTML document, but we will not be able to render it (remember that TELNET is a simple text-based terminal application). Therefore, we have included the HTML source contained in `telnet_doc.html` in Figure 5–11 so that you can compare it with the TELNET results.

Exercise 5-1

```
1    [pshafae@liszt pshafae]$ telnet liszt.toolsofcomputing.com 80
2    Trying 10.10.10.2...
3    Connected to liszt.toolsofcomputing.com.
4    Escape character is '^]'.
5    GET /wpltest/telnet_doc.html HTTP/1.0
6
7    HTTP/1.1 200 OK
8    Date: Sat, 02 Dec 2000 17:36:34 GMT
9    Server: Apache-AdvancedExtranetServer/1.3.12   (NetRevolution/Linux-
Mandrake) PHP/3.0.16 mod_perl/1.22
10   Last-Modified: Sat, 02 Dec 2000 16:42:16 GMT
11   ETag: "33aee-5a-3a292668"
12   Accept-Ranges: bytes
13   Content-Length: 90
14   Connection: close
15   Content-Type: text/html
16
17   <HTML>
18   <BODY>
19   <H1>Welcome!</h1>
20   You have obtained a simple HTML document.
21   </BODY>
22   </HTML>
23   Connection closed by foreign host.
```

1	At the command prompt, use TELNET to connect to the Web server. Notice that we must provide the well-known port number for the Web server. TELNET is a generic terminal application and by default it will contact the TELNET daemon, listening to the well-known port number 23.
2–4	Basic connection response received from the Web server on liszt. The Web server is now ready for an operation.
5	Basic GET request header. It contains a single header field referred to as the method field. GET identifies the request operation to be performed. The path /wpltest/ telnet_doc.html is the resource identifier and it identifies the relative path and file name of the document that the operation will be performed on. Finally, the last argument (which is not required by all Web servers) identifies the protocol name and version that the client (our TELNET session) expects to use.
6	Blank line consisting of CRLF. We simply pressed the Enter key without typing any other characters. This indicates to the Web server that the request header is completed and it is time to process the request.
7–15	Server response header. Contains a list of response fields set by the server. We will cover the significance of each response field shortly.
16	A blank line containing the CRLF character. This indicates to the client (in our case, the TELNET session, but normally the Web browser) that the end of the response header has been reached and that the response body follows.
17–22	Body of the server response containing the HTML stored in the requested document /wpltest/telnet_doc.html. Comparing this with Figure 15–11 reveals that the two documents are identical.
23	TELNET message indicating that the server has terminated the session. As you may recall, HTTP is a single-transaction protocol. Since we have completed the transaction, the server closes the connection.

This exercise clearly illustrates the simplicity of HTTP. We were able to request and obtain an HTML document by constructing a one-line request header. There are several optional request header fields that can be used to customize the request. Table 5–4 summarizes the request fields available in the current version of HTTP.

Table 5–4
HTTP Request Header Fields

Accept: <type/subtype, type/subtype...>	List of MIME types that the client is willing to accept
Accept-Charset: <charset1, charset2, ...>	List of character sets that the client can work with
Accept-Encoding: <type1, type2, ...>	List of data-encoding types that the client is willing to work with, such as x-compressed and x-gzip
Accept-language: <language name1, language nam2,...>	Names of languages that the client is willing to accept. This limits the message sent back by the server based on the name of the language.
Authorization: <scheme> <additional information>	Defines the user authentication scheme and information; used for accessing various directory, file, and CGI resources.
Connection: <state of connection>	Used to perform mutliple transactions by keeping the conection open in a "keep-alive" state. The server will not close the connection when the transactions are completed. This speeds up Web access when multiple resources are to be retrieved.
Content-language: <language name>	Language name that the data is authored in
Content-length: <length of message in bytes>	Size of data, in bytes, contained in the request body
Content-type: <MIME type/subtype optional parameters;>	MIME type and subtype encoding of the request body
Cookie: <list of available cookies>	A list of all cookies available. Remember that only cookies set by the particular server are sent back. Cookies set by other servers (identified by the server's domain name) will not be returned.
Date: <date/time format>	Date and time of the transaction

Table 5–4
HTTP Request Header Fields (Continued)

From: <e-mail address>	E-mail address of the user; not commonly used.
Host: <domain:port>	Domain and port information of the Web server that the request is destined for. Mainly used in environments where proxy servers pass requests to back-end Web servers.
If-Modified-Since: <date/time format>	Used to filter resources based on modification date and time. The server will not return the resource if it has not been modified since the listed date and/or time.
Referrer: <URL>	URL of the document from which the request originated.
User-Agent: <name/version>	Name and version of the client application making the request. Some CGI applications use this information to customize the format of the resulting document.

The server's response header contains a number of fields that provide information about the server and the document requested. Table 5–5 lists some of the possible server response fields. A detailed discussion of the client and server header fields is beyond the scope of our discussion, but understanding the meaning of these fields is invaluable in learning how different types of media can be reliably transported using HTTP.

Table 5–5
HTTP Server Response Header Fields

Allow: <method1, method2, ...>	Reports the possible HTTP methods that can be performed on a specified resource. Included in the error response generated to a bad HTTP call.
Content-encoding: <data encoding>	Describes how the data are encoded; valid types include x-compress and x-gzip.
Content-length: <number of bytes>	Length, in bytes, of the message being returned.
Content-type: <MIME type/subtype optional parameters;>	MIME encoding type that best describes the data being sent back.

Table 5–5
HTTP Server Response Header Fields (Continued)

Content-version: <version>	Resource version control number. If supported, the server will retain version information about documents using a version control system such as CVS, RCS, etc.
Date: <date/time format>	Date and time of the request.
Expires: <date/time format>	Date and time at which the returned resource will be considered invalid.
Last-modified: <date/time information>	Date and time when the resource was last modified.
Link: <link information>	Provides information about the relationship of the resource to other resources; used for cataloging.
Location: <redirect URL>	URL that the client is redirected to. If present, your browser will automatically visit the listed URL.
Public: <method1, method2...>	HTTP methods supported by the server.
Retry-after: <date/time format>	Date and time at which the client should try again to request the resource. Set when the server is unavailable.
Server: <application name and version>	The name and version of the Web server.
Set-cookie: <cookie>	Instructs the browser to store a cookie. The cookie information must follow a specific format.
Title: <document title>	Description of the document based on the TITLE HTML tag. Returned as a result of HEAD requests.
WWW-authenticate: <auth. scheme> <addl. information>	Provides authentication and encryption schemes that the server will use for directory, file, and CGI access.

Review of HTML Tags Associated with HTTP Requests.   The AREA and FORM tags are the two HTML tags used to perform requests. AREA (A for short) is used to create a hyperlink. The A tag contains an HREF attribute that defines the address to the resource that the linked area references. When the user selects the linked area, an HTTP request header (a GET request header, to be more specific) is created using the value of the HREF attribute. Shortly we will see how the AREA tag can be used to interact with Web applications.

The FORM tag is used to create a Web form. FORM has ACTION, METHOD, and ENCTYPE attributes. The ACTION tag serves the same purpose as the HREF attribute of the AREA tag. The METHOD and ENCTYPE attributes specify the HTTP method and encoding details of the request. (We will cover the importance of these attributes when discussing the details of POST.) There can be any number of input fields in the body of the FORM tag. There are several types of input fields, ranging from selection boxes to text fields and buttons. Forms can contain a special type of input field called "submit." It is rendered as a button and upon selection, the browser performs the HTTP request.

There are a number of idiosyncrasies with respect to the FORM tag that are worth mentioning. First, all empty form fields are *not* sent to the Web server. For example, if your form contains a text box named "first_name" and the user leaves this field blank, the targeted Web application will not receive any information regarding the existence of the FORM field. This is unusual: One would expect the browser to set the value of an empty field to an empty string. As a consequence, your Web application cannot depend on any form field information sent by the browser. Later we will introduce programming techniques that help you overcome this limitation.

Second, input fields can share the same value for the NAME attribute. For example, your form may contain a number of check boxes or radio buttons all named "my_check_box." Upon submission, the values of the boxes and buttons are grouped as a list of values assigned to a single field name. Your Web application will need to know ahead of time if an input field does not have a unique name, in order to work correctly with the data obtained. As we will see shortly, you can take advantage of field name sharing to create a group of check boxes or radio buttons that are logically related but that have unique values.

Finally, each form can interact with only one Web application. Situations will arise in which it is desirable to have different operations performed on the same form. As an example, a Web-based address book may have a single form for entering new contact information as well as searching for existing contacts. In the former operation, the form data are newly entered in the address book, while in the latter the data are used as search criteria to locate matching records. Several different options are available for dealing with such scenarios; we will examine them in future sections.

Now that we have covered the mechanics of the HTTP protocol, we will explore the details of GET, POST, and HEAD. The difference between the GET and POST semantics greatly affects the design and implementation of your Web application. Always keep in mind that your Web applications are bound by the limitations of the HTTP protocol, making the HTTP request operations the foundation of your design. Having a strong understanding of HTTP will give you more control over the design and implementation of enterprise-grade Web applications.

GET and Web Queries.   GET is the most frequently applied HTTP method. As its name implies, it is used to retrieve a resource. As we saw in Exercise 5–1, every time you select a hyperlink, you are performing a GET request on a document or resource. GET can also be used to perform a Web query. A query is a request for information based on data supplied by the client. Unlike basic requests, queries do not retrieve static documents. Instead, they are used to interact with a Web application that lives on the server. In almost all cases, the result of a query is a dynamically generated document.

GET queries can be formed with both FORM and AREA tags. The popular Web search engines provide the best example of how GET queries are used in forms. Almost everyone on the Web has used a search engine such as Excite or AltaVista to locate a document. The simplest search engine has a single input field used to collect keywords for the search. When the submit button is pressed, the browser assembles a GET query request header that contains the value of the input field as a name/value pair.

Name/value pairs are constructed using an equals sign "=" to bind the data entered into the input field (the value of the input field) to the name of the input field. Multiple name/value pairs are concatenated using an ampersand to form a name/value list. This list is then appended to the identifier component of the GET request header using a question mark. Recall that the identifier component contains the relative path and filename of the document that we are attempting to retrieve. In the case of a query, the identifier contains the relative path to the Web application that will process the query. The following is an example of a GET request header used to perform a query operation with several named parameters:

```
GET /cgi-bin/webapp.py?param1=value1&param2=value2&param3=value3 HTTP/1.0
```

```
<FORM METHOD="GET" ACTION="http://liszt.toolsofcomputing.com/cgi-bin/
wpltest/simple_search.py" >
Search string: <INPUT TYPE="text" NAME="search_string" SIZE="25" ><BR>
<INPUT TYPE="submit" VALUE="Search" >
</FORM>
```

Figure 5–12
HTML Form for `simpl_search.py`

Upon receipt of a query request, the server invokes the identified Web application. The name/value list is then passed to the Web application by the server. It is the responsibility of the Web application to parse the name/value pairs and use the information to perform the desired task. In the case of the Web search, the application will search for documents that contain the query string. The response will be a dynamically generated HTML page that reports the results of the search. The search application must dynamically construct the resulting document, as each result varies depending on the query string used.

We will use TELNET to illustrate a query operation. As before, we will play the role of the Web browser in processing a simple HTML form. The form portion of the HTML code is listed in Figure 5–12. We will assume that the user has typed the string "Hello" into the form's text box and pressed the submit button. Using the TELNET session, we will perform all of the operations that the browser would perform to prepare the request header and perform the query. As before, the exercise is a line-by-line description of the events that took place.

Exercise 5-2

```
1   [pshafae@liszt pshafae]$ telnet liszt.toolsofcomputing.com 80
2   Trying 10.10.10.2...
3   Connected to liszt.toolsofcomputing.com.
4   Escape character is '^]'.
5   GET /cgi-bin/wpltest/simple_search.py?search_string=Hello HTTP/1.0
6
7   <HTML><BODY><H1>Congratulations!</H1>
8           You tried to search for documents with the following search
string 'Hello'.</BODY></HTML>
9   Connection closed by foreign host.
```

5   GET method field with identifier `/cgi-bin/wpltest/` `simple_search.py`. Appended to the identifier is name/value list created when the "Search" button is hit. The browser assembles the parameter/value list using the name and value of the input fields that appear in the form. The browser would also send the name value of the "submit" input field, which we have omitted to do here.

7–9   Query response obtained from `simple_search.py`. This is a dynamically generated document, as it includes the value of the search_string parameter we submitted.

You can also perform GET queries using the AREA tag. All of the parameters intended for the script can be defined using the name/value pair syntax discussed earlier. For example, the following AREA tag will invoke the same search application discussed above with the predefined search string "animals":

```
<a href="http://liszt.toolsofcomputing.com/cgi-bin/wpltest/
simple_search.py?search_string=animals">Search for animals</a>
```

This technique is not useful for queries that rely on user input, such as search queries. As you will see in later chapters, there are many instances in which the parameters passed to the server are predetermined and the use of FORM tags limits the glamour of the page. For example, some Web sites use fancy images for navigating the results of a query. All of the parameters needed to perform the navigation operation are packed in AREA tags that surround fancy images. By selecting the image, the user is performing a query operation similar to our predetermined search query for "animals." Here the use of FORM tags would discount the appearance and layout of the navigation system.

All data sent to the server via a GET query is encoded in the GET request header. This limits the amount of information that can be sent in a single request, since there is a maximum byte limit on request headers. At first this appears to be a big limitation, but it is offset by the fact that hyperlinks (AREA tags) can be used to perform GET queries. As we will see in the next section, the POST operation allows us to overcome the size limitations of GET, but at the cost of using only FORM tags, which makes it impossible for users to bookmark the result of a query.

```
<FORM METHOD="POST" ACTION="http://liszt.toolsofcomputing.com/cgi-bin/
wpltest/simple_contact.py" >
First Name: <INPUT TYPE="text" NAME="first_name" SIZE="25" ><BR>
Last Name: <INPUT TYPE="text" NAME="last_name" SIZE="25" ><BR>
Email Addres: <INPUT TYPE="text" NAME="email" SIZE="25" ><BR>
<INPUT TYPE="submit" VALUE="Search" >
</FORM>
```

Figure 5–13
Simple Personal Contact Form

POST. The POST operation is used to submit an HTML FORM to a Web-based application. Unlike GET, POST cannot be used to retrieve documents. The method is specialized for packing and sending large quantities of information to a Web application. You may be wondering how POST is able to do this if there is a limit on the header size. A POST operation does *not* pack FORM data in the request header. Instead, the data are packed in the request body. As a result, two additional header fields, Content-Type and Content-Length, are set so that the Web server can discern the type and length of data presented in the request body. Unfortunately, POSTs can only be performed using FORM tags, because the AREA tag does not provide any attributes for specifying the request method and always defaults to GET.

We will now use a TELNET session to illustrate the mechanical differences between GET and POST. The HTML code for the form is listed in Figure 5–13.

Exercise 5–3

```
1    [pshafae@liszt pshafae]$ telnet liszt.toolsofcomputing.com 80
2    Trying 10.10.10.2...
3    Connected to liszt.toolsofcomputing.com.
4    Escape character is '^]'.
5    POST /cgi-bin/wpltest/simple_contact.py HTTP/1.0
6    Content-type: application/x-www-form-urlencoded
7    Content-length: 57
8
9    first_name=John&last_name=Shafaee&email=pshafae@yahoo.com
10   HTTP/1.1 200 OK
11   Date: Sun, 03 Dec 2000 23:40:36 GMT
12   Server: Apache-AdvancedExtranetServer/1.3.12
     (NetRevolution/Linux-Mandrake) PHP/3.0.16 mod_perl/1.22
13   Connection: close
14   Content-Type: text/html
```

```
15
16   <HTML><BODY><H1>Congratulations!</H1>
17   New contact information added to contact list.
18   <P>
19   <UL>
20   <LI>First name: 'John'
21   <LI>Last name: 'Shafaee'
22   <LI>Email: 'pshafae@yahoo.com'
23   </BODY></HTML>
24   Connection closed by foreign host.
```

5   POST method field with identifier `/cgi-bin/wpltest/ simple_contact.py`. Notice that no name/value pairs are appended to the identifier.

6   `Content-type` field header. If you recall from our discussion of HTTP, this field specifies how the data in the body of the request are encoded. The value of the field is a MIME type, specifying that the data in the request body are encoded as a name/value pair originating from a form.

7   `Content-length` field header. As you may recall from earlier discussions, this field specifies the length of the request body in bytes. In our example this is set to 57, as there are 57 different characters in our message body. The server will not start processing the request until all 57 bytes have been received.

8   Blank line containing only the CRLF character combination. Indicates to the server that the end of the request header has been reached and that what follows is the request body.

9   List of name/value pairs that are to be processed. The browser would essentially create the list using the completed input field names and values of the form.

10–23   Dynamic document generated by the script.

The value of the `Content-type` field is set to one of several Multipurpose Internet Mail Extension (MIME) types. The `Content-type` field is used by the receiving application to decipher how the transferred data are encoded. MIME is a generic set of guidelines used to encode data. MIME types are used throughout the Internet by almost all message-based services, including e-mail and news. The MIME type `x-www-form-urlencoded` used in our example indicates that the POST request body contains data originating from an HTML form. In some cases, such as when transferring a file in an upload operation, you will want to use a different MIME type, such as `multipart/form-data`, to indicate a more complex request body structure.

As you may recall, the HTML FORM tag provides an ENCTYPE attribute that can be used to specify the MIME encoding of the request. If not explicitly set, the default value of `x-www-form-urlencoded` is used. In later examples we will explicitly change this attribute to facilitate file uploads. Several different RFCs provide detailed discussions of MIME. These are beyond the scope of our discussion, but we encourage you to review them on your own.

As with GET, it is perfectly legal to pack additional name/value pairs at the end of the resource identifier. For example, the following FORM results in a POST request header that has name/value pairs following the resource identifier:

```
<FORM METHOD="POST" ACTION="http://liszt.toolsofcomputing.com/cgi-bin/
wpltest/post_test.py?param1=value1&param2=value2"></FORM>
```

The name/value pairs would be passed to the Web application as if they originated from input fields. Note, however, that the body of this example FORM is empty. If input fields were included in the body of the form, the name/value pairs following the question mark would be *ignored* and only the values of the input fields would be sent. This is an important consequence to remember, as it can lead to many programming pitfalls when programming queries with a mixture of hyperlinks and FORM tags.

HEAD. The HEAD request allows a browser to obtain only information about a document, as opposed to the document itself. The main purpose for using HEAD is to make Web interactions more efficient. By issuing a HEAD request, the browser can retrieve limited information about the type and configuration of the Web server, the type and length of data stored in a document, and the date that the document was last modified.

Your browser can use this information to facilitate a caching strategy. For example, most browsers cache the most recent Web pages visited. When you attempt to load a recently visited page, the browser can make a HEAD call to see if the locally cached page has been modified. If so, the browser will perform a GET request to obtain the most recent version of the page. Otherwise, the local copy can be used, saving the cost of an HTTP transaction.

Using `Lynx` and `httplib` Instead of TELNET

Thus far, in all of the exercises, we used TELNET to connect to Web servers and perform an HTTP operation. This works well when you are learning the details of HTTP, but is rather complicated and inconvenient when attempting to debug your CGI application. Debug CGI applications via Web requests? Yes, in some situations you may need to connect to the Web server and verify that the returned response header includes a particular attribute such as a cookie or a MIME type.

An alternative to TELNET is `Lynx`. Lynx is a text-based Web browser that is available on Linux. Typing `Lynx` at the command line will load `Lynx` in interactive mode to be used to surf the Web. Since Lynx is strictly a text-based browser, it removes all images and fancy word formats found on the Web page. The Web page may look unfamiliar at first, but closer inspection will reveal that the content is preserved.

Lynx can also be used in noninteractive mode to perform certain Web operations. A number of command line options can be used to perform GET and POST requests on Web forms. All you provide is the data that is sent to the server, and `Lynx` handles creating a properly formatted HTTP request. For example, the following command uses `Lynx` to send username and password data to a login form:

```
echo 'username=john&password=johnpassword' | lynx -source -post_data
-mime_header http://www.toolsofcomputing.com/cgi-bin/simple_login.cgi
```

We use `echo` to express the data that would normally be encoded by the browser in a POST operation. Notice that we have followed the same encoding rules. The `Lynx` command takes options to display the source of the resulting page (otherwise the page would be rendered), perform a POST request, and display the full server response including MIME headers. The last argument to `Lynx` is the CGI application that is the target of the POST operation. This is much simpler than using TELNET; we simply provided the data and let `Lynx` create the appropriate request header and body. Similarly, you can use the `-get_data` option to perform a GET request. Make sure to read through the `Lynx` manual pages for a full description of how `Lynx` is used and a listing of additional command line options.

The Python `httplib` module provides yet another alternative to using TELNET. The following example depicts how it can be used to perform the same login operation as performed previously with `Lynx`:

```
import httplib
params = "username=john&password=johnpassword"
con= httplib.HTTP("www.toolsofcomputing.com:80")
con.putrequest("POST", "/cgi-bin/simple_login.cgi")
con.putheader("Content-type", "application/x-www-form-
urlencoded")
con.putheader("Content-length", "%d" % len(params))
con.endheaders()
con.send(params)
(reply, message, headers) = con.getreply()
print header
print conn.getfile().read()
```

This is a little more complicated than using Lynx, but provides a means to perform HTTP operations from within a Python application. You can take advantage of `httplib` and many other Python Internet modules to access and work with Web resources. Review the Python module documentation for a more in-depth discussion of `httplib`.

Differences between HTTP 1.0 and 1.1

HTTP 1.0 set the stage for a simple yet powerful information exchange protocol. However, over time, users and developers discovered that many minor optimizations can be made to speed up HTTP transactions and improve Web performance in general. These optimizations led to the release of version 1.1 of the HTTP protocol.

The biggest improvement made in HTTP 1.1 is the concept of the connection "Keep-Alive." As you may recall, HTTP is a single-transaction, stateless protocol. This means that when a browser accesses a Web page with several images, it must open and close a TCP connection to the server once per image. TCP connection initialization and teardown is a relatively expensive operation. Based on Web usage patterns, it was evident that most of the images linked on a Web page resided on the same server. As a result, the HTTP protocol was extended to allow a single TCP connection to be used to perform multiple HTTP operations. This drastically decreases the time it takes to obtain all of the items needed to render a page.

Another important HTTP improvement was in data compression. HTTP 1.1 extends the 1.0 protocol to allow basic data compression to be used by both the client and the server, in order to decrease the actual size of the data transferred. Fewer bytes transmitted logically result in improved performance and faster transfer times.

The 1.1 protocol also provides additional extensions used to improve document caching. The browser can take advantage of these extensions when caching static documents or when checking the freshness of a cached document. Since most Web pages are supported by static files, page caching is still one of the biggest performance optimizations allowed by HTTP, because in many cases it drastically reduces the amount of data transmitted between the browser and server. When a page is cached, the browser only needs to obtain the page header from the server to validate the freshness of the page. There is no need to transfer the entire document, which may contain many references to additional resources such as images.

Several other minor revisions were made, which are not covered here. The take-home message is that HTTP 1.1 is mainly a performance-intensive revision. All of the changes made are centered on speeding up access times and decreasing the amount of data that is transmitted between the browser and server. These changes are especially important for users who access Web pages via a modem over a 56K connection.

Uniform Resource Identifier (URI)

Throughout the second half of this chapter, we have used URLs to locate documents and Web applications. The URL (Uniform Resource Locator) is a special address used to identify a specific Web resource. There are a number of other protocols that use a variation on the URL scheme to locate resources. All such locators are descendants of the URI (Uniform Resource Identifier). URI outlines all of the parts required for a uniform locator. All addressing schemes that conform to the URI standard are guaranteed to uniquely address any network distributed resource. In this section we will dissect the URL and investigate the role of each component.

Dissecting a URL.   A URL is composed of several subcomponents. Figure 5–14 is an example URL that provides the address to a static HTML page. We have labeled each distinct component by the component name. The component names are referenced below, along with a detailed description of the component's role in the scope of addressing the resource.

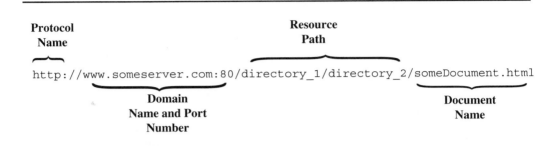

Figure 5–14
A Simple Uniform Resource Locator (URL)

Protocol Name • The first part of the URL is the protocol name. The protocol name identifies how the desired resource is to be obtained. Resources served by a Web server are obtained using the HTTP protocol, identified by the protocol name "http." A number of other protocol names are available for communicating with different resource servers. For example, you can use "ftp" to obtain a file from an FTP server. Table 5–6 lists several popular protocols along with brief descriptions.

Table 5–6
URL Protocols

http	Hypertext Transport Protocol. Obtain static HTML pages and interact with applications served by a Web server.
https	Secure Socket Layer (SSL) transport. This is basically the HTTP protocol made more secure with encryption technology. Data transmitted to and from the server is encrypted and not easily accessible by untrusted Web users.
ftp	File Transfer Protocol. Retrieve files served by an FTP server.
ldap	Lightweight Directory Access Protocol. Obtain directory listings from an LDAP server.
news/nntp	Retreive news threads from a news or discussion server.
mailto	Send an e-mail using a local e-mail client.

Domain Name and Port Number • The next URL component defines the domain name of the host serving the resource. In the first section of this chapter we learned that domain names map to IP addresses, which in turn uniquely identify hosts in the network. The domain name is separated from the protocol name by a semicolon and two forward slashes (://) and ends at the next forward slash. Any valid domain name may be used, including the IP address of the domain.

There are two additional parameters that may be used with the domain name. First, you may specify a port number. By default, the browser will contact the well-known port for the specified protocol. When using "http," the well-known port number is 80. If the Web server that you are trying to contact is configured to use another port, you can specify this by appending the port number to the domain name using a colon. You should generally be able to rely on the well-known port number for accessing a resource. If you do encounter difficulties, check with the Web site administrator to ensure that you are using the correct domain name and port number combination.

Second, you can include a username and password to use when accessing a resource on a particular host. The username and password combination precede the host's domain name and are separated by an at sign (@). The following is a modified version of the URL presented in Figure 5–14 that takes advantage of the username and password encoding:

```
http://john:my_pass@www.someserver.com:80/directory_1/directory_2/
someDocument.html
```

Usernames and passwords are useful only when accessing resources that have been explicitly secured by the Web server. You can get more information on this topic by looking at the Apache user manual. You should typically try to avoid the use of this feature, as the username and password values are sent as clear text over the Internet. This allows malicious users to gain easy access to restricted resources. You should attempt to include access control logic within your Web application and use Secure Socket Layer (SSL) transfer protocol for working with secured data. SSL will ensure that the data sent over the Internet is encrypted and not easily accessible to malicious users.

Resource Path and Document Name • The protocol name, domain name, and port number uniquely identify the host serving the resource, but we will need a directory path and document name to access the unique resource on the specified host. This information is the third URL component and follows immediately the domain name/port number component, separated by a forward slash. Based on the the URL in Figure 5–14, we can state that we are referencing a static

HTML document named someDocument.html that is physically stored in the directory path /directory_1/directory_2. Well, this is mostly true. The document name is in fact someDocument.html, but the path is relative to some server-side setting and not the root of the host's file system. In Chapter 6, you will learn how to configure the Apache Web server to use a custom document root that will be used as a relative path to all files and directories served by the Web server.

Static documents may also contain any number of location fragments. Location fragments are set using the <a> HTML tag and are used to mark a particular location within an HTML page. Location tags were popular when HTML was in its infancy. Typically, the HTML author would include long text pieces organized by sections in a single HTML document. The sections would be tagged with a fragment name. The author could then create a page-level table of contents at the top of the page that the user could use to access a section quickly without having to scroll aimlessly down the page. Figure 5–15 depicts our original example URL modified to access a location fragment named location_a. As you can see, the location fragment is separated from the document name in the URL by a pound sign (#). This tag only has relevance when accessing static HTML pages.

The URL in Figure 5–14 is the simplest and most common form. There are several additional components that follow the document path and document name and play an important role when interacting with dynamic data generated by server-side applications such as CGIs. Figure 5–16 lists three extended URLs that contain these components.

The first of the three listed URLs is probably the most confusing. When the www.someserver.com host is contacted with this URL, it will parse the URL into the directory and document name components and incrementally locate the selected resource. In this example, the

---

http://www.someserver.com:80/directory_1/directory_2/someDocument.html#location_a

Location Tag

Figure 5–15
URL with Location Tag

server will discover that there is a resource called my_app.cgi that

Figure 5–16
Extended URLs

lives in `/directory_1/directory_2`. The additional path information following the resource name is then considered extra and passed to the resource. The extra path information is subtle, but very important. Extra paths are useful for passing path data to a CGI application. In Chapter 13, we depict how the extra path information can be used by a CGI application to locate and dispatch additional Python code that is organized in subdirectories.

The second URL listed in Figure 5–16 depicts how command line arguments, commonly referred to as ISINDIX style arguments, can be passed to a server-side application. Notice that the arguments are separated from the CGI application name by a question mark. Each argument is separated by a plus sign. Before the Web server executes the referenced CGI, all of the data following the question mark are transformed into command line arguments. CGI applications that use ISINDEX style arguments can be easily tested at the shell level by executing the application with any number of command line arguments. For example, we could test the `my_app.cgi` application at the shell by performing the following operation: `./my_app.cgi arg1 arg2 arg3`. Here we assume that you are already in the relative directory path of the CGI application.

ISINDEX style arguments are very easy to program with and provide an easy method for passing simple arguments to a CGI application. However, Web forms offer a greater level of complexity with respect to the data that can be obtained from the user. For example, a single Web form can contain a number of input fields of varying types, such as text fields and selection boxes. Each field is identified with a field name, creating a parameter/value pair. This information would be difficult to convey to a CGI application using the ISINDEX style encoding, because ISINDEX arguments are position-sensitive and do not allow you to encode anything beyond the value of a field.

This leads us to the third URL listed in Figure 5–16. Here we encode parameters as parameter/value pairs using the equals sign to associate parameter names to parameter values and using ampersands to separate the pairings. As with ISINDEX style encoding, all of the parameter/value pairs are separated from the application name by a question mark. However, the parameter/value pairs are not position-sensitive because they are not passed in as command line arguments. Instead, the parameters/value pairs are passed to the application via the standard input stream. The Web server passes the encoding as is to the application, and it is the application's responsibility to parse the encoding into a data dictionary. As we saw in earlier sections of this chapter, the parameter/value pair encoding is performed by the POST operation and the data are passed to the server in the body section of the HTTP request. This is important when passing in large amounts of data to a server, such as when a file is uploaded, since there is a limit on the size of a request header.

The Python CGI module can be used to parse the parameter/value pairs passed into a Python CGI application by the Web server. In Chapter 7, we cover the use of the cgi module in more detail, but it is important to note that unlike ISINDEX style URL encoding, additional processing must be performed by the CGI in order to access the user's data. You may be wondering how the URL can be used to pass in parameters whose values contain equal signs, plus signs, and ampersands. Such values are considered reserved and must be escaped when creating a URL. You can look up the escape sequence for each character in any popular HTML reference manual.

As highlighted earlier, there is an unexpected side effect when using parameter/value URL encoding to specify a form action URL. The URL encoded data will *not* be passed to the CGI application.

Instead, only the form field data will be encoded and passed in via the standard input stream. The following is an example depicting this:

```
<form action="http://www.someserver.com/cgi-bin/
my_app.cgi?param1=value1">
<input type="text" name="text1" >
<input type="hidden" name="hidden1" >
</form>
```

The parameters `text1` and `hidden1` will be passed into `my_app.cgi`, but the `param1` parameter is silently ignored. Alternatively, you can use ISINDEX-style URL encoding when working with Web forms.

It is also important to note that you can combine the extra path component with either the ISINDEX or parameter/value style data encoding. This is quite useful, as it alleviates the need to escape and pass in a path as an argument or a parameter.

Summary

Computer networks, like hardware design, will always comprise an intense and rapidly changing area of study. Looking at the history of computer networks and network protocols such as TCP/IP, it is clear that the most popular protocols used today are built entirely on top of older models and experimental concepts. By learning the basic concepts of IP numbers, the TCP/IP stack, and DNS, one can take full advantage of the Internet to develop powerful applications that solve practical business problems.

As evidenced by the popularity of the World Wide Web, the future of computing is without a doubt in information-sharing over networks. Although the World Wide Web is still in its infancy, it has provided the perfect platform for developing powerful applications that can be accessed from anywhere in the world. Web forms allow users in the United States to subscribe to services provided by companies based in Europe. There is no longer a need to have a computer science degree to share information over the Internet. The Hyper Text Markup Language (HTML) allows almost anyone with minimal computer knowledge to develop stunning and powerful content pages that include forms for interacting with users.

In this chapter, we have covered a number of topics that are typically spread over several textbooks. Beside serving as a review of computer networks and HTTP protocol, we hope that this chapter has encouraged you to investigate privately and study the topics presented here in much greater depth.

6

Network Setup and Apache Configuration

While Web development *can* be done with minimal knowledge of network administration, we feel strongly that the Web developer on Linux will be somewhat constrained by focusing strictly on Web programming, without having knowledge of how to configure networking to *support* the Web development process. This might appear at first to be a circular statement; however, we will make a strong case that doing one activity (Web development) without the other (network configuration) in the end puts the Web developer at the mercy of a system administrator. We believe that administration will be highly relevant to a Linux- (or Unix-) based Web developer and thus we have chosen to spend a number of pages discussing it.

In addition to basic network administration activities, it is essential that the Linux-based Web developer have knowledge of the basics of configuring the Apache Web Server and the many options that are provided to support virtual hosting.

This chapter is not a full reference on network administration and Apache Web Server administration; reference material is provided in the Bibliography. This chapter provides a goal-oriented discussion with the intention of getting results fairly quickly by considering a number of common use cases.

Introduction

This chapter covers both network and Apache Web configuration. We will first present an overview of the three typical development environments and discuss how you can configure networking to support each of these environments. Then we will address the basic installation and configuration of the Apache Web Server. We strongly encourage you to follow the guidelines here, especially if you are new to Web programming or have not done any administration on Linux.

Assumptions

In this chapter, we assume that you have gotten Linux up and running on your system. The discussion here should work with all recent and current releases of Linux.[1] With some additional work (mainly for configuring network interfaces), you should be able to get this working under other popular Unixes, such as Solaris, AIX, etc.

Part of this discussion does depend on your hardware configuration. In particular, we recommend that you at least have a network card installed in your computer. Network cards can be had quite cheaply, and many of the cheapest no-name brands will be detected properly under Linux.[2] Even if you do not plan to connect your computer via Ethernet (i.e., you're using dial-up networking), you might still want networking on your computer to participate in a private network. One of our use cases specifically covers Web development in an intranet setting, with no assumption of a connection to a wide-area network.

Since we show some use cases that involve an actual network, you might also want to acquire a network hub or switch. This will allow you to connect two or more computers to form a network.[3] We encourage you to consider setting up a network at home. Having a network will give you a sense of how your Web application (and Web site) responds from a remote machine (as opposed to the machine where your application is being hosted), as well as point out any other assumptions that may not be correct (e.g., failing to use relative links in HTML).

---

1. We recommend kernel 2.x and beyond. Red Hat and Mandrake are two of our favorite distributions; however, we have chosen not to rely on any features that could make our lives easier, as these tend not to be portable between different versions of Linux. The ideas we are discussing here can be applied to other Unices, such as Solaris. When possible, we try to tell you what to do or (at a minimum) whether what we are discussing will or will not work on your favorite version of Unix.

2. If not using Linux, please stick with fairly conventional cards such as 3Com and Intel. We do not ordinarily make recommendations of specific products but feel compelled to make you aware of potential troubles on alternate platforms.

3. Before you write to us, yes, we do know that you can connect two computers point-to-point using a null cable. We'll not be covering this case as it is a special case of a hub and will in the end not be as good a solution. Get a network hub/switch and travel first class!

Finally, we assume that you know a thing or two about basic system administration. In particular, you should (at this time) recall how to become the `root` user (superuser) using the "`su`" command. Everything we are showing here requires the ability to become the root user. In general, you should do *as little as possible* as the root user. While you are trying to repeat the steps that we present here in the remaining sections, please do things as root that truly need to be done as root. To this end, we recommend that you keep a second window open on your desktop and `su` to user `root`.

Use Cases

Enough about assumptions. Let us get to the good stuff.[4] As a developer, you need to think about your efforts by considering the development environment and the production environment. This has always been true in software development, but is more important than ever in the context of Web development. Toward the end of the chapter, we will discuss some traps and pitfalls that are encountered in Web development. We will consider three development environments, focusing only on the networking issues themselves. These environments are presented in Table 6–1. This table is an idealization but is nonetheless relevant to those who will be using this book to develop Web applications.

Table 6–1
The Typical Development Environment

Short Name	Salient Features
Stand-alone	Single computer, either non-networked or transiently networked (typical of dial-up connections)
Private	Multiple computers connected on a private LAN or one computer transiently networked and on the private LAN but with no permanent network connection
Internet	Similar to the private network, but one or more computers exposed to the Internet and able to "serve"

---

4. We find this to be among the most fun stuff you will ever work on. Once you get it going, you feel a tremendous sense of satisfaction, despite its all being fairly simple. If you have multiple domains to host/maintain, the material in this chapter will give you a good start.

Let us now consider these configurations in slightly greater detail. Each of the cases increases in sophistication, and some of the issues for a simpler case sometimes apply to the more complex case. You should read all of them to understand the similarities and differences.

Stand-Alone

The vast majority of new developers have a stand-alone configuration of Linux.[5] That is, Linux has been installed on a computer that is not permanently connected to the Internet. By "not permanently connected," we mean a dial-up configuration or any connection that is not transparently brought up on demand. We also include any computer that relies on DHCP (dynamic host configuration protocol) for the network interface used to reach the Internet. This applies to you if you are using a cable modem or DSL connection and you have not been given a fixed IP number by your provider. If you find any of this terminology confusing, Chapter 5 will bring you up to speed.

Intranet

A private network setup is similar to the stand-alone configuration. The difference, of course, is that you have a local area network (LAN) with more than one computer; however, you have no intention of exposing your private network to the Internet and intend to run your Web server internally.

In this configuration, we note that one machine may be exposed to the Internet; however, the machine running your Web server is not exposed to the Internet. We will not be addressing in any detail the requirements to configure a firewall to protect your private network. We provide references in the Bibliography to assist you in shielding your privacy.

Larger companies use a combination of private (so-called intranets) and Internet-style networking. If you are fortunate to be in such a position, you have probably marched into the later chapters, as someone has already configured the network for you. Nevertheless, you will find this discussion useful in the event you need certain features enabled for you within your company.

---

5. At this point we will be referring only to Linux, dealing with the issues involved in moving to other versions of Unix as special cases when appropriate. Linux is our preferred environment (and we think it will be yours). We'll offer as many tips as we can to help you perform similar steps on other notable versions of Unix that run on Intel hardware (Solaris).

The Internet

The Internet is your ultimate destination. With a little extra work, you can enable one or more machines running on your private network to participate on the Internet. To that end, we will discuss how you can use the `ipchains` software to forward requests to your internal Web server.

Networking and the DNS Setup

Regardless of the kind of setup you are performing, it will be necessary to perform one or more of the steps shown in this section. In describing the use cases, we have focused on the general activities that must be performed in order to execute the use case successfully. We have identified a number of general activities for which use case(s) the activity applies (Table 6–2).

Table 6–2
Configuration Activities

Activity	Use Case(s) Where Activity Must Be Performed (Items in italics are optional.)
Host File Configuration (page 263)	Stand-alone, *Intranet, Internet*
Caching the DNS Setup (page 265)	Internet
Configuring Your Intranet (page 272)	Intranet
Name Resolution	Intranet, Internet
Using DNS to Maintain Your Intranet Host Information (page 279)	*Stand-alone, Intranet, Internet*
Network Address Translation	*Intranet, Internet*

Host File Configuration

This activity generally applies to all of the use cases that were presented in the previous section. (See "Use Cases" on page 261.) In a stand-alone configuration (the configuration in which there is a single computer not participating in a local area network), this activity will be necessary only if you intend to support virtual hosting.

Host file configuration is the most primitive form of getting hostnames resolved on your local area network. For example, when you use TELNET to access a particular host (e.g., `telnet snoopy`), you see the `/etc/hosts` file:

```
127.0.0.1               liszt localhost.localdomain localhost
209.246.58.1            gateway
209.246.58.59           liszt-dsl
10.10.10.1              router
10.10.10.2              liszt
10.10.10.3              mail
10.10.10.4              rachmaninov
```

Accessing the `/etc/hosts` file is definitely better than memorizing each computer on the network by its IP address(es), but not without shortcomings. First, it is a single file maintained on a single computer. In a real computer network, where there are multiple machines, this single file would have to be replicated among multiple machines, and thus quickly presents a maintenance nightmare. There are many clever approaches that have been used to replicate the file to different machines; however, there are always a few entries that might well be different. We recommend using `/etc/hosts` only to maintain two or fewer computers that are (for all practical purposes) rarely connected to the Internet.

There are some environments in which the `/etc/hosts` file will prove useful[6]; however, they are for the developer wanting to set up a LAN environment at home and to support development of Web applications. We will not consider them here.

DNS provides all that is required to support seamless and transparent naming of resources. We recommend, especially on your own private network, sticking with one naming service to avoid confusion. Entries in `/etc/hosts` may (depending on your `nsswitch.conf` file) lead to confusion of name query results.

---

6. Most notably, NIS and NIS+. NIS+ is more or less exclusive to Sun. Our experience with NIS and NIS+ on Linux has not been favorable. We recommend for small networks at home or business that you forego NIS and NIS+ unless you are supporting several users and want to create a totally seamless environment. We are assuming here that you'll perhaps be doing Linux development in a heterogeneous Windows–Linux environment. You might also want to consider setting up Samba to share files between the Windows clients and your Linux server; this will not be covered here.

Caching the DNS Setup

Caching DNS is a generally useful feature that should be enabled, especially if you are connected to the Internet permanently and have been given access to external DNS servers maintained by an ISP, which are often overloaded with requests from customers. The notion of caching allows the answers to DNS queries to be memorized.

Before we go too far with this discussion, there are a few preliminaries. DNS is supported on Linux using the Bind software and is available, when installed, via the `named` daemon. It is possible that this software is not installed, depending on how you set up your computer. You will want to add this software using the `rpm`, or you can download the Bind software distribution and install it yourself. We will not cover the installation via any method except `rpm`, but we list how to download and install it yourself on our Web site.[7]

Here is how you can check for the installation of `bind`:

```
$ rpm -q -a | grep bind
bind-utils-8.2.2P5-5mdk
bind-8.2.2P5-5mdk
```

What you see here might be somewhat different, depending on the Linux OS where you issued this command.[8] You need both of these packages in order to follow the discussion in this chapter. The "*bind-utils*" package includes the client interface to DNS (e.g., `nslookup` and others), while "`bind`" includes the server-side component (`named` and the `ndc` convenience utility for managing `named` as an `/etc/rc.d/init.d` style script). Depending on how you installed your operating system, these packages may not actually be installed. You will need to do one of two things:

1. Download the Bind code and rebuild it. (This is not difficult, but may force you to read the documentation.)
2. Download the `rpm` files for your distribution of Linux[9] and install using `rpm -Uvh package-name.rpm`, where `package-name`

---

7. This, of course, needs to be done.
8. This was done on Mandrake 7.2. Mandrake names its packages like RedHat (on which it is based), but appends `mdk` to the package name.
9. Other Linux distributions use a different package manager. Debian GNU/Linux has `.deb` files. We cannot cover all of these different formats. You need to extrapolate what to do if you insist on using a Linux distribution that does not support `rpm` for package management.

is similar to the ones mentioned above. Usually, these files can be found in the RPMS directory on your distribution CD.

At this point we assume you have the bind software installed on your computer. The rest of the discussion can be followed without going through the mechanics of setting everything up now; however, the greatest impact will be experienced by following along and creating your own domain and, accordingly, editing the files that we are discussing.

A typical setup of DNS involves the /etc and /var/named directories on your Unix box. The /etc directory is where you find just about everything configuration-related on Linux. The /var directory is used to maintain the details for things that are changing more frequently,[10] usually after a particular service has been started.

In addition to the DNS setup files, there are some files you need to adjust to ensure proper name resolution takes place (see Table 6–3).

Table 6–3
Some Highly Relevant Configuration Files

Format Name	How It Works
/etc/named.conf	The top-level configuration file for named (the DNS service) to do anything useful. You put configuration options and zone information (that is, information on how to locate the zone maps) in this file. For the most part, this file can be left alone, as long as it is present.
/etc/resolv.conf	This file allows you to configure what nameservers are used to perform name resolution. After getting our caching DNS server set up, we'll adjust this file to point to our new nameserver.
/etc/nsswitch.conf	It is often necessary to make adjustments to this file. This file, which has its origins in Solaris, allows you to set a number of parameters for how various entities are looked up, including hostnames, password information, group information, etc. Sometimes this file in its default form is not configured to allow hostnames to resolve using DNS.

---

10. Contrary to public opinion, many of the directories on Unix systems have been intelligently thought out. /var stands for the "variable" partition. Among things you find here are spool directories (mail, printing), system logs, and the DNS zone files (what we're discussing now).

The file `/etc/named.conf` is used to perform the top-level configuration of DNS. Let's take a look at a particular setup of DNS from one of our home machines:

```
options {
    directory "/var/named";
};

zone "." {
    type hint;
    file "root.hints";
};

zone "0.0.127.in-addr.arpa" {
    type master;
    file "pz/127.0.0";
};

zone "quillscape.com" {
    notify no;
    type master;
    file "pz/quillscape.com";
};

zone "10.10.10.in-addr.arpa" {
    notify no;
    type master;
    file "pz/10.10.10";
};
```

We will be using this file to supplement the discussion in a number of the sections related to DNS. Boldface will be used to illustrate what section is relevant to the present discussion.

The basic setup of DNS is relatively straightforward, despite the widespread perception that it is complicated. Much of that perception is due to the fact that the rules for writing the files must be followed religiously. Errors can result in problems that are virtually impossible to troubleshoot.[11]

As shown, a typical setup consists of `options` and a number of `zone` entries. The options section here indicates that the *directory /var/named* will be used to locate zone configuration information. Zones are essential to the operation of DNS, since they allow the Internet as well as your own DNS namespace to be partitioned hierarchically. The items shown in bold-

---

11. A number of these Unix configuration files would be ideal candidates for an overhaul using XML.

face (the options and the first two zone entries) are essential to the present discussion: how to set up a caching DNS server.

Installing a caching DNS server is a great way to become familiar with the DNS operation. Once you have this in place, you can extricate yourself from those slow DNS servers that your Internet provider has given you. Additionally, having your own caching DNS server allows you to get the most reliable DNS information, since it works by contacting a number of root servers, which are updated frequently about all of the domains in existence.

Returning to the discussion of the /etc/named.conf file: There is more than a good chance that this file is already on your system, if you have the Bind software installed. If for some reason it is not installed, go ahead and type in all text that appears in bold.

Configuring Root Hints • The following entry in /etc/named.conf shows the configuration of the root zone:

```
zone "." {
    type hint;
    file "root.hints";
};
```

This zone entry from /etc/named.conf tells you how to find the root zone information (the so-called *hints)* shown in Table 6–4. The type (set to hint) property indicates that the zone is built by consulting the root DNS servers to obtain answers to queries.[12] The file property indicates the name of the hints file as root.hints. This file can have any name but has been named this way to be consistent with how network administrators often name it. This file is actually found in /var/named/root.hints, because the configuration directory /var/named was specified in the options section. How do you actually get this file? You generate it using a program called Dig. You can always find the latest hints on the Internet.[13]

12. Yes, you must be connected to the Net at this point. Please do so now!
13. http://rs.interniconet/domain/named.root is one of the official links to obtain the list of root servers.

Table 6–4
/var/named/root.hints - Where the Root Server Information Was Configured

```
 .                       6D  IN  NSE.ROOT-SERVERS.NET.
 .                       6D  IN  NSD.ROOT-SERVERS.NET.
 .                       6D  IN  NSA.ROOT-SERVERS.NET.
 .                       6D  IN  NSH.ROOT-SERVERS.NET.
 .                       6D  IN  NSC.ROOT-SERVERS.NET.
 .                       6D  IN  NSG.ROOT-SERVERS.NET.
 .                       6D  IN  NSF.ROOT-SERVERS.NET.
 .                       6D  IN  NSB.ROOT-SERVERS.NET.
 .                       6D  IN  NSJ.ROOT-SERVERS.NET.
 .                       6D  IN  NSK.ROOT-SERVERS.NET.
 .                       6D  IN  NSL.ROOT-SERVERS.NET.
 .                       6D  IN  NSM.ROOT-SERVERS.NET.
 .                       6D  IN  NSI.ROOT-SERVERS.NET.

;; ADDITIONAL SECTION:
E.ROOT-SERVERS.NET.5w6d16h  IN  A192.203.230.10
D.ROOT-SERVERS.NET.5w6d16h  IN  A128.8.10.90
A.ROOT-SERVERS.NET.5w6d16h  IN  A198.41.0.4
H.ROOT-SERVERS.NET.5w6d16h  IN  A128.63.2.53
C.ROOT-SERVERS.NET.5w6d16h  IN  A192.33.4.12
G.ROOT-SERVERS.NET.5w6d16h  IN  A192.112.36.4
F.ROOT-SERVERS.NET.5w6d16h  IN  A192.5.5.241
B.ROOT-SERVERS.NET.5w6d16h  IN  A128.9.0.107
J.ROOT-SERVERS.NET.5w6d16h  IN  A198.41.0.10
K.ROOT-SERVERS.NET.5w6d16h  IN  A193.0.14.129
L.ROOT-SERVERS.NET.5w6d16h  IN  A198.32.64.12
M.ROOT-SERVERS.NET.5w6d16h  IN  A202.12.27.33
I.ROOT-SERVERS.NET.5w6d16h  IN  A192.36.148.17
```

We will not be covering the details of how this file is structured. You'll be able to find more detail on the precise structure of hints and zone files by consulting any reputable reference on DNS and Bind.[14]

An interesting question is: Why are there so *many* of these root servers? Another interesting question might be: Why are there so *few* of them? The answer does get a bit involved for inclusion in a Web book. The lowdown is that on the Internet, two things are of utmost importance: maintaining connectivity and being able to find names. The magic of DNS is that it is able to guarantee sufficient availability, which is achieved by guaranteeing with fairly high probability that at least a

---

14. The O'Reilly reference on DNS and Bind covers everything here in great detail. See Bibliography.

handful of root servers can be reached at any time. The additional magic is that queries to the root servers are likely to be distributed uniformly and occur relatively infrequently. This explanation will have to suffice for this book, but should give you a pretty good handle on the basic workings of DNS.

Once the root hints are in place, we are essentially done with the caching DNS setup.

Starting, Stopping, or Checkin Status of `named` **(the DNS service on Linux)** • DNS may or may not already be running on your system. If it is running, you'll be able to inspect this readily by running `ps`.[15] Note here that we assume you are working as the root user, since much of what is being done here requires superuser privileges to be carried out successfully.

In general day-to-day work with DNS, the third case is most commonly used. You should try to run this command at this time. If all goes well, you will see a message indicating the new `pid` of the `named` daemon. If it doesn't go well, all you need to do is find the `named` command (usually in `/usr/sbin/named`) and explicitly start it after killing the existing process, if it is running already.

Resolving DNS Queries • Merely starting the `named` daemon does not imply that name resolution will work immediately. You will need to update the `/etc/resolv.conf` file to point to your new nameserver. Since the assumption has been that you are working on a single machine at this time, we are using the same machine both to run the DNS server and to resolve DNS queries. You will want to do the following:

- Copy `/etc/resolv.conf` to `/etc/resolv.conf-backup`. You might need to switch back to whatever you were using previously for resolving DNS queries (e.g., your ISP's name servers) in case something doesn't work.
- Make the following the content of `/etc/resolv.conf`:

  `nameserver 127.0.0.1`

Making these changes to /etc/resolv.conf results in the "localhost" being used to resolve DNS queries. The question now is: How do you know whether it is working?

---

15. Note that on Solaris or System V derived Unix systems, you might be getting a version of ps that accepts different options. **ps -ef** usually works in place of what you see here.

▶ **TIP: Stopping and Restarting DNS under Linux**

To check whether `named` is already running before killing it (what we usually do):

```
# ps auxww | grep named
root 464 0.0 0.7 2652 1840 ? S Feb09 0:07 named
```

On Linux you can use the `killall` command to stop a particular daemon as follows:

```
# killall named
```

If you do not have this command, you can just look up the `pid` for the `named` process that is running and kill it that way. The polite way to kill it is as follows (replace 464 with what was reported by `ps` above):

```
# kill 464
```

The Bind software comes with a command that can be used as an "init" script to automate starting, restarting, and shutting down the `named` daemon. The command is called `ndc` and is used as follows:

```
# ndc start
```

This starts `named`.

```
# ndc stop
```

This stops `named`.

```
# ndc restart
```

This restarts `named`.

The `nslookup` command is used to allow you to interact with DNS directly instead of having to launch a TCP/IP-aware client such as TELNET or your Web browser. You can use it as follows:

```
$ nslookup
```

You may run into problems. Despite having made changes to the `/etc/resolv.conf` file, you will be left with the impression that the change you made to point the nameserver at `127.0.0.1` has been ignored. This is not the case. Another configuration file, `/etc/nsswitch.conf`, may also need to be updated. This file contains a line for how to resolve "hosts." You'll be able to identify it by looking for the following line:

```
hosts: files
```

Other entries may also appear on that line. Permitted values include `nis`, `nisplus`, and `dns`. If your attempt to look up names with `nslookup` is unsuccessful, it is more than likely because the value `dns` is not present on this configuration line. You should update it to include DNS for resolving host names:

```
hosts: files dns
```

This indicates that host name resolution is to be done first by checking "files," which is kind of cryptic but means that the standard "hosts" file `/etc/hosts` is to be consulted. After checking the hosts file, DNS is to be used. This means that the information in `/etc/resolv.conf` will be used to figure out what nameserver(s) to contact to look up a given host (that is, if it was not found in `/etc/hosts`). You might be wondering why one would ever want to use anything but DNS. In practice, the `/etc/hosts` file and other naming services (such as NIS, NIS+, and Active Directory) are used to look up local host information. You will probably not need any of these alternative naming services in a home environment, unless you are trying to build a seamless network similar to those in large corporations.[16]

Once you have modified the `/etc/nsswitch.conf` file, the caching DNS setup is complete.

Configuring Your Intranet

In this section we will cover how to look up names on your intranet. An intranet is basically a network of machines that is more than likely connected to the Internet but is often restricted in terms of what services and individual machines are exposed.

In this section, we assume that you'll be configuring a server that has two network interfaces and is acting as a router. One of the network

---

16. NIS, NIS+, and Active Directory are used to create such seamless networks. NIS and NIS+ are used primarily in a Unix environment, while Active Directory is the Microsoft offering. Using these technologies, you can centralize authentication, file systems, and other shared resources to create a uniform setup on all machines on a LAN. We won't be covering this here; our discussion is focused on seamless access to host names.

interfaces is your gateway to the Internet. The other interface represents your gateway to the LAN. Network interfaces on the LAN are accessed using private network addresses. Figure 6–1 and the discussion that follows should make this clear.

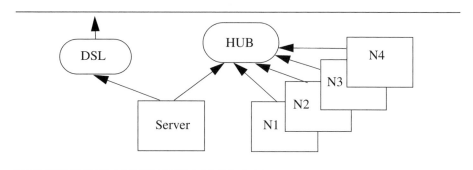

Figure 6–1
An Intranet

Item	About
DSL	This could also say Cable Modem or ISDN. The key is that this oval represents a box that represents your connection to the WAN (Wide Area Network). Increasingly, this box is becoming a DSL or cable modem. We assume that your connection to the WAN is coming by way of a service provider that limits you to a single IP address.
Hub	This could also be a switch. The Server and the various network clients N1...Nn are all connected to the hub. If the hub is a switch, this means that it could have a number of capabilities, including support for faster peer-to-peer communication (switches help to reduce unnecessary Ethernet broadcasts when communication is taking place between two specific IP addresses), network address translation, etc. If your hub and DSL box are one in this drawing, you will not need to do anything special to translate private network addresses when connections are made to the WAN.

Item	About
Server	The machine that will act as your router. Your Linux system (and many other Unix systems) can act as a dedicated router out of the box. Among other things, this allows all of your machines on the network to share a common connection to the Internet.[a] The term *server* is almost a misnomer (but not quite), since any of these machines at one level or another is a server because various networking daemons are installed on all machines in the network (at least on the Linux machines). Windows machines may also be present on the network, and client configuration is trivial.
N1, N2, ...	The other machines on your network. Often these machines will be referred to as clients. This is not necessarily the case. It might be that there is a client/server relationship with "Server" in this picture; these machines could also be completely autonomous in most regards. That is, none of the resources of the Server are being used (e.g., no shared file systems, no printer access, etc.). These machines represent the unexposed part of your network.[b]

a. For DSL and cable modem users, there are boxes on the market that already do what we are describing here. These boxes are excellent but lack the configurability of a Linux-based solution. With Linux you can exercise very fine control over port forwarding, port blocking, and general firewalling.

b. The setup we will be describing leaves all of the machines, Ni ... Nn, unexposed. It is possible to expose individual machines to the Internet using port forwarding. As this feature will not be needed for our discussions in this book, it will not be covered.

These assumptions are pretty reasonable for a home setup based on DSL, cable modems, or ISDN, all of which represent more or less permanent connections to the Internet. If your environment is not similar to this, we highly recommend that you add the missing components, which are likely to be listed in Table 6–5.

We will discuss how to configure a server and one additional machine. Once both have been configured and basic connectivity has been established, we will extend the caching DNS server to act as a local DNS server. At the end of this discussion, everything will be in place for you to do Web development and testing from anywhere on your LAN.

Table 6–5
Things You May Not Yet Own But Should Acquire ASAP

Item	About
Second Ethernet controller	This is needed only if you want to configure your server as a router for your network. Routers allow traffic to get from one network to another, so this is a useful thing. It may be the case that your connection to the WAN (or Internet) already does routing and network address translation, in which case you do not need to configure a router. However, configuring your own router will give you the best control over your network (and ultimately, with some work, the greatest security).
Hub	Many people we know have only two machines and suggest that you can get by without a hub, since a null modem connection can be used between the server and the second machine (which would just be the picture presented in Figure 6–1 with only N1 present). This is academically correct, but is penny-wise and pound-foolish. The cost of a hub is minimal. It does cost more than an Ethernet controller, but the cheapest are less than three times the cost of a cheap Ethernet card. If you choose to add a third machine, you will no longer need the null modem cable and will be forced to buy a hub. (This has happened to all of the authors rather quickly; it doesn't take long if you have two desktops and a notebook is thrown into the picture). Get the hub and avoid feeling sorry later.

Configuring the Server's Network Interfaces • It is likely that the overall experience of doing this work is going to force you to *think* about how you want your network to be set up. It is even more likely that when you move to an Internet configuration (i.e., when some of your intranet machines become exposed as public servers), you may need to do a second round of thinking.

When configuring your server to act as a router, you will be doing something that is known as a *dual-homed* setup, which means that this computer has two network homes: the private network and the public (the Internet, a.k.a. the WAN) network.

In order to have a dual-homed setup, there is an explicit requirement that you have two network interfaces (assumed here to be Ethernet) present on your computer as shown in Figure 6–1.[17] Based on the assumptions stated in footnote 17, you can inspect that two are actually detected in Linux by viewing the `/proc/pci`[18] file.

▸ **TIP**

> The `/proc/pci` file provides information about the PCI devices available on your system. (Note that similar files are provided for other bus standards, including ISA and SCSI.) This file is shown in an abbreviated form.
>
> ```
> PCI devices found:
>   Bus  0, device   0, function  0:
>     Host bridge: Intel 82437 (rev 1).
>
>   Bus  0, device   7, function  0:
>     ISA bridge: Intel 82371FB PIIX ISA (rev 2).
>
>   Bus  0, device   7, function  1:
>     IDE interface: Intel 82371FB PIIX IDE (rev 2).
>
>   Bus  0, device  17, function  0:
>     SCSI storage controller: Adaptec AIC-7871 (rev 3).
>
>   Bus  0, device  18, function  0:
>     Ethernet controller: LiteOn Unknown device (rev 37).
>
>   Bus  0, device  19, function  0:
>     Ethernet controller: LiteOn Unknown device (rev 37).
>
>   Bus  0, device  20, function  0:
>     VGA compatible controller: Matrox Mystique (rev 3).
> ```
>
> Note that both Ethernet controllers are bolded above. If you see only one occurrence of Ethernet, then only one controller has been detected and you will not be able to configure your computer as a router.

---

17. We are going to assume that you are using a reasonably modern computer that has a PCI bus, and that PCI network cards are installed in all machines on your network. The setup for ISA would be similar, but requires much more proficiency in resolving interrupt conflicts and other sordid details that end up wasting a lot of time. Consider investing in a more modern machine (it doesn't need to be the fastest CPU, but should be PCI architecture for peripherals at a minimum).

18. The `/proc filesystem` is available on Linux and Solaris. On Linux it is replete with information about your entire computer setup and is an excellent diagnostic tool that can help you to figure out why things don't appear to be working. We refer you to the HOWTO documents at http://linux.org.

If all has gone well, as pointed out in the Tip, you'll see two Ethernet entries. (The output may vary based on the Ethernet controller vendor.) You are now ready to configure the interfaces. We summarize the configuration to be done in Table 6–6. Essentially, there are three files that must be modified: `/etc/sysconfig/network`, `/etc/sysconfig/ifcfg-eth0`, and `/etc/sysconfig/ifcfg-eth1`.

Table 6–6
Interface Configuration for `eth0` and `eth1` in `/etc/sysconfig`

File	Content

network
(relative to `/etc/sysconfig`)
	`GATEWAYDEV=eth0`
	`FORWARD_IPV4=true`
	`GATEWAY=209.246.58.1`

`network-scripts/ifcfg-eth0`
(relative to `/etc/sysconfig`)
Make sure the cable for this is connected to your DSL or other modem LAN port.
	`BOOTPROTO=none`
	`DEVICE=eth0`
	`ONBOOT=yes`
	`BROADCAST=209.246.58.255`
	`NETMASK=255.255.255.0`
	`NETWORK=209.246.58.0`
	`IPADDR=209.246.58.59`

`network-scripts/ifcfg-eth1`
(relative to `/etc/sysconfig`)
Make sure the cable for this is connected to your hub.
	`BOOTPROTO=none`
	`DEVICE=eth1`
	`ONBOOT=yes`
	`NETWORK=10.10.10.0`
	`BROADCAST=10.10.10.255`
	`NETMASK=255.255.255.0`
	`IPADDR=10.10.10.1`

In this example, which came from one of our servers, `eth0` and `eth1` are the two Ethernet interfaces on the system. The first interface, `eth0`, is directly connected to the Wide Area Network (the WAN), which could be a DSL, cable, or other dedicated connection to the Internet. In this example, `eth0` is assigned the IP address `209.246.58.59`. Note that `209.246.58.1` is the gateway assigned by the ISP for routing purposes. (You cannot just make up a random IP number for GATEWAY and IPADDR. These numbers must be assigned to you and configured in your ISP's router!) The number must be one that was assigned by your Internet Service Provider (ISP). The second interface, `eth1`, is connected to the hub (along with other client machines), which represents the private network. This is where you have some freedom: You can choose any non-routable IP subnet and assign addresses within this subnet to this machine and other clients connected to the hub. Here we have chosen the `10.10.10.` as a class C subnet and are numbering the clients (beginning with this machine) as `10.10.10.1, 10.10.10.2`, etc.

Once you have made the changes to the three files mentioned in Table 6–6, there is no need to reboot your computer. Unlike many other operating systems (most notably, Windows), Linux does not usually have to be rebooted, unless you are actually installing new hardware. You do, however, need to bring up networking again. The easiest way is to run the script `/etc/rc.d/init.d/network` as follows:

```
# /etc/rc.d/init.d/network restart
```

One additional point about the IP configuration shown in Table 6–6 is in order: The `/etc/sysconfig/network` file has an option for doing IP forwarding. IP forwarding enables IP packets originating anywhere on the `10.10.10.x` private network to appear to have originated from the IP address `209.246.58.59` (this should be replaced with the IP address assigned by your Internet Service Provider). This option may only work on systems running on Red Hat Linux. If you encounter trouble when trying to configure a client elsewhere on the network to share the Internet connection, you may want to try the following:

```
# echo "1" > /proc/sys/net/ipv4/ip_forward
# /sbin/ipchains -P forward DENY
# /sbin/ipchains -A forward -i eth0 -j MASQ
```

Once IP forwarding is enabled, all of the machines on the private network will be enabled to communicate on the Internet, provided you configure the network settings on each of the other clients correctly. If those machines are Linux machines, it is simply a matter of replicating the setup for the `eth1` interface for each client's `eth0` interface. This is summarized in Table 6–7.

These settings must be done for each client on the private network; that is, each of the machines connected to the hub (or switch) in the original figure. Each of the machines must be assigned a distinct private address (`10.10.10.X`, where X `!=` 1). You must take care to ensure that the IP address placed here is not the same as the dual-homed machine (the one acting as your network router) and that no two machines on your LAN have the same IP address. Otherwise, nothing will appear to be working. Once you have configured the client, as with the router, you must restart networking. In the case of client setup, there is no need to forward `IPv4`, so you should not perform this step as part of client configuration.

Table 6–7
Interface Configuration for `eth0` on other Linux clients

File	Content

`network-scripts/ifcfg-eth0` (relative to `/etc/sysconfig`) Make sure the cable for this interface is connected to your hub.	`BOOTPROTO=none`
	`DEVICE=eth0`
	`ONBOOT=yes`
	`NETWORK=10.10.10.0`
	`BROADCAST=10.10.10.255`
	`NETMASK=255.255.255.0`
	`IPADDR=10.10.10.X where X != 1`
	`GATEWAY=10.10.10.1`

A final word about networking setup: We do not cover Windows or other operating systems' configuration here; however, you can easily configure Windows or Macintosh clients by supplying the `IPADDR`, `NETWORK`, and `GATEWAY` values in the appropriate networking control panel dialog. It is fairly straightforward, and the information in the table with this description should be sufficient for you to perform the setup on your own.

Using DNS to Maintain Your Intranet Host Information

Forward Lookups • The forward lookup zone is needed to resolve queries for a domain. There can be any number of forward lookup zones configured in the `/etc/named.conf` file. We will show only one here for our private network, quillscape.com, but others can easily be added. We'll discuss what needs to be done toward the end of this section.

Below is a copy of the forward lookup zone for quillscape.com. Glance over it briefly; a line-by-line summary of what is going on is provided.

```
1   @     IN      SOA     liszt.quillscape.com. hostmaster.quillscape.com. (
2                         199802151        ; serial, todays date + todays serial #
3                         8H              ; refresh, seconds
4                         2H              ; retry, seconds
5                         1W              ; expire, seconds
6                         1D )            ; minimum, seconds
7   ;
8                 NS      liszt
9                 MX      10 mail.quillscape.com.
10                MX      20 mail2.quillscape.com.
```

```
11   ;
12   localhost       A      127.0.0.1
13   liszt           A      10.10.10.2
14   mail            A      10.10.10.2
15   mail2           A      10.10.10.3
16   rachmaninov     A      10.10.10.4
17   ravel           A      10.10.10.7
18   schubert        A      10.10.10.8
19   intranet        A      10.10.10.50
20   loyola          A      10.10.10.150
21   tools           A      10.10.10.151
22   jhpc            A      10.10.10.152
23   nina            A      10.10.10.153
24   george          A      10.10.10.154
25   www             CNAME  liszt
```

Here is what is going on:

1   Start of Authority (SOA) configuration. This indicates that this is the beginning of the configuration for "authoritative information" about the domain `quillscape.com`. This line indicates that liszt.quillscape.com (where `named` is running) is where the SOA is configured. Queries about the domain can be sent to hostmaster@quillscape.com.

2   Serial number. This can actually be anything but is usually based on a date, plus some serial number (or displacement). When you change this file, it is a good idea to bump the serial number.

3–7   `refresh`, `retry`, `expire`, and `minimum` are parameters to control the caching behavior. For additional information, please see the Bind documentation in the Bibliography.

8   `NS` record to indicate that `liszt` is a name server.

9–10   `MX` records are used to get inbound mail to the "right place", e.g., mail sent to `george@quillscape.com` actually needs to go to an internal mail server, which runs on mail.quillscape.com. (Mail can be sent there directly, of course, but this provides a useful convenience for your customers.) There are two `MX` records (more can be added), with priorities 10 and 20. The lower the value, the higher the priority. This means that the preference is to always use `mail.quillscape.com` first.

12–25   A number of A records. These records are used to associate a name with an IP number. This is the most common kind of record to be placed in the forward lookup zone configuration file. Each of these records is made relative to quillscape.com (the zone being configured).

26   A CNAME record can be used for aliasing other records. Here an alias has been created from www to liszt.

Clearly, in managing DNS, it is imperative that you devise a good process for managing (and keeping track of) all those IP numbers. In the example for quillscape.com, not all of the IP numbers correspond to physical network addresses. By convention only, this network (which is going to remain small for the foreseeable future) uses the range 10.10.10.1–10.10.10.50 for private network addresses[19] and uses 10.10.10.100 and higher for virtual interfaces. This is not a requirement; you might choose to organize things differently. In a larger corporation (or even a small or medium-size company), it might be advisable to do more planning, such as using one subnet (say, 10.10.10.*) for clients and another (10.10.13.*) for virtual hosts. Perhaps another would be appropriate for serving dynamic IP with DHCP (10.10.10.14). Whatever the case, planning a more complicated network is beyond the scope of this book, and our intent has been to get you primed with a very usable private DNS setup. You can actually make up your own domain and (more or less) search and replace to get the ball rolling for your private network.

There are a few things we cannot show here in the interests of space, focus, and time:

- **Dynamic Update Protocol**–This aspect of DNS (covered by a separate IETF RFC) allows dynamically assigned IP addresses to be mapped on the fly. This tends to be useful, say, with transiently connected devices (e.g., palms, notebooks, etc.) This is something you can learn about independently and set up after you get the basic setup completed, which we are advocating here.
- **Mapping Multiple IP Numbers from a Single Entry**–This is pretty straightforward, as you simply list the IP numbers you want in addition to the one already specified.

---

19. The author of this chapter would have a very difficult time convincing his wife that having 50 computers around is acceptable. Though it would be cool, it would likely infringe on domestic tranquillity.

- **Revolving (or Round-Robin) DNS**–This is a technique used to cycle through a list of IP numbers to address load-balancing considerations. Many Web sites actually make use of this facility to distribute the requests to a Web server among a cluster of servers. Our Web framework is actually able to address load distribution, though this topic is not covered in this introductory text.

Reverse Lookups • The forward lookup zone is used to map a name to one or more IP numbers, which is very useful for most of what you will ever need to do, particularly for the topics in this book. There are times, however, when you are given an IP number and need to determine the host name. DNS does not do this automatically for you based on the forward lookup information. The short explanation for this is that it is not entirely possible to do so, based on the example presented in the previous section. Consider the names `liszt` and `mail`. Both of these names are mapped to 10.10.10.2. So what should the reverse entry be? This is analogous to a question in math: Given $y = x*x$, where $y = 4$, what is x? There are two values of x (–2 and 2) that produce the mapping to 4. Looking at the forward lookup zone, we know that 10.10.10.2 has an inverse mapping to `liszt` and `mail`, but which should be returned?

DNS has been carefully designed to address the issue of inverse mapping and uses a reverse lookup zone to achieve this. The reverse lookup zone is named after any reasonable subnet within your network. Recall from our earlier discussion about the zone configuration file the definition of `10.10.10.in-addr.arpa` for the reverse zone. This naming convention, while appearing cryptic, is actually comprehensible. (The `10.10.10.*` network follows the original ARPA IP addressing framework.) This allows for the posibility of a future addressing scheme in which there are more than four octets used to represent the IP address.[20]

In many respects, the reverse lookup file looks like the forward zone configuration file with an `SOA` section (configured here exactly the same as in the forward zone configuration file) and NS records. You want to make sure these items are in every zone file. The notable difference is the presence of pointer (`PTR`) records. `PTR` records are used to map an IP number (which is taken relative to the subnet that has been used to name the file, hence the importance of naming this file correctly) to a hostname. This mapping is the reverse mapping we have discussed:

---

20. A possibility that has been foreshadowed but is yet to be realized.

```
@        IN      SOA     liszt.quillscape.com. hostmaster.quillscape.com. (
                         199802151 ; Serial, todays date + todays serial
                         8H        ; Refresh
                         2H        ; Retry
                         1W        ; Expire
                         1D)       ; Minimum TTL
                 NS      liszt.quillscape.com.

2                PTR     liszt.quillscape.com.
3                PTR     mail2.quillscape.com.
4                PTR     rachmaninov.quillscape.com.
7                PTR     ravel.quillscape.com.
8                PTR     schubert.quillscape.com.
50               PTR     intranet.quillscape.com.
150              PTR     loyola.quillscape.com.
151              PTR     tools.quillscape.com.
152              PTR     jhpc.quillscape.com.
153              PTR     nina.quillscape.com.
154              PTR     george.quillscape.com.
```

The reverse entries must correspond to a proper name that is already mapped (presumably by a forward entry in the forward zone configuration file). Great care must be exercised to ensure that the mapping is not treated as a relative mapping. Omitting the trailing dot from the entries is one of the classic mistakes made during the configuration of this file, and it can be very difficult to identify. The reason relative names are supported here is that you might actually want to assume "quillscape.com" (the domain of interest) is used as a base. Don't assume anything. The best approach is to be explicit about the inverse mapping by listing the canonical name of the host as opposed to the hostname itself (e.g., `liszt.quillscape.com.` is preferred to `liszt`).

Note that you will more than likely configure two reverse lookup zones for your setup. You want one reverse lookup zone for each subnet and one for the loopback family of addresses, which should be named `0.0.127.in-addr.arpa.` You can download our configuration from the Internet.

A Quick Sanity Check • At this point there are a number of things you should check. We summarize these in Table 6–8 and tell you how to determine whether there is a problem. Keep in mind that it is impossible to foresee every problem that you might encounter in deploying your own DNS server; our hope is that this is a reasonably complete start to ensure the smoothest possible deployment for what you will need to work with this book in a networked setting.

Table 6–8
Basic Test Cases

Test Case	Trying It Out (Using Nslookup)
Caching	> `server 10.10.10.1` > `www.prenhall.com` Hopefully, you will get a response. > `www.prenhall.com` You will get a response that differs by printing a nonauthoritative response. **Resolution**: Check the `/etc/named.conf` file to ensure that the root `hints` file appears. Check `/var/named/root.hints` to ensure the existence of the file.
Forward lookups	> `server 10.10.10.1` > `set domain=quillscape.com` > `george` Should respond with the correct IP number. > `george.quillscape.com` Similar. **Resolution**: If you get any errors here, it is most likely due to a file that is not named the way it was spelled in the `/etc/named.conf` configuration file. It is also possible that there is an error in the file itself. You can check `/var/log/messages` to see if any errors have been generated by `named`.
Reverse lookups	> `server 10.10.10.1` > `10.10.10.1` This should return the name of the nameserver (`liszt` in our example). This is necessary for some `nslookup` clients to allow your nameserver to be used. > `10.10.10.50` Should return intranet.quillscape.com. **Resolution**: Reverse lookups can fail if the file is not named the way it was typed in the `/etc/named.conf` configuration file. The file must also be named `subnet.in-addr.arpa`, where subnet is a valid class A, B, or C subnet reference (10.10.10 is used in our examples). You must also check whether reverse entries are indeed taken relative to root level, which means the fully qualified hostname followed by a period (.), e.g., `liszt.toolsofcomputing.com.` was used in our discussion. *(Do not forget the trailing period.)* .

Table 6–8
Basic Test Cases (Continued)

Test Case	Trying It Out (Using `Nslookup`)
Loopback interface IP number reverse lookup	`> 127.0.0.1` This should return the proper name, `localhost`. It is tempting to say "I don't need that stinking name `localhost`," but many commands and useful tests can be performed when it resolves correctly (both forward and in reverse) via DNS. For example, we tend to use it in examples whereby we test the Web server in the Apache configuration sections that appear shortly.

Apache Web Server Configuration

We dedicate the remainder of this chapter to getting the Apache Web Server (AWS) set up correctly on your Linux system. We will discuss the following:

- How to uninstall your current Apache (if present)
- How to know whether it is actually installed
- The use of `rpm`, `wget` (a text-based tool for getting documents from the Web), and `lynx` (a similar tool)
- Downloading, configuring, compiling, and installing AWS
- Performing postinstallation tailoring of the setup
- Performing more exotic setups, in particular virtual hosting and SSL configuration

Unconfiguring Preinstalled Apache

The very first thing we usually do, regardless of the Linux system we are using, is to conduct our own setup of the Apache system. We also recommend uninstalling Apache either if it has been preconfigured on your system, or if you have added it because you thought it would be difficult to install it from scratch.

```
$ rpm -q -a | grep apache
apache-1.3.12-2
```

The output you see here indicates that the package is already installed. It is fairly straightforward to uninstall the package by using `rpm—erasefiles apache`. We recommend that you do this if you think there is any chance you will get confused between a new installation of Apache and the preinstalled version.

Reinstalling Apache

Reinstallation of Apache is fairly straightforward. For the purposes of this book, we recommend that you work with the latest 1.x release of the Apache Web Server; this can be obtained from `http://www.apache.org`. Please note that in the interest of keeping the book general, we list only the current version by example. This version may have changed, and you should download an appropriate version in case any security enhancements or critical updates have been made.

There is a convenient little package that comes with most versions of Linux, called `wget`. This allows you to get something from the Web without having to go to the graphical browser, which is still clunky and inefficient to use under Linux. There is also lynx, which provides an acceptable browser for browsing simple Web sites. Here is the approximate package name you should look for, based on the results of a search using `rpm` on my system:

```
$ rpm -q -a | grep lynx
lynx-2.8.3dev.22-2mdk
$ rpm -q -a | grep wget
wget-1.5.3-8mdk
```

If `wget` and `lynx` are not installed, taking the time to install them now will alleviate your having to work with the slow Web browsers on the Linux platform.[21] As mentioned earlier in this chapter, we will assume that you now know how to locate packages such as these in the RPMS directory on your OS installation CD or from the Internet. We will further assume that you now have these utilities installed, as we intend to use both of them shortly to install and inspect the overall setup.

At the time of writing, the current version of Apache is 1.3.14 (on the 1.x development line). Here is how `wget` can be used to acquire this package easily from the command line:

---

21. This author remains convinced that Linux is better positioned to become a killer server platform than a killer desktop platform. In spite of the hard work people are doing to make it a killer desktop platform, we don't find the overall experience pleasant compared to Windows or Macintosh. Learn to use the command line utilities if possible—they work beautifully!

```
$ wget http://httpd.apache.org/dist/'apache_1.3.17.tar.gz
--10:52:42--  http://httpd.apache.org:80/dist/apache_1.3.17.tar.gz
           => apache_1.3.17.tar.gz'
Connecting to httpd.apache.org:80... connected!
HTTP request sent, awaiting response... 200 OK
Length: 1,813,581 [application/x-tar]

    0K -> .......... .......... .......... .......... [   2%]
   50K -> .......... .......... .......... .......... [   5%]
  100K -> .......... .......... .......... .......... [   8%]
... Much output suppressed for concise presentation!
 1700K -> .......... .......... .......... .......... [  98%]
 1750K -> .......... .......... .......... .......... [ 100%]

10:53:28 (39.02 KB/s) - 'apache_1.3.17.tar.gz' saved [1813581/1813581]
```

So how did we know what file to get? The answer is surprisingly clever and involves a brief digression. This author typically uses both Windows and Linux in his day-to-day work. When visiting the Apache Web site, you will ultimately be following a link that takes you to a download area as shown in Figure 6–2.

▶ **TIP: To be graphical or nongraphical? It isn't a question.**

We have been taking care not to assume that you are using a graphical desktop, especially on the server where you will be running Web applications. This might frustrate you at first, but this is the way that most Linux developers work. Even those who have a graphical desktop can be spotted with myriad terminal windows running on their desktops, sometimes in virtual window managers. From our experience, this speaks volumes for not assuming you are working in a graphical context. Surprisingly, this assumption actually works to your advantage. Working from the command line in Linux (unlike in Windows) is not the equivalent of traveling in coach class by air.

In this case, you should note that the commands we have shown can all be run on the server, which eliminates the need to ftp or scp (secure copy) the files from your Windows or Linux desktop to another system, if that system happens to be remote. Learning the command line way will save you time. You might even surprise your friends who try doing it on Windows and end up having to go through extra steps to get the files where they need to be.

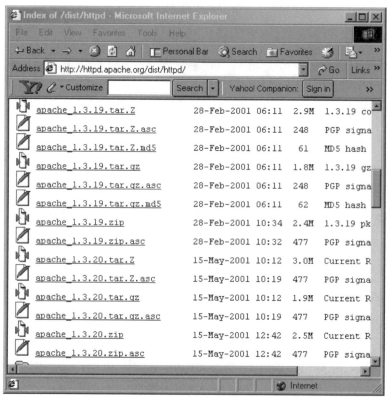

Figure 6–2
Download Window

Then you can hover over the appropriate link (here, `apache_1.3.17.tar.gz` is the highest numbered release), right-click, and copy shortcut. This copies the actual text of the URL that will get `apache_1.3.17.tar.gz`. Then go to the terminal window and paste it (usually **control-v** or **shift-ins**).

In Figure 6–3, the text for the URL was pasted. All that had to be done was to make sure the window was selected (a mouse click on the title bar usually does the trick), then type `wget` (without hitting Enter), and then right-click in the terminal window and choose Paste. Bear in mind that this operation should be done precisely as specified. After typing `wget`, be sure not to hit the Enter key, as you want the paste operation to paste the text immediately following the `wget`. (It's okay to go ahead and put a space after `wget`, although it is also okay just to let the text paste immediately following it and use the `bash` shell to edit the command to have appropriate spacing.)

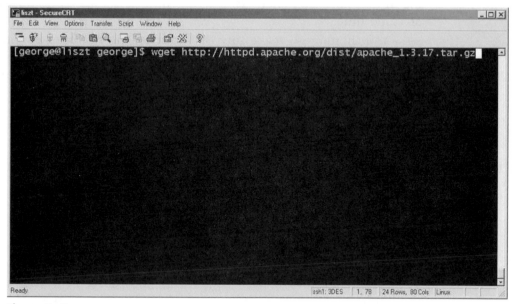

Figure 6–3
Pasted URL

If all has gone according to plan, you will have a copy of the `tar` file containing the Apache source code. Now you will want to unpack this code. Unpacking gzipped `tar` files under Linux is straightforward, due mostly to having a proper version of `tar` installed that supports the "z" option to do transparent decompression when unpacking archives:

```
$ tar xzf apache_1.3.17.tar.gz
```

This usually results in a subdirectory `apache-1.3.17` being created relative to the current working directory.

A few words are in order about goals. Our goal with respect to Apache configuration is to get a highly usable setup completed for the purposes of development. We will do this and then do some tailoring to make the setup more flexible, especially if you plan to deploy in a multiuser environment. Toward that end, we will show how to evolve the setup to support HTTP over secure sockets–the so-called HTTPS setup. It could all be done now, but is being done in two phases to give you the opportunity to do a basic setup and proceed to the development chapters, then consider the more advanced setup later. This especially applies to our readers who may not be so advanced. If you are in this category, get the basic setup going and do the HTTPS setup after working through the later chapters. There is no harm done by going secure at a later time.

You should also make sure that your system has been configured as a development environment. Among other things, this means that both make and the gcc compiler are present. You can inspect this by checking as follows:

```
$ rpm -q -a | grep ^make
make-3.79-2mdk
$ rpm -q -a | grep ^gcc
gcc-cpp-2.95.2-7mdk
gcc-2.95.2-7mdk
gcc-c++-2.95.2-7mdk
gcc-g77-2.95.2-7mdk
gcc-java-2.95.2-7mdk
gcc-objc-2.95.2-7mdk
gcc-colorgcc-2.95.2-7mdk
gcc-libgcj-2.95.2-7mdk
gcc-chill-2.95.2-7mdk
```

This is what you can expect to see on a Mandrake system. Other Linux systems may not have the trailing "mdk," but will be similar. In any event, here is where we have to draw the line. When you set up Linux for the first time, you can choose to configure a development system. This will install tools that are needed in order to build packages such as Apache Web Server (which are usually written in C–a situation that is slowly changing). So you still need to have that C compiler around. Your RPMS directory can help you find all of the needed components.

We can now rebuild AWS. Like many other open-source packages developed in C, there is a configure script that must be run, followed by make.

```
$ cd apache_1.3.17
```

When working with any package such as Apache, it is a good idea to be cognizant of the many configuration options at one's disposal. This can be determined as follows (a plethora of output is generated; it is abbreviated here to highlight the most useful options for getting started):

```
$ ./configure --help
```

This will display a usage message.

Table 6–9 summarizes some of the useful options for those just getting started and an explanation of why you would want to consider their use.

Table 6–9
Useful Configuration Options for Proper Initial Configuration

Option	Description and Why You'd Even Consider It	Do I need to worry about this now?
`--help, -h`	To obtain help for all of the options that we're not presenting here	**Yes**, in case you have an advanced need later on.
`--prefix=PREFIX`	Install architecture-independent files in PREFIX. Here you are expected to replace PREFIX with the parent directory where you want to install AWS. We recommend installing third- party software according to the established Unix convention of directory `/usr/local`, e.g. `/usr/local/apache`. Example: `--prefix=/usr/local/apache`	**Yes**, you want to install to a separate directory to make it easy to remove the software later, or simply to add another version. It is okay to have as many copies of Apache running as you like (even from different directories). Beginners, please install to `/usr/local/apache` if this is your first time.
`--htdocsdir=DIR`	Install read-only document files in DIR. Example: `--htdocsdir=/home/httpd/html`	**No**. Consider this option only if you absolutely must put the documents somewhere else. Many Linux systems have already created a directory `/home/httpd/html`.
`--cgidir=DIR`	Install read-only `cgi` files in DIR. Example: `--cgidir=/home/httpd/cgi-bin`	**No**, for reasons similar to those given for `--htdocsdir`.

Table 6–9
Useful Configuration Options for Proper Initial Configuration (Continued)

Option	Description and Why You'd Even Consider It	Do I need to worry about this now?
`--iconsdir=DIR`	Install read-only icon files in DIR. Example: `--iconsdir=/home/httpd/iconsdir`	**No**, for reasons similar to those given for `--htdocsdir`
`--with-port=PORT`	Run the server on an alternate port. This is important if you are already using port 80 to run a Web server. Example: `--with-port=8080`	**Yes**. You can always change your mind later and edit `httpd.conf`. If you are reluctant to remove your existing AWS setup on your Linux distribution, you can use this option to avoid it. We recommend sticking with ports such as 8000 and 8080 that are easy to memorize and are not likely to be in use.

`--server-uid=UID`	Set the user ID to the one on which the Web server should be run. By default, as the `--help` option tells you, user `nobody` is chosen. You almost never want this user to be used. In fact, for this book, you will want to use yourself.
	
	Examples:
	`--server-uid=gkt`
	`--server-uid=500`
		Yes. You can always change your mind later and edit `httpd.conf`.
		
		However, this convenience option should be pursued now. Consider creating a user named `apache` on your system or use your own user name. This will make it easy for you to maintain the document (`htdocs`) and script (`cgi-bin`) directories.

Table 6–9
Useful Configuration Options for Proper Initial Configuration (Continued)

Option	Description and Why You'd Even Consider It	Do I need to worry about this now?

`--server-gid=GID`	Set the group ID of which the user ID (chosen above) is a member. This option should be used with `--server-uid`. Make sure the user specified with `--server-uid` is actually a member of GID.
	
	Examples:
	`--server-gid=staff`
	`--server-gid=100`
	
	Use the `groups` command to ascertain whether a user is a member of a group as follows:
	`$ groups george`
		Yes. You can always change your mind later and edit `httpd.conf`.
		
		If you choose to use this, use `--server-gid` as well.

This table has been organized to include the most essential options. Toward the end of this chapter, we will consider options that pertain to CGI script execution that will prove useful mostly to intermediate and advanced readers (and those who care about security).

Here is an example of configure command line and an explanation of what would occur as a result:

```
./configure --prefix=/usr/local/apache
```

Configure AWS for installation in /usr/local/apache. All content (HTML) and CGI scripts will be served out of subdirectories relative to /usr/local/apache (htdocs and cgi-bin, respectively.) This is okay but will probably force you to make the most changes to your configuration in /usr/local/apache/conf/httpd.conf later.

With a little more work, you can get a better setup and minimize your interactions with the configuration file (and avoid having to do most things as the `root` user.) Here is another command that does a lot more (especially in the typing department):

```
./configure --prefix$HOME/apache \
    --htdocsdir=$HOME/Web/htdocs \
    --cgidir=$HOME/Web/cgi-bin --iconsdir=$HOME/Web/icons \
    --with-port=8080 --server-uid=george --server-gid=george
```

This configuration command makes use of all of the options mentioned above. The difference is that we have configured AWS to obtain all of the content from `$HOME/Web`. (`$HOME` expands to `/home/george` for user `george` on most Linux distributions and is usually set correctly by the various shells available on Linux.) The actual AWS binaries and needed configuration files are installed to a subdirectory named `$HOME/apache`. So, for clarity, there are two directories being created here:

- `/home/george/apache`: This is where the binaries and configuration settings for AWS are stored.
- `/home/george/Web`: This is where the static content (`htdocs`), executable scripts (`cgi-bin`), and icons (`icons`) are stored.

Why are we putting things in two directories? First, we do this to show that you can actually run the Web server as your own user id. Second, you can separate content from the actual Apache-specific code and configuration files. This will prove useful later when you may want to go into production mode. All you have to do is run AWS as root and point to a slightly modified configuration file that (among other things) will start on the standard HTTP port (80) instead of on port 8080.

Using the much improved configuration line is a very practical way to go as a developer. It allows you to work on getting your site up and running and helps you avoid the problems that occur when working with the default setup, such as your user id not being able to access (for read and write) the Web document and scripts directories. This inconveniences you by either forcing you to do your development as the Web user (`nobody`) or requiring you to switch frequently between your username (here `george`) and the Web user (`nobody`). Later we will see that the static and dynamic content directories can easily be migrated to another directory, if desired. This may be important when your development actually becomes the production release and you need to get other developers involved (a case when you will no longer want the apache/htdocs and apache/cgi-bin directories lingering in your home directory, but you will want all of your group members to have access).

When you run configure, some time will elapse before you are able to actually run make. This is because the configure process generates a number of make files and ascertains a number of platform-specific configuration settings to perform the compilation successfully.

```
[george@liszt apache_1.3.14]$ sh config.george
Configuring for Apache, Version 1.3.14
 + using installation path layout: Apache (config.layout)
Creating Makefile
Creating Configuration.apaci in src
Creating Makefile in src
 + configured for Linux platform
 + setting C compiler to gcc
 + setting C pre-processor to gcc -E
 + checking for system header files
 + adding selected modules
 + checking sizeof various data types
 + doing sanity check on compiler and options
Creating Makefile in src/support
Creating Makefile in src/regex
Creating Makefile in src/os/unix
Creating Makefile in src/ap
Creating Makefile in src/main
Creating Makefile in src/lib/expat-lite
Creating Makefile in src/modules/standard
```

It is not possible to cover the details of configure scripts without going beyond the scope of this chapter. You can see from the output that an important outcome is for several Makefiles to be created at different levels. The Apache Web Server is a significantly large and complex piece of software that consists of many components. Each of these components must be built (recursively) in order for the entire AWS build to succeed. On most platforms, Linux and Solaris included, the build tends to go very smoothly. The problem that is most likely to cause trouble is the detection of the gcc compiler (which may fail if you did not install it correctly or it is not found in any of the expected places). Another problem may occur when "doing a sanity check on compiler and options." We strongly recommend that you always work with a recent (and stable) release of the gcc compiler, regardless of the version of Linux (or Unix) being used.

Once configuration is complete, you can run `make`.

```
$ make
```

A great deal of output will appear. In general, the process involves a recursive descent into the directories to compile the various source files that are present. In the past, successful configuration sometimes resulted in unsuccessful compiles. This seldom happens today. If you encounter problems during the `make`, you might want to consider a few possibilities:

- Your compiler, C header files, and/or libraries may be out of date. This usually can be solved by upgrading your installation with the latest RPM files. The packages to investigate are `gcc*.rpm`, `glibc*.rpm`, etc.
- Consider downloading a slightly older (or newer) point release. Occasionally, releases of free software are rushed out the door, despite every attempt to test the code. It might seem hard to believe but true: A release can be replaced by a new release minutes later. Check back to the Apache Web site often if you encounter trouble.
- Consider working with a prebuilt binary release of Apache. If you go this route, read the next section on postinstallation configuration, which covers how to configure some of the options we covered at runtime only. We do not generally encourage this, because the prebuilt releases tend to create directories and files that a particular *vendor* thought would be appropriate. Usually, the decisions made appear to be almost arbitrary (e.g., not putting the binaries in a separate directory under `/usr/local`, putting the Web content in `/home` instead of `/Web`, and not setting UID/GID meaningfully.) You will find that the greatest configurability is achieved when you go through the process of building AWS yourself and configuring it as appropriate for your site.

Once AWS has been compiled successfully, it must be installed using `make install`. Note that if you configured without using the `--with-port` option and specified `$HOME/apache` as the target directory, it will more than likely be necessary to `su` to become super user. (This is easy: Type `su` at the command line and enter, then type the root password when prompted.) If you cannot become root for any reason, you may need to reconfigure with a different `--prefix`.

(We suggest `--prefix=$HOME/apache`, in which case all binaries and content end up in your home directory `$HOME` in a subdirectory named `apache`.)

```
$ su
password: XYZPDQ
$ make install
```

Again, a great deal of output will ensue as files are copied into the installation directories. You may run into problems if you took too much liberty with the options just presented. In particular, if you have configured to install in the `/usr/local` directory, you probably need to run as root. If everything was done relative to `$HOME` as prescribed, the install should be a breeze.

Now you can start the Web server:

```
[george@intranet bin]$ cd $HOME/apache/bin
[george@intranet bin]$ ./apachectl start
./apachectl start: httpd started
```

Seeing the words "`httpd started`" is reassuring. However, if you don't always believe what you read, you can check this out by checking the output of `ps`. Here is the output on one of our systems:

```
[george@intranet bin]$ ps auxww  | grep ^george
george   3506  0.0  0.5  1756 1012 pts/0    S   11:32   0:00 -bash
george   6645  0.0  0.4  2060  944 ?        S   14:11   0:00 /home/george/apache/bin/httpd
george   6646  0.0  0.4  2072  932 ?        S   14:11   0:00 /home/george/apache/bin/httpd
george   6647  0.0  0.4  2072  932 ?        S   14:11   0:00 /home/george/apache/bin/httpd
george   6648  0.0  0.4  2072  932 ?        S   14:11   0:00 /home/george/apache/bin/httpd
george   6649  0.0  0.4  2072  932 ?        S   14:11   0:00 /home/george/apache/bin/httpd
george   6650  0.0  0.4  2072  932 ?        S   14:11   0:00 /home/george/apache/bin/httpd
george   6652  0.0  0.3  2332  704 pts/0    R   14:13   0:00 ps auxww
george   6653  0.0  0.2  1368  536 pts/0    S   14:13   0:00 grep ^george
```

The output appears somewhat convincing. There are a bunch of processes owned by user `george`.[22] The implementation of AWS is a concurrent server. By default, a minimum of five "spare" servers are created to serve HTTP requests.

Although the server is running, the final test is whether pages can actually be viewed through the browser. You can use the TELNET method shown in Chapter 5 to connect directly to the Web server you have started. (On this system, `intranet.quillscape.com`, the names `intranet` or `intranet.quillscape.com` can be used as the hostname or

---

22. Ordinarily we try to keep secret who wrote what chapters, but a pattern is beginning to emerge here.

localhost.) One thing to keep in mind is that during configuration, we set the port to 8080; this port must be used as part of the contact URL. Here are the ways you can refer to the freshly installed server:

```
http://intranet.quillscape.com:8080
http://intranet:8080
http://localhost:8080
```

To approximate your environment as closely as possible, we will stick with the third form for the time being. If you have gone about setting up a LAN environment as described in the first half of this chapter, you will probably want to test the other two cases from other machines (e.g., Windows, Macs) on your network.

Let's test on the machine itself first. There are some nice text-based browsers that allow you to get the home page from the command line without having to bring up a full Web browser, etc. We will show both wget and lynx. These commands are extremely useful, especially if you are configuring a remote Web server and do not have a full graphical desktop view of the remote system. We show lynx this time around:

```
$ wget http://localhost:8080
$ wget http://intranet:8080
$ wget http://intranet.quillscape.com:8080
```

You will probably be using different hostnames on your system. The first form, which uses localhost, should work on your setup, provided an entry appears in your /etc/hosts file to map localhost to 127.0.0.1 (which is usually the case). If for any reason you are unable to connect, it is likely due to a problem with host name resolution, or may be due to a minor configuration problem. The next section focuses on essential configuration needs and explains what may have gone wrong in the initial configuration.

Postinstallation Configuration Options

Even when Apache has been installed, you are not necessarily done. In this section, we will discuss some of the issues that are likely to be important for even your most basic development needs.

Several things might need to be changed. In the current version of Apache, everything is done in /usr/local/apache/conf/httpd.conf.

ServerName • The ServerName option is used, optionally, to config-ure the name by which the server is intended to be accessed. The Apache documentation admonishes you:

"Note: You cannot just invent host names and hope they work."

We'll go a bit further. ServerName must be set to a name that ultimately resolves by DNS, especially if you are deploying on the Internet. At a minimum, you should make sure the server can be found on your private network. This means that you must make entries in /etc/hosts (if doing a stand-alone setup) or in one of your DNS zone files.

Whatever you choose as the ServerName should be reachable either by one of the standard TCP/IP commands (such as TELNET) or via nslookup. For example, our private network, intranet.quillscape.com, is the name of our intranet host that is used to provide Web service. ServerName, accordingly, is set to intranet.quillscape.com. When performing a DNS query, this name comes up (and matches the IP number for the machine the server is running on.)

```
$ nslookup intranet
Server:   liszt.quillscape.com
Address:  10.10.10.2

Name:     intranet.quillscape.com
Address:  10.10.10.50
```

One other detail: You cannot specify the ServerName to any ran-domly chosen host on your network. The address reported above must match exactly the address of at least one network interface on your computer. On intranet.quillscape.com, this is the case, as shown by the output of ifconfig:

```
$ ifconfig

eth0      Link encap:Ethernet  HWaddr 00:A0:CC:26:E1:7C
          inet addr:10.10.10.50  Bcast:10.10.10.255
          Mask:255.255.255.0
          UP BROADCAST RUNNING MULTICAST  MTU:1500  Metric:1
          RX packets:103347 errors:0 dropped:0 overruns:0 frame:0
          TX packets:49180 errors:0 dropped:0 overruns:0 carrier:0
          collisions:0 txqueuelen:100
          Interrupt:9 Base address:0xf800

eth0:0    Link encap:Ethernet  HWaddr 00:A0:CC:26:E1:7C
          inet addr:10.10.10.150  Bcast:10.10.10.255
```

```
Mask:255.255.255.0
          UP BROADCAST RUNNING MULTICAST  MTU:1500  Metric:1
          Interrupt:9 Base address:0xf800


lo        Link encap:Local Loopback
          inet addr:127.0.0.1  Mask:255.0.0.0
          UP LOOPBACK RUNNING  MTU:3924  Metric:1
          RX packets:54 errors:0 dropped:0 overruns:0 frame:0
          TX packets:54 errors:0 dropped:0 overruns:0 carrier:0
          collisions:0 txqueuelen:0
```

There are several interfaces on this computer: eth0, eth0:0, and lo (as well as a few others we have eliminated to keep this brief). Note that eth0 (the primary interface) is bound to 10.10.10.50, which matches the address found for intranet.quillscape.com.

The other interfaces are not of particular relevance. You can start the Web server on either of these interfaces. lo is the loopback interface and usually is mapped from the name localhost. If you aren't connected to a network and want to go totally stand-alone, you can specify localhost as the server name. We think this is unlikely to be of interest and strongly recommend that you be connected to the network in some way, even if only a private network. eth0:0 is one of several *virtual* interfaces that we have configured. Virtual interfaces allow multiple IP numbers to be bound to a specific network interface. We will be discussing this in greater detail when we discuss *virtual hosting*.[23]

▶ **TIP: Example of ServerName Directive**

> ServerName intranet.quillscape.com
> Specifies that the ServerName is intranet.quillscape.com. Note that the primary interface must actually have the same IP number as intranet.quillscape.com.

Port • The port directive allows you to serve Web requests on an alternate port. By default, the Web server is configured to run on port 80.[24]

---

23. Companies that provide virtual hosting solutions use this feature extensively to serve multiple domains via a single server.

24. If you did not uninstall or disable the Apache service as instructed earlier, it is possible the port will be set to 8080 instead of 80. This is harmless, but means that another Web server was detected to be running. You want to take down the other one as soon as possible unless you know precisely what is going on; otherwise, confusion is likely to ensue.

It is also possible to run many instances of the Apache Web Server simply by running the version you built with different configuration files.[25]

To be more productive, you will want to stick with port 80. Among other things, you will not have to type `http://hostname:port` instead of `http://hostname`. Port 80 is the standard, well-known port for accessing HTTP service. (HTTPS is 443.) If you have any intention of going public, stick with the standard port numbers.

There are practical uses for alternate port numbers, for example if you are working with a Linux (or another Unix) system for which you do not have `root` access. Root access is required to install any TCP/IP service that listens on a well known port. The Apache Web Server can be run on higher numbered ports (greater than or equal to 1024) by any user.

> ## TIP: Usage of Port Directive

```
Port 8765
```
This would start AWS on Port 8765, provided this port number is not already in use.

User and Group • Inevitably you will want to know about the User and Group directives.

Block Directives and `<Directory>...</Directory>` • Increasingly, Apache Web Server releases are taking greater advantage of quasi-XML syntax for configuring the server. We say quasi-XML because most of the configuration options are not expressed with XML syntax. When the quasi-XML syntax is used, it is used primarily for what are referred to in the Apache documentation as *block directives*. A block directive is used to define a context where certain options can be applied.

The `<Directory>` tag is used to specify a block directive that applies to a directory (either an exact name or a pattern that matches one or more directories). The directive applies to the directory and all subdirectories unless another directive appears that applies to a subdirectory.

It is beyond the scope of this book to cover every nuance of the configuration file syntax and this directive; however, a basic knowledge is necessary to configure your server for proper operation in a multiuser

---

25. In the interest of getting going, you should view this as an advanced usage that will not be covered here. You might actually want to do it someday. All you have to do is to create a different configuration file and start up the Web server with an alternate configuration file.

environment, especially if you have fantasies of one day developing the setup to go to a team development effort. Let's take a look at a few examples at a high level and explain why you might care about them. It is likely you will need to apply one or more of these cases in the future.

Top Level Directory Access Control • The following use of the Directory directive illustrates how to configure the access control for all directories on your system. This directive applies to "/" and everything beneath "/", unless another Directory directive appears.

```
<Directory />
    Options FollowSymLinks
    AllowOverride None
</Directory>
What does this entry tell you?
```

- Options can be construed as a capability that indicates what can be done within the scope of this directive. The only capability being granted is FollowSymLinks (follow symbolic links). Aside from that, nothing else may be done.
- There are no default values for Options. If you do not provide an option, it is not available. As will be shown, options are inherited. So any Directory directive will inherit whatever "/" provides, unless the option has been removed.
- AllowOverride None indicates that if this directive is applied, the .htaccess file may not be used in a directory to override the access control mechanism. The .htaccess file is useful to support user-level access control for a particular directory or directories (as opposed to requiring root to do everything).

In a general sense, when AWS is configured, built, and installed, you can rest assured that this top-level Directory access control has been done correctly. However, you should ensure that the directory "/" entry is as restrictive as shown here. This one entry provides a great deal of protection for your system, as it virtually assures you that a directory is not exposed to the outside world unless an explicit Directory entry exists for it.

Document Directory Access Control • The following Directory directive shows how to configure the default htdocs (or HTML) directory, which is where all of your site's static Web pages are likely to be placed. This directory is the one that was specified using --withhtdocs and/or the DocumentRoot directive. You especially want to be cognizant of this directive if you plan to migrate your htdocs directory to a different location.[26]

```
<Directory /usr/local/apache/htdocs>
    Options Indexes FollowSymLinks MultiViews
    AllowOverride None
    Order allow,deny
    Allow from all
</Directory>
```

It is important that this entry be specified correctly. Here is what the fragment is doing:

- Enabling the Indexing option. Indexing is what allows the contents of /usr/local/apache/htdocs to be indexed (or, more precisely, listed). It is also what allows the index.html file to be loaded from a directory, as opposed to listing the directory's contents. If your pages are not loading, you need to make sure that the correct directory has been listed here.
- Enabling symbolic links to be followed.
- Enabling MultiViews.
- Enabling access from the world. The Order allow,deny policy says "First check what is allowed by Allow, then what is denied by Deny." As Allow from all has been specified, the deny policy will not be applied.

User Directories Access Control • This can be quite frustrating for new users of the Apache Web Server. When AWS is configured, the default configuration prohibits access from user directories, as this is considered a security risk. (Odd, considering that most users do not have a public_html subdirectory in their home directories initially.) The following shows what you need to do to enable user directories to serve their own content and to run CGI scripts. That is, when someone from the outside wants to reach http://your-domain.com/~username, they will not be rudely greeted with an access denied message:

```
1    <Directory /home/*/public_html>
```

---

26. In the configuration example, the htdocs directory is /home/george/apache/htdocs. If you performed a similar configuration, what you see here would more than likely be different.

```
2        AllowOverride FileInfo AuthConfig Limit
3        Options ExecCGI MultiViews Indexes SymLinksIfOwnerMatch IncludesNoExec
4        <Limit GET POST OPTIONS PROPFIND>
5            Order allow,deny
6            Allow from all
7        </Limit>
8        <LimitExcept GET POST OPTIONS PROPFIND>
9            Order deny,allow
10           Deny from all
11       </LimitExcept>
12   </Directory>
```

Here is what is going on:

1   Apply to /home/*/public_html. In practical terms, this is what allows your home directory to be served by AWS. The "*" will match any user on the system, e.g., george typically has a directory /home/george/public_html.

2–3   You can read the AWS online documentation to learn more about these options. Basically, in Web programming with AWS, you want to ensure that ExecCGI appears here, and the other options. It is also possible to write this line more concisely as follows:
Options All MultiViews
This will enable just about everything to be done in user directories. Do this only after you have read the AWS documentation and fully understand the security ramifications.

4–7   The <Limit> block directive shown here enables GET, POST, OPTIONS, and PROPFIND with all rights and privileges thereof.

8–11   The <LimitExcept> block shown here disables all directives beside GET, POST, OPTIONS, and PROPFIND.

Renaming "public_html" to "www" • By default, user documents are served from $HOME/public_html, where $HOME refers to the home directory for a particular user (e.g., user george would have directory /home/george/public_html on a typical Linux configuration).

Although `public_html` is a perfectly good directory name, it is somewhat less than ideal, considering that the directory could be serving non-HTML content and even CGI scripts may execute therein. A preferable name would be www, to indicate that Web content is being served.

```
<IfModule mod_userdir.c>
    UserDir www
</IfModule>
```

It is here that we begin to see something that is a bit odd: the `<IfModule>` directory. As the AWS has grown more popular, there has been an accompanying desire to extend it with new functionality. The Apache team went to a module-based scheme, wherein new features could be added using modules. Most of the newer features are supported using modules, including the ability to customize the user directory. The way to read the above example is, "If the module `mod_userdir.c` has been loaded, then set the property `UserDir` to www."[27]

For the remaining configuration options, we will be discussing those that require the `<IfModule>` directive. You should not be intimidated by the presence of these directives in the configuration file; they are designed to make your life easier. You will find that their meaning is quite intuitive when the day comes when you want to add a feature to AWS, such as `mod_perl`, `mod_python`, or `mod_php`. We will not rely upon such features for this book, but want to convince you that these directives exist for a reason.

ScriptAlias and CGI Script Redirection • In order for directories such as "`icons`" and "`cgi-bin`" to be used, there must be aliases for reaching these directories. You will be more or less okay with these for basic needs. For more advanced needs, such as virtual hosting, these options take on a higher degree of importance, as each virtual host needs to have its own `scripts` directory.

---

27. Note that it is not sufficient simply to indicate that the user directory is www. You may also need to make a change to enable proper access (shown in the preceding section), and make sure your users know that this is the name of the directory (as opposed to `public_html`) to be created.

This is what is meant by this block of code you will find in `httpd.conf`:

```
1    <IfModule mod_alias.c>
2        Alias /icons/ "/usr/local/apache/icons/"
3        <Directory "/usr/local/apache/icons">
4            Options Indexes MultiViews
5            AllowOverride None
6            Order allow,deny
7            Allow from all
8        </Directory>
9        ScriptAlias /cgi-bin/ "/usr/local/apache/cgi-bin/"
10       <IfModule mod_dir.c>
11           DirectoryIndex index.html
12       </IfModule>
13       <Directory "/usr/local/apache/cgi-bin">
14           AllowOverride None
15           Options None
16           Order allow,deny
17           Allow from all
18       </Directory>
19   </IfModule>
```

Here is what is going on:

2   Allows `http://www.your-domain.com/icons` to work.

3–8   Usual assortment of options to allow everyone to get this directory.

9   Allows `http://www.your-domain.com/cgi-bin/myscript.cgi` to work.

10–12   Allows you to change the "`index`" document. Many sites (especially those with content authored on a Microsoft platform and copied to Unix) rely on "`index.htm`" due to the (annoying) 8.3 file format of MS-DOS.

13–18   Usual assortment of options to allow everyone to get to the CGI directory.

Sanity-Checking Your Setup

Once your Apache Web Server has been built and properly configured, start the server and perform a sanity check of the setup. Here is a list of steps that will be performed, in order:

- Restarting the server (`apachectl restart`)
- Making sure you can serve static content from your `htdocs` directory
- Making sure you can run CGI scripts
- Making sure you can run a Python CGI script

- Optionally, making sure you can serve content from a user directory
- Optionally, making sure you can run CGI scripts from a user directory

Restarting the Server • If you made any changes to the `httpd.conf` configuration file, the server must be restarted. You can do this easily with the `apachectl` script found in `apache-dir/bin`.

```
$ apache-dir/bin/apachectl restart
```

If you have not yet started the server, the `start` option should be used instead.

Serving Static Content • Changes to the DocumentRoot, the Directory directives, and others can cause your Web server no longer to be able to serve static content. We've used the `lynx` browser before. This time, we will use `wget` with the `-S` option to get detailed status messages indicating whether everything is okay.

```
$ wget -S http://localhost
--15:50:13--  http://localhost/
           => `index.html'
Connecting to localhost:8080... connected!
HTTP request sent, awaiting response... 200 OK
Date: Sun, 25 Feb 2001 21:50:14 GMT
Server: Apache/1.3.14 (Unix)
Content-Location: index.html.en
Vary: negotiate,accept-language,accept-charset
TCN: choice
Last-Modified: Sat, 20 Nov 1999 21:29:40 GMT
ETag: "2094b7a1-54e-383712c4;3a973664"
Accept-Ranges: bytes
Content-Length: 1358
Connection: close
Content-Type: text/html
Content-Language: en
Expires: Sun, 25 Feb 2001 21:50:14 GMT


    OK -> .                              [100%]
```

wget is a very powerful command. It shows the essential details of the transaction performed with the Web server running on local-host. Using -S allows us to look at the complete status information, including the return code (here 200, meaning that the request was successful). If all goes well, the document "index.html" will be returned and appear in your current working directory.[28]

CGI Scripts/Dynamic Content • Once you have ascertained that the static content is being served properly, a similar test can be used to check whether the CGI scripts are working. The Apache Web Server comes with a basic test CGI script written in the shell programming language. This file is copied into your *apache-dir*/cgi-bin upon installation.

```
$ wget -S http://localhost:8080/cgi-bin/test-cgi
--16:04:19--  http://localhost:8080/cgi-bin/test-cgi
           => `test-cgi'
Connecting to localhost:8080... connected!
HTTP request sent, awaiting response... 200 OK
Date: Sun, 25 Feb 2001 22:04:19 GMT
Server: Apache/1.3.14 (Unix)
Connection: close
Content-Type: text/plain

   OK ->

16:04:19 (40.82 KB/s) - 'test-cgi' saved [418]
```

Here, the GET method is being used to get the content produced by executing test-cgi. This is a reasonably complete test of whether CGI scripts will work but does not test the POST method, which is used by form submissions. You can proceed confidently, provided your <Limit> access control directive includes both GET and POST.

---

28. Although we don't expect anyone to do this, you should make sure to run this in a directory such as /tmp that doesn't contain important files that you might need later. wget is pretty careful not to delete anything, but you might find the results somewhat unintuitive if the file already exists in your directory.

Running Python CGI Scripts • You might also want to ensure that Python CGI scripts run properly from the *apache-dir*/cgi-bin directory. This involves creating a script in the directory. Here is an example (`test-python`) that you can type in quickly to test things out:

```
#!/usr/local/python-1.6/bin/python

print "Content-type: text/html";
print "\n\n";

print "Hi, I am Python!"

import cgi
print dir(cgi)
print "<title>This is a test</title>";
print "<h1>Does it work?</1h>";
```

Make sure the program is named `test-python` and make sure to set the permissions to 755 as follows:

```
$ chmod 755 test-python
```

Note that you can't just type this program in blindly; the first line must contain the "#!", followed by the full path to reach your Python interpreter. What you place there must be the actual path to the Python interpreter as it would be typed on the command line:

```
$ /usr/local/python-1.6/bin/python
Python 1.6 (#21, Feb 24 2001, 15:33:54)   [GCC 2.95.2-6
19991024 (cygwin experime
ntal)] on cygwin_nt-5.01
Copyright (c) 1995-2000 Corporation for National Research
Initiatives.
All Rights Reserved.
Copyright (c) 1991-1995 Stichting Mathematisch Centrum,
Amsterdam.
All Rights Reserved.
>>>
```

If you do not see a similar message after issuing this command, check for the location of your Python interpreter[29] and try a different location. Once the location of Python has been determined, make sure the program `test-python` can actually be run properly from the command line:

```
$ ./test-python
```

You will see output. If there are any errors, there is probably a problem with your Python installation. (Either it is not installed or it is not installed correctly.) Here is the output to be expected:

```
$ ./test-python
Content-type: text/html

Hi, I am Python!
['FieldStorage', 'FormContent', 'FormContentDict', 'InterpFormContentDict', 'Min
iFieldStorage', 'StringIO', 'SvFormContentDict', '__builtins__', '__doc__', '__f
ile__', '__name__', '__version__', 'dolog', 'escape', 'initlog', 'log', 'logfile
', 'logfp', 'maxlen', 'mimetools', 'nolog', 'os', 'parse', 'parse_header', 'pars
e_multipart', 'parse_qs', 'parse_qsl', 'print_arguments', 'print_directory', 'pr
int_environ', 'print_environ_usage', 'print_exception', 'print_form', 'rfc822',
'string', 'sys', 'test', 'urllib']
<title>This is a test</title>
<h1>Does it work?</1h>
```

This test is a little more than a basic test. It ensures that output is sent and the built-in Python support for `cgi` can be loaded. Now let us test whether the script can actually be run through the AWS, again using the `wget` command:

```
$ wget -S http://localhost:8080/cgi-bin/test-python
--16:20:03--  http://localhost:8080/cgi-bin/test-python
           => `test-python'
Connecting to localhost:8080... connected!
HTTP request sent, awaiting response... 200 OK
2 Date: Sun, 25 Feb 2001 22:20:03 GMT
3 Server: Apache/1.3.14 (Unix)
4 Connection: close
5 Content-Type: text/html
6

   OK ->

16:20:04 (28.66 KB/s) - 'test-python' saved [587]
```

---

29. Usually, this means `/usr/bin`, `/usr/local/bin`, `/usr/local/python<version>/bin`, etc.

If all goes well, again the return status of 200 OK message will be seen. Additionally, the output from executing the script (i.e., the resultant Web page) will be saved to a file named after the script specified after cgi-bin. You'll see a file in your directory named test-python. The output can be viewed as follows:

```
$ cat test-python
```

This file will contain the same content that appeared on standard output when you ran the test-python script manually above, with the exception of the initial "Content-type: text/html" header, which is stripped away by the browser.

Summary

This chapter has covered a lot of ground. We have endeavored to balance the discussion between networking topics and configuring your Web server in order to do actual Web development. It is very difficult to do anything with the Web without knowing the context in which it takes place. The previous chapter addressed at a high level what takes place on the Internet to make it possible for you to visit http://www.*mydomain*.com. This chapter addressed how to actually configure http://www.mydomain.com (as well as mydomain.com) and the Web server, with the hope that you can ultimately get a meaningful and useful development and production environment up and running.

One aspect of Web configuration that we did not address in this chapter is security; in particular, how one configures a secure Web server. Instead, we have placed this material in the Appendix. It is an important topic that can, indeed, be mastered after gaining a solid foundation in how to build a Web application. The foundation classes provided in our book are designed to make the use of SSL transparent and even to make it possible to use SSL only when needed, as it causes performance problems in actual use. If you want to set up Apache and SSL, please see the Appendix.

7

CGI Programming in Python

CGI programs are programs executed by the Web server when browsers connect to their program files. They are most commonly executed when the user submits data in a form.

Overview

Let us review HTTP, the protocol used by Web servers and browsers. Web pages are typically written in Hyper Text Markup Language (HTML). This language tells a browser how to display the page. The pages can contain links to other pages, so that by clicking on the link, the user can have the browser load another page.

Pages can also contain some interactive elements, for example, *forms* that allow the user to send information to a Web server. For this information to be used, the Web server must run a program and pass the information to it. These programs are called Common Gateway Interface (CGI) programs. It is these CGI programs that concern us in this chapter.

The basic work cycle of HTTP is this: The browser sends a request; the server sends a response; and the connection is dropped. Since the connection is not maintained, one of the problems to be solved is how to remember the user from one interaction to the next. As an optimization, the browser can ask the server to keep the connection open, but the server is not required to do so. The interactions must be programmed as if each one were isolated from the others.

HTTP communications are at least partly in plain text. Humans can read the contents of the messages. Other than a header line, the communication is in Multipurpose Internet Mail Extensions (MIME) format: There is a header part separated from the optional body part by a blank line. The header lines have the general format:

```
attribute: value ; optional additional parameters
```

Your browser will format the messages it sends to the server in MIME. When you write a CGI program, however, you are responsible for formatting your response in MIME. This leads to a number of questions:

Q. When you send data to a Web server, how does it know which CGI program to run?

A. It knows in the same way it would know which Web page to send back. You specify a URL; the URL leads to the file of a CGI program; the server puts the query information where the CGI program can find it and runs the program.

Q. How does your browser send the information it gets from an HTML form?

A. There are two ways. In an HTML form, you can tell the browser to use either a `GET` or a `POST` method. The `GET` method attaches the information to the URL after the path to the file to execute. The amount of information that can be sent that way is limited; URLs must not be too long. The `POST` method can send the data as a multi-part file to the server, which can be of any length.

Q. How does the server give this data to the CGI program?

A. When the server runs a CGI program, it puts a lot of information in the environment variables. If the browser sent a `GET` message, all the information is placed in the environment variables. The data from the form is placed in variable `QUERY_STRING`. For a `POST` message, the data from the form is given to the CGI program on its standard input stream.

Installing CGI Programs

There are a number of things that can go wrong when you try to install a Python CGI script on a Linux system. Here is the procedure, with remarks on what can happen.

1. Make sure the Python interpreter exists on the machine. Find its absolute address, e.g., type `which python` to `bash`. Make sure it can be executed by others as well as you.

2. Put a script comment as the first line in your Python program, telling it to execute the Python interpreter. If Python is in directory `/usr/local/bin`, the line would read:

```
#!/usr/local/bin/python
```

The path to use is shown by the `which python` you typed in step 1.

3. Put your script in the proper directory for CGI scripts. Here we'll assume it is `/usr/local/apache/cgi-bin`. If someone else is the system administrator, you may need to ask where the scripts should be put. If you can't log in as `root`, you may need to be placed in a group that has access to the `cgi-bin` directory and use `newgrp` to be able to access it.

4. Make sure your script is executable by others. The CGI processes usually belong to user `nobody`. If you are testing your script just by executing it directly yourself, you can't be sure that it can be executed by "nobody." So set the protections with

```
chmod a+x
```

5. If your script is going to access other files or directories, make sure they are accessible to others. Set the permissions for others to readable, writable if necessary, executable for programs, and searchable for directories. Again, even if you can access them yourself, you must make sure that "nobody" can access them.

6. Don't assume that the environment variables are set the same way they are in your shell. The important variables, PATH and PYTHONPATH, may not be set correctly. If you are planning to execute other programs, you should probably use absolute paths to them. You can fix PYTHONPATH so that Python can find your extra modules by adding directories to its search path:

```
import sys
sys.path.insert(0,absPathToDirectory)
```

7. You can test your understanding of these rules by installing `cgi.py` in the `cgi-bin` directory and executing it from your browser, e.g., by typing:

```
http://localhost/cgi-bin/cgi.py?a=1&b=2
```

replacing *localhost* with the name of your host and `cgi-bin`, if necessary, with the path Apache will take to the CGI directory.

Script `cgi.py` will write out an HTML page with the information that it was called with. If you get this page, you understand the procedure for installing scripts. If you get a 404 error, the server can't find your script. Maybe it should be in a different directory. Other errors hint at other problems.

Now we are ready to examine CGI programming more closely.

GET Method

Running CGI Programs

You don't have to use an HTML `<form>` tag to invoke a CGI program. You can try to fetch it the same way you would a Web page. Consider the CGI program in Figure 7–1.

We put it on the Web server on our local network in file `HiPlain` in the `cgi-bin` subdirectory of our Apache Web server. Then we pointed a browser to it with the URL:

```
http://192.168.1.1/cgi-bin/HiPlain
```

Here, the `192.168.1.1` is the address of host number one on the local network. Don't try getting to it by typing that URL into your browser. Host addresses of the form `192.168.1.*` are known only within a local network. The Internet will not pass those addresses between networks.

The subdirectory `cgi-bin` is used on our server as the directory in which to place CGI programs. When it finds a URL indicating an executable file in that directory, Apache will execute it as a CGI program. On other servers there may be other conventions for recognizing CGI programs.

```
#!/usr/bin/python
print "Content-type: text/plain"
print

print "Hello, world"
```

Figure 7–1
`HiPlain`, a CGI Program to Say "hello, world" in Plain Text

Now look at HiPlain itself. It is a Python script. In the comment in the first line, it tells the system where to find the Python interpreter to run it. It begins by writing out a MIME header. The content-type header line is required. We have to tell the browser how to handle the file we are writing. We tell it that the file is just text, without any formatting. That is the only header line we are using, so we end the header by writing an empty line.

The final print statement writes out the line that the browser will display. So when we type the URL

```
http://192.168.1.1/cgi-bin/HiPlain
```

into our browser, it loads a page saying, in small print at the top left,

```
Hello, world
```

For attractiveness of output, we should probably use HTML. Figure 7–2 gives a version of the "Hello, world" program that writes its message in HTML. In this case, the content-type line specifies text/html to tell the browser how to format the file. The rest needs some explaining if you don't know HTML, so let's pause and describe it.

HTML contains text and tags. The tags are enclosed in angular brackets <...> and tell the browser how to format the text. The tag begins with a string identifying the tag. Case is not significant in tag names.

There are generally two kinds of tags: those that appear alone and those that appear as pairs enclosing other HTML text. In this example, all the tags are paired. The paired tags begin <tagname...> and end with </tagname>. The <tagname...> can contain a number of attributes of the form attributename=value. We'll see some later.

```
#!/usr/bin/python
print "Content-type: text/html"
print

print "<html><head><title>Hi in HTML</title></head>"
print "<body>"
print "<h1>Hello, world</h1>"
print "</body></html>"
```

Figure 7–2
CGI Program to Say "Hello, world" in HTML

HTML code properly begins with <html> and ends with </html>. Many browsers are lax in their enforcement of the rules of HTML and will accept HTML code not enclosed between <html> and </html> brackets. The HTML code is broken into two parts, the head and the body. The head contains information about the page while the body contains information to display. In the head, the title gives the name of the page for the browser to display at the top of its window. In the body, <h1>...</h1> tags bracket a top-level heading. The text between will be formatted large and bold.

So when we typed into our browser the URL

```
http://192.168.1.1/cgi-bin/HiHtml
```

it displayed a page with a large

Hello, world

Table 7–1 lists the HTML tags we will be using in this chapter.

Table 7–1
Selected HTML Tags

Tag	Explanation
<html>...</html>	Surrounds HTML text.
<head> ... </head>	Surrounds head section of HTML text.
<body>...</body>	Surrounds body section of HTML text.
<h1> ... </h1> ... <h6> ... </h6>	Formats the enclosed text as a heading, <h1> for top-level, largest font heading.
<p> ... </p>	Formats the enclosed text as a paragraph. It will also work just to separate paragraphs with a single <p>.
<a href=url> linktext </a>	A link to the page indicated by the url. The text between the opening and closing tags is highlighted as the link. Clicking it loads the page given by the url. An <image> as a link can be used as an image map.

Table 7–1
Selected HTML Tags (Continued)

Tag	Explanation
`<img src=`*url*` width=`*num* `height=`*num* *ismap* `>`	Includes an image in the displayed Web page. The image is requested for the source `url`. The browser is told to allocate `width` by `height` pixels for it. As discussed below, the optional parameter *ismap* indicates the image is to be treated as an input field. See "Image Maps" on page 326.
`<form action=`*url* `method=`*GETorPOST* `enctype=`*encoding* `>` `...` `</form>`	The `<form>` tags surround a query submission form. The action `url` indicates a CGI program to receive the query. The method indicates how the query is to be sent, either as part of the URL (method=`GET`) or as a file (method=`POST`). The optional parameter `enctype` is only relevant for `POST` methods, and is discussed at length in "`POST` Method" on page 336. The `<input>` and `<textarea>` tags are associated with the surrounding `<form>`.
`<input type="text"` `name=`*string* `value=`*string* `size=`*num* `maxlength=`*num*`>`	Displays a text field. The field will be given to the server with the indicated `name`. The `value` is an optional initial value for the field. The field is displayed as `size` wide, but can be scrolled up to the maximum length.
`<input type="submit"` `name=`*string* `value=`*string* `>`	Displays a submit button. If `name` is present, the `value` is sent to the server when the button is clicked. The `value`, which defaults to "Submit Query," is displayed on the button.
`<input type="password"` `name=`*string* `value=`*string* `maxlength=`*num* `size=`*num*`>`	A `password` input is the same as `text`, except that the text typed into it is not displayed on the browser's screen. Instead, each character is displayed as a star.
`<input type="checkbox"` `name=`*string* `value=`*string* *checked*`>`	A `checkbox` input item displays a check box on the screen. The optional `checked` parameter, if present, indicates that the check box is initially checked. If the check box is checked when the form is submitted, the `name` will be sent with its assigned `value`. If `value` is absent, it defaults to `on`. If several check boxes have the same name, the name is sent with each checked value, requiring the CGI program to be able to handle multiple values for a name.

Table 7–1
Selected HTML Tags (Continued)

Tag	Explanation

`<input type="radio"`
`name=string value=string`
`checked>`
	Radio buttons are similar to check boxes, but all those with the same name are grouped so that at most one of them can be checked at a time.

`<select name=string`
`size=num > ...`
`</select>`
`<option selected`
`value=string > ...`
`</option>`
	The `<select>` tags surround a list of `<option>` tags. It will display a field `size` items high. The text between `<option>` and `</option>` is displayed in the field for that option. These behave like radio buttons. The user selects an option and its value is sent as the value for the name in the `select` tag.

`<input type="file"`
`name=string maxlength=num`
`size=num >`
	The file input displays a text field with a BROWSE button beside it. The user types a file name in the text field, or browses through the directories for it. If the field is filled in, the browser tries to send the file. The contents of the file are sent if the form's method is `POST` and the `enctype` is `multipart/form-data`. If the file doesn't exist, or is a directory, or has some other problem, an empty, zero-length file is sent. If the method is `GET` or `enctype` is not `multipart/form-data`, only the file's name is sent.

`<textarea cols=num`
`rows=num name=string`
`wrap=wrapStyle > initial`
`contents`
`</textarea>`
	A text area is like a two-dimensional text field. The `cols` and `rows` indicate the size to be displayed. The optional `wrap` attribute indicates that lines are automatically to be wrapped when they would extend beyond the edge of the area.

`<input type="hidden"`
`name=namestring`
`value=valuestring>`
	A hidden input item does not display anything, but sends the `name` and `value` to the server when the form is submitted. It is used to remember information the user has supplied. A CGI program responding to one form writes out a page that contains another form containing information from the previous form in hidden fields.

Passing Information to a CGI Program

Usually when we run a CGI program, we pass it some data from the browser. This data is read by the CGI program from its environment variables and, if it is called with a POST method, its standard input file.

Since we must provide both the CGI program and the HTML pages that reference the CGI programs, we will have to debug simultaneously the sending and receiving ends. A CGI script like printquery, shown in Figure 7–3, helps us check that the CGI program is receiving the parameters properly.

The printquery script first gets a list of all the items, key and value pairs, in its environment, sorts them, and writes them out. Then it writes out the contents of its input file.

An HTML file, printquery.html, shown in Figure 7–4, contains a link to the printquery CGI script. When we click on the text

```
http://192.168.1.1/cgi-bin/printquery/A/B?x=1&y=2
```

```python
#!/usr/bin/python
import cgi
import os,sys
import string
print "Content-type: text/plain"
print

print "environment variables"
print "--------------------"
env=os.environ.items()
env.sort()
for v in env:
    print v[0],'=',repr(v[1])
print "----------"
print "input file"
print "----------"
s=sys.stdin.readline()
while s:
    print s
    s=sys.stdin.readline()
print "----------------"
print "end of input file"
```

Figure 7–3
The printquery CGI Script

```
<html>
<head>
<title>Print Query</title>
</head>
<body>
<h1>click the link to GET the URL</h1>
<a href="http://192.168.1.1/cgi-bin/printquery/A/
B?x=1&y=2">
http://192.168.1.1/cgi-bin/printquery/A/B?x=1&y=2
</a>
</body>
</html>
```

Figure 7–4
Link to printquery

it will link to the printquery program and pass the parameters indicated. What parameters? There are two sets: extra path parameters and query parameters. The URL actually breaks down into five parts:

1. The protocol part, http://
2. The host address, 192.168.1.1[1]
3. The path, /cgi-bin/printquery, that leads to the CGI program
4. The extra path parameters, /A/B. This will be contained in environment variable PATH_INFO and will be attached to the server's default document directory in PATH_TRANSLATED.
5. The query string, x=1&y=2. These will be in environment variable QUERY_STRING if you are using the GET method.

The part of the URL following the protocol and host address will be in environment variable REQUEST_URI. Table 7–2 lists the environment variables.

The extra path parameters look like a continuation of the path past the CGI program. They are written in the HTML as part of the URL, so they do not vary. The query string is usually attached to the URL by the browser from the user's input, so its content will normally vary from use to use. In our example, however, we have filled it in ourselves.

You can find useful functions in module urlparse for those occasions when you need to break down URLs into their parts or put their parts together.

What is the point of the extra path parameters? You can use them for anything you want, of course, but the assumption is that they will refer to a document file. The PATH_TRANSLATED environment variable

---

1. Remember, if you are doing this on your own machine, you will need to substitute your machine's name or IP address for 192.168.1.1.

Table 7–2
Important CGI Environment Variables (Not always present)

Environment Variable (Not always present)	Explanation
CONTENT_LENGTH	For POST method requests, the length of the input to be read from stdin. See "POST Method" on page 336.
CONTENT_TYPE	For POST method requests, the encoding of the input in stdin. The options are "application/x-www-form-urlencoded" and "multipart/form-data." See "POST Method" on page 336.
DOCUMENT_ROOT	The top of the tree of directories directory containing the Web pages the server will deliver.
HTTP_COOKIE	Information that has been stored on the client at the request of a CGI program, to be sent back when the client connects to this site. It is used to maintain continuity across several client requests. Otherwise, each request is separate from those that have come before. See "Maintaining Context" on page 354.
HTTP_REFERER	The URL of the document that contained the reference to this CGI program.
PATH	As usual, the search path for programs. It probably won't be set to what you need.
PATH_INFO	The extra information in the URL path. The extra directory and file names after the path to the CGI program.
PATH_TRANSLATED	Equals DOCUMENT_ROOT followed by PATH_INFO. It assumes that the PATH_INFO leads to a document file on the server.
QUERY_STRING	For a GET method query, the parameters following the "?" in the query URL. See "GET Method" on page 316.
REMOTE_ADDR	The IP address of the user's machine.
REQUEST_METHOD	"GET" or "POST."

will contain the PATH_INFO interpreted as a path to a document on the server. This suggests a couple of uses. You could have the CGI program log some information, such as the page that linked to it, HTTP_REFERER, and the address of the machine making the request, REMOTE_ADDR, and then just deliver the PATH_TRANSLATED file to the requester as a Web page. Or you could have the CGI program encode the PATH_TRANSLATED file in some fashion before passing it on, e.g., compressing it.

When we load the printquery.html page and click on the link, we get a page with the contents shown in Figure 7–5.

```
environment variables
---------------------
DOCUMENT_ROOT = '/usr/local/apache/htdocs'
GATEWAY_INTERFACE = 'CGI/1.1'
HTTP_ACCEPT = 'image/gif, image/x-xbitmap, image/jpeg, image/pjpeg,
application/msword, */*'
HTTP_ACCEPT_ENCODING = 'gzip, deflate'
HTTP_ACCEPT_LANGUAGE = 'en-us'
HTTP_CONNECTION = 'Keep-Alive'
HTTP_HOST = '192.168.1.1'
HTTP_REFERER = 'http://192.168.1.1/~tc/printquery.html'
HTTP_USER_AGENT = 'Mozilla/4.0 (compatible; MSIE 5.5; Windows NT 5.0)'
PATH = '/sbin:/usr/sbin:/bin:/usr/bin:/usr/X11R6/bin'
PATH_INFO = '/A/B'
PATH_TRANSLATED = '/usr/local/apache/htdocs/A/B'
QUERY_STRING = 'x=1&y=2'
REMOTE_ADDR = '192.168.1.6'
REMOTE_PORT = '1064'
REQUEST_METHOD = 'GET'
REQUEST_URI = '/cgi-bin/printquery/A/B?x=1&y=2'
SCRIPT_FILENAME = '/usr/local/apache/cgi-bin/printquery'
SCRIPT_NAME = '/cgi-bin/printquery'
SERVER_ADDR = '192.168.1.1'
SERVER_ADMIN = 'gkt@toolsofcomputing.com'
SERVER_NAME = '999.999.999.999'[a]
SERVER_PORT = '80'
SERVER_PROTOCOL = 'HTTP/1.1'
SERVER_SIGNATURE = '<ADDRESS>Apache/1.3.12 Server at 999.999.999.999[a]
Port 80</ADDRESS>\012'
SERVER_SOFTWARE = 'Apache/1.3.12 (Unix) mod_ssl/2.6.2 OpenSSL/0.9.4'
-----------------
input file
-----------------
-----------------
end of input file
```

a. Server's Internet address purposely obscured.

Figure 7–5
Output from printquery

```
<html>
<head>
<title>Test coming from page</title>
</head>
<body>
<h1>Choose destination</h1>
</body>

<p><a href="http://192.168.1.1/cgi-bin/printquery" >
 See all environment variables
</a></p>
<p><a href="http://192.168.1.1/cgi-bin/youcamefrom" >
 See your address and referring page
</a></p>
</html>
```

Figure 7–6
comefrom.html

Rather than linking from http://192.168.1.1/~tc/
printquery.html, we could just type the URL http://
192.168.1.1/cgi-bin/printquery/A/B?x=1&y=2   directly
into the browser. We would get most of the same output. If you do it,
however, the HTTP_REFERER variable will not be defined. It is the
URL of the page containing the link we followed, but if we type the
link directly into the browser, there is no such page.

Here is an example of a page that will let us see where we are
accessing the server from. The HTML page is comefrom.html,
shown in Figure 7–6. It links to the CGI script youcamefrom shown in
Figure 7–7. The youcamefrom script will write out the URL of the
referring page, if there was one, and the Internet address of the machine
the user is browsing on.

```
#!/usr/bin/python
import os
print "Content-type: text/html"
print

print "<html><head><title>You came from</title></head>"
print "<body>"
print "<h1>Hello</h1>"
r=os.environ.get('HTTP_REFERER')
if r:
                print '<p>You were referred by page',r,'</p>'
print '<p>Your internet address is',os.environ.get('REMOTE_ADDR'),'</p>'
print "</body></html>"
```

Figure 7–7
youcamefrom Script

Rather than writing out all environment variables with `printquery`, we can write other scripts to show only the most relevant environment variables. Since we are interested mostly in the parameters, we will usually use the CGI program `printparams`, shown in Figure 7–8.

```python
#!/usr/bin/python
import cgi
import os,sys
import string
print "Content-type: text/plain"
print

if os.environ.has_key('CONTENT_LENGTH'):
                print 'CONTENT_LENGTH
=',repr(os.environ['CONTENT_LENGTH'])
if os.environ.has_key('CONTENT_TYPE'):
                print 'CONTENT_TYPE
=',repr(os.environ['CONTENT_TYPE'])
print "QUERY_STRING =",repr(os.environ.get("QUERY_STRING"))
print "REQUEST_METHOD =",repr(os.environ.get("REQUEST_METHOD"))
print "REQUEST_URI =",repr(os.environ.get("REQUEST_URI"))
print "PATH_INFO =",repr(os.environ.get("PATH_INFO"))
print "PATH_TRANSLATED =",repr(os.environ.get("PATH_TRANSLATED"))

if string.upper(os.environ.get("REQUEST_METHOD"))=="POST":
                print "-----------------"
                print "input file"
                print "-----------------"
                s=sys.stdin.readline()
                while s:
                  print s,
                  s=sys.stdin.readline()
                print "<----------------"
                print "end of input file"
```

Figure 7–8
printparams

Image Maps

An image map is an image that allows the user to click at a position on the image and load another page. The position of the click determines which other page is loaded. HTML allows image maps to be handled either on the server or on the client. Since we're interested in CGI programming, we will only consider the server-side image maps.

Pages are loaded when the user clicks on anchored text or image, i.e., between an `<a...>` and a `</a>` tag. The form for an image map is:

```
<a href="URLforCGIprogram"> <image src=urlForImage ismap width=m height=n> </a>
```

The `href` attribute specifies the page to load or CGI program to run. For an image map, it will be a CGI program. The image tag says that the image is to come from the `urlForImage` given in `src`, that it is m pixels wide and n pixels high (numbers, of course), and that it is an image map (`ismap`).

The pixels within the image are numbered by their horizontal and vertical distance from the upper left corner, which is (0,0). When the user clicks within the image, at position i pixels right from the upper left corner and j pixels down, a GET connection is made to `URLforCGIprogram` with the query string `?`i,j.

Figure 7–9 shows the contents of file `pokeleaf.html`. When we browse this file, we get a screen somewhat like Figure 7–10. It says to execute the CGI program `printparams` when the image is clicked. Clicking on the leaf gave us a page with the contents shown in Figure 7–11.

Notice that the query string is the position of the click within the image of the leaf.

If we had left out the `ismap` attribute of the image, it would still run the same CGI program when we click it, but it wouldn't pass the position of the click.

```
<html>
<head>
<title>Test Document</title>
</head>
<body>
<h1>This is a test</h1>
</body>

<a href="http://192.168.1.1/cgi-bin/printparams" >
 <img src="lightleaf.gif" ismap width="200" height="196">
</a>
</html>
```

Figure 7–9
HTML Page for `pokeleaf.html`

Poke the leaf somewhere

Figure 7–10
Browser Display for Page `pokeleaf.html`

```
QUERY_STRING = '116,47'
REQUEST_METHOD = 'GET'
REQUEST_URI = '/cgi-bin/printparams?116,47'
PATH_INFO = None
PATH_TRANSLATED = None
```

Figure 7–11
Example Output of `pokeleaf` CGI Program

Data Entry Forms

You usually use forms to allow the user to submit data. A form contains a number of buttons and text entry fields. The user toggles the buttons and enters text, and then pushes a submit button to send the contents of the form to the CGI program.

When you submit a form, the CGI program will run. It will be given the contents of the form as a collection of *name=value* pairs. For a GET method, these pairs will be listed in the query string.

You write a form in HTML between <form...> and </form> tags. The actual input buttons and fields are specified with <input...> tags.

You can specify three attributes for the `<form>` tag:

```
<form action=url method=GETorPOST enctype=encoding>
```

The `action` attribute is required. It gives the URL of the CGI program to run. The `method` attribute is also required. It is either `GET` or `POST`. In this section we will consider the `GET` method and put off discussing the `POST` method until later.

The `enctype` attribute is optional. For the `GET` method, it will always be the string `application/x-www-form-urlencoded`, which it defaults to. That encoding method also works with the `POST` method.The only alternative is `multipart/form-data`, which will only work with the `POST` method.

An essential input tag is a submit button, to make the browser send the contents of the form to the CGI program. It is written:

```
<input type="submit" name=namestring value=valuestring>
```

where the `name` and `value` attributes are optional, so you can get away with

```
<input type="submit">
```

The `submit` input tag tells the browser to display a button. If you specify a `value` attribute, it labels the button with the *valuestring*; otherwise, it uses the label `Submit Query`. If you include the `name`, then it will include *namestring*=*valuestring* in the CGI program's parameters. This allows you to have several different kinds of submission, e.g., placing an order for overnight delivery or for ground delivery.

The way you specify a text field is

```
<input type="text" name=namestring value=valuestring maxlength=n size=m>
```

This tag will have the browser display a text entry field. It is one line high and `size` (*m*) characters long. The actual number of characters it can hold are `maxlength` (*n*). If `maxlength` exceeds `size`, then the user will have to scroll the field left and right to access all the characters.

If the `value` attribute is present, its string is the initial contents of the text field. If absent, the field will initially be empty.

There is another option for text fields: You can specify a `password` field. It's just a text field, but all the characters the user types in it are displayed as stars. Otherwise it is the same as a text field:

```
<input type="password" name=string value=string maxlength=n size=n>
```

Although it obscures the text on the screen, it doesn't encrypt it. It is sent to the server as plain text and hence is only as secure as the connection. You should be using HTTPS (secure HTTP) or SSL (Secure Socket Layer) if security is important.

Figure 7–12 gives an HTML file to display the behavior of a text field. You fill in a text field and submit it, and it passes the parameters to the `printparams` CGI script to write them out.

Figure 7–13 shows the output of `textfield.html` for the message "Hello, world." Environment variable `REQUEST_URI` shows the contents of the URL the browser sent with the protocol and host information removed. The query string itself, contents of environment variable `QUERY_STRING`, is `msg=Hello%2C+world&submission=Submit+Query`. There are a couple of things to notice. There are two names in the form, `msg` for the text field and `submission` for the submit button. Both are given values here in *name=value* pairs. The two are separated by an ampersand. No quotes are included around either names or values. There is no white space. The default value of the submit button is `Submit Query`, but in the query string it is replaced by `Submit+Query`. The message `Hello,  world` was translated to `Hello%2C+world`. The comma was replaced with `%2C` and the blank with `+`.

```
<html>
<head>
<title>Text Field</title>
</head>
<body>
<h1>This is a test</h1>
</body>
<form action="http://192.168.1.1/cgi-bin/printparams"
                method="GET">
Message: <input type="TEXT" name="msg" size="20" maxlength="40">
<input type="SUBMIT" name="submission"  >
</form>
</html>
```

Figure 7–12
Text Field Input: `textfield.html`

```
QUERY_STRING = 'msg=Hello%2C+world&submission=Submit+Query'
REQUEST_METHOD = 'GET'
REQUEST_URI = '/cgi-bin/
printparams?msg=Hello%2C+world&submission=Submit+Query'
PATH_INFO = None
PATH_TRANSLATED = None
```

Figure 7–13
Parameters Submitted for Message "Hello, world" in `textfield`

URL Encoding

The reason for the translation of blank and comma shown in Figure 7–13 is that blanks and many other special characters would confuse the parsing of the URL. So blanks are replaced with plus signs and other special characters are replaced with percent signs followed by their hexadecimal code.

There are two kinds of characters that should be encoded: characters that delimit parts of the URL and characters that might have significance in the context in which the URL is used. Python has modules with functions for handling URLs, encoding and decoding them.

Module `cgi` contains function `parse_qs()`, which you can call in any of the following ways:

```
parse_qs(s)
parse_qs(s,keepBlankValues)
parse_qs(s,keepBlankValues,strict)
```

The `parse_qs()` function returns a dictionary mapping the names into *lists* of their values. Although most names will have at most a single value, some may have many values, so just in case, it uses lists for all names. The values in the lists are decoded from their URL encoding. In the calls of `parse_qs()`, s is the query string. Parameter `keepBlankValues`, if true, tells the function to include blank values as empty strings in its output. And `strict`, if true, tells it to raise a `ValueError` exception if s is malformed, rather than just ignoring it. "Example: Pizza Orders" on page 336 shows a use of the `parse_qs()` function.

Module `urllib` contains function `quote_plus(s)` that encodes a string for inclusion in a URL query. It replaces the blanks in string s with pluses and replaces special characters with their hexadecimal encoding. It leaves letters and digits and the characters comma, dot, hyphen, underscore, and slash (`,` `.` `-` `_` `/`) as is. *Note*: You would not encode an entire query or an entire URL with this function. It would translate characters that have special meaning, such as & and =, to the hexadecimal form, which would make them lose their special significance. Module urllib's function unquote_plus(s) is the inverse of quote_plus().

The urllib module's functions quote(s) and unquote(s) are similar to quote_plus() and unquote_plus(), but they replace blanks with their hexadecimal encoding rather than with plus signs.

Why should you want to encode URL strings? Module urllib also allows you to make HTTP or FTP connections to other computers to download files or run CGI programs.

Module urlparse contains the function urlparse() that you can use to break URLs into their components.

Example: CGI Program to Send an Image

CGI programs are not restricted to delivering new pages for display. The same HTTP protocol is used to pass other kinds of values. For example, if a Web page contains an <image> tag, the image tag contains an src attribute that specifies the URL of the image to display. The browser will request the image just the way it requests a Web page. The src URL can specify a CGI program. Figure 7–14 shows a CGI program, sendleaf, that was used to send a GIF file.

```
#!/usr/bin/python
print "Content-type: image/gif"
print

f=open("/home/tc/public_html/lightleaf.gif","rb")
s=f.read()
print s,
```

Figure 7–14
CGI Program to Send an Image File

Selections

There are several kinds of <input> tags in HTML to allow the user to make a choice among several options. There are *check boxes, radio buttons*, and *selection lists*. Figure 7–15 shows a Web page containing these components. Figure 7–16 shows HTML for the page. Figure 7–17 shows the parameters sent when the default values are sent by pressing the submit key on the page, and Figure 7–18 shows the parameters submitted with different selections.

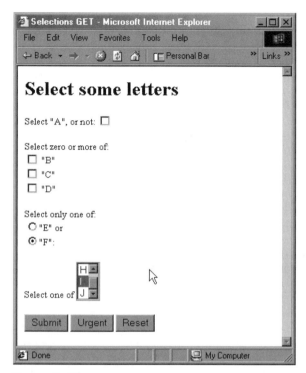

Figure 7–15
Display of `selections.html`

The HTML code in Figure 7–16 is divided into five sections, each a paragraph. The first two create check boxes; the third, radio buttons; the fourth, a selection list; and the fifth, submit and reset buttons.

Check boxes are indicated by `<input>` tags of the form:

```
<input type="checkbox" name=string value=string checked>
```

The `value` and `checked` attributes are optional. If present, the `checked` attribute says the check box is to be checked by default.

The first section consists of a single check box with name a and value A. It has no `value` attribute. By default, it is not checked. In Figure 7–17, submitted with default values, it doesn't appear in the query string. In Figure 7–18, it was checked. Since the input tag doesn't specify a different `value` attribute, the value on is used.

The second section is composed of three check boxes, all of which have the name bcd and which have the respective values B, C, and D. In Figure 7–17, none of them are passed in the query string since none

```
<html>
<head>
<title>Selections GET</title>
</head>
<body>
<h1>Select some letters</h1>
<form action="http://192.168.1.1/cgi-bin/printparams"
                method="GET">
<p>Select "A", or not: <input type="CHECKBOX" name="a"> </p>
<p>
Select zero or more of:
<br><input type="CHECKBOX" name="bcd" value="B">  "B"
<br><input type="CHECKBOX" name="bcd" value="C">  "C"
<br><input type="CHECKBOX" name="bcd" value="D">  "D"
</p>
<p>
Select only one of:
<br><input type="RADIO" name="ef" value="E">"E" or
<br><input type="RADIO" checked name="ef" value="F">"F":
</p>
<p>
Select one of <select name="ghij" size="3">
<option value="G"> G </option>
<option value="H"> H </option>
<option value="I" selected> I </option>
<option value="J"> J </option>
</select>
</p>
<p>
<input type="SUBMIT" name="submission" value="Submit">
<input type="SUBMIT" name="submission" value="Urgent">
<input type="RESET">
</p>
</form>
</body>
</html>
```

Figure 7–16
Buttons and Selections

of them are checked by default. To submit the form for Figure 7–18, the check boxes with values B and D were checked. Note that both of them are listed in the query string.

From these, you can see problems for CGI programs. Check box names may not appear at all or they may appear more than once.

Radio buttons are specified by input tags:

```
<input type="radio" name=string value=string checked>
```

```
QUERY_STRING = 'ef=F&ghij=I&submission=Submit'
REQUEST_METHOD = 'GET'
REQUEST_URI = '/cgi-bin/printparams?ef=F&ghij=I&submission=Submit'
PATH_INFO = None
PATH_TRANSLATED = None
```

Figure 7–17
Submission with Defaults

where attribute checked is optional and should be specified for one of the buttons at most.

The third section of the HTML contains two radio buttons with name ef and values E and F. With radio buttons, at most one of the buttons with the same name can be selected at a time. In this example, button F is checked by default.

A selection list allows you to scroll through a list of options to select one. The list appears between a <select> and a </select> tag. Each of the options is written with <option> and </option> tags.

The form of a select tag is

```
<select name=string size=n >
```

where the size attribute specifies how many selection options will be visible at one time. The form of the option tag is:

```
<option selected value=string >
```

where the selected attribute is optional. If present, it indicates which option is selected by default.

In the HTML code, the selection component has the name ghij. The options have values G, H, I, and J. They also have those letters as the names they will be displayed as. The strings between <option> and </option> are the strings displayed in the selection box.

```
QUERY_STRING = 'a=on&bcd=B&bcd=D&ef=E&ghij=G&submission=Urgent'
REQUEST_METHOD = 'GET'
REQUEST_URI = '/cgi-bin/
printparams?a=on&bcd=B&bcd=D&ef=E&ghij=G&submission=Urgent'
PATH_INFO = None
PATH_TRANSLATED = None
```

Figure 7–18
Other Selections

The final section of the HTML code has two submission buttons, which have already been explained, and a *reset* button. When the user clicks that, all the components of the form are reset to their default values.

Example: Pizza Orders

In this example, we use a GET QUERY_STRING to gather information in a tiny prototype pizza ordering system whose Web page is shown in Figure 7–19 and whose response to the selections is shown in Figure 7–20. Its HTML code is in Figure 7–21 and its CGI program is in Figure 7–24.

We get the QUERY_STRING environment variable and parse it into variable q with the

```
s=os.environ['QUERY_STRING']
q=cgi.parse_qs(s)
```

lines. The 'size' key is guaranteed to be present and to have exactly one value since it is a radio button with 'large' selected by default, so q['size'][0] is what we want. The code to write the toppings first has to check to see if any toppings were ordered. If none were checked, q will have no 'toppings' key, so we report that a cheese pizza was ordered. Otherwise, q['toppings'] is a list of all the toppings.

POST Method

In the preceding section, we considered only the GET method for forms. The big problem with GET is that all the form data are attached to the URL used to invoke the CGI program. This can be a problem if there are a lot of form data. Systems may have limits on how long a URL can be; the POST method lifts this restriction.

What POST Method Does

The POST method passes the query in a stream of characters (equivalent to a file) in a connection to the Web server, rather than just in the URL. This stream can be of any length. The POST method allows Web browsers to send files to CGI programs, potentially much too long ever to include in a URL.

The stream of characters the POST method sends becomes the CGI program's standard input, so instead of finding all of its input in

Figure 7–19
Web Page for Pizza Order

Figure 7–20
CGI Response to Pizza Order

```
<html>
<head>
<title>Order a pizza</title>
</head>
<body>
<h1>Order a pizza</h1>
<form action="http://192.168.1.1/cgi-bin/pizzaorder"
                  method="GET">
<p>
What size?
<br><input type="RADIO" name="size" value="small">"Small" or
<br><input type="RADIO" name="size" value="medium">"Medium" or
<br><input type="RADIO" checked name="size" value="large">"Large":
</p>


<p>
Select Toppings:
<br><input type="CHECKBOX" name="toppings" value="garlic">  "garlic"
<br><input type="CHECKBOX" name="toppings" value="anchovy"> "anchovy"
<br><input type="CHECKBOX" name="toppings" value="onion"> "onion"
</p>

<p>
<input type="SUBMIT" name="submission" value="Submit">

<input type="RESET">
</p>
</form>
</body>
</html>
```

Figure 7–21
HTML for Pizza Ordering System

environment variables, the CGI program must find its query string in the input.

But there are two options with the POST method for the encoding of the data in the input stream. The encoding is specified in the form tag with the enctype attribute.

The default encoding for form data is written as enctype="application/x-www-form-urlencoded" and it is the same for both GET and POST methods; for the GET method, it is passed as part of the URL; and for the POST, it is passed in the CGI program's input stream.

To show what the CGI program gets from a POST method, we created a file textfieldPostUrlenc.html identical to

```
#!/usr/bin/python
import cgi
import os,sys
import string
print "Content-type: text/html"
print

print "<html>"
print "<head>"
print "<title>Your pizza order</title>"
print "</head>"
print "<body>"
print "<h1>Thank you for your pizza order</h1>"
s=os.environ['QUERY_STRING']
q=cgi.parse_qs(s)
print 'You ordered a',q['size'][0]
if not q.has_key('toppings'):
                print 'cheese pizza.'
else:
                print 'pizza with '
                toppings=q['toppings']
                if len(toppings)==1:
                  print toppings[0]+'.'
                else:
                  for i in range(len(toppings)):
                    if i<len(toppings)-2:
                      print toppings[i]+','
                    elif i==len(toppings)-2:
                      print toppings[i],'and'
                    else:
                      print toppings[i]+'.'


print "</body>"
```

Figure 7-22
CGI for Processing Pizza Order QUERY_STRING

textfield.html (Figure 7–12) except that it uses the POST method rather than GET. Figure 7–23 shows its form code. Its CGI program, printparams, gets the input shown in Figure 7–24. A comparison to Figure 7–13 shows that the query string is in the input file for POST. The "<---------------" at the end of the query string indicates there is no line termination following it. Also, there is no "submission=..." here. We hit the enter key in the text field, which submitted the text without use of the submit button.

```
<form action="http://192.168.1.1/cgi-bin/printparams"
                method="POST">
Message: <input type="TEXT" name="msg" size="20" maxlength="40">
<input type="SUBMIT" name="submission" >
</form>
```

Figure 7–23
Form from `textfieldPostUrlenc.html`

```
CONTENT_LENGTH = '18'
CONTENT_TYPE = 'application/x-www-form-urlencoded'
QUERY_STRING = ''
REQUEST_METHOD = 'POST'
REQUEST_URI = '/cgi-bin/printparams'
PATH_INFO = None
PATH_TRANSLATED = None
----------------
input file
----------------
msg=Hello%2C+world <----------------
end of input file
```

Figure 7–24
Parameters Passed to CGI Program from `textfieldPostUrlenc.html`

The other option is `enctype="multipart/form-data"`. With this option, the stream is divided into parts, one per parameter. The form of the stream is a multipart file, each part consisting of a MIME header and a body, and the sections are separated by separator lines.

Figure 7–25 shows the form component of file `textfieldPost.html`, which is the same as in `textfieldPostUrlenc.html` except that it specifies `enctype="multipart/form-data"`. Figure 7–26 shows the stream it sends to `printparams`, the CGI program.

```
<form action="http://192.168.1.1/cgi-bin/printparams"
                method="POST" enctype="multipart/form-data">
Message: <input type="TEXT" name="msg" size="20" maxlength="40">
<input type="SUBMIT" name="submission" >
</form>
```

Figure 7–25
Form from `textfieldPost.html`

```
CONTENT_LENGTH = '258'
CONTENT_TYPE = 'multipart/form-data; boundary=------------------------
--7d0d713202e0'
QUERY_STRING = ''
REQUEST_METHOD = 'POST'
REQUEST_URI = '/cgi-bin/printparams'
PATH_INFO = None
PATH_TRANSLATED = None
----------------
input file
----------------
---------------------------7d0d713202e0
Content-Disposition: form-data; name="msg"

Hello, world
---------------------------7d0d713202e0
Content-Disposition: form-data; name="submission"

Submit Query
---------------------------7d0d713202e0--
<---------------
end of input file
```

Figure 7–26
Output of `textfieldPost.html` with "Hello, world"

The parameters are in a multipart file with separator lines:

```
---------------------------7d02d22c4007a
```

If the form is being submitted with the POST method and enctype="multipart/form-data", the environment variable REQUEST_METHOD is 'POST' and the environment variable CONTENT_TYPE is 'multipart/form-data; boundary=*boundary-string*'. The boundary string is part of the separator line between the parts of the multipart file.

The separator line occurs as the first line in the file. Its next occurrence separates the parameters. The final occurrence contains two hyphens at the end:

```
---------------------------7d02d22c4007a--
```

This indicates it is the end of the file. Although it is difficult to see here, the boundary string in the content-type line is two characters shorter than the separator lines. All separator lines are supposed to begin with at least two hyphens. The separator line is the boundary with two initial hyphens in front.

What does the content of the boundary string mean? Actually, it is supposed to be chosen randomly so as to make the probability of a separator line occurring anywhere in the data by chance vanishingly small.

Remember, MIME headers are composed of a sequence of lines of the form `linetype: data` followed by an empty line. For the form parameters in Figure 7–26, each parameter's MIME header consists of a single `Content-Disposition` line. These lines are of the form

```
Content-Disposition: form-data; name=...
```

or

```
Content-Disposition: form-data; name=...; filename=...
```

The `name` gives the name from the input component. The `filename` applies to file input, which we'll discuss later. The body of that section of the multipart file is the value associated with variable `name`. For example, the first section gives the value

```
Hello, world
```

for the variable `msg`. Notice that, in contrast to Figure 7–24, the submitted string is *not* URL-encoded.

File Input

You can create an input tag that allows files to be sent from the user's computer to the server. The input tag to submit files has the form:

```
<input type="file" name=string  maxlength=n size=n >
```

It displays a text field for the file's name with a browse button beside it. Pushing the browse button throws up a file dialog box.

File input only works with forms that specify `method="POST"` and `enctype="multipart/form-data"`. If you use the GET method, or POST with `enctype="application/x-www-form-urlencoded"`, the file tag behaves like a text tag: The name of the file is sent, not its contents.

Figure 7–27 shows HTML code for a page to submit a file to our `printparams` CGI script. Using it to submit the file `SayHi.py`, we get the input shown in Figure 7–28. The section of the multipart file containing the file itself has the MIME header:

```
Content-Disposition: form-data; name="TheFile";
filename="c:\Downloads\SayHi.py"
    Content-Type: unknown
```

```
<html>
<head>
<title>File field with a POST</title>
</head>
<body>
<h1>Send a file</h1>
<form action="http://192.168.1.1/cgi-bin/printparams"
                enctype="multipart/form-data"
                method="POST">
Submit a file: <input type="FILE" name="TheFile" size="20"
maxlength="40">
<input type="SUBMIT" name="submission" value="Submit">
</form>
</body>
</html>
```

Figure 7–27
fileWithPost

```
CONTENT_LENGTH = '336'
CONTENT_TYPE = 'multipart/form-data; boundary=------------------------
--7d01a47202e0'
QUERY_STRING = ''
REQUEST_METHOD = 'POST'
REQUEST_URI = '/cgi-bin/printparams'
PATH_INFO = None
PATH_TRANSLATED = None
----------------
input file
----------------
---------------------------7d01a47202e0
Content-Disposition: form-data; name="TheFile";
filename="C:\Downloads\SayHi.py"
Content-Type: text/plain

#!/usr/bin/python
print 'Hello'
---------------------------7d01a47202e0
Content-Disposition: form-data; name="submission"

Submit
---------------------------7d01a47202e0--
<---------------
end of input file
```

Figure 7–28
SayHi.py Submitted with POST

The `Content-Disposition` line gives the name used in the file input tag, `TheFile`, and the name of the file that was submitted.

What if the user types in the name of a file that doesn't exist? How is the CGI program informed of the error? It isn't. It just receives an empty file. It is the same if the user selects a directory. The CGI program receives an empty file. It is up to you to check that you got a non-empty file and give the user another chance to submit it if it was empty.

Text Areas

Another input field that probably requires a `POST` method with `enctype="multipart/form-data"` is the text area. The text area is a two-dimensional space in which the user can enter text. Its tag is:

```
<textarea cols=n rows=m
    name=string wrap=wrapStyle >...</textarea>
```

Of course, the text area needs a `name` to be referenced by in the CGI program. The text area will have n columns and m rows. The text between the `<textarea>` and `</textarea>` tags will be the default value that the text area is initialized to.

The text in the text area is sent to the server program with carriage-return/line-feed pairs between the lines. The `wrap` attribute specifies whether there will be word-wrapping and how the text will be transmitted. The default action is no text wrapping: The text will flow to another line only when the user types return. You can get the default action explicitly with `wrap=off`. In Netscape, if you specify `wrap=physical`, text will wrap onto the next line whenever a word would extend beyond the end of a line. When the text is sent to the server, the browser will send a carriage-return/line-feed pair between each line visible in the text area, i.e., it will insert the line-termination characters wherever it wrapped a line. If you set `wrap=virtual`, the browser will wrap the text in the text area the same as with the physical wrapping, but it will send line-termination characters only where the user typed Enter. Don't count on all browsers handling these options the same way.

Processing the Input Stream

As we mentioned, for the `GET` method you can use the `cgi` module's function `cgi.parse_qs()` to get a dictionary of the form's variables and values. The questions with `POST` inputs are: What can we use to read in the variables and values? And what do we do about file uploads? Files need to be treated specially so as not to have the entire contents in memory all at once.

Do It Yourself

There are modules you can use to handle POST input yourself. As we will see later, you probably won't need to program it yourself, but if you do, here are some modules to look at:

- multifile–The multifile module has tools for reading multifile streams, breaking them into the sections indicated by the separator string. It allows you to push and pop separators to handle multifiles nested within sections of other multifiles.
- mimetools–The mimetools module helps you read and parse the MIME headers of the sections of the multipart files. It also contains functions to help you translate files to and from common transmission encodings, e.g., base64.
- mimetypes–The mimetypes module helps you keep track of file content types, including tables for guessing the MIME type for file extensions and file extensions for MIME types.

Module cgi's Parsing Functions

The cgi module has functions that allow you to parse queries, whether they are URl-encoded or multipart files. All these functions parse queries into dictionaries that map the names of query variables into *lists* of values. You can use the same name more than once in input tags and get more than one value, so the dictionaries use lists to anticipate that possibility, even when you aren't using it.

The cgi functions and object classes used to decode queries are listed in Table 7–3.

Table 7–3
Module cgi Query Parsing Functions and Classes

Function/Class	Used For
parse_qs(qs, keepBlankValues, strict)	Parses a query string, qs, into a dictionary mapping the form variables' names into lists of their string values. Variables that have an empty value to the right of the equals sign are omitted unless keepBlankValues is true. The strict parameter, if true, will raise a ValueError exception if the query string is malformed. The default action is to ignore these errors.

Table 7–3
Module cgi Query Parsing Functions and Classes (Continued)

Function/Class	Used For
parse_multipart(fp,dict)	Parses the multipart form from file fp and with the environment indicated by dictionary dict. These default to sys.stdin and os.environ. It returns a dictionary mapping the names of the form variables into lists of their values. It is not appropriate if there are file inputs, since it would read the entire file into memory and put it as a string in the value list. Use FieldStorage instead. (See "Module cgi's FieldStorage Objects" on page 347.) This doesn't handle nested multipart forms, i.e., multipart files as values of variables in a multipart form.
parse()	Parses the query string or a multipart file contained in the environment and/or sys.stdin as determined by environment variables REQUEST_METHOD and the contents of the input file. It returns a dictionary mapping the names of query variables into lists of their values. It is not appropriate if there are file inputs since it would read the entire file into memory and put it as a string in the value list. Use FieldStorage instead. (See "Module cgi's FieldStorage Objects" on page 347.)
FieldStorage()	Creates an instance of the FieldStorage class that contains within it information about all the query variables. These variables are represented themselves by instances of the FieldStorage class or the MiniFieldStorage class. Unless you try to access the value of a file input variable, the file is not loaded into memory but rather is represented by an open file object from which the contents of the file can be read.

The general method for parsing the query into a dictionary of variables and their values is the parse() function. It will parse the query whether it is a GET, POST URL-encoded, or POST multipart form. It returns a dictionary mapping each variable from the form into a list of the values assigned to it. If the variable is assigned a single value in the form, it still gets a list in the dictionary. There are two other parse functions that work explicitly on URL-encoded or multipart forms. You can call them directly if you know what you've got.

The problem with all these parse functions is that they read the values of a variable into memory as strings. This means that a file input would result in the entire file being loaded into memory. If there is file input, you should use the `FieldStorage` class, which does not read an entire file as a string unless you request it.

Module `cgi`'s `FieldStorage` Objects

The preferred way to use the `cgi` module is to use the `FieldStorage` class. Consider the form variables or the sections of a multipart file object to be "fields," and you get the name. You create a single instance of the `FieldStorage` class:

```
form=cgi.FieldStorage()
```

The class's initialization code will read the entire query (including `sys.stdin`) and attach it to the object it returns. Don't try instantiating more than one: There won't be anything left to initialize the subsequent ones.

The `FieldStorage` class has two uses: The top-level use represents the entire form. It can also occur within a form to represent part of a multipart form. These two uses are somewhat different. They use some different object attributes. The major reason for allowing `FieldStorage` objects to represent parts of multipart forms is to allow multipart files to be nested within other multipart files, more a theoretical than a practical reality at the moment.

There is also a `MiniFieldStorage` class that is used to represent simple fields, query variables with small string values.

The top-level `FieldStorage` will have an attribute, `list`, that contains a list of all the fields contained in the query. Each of these will be a `FieldStorage` or `MiniFieldStorage` object. The top-level `FieldStorage` will also behave like a dictionary in that:

- You can ask if a name, `key`, is assigned one or more values in the query by calling the function

```
form.has_key[key]
```

which behaves the same as for a dictionary.

- You can get a list of all the names assigned values in the form by calling:

  `form.keys()`

- You can subscript with the name, `key`, and get the value or values associated with key:

  `form[key]`

  But this does not give you the value directly. It will either give you a `FieldStorage` or `MiniFieldStorage` object for the field, or it will give you a list of such objects representing all the values for the name.

The contained `FieldStorage` and `MiniFieldStorage` objects have these attributes:

- `name`—The name of the field, or if you prefer, the name of the query variable. If you get at the inner object by subscripting the top-level `FieldStorage`, which we're calling `form`, this name may seem redundant, but if you get at this contained object from `form`'s `list` attribute, you'll need the name.
- `value`—The value of the field. For everything except a file input, this is what you want. It does not have the contents of a file input assigned to it initially, but if you try to access it, the entire file will be read into memory as a string. So don't touch it unless you're sure the field is not a file.
- `filename`—If the field corresponds to a file input, `filename` is the name of the file on the browser's machine, and it will test as true in `if` statements. If the field is not a file upload, this attribute will test as false.
- `file`—If the field corresponds to a file input, the `file` attribute is an open file object that can be used for reading the file, in which case it will test as true. Otherwise it tests as false in `if` statements.

From all this, we can derive some programming conventions for use with `FieldStorage`. First, remember that you create a single `FieldStorage` object and assign it to a variable. We will call the variable `form`.

To get the value of a field, you have to consider several possibilities:

1. The `form` variable may not have any value assigned.
2. The `form` variable may have exactly one value assigned.
3. The `form` variable may have more than one value assigned.

Moreover,

1. A value may be a string.
2. A value may be a file.

Each combination of these requires different code. First consider what to do depending on how many values the variable, id, has. You will need something like the following:

```
if form.has_key(id):
    v=form[id]
    if type(v) is types.ListType:
      #handle multiple values
      for x in v:
        val=x.value
        . . .
    else:#handle single value
      val=v.value
      . . .
else:
    #handle no value
```

If you are sure the form variable has exactly a single value assigned to it, you can write form[key].value to get it. If you are not sure how many values the key has, you can instead use the method form.getvalue(key,d), which will get the value of the key, if there is one, or return the value d if there is none. Parameter d defaults to None. If the key has more than one value, you will get a list of the values.

If the field is a file input field, you do not want to access its value attribute. Instead, you will want to do something like this:

```
if form.has_key(id):
    f=form[id]
    if f.file:
      #read the file from f.file
      . . .
    else: #something's wrong. The field's not a file.
      . . .
else:
    #handle the absence of the file upload
```

Example: File Submissions

In this example, we create an HTML page and CGI script to allow people to submit files. This could be used to submit articles to a newsletter, to submit papers for a conference, or to submit homework in a class.

The form provides space for the name and e-mail address of the person submitting the file, a text area for remarks about it (in effect, a cover letter), and of course, the file input item. If the file arrives empty, the user is informed and given a chance to try again. Simply backing up to the HTML page works nicely in Netscape and Internet Explorer; the text fields and text area still have the contents the user typed in to them.

Upon successful completion, the CGI program will give the user an identification code to refer to the submission by in any further communications about the submission.

The trick is to put each submission in its own subdirectory. The directory will be created when the submission is made. It will have a generated name (intended to be unique). It is the name of this directory that will be returned to the user as the identification code.

The submission's subdirectory will have two files in it. The file submission will contain the file that was submitted. The file info will have the other information that the user provided.

Figure 7–29 shows the HTML code submitFile.html. It is a relatively straightforward form. It provides text filed inputs named LASTNAME, FIRSTNAME, and EMAIL, a text area COVER for the "cover letter," and a file input FILE for the file being submitted. It invokes the CGI program submitfile, Figure 7–30, with a POST method and multipart/form-data encoding.

The submitfile script begins by writing out the header for an HTML response. Then it reads in the form by calling cgi.FieldStorage(). It then checks to see if the required fields, LASTNAME, EMAIL, and FILE, are present. If any are absent, the response to the user will say that it is required and the user should try again.

If the required fields are present, it generates a name, docId, for the directory that the submission will be placed in. It assigns to docId the string IDpid-time, where *pid* is the script's process id and *time* is the current time in seconds since the beginning of the epoch (January 1, 1970). Both the process id and the time are converted to hexadecimal.

The directory is created as a subdirectory of /home/tc/wp14/submissions/[2] and its protections are set to allow the owner and anyone in the same group to read, write, or look into it. The protections are important and require a bit of thought.

---

2. If you are trying out this code, of course, you will need to specify a different directory to put the submission's directory into.

```
<html>
<head>
<title>Submit a file</title>
</head>
<body>
<h1>Submit a file</h1>
<form action="http://192.168.1.1/cgi-bin/submitfile"
                    enctype="multipart/form-data"
                    method="POST">
<h2>Main author</h2>
<p>
Family name:<input type="text" name="LASTNAME" size="30" maxlength="40">
</p>
<p>
Given name:<input type="text" name="FIRSTNAME" size="30" maxlength="40">
</p>
<p>
E-mail:<input type="text" name="EMAIL" size="50" maxlength="70">
</p>
<p>
<h2>Document</h2>
<p>
The file: <input type="FILE" name="FILE" size="20" maxlength="40">
</p>
<h2>Cover note</h2>
<p>
<textarea  name="COVER" cols="40" rows="8" wrap="physical"></textarea>
</p>
<input type="SUBMIT">
</form>
</body>
</html>
```

Figure 7–29
HTML Page submitFile.html for File Submission Example

The CGI program is going to run as user nobody and in the group nobody. I, who will use this information, am a different user. I need to make sure that the CGI program can create the directory and files it needs to, and that I can access them. So here's how I did it.

I made myself a member of the nobody group. I created the submissions directory, which made me its owner and my login group its group. I changed the group of the submissions directory to nobody. (I had to execute newgrp nobody before chgrp nobody submissions would work.) I set the protections on the directories tc and wp14 so that anybody can include them on a path, which allows the CGI program to get to the submissions directory. I set the permissions on the submissions directory to allow anybody in its group to do anything with it. Because the CGI program's group is the same as the directory's, the CGI program can create the subdirectories in it. The CGI program creates the subdirectory, dir

```
#!/usr/bin/python
import cgi
import os,sys
import types
import time
import shutil

print "Content-type: text/html"
print
print
print '<html><head><title>File upload'
print '</title></head><body>'

fs=cgi.FieldStorage()

okay=1
if not fs.getvalue('LASTNAME'):
                if okay: print '<h1>Problem</h1>'
                print '<p>Family name is required.</p>'
                okay=0
if not fs.getvalue('EMAIL'):
                if okay: print '<h1>Problem</h1>'
                print '<p>Email address is required.</p>'
                okay=0
if not fs.getvalue('FILE'):
                if okay: print '<h1>Problem</h1>'
                print '<p>File is required.</p>'
                okay=0
if not okay:
                print '<p>Please try again.</p>'
                print '</body></html>'
                sys.exit()

docId='ID'+hex(os.getpid())[2:]+'-'
docId=docId+hex(long(time.time()))[2:-1]
dir='/home/tc/wp14/submissions/'+docId
os.mkdir(dir)
os.chmod(dir,0775)
file=fs["FILE"].file
dst=dir+'/submission'
dstfile=open(dst,'wb')
shutil.copyfileobj(file,dstfile,1024)
dstfile.close()
```

Figure 7–30
CGI Program submitfile

```
filesize=os.path.getsize(dst)
if filesize==0:
                print '<h1>Problem</h1>'
                print "<p>The file didn't come through. "
                print 'Make sure it exists and is not '
                print 'a directory, and try again.</p>'
                print '<p>Please try again.</p>'
                os.remove(dst)
                os.rmdir(dir)
                print '</body></html>'
                sys.exit()
os.chmod(dst,0664)
info=open(dir+'/info','w')
info.write('Last: '+fs['LASTNAME'].value+os.linesep)
if fs.getvalue('FIRSTNAME'):
                info.write('First: '+fs.getvalue( \
                    'FIRSTNAME',"")+os.linesep)
info.write('Email: '+fs['EMAIL'].value+os.linesep)
info.write('Filename: '+fs['FILE'].filename+os.linesep)
info.write(os.linesep+fs['COVER'].value+os.linesep)
info.close()
os.chmod(dir+'/info',0664)
print "<h1>Thank you for your submission</h1>"
print "<p>Your submission's ID is:",docId+"."
print "Please refer to it in all communications.</p>"
print '<p>You submitted file',fs['FILE'].filename
print 'which was',filesize,'bytes long.</p>'
print "</body></html>"
```

Figure 7–30
CGI Program submitfile (Continued)

(/home/tc/-wpl4/submissions/*docId*), and sets its protections to allow other members of its group to do anything they want to it. That will be me.

Next, the CGI program gets the input file object, opens an output file /home/tc/wpl4/submissions/*docId*/submission, and copies the input file into it. Once it has copied the file, it has to see if there really was an input file. If the file the user tried to submit was a directory or the file name was misspelled, there is no error indication. It's just sent as an empty file. So if the file size is zero, the file was not successfully transmitted. In that case the CGI program removes the file and directory, writes out an error message, and terminates.

If a file was received, the CGI program goes on to write file info containing the other information the user sent. We use a MIME-like header for the text fields. Since the FIRSTNAME is optional, we don't write it if it wasn't specified. We write the cover-letter text as the body.

These two files will be owned by nobody and belong to the nobody group. The protections are set to allow the other members of the group to access them.

After successfully saving the file and other information, we write out a response to the user, saying that the file has been successfully received and giving its directory name as its identification code.

Maintaining Context

Since each browser–server interaction is a separate interaction, there is a problem maintaining a context, a continuity over a longer interaction (e.g., keeping a shopping cart). We don't want to force the user to retype information. There are several ways to accomplish this.

One way is to have the CGI programs write new HTML pages back to the user that have the context information embedded in them, where it will be submitted with the next form. Or at least have a key embedded that can be used to look up the information in a database.

Another way is to store a cookie on the user's computer. The cookie contains the needed information and will be automatically sent in the HTTP header in subsequent transactions.

Hidden Text • One way to store information in HTML pages is with the "hidden" input tag. The hidden input is like text-filed input, but it does not display anything in the form or allow the user to type text. The hidden type input has the form:

```
<input type="hidden" name=string value=string>
```

It simply submits the value with the name. To use hidden input to maintain context, a CGI program can take the information submitted in a form and put it into a hidden input tag in the form of the HTML page it writes back to the user. This information will be sent back when the user submits the next form. This can continue through a series of forms. Of course, if the information becomes too voluminous, it can be stashed in a temporary file and the file name included in the form. Another program can sweep up the older temporary files every so often.

As an alternative to using a hidden field, especially if you are using a temporary file, you could just as well include the file name in the extra path information of the CGI program's URL in the form tag.

Cookies

A cookie is information stored on the user's machine at the server's request that the browser automatically sends back to the server in subsequent HTTP connections. Cookies are handled in the headers of HTTP messages, not in the query strings. They work as follows.

A CGI program needs to save some context for further communications, so when it sends a page back to the browser for display, it includes a line in the MIME header saying:

```
Set-cookie: name=value; options
```

The browser will store the cookie in its local memory. When it connects again, it will include in the MIME header of its query a cookie line:

```
Cookie: name=value ; name=value ; ...
```

The line contains all the names and values for the relevant cookies. The server will supply these to a CGI program in the `HTTP_COOKIE` environment variable. The value must not contain a space, tab, or semicolon. URL encoding would work for the value. Module `urllib`, recall, contains functions to create and decode URL-encoded strings.

What are the "relevant" cookies that will be sent back? Cookies are associated with locations on the Web. If you send a `set-cookie` and don't restrict it otherwise, the cookie will only be sent back to you, i.e., it will be sent when the browser connects again to your URL.

If you put in the option `path=directories`, the cookie will be sent when a connection is sent to your host and its path on your host begins with *directories*. Actually, the path is not absolute. It is relative to a base directory the Web server uses. But the path you specify looks absolute. It starts with a /. If it is /, the cookie will be sent whenever a connection is made to anywhere on your URL.

If you specify the option, `domain=domainName`, the cookie will be sent to hosts in the domain. If you specify, for example, `domain=.y.z.com`, the cookie would be sent to hosts `x.y.z.com` and `w.y.z.com`, but not to `v.z.com`. Notice that the specified domain begins with a dot. If it doesn't begin with a dot, it specifies a particular host.

You can specify when a cookie will expire. The option has the form:

```
expires=weekday, dd-mm-yy hh:mm:ss GMT
```

The cookie will not be sent back after that time. Only GMT may be used. The weekdays are spelled out entirely, for example:

```
Wednesday, 13-Dec-2000 17:36:03 GMT
```

The year can be written with either two or four digits. If you don't specify an expires option, the cookie is stored only in the browser and will persist only until the browser exits.

A way to create a time field in the proper format is:

```
import time
secs=time.time()
ttuple=time.gmtime(secs+48*60*60)
date=time.strftime('%A, %d-%b-%Y %H:%M:%S GMT',ttuple)
```

The time module has functions for calculating and formatting times. Its time() function returns the number of seconds since the start of the "epoch," January 1, 1970. The gmtime() function converts the seconds into a tuple of fields giving date, time, day of the week, etc. Here we add the number of seconds in two days to the current time as the expiration time for a cookie. The strftime() function formats the tuple into a string. The %letter elements, of course, specify which component of the time tuple is to replace them and how it is to be formatted.

Figure 7–31 shows the HTML for a page that requests a text field and submits it to a CGI program, storeCookie, that will store it. Program storeCookie, Figure 7–32, sends the cookie back in its response header and provides an HTML page asking the user what to do next. The options are to invoke CGI program showCookie, Figure 7–33, to display the cookie, or to invoke the printQuery program to show all the environment variables. In either case, the cookie is sent back from the browser to the server and passed to the CGI program in the HTTP_COOKIE variable.

```
<html>
<head>
<title>Text Field</title>
</head>
<body>
<h1>Save as a cookie</h1>
</body>
<form action="http://192.168.1.1/cgi-bin/storeCookie"
                method="GET">
Message: <input type="TEXT" name="MEMO" size="20" maxlength="40">
<input type="SUBMIT" name="submission" >
</form>
</html>
```

Figure 7–31
HTML Providing a Cookie to Be Stored

```
#!/usr/bin/python
import os
import cgi
qs=os.environ['QUERY_STRING']
qdict=cgi.parse_qs(qs)
memo=qdict.get("MEMO",['nothing+to+remember'])[0]

print "Content-type: text/html"
print "Set-cookie: remembering="+memo
print

print "<html><head><title>Remembering</title></head>"
print "<body>"
print "<h1>Where next?</h1>"
print "<p><a href='http://192.168.1.1/cgi-bin/showCookie'>"
print "Show cookie"
print "</a></p>"
print "<p><a href='http://192.168.1.1/cgi-bin/printquery'>"
print "print CGI parameters "
print "</a></p>"
print "</body></html>"
```

Figure 7–32
CGI Program storeCookie

```
#!/usr/bin/python
import os
import cgi
qs=cgi.FieldStorage()
print "Content-type: text/html"
print

print "<html><head><title>Remembering</title></head>"
print "<body>"
print "<h1>The cookie</h1>"
print os.environ['HTTP_COOKIE']
print "</body></html>"
```

Figure 7–33
CGI Program showCookie

More Notes on Debugging

We already mentioned some debugging considerations in "Installing CGI Programs" on page 314. There we discussed the problems you will have just getting CGI programs installed on your system. Clearly, you will have to get past that before you can even consider debugging your actual code.

You will benefit by using several windows, or several simultaneous ssh sessions, while debugging these scripts. I [TC] used a window in the ~tc/public_html directory to examine and debug the HTML pages, a window in another directory where I was developing the CGI programs, another window with root access to copy the CGI programs to /usr/local/apache/cgi-bin/, a browser window, and a window executing

```
tail -f /usr/local/apache/logs/error.log
```

to show the Apache server's error log file.

You can try executing your script from the command line in your own directory. The environment variables won't be set correctly and the input file won't be correct, but it will check to see if you have syntax errors. This works best if everything is contained in functions except a final line calling a main program function. You can call sys.exit() just before that if your program might do some harm if it runs in the wrong context.

Since you will be debugging both your HTML form and your CGI program, you will need to be sure that the form is sending the correct information to the CGI program. You can install `printquery` (Figure 7–3), `printparams` (Figure 7–8), or `cgi.py` from the Python library and have your form send its query to that script. It will tell you if the query is getting through at all, and if so, what's in it.

When you get ready to install your script in `cgi-bin`, you can make the first executable lines be:

```
import cgi, sys
cgi.test()
sys.exit()
```

The `cgi.test()` will make your script behave as if it is running the `cgi.py` module as a script. It will write out what your program is receiving, formatted in an HTML page. The `sys.exit()` will stop execution. Once you are sure it is being executed, you can remove the test and exit calls.

Then you may wish to start your script with:

```
print "Content-type: text/plain"
print
sys.stderr=sys.stdout
```

This will cause all your program's output to be sent to the browser as a plain text file. You will be able to see precisely what you are writing out, header and body. And you will be able to see the error messages Python writes out when your code crashes. (Otherwise, you will have to watch Apache's error log file for them.)

Once the thing seems to be working, you will remove the `print` statements and let your CGI program write out its own header lines. If you are writing `text/html` content, you may still need to look at the information your program is getting. The `cgi` module provides functions to format and write out in HTML some of this information:

- `print_environ()` formats and writes the shell environment variables in HTML.
- `print_form(form)` prints the contents of the form in HTML where `form` is the `FieldStorage` you read from the input.
- `print_directory()` prints the current directory formatted in HTML, allowing you to check that you have gotten to the right directory and the right files are present.

Still, whatever you do, debugging CGI programs can be a real pain.

Summary

In this chapter we explored writing CGI programs, programs that are invoked by a Web server for forms the user submits, and possibly for other requests as well.

There are problems with installing CGI programs. There are problems debugging them. A lot of these come from the programs being installed in a directory away from your own home directory; the program being executed at the command of the Web server running as a user, nobody, without your privileges; and the programming running without the PATH variables being set properly.

The CGI programs themselves can receive the user's query in one of three forms: GET, POST URL-encoded, and POST multipart-form-encoded. Variables from the form may or may not be present and may or may not have multiple values. File uploads call for special handling so as not to load the entire file into memory at once.

Since each browser request is a separate interchange with the server, there is a problem remembering where you are in a communication, e.g., remembering what's in a shopping cart. You can use hidden fields or cookies to keep track of what has gone on before.

Problems

7.1 Modify the code in Figure 7–27 to submit a textarea rather than a file. Experiment with the wrap attribute and observe its effects under Netscape and Internet Explorer.

7.2 Use the HTML page of Figure 7–27 to submit a directory and to submit a file that doesn't exist. Observe what the CGI program gets.

7.3 Use a hidden field to maintain context.

7.4 Write a CGI program to send a zip (or gzip) file to the user. Provide an HTML page with a link that will cause the CGI program to send the file.

7.5 Reconsider the file submission program. (See "Example: File Submissions" on page 349.) Are the generated identification codes guaranteed to be unique? If there is reason to worry that they might not be, what can be done to make them so?

8

Database Essentials Featuring MySQL

In many respects, database technology has been one of the unsung heroes of the Internet. During the explosive period of growth of Web technology on the Internet, many Web proponents seemed almost content to ignore database technologies and many fundamental issues known to be important for a long time. Some went so far as to predict the eventual demise of database technology. Even now, many Web sites fail to understand the importance of issues such as data modeling, data integrity, and transactions.

This chapter will acquaint you with the basics of working with databases, with a focus on MySQL. We have chosen MySQL for this particular book, first because it is free and works on all platforms, including Linux and Windows. Second, it is relatively painless to administer: It is one of the easiest databases to set up and has reasonably good security. Third, it is pretty well supported in Python. For our readers who use Postgres, the code we discuss toward the end of this chapter will work with Postgres.

We'll begin with a discussion of database design principles. Then we'll discuss the basics of working with tables, followed by a discussion of how to use the WPL and Python database classes to interact with MySQL.

Entities and Relationships

An important first step in working with databases is to identify the key entities and relationships between them. This is quite often done as an afterthought, which creates havoc for the entire development team. The

Entity/Relationship (E/R) model was the first major framework to be proposed for doing basic database design, and remains one of the best due to its simplicity and minimalist focus. There are other modeling frameworks of notoriety, including the object/relational model and object-oriented data modeling. We definitely think these modeling techniques and associated technologies have a bright future but will not be covering those here. MySQL is a relational database, hence our focus on relational principles.

Before proceeding with a discussion of the building blocks of database design, it is worth noting that all design models in current use (e.g., UML) make use of concepts similar to entities and relationships. The E/R approach is focused primarily on modeling data and the relationships among data. It is not concerned so much with processing the data; this is a good thing.

Entities • Entities are the nouns in your database. For every thing in your system, there is more than likely going to be a table to represent that thing. Examples of entities include Customer, Supplier, Part, Product, and so on. As with object-oriented programming, some entities can have an intangible nature.

As with object-oriented programming, entities have *attributes*. Attributes are represented by a name and an associated type. In traditional relational modeling, the type system is not extensible and is limited primarily to primitive types (such as integer and float) and text.

What Are Relationships? • Relationships are the verbs in your database. Typically, relationships are only considered between any pair of entities. There are many examples of relationships. Employee "works for" a Department. Supplier "supplies" a Part. The concept of relationships is found in object-oriented programming as well.

Relationships in the entity/relationship model differ somewhat from the same notion found in object-oriented programming, specifically, in the modeling techniques. The relationships in OOP typically do not include attributes. In the E/R model, relationships can be decorated with attributes. For example, an Employee "works for" a Department for 40 hours per week. In a database, a relationship "works for" would appear as a table with fields for the Employee key field, the Department key field (both of which collectively form a key), and an additional field for the number of hours.

It is often claimed in the literature that advanced modeling techniques, such as UML, superseded the E/R model. We are not convinced.

Data modeling and object modeling really address different consider-ations: Object modeling is more concerned with behavioral aspects of a system; the E/R model is more concerned with information aspects of a system. These two aspects are not entirely *unrelated*, and each does its task well. We further note that if object modeling clearly supersedes data mod-eling, it is worth pondering why object databases have not superseded relational databases. In fact, object/relational databases (a hybrid approach) have also failed to make a significant impact in most practical database applications, leading us to believe that E/R modeling is still of great importance. E/R modeling is an important ingredient of good data-base design. By thinking about your data, you are likely to maintain a design that is both scalable and comprehensible.

Cardinality • Cardinality is an important aspect of all relationships in an E/R design. There are three general kinds of cardinality: 1 to 1 (one to one), 1 to N (one to many), and M to N (many to many). 1-to-1 and 1-to-N relationships are fairly straightforward to model. In a 1-to-1 rela-tionship, it is possible to avoid the creation of a table to maintain the relationship, provided there are no additional attributes. A table can make use of something called a foreign key to codify a relationship between two entities.

An employee working for a department is an example of a 1-to-1 relationship. If employee information were maintained in a table, a for-eign key could be used to refer uniquely to a specific department. If an employee works for many departments as in a 1-to-N relationship, how-ever, it will be necessary to create an additional entity to relate the employee to multiple departments. This intermediate table might be named "works for" and would have at least two attributes: the employee and the department key fields.

Many-to-many relationships present some difficulty when it comes to mapping an E/R diagram into relational database tables. In general, it is necessary to split such relationships into two (or more) one-to-many relationships. This is generally done by creating a *junction* table and then relating each of the tables for a given entity to the junction table by a one-to-many relationship. The junction table consists of a key field that comprises the keys of each table being linked by a one-to-many relationship.

In short, learning databases requires you ultimately to dedicate some time to modeling. It is possible to design databases and normalize them (something we will not be covering here) without knowing any of the theory; however, not knowing the theory will result in a database design that appears to have been done in an amateur fashion.

Some No-Nos • In database design, there are many techniques that are regarded to be bad form. Some of those we have observed that are particularly troublesome are:

- *Computed* columns are those where the value is derived from other column values; these account for major database bugs in practice. What looks like performance optimization will later will be your worst nightmare. In general, it is very difficult to protect against changes to fields and to guarantee that the computed field is recomputed.
- *Multivalued columns* are generally not considered to be good design. This is because a one-to-many relationship is being encoded in a single table, effectively breaking normalization. A better approach is to break out such columns into a separate table as described above.
- *Interpreted columns* are considered bad form. Sometimes, certain fields are used as flags or bitmasks. Sometimes comma-delimited data (such as CSV) are maintained to get around the need to partition one-to-many relationships. There is a disadvantage to this approach: The natural checking and validation provided by the database is lost.
- *Chains* are used as a work-around to the one-to-many problem. Effectively, a set of rows is linked to one another by having a foreign key that refers to the primary key of the same table. This is best solved by splitting into multiple tables.

Now we turn our attention to MySQL.

Getting Started with MySQL

Before we get into the basics of working with tables and using database queries, it is necessary to immerse oneself in some administrative activities. This is true of all databases. Despite MySQL's attempt to make it utterly simple and comprehensible, it still involves some pain, mostly with respect to access control. The intention here is to bootstrap a working database setup so we can get to the good stuff, which involves building a first database and being able to connect to it from Python.

Checking Your Installation and/or Installing MySQL

Linux uses the RPM system to install packages and to perform other package management functions. Recall that we encouraged you to compile, install, and configure Apache Web Server from scratch because of a number of distributions on the market that take excessive liberties with respect to configuration. Fortunately, this is not true of MySQL. You will want to use RPM to determine whether MySQL was already installed on your system and (if necessary) install from the mysql*.rpm files or do what was shown for Apache Web Server (install it from scratch).

To check whether it is installed, use RPM as follows:

```
$ rpm -q -a | grep mysql
```

If no lines of output are shown, MySQL is probably not installed on your system. If two lines are shown, it is probably installed correctly. MySQL is usually distributed as two RPM files, because the client tools and server are bundled as separate binaries. This might seem a bad idea at first but makes sense where an environment needs to run a server only on a single machine (or few machines), but needs the client and development tools installed everywhere.

If not installed, the RPM files need to be. These are usually found on the installation CD and can also be obtained from the Internet site of your favorite Linux vendor. Binary distributions are also provided on the MySQL home page at http://www.mysql.com. There are binaries for Linux as well as other operating systems, including Windows. We have actually used MySQL on Linux, Solaris, and Windows and can personally attest to the fact that it is a bona fide cross-platform database solution. If desired, source code is provided at the same site, allowing you to perform the installation from scratch.

Starting the Server

In order for MySQL to be used, you must start the server. This can be done in one of two ways, depending on how MySQL was installed. If it was installed from RPM, it is likely the case that an appropriate start script was copied into the `/etc/rc.d/init.d` directory. This is the best one could hope for; starting the server will be easy. As the root user,[1] run the `mysqld init` script:

```
# /etc/rc.d/init.d/mysqld start
```

If you cannot locate this script or a similar one, it will be necessary to find the MySQL installation directory (`/usr/local/mysql`, if MySQL is built from the source distribution). In the bin subdirectory, there is a script to be executed in order to start the server, which is named `safe_mysqld`. You will be tempted to run it, but wait. If you just built and installed MySQL from source, it is absolutely necessary to "seed" the database and get some initial access control entries. This is done with another script, named `mysqlinitdb`. Make sure this is done; otherwise, you cannot do anything.

```
# /usr/local/mysql/bin/mysqlinitdb
```

Then you can run the actual MySQL database server, `mysqld`. The "d" here signifies that the program is a daemon, which theoretically runs forever.

```
# /usr/local/mysql/bin/safe_mysqld &
```

You can set things up so the MySQL daemon will always be available upon system startup. The best way to do this, provided you are careful, is to put the following lines somewhere (near the bottom) of the `/etc/rc.d/rc.local` file:

```
if [ -f /usr/local/mysql/bin/safe_mysqld ]; then
     /usr/local/mysql/bin/safe_mysqld &
fi
```

There is a great temptation to just copy and paste the line into the file and assume everything will work. The single most common (and frustrating) mistake is to omit the & from the above fragment. In the case of the MySQL daemon, it blocks itself and waits forever. It needs to be run in the background.

---

1. In this chapter, we ask that you either be or are able to locate the system administrator (the root user). Once you have gotten things properly set up, it is possible to continue without being the root user, provided you create appropriate access control entries in the database.

If you are experienced in writing start/kill scripts, an alternative is to create a script in the /etc/rc.d/init.d directory.

Basic Administration

To do anything with MySQL, one must become familiar with basic database administration. Horror stories about database administration abound, mostly originating with enterprise-class database servers available at astronomical prices. These products have a great deal going for them, but ease of configuration is not one of their features. Luckily for the MySQL user, administrative complexity pales by comparison.

When MySQL is first set up, it must be possible to connect to it and manage it as the root user. On Unix systems, the database is pre-configured to allow the root user to log in without a password. After becoming the root user (with the su command as discussed earlier), you can do the following:

```
# mysql -u root
Welcome to the MySQL monitor.  Commands end with ; or \g.
Your MySQL connection id is 8 to server version: 3.23.28

Type 'help;' or '\h' for help. Type '\c' to clear the buffer
mysql>
```

If all has gone well, you will see a command prompt labeled mysql. This is an indication that you have been successfully authenticated and the monitor is now prepared to accept SQL statements.

Creating Your Own Account

The first thing you should do is to ensure you have an account. This is especially important if you are trying to convince a grumpy system administrator to install MySQL on a system where you will not have root privileges. And it is important that you get an account set up whereby you will have sufficient privileges to do basic database administration, which includes the ability to create databases and tables.

Once logged in as described in the preceding section, you will need to use the MySQL database to create some access control entries for yourself. The interesting aspect of MySQL is that it cleverly uses a database and tables within the database to address the issue of access control. It is particularly elegant and is much better than having to deal with flat files, as often required with other Unix services. Suppose your username is gkt. You need to do the following:

Choose the mysql database:

```
mysql> use mysql
Database changed
```

Create an entry in the user table:

```
mysql> INSERT INTO user VALUES (
-> '%','gkt',password('go.cubs'),
-> 'Y','Y','Y','Y','Y','Y','Y','Y','Y','Y','Y','Y','Y','Y');
```

We have intentionally entered this using multiple input lines to show you that SQL can be entered on multiple lines. When the SQL statement is terminated with a "`;`" the command is completed and will be fed into the SQL interpreter.

The above statement creates an entry for user gkt with an encrypted password 'go.cubs'. The % indicates that this user can log in from any host. The long string of Ys indicates what general privileges the user gkt has been given. Having set all of these columns to 'Y' gives user gkt all privileges to manage this instance of MySQL from any network host. This obviously is not secure but is okay if you are working on a private network. To tighten things up, you can replace % with a specific hostname (or pattern), as well as create entries involving IP numbers.

Finally, you need to force the server to reload the access control information. This is done by using the flush privileges statement:

```
mysql> flush privileges
```

You might want to open a second window on your terminal to test whether the privileges have been successfully applied. Do the following:

```
$ mysql -u gkt -p
password: go.cubs
```

You will want to replace gkt and go.cubs with the username and password of your choice. If permission is denied, you'll need to go back and check everything twice. Be sure you flushed the privilege information to force the server to reload privilege information and make use of it for authentication and other access control issues.

Creating Your Own Database

Once logged in, it is possible to create a database and make sure the privileges that have been assigned work as advertised. You should be able to create any number of databases, given the full privileges we enabled in the preceding section.

Creating a database is actually straightforward:

```
mysql> create database cubs2001
```

Aside from wishful thinking, this creates a database named cubs2001. A database is nothing more than a place where tables live. Where the tables live in terms of actual directories and files depends to a great extent on how MySQL was configured. When installed from RPM packages, the directory is usually /var/mysql; when building from scratch, it is /usr/local/mysql/var.

Once you have created a database, you are not done. The new database will be accessible to you; however, it may not be accessible to others. You will need to add entries to the user and db tables in the MySQL database.

Creating Some Sample Tables

Once you have created a database, you will want to create some initial database tables. We have actually gone through the pains of developing some actual databases that can be used with the portal applications covered toward the end of this book. You can download the dump file for our databases, which are named shop.sql and wiki.sql, from our book website.

Thus far we have been interacting with the mysql command line client. This client is much more than the typical dumb client found in some database systems. It supports a lot of features and can even do many useful database functions without even entering the monitor mode to interactively type SQL statements, etc. We show the use of the mysql client to create a database:

```
$ mysql -u gkt -e "create database gkt1"
```

Here is a sample (abbreviated) dump file, which was created using mysqldump --databases shop, where shop is the shopping portal database. We will use it to pipe a series of SQL statements to the MySQL client.

```
# MySQL dump 8.11
#
# Host: localhost    Database: shop
#-------------------------------------------------------
# Server version 3.23.28-gamma

#
# Current Database: shop
#

CREATE DATABASE /*!32312 IF NOT EXISTS*/ shop;

USE shop;

#
# Table structure for table 'adminuser'
#

CREATE TABLE adminuser (
  id int(11) NOT NULL auto_increment,
  username varchar(25),
  password varchar(25),
  PRIMARY KEY (id)
);

#
# Dumping data for table 'adminuser'
#

INSERT INTO adminuser VALUES (1,'shopper','shopper');

#
# Table structure for table 'customer'
#

CREATE TABLE customer (
  id int(11) NOT NULL auto_increment,
  first_name varchar(50),
  last_name varchar(50),
  street1 varchar(100),
  street2 varchar(100),
  city varchar(100),
  state varchar(100),
  country varchar(100),
  zip varchar(25),
  username varchar(50),
  password varchar(50),
  cc_number varchar(20),
  cc_exp_month char(2),
  cc_exp_year varchar(4),
```

```
    PRIMARY KEY (id)
);

#
# Dumping data for table 'customer'
#

INSERT INTO customer VALUES (1,'John','Shafaee','555 West
Madison','Suite
4003','Chicago','IL','US','60660','pshafae','pshafae','4111111111111111
','02','2002');
INSERT INTO customer VALUES (2,'George','Thiruvathukal','655 W. Irving
Park','','Chicago','IL','USA','60613','gkt','wnua95.5','373722222222222
','07','2005');

#
# Table structure for table 'product'
#

CREATE TABLE product (
  id int(11) NOT NULL auto_increment,
  product_id varchar(25) DEFAULT '' NOT NULL,
  name varchar(25),
  description text,
  price float(10,2),
  in_stock tinyint(4),
  img_link text,
  PRIMARY KEY (id),
  UNIQUE product_id (product_id)
);

#
# Dumping data for table 'product'
#

INSERT INTO product VALUES (9,'java.threads','High-Performance Java
Pla','Thomas W. Christopher, Evanston, Illinois\r\nGeorge K.
Thiruvathukal, Chicago, Illinois \r\nCopyright 2001, 432 pp.\r\nPaper
format\r\nISBN 0-13-016164-0\r\n',49.95,1,'<img src=\"http://
vig.prenhall.com/coverimage/0130161640.jpg\" border=1 hspace=0 vspace=0
alt=\"\">');

#
# Table structure for table 'transaction'
#

CREATE TABLE transaction (
  id int(11) NOT NULL auto_increment,
  date_and_time datetime,
  customer_id int(11),
```

```
  product_id varchar(50),
  quantity int(11),
  total float(10,2),
  PRIMARY KEY (id)
);


#
# Dumping data for table 'transaction'
#

INSERT INTO transaction VALUES (1,NULL,1,'ProdC1',4,55.25);
INSERT INTO transaction VALUES (2,'2001-03-20
03:22:52',2,'ProdC1',1,125.00);
```

This dump can be directly used to rebuild the database on your installation of MySQL by piping the content directly into the mysql client. This is done as follows:

```
$ cat shopdump.sql | mysql -u gkt
```

In the blink of an eye, a database has been created on your system and populated with some initial content. We are seeding you with a sample database that serves two important objectives:

- You can see at a glance how SQL is actually used. The dump file shows database creation, database selection, table creation, and a set of inserts into the various tables.
- It allows us to bootstrap you with some content to provide you a basic SQL primer and a "sandbox" where you can experiment with SQL and do some practice queries.

After the above command has been executed to bootstrap the database, it is important that it proceed without errors. Assuming that you have created a proper user and the user access control entry as we requested, there should be no errors. If no output is observed, the import was more than likely a success.

Of course, it is easy to check:

```
$ mysql -u gkt -p -e "show databases"
+----------+
| Database |
+----------+
| mysql    |
| shop     |
| test     |
+----------+
```

If shop does not appear in the list of databases, you'll have to go back and check everything. This is a showstopper.

It is also advisable to check whether the tables were created properly. This is done as follows:

```
mysql> use shop
mysql> show tables
```

This should show you a handful of tables:

```
mysql> use shop
Database changed
mysql> show tables;
+----------------+
| Tables_in_shop |
+----------------+
| adminuser      |
| customer       |
| product        |
| transaction    |
+----------------+
4 rows in set (0.00 sec)
```

The tables you see may vary; there should be at least one if the import was successful.

More Advanced Access Control

What we have covered thus far is ideal for doing Web development. In actual production environments, companies and organizations seldom expose their database systems to the outside world, making it possible more or less to stop here. This can be less than ideal in a medium-size to large organization, where the need-to-know rule may dictate that not necessarily everyone needs to know. There are other pragmatic considerations: The more people who have direct access to the database, the more likely database problems will occur. Databases are the lifeline of most companies and therefore one of their most protected assets.

For these reasons, it is necessary to think about security. Earlier, we did something that might not be best for your particular organization:

```
mysql> INSERT INTO user VALUES (
    -> '%','gkt',password('go.cubs'),
    -> 'Y','Y','Y','Y','Y','Y','Y','Y','Y','Y','Y','Y','Y','Y');
```

We wanted to get the process rolling without being saddled with all details of the MySQL privileges system. Now it is necessary to go into some detail about this.

The theory on which MySQL's privilege system is based is known in operating systems literature as *access control and capability lists*. This is very important in any security context. Many of the original ideas go as far back as the Hydra operating systems project, which introduced the notion of capabilities. In MySQL, every capability is named (usually as a column). Three tables are used in different situations to determine whether a particular user has access or not. The table rows themselves are being used to maintain the access control lists. It is a form of hierarchical access control, where the policies for access are actually layered as well.

The "user" Table • The user table meets two responsibilities: user authentication and general-purpose access control.

The user table has the following structure-based on a dump of the MySQL database schema:

```
Host char(60) DEFAULT '' NOT NULL,
User char(16) DEFAULT '' NOT NULL,
Password char(16) DEFAULT '' NOT NULL,
Select_priv enum('N','Y') DEFAULT 'N' NOT NULL,
Insert_priv enum('N','Y') DEFAULT 'N' NOT NULL,
Update_priv enum('N','Y') DEFAULT 'N' NOT NULL,
Delete_priv enum('N','Y') DEFAULT 'N' NOT NULL,
Create_priv enum('N','Y') DEFAULT 'N' NOT NULL,
Drop_priv enum('N','Y') DEFAULT 'N' NOT NULL,
Reload_priv enum('N','Y') DEFAULT 'N' NOT NULL,
Shutdown_priv enum('N','Y') DEFAULT 'N' NOT NULL,
Process_priv enum('N','Y') DEFAULT 'N' NOT NULL,
File_priv enum('N','Y') DEFAULT 'N' NOT NULL,
Grant_priv enum('N','Y') DEFAULT 'N' NOT NULL,
```

```
References_priv enum('N','Y') DEFAULT 'N' NOT NULL,
Index_priv enum('N','Y') DEFAULT 'N' NOT NULL,
Alter_priv enum('N','Y') DEFAULT 'N' NOT NULL,
```

MySQL uses a network-centric model for authentication. It is assumed that a user wants to access MySQL from a particular remote host. This allows credentials and privileges to be different based on each host from which a user is connecting. This strategy allows you to tighten up security in one respect: You can limit access from particular machines (say, developer machines). This will likely be important when you or a group are distributed across the Internet and jointly working on a Web project, as we happen to be doing.

Once a user is authenticated using the first three columns (Host, User, Password), the remaining columns indicate what capabilities the user will be enabled. These are general permissions that can be overridden by entries in the "db" table. Thus, it is best to think of entries in the "user" table as universal permissions that are applied.

There are many privileges. Select, insert, update, and delete all refer to the ability to issue the corresponding SQL statements (which all have the same keywords) on tables *within* databases. Create and drop privileges refer to the ability to create and drop entire databases. These privileges must be given out with care, as any user who has them essentially has the ability to instantly wipe out a collection of tables within a database. There are other privileges here, such as reload and shutdown, that are clearly the kind of superuser privileges almost nobody should ever have; we recommend setting all of these to N. There are other privileges that allow indices and table structure to be altered; these can safely be set to Y.

Note that for most options, the default policy is to disable all privileges. It is perfectly acceptable to do this as an administrator and grant specific permissions on a per-database basis. This has the net effect of creating more work for yourself in the long run, as it will be your responsibility to create entries anytime someone needs a database.

At this point we must say something about the way hostnames are specified. You can specify either the local name, the fully qualified name, or the IP number of a host. Wildcards may also be used to allow access from a collection of related hosts. The % can be used to indicate a sort of match-all condition, which should not be confused with the * of regular expressions. If % is used as the host name, the entry will match all hosts.

Let's take a look at a few cases, summarized in Table 8–1. For the purpose of this discussion, we will be considering hypothetical users named tc and pshafaee.

Table 8–1
User Table Administrative Cases

Case	SQL and Commentary

Power user `tc` on trusted network	`INSERT INTO user VALUES ('%','tc',password('cubs.2001'),`
	`'Y','Y','Y','Y','Y','Y','Y','Y','Y','Y','Y','Y','Y','Y');`
	
	This should only be done if you are keeping the database port 3305 totally unexposed on the Internet.

Power user `tc` on local host only	`INSERT INTO user VALUES`
	`('localhost','tc',password('cubs.2001'),`
	`'Y','Y','Y','Y','Y','Y','Y','Y','Y','Y','Y','Y','Y','Y');`
	`INSERT INTO user VALUES`
	`('127.0.0.1','tc',password('cubs.2001'),`
	`'Y','Y','Y','Y','Y','Y','Y','Y','Y','Y','Y','Y','Y','Y');`
	
	Why two entries? In some releases of MySQL, we have noticed that `localhost` and `127.0.0.1` seem to be confused for being different things.

General user `pshafaee` with no administrative functions, but able to perform most traditional queries on tables (local host only)	`INSERT INTO user (Host, User, Password,  Select_priv,`
	`Insert_priv, Update_priv, Delete_priv) VALUES`
	`('127.0.0.1','pshafaee',password('cubs.2001'),`
	`'Y','Y','Y','Y');`
	SQL allows you to specify just the columns to be inserted. The `values` clause must contain as many items as specified.

Same as previous case, but with the ability to access from anywhere in the local domain, `quillscape.com`	`'INSERT INTO user (Host, User, Password,  Select_priv,`
	`Insert_priv, Update_priv, Delete_priv) VALUES`
	`('%.quillscape.com','pshafaee',password('cubs.2001'),`
	`'Y','Y','Y','Y');`
	
	Note: We have observed that reverse DNS must be working correctly in order for this to work. If your reverse zone is not configured, you'll potentially need an entry as follows:
	
	`INSERT INTO user (Host, User, Password,  Select_priv,`
	`Insert_priv, Update_priv, Delete_priv) VALUES`
	`('192.168.%.%','pshafaee',password('cubs.2001'),`
	`'Y','Y','Y','Y');`

The user table is used to define a maximal set of privileges a user will have on the server. It is possible further to restrict these privileges by making entries in the other tables. Now we turn to a discussion of these other tables.

The "host" Table • The host table is used to limit access to specific hosts. It is very important to have proper entries in this table; otherwise, the "user" and "db" tables will appear to have no effect. If you refer to a hostname (or hostnames, when using a wildcard) it is necessary to have equivalent entries for every host that has been used in this table. It is strongly recommended that you have a catchall entry for %, which will allow access from any host, provided appropriate entries exist in the "user" and "db" tables. The general structure of the "host" table is shown in the following SQL create statement:

```
CREATE TABLE host (
Host char(60) DEFAULT '' NOT NULL,
Db char(64) DEFAULT '' NOT NULL,
Select_priv enum('N','Y') DEFAULT 'N' NOT NULL,
Insert_priv enum('N','Y') DEFAULT 'N' NOT NULL,
Update_priv enum('N','Y') DEFAULT 'N' NOT NULL,
Delete_priv enum('N','Y') DEFAULT 'N' NOT NULL,
Create_priv enum('N','Y') DEFAULT 'N' NOT NULL,
Drop_priv enum('N','Y') DEFAULT 'N' NOT NULL,
Grant_priv enum('N','Y') DEFAULT 'N' NOT NULL,
References_priv enum('N','Y') DEFAULT 'N' NOT NULL,
Index_priv enum('N','Y') DEFAULT 'N' NOT NULL,
Alter_priv enum('N','Y') DEFAULT 'N' NOT NULL,
PRIMARY KEY (Host,Db)
);
```

The "host" table has two important columns: Host and Db. Entries can be made for every Host and Db combination. As with the user table, you can configure general privileges to be applied.

The Db column can also make use of wildcards. This turns out to be a real time-saver, as our experience suggests that you do not want to put anything in the Db field beside %. This is because you can configure specific privileges for every combination of (User, Db) that typically should not be different based on the Host. In practice, this table typically consists of entries that are very restrictive. Basically, the rule of thumb is: Make an entry that allows access to any database from any host; the default policy is to allow no access and force MySQL to consult the Db table to determine the actual privileges.

In summary, the "host" table is essential for allowing databases to be accessed (regardless of which user is accessing them) from a number of hosts. It should be set up with very general entries for all hosts from which access would be needed, and it is essential that you provide a meaningful catchall entry as shown in the table. It is seldom desirable to maintain this table and it can end up creating a lot of headaches if set up incorrectly.

The "db" Table • The "db" table is what brings hosts, users, and databases together. This table is used to further restrict the operations that a particular user can do on a particular database. This table is very similar to the other two tables; we present its structure and a few cases for its use below:

```
Host char(60) DEFAULT '' NOT NULL,
Db char(64) DEFAULT '' NOT NULL,
User char(16) DEFAULT '' NOT NULL,
Select_priv enum('N','Y') DEFAULT 'N' NOT NULL,
Insert_priv enum('N','Y') DEFAULT 'N' NOT NULL,
Update_priv enum('N','Y') DEFAULT 'N' NOT NULL,
Delete_priv enum('N','Y') DEFAULT 'N' NOT NULL,
Create_priv enum('N','Y') DEFAULT 'N' NOT NULL,
Drop_priv enum('N','Y') DEFAULT 'N' NOT NULL,
Grant_priv enum('N','Y') DEFAULT 'N' NOT NULL,
  References_priv  enum('N','Y')  DEFAULT  'N'  NOT
NULL,
Index_priv enum('N','Y') DEFAULT 'N' NOT NULL,
Alter_priv enum('N','Y') DEFAULT 'N' NOT NULL,
```

In this table, you have the ability to create triples of (Host, User, Db) to restrict access. In practice, we use a wildcard for the Host, figuring that if an appropriate entry exists in the user table, there is no particularly good reason to further restrict access by the Host. Observe that the capabilities are the same for all tables.

A few cases are shown in Table 8–2.

Table 8–2
Database Table (db) Administrative Use Cases

Case	SQL and Commentary
Expand `pshafaee`'s privileges to allow full control over that user's own database	`INSERT INTO db VALUES ('%','pshafaee','pshafaee','Y','Y','Y','Y','Y','Y','Y','Y','Y','Y');` Recall from Table 8–1 that `pshafaee` was not a power user and was given fairly limited privileges. Here we can expand the privileges for the user's own database.
Similar, but use wildcards to match several database names	`INSERT INTO db VALUES ('%','pshafaee%','pshafaee','Y','Y','Y','Y','Y','Y','Y','Y','Y','Y');` Here, user `pshafaee` will have full control over any database with name beginning with `pshafaee`.

In any event, the access control framework of MySQL offers a great deal of flexibility. It is possible to exert coarse and fine-grain control as a database administrator. We stress that in a Web context it is more sensible to exert coarse-grain control, unless you are in a very large organization where there is a need to be obsessed with how many individuals are accessing the database.

We summarize by suggesting that you take a look at some of the classic operating systems textbooks, which cover access control lists and capability systems.[2] Such systems offer the most flexibility when it comes to security, but have seldom been used in operating systems since they were introduced, so it is good to see them reemerging on the computing scene. This flexibility must be managed very carefully. One of the major criticisms leveled against ACL schemes is the overhead of storing information. In a database there is typically little reason to care about overhead for storing this information. (If overhead matters more than convenience, you probably should be using a low-level programming library to access ISAM/VSAM files or some form of Persistent B-Tree, and not a database.) Nevertheless, it is imperative to keep the number of entries in the `host` and `user` tables to a minimum.

---

2. Silberschatz and Galvin provide an excellent starting point.

SQL Basics

SQL was designed to be a language that resembled natural languages as spoken by humans. Until the advent of programming, SQL in many respects was a shining example of how to design languages: The ideas were clear and the functions performed were coherent. It did not attempt to be a full programming language. Over time, as more and more purveyors of databases entered the fray, SQL began to evolve in different directions, with many de facto standards (e.g., Oracle's design) and few attempts to devise a coherent standard. This has resulted in a number of different SQL implementations; every database purveyor has some deviation from the SQL standard. The standard by which most databases swear compliance is ANSI SQL 92.

This section will cover SQL at a very basic level with clarifying examples. We will explore basic database manipulation statements, table manipulation, table query operations, join operations, and how to access table metadata.

Database Management Operations

Standard SQL provides direct support for creating and destroying databases. To create a database, the `create database` syntax is used:

```
mysql> create database database_name
```

The database name must be a valid identifier. Note that *database_name* must be a valid identifier as in Python, C, or Java, and that it will be handled in a case-insensitive manner. So databases named `gkt` and `GKT` refer to the same database.

While we are on the subject of case insensitivity, as a general rule SQL is mostly case-insensitive, so the actual SQL keywords can be typed in any case.

When a database is created, the effect is to create a totally separate namespace in which tables can be manipulated. We will cover these table manipulation operations in the next section.

Table Management Operations

General Table Principles • Most of SQL is dedicated to working with tables. The concept of tables comes from a ledger, wherein data are arranged as *rows* of data along named *columns*. Within a column, only a certain kind of datum may be placed, hence the notion of a *data type* is important to define what is permitted within a column.

Similarities with a typical ledger end with the essentials of rows and columns. Nonetheless, the analogy is still useful for introducing some other terms:

Nullable Columns • The concept of a nullable column allows the column to have no value instead of the type it is declared to hold. When do you need this? Consider a professor (who shall remain nameless) who has given an exam to a class of 40 students. A few students miss the exam and will probably not have a grade entered. A null value allows you to provide a value for the exam grade that makes it clear that no value has yet been assigned. An early mistake often made in database design is not making use of null values effectively. This results in arbitrary values (numbers such as "0" and "–1" are common for numeric fields) being used to indicate that the grade has not been entered yet.

Null values can be very helpful for formulating queries and for effectively using aggregate functions. Consider the quiz example again; suppose this same professor wants to report the average, max, and min for a quiz based on the data as it currently stands:

```
select avg(grade) from grade where name="quiz1" and grade not null;
select max(grade) from grade where name="quiz1" and grade not null;
select min(grade) from grade where name="quiz1" and grade not null;
```

These SQL queries show the power of aggregate functions, which work by taking all of the column values found in a particular selection of rows and applying the function to these values collectively. The use of null values makes such a query much cleaner than relying upon "flag values," which often are set incorrectly. In fact, as we'll see when discussing the `create statement` syntax, null values can be the default value for a field such as the "grade" field, which is a non-key field.

Keys • The notion of a key is very similar to the same notion found in a Python dictionary data structure. The difference in a database is that the key may actually be more than one column. Most databases do not have a notion of objects, so keys typically involve more than one field when it comes to the modeling of relationships between two or more entities.

Deciding what is or is not a key is part science and part art. In practice, it is difficult to find a set of keys that is unique when the entire spectrum of values is examined. And more often than not, a number of tables are created with a computed key field. Most sophisticated databases provide support to one degree or another for something called a key generator. This facility tends to travel by different names in databases. In MySQL, it is called an *auto-increment* type; in Postgres, the *serial* type. Whatever the type is named, it is indispensible for working with databases involving many tables and on a large scale and eliminates the need to invent your own arbitrary scheme for computing unique keys. Furthermore, due to concurrency issues, it is necessary to have a unique value assigned at the time of insertion that happens automatically. MySQL supports this notion via the INSERT SQL statement, which can be used to assign (and fetch) a unique key for a new row of data—all at once.

Basic Data Types

MySQL supports most of the primitive data types that you would expect to find in a programming language, and a few more interesting ones that would be nice additions to most programming languages, including Python. These types include:

- Integers
- Floating point values
- Fixed decimal values
- Text values
- Dates and times
- Blobs—very large objects
- Enumerations
- Sets

There are also many functions that can be used directly in SQL statements. We will address some of these later.

Integer Types • MySQL supports many forms of integer. The general form of the type is:

```
<int-type> ::= <type-name> [<display-size>] [ UNSIGNED ] [ ZEROFILL ]
<type-name> ::= TINYINT | SMALLINT | MEDIUMINT | INT | INTEGER | BIGINT
<display-size> ::= '(' num ')'
```

This fragment of BNF grammar says that an integer type is a type name, followed by an optional display size, followed by option modifiers UNSIGNED or ZEROFILL. There are several basic integer types, summarized in Table 8–3. The display size refers to how values are printed and has nothing to do with the precision of the data type. For information on precision, please see Table 8–3.

Integer types obviously prove to be very useful in database development, especially to support the auto-increment key concept discussed earlier. When relying upon integers for keys, use only unsigned values and the larger integer types. It is somewhat unfortunate, even if only from a theoretical point of view, that the BIGINT class is not of unlimited precision. This means that there is no real way to keep generating keys without having to worry some day.

What are the UNSIGNED and ZEROFILL qualifiers all about? C programmers will undoubedly recall that unsigned quantities are numbers without the sign bit being used. The net effect of using UNSIGNED

Table 8–3
The Integer Types of MySQL

Integer Type	Signed Range	Unsigned
TINYINT An 8-bit integer quantity (byte)	-128 .. 127	0 .. 255
SMALLINT A 16-bit integer quantity (short)	-32768 .. 32767	0 .. 65535
MEDIUMINT A 24-bit integer value (this is very curious)	-8388608 .. 8388607	0 .. 16777215
INT A 32-bit integer quantity (long)	-2147483648 .. 2147483647	0 .. 4294967295
INTEGER Same as INT	-2147483648 .. 2147483647	0 .. 4294967295
BIGINT A very large (but not infinitely large) integer	-9223372036854775808 .. 9223372036854775807.	0 .. 18446744073709551615

is to double the non-negative range of numbers and to eliminate the negative range. The notion of ZEROFILL has to do with formatting done when using SQL. It will result in numbers being padded with zeroes to fill the "width" of the column. We do not recommend using this option, as formatting information will be ignored when selecting rows in the Python program. Using ZEROFILL causes the integer to be treated as an UNSIGNED. A few integer types are shown in Table 8–4.

Table 8–4
Some Example Integer Type Declarations

Example	Explanation
INT	An integer quantity with no display width specified. By default, 11 is assigned in MySQL.
BIGINT	A large integer. By default, display width is 11.
INT(10)	An integer with display width of 10
INT(10) UNSIGNED	An unsigned integer with display width of 10

Floating Point Types • Floating point numbers also come in many flavors and sizes. Much like integer types, the ranges are limited to a finite size. Similar to the floating point types found in Python and on any given microprocessor, the precision (number of decimal places of accuracy) is also limited. The general form of a floating point number is summarized again using a BNF grammar:

```
<float-type> ::= <float-type-name> [ <precision> [, <display-width>] ] [ ZEROFILL ]
<float-type-name> ::= FLOAT | DOUBLE | DOUBLE PRECISION | REAL
```

There are only two kinds of floating point types (FLOAT and DOU-BLE), because the other two types are aliases for the DOUBLE type. These types are distinguished from another type, called a fixed decimal type, which gives you total control over size and precision; we will discuss it shortly. Table 8–5 summarizes the floating point types.

In general, if space is not a major consideration, use DOUBLE. It is the most general of the floating point types and the extra accuracy of the decimals is probably worth the overhead. Some examples are given in Table 8–6.

Table 8–5
Floating Point Types in MySQL

Float Type	Range
FLOAT	-3.402823466E+38 to -1.175494351E-38, 0, and 1.175494351E-38 to 3.402823466E+38 Note that if a FLOAT type is defined with a precision greater than 24, it is automatically treated as a DOUBLE. All floating point types are prohibited from being unsigned, which is an artifact of the IEEE standard for floating point.
DOUBLE	-1.7976931348623157E+308 to -2.2250738585072014E-308, 0, and 2.2250738585072014E-308 to 1.7976931348623157E+308 Note that FLOAT(precision > 24, *) is equivalent to DOUBLE(precision, *).
DOUBLE PRECISION	Alias for DOUBLE
REAL	Alias for DOUBLE
DECIMAL and NUMERIC	These are really just DOUBLE types in disguise. Although it is possible to specify the number of decimal positions, the types are implemented as DOUBLE precision and (thus) are subject to the same limitations.

Table 8–6
Example Floating Point Type Declarations

Example	Explanation
FLOAT(10)	Creates a floating point type with precision of 10 decimal places.
FLOAT(25)	Similar but with a precision of 25 decimal places.
FLOAT(10, 10)	Creates a floating point number with precision of 10 decimal places and display width of 10.
FLOAT(10, 25)	Similar to FLOAT(10,10) but with a display width of 25.

Table 8–6
Example Floating Point Type Declarations (Continued)

Example	Explanation
DOUBLE(10, 40)	Similar to FLOAT(10, 10) but DOUBLE precision and a display width of 40.
DOUBLE PRECISION (10, 25)	Same as DOUBLE(10, 40) with precision of 10 places and display width of 25.
REAL(10, 25)	Same as DOUBLE(10, 25) or DOUBLE PRECISION(10, 25).

Text Values • A number of types are dedicated for holding character data (text) as well as binary data (blobs). The text types are CHAR(n), VARCHAR(n), TINYTEXT, TEXT, MEDIUMTEXT, and LONGTEXT. As with integer types, the difference between one type and another is the maximum length of the text. CHAR(n) and VARCHAR(n) are for a fixed-length string and variable-length string, respectively, but are limited to "n" characters at most. The types are from the early SQL standard but are considerably less useful than the TEXT types for which the length need not be specified. TINYTEXT, TEXT, MEDIUMTEXT, and LONGTEXT can have as many characters as defined by the corresponding unsigned INT types (e.g., TINYTEXT can hold 255 characters, TEXT can hold 65,535 characters, etc.).

The blob types are named similarly and can be used to hold binary data. You will certainly want to know about blobs to store images and other binary data in the database. (Textual data can also be stored as blobs, which might be desirable if you are worried about international characters.)

Enumerations • Enumerations are used to provide a list of permitted values that are textual but actually stored as integers (at least internally). Enumerations are implemented internally as regular integers (the INT type) and can be used meaningfully in many numeric contexts, such as comparison.

Enumerations are defined as summarized in the following BNF rule:

```
<enum-type> ::= ENUM '(' <string-literal-list> ')'
<string-literal-list> ::= <string> { ',' <string> }*
```

Here is an example of an enumeration (shown earlier in the structure for the MySQL privilege system):

```
ENUM("Y","N")
```

This indicates that the values "Y" and "N" may be assigned in any column using this data type. Internally, "Y" is represented as 1, while "N" is represented as 2. It is unclear whether this mapping is really a good one to rely upon, as Boolean values such as yes and no (or true and false) tend to be assigned 1 and 0 in practice. There is no way actually to do this with the enumeration concept supported in MySQL, because all enumerations begin numbering the user-defined values in the `<string-listeral-list>` at 1. The empty string `""` is implicitly added to any defined enumeration with value 0.

One important note about enumerations: From the MySQL documentation, any column having an enumeration value cannot be directly obtained as an integer; you must use SQL to convert an enumeration value to an integer. SQL supports full arithmetic in the `SELECT` class, and it is a matter of taking the column name (having an enumeration type) and adding 0 to it.

Sets • A limited but potentially useful set type is supported in MySQL. The syntax for a set is similar to that of an enumeration and differs only in the presence of a `SET` keyword.

Sets are implemented as large integers internally, 64 bits in length. This means that a set consisting of 64 elements can be directly supported with this type.

The SQL syntax as supported in MySQL has been extended to accommodate the set type. Using the `FIND_IN_SET(member, column-having-set-type)` function, it is possible to test for set membership in a query.

As with enumerations, each value in an enumeration is assigned a set value. Suppose you wanted to use the set types to support the design of an access control framework with a number of capabilities. You might devise a scheme as shown in Table 8–7.

There is a fixed set of access privileges (or capabilities) that is available. These privileges are either set or not set for a particular user. The

Table 8–7
Example Use for the SET Type

User	Password	Access Rights
`gkt`	Encrypted text	`CreatePage, EditPage, DeletePage, ViewIndex, ViewPage`
`tc`	Encrypted text	`CreatePage, EditPage, ViewPage`
`pshafaee`	Encrypted text	`ViewPage, ViewIndex`

set concept allows you to use a single column (as shown in Table 8–7) to maintain the list of access privileges for each user.

Even the possibility of using a field to keep track of a set of capabilities goes squarely against something that is taught in most database courses regarding multivalued or computed fields. Without the set type, a column (probably of type integer) would have to be created for each capability. Although this would be cleaner database design, the storage overhead can be significant (one integer per capability) for a practical access control framework.

To support the access control scheme, a simple set type would be defined as follows, where all of the capabilities are listed:

```
SET("CreatePage","EditPage","ViewPage","DeletePage","ViewIndex")
```

As new capabilities are envisioned, as often occurs in practical applications, it is a matter of augmenting the set type with additional capabilities.

Date and Time

MySQL supports a number of column types that are used for maintaining date and time information. These types are summarized in Table 8–8. In the interest of keeping things basic, we will not say more about these types apart from the explanations of each given in the table. We will be making use of DATETIME in one of the portal applications, when more detail will be provided.

Table 8–8
Date Data Types

Date Data Type	Description and Commentary
DATETIME	The DATETIME column type is used for values for which complete date and time information, down to the second, is required. Only dates in the range 1/1/1000 to 12/31/9999 (one second before midnight) are supported. Dates outside this range might be allowed as entries, but may cause certain intrinsic functions that operate on dates to fail.
DATE	The DATE type is used when you need only a date value, without a time part, subject to the limitations of the DATETIME column type.
TIMESTAMP	The TIMESTAMP column type is used to mark INSERT and UPDATE operations automatically in the same format as the DATETIME column type. Only the first column defined to have a timestamp will actually be updated as the result of an INSERT or an UPDATE. We seldom offer strong opinions on features, but this is a data type you should not use at all. It is unlikely to be meaningful when there are concurrent updates going on, and it cannot be relied on in a transactional setting. It is unfortunate that this type has no qualifiers (e.g., INSERT TIMESTAMP, UPDATE TIMESTAMP, etc.) to allow each type of SQL operation to be timestamped separately. Avoid this like the plague; it could kill you.

Essential Table Operations in SQL

Armed with a summary of available data types and their reasons for existing, we proceed to a discussion of essential SQL. This discussion is very goal-oriented and is focused on the kinds of queries you are likely to perform when working with SQL. It is not intended to be complete, although we have striven to come up with a representative set of tasks you are likely to encounter.

Creating Tables (CREATE)

To do anything useful in SQL requires that a few tables have been created beforehand. The SQL CREATE statement is used to create database tables within a database. To create a table, it is necessary first to be *using* a database (the USE statement), which was introduced in our discussion of basic database management operations. The general form of the create statement is:

```
CREATE [TEMPORARY] TABLE [IF NOT EXISTS] tbl_name
[(create_definition,...)]
[table_options]
[select_statement]
```

The general form can be simplified a bit for the purpose of this discussion:

```
CREATE TABLE tbl_name [ (create_definition, ...)]
```

A create_definition is:

```
col_name type [NOT NULL | NULL] [DEFAULT default_value] [AUTO_INCREMENT]
[PRIMARY KEY] [reference_definition]
or PRIMARY KEY (index_col_name,...)
or KEY [index_name] (index_col_name,...)
or INDEX [index_name] (index_col_name,...)
or UNIQUE [INDEX] [index_name] (index_col_name,...)
or FULLTEXT [INDEX] [index_name] (index_col_name,...)
or [CONSTRAINT symbol] FOREIGN KEY index_name (index_col_name,...)
[reference_definition]
or CHECK (expr)
```

There are a lot of different ways to write a create_definition; however, only the first possibility is truly needed. We will focus on the clauses that address column definition, which is the essential building block for any interesting table:

```
col_name type [NOT NULL | NULL] [DEFAULT default_value]
```

Now we can put everything together to come up with a form of creation that will be useful for anything we have to do in this book:

```
CREATE TABLE tbl_name [ (create_definition, ...)]
```

A `create_definition` is:

```
[AUTO_INCREMENT]
[PRIMARY KEY] [reference_definition]
col_name type [NOT NULL | NULL] [DEFAULT default_value]
```

We have gone to this trouble to reduce the general syntax to this form in order to cover the basics of the SQL `create` statement, leaving many advanced features for further study. What exactly have we left out?

1. The `TEMPORARY` keyword used to create temporary tables. This has some practical value, but is not necessary for learning SQL.
2. Clauses related to indexing. It might look like we have done something bad by removing some clauses, but we only removed things that are not commonly used in SQL. We junked all clauses that related to indexing, important for optimizing and/or tuning database performance but not strictly necessary for learning to work with them effectively.
3. Some clauses related to integrity checking, which isn't supported in MySQL yet anyway.

Let's take a look at the `CREATE` statement in action. We will be making use only of the simple form that we derived from the general syntax presented in the MySQL manual. To summarize our derived syntax: A `CREATE` statement requires a `table_name` to be specified. Within the parentheses, we must have a series of `create_definitions`, each of which requires a column name, an optional nullable clause, and a default value clause. Note that "primary key" and "auto_increment" are considered to be separate `create` definitions. This is a bit odd, since these two clauses do not in fact create anything; they really refer to a previous occurrence of a column definition. So the parser for SQL must actually do some analysis to see whether the parsed list of `CREATE` definitions actually makes sense.[3]

Let us consider a practical example, which we will be using to demonstrate the power of SQL. It is a famous example from classic database books that will help later to illustrate some of the problems

---

3. It is a sad disconnect in computing history, but database implementors and language people could have worked a little harder to make sure their grammars were well written and didn't contain such blatantly context-sensitive constructs. Hopefully, examples will make this clear!

that arise in working with SQL table operations (in particular, updates and deletes). The example is a very simple one. There are three tables:

- Employee
- Department
- WorksFor

Employee has the following attributes:

- **id**–A unique identification code
- first, middle, and <u>last</u> names–All small text fields
- address1, address2, city, state, and zip code–More small text fields
- salary–A floating point number
- <u>gender</u>–Male or female

Department has the following attributes:

- **id**–A unique identification code
- <u>name</u>–Small text field to identify the department
- description–Medium text field to provide some additional detail
- <u>manager_id</u> – The employee who manages the department

WorksFor has the following attributes:

- **employee_id**–The id of an employee
- **department_id**–The id of a department
- hours–Number (int) of hours/week the employee is supposed to work for the department

This is a very simple example, so we did not go through the normal process of making an E/R diagram. For the moment, our goal is to get some basic tables created to be set up to do a tour of queries in SQL.

One thing to consider for each table is: What are the keys? In the case of Employee and Department, we assume there is an ID that can be guaranteed to be unique. This means that the id column in both Employee and Department will be a primary key in each of those tables. What about the WorksFor table? If you could assume that every Employee works for only one Department, it would be possible to use the Employee id as the key. Of course, that would defeat the purpose of having a separate table to maintain the WorksFor relationship (i.e., you would just have `dept_id` listed in Employee in this case). The combination of an `employee_id` and `department_id` will be sufficient to guarantee uniqueness of every row of data entered into the WorksFor table. We have indicated in bold all primary keys for each table.

Another aspect that must be considered is: What are the nullable fields? Additionally, should some fields have a default value associated with them in the event a null value is used? Key fields, by their nature, may not contain null values. In looking at what fields are allowed to be null, it is sometimes easier to consider what fields *should not* be null. We have underlined the fields that should not be null under any circumstances. We have only underlined a few things. In the Employee table, we require the last name to be present, because at least one name component is present for every individual out there. The gender field is also one that cannot be null. For department, we require that the name and the manager_id are not null.

Now we are in a position to write some SQL CREATE statements to do the work:

```
drop database introsql;
create database introsql;
use introsql;

create table Employee (
    id int auto_increment primary key,
    first tinytext,
    middle tinytext,
    last tinytext not null,
    address1 tinytext,
    address2 tinytext,
    city tinytext,
    state tinytext,
    zip tinytext,
    salary float,
    gender enum("male", "female") not null
);

create table Department (
    id int auto_increment primary key,
    name tinytext,
    description text,
    manager_id int not null
);

create table WorksFor (
    employee_id int not null,
    department_id int not null,
    hours int default 0,
    primary key (employee_id, department_id)
);
```

These SQL statements can be used to create the database just described. The syntax pretty much falls out of the hat, based on our simplification shown earlier. One thing to note is the WorksFor table, which requires a separate primary key clause to support the notion of multiple column names acting as a single key. It is a requirement of SQL that when multiple columns are used to form a key, the "not null" or "unique" clause appears. The difference between the two is that unique allows the possibility of a null value. We think that null values should be used sparingly, and never in keys. (In fact, we have intentionally omitted UNIQUE, which seems to be a kludge in the SQL standard.)

Once you have created the tables, it is a good idea to verify that both the database introsql and its tables have been created successfully. This was shown when we showed how to import the shop database from an SQL dump file (see "Creating Some Sample Tables" on page 369).

Populating Tables with Data (INSERT)

Once some tables are created, the next thing to do is to populate them with actual data. We will create a few Employees, Departments, and WorksFor entries. The INSERT statement is the primary mechanism that can be used to populate tables. In its basic form, one simply does:

```
INSERT INTO table_name VALUES (list-of-values);
```

We created a basic database with a number of employees working for a number of departments. Observe that the department table has references to managers in the manager_id column.

```
INSERT INTO department VALUES
(null,'Sales','The Sales Department',5);

INSERT INTO department VALUES
(null,'Technical Support','Technical Support Dept.',3);

INSERT INTO department VALUES
(null,'Domestic','Domestic issues, Cooking and Cleaning',1);

INSERT INTO employee VALUE
(null,'George','K','Thiruvathukal',
'1 Main Street',NULL,'Chicago','IL','60601',25000,'male');

INSERT INTO employee VALUES
(null,'George','J','Thiruvathukal','21 W. Elm Street',
```

```
NULL,'Chicago','IL','60606',28000,'male');

INSERT INTO employee VALUES (null,'Nina','A','Wilfred',
'1 Main Street',NULL,
'Chicago','IL','60601',100000,'female');

INSERT INTO employee VALUES (null,NULL,NULL,'Smith',
'1 Sunset Blvd',NULL,
'Hollywood','CA','90025',1e+007,'female');

INSERT INTO employee VALUES (null,NULL,NULL,'Jones',
'1 Eternal Place',
NULL,'Heaven','Universe','00000',1e+009,'female');

INSERT INTO worksfor VALUES (3,1,40);
INSERT INTO worksfor VALUES (4,1,40);
INSERT INTO worksfor VALUES (5,2,40);
```

As a result of this series of insertions, the database contains a number of entries that can be used to perform some interesting queries. As you can see, numeric data (literals) are handled in much the same way as in C or Python. String literals must be surrounded with single quotes. Quotes may be included within quotes using escapes, etc. In any event, reading the documentation will clarify the rules, if you are doing all of this interactively. If you use our database module within a Python program, the code takes care of all of the details of cleaning up text before performing an insert or interpolation operation. This gives you confidence that your database insert (or any other query) will proceed successfully.

How to Ensure Use of `auto_increment` • Before continuing, it is necessary to pause briefly to consider columns that have `auto_increment` type. First, such a column may occur once and only once in any table definition. In the `insert` statements shown for the employee and department tables, observe the boldface **null** reference. The use of a null value in an `auto_increment` column (id) results in the next unique integer (starting at 1) being assigned for that column's data. Note further that the `auto_increment` values are distinct for each table: Each table has a column named `id` with a unique `auto_increment` counter available to it. This is what makes it possible for employee and department id codes to be assigned uniquely for each table.

Selecting Rows

To retrieve a list of rows from a table requires the SELECT statement. This statement comes in many forms with many options. In its basic form you simply do one of:

```
SELECT column-list FROM tables WHERE conditions;
SELECT * FROM table WHERE condition;
```

The first form is used when you have specific columns to select from multiple tables, typically some form of a *join* operation. Joins are essential for doing just about anything interesting with databases (for more on joins, see "Performing a Basic Join on Two Tables" on page 407).

The second form is used typically when you wish to see the entire contents of a table. In the preceding section we created a set of tables.

Selecting All Rows and All Columns

```
mysql> select * from worksfor;
```

```
+-------------+---------------+-------+
| employee_id | department_id | hours |
+-------------+---------------+-------+
|           3 |             1 |    40 |
|           4 |             1 |    40 |
|           5 |             2 |    40 |
+-------------+---------------+-------+
```

Selecting All Rows and Specific Columns from One Table • To see this, break up the select into two different selects:

```
mysql> select employee.id, employee.name from employee;
```

```
+----+---------------+
| id | last          |
+----+---------------+
|  1 | Thiruvathukal |
|  2 | Thiruvathukal |
|  3 | Wilfred       |
|  4 | Smith         |
|  5 | Jones         |
+----+---------------+
5 rows in set (0.00 sec)
```

Selecting Columns from Multiple Tables

```
mysql> select employee.id, department.id, employee.last,
department.name from employee, department;
```

```
+----+----+---------------+-------------------+
| id | id | last          | name              |
+----+----+---------------+-------------------+
|  1 |  1 | Thiruvathukal | Sales             |
|  2 |  1 | Thiruvathukal | Sales             |
|  3 |  1 | Wilfred       | Sales             |
|  4 |  1 | Smith         | Sales             |
|  5 |  1 | Jones         | Sales             |
|  1 |  2 | Thiruvathukal | Technical Support |
|  2 |  2 | Thiruvathukal | Technical Support |
|  3 |  2 | Wilfred       | Technical Support |
|  4 |  2 | Smith         | Technical Support |
|  5 |  2 | Jones         | Technical Support |
|  1 |  3 | Thiruvathukal | Domestic          |
|  2 |  3 | Thiruvathukal | Domestic          |
|  3 |  3 | Wilfred       | Domestic          |
|  4 |  3 | Smith         | Domestic          |
|  5 |  3 | Jones         | Domestic          |
+----+----+---------------+-------------------+
15 rows in set (0.00 sec)
```

Recall that we had entered five names and three departments. What this query shows is the nature of selections involving multiple tables. This is called a Cartesian product. You will get the cross of all rows returned by selecting separately on employee and all rows returned by selecting separately on department.

To see this, break up the `select` into two different selects:

```
mysql> select employee.id, employee.name from employee;
```

```
+----+---------------+
| id | last          |
+----+---------------+
|  1 | Thiruvathukal |
|  2 | Thiruvathukal |
|  3 | Wilfred       |
|  4 | Smith         |
|  5 | Jones         |
+----+---------------+
5 rows in set (0.00 sec)
```

```
mysql> select department.id, department.name from
department;

+----+-------------------+
| id | name              |
+----+-------------------+
|  1 | Sales             |
|  2 | Technical Support |
|  3 | Domestic          |
+----+-------------------+
3 rows in set (0.00 sec)
```

You can observe that these two selections return five rows and three rows, respectively. When crossed together, the net effect is to return 15 rows.

The WHERE clause can be used to filter rows that are not of interest. The WHERE clause consists of a Boolean expression involving the names of the columns. For example, to select only employees having the last name "Thiruvathukal," you can do the following:

```
mysql> select id from employee where name =
'Thiruvathukal';

+----+---------------+
| id | last          |
+----+---------------+
|  1 | Thiruvathukal |
|  2 | Thiruvathukal |
+----+---------------+
2 rows in set (0.00 sec)
```

You are not limited to testing a single condition. Suppose you wanted to check for last names being Thiruvathukal or Wilfred. You can do this:

```
mysql> select id, last from employee where
last='Thiruvathukal' or last='Wilfred';

+----+---------------+
| id | last          |
+----+---------------+
|  1 | Thiruvathukal |
|  2 | Thiruvathukal |
|  3 | Wilfred       |
+----+---------------+
3 rows in set (0.00 sec)
```

Basically, most relational operators that you would expect to find for the purposes of comparison are provided. It is also possible to test against a set of values (not to be confused with the set type that was discussed earlier) instead of having to perform multiple tests for equality. This ends up being useful in many situations.

```
mysql> select id, last from employee
where last in ('Thiruvathukal','Wilfred','Beethoven');

+----+---------------+
| id | last          |
+----+---------------+
|  1 | Thiruvathukal |
|  2 | Thiruvathukal |
|  3 | Wilfred       |
+----+---------------+
3 rows in set (0.01 sec)
```

Observe that it is okay to test for membership in a set of values where some (if not all) are not present in the column being tested. Beethoven is clearly not present as a last name for any row; however, Thiruvathukal and Wilfred both are.

Grouping and Ordering

SELECT statements in SQL (and MySQL) may be qualified with ORDER BY and GROUP BY clauses. The ORDER BY clause allows you to establish an ordering of selected rows based on one or more columns.

We present just a few examples here. To see all employees in ascending alphabetical order:

```
select id, last from employee order by last;
```

The ASC and DESC modifiers can be used after each column being ordered to allow a mix of ascending and descending orderings to be chosen arbitrarily.

```
select id, last from employee order by last desc;
```

reverses the ordering.

```
mysql> select id, last, first from employee order by last
desc, first asc, middle desc;

+----+--------+--------+---------------+
| id | first  | middle | last          |
+----+--------+--------+---------------+
|  3 | Nina   | A      | Wilfred       |
|  1 | George | K      | Thiruvathukal |
|  2 | George | J      | Thiruvathukal |
|  4 | NULL   | NULL   | Smith         |
|  5 | NULL   | NULL   | Jones         |
+----+--------+--------+---------------+
5 rows in set (0.00 sec)
```

Here we order by last name in descending order. When two or more rows share a common last name, we order them by first name in ascending order. If two or more within this set share a common first name, they are further reordered using the middle name in descending order. This table is not necessarily indicative of the power of ORDER BY but does demonstrate that SQL is smart enough to get any ordering you would want.

GROUP BY is used to organize a set of rows based on a common column value. The key aspect to understand is that the notion of grouping does what you might expect. It presents the rows in such a way that each column value being grouped appears only once between the groups. It can be a bit unintuitive, so we'll consider a couple of examples. Let's take a look at what happens when we group all employees in a selection by last name:

```
mysql> select id, last from employee group by last;
+----+---------------+
| id | last          |
+----+---------------+
|  5 | Jones         |
|  4 | Smith         |
|  1 | Thiruvathukal |
|  3 | Wilfred       |
+----+---------------+
4 rows in set (0.01 sec)
```

Here you can observe that the employee having id 2 does not appear. This is because his last name is also Thiruvathukal. Now if another column is added to the selection, the salary, the value will only be shown for the employees you see here:

```
mysql> select id, last, salary from employee group by last;
+----+---------------+--------+
| id | last          | salary |
+----+---------------+--------+
|  5 | Jones         | 1e+009 |
|  4 | Smith         | 1e+007 |
|  1 | Thiruvathukal |  25000 |
|  3 | Wilfred       | 100000 |
+----+---------------+--------+
4 rows in set (0.01 sec)
```

None of this seems to be particularly useful—yet. The notion of grouping appears to have been created with the idea of preparing reports quickly. A concept that we have not introduced and only intend to cover briefly—aggregate functions—can be combined with this to do some powerful things without writing any code. Let's take a look at how an aggregate function can be used to show the sum of salaries *by group*:

```
mysql> select id, last, sum(salary) from employee group by
last;
+----+---------------+-------------+
| id | last          | sum(salary) |
+----+---------------+-------------+
|  5 | Jones         |  1000000000 |
|  4 | Smith         |    10000000 |
|  1 | Thiruvathukal |       53000 |
|  3 | Wilfred       |      100000 |
+----+---------------+-------------+
4 rows in set (0.00 sec)
```

What happens if you omit the GROUP BY clause from the above?

```
mysql> select id, last, sum(salary) from employee;
ERROR 1140: Mixing of GROUP columns
(MIN(),MAX(),COUNT()...) with no GROUP columns is illegal
if there is no GROUP BY clause
```

Updating Rows in a Table

The UPDATE statement is used to alter the contents of one or more rows and has the following general form:

```
UPDATE table-name
SET c1=e1, c2=e2, etc.
WHERE condition;
```

The WHERE clause is optional, as in an INSERT statement. The SET clause is used to indicate the names of columns that should be set to new values. In the general form, we mention e1, e2, etc., to indicate that any reasonable expression may occur here. Consider an example where we want to increase everyone's salary by 10%:

```
mysql> update employee
    -> set salary = salary * 1.10
```

We have already shown a number of examples where the old salary values were displayed, so we show just the new salaries here:

```
mysql> select id, first, middle, last, salary from
employee;
+----+--------+--------+---------------+----------+
| id | first  | middle | last          | salary   |
+----+--------+--------+---------------+----------+
|  1 | George | K      | Thiruvathukal |    27500 |
|  2 | George | J      | Thiruvathukal |    30800 |
|  3 | Nina   | A      | Wilfred       |   110000 |
|  4 | NULL   | NULL   | Smith         | 1.1e+007 |
|  5 | NULL   | NULL   | Jones         | 1.1e+009 |
+----+--------+--------+---------------+----------+
5 rows in set (0.00 sec)
```

One thing that may not be apparent from the general form is the ability to set the values along a particular column to a common value. Suppose we want to reset everyone's salary to $45,000. We could do the following:

```
mysql> update employee set salary=45000;
Query OK, 5 rows affected (0.01 sec)
Rows matched: 5  Changed: 5  Warnings: 0

mysql> select id, first, middle, last, salary from
employee;
+----+--------+--------+---------------+--------+
| id | first  | middle | last          | salary |
+----+--------+--------+---------------+--------+
|  1 | George | K      | Thiruvathukal |  45000 |
|  2 | George | J      | Thiruvathukal |  45000 |
|  3 | Nina   | A      | Wilfred       |  45000 |
|  4 | NULL   | NULL   | Smith         |  45000 |
|  5 | NULL   | NULL   | Jones         |  45000 |
+----+--------+--------+---------------+--------+
5 rows in set (0.01 sec)
```

Now everyone has the same salary. As mentioned in the discussion of the general syntax for UPDATE, you can also use a WHERE clause to restrict an update to certain rows. Suppose we want to change Jones's salary to $99,000. This can be achieved as follows:

```
mysql> update employee set salary=99000 where last='Jones';
Query OK, 1 row affected (0.00 sec)
Rows matched: 1   Changed: 1   Warnings: 0
```

We will not be showing the effect of every query. MySQL conveniently gives you useful information about whether an operation succeeded. Here you can see that one row was matched and that same row was changed as a result of the UPDATE query. If you are still not a believer, you can check Jones's salary.

```
mysql> select id, first, middle, last, salary from employee
where last='Jones';
+----+-------+--------+------+--------+
| id | first | middle | last | salary |
+----+-------+--------+------+--------+
|  5 | NULL  | NULL   | Jones| 99000  |
+----+-------+--------+------+--------+
1 row in set (0.00 sec)
```

If you set multiple columns in an UPDATE statement, be advised that the expressions in the SET clause are evaluated from left to right. Suppose you wanted to give each employee a 10% raise and a 5% bonus after the raise is factored in. You could do the following:

```
update employee set salary = salary * 1.10,
                    salary = salary * 1.05;
```

Functions

Functions may be used in many contexts in MySQL. They can be used in the SELECT clause to perform, say, a calculation involving the columns. They can also be used in the WHERE clause. As shown earlier, when performing an UPDATE, functions can even be used to compute a new value for a column. A special function, called an aggregate function, can be used to operate on all or a subset of rows (known as a group), typically using the values in a particular column.

In the interest of space, we will present just a few examples that should demonstrate the utility of functions. In MySQL, it is possible to extend these functions. Databases such as Postgres and Oracle support the notion of stored procedures, which can be used to provide custom functions that are evaluated using the database itself.

**Selections Involving a Function on One Row's Columns • ** Consider the employee example again. It would be nice if the names of all employees could be printed as a single column. For example, the component names George, K., and Thiruvathukal would all be concatenated to form a single name column when selected. A built-in function, CONCAT, can be used for this purpose. Let's take a look at how it works.

```
mysql> select concat(first, ' ', middle, ' ', last)
from employee;
+---------------------------------------+
| concat(first, ' ', middle, ' ', last) |
+---------------------------------------+
| George K Thiruvathukal                |
| George J Thiruvathukal                |
| Nina A Wilfred                        |
| NULL                                  |
| NULL                                  |
+---------------------------------------+
5 rows in set (0.01 sec)
```

The rows having non-null entries in the first, middle, and last names are all concatenated to form the "full name" of the various employees. Observe, however, that Smith and Jones end up being null. This is not quite what was intended. It is possible to get it right with a little research into other available functions.

```
mysql> select concat(
                ifnull(concat(first, ' '), ''),
                ifnull(concat(middle, ' '), ''),
                ifnull(last, ''))
        as full_name from employee;
+------------------------+
| full_name              |
+------------------------+
| George K Thiruvathukal |
| George J Thiruvathukal |
| Nina A Wilfred         |
| Smith                  |
| Jones                  |
+------------------------+
5 rows in set (0.00 sec)
```

Amazing but true, it is possible with the help of the ifnull() function in SQL. The way this function works is as follows. When the first value passed to it evaluates null, the second value will be returned as the value; otherwise, the first value itself is returned. Having learned in the first version of this that concat(*anything*, null) or concat(null, *anything*) returns null means that we can blindly attempt to concatenate the first and middle names with a blank space. If this result is null, then we return an empty string to be concatenated with the overall result. (If a name component is null, we don't want extra leading spaces to be introduced; this helps avoid the problem altogether.)

Aggregate Functions • Aggregate functions are functions that are applied to an entire selection of rows or a collection of rows selected with a GROUP BY clause. Let's take a look at such a function being used in a GROUP BY context:

```
mysql> select last, count(last) from employee group by
last;
+----------------+-------------+
| last           | count(last) |
+----------------+-------------+
| Jones          |           1 |
| Smith          |           1 |
| Thiruvathukal  |           2 |
| Wilfred        |           1 |
+----------------+-------------+
4 rows in set (0.01 sec)
```

This shows how to produce a report of the number of people having a particular last name. Observe that the function count(last) computes the number correctly for each group.

An aggregate function can also be applied to an entire selection of rows. We could use this to find the the salary of the highest-paid employee in the company at the moment:

```
mysql> select max(salary) from employee;
+-------------+
| max(salary) |
+-------------+
|       99000 |
+-------------+
1 row in set (0.00 sec)
```

Of course, this does not tell you the details about who the highest-paid employee is. And furthermore, the highest-paid employee might be *more than one* employee. Unfortunately, this is not very easy to achieve by relying exclusively on the SELECT syntax and aggregate functions, for two reasons. The first has to do with MySQL's omission of a *nested* SELECT statement, which allows a selection to be performed based on the result of another selection. The second reason is that aggregates cannot be used in the WHERE clause. Of course, there is a point at which it is unreasonable to expect the database to do something when a (better) programming language like Python is at your disposal. In Python, you can do the query to obtain the result of the aggregate function, save the result in a Python variable, and then issue another query to find the employee(s) having the salary.

There are many useful aggregate operators in MySQL (and standard SQL as well). They are summarized in Table 8–9.

Table 8–9
Some Commonly Used Aggregate Functions (Not an all-inclusive set)

Function	Description and Example

COUNT(expr)	Returns the number of rows for a particular expression where the expression is not null.
	`select COUNT(last) from employee where salary > 10000;`
	`select COUNT(last) from employee group by last;`

COUNT(DISTINCT expr,[expr...])	Returns the number of rows for a particular expression where the expression is not null and has a unique value. `select COUNT(DISTINCT last) from employee` will return the number of unique last names.
AVG(expr)	Returns the average of a particular expression. This is only applicable to numeric fields. `select avg(salary) from employee;`
MIN(expr) MAX(expr)	Returns the minimum or maximum of a given expression and is only applicable to numeric fields. `select min(salary), max(salary), avg(salary) from employee;`

Table 8–9
Some Commonly Used Aggregate Functions (Not an all-inclusive set) (Continued)

Function	Description and Example
SUM(expr)	Returns the sum of an expression. `select sum(salary) from employee`

STD(expr)
STDDEV(expr)
	Returns the standard deviation for an expression.
	`select avg(exam1), std(exam1) from`
	`student_grades;`

Performing a Basic Join on Two Tables

A join operation is used to merge two or more tables having common columns. The most basic form of join can be achieved using a SELECT statement involving two or more tables and a WHERE clause having a condition that performs a test on a common column name (or names). So the question is: Why do we need joins?

In the course of database development, a database design results in the identification of entities and relationships. A process called normalization results in tables that have very crisply defined functional dependencies, wherein (the lowdown) there are no transitive functional dependencies and the key is the only thing that functionally determines the rest of the columns in the table. This tends to work very well, but also presents a problem. Tables frequently should be combined to do anything useful, especially when it comes to reporting and presenting the information in a manner that is intuitive to the user (as opposed only to the database).

Let's consider an example. Earlier we constructed a department table that contains all information about a department. It also contains information about who manages the department. Now suppose we want to get a report of who this person actually is. In other words, we want to combine this result:

```
mysql> select id,name,manager_id from department;
+----+--------------------+------------+
| id | name               | manager_id |
+----+--------------------+------------+
|  1 | Sales              |          5 |
|  2 | Technical Support  |          3 |
|  3 | Domestic           |          1 |
+----+--------------------+------------+
3 rows in set (0.00 sec)
```

with this result, which was shown earlier:

```
mysql> select id, concat(
    ->                         ifnull(concat(first, ' '), ''),
    ->                         ifnull(concat(middle, ' '), ''),
    ->                         ifnull(last, ''))
    ->             as full_name from employee;
+----+------------------------+
| id | full_name              |
+----+------------------------+
|  1 | George K Thiruvathukal |
|  2 | George J Thiruvathukal |
|  3 | Nina A Wilfred         |
|  4 | Smith                  |
|  5 | Jones                  |
+----+------------------------+
5 rows in set (0.00 sec)
```

to produce a report of all departments and the full name of the managers who are managing the departments. It can be done using a `select` statement and doing an equality test on the id columns from each table, as follows:

```
mysql> select department.id,name, employee.id, concat(
    ->    ifnull(concat(first, ' '), ''), ifnull(concat(middle, ' '), ''),
    ->    ifnull(last, '')) as full_name from employee,department
    -> where employee.id = department.manager_id;

+----+-------------------+----+------------------------+
| id | name              | id | full_name              |
+----+-------------------+----+------------------------+
|  1 | Sales             |  5 | Jones                  |
|  2 | Technical Support |  3 | Nina A Wilfred         |
|  3 | Domestic          |  1 | George K Thiruvathukal |
+----+-------------------+----+------------------------+
3 rows in set (0.00 sec)
```

The use of a join operation is fundamental to working with SQL. Joins themselves happen frequently in the course of database development. In looking at the results of a join, it is clear that any selection performed on database tables itself appears to be a table. Many databases support the notion of a view, which is a special form of table definition that is based on a query. Views are a very powerful feature, but missing from MySQL. A view can be emulated using a special form of the CREATE statement (shown in the earlier syntax) known as a temporary table; however, this emulation is less than perfect. The notion of a view is one that is always coherent with respect to the underlying tables. Creating a temporary table in effect represents a cached view that must be regenerated every time a view is needed. Databases such as Postgres and Oracle support this notion.[4]

One issue to consider when working with joins is the potential for inefficiency. Joins performed in the manner shown happen quickly due to the small number of rows being present in each table, but as the number of rows increases, so does the cost of a join. MySQL claims to have a good optimizer; however, in the worst case, a join is handled purely as a cross-product of rows and the rows not satisfying the join condition are eliminated. MySQL and standard SQL both provide special syntax for more optimal join operations.

```
mysql> select table1.* from table1
LEFT JOIN table2 ON table1.id=table2.id
where table2.id is NULL;
```

such features of joins are likely to be important only in large applications.

Distinct Clause

When performing queries involving a projection of specific columns, it is possible to obtain what appear to be duplicate results. SQL provides standard syntax for coping with this: The DISTINCT modifier can be used to eliminate any duplicate results that are returned.

Suppose you want to generate a listing of all last names in the company. The DISTINCT clause can be used to eliminate any row in the selection that contains duplicates:

```
mysql> select first,last from employee;
+--------+---------------+
| first  | last          |
+--------+---------------+
| George | Thiruvathukal |
| George | Thiruvathukal |
| Nina   | Wilfred       |
| NULL   | Smith         |
| NULL   | Jones         |
+--------+---------------+
5 rows in set (0.00 sec)
```

---

4. MySQL allows you to get your foot in the door. More sophisticated features exist in other databases, but we think the balance of simple administration and configuration offsets the few missing features.

```
mysql> select distinct  first,last from employee;
+--------+---------------+
| first  | last          |
+--------+---------------+
| George | Thiruvathukal |
| Nina   | Wilfred       |
| NULL   | Smith         |
| NULL   | Jones         |
+--------+---------------+
4 rows in set (0.01 sec)
```

The distinct modifier is pretty clever. It is able to eliminate duplicates even when multiple columns are involved.

You need to exercise caution and not rely upon DISTINCT in general, especially when it comes to float and double column data. Floating point cannot precisely represent a floating point number; there is always an error term. Thus 2.0 and 2.0000000000000001 would not compare equally. You can pretty much count on text and integer data comparing properly (other types such as enumerations and sets are handled as integers), but should never rely on floating point comparison in any language when it comes to the equality test.

Column Aliasing

We have already taken the liberty of showing this in a number of examples. The AS clause is used in a SELECT statement to form an alias for a particular column. The intention of the AS clause is to provide a meaningful header when preparing the output. In MySQL it can also be used to give the column a label that will be returned correctly to Python as a record. We will be covering this in our discussion of the Record class, which is part of the WPL programming library.

Creating Temporary Tables

Temporary tables are a unique feature of MySQL that prove to be very useful. They can be created using the syntax that was shown earlier for the CREATE statement by adding the word TEMPORARY immediately following the CREATE keyword and defining the structure accordingly.

The most interesting use of this concept is to create a table based on a selection. The MySQL folks intimate the possibility of this feature one day supporting a view mechanism. This sneak preview allows the possibility of working with a copy of a table to see whether a query we want to do (such as an UPDATE or DELETE) will work properly. We will create a copy of the employee table:

```
mysql> create temporary table employee_clone select * from employee;
Query OK, 5 rows affected (0.04 sec)
Records: 5  Duplicates: 0  Warnings: 0
```

And we can determine whether it has the same structure using the DESCRIBE statement:

```
mysql> describe employee_clone;
```

This produces a fairly large table, which has not been copied here in the interest of keeping the presentation concise. You can do this yourself and verify that, indeed, the table descriptions are identical.

The nice thing about temporary tables is that they do not persist beyond the session; when the mysql command-line client is exited, the temporary tables are dropped. It is also worth noting that the result of any select statement can be turned into a temporary table. If you are creating a table such as the one we showed earlier in which all of the name components (first, middle, and last) were concatenated to form the full name, you must create an alias if you ever hope to access the column data. This is because MySQL will literally name the field after the expression you selected. To make this clear, here is the example again, this time selected and used to create a temporary table:

```
mysql> create table full_employee_names select id, concat(
    ->                        ifnull(concat(first, ' '), ''),
    ->                        ifnull(concat(middle, ' '), ''),
    ->                        ifnull(last, ''))
    ->            as full_name from employee;
Query OK, 5 rows affected (0.05 sec)
Records: 5  Duplicates: 0  Warnings: 0
```

And here is what happens when all records are selected from the temporary table full_employee_names:

```
mysql> select * from full_employee_names;
+----+------------------------+
| id | full_name              |
+----+------------------------+
|  1 | George K Thiruvathukal |
|  2 | George J Thiruvathukal |
|  3 | Nina A Wilfred         |
|  4 | Smith                  |
|  5 | Jones                  |
+----+------------------------+
5 rows in set (0.00 sec)
```

Here you can observe that everything has worked as intended! An interesting question is: What is the structure of this table, since it is more compact than the employee table itself? Let's take a look at the results of describing it:

```
mysql> desc full_employee_names;
+-----------+------------+------+-----+---------+-------+-----------------------
----------+
| Field     | Type       | Null | Key | Default | Extra | Privileges
          |
+-----------+------------+------+-----+---------+-------+-----------------------
----------+
| id        | int(11)    |      |     | 0       |       | select,insert,update,references
| full_name | mediumtext |      |     |         |       | select,insert,update,references
+-----------+------------+------+-----+---------+-------+-----------------------
----------+
2 rows in set (0.00 sec)
```

It is somewhat hard to see, as the output lines are longer than 80 characters and tend to wrap. The table description (correctly) has an `id` of `int` type and `full_name` as `mediumtext`.

Deleting Rows from a Table

This is an appropriate time to introduce the DELETE statement. This author is particularly conservative about deletions from a database, especially during development against a live database. The ability to create temporary tables allows one to copy all tables that are involved and work exclusively on copies. If something goes wrong, the copies can be regenerated from a known good state of the database tables until new code has been demonstrated (and tested) to work.

SQL supports deletion using the DELETE FROM clause. The DELETE FROM clause can only operate on a single table and has the following general form:

```
DELETE FROM table-name
WHERE condition;
```

The general form says that entries are deleted from a table where a condition applies. The WHERE clause (as in the SELECT and UPDATE statements) is optional and can be used to delete all rows.

We will work with a copy of the employee table as shown in the previous section. Let's delete all users having Thiruvathukal as the last name.

```
mysql> delete from employee_clone
       where last = 'Thiruvathukal';
Query OK, 2 rows affected (0.00 sec)
```

By now, we think you will believe us when we say that both of the entries have been deleted. We happen to know that there are only two such people in the database, and the output demonstrates that precisely two rows were affected, thereby deleting these two (unfortunate) employees from the company.

A Few Words about Referential Integrity • Referential integrity is a problem that arises in databases in a number of contexts. Typically it is the result of a deletion. In the interest of brevity and to keep the discussion focused, we do not cover it in detail. That said, it is important to us that you are aware of the problem and know that MySQL does not provide a framework for addressing it. We will ultimately leave it to you to decide whether referential integrity is a problem or whether you can make an intelligent design decision to address the issue.[5]

So what exactly is referential integrity? Let us consider again the world-famous example of an employee (with id E1) who works for a department (with id D1). One day, the employee decides to leave the company (a common occurrence). In one database design, the employee could be deleted from the database. What are the consequences? Well, if the employee E1 is removed from the employee table, any entries in the WorksFor table should also be cleaned up. In the case of the WorksFor table, there would be an entry for the foreign keys E1 and D1. Thus, this entry would be deleted. A database is said to follow referential integrity if, for any foreign keys, the key exists in the relevant table. Similarly, if a key is not present in a table (as is now the case with E1), there should be no table containing a row in which the key is used as a foreign key.

The conventional school of databases provides a wealth of theory on how to enforce referential integrity. One of the methods, which is found in Postgres, is known as a trigger. Triggers can be defined to automate the process (to some extent) of ensuring that referential integrity is maintained throughout the database. Triggers can be defined for any

---

5. We tend to be of the persuasion that deletions are something that should rarely be done in a database. For example, we would never delete an employee. Instead, we would mark an employee as *inactive*. Why? Because you might want to get information about that employee later. There are situations in which it is probably desired to delete something in a database; however, in our experience, these situations almost always can be replaced with a design that simply deactivates the record instead of deleting it.

kind of SQL statement, including `INSERT`, `UPDATE`, and `DELETE` statements. In the case of a `DELETE` statement, you can write a rule such as the following (expressed in pseudocode):

```
when deleting an employee E1 from the employee table,
delete entries from the worksfor table, where the employee = E1
```

This integrity rule, if you could write it in MySQL, would in fact guarantee referential integrity. But there is a real question: Is this something that you necessarily want? There are several reasons to believe in general that you might not want this:

- **Performance**: Integrity rules can result in a phenomenon known as the cascading of deletes (or cascading of any operation). In a cascade, an operation that you thought would take a short amount of time (as a delete normally does) ends up taking a long time. This is because a query is no longer performing a single operation. Instead, multiple operations are performed. In the preceding example, two delete operations are performed. In real databases, the number of operations could be significantly larger.
- **Loss of Important Information**: Integrity may be achieved but the information about the employee is lost forever (unless it was backed up). In the case of an employee, there are many reasons that you wouldn't want to actually delete him or her from the system, one of which is obvious: What if the employee comes back to work for the company again someday?
- **Semantics**: The semantics of the delete statement are no longer clear. This can make it very difficult to debug the database and any code that touches it. Furthermore, the general triggering mechanism allows you to define strange triggers. For example, you could define a trigger to insert an employee into the `old_employee` table upon deletion. Needless to say, confusion can abound.
- **Stored Procedures a Better Fit?**: When you think of what a trigger is, it is more like a procedure for "what to do when an employee is deleted from the database." Having a `delete_employee(emp)` procedure would be a better interface for users of a database than triggers, and doesn't suffer from the disadvantage of breaking the transparency of the `DELETE` (or any other) SQL operation.

So the issue is, how does one rework the employee-worksfor-department trinity of tables to make use of a passivation scheme instead of deletion? We summarize this below:

- Add a column to the employee table active with values 'yes' and 'no.' By default, any employee is created with active = 'yes.'
- On deletion, set active='no.' No other change is made to the employee's record.
- Now there is another interesting problem: How does one find the list of employees working for a particular department? The short answer is that a join must be performed with the employee table to check whether each employee in the department is active or not. For performance, an active column can be kept in each table using employee id as a foreign key. Of course, this is perhaps more bookkeeping than you want to do. For a small number of tables using a foreign key, performing the join is probably the way to go.

In short, referential integrity as a principle is something you should care about in designing a database. Whether you need the horsepower of a triggering mechanism (as found in Postgres or Oracle) or not is a subject of debate that has been raging for years. If after reading this you are convinced that you absolutely and positively cannot live with the argument presented here, we suggest that you migrate to Postgres or Oracle.

Null Testing in the WHERE Clause

One thing we have avoided up to this point is the ability to do null testing in a condition. The IS NULL and IS NOT NULL clauses can be used to perform a test for the null value (or a non-null) value in an query (INSERT, UPDATE, or DELETE). Suppose we wanted to see a report of employees who have single-word names:

```
mysql> select id, last from employee where first is null
and middle is null;
+----+---------+
| id | last    |
+----+---------+
|  4 | Smith   |
|  5 | Jones   |
+----+---------+
2 rows in set (0.42 sec)
```

As expected, only Jones and Smith show up in the list. Similarly, we can find a report of all people having all parts of a "typical" name present:

```
mysql> select id, concat(first, ' ', middle, ' ', last)
          from employee where first is not null
                    and middle is not null
                    and last is not null;
+----+--------------------------------------+
| id | concat(first, ' ', middle, ' ', last) |
+----+--------------------------------------+
|  1 | George K Thiruvathukal               |
|  2 | George J Thiruvathukal               |
|  3 | Nina A Wilfred                       |
+----+--------------------------------------+
3 rows in set (0.00 sec)
```

Clearly, the ability to test for nulls made the formatting of full names easier, because our call to `concat()` can now assume that everything being concatenated is not null and, therefore, we can safely assume that blank spaces should be included in the concatenated name.

Altering Table Structure

Feature creep is no stranger to database design. After settling into widespread use, questions arise such as, "How hard would it be to add a new field X1 to an existing table X?" Luckily, the ability to change a table's structure is supported as part of SQL and happens to work very well in MySQL, specifically. The ALTER TABLE syntax is used to support such alterations. We will cover the ALTER TABLE syntax briefly and present examples of the syntax that you are likely to use in practice.

The general syntax of the ALTER TABLE SQL statement looks like this:

```
ALTER [IGNORE] TABLE tbl_name alter_spec [, alter_spec ...]

alter_specification:
        ADD [COLUMN] create_definition [FIRST | AFTER column_name ]
  or    ADD [COLUMN] (create_definition, create_definition,...)
  or    ADD INDEX [index_name] (index_col_name,...)
  or    ADD PRIMARY KEY (index_col_name,...)
  or    ADD UNIQUE [index_name] (index_col_name,...)
  or    ADD FULLTEXT [index_name] (index_col_name,...)
  or    ADD [CONSTRAINT symbol] FOREIGN KEY index_name (index_col_name,...)
            [reference_definition]
  or    ALTER [COLUMN] col_name {SET DEFAULT literal | DROP DEFAULT}
  or    CHANGE [COLUMN] old_col_name create_definition
```

```
or      MODIFY [COLUMN] create_definition
or      DROP [COLUMN] col_name
or      DROP PRIMARY KEY
or      DROP INDEX index_name
or      RENAME [TO] new_tbl_name
or      ORDER BY col
or      table_options
```

It is obviously not a good idea to try to remember the exact syntax of this statement. Basically, the way to parse this definition is as follows. To alter a table, there are typically different kinds of alterations that are required. These are:

- Adding a Column (ADD clause): Take an existing table definition and add something that is not part of the current definition. The most common thing you might have to do in practice is to add a column to a table.

- Changing a Column (ALTER, CHANGE, or MODIFY clause): Take an existing column definition within a currently defined database table and change it in some way. It might seem silly to have keywords that all allow you to achieve the same (or a similar) result. Bear in mind that SQL was invented to be close to natural language. Often in the SQL syntax, you can find more than one way to "say" what you want done.

- Getting Rid of a Column (DROP clause): Remove something. You can remove column definitions, key information, and indexes (not covered in this chapter). Bear in mind that removing a column from a table definition also removes whatever data is presently in the table (for that column only). In general, such database changes should be made only if a mistake has been made during development, and almost never on a production system unless you are really sure you know what you are doing.

Consistent with the rest of our discussion thus far, syntax diagrams are not for everyone, and we provide a goal-oriented discussion of how to use the ALTER TABLE construct.

For the examples shown, you can assume that we'll be working with a new employee table named employee and defined as follows:

```
create table employee (
id int4 auto_increment primary key,
first text,
middle text,
last text);
```

In the examples presented, we may show the effects of altering a table. So here is a selection of all records that have been used to populate the table initially:

```
mysql> select * from employee;
+----+--------+--------+---------------+
| id | first  | middle | last          |
+----+--------+--------+---------------+
|  1 | George | K      | Thiruvathukal |
|  2 | George | J      | Thiruvathukal |
|  3 | Thomas | W      | Christopher   |
|  4 | John   | P      | Shafaee       |
|  5 | Nina   | A      | Wilfred       |
+----+--------+--------+---------------+
5 rows in set (0.00 sec)
```

Adding a Column • The first example to be considered is the addition of a single column, ssn (for Social Security number) to the employee table.

```
mysql> alter table employee add ssn varchar(9) after id;
Query OK, 5 rows affected (0.01 sec)
Records: 5  Duplicates: 0  Warnings: 0
```

This will add the column after the column named id in the employee table definition. Note that when the change is made (as with all changes covered in the remaining discussion), the existing rows of the table are revised to reflect the change made. The values for column ssn will all appear to be null, if no default value has been supplied in the creation clause [ADD COLUMN ssn VARCHAR(9)].

Here is the outcome of executing this statement:

```
mysql> select * from employee;
+----+------+--------+--------+---------------+
| id | ssn  | first  | middle | last          |
+----+------+--------+--------+---------------+
|  1 | NULL | George | K      | Thiruvathukal |
|  2 | NULL | George | J      | Thiruvathukal |
|  3 | NULL | Thomas | W      | Christopher   |
|  4 | NULL | John   | P      | Shafaee       |
|  5 | NULL | Nina   | A      | Wilfred       |
+----+------+--------+--------+---------------+
5 rows in set (0.00 sec)
```

To make `ssn` the first column, the following ALTER TABLE statement could be executed instead:

```
mysql> alter table employee add ssn varchar(9) first;
```

Here, `ssn` will become the first column. This is not shown, as the results would be similiar to the preceding example with the only difference being that the first column would be named `ssn` and would have NULL values listed.

Setting a Default Value for a Column • Often when creating a column definition, it becomes apparent that null values are not desired, as shown in the preceding example.

Let us alter the table definition so that the insertion of a null `ssn` will result in a default value being assigned:

```
mysql> alter table employee alter column ssn set default '000000000';
Query OK, 5 rows affected (0.01 sec)
Records: 5   Duplicates: 0   Warnings: 0
```

Assuming the following insertion takes place:

```
mysql> insert into employee (id,first,middle,last) values (null, 'Smith',null,null);
Query OK, 1 row affected (0.00 sec)

mysql> select * from employee
    -> ;
+----+-----------+---------+--------+---------------+
| id | ssn       | first   | middle | last          |
+----+-----------+---------+--------+---------------+
|  1 | NULL      | George  | K      | Thiruvathukal |
|  2 | NULL      | George  | J      | Thiruvathukal |
|  3 | NULL      | Thomas  | W      | Christopher   |
|  4 | NULL      | John    | P      | Shafaee       |
|  5 | NULL      | Nina    | A      | Wilfred       |
|  6 | 000000000 | Smith   | NULL   | NULL          |
+----+-----------+---------+--------+---------------+
6 rows in set (0.00 sec)
```

Observe that the new entry for Smith results in a default value being assigned for her `ssn`, because `ssn` now has a default value of `'000000000'`.

Of course, upon making this change, you realize that '000000000' is not exactly a reasonable Social Security number. In fact, the original decision to allow it to be null was more sensible. So you wish to turn it off. This is easily done by making the following table alteration:

```
mysql> alter table employee alter column ssn drop default;
Query OK, 6 rows affected (0.00 sec)
Records: 6  Duplicates: 0  Warnings: 0
```

This results in subsequent insertions into the employee table, where ssn is omitted or null, having null as the column value. Again in the interest of brevity, we assume this makes sense and proceed to examples of other features.

A Few Short Takes • There is quite a bit one can do with the table alteration syntax of SQL. Here we provide a few short takes on how some of the other syntax works, mostly by documenting a typical session at the mysql command prompt.

Let's get rid of the ssn column:

```
mysql> alter table employee drop column ssn;
Query OK, 7 rows affected (0.00 sec)
Records: 7  Duplicates: 0  Warnings: 0

mysql> select * from employee;
+----+---------+--------+---------------+
| id | first   | middle | last          |
+----+---------+--------+---------------+
|  1 | George  | K      | Thiruvathukal |
|  2 | George  | J      | Thiruvathukal |
|  3 | Thomas  | W      | Christopher   |
|  4 | John    | P      | Shafaee       |
|  5 | Nina    | A      | Wilfred       |
|  6 | Smith   | NULL   | NULL          |
+----+---------+--------+---------------+
6 rows in set (0.00 sec)
```

Let's add the ssn definition again and then perform a change to alter the name ssn to social and its definition from varchar(9) to varchar(11):

```
mysql> alter table employee add ssn varchar(9) after id;
Query OK, 6 rows affected (0.01 sec)
Records: 6  Duplicates: 0  Warnings: 0
```

Here is where we realize that we wanted `varchar(11)` to accommodate up to 11 characters (for the two hyphens in the Social Security number). We also use the `change` clause to completely change the definition. That is, we change the structure and the name as well, as follows:

```
mysql> alter table employee change ssn social varchar(11);
Query OK, 6 rows affected (0.00 sec)
Records: 6  Duplicates: 0  Warnings: 0
```

And here is what we get:

```
mysql> select * from employee;
+----+--------+--------+--------+---------------+
| id | social | first  | middle | last          |
+----+--------+--------+--------+---------------+
|  1 | NULL   | George | K      | Thiruvathukal |
|  2 | NULL   | George | J      | Thiruvathukal |
|  3 | NULL   | Thomas | W      | Christopher   |
|  4 | NULL   | John   | P      | Shafaee       |
|  5 | NULL   | Nina   | A      | Wilfred       |
|  6 | NULL   | Smith  | NULL   | NULL          |
+----+--------+--------+--------+---------------+
6 rows in set (0.00 sec)
```

After all the trouble, suppose we want to get rid of the column again. The following `alter` statement achieves this result:

```
mysql> alter table employee drop column social
    -> ;
```

As a final short take, suppose we want to rename the table from `employee` to `employees`. It is easy:

```
mysql> alter table employee rename to employees;
```

The `ALTER TABLE` statement can do much more than has been shown here. We encourage you to study it further to understand the more advanced features. This should cover most of the kinds of alterations you are likely to make when designing and implementing a serious database, all from the comfort and safety of the command line.

The WPL Database Classes

This section focuses only on making it easy to connect to one or more database providers using configuration files. The second aspect is support for record set processing in a manner that best utilizes the metaprogramming facilities of Python. The third aspect is to make it possible to connect to other providers, such as Postgres. It is our hope to participate in the Python database Special Interest Group (SIG) to make a number of these ideas become available to all database API's in Python; we have found them to be very useful, especially when migrating from one database provider to another.[6]

The Record Class

The `Record` class is one of the bread-and-butter classes of the WPL database module (`wpl.db`). The concept of a record is the same one encountered in most modern programming languages. It is based on the intrinsic `UserDict` class found in Python.

The notion of a record type was introduced in the Icon programming language:

```
record employee(id, first, middle, last)
```

Records in Icon could be created on demand as follows:

```
e := employee(100, "George", "K.", "Thiruvathukal")
```

This would create an employee record for which the fields id, first, middle, and last are initialized to the values 100, George, K., and Thiruvathukal, respectively. In addition to being able to define records, the fields of a record could appear freely on the left- and right-hand sides of assignment statements, as follows:

```
write("The writer's first name is", e.first)
e.id = 101
```

---

6. We have a number of activities planned in the area of database transparency; for the latest information, please visit our book's Web site.

One might be inclined to dismiss the record concept as nothing more than the Python class concept. And we would agree, were it not for a few issues:

- Most uses of a record abstraction have no need for the class concept.
- Using a class would require a definition mechanism (class) and an initialization mechanism [an __init__() method] each time a new record is to be made. This would be less than ideal, since much repetitive work needs to be done that could be achieved using a general-purpose class (which, we hope, will one day lead to a language extension).
- Records are easily implemented using dictionaries, anyway.

The notion of a record can be supported easily in Python by overloading the __getattr__() and __setattr__() methods. These methods are syntactic hooks that allow instances to access attributes (or fields) transparently. Here we have overloaded these methods to override access to the fields. Instead of providing access to the attributes defined in the class, we provide access to attributes found in the underlying dictionary. The general structure of the Record class is shown below.

```
1    class Record(UserDict):
2        def __init__(self,dict, read_only=1):
3            self.read_only = read_only
4            UserDict.__init__(self, dict)
5
6        def __getattr__(self,name):
7
8        def __setattr__(self, name, value):
9
10       def __repr__(self):
11
12       def __str__(self):
```

It is clear that the Record class is implemented as a proper subclass of UserDict. Subclasses of this class will be able to do whatever a UserDict can do, with the added ability to support the record features shown in the Icon example.

Records are constructed by specifying a dictionary reference and an optional read-only attribute. Read-only is the default policy, which means that fields in a record may be read but not written (mutated).

As mentioned, the methods __getattr__(self, name) and __setattr__(self, name, value) are key to building the Record class. These methods will be discussed shortly.

The constructor is straightforward. The UserDict superclass is initialized with the supplied dictionary dict, and the read_only flag is set.

```
1       def __init__(self,dict, read_only=1):
2               self.__read_only = read_only
3               UserDict.__init__(self, dict)
```

The __getattr__() method is defined as follows:

```
1       def __getattr__(self,name):
2               if self.data.has_key(name):
3                   return self.data[name]
4               else:
5                   raise AttributeError(name)
```

Implementing the __getattr__() method is fairly straightforward because of its semantics. The way it works is as follows. If name is found in the dictionary, return this value. Otherwise, raise an AttributeError exception. Now if __getattr__() returns an AttributeError, the name will still be looked up in the current object (self's) namespace. This turns out to be an important detail. When overriding __getattr__() and __setattr__(), it is possible to make a real mess of things. This will become more apparent as we discuss the __setattr__() method, shown below:

```
1       def __setattr__(self, name, value):
2           if name in ['data', '__read_only']:
3               if not self.__dict__.has_key('data'):
4                   self.__dict__[name] = value
5               elif not self.__dict__.has_key('__read_only'):
6                   self.__dict__[name] = value
7               else:
8                   raise AttributeError(name)
9           else:
10              self.__dict__[name] = value
11
12          if self.__dict__.has_key('data'):
13              if self.__dict__.has_key('read_only'):
14                  read_only = self.__dict__['__read_only']
15                  data_ref = self.__dict__['data']
16                  if read_only:
17                      return
18                  else:
19                      data_ref[name] = value
```

The __setattr__() method must be overridden with even greater care. Any mistake here can can leave you with the impression that Python has somehow gotten broken, when nothing could be further from the truth. The __setattr__() method is used to allow record-like assignments to be made (that is, rec.field = value). Allowing such assignments does present some challenges. First, overriding __setattr__() can prevent access to the object self altogether. The prime consideration is that the attributes data and __read_only must be accessible at all times in order for anything to work (e.g., data is the dictionary where all of the record's fields are stored.)

In lines 2–8, this code allows a one-time initialization of the data and __read_only attributes. Any subsequent attempt to change these attributes will result in an AttributeError. In fact, this allows the UserDict initializer to set the data field, after which this field cannot be modified. The else clause on lines 9–10 ensures that any attribute set is actually written to self. Note that this does not necessarily write through to the underlying dictionary (self.data); this depends on whether self.__read_only is set.

Before we complete the discussion of this method, note that self.__dict__ is used to access the fields of self. Why? The answer is not obvious. If you directly access any field of self at this point (e.g., self.data), big trouble will ensue. A recursive call will be made to __setattr__(), and it will not be long before Python reports that the stack space has been exhausted.

This discussion should make it clear why the code in lines 12–19 is treated so gingerly. The values are fetched from the dictionary and bound to local names, which liberates us from the effects of any potential __setattr__() recursion. After all that trouble, we simply test the local value of read_only and set the value in the underlying dictionary only if the self.__read_only flag is not set.

DataAccess

The DataAccess class is provided as a simplified interface to the underlying database APIs found in Python. Database support for Python is fairly extensive, primarily due to excellent C language support found in most databases. There is a special interest group (SIG) in Python that is dedicated to making database access ubiquitous (as ODBC is for Microsoft and JDBC is for Java). Our DataAccess framework exists only to simplify the current process of connecting to databases using the MySQL and Postgres programming interfaces and is not intended to be the all-inclusive and all-encompassing framework. We believe significant community effort and support of database vendors (both free and commercial) will be necessary to make this possible. Our framework addresses the following issues:

- **Configuration Files**: We are not advocates of hard-coding of any kind. The `DataAccess` framework processes configuration files to allow us to configure different databases (and providers) simply by updating a single (or multiple) clearly identifiable file(s).

- **Strategies**: A major advantage provided by JDBC is the notion of a driver, which is fundamentally an implementation of the *strategy* design pattern. Our use of strategies involved the identification of essential database functions and then using the MySQL (or Postgres) strategy to support the strategy.

- **Error Handling**: When working with different database strategies, we have noticed that different exceptions tend to percolate upward to the application code. This tends to make troubleshooting very difficult. As well, it is not desirable from an application programmer's perspective. Exceptions generated in the underlying database access module are caught and raised as more comprehensible exceptions. In our current implementation, regardless of whether MySQL or Postgres is used, a meaningful and consistent exception is thrown in both strategies whenever an exception occurs in the lower-level database access code.

- **Record Set (Result Set) Processing**: There is still a great deal of thrashing going on in the database driver development for Python. Some of the implementations provide record-like access to individual rows retrieved in a selection, while others provide no such access. For example, `e['first']` would be used to access the first name of a retrieved employee. The ability to support this access depends on access to database metadata, which is supported fully by all of the good databases (MySQL, Postgres, and Oracle). We have integrated support for the `Record` class (discussed in the immediately preceding section) with the `DataAccess` framework.

In the interest of brevity and due to continuing evolution of the Python database APIs, we show how to use our `DataAccess` without the in-depth coverage of the implementation provided in our other frameworks.

In order to use the `DataAccess` class, you must create a configuration file. This file allows you to supply the database connection information outside of the code itself. It also allows you to connect to more than one database by creating separate configuration files (not shown here).

```
[Database]
db=book2
user=root
host=127.0.0.1
password=root
mysqldb=MySQLdb
```

The syntax of this file is straightforward. It is actually the same as that used in the `ConfigParser` class, which is a standard Python module for supplying properties (similar to the Properties concept of Java). But in Python, the properties can be organized into sections (similar to the Windows `.ini` file concept). Here you are required to have a section named "Database" and supply the name of the database (`db`), the user name (`user`) and password (`password`) to connect to the database, and the hostname or IP# (`host`). Note that if your MySQL configuration is not running on the standard port for MySQL (3308), you can also specify the port number (`port`). The last property (`mysqldb`) indicates that Python's intrinsic `MySQLdb` module is to be used to interact with the database. Once this file is created, it is possible to connect to the database. We show this below and provide in-line explanations:

```
>>> from wpl.db.DBFactory import DataAccess
>>> db = DataAccess()
```

The `DataAccess` class is provided as part of the `wpl.db.DBFactory` module. Assuming that the configuration file has been created, no parameters need be passed to the constructor.

```
>>> db
MySQL Strategy -> db=book2 host=127.0.0.1 user=root
password=****
```

The above is what you should see if all has gone well. The most important thing to note is that "`MySQL Strategy`" or something equivalent must appear here. The rest of the information is basically what you saw in the configuration file. You won't see anything if an exception occurs when trying to connect.

Assuming this has gone well, let's try to issue some queries through the database:

```
>>> db.execute('show databases')
>>> for r in db.getRecords():
...     print r
```

Here we issue the query to show the databases and then use the getRecords() method to obtain the list of records (a record or result set), which are then iterated in a loop and printed. Observe the output below, which is written in an XML-like syntax.[7]

```
<Record>
 <Field name="Database" value="biztools"/>
</Record>
<Record>
 <Field name="Database" value="book2"/>
</Record>
<Record>
 <Field name="Database" value="wiki"/>
</Record>
<Record>
 <Field name="Database" value="wiki2"/>
</Record>
```

Here is a query that gets all of the employee records:

```
>>> db.execute("select * from employees")
>>> for e in db.getRecords(): print e
<Record>
 <Field name="first" value="George"/>
 <Field name="id" value="1"/>
 <Field name="last" value="Thiruvathukal"/>
 <Field name="middle" value="K"/>
</Record>
<Record>
 <Field name="first" value="George"/>
 <Field name="id" value="2"/>
 <Field name="last" value="Thiruvathukal"/>
 <Field name="middle" value="J"/>
</Record>
<Record>
 <Field name="first" value="Thomas"/>
 <Field name="id" value="3"/>
```

---

7. This is something still under development and, unfortunately, cannot be commented upon in detail. Please check the Web site to see our latest developments related to XML.

```
<Field name="last" value="Christopher"/>
<Field name="middle" value="W"/>
</Record>
<Record>
 <Field name="first" value="John"/>
 <Field name="id" value="4"/>
 <Field name="last" value="Shafaee"/>
 <Field name="middle" value="P"/>
</Record>
<Record>
 <Field name="first" value="Nina"/>
 <Field name="id" value="5"/>
 <Field name="last" value="Wilfred"/>
 <Field name="middle" value="A"/>
</Record>
<Record>
 <Field name="first" value="Smith"/>
 <Field name="id" value="6"/>
 <Field name="last" value="None"/>
 <Field name="middle" value="None"/>
</Record>
```

Note that each of these records can be examined just like a regular Python dictionary, as follows:

```
>>> r0 = db.getRecords()[0]
>>> r0
Record: {'first': 'George', 'id': 1, 'last':
'Thiruvathukal', 'middle': 'K'}
>>> print r0['first']
George
>>> print r0['id']
1
>>> for x in r0.keys():
...    print x, r0[x], type(r0[x])
...
first George <type 'string'>
id 1 <type 'int'>
last Thiruvathukal <type 'string'>
middle K <type 'string'>
```

In the above, r0 refers to the first record in the record set. When examining r0, observe the field names. They all match the column names used in the earlier employee table example. Each record returned by getRecords() looks like a Python dictionary object, so the fields of the record can be examined simply by using the dictionary interfaces. Subscript is used to obtain a field (r0['first'] gives the first field's value). `r0.keys()` returns all of the column names. Observe that the fields, when examined for their type, are converted to an appropriate Python type. `TEXT` and `VARCHAR(n)` are converted to Python `string` types; `INT` is converted to a Python `INT` type; and so on.

In summary, the WPL provides code for simplified database access. The process is simple: Make a configuration file, create the `DataAccess` instance, issue queries, and work with result sets. In the Slither applications chapter (and associated code), we will be showing interactions with databases via a `DataAccess` object. For all practical purposes, Slither application developers can connect to MySQL or Postgres databases without knowing the details of how the database API works. This is how it should be.

Summary

Databases no longer require you to spend all of your company's profits. This chapter has advised you of the importance of understanding the basics of database design and the potential pitfalls. We covered the use of MySQL from both a management and a usage perspective. Our approach focused on immersing you in actual database usage, rather than abstract rules and complicated examples. We concluded with an overview of our `Record` and `DataAccess` classes, which are supplied in the `wpl.db` module. These classes allow you to work with databases without having to understand all of the details of using the `MySQLdb` module, which provides you with a great deal of control but is also very much a work in progress. Using the supplied `wpl.db` module, you can do database processing in Python and MySQL without worrying about all of your code having to be rewritten later.

Part 2

WPL MODULES

odules are primarily what makes Python "Python." At first glance, one might be inclined to think, "So what? Modules are in every programming language. Python can't possibly be different." We beg to differ. The concept of a module in Python is cleverly integrated with the namespace theme that pervades the Python language design. This makes it very easy for you to "grow the language"[1] using either C or Python as the development language. We have stuck to using Python, but as you explore Python further, you will find that many of the intrinsic modules are actually written in C.

Here we will discover the WPL (Web Python Linux) modules. The name might appear strange. But when we first began discussing a possible book with our editor, Mary Franz, we talked about how great it would be if there were a Web book out there that focused on Linux and a "cool language" like Python. When coding actually began, we settled on WPL as the top-level namespace for our programming modules. The name stuck.

---

1. We first heard this term used by Guy Steele in a discussion about Java language features. He has even written a paper with this phrase in it's title.

9

Template Processing with the WriteProcessor

Web programming is mostly a story about processing text documents. Yes, we are just kidding–there really is more to it. However, a great deal of the complexity of Web development is attributable to having to deal with processing HTML on the server side and returning it to the client. More complexity is added when you consider the possibility of doing client-side scripting (used to make more "active" interfaces) and server-side scripting (usually to connect to your database and other enterprise-level services).

In this chapter, we talk about how to process text. In typical CGI programming, you will find by studying source code that most of the scripts are an incomprehensible blob of code. Compared to the old days of spaghetti codes (developed in BASIC, FORTRAN, and other languages), some of today's scripts (many in Perl) can give those old dusty deck applications a run for their money. The comprehension problem has much to do with the mentality that "There is no reason to clean up the code, since we are only going to use this once." The typical CGI script reads in the variables of a form, reads in some environment variables, and then does a mix of processing and HTML generation. In this chapter and the next, we will address how to do CGI programming with something called WebForm, which is a class library and design pattern for making CGI scripts.

Here we will focus on how to evolve a framework for generating the HTML. First we'll talk about the core language mechanisms of Python (even mentioning some things about Perl) for doing something called string interpolation. We'll address how string interpolation is a problematic mechanism, especially for working with HTML text, and then discuss the SimpleWriter class, which is designed to be a more sophisticated framework for string interpolation. Then we'll discuss the WriteProcessor, which is designed to augment SimpleWriter for use on entire files, working one line at a time. The WriteProcessor supports the ability to include other files, similar to what the C preprocessor (and other macroprocessors) can do. Additionally, the WriteProcessor has the ability to operate on a given input line multiple times. Finally, we will discuss the benefits of SimpleWriter and WriteProcessor that are not provided by relying on the built-in language features or `printf()`-like functions found in Perl and C.

String Interpolation

String interpolation is a dominant feature of the shell[1] and Perl programming languages that allows variables to appear in character string data and be substituted when the value of the string is needed. The term *interpolation* is found most commonly in mathematics and is usually used to estimate a value between two endpoints. Its use in programming languages is a bit of a misnomer, and we regret that it has come into common use. We prefer the term "interpretation" or "expansion," but will accept the fact that history has more to do with the meaning of the word than the definition itself.

Let's consider the essentials of how string interpolation is supported in these different environments, since much of what we will discuss in the SimpleWriter class owes a partial debt to what is found in the shell and Perl languages.

---

1. Whenever the term "shell" is mentioned in this book, we mean the Bourne, C, Korn, or Bourne-Again shells found in the various Unix operating systems. `bash`, the Bourne-Again shell, will be the shell of choice in this book.

The shell provides support for scalar and array variables. These variables can be defined at any time (just like Python) and can be used just about anywhere, most notably in strings.

```
x=25
print "The number $x is my favorite number."
```

If you were to run this example using the shell, you would see the following output:

```
The number 25 is my favorite number.
```

This represents a very simple example. It is done almost identically in Python with the interpolation operator (%).

```
x=25
print "The number %d is my favorite number." % (x)
```

The Python syntax is reminiscent of the C syntax for the `printf()` function, with a notable difference. In C it is possible to call the `printf()` function with the wrong number of arguments, resulting in a significant programming error and sometimes costing many minutes or hours of debugging effort. Languages such as Python (as well as the shell and Perl) are able to protect you because they have more control of the runtime environment. In the case of Python, the interpolation operator is able to check that the tuple expression on the right of the % matches the expectations of the string on the left of the %. In the example above, the %**d** is supposed to be paired up with a matching value that can be converted into an integer. (The %**d** indicates that the value is expected to be a **decimal** one.) There are myriad formatting characters available.

In any event, Python will throw an exception if one of two things happen:

- The number of elements in the tuple does not match what is expected. (In the example, at least one value is expected to appear.)
- The values mentioned in the tuple cannot be converted to the format that is expected.

Let's take a look at how the basic interpolation mechanism works in Python and how these two common errors are addressed.

```
1    Python 2.0b1 (#4, Sep  7 2000, 02:40:55) [MSC 32 bit (Intel)] on win32
2    Type "copyright", "credits" or "license" for more information.
3    IDLE 0.6 -- press F1 for help
4    >>> x=10
5    >>> y="This is a test."
6    >>> z="George"
7    >>>
8    >>> text = "Hi, %s, %s The magic number is %d" % (z, y, x)
9    >>> print text
10   Hi, George, This is a test. The magic number is 10
11   >>> text = "Hi, %s, %s The magic number is %d" % (z, y)
12   Traceback (innermost last):
13     File "<pyshell#6>", line 1, in ?
14       text = "Hi, %s, %s The magic number is %d" % (z, y)
15   TypeError: not enough arguments for format string
16   >>> extra  = 25
17   >>> text = "Hi, %s, %s The magic number is %d" % (z, y, x, extra)
18   Traceback (innermost last):
19     File "<pyshell#8>", line 1, in ?
20       text = "Hi, %s, %s The magic number is %d" % (z, y, x, extra)
21   TypeError: not all arguments converted
22   >>> text = "Hi, %s, %s The magic number is %d" % (z, y, y)
23   Traceback (innermost last):
24     File "<pyshell#9>", line 1, in ?
25       text = "Hi, %s, %s The magic number is %d" % (z, y, y)
26   TypeError: an integer is required
27   >>>
```

This is an interactive session with the Python interpreter. Each line of input and output is numbered; this allows for easy explanation of what is going on. Every attempt has been made to ensure that something being typed into the interpreter (usually at the >>> prompt) is set in boldface. Everything else (in particular, interpreter output) is set in normal type.

Here is a summary of what is happening above. (In this and all subsequent code examples in this book, we will make use of line numbers and explanations as shown below. It isn't possible to explain every nuance of every line, so we often explain a group of lines, saving explanations of individual lines for instances of significant complexity.)

4–6   Three variables are defined for the example: an integer (x) and two strings (y and z).

8   A string variable (text) is defined and interpolated. The %s, %s, and %d references are used to indicate how the values that appear in the tuple will be formatted. Variables y, z, and x are substituted.

9–10   This is what happens when all goes well. The string is formatted with all of the values that appeared in the tuple having been substituted successfully.

11–14   Here one of the elements of the tuple is removed, causing an exception because there are not enough values to be formatted. The same error in C would result in somewhat indeterminate behavior. In Python, the rules are very precise: You cannot perform an interpolation without the exact number of values.

17–21   Another safeguard built into Python's mechanism is the ability to ensure that every value that appears in the tuple has a matching format reference in the string on the left-hand side. We introduce a variable (extra) here to cause this to happen. Python politely informs us that not all of the arguments have been converted.

22–26   Finally, we complicate things a bit by trying to print something that cannot be printed as a decimal. This causes an appropriate error message that indicates that an integer is required.

A few comments are in order about the Python string interpolation mechanism. It is certainly an improvement over the same mechanism found in the C programming language. It is very safe and provides a great deal of runtime checking. That said, the basic form of Python string interpolation is not without disadvantages. It still has the flavor of C, since formatting codes (such as %s and %d) must be matched explicitly with values that can convert to those types. Unlike the shell and Perl, the basic form does not permit variables in the current scope to appear directly in the string. Many errors can still arise, because the values in the tuple may be inadvertently listed in the wrong order.

Python is able to overcome this limitation by allowing a *dictionary* to be the subject of the interpolation. Since the entire Python language is predicated on namespaces (which are dictionaries), this turns out to be a powerful improvement. The formatting sequences are augmented with the ability to make a reference to an entry (key) in the dictionary. Let's take a look at how the previous session can be written more elegantly using this capability.

```
1    >>> dict = { 'x' : 10, 'y' : 'This is a test.', 'z' : 'George' }
2    >>> text = "Hi, %(z)s, %(y)s The magic number is %(z)d." % dict
3    Traceback (innermost last):
4      File "<pyshell#20>", line 1, in ?
5        text = "Hi, %(z)s, %(y)s The magic number is %(z)d." % dict
6    TypeError: an integer is required
7    >>> text = "Hi, %(z)s, %(y)s The magic number is %(x)d." % dict
8    >>> print text
9    Hi, George, This is a test. The magic number is 10.
10   >>> del(dict['z'])
11   >>> dict
12   {'x': 10, 'y': 'This is a test.'}
13   >>> text = "Hi, %(z)s, %(y)s The magic number is %(x)d." % dict
14   Traceback (innermost last):
15     File "<pyshell#25>", line 1, in ?
16       text = "Hi, %(z)s, %(y)s The magic number is %(x)d." % dict
17   KeyError: z
18   >>> dict['z'] = 'John'
19   >>> text = "Hi, %(z)s, %(y)s The magic number is %(x)d." % dict
20   >>> print text
21   Hi, John, This is a test. The magic number is 10.
22   >>> dict['extra'] = 'Hippo'
23   >>> text = "Hi, %(z)s, %(y)s The magic number is %(x)d." % dict
24   >>> print text
25   Hi, John, This is a test. The magic number is 10.
```

1   A dictionary is created (dict) with the same entries as the variables we used in the previous example.

2   An interpolation is performed again. This time, the formatting codes are written differently: %(z)s, %(y)s, and %(z)d. This indicates that values z, y, and z are expected to appear in the dictionary (dict) and will be formatted as string, string, and integer, respectively. (Yes, the last item listed has been intentionally mistyped!)

3–5   An exception occurs because 'z' cannot be formatted as an integer. Notice that the exception is a bit disappointing. It would be nice if the exception more accurately indicated what caused the problem (e.g., name 'x' cannot be formatted '%d'– '%(x)d'.) Nevertheless, the error is still better than what C would have done in this situation.

3–6   TypeError is a built-in exception that is thrown due to a type not being convertible. String cannot be converted to integer without an explicit conversion.

7–9   The problem is corrected, resulting in a better outcome.

10–17 The name 'z' is removed from the dictionary and the same interpolation operation is performed. This time, the error message more clearly indicates what caused the problem.

18–21 The name 'z' is defined in the dictionary (`dict`) again, and everything works as it did before.

22–25 As in the previous example, we add a variable (`extra`). This time, the interpolation operation succeeds. At first, this might seem like a violation of the rules. As it turns out, this is a feature. We will talk about this when we consider a special dictionary in Python (available via the `vars()` built-in function).

This example demonstrates that the dictionary is the clearly superior way to work with string interpolation in Python. The potential for making errors is significantly lowered, as the formatting sequence and the name of the variable are part of the same syntax. That said, it still could be better; this flexibility came at a cost. A dictionary first had to be constructed; then the dictionary could be the subject of the interpolation operation. Certainly there must be a better way–luckily, there is. As mentioned, Python is a language built entirely around the concept of namespaces. As pointed out by the old gentleman in the movie *City Slickers*, in life you really need to go after that one thing.[2] Namespaces are central to Python. Let's take a look at how they work. Then we will return to interpolation and address how to avoid creating that dictionary (in what appears to be an unwanted step).

In Python, you are always working in a namespace. Let's take a look at how the namespace concept works when it comes to handling variables in a particular context.

---

2. What really makes a language great is the presence of that "one great thing." Consider the many languages before us today. Visual Basic introduced components. Perl introduced powerful reporting capabilities (and text processing). C introduced high-level syntax but had (and still has) a good mapping to the hardware to exploit performance. Languages that succeed have that one great thing that no other language does better, and Python has namespaces.

```
1     Python 2.0b1 (#4, Sep  7 2000, 02:40:55) [MSC 32 bit (Intel)] on win32
2     Type "copyright", "credits" or "license" for more information.
3     IDLE 0.6 -- press F1 for help
4     >>> vars()
5     {'__doc__': None, '__name__': '__main__', '__builtins__': <module
'__builtin__' (built-in)>}
6     >>>
7     >>> x = 25
8     >>> y = 35
9     >>> vars()
10    {'y': 35, '__doc__': None, 'x': 25, '__name__': '__main__',
'__builtins__': <module '__builtin__' (built-in)>}
11    >>> def min(a, b):
12            if a < b: return a
13            else: return b
14
15    >>> vars()
16    {'y': 35, '__doc__': None, 'min': <function min at 00A1A154>, 'x': 25,
'__name__': '__main__', '__builtins__': <module '__builtin__' (built-in)>}
17    >>> z = "George"
18    >>> vars()
19    {'__doc__': None, 'z': 'George', 'x': 25, 'y': 35, 'min': <function min
at 00A1A154>, '__builtins__': <module '__builtin__' (built-in)>,
'__name__': '__main__'}
```

4   vars() is a Python built-in function. It is a dictionary of name bindings for the current environment. When you start up the interpreter, the current environment is not completely empty. There are some bindings present: __name__, __doc__, and __builtins__. These are actually references to Python objects.

7–10   Variables are defined (x and y). The vars() function is called again. Notice that the original list of bindings is augmented with entries for x and y.

11–16   A function is defined (min) to show the effect on the environment. vars() is called again. This time, a new entry appears in the dictionary. Next to 'min' appears the textual "representation" of the function. Everything in Python is really an object. So when you 'def' a function, it is actually constructing an object (for all practical purposes, you can read "def min" as "min = create a function object").

17–19   Another variable is added to the environment.

This shows that just about everything being done in your Python program is effecting a change in the current namespace. The current namespace, always accessible via vars(), is in fact just a dictionary. Just look at what happens when vars() gets printed. (We did not call print() explicitly, since Python will always attempt to print anything that does not do an assignment but produces a result. It is permitted to do so, however, and would result in the same text being printed.) We have only shown the one-way usage for vars(); you can mutate existing variables or create new ones through a reference to vars() itself.

The first two sessions we have shown to do interpolation can be combined. We can assign the variables (x, y, z, etc.) and get a dictionary for the purpose of interpolation.

```
1     >>> x = 25
2     >>> y = 35
3     >>> vars()
4     {'y': 35, '__doc__': None, 'x': 25, '__name__': '__main__',
'__builtins__': <module '__builtin__' (built-in)>}
5     >>>
6     >>> def min(a, b):
7             if a < b: return a
8             else return b
9     >>> vars()
10    {'y': 35, '__doc__': None, 'min': <function min at 00A1A154>, 'x': 25,
'__name__': '__main__', '__builtins__': <module '__builtin__' (built-in)>}
11    >>> z = min(x, y)
12    >>> print "The minimum of %(x)d and %(y)d is %(z)d." % vars()
13    The minimum of 100 and 35 is 35.
```

1–10   This code was explained earlier. It has been copied to help avoid page turning.

11   The minimum function is called; the result is stored in 'z'.

12   Interpolation is performed on a dictionary: vars(). The variables x, y, and z have all been defined in the current environment. Therefore, calling vars() results in all of the current values for these variables being substituted.

13   It works like a charm.

That is all there is to string interpolation. As we have seen, there are two ways to use it: with tuples or with dictionaries. The method involving dictionaries is much better, because it is the closest thing you will find to being able to embed the variable name directly in the string (in Python). And the formatting codes can still be specified, much like printf(). It has not been explicitly stated until now: With Python, string interpolation and formatting take place on strings. You do not need to use the print() (or a printf() function) in order to take advantage of interpolation.

The ability to do string interpolation is essential to the development of Web applications. Although the introduction of XML is causing a transformation on the Web today, a great deal of Web development is still done by creating and/or generating HTML code directly, using CGI scripts.

Analysis of Python String Interpolation with Respect to the Web

The interpolation framework of Python is powerful for doing basic formatting of output. Problems arise when it comes to using this framework for Web programming.

The first problem pertains to the strict semantics of the interpolation mechanism. Any reference to a variable must appear in either the tuple or the dictionary. This is significantly different from how shell and Perl languages work, where a variable that has not been defined is assigned a default value. Of course, this owes much to how variables are defined. In the shell, all variables (by default) are of the string type. The meaningful default value for a variable is the empty string. In Perl, every variable is *typed.* That is, variables beginning with $x are scalars (assumed to be string). Variables beginning with @x are lists. Python does not have typed variables; all typing is done at runtime only. If a variable is undefined, any attempt to get its value results in a NameError, which means that the name could not be found in the current environment. In Web programming, especially CGI, this can be cumbersome when coding the logic for forms, wherein a form field is given either a default value or the value that was last filled in without errors.

A second problem with the interpolation mechanism is the lack of an object behind the formatting string itself. It would be nice to have the ability to "discover" information in the string, such as the variables that are used in the string, how they are to be formatted, etc. Unfortunately, this is not possible with the current syntax (at least not in a very programmer-friendly way) because it is not required to have a name behind a formatting sequence. For example, %d and %(x)d are both valid formatting options. The %d indicates that an integer is expected but does not require a specifically defined variable, as in the second form %(x)d. In fact, there is nothing that legislates that the value to be formatted must be a variable in the first case—it could be any Python expression that evaluates to an integer. Discovery is very important in the case of the Web, and it has much to do with why XML was created.

The final problem with the interpolation mechanism is that it is really intended to do formatting only. There is a very real need (related to the first problem) to have the ability to do conditional substitutions when it comes to text processing, especially when you want the ability to separate the business logic from the formatting of output. In many programming languages (the shell is just one of them), the variable syntax provides support for conditional evaluation. For example, the shell has the ability to test whether a variable is set. If not, a default value can be returned. There are many other features found in the shell variable syntax, such as pattern matching, etc.

Of course, the limitations of the Python interpolation mechanism are partly by design. Remembering the syntax of the shell and Perl languages is very difficult; going back to read programs written in these languages at a later point is even more difficult. (Python programs are very readable, because of its very lean syntax.) And being forced to do proper indenting of block structure makes it even more difficult to write a program that can be read and comprehended at a later date. The interpolation mechanism and the language itself are not perfect; you need to build a more sophisticated interpolation framework for Web programming. We have done just that by building the `WriteProcessor` Framework. As the intrinsic mechanism for interpolation has much to offer, we use it to delegate the work done by our interpolation framework.

SimpleWriter

The core of the WriteProcessor framework is the SimpleWriter class. The class was designed with a number of goals in mind:

- **Clarity**–A key requirement of design was that the mechanism must not leave open the possibility of being misused. For example, Python allows a formatting sequence to be specified without mentioning a variable name. While this is useful in some situations, it isn't good for the Web. Variable names always need to be mentioned to perform meaningful substitutions into templates.
- **Safety**–The interpolation mechanism in Python is very safe, despite the lack of clarity. SimpleWriter will not allow any undefined variable to be expanded. However, there is a key design difference. SimpleWriter variables can provide failure values (i.e., a value to be produced if the variable is either undefined or cannot be formatted) as part of a variable definition.
- **Formatting**–Formatting sequences are still permitted with exactly the same syntax permitted in Python string interpola-

tion. The difference is that formatting sequences may not opt out of listing the name of a variable that is expected.

- **Dictionary Enabling**–Interpolation always takes place against a dictionary, which we often choose to call an *environment* for evaluation of the string. The tuple syntax is not supported. (It is trivial to support it but we have yet to find compelling reasons for having it, and it does not mesh well with the first design goal, especially.)
- **Introspection**–At the heart of Python is the ability for everything within the language to be examined and altered. Introspection is the term (part of the vernacular of psychologists) that refers to the ability to look into oneself. The interpolation string, now an instance of SimpleWriter, has the ability to answer questions about itself, such as "What variables are defined in the string?" The knowledge of this can be very useful, especially when you have read the interpolated string from a file, which is the case when it comes to processing HTML templates.

These goals motivated the design of the SimpleWriter string interpolation framework. As it turns out, there were many other noble goals that were achieved as a consequence of addressing these.

Syntax

SimpleWriter variables have a syntax that appears to have originated with the Web. Variable definitions are surrounded with << and >>.[3] This does not prevent these characters from being included in the string, but may require the use of an escape sequence.[4] The general syntax is described by:

```
variable ::= << identifier [ % format ] [ | fail value ] >>
```

---

3. It is also permitted to specify alternative openers and closers, subject to our esthetics. We also permit [[and]] as well as {{ and }}.
4. When processing HTML fragments, < and > can be used to cause < and > to be displayed literally. The choice of << and >> is particularly appropriate for HTML, since << and >> do not correspond to any particular HTML markup tags.

This reads as: A variable definition is

- An opener `<<`
- Followed by an optional formatting sequence, which is `%` followed by Python's standard formatting characters
- Followed by an optional failure sequence, which is "`|`" followed by any characters
- Followed by the closer `>>`

The following represent a few valid examples of variables in the above syntax:

- `<<x>>`—Substitute the value of "x" if it is defined. Otherwise, an error occurs.
- `<<x|x is not defined>>`—Substitute the value of "x" if defined. If not defined, substitute the text following the "`|`", which is "`x is not defined.`" Quotes will not be substituted, only the content between the quotes.
- `<<x| >>`—Substitute the value of "x" if it is defined. If not, substitute the empty string. This is actually a special case of the preceding one and allows us to mimic the semantics of shell or Perl variables. Anything can be a failure value, because string interpolation always has the ultimate goal of producing text (i.e., character string data).
- `<<x%d>>`—Substitute the value of "x" if it is defined. Format the result as an integer. If it cannot be formatted, an attempt will be made to format it as a string. (We added this feature, since most Python objects can be converted to string using the `str()` and/ or `repr()` functions.) If neither conversion can be performed, an error occurs.
- You can combine the formatting and failover operators. Just keep in mind that the fail value is applied only if the variable is undefined and cannot be formatted according to the specified format or string. (The probability of both conversions not being possible in general is pretty minimal, so the fail value should only be expected when the variable is not defined.)

Basic Design

Let's take a look at the basic interface provided by the SimpleWriter. Then we will discuss the implementation of this class in detail.

```
1    import re
2
3    from Emitter import Emitter, ListEmitter
4    from UserDict import UserDict
5
6    class Variable(UserDict):
7            def __init__(self, dict):
8            def __str__(self):
9            __repr__ = __str__
10
11   class SimpleWriter:
12           def __init__(self, emitter=Emitter()): ...
13               self.emitter = Emitter()
14               self.wpPat = re.compile("""
15               self.defaultEmitter = Emitter()
16               self.rep = []
17               self.varList = []
18
19           def compile(self, line): ...
20           def evaluate(self, evalEnv): ...
21           def emit(self, evalEnv): ...
22           def getRep(self): ...
23           def getVars(self): ...
24           def hasVar(self, var): ...
25       def __repr__(self): ...
```

The SimpleWriter classes are all part of the SimpleWriter module, which is kept in SimpleWriter.py. The implementation comprises SimpleWriter, Variable, and Emitter (an implementation of the strategy design pattern, which allows the output to be generated to different destinations). SimpleWriter is the only class that needs to be mastered from a programmer's perspective, since it provides the entire API for doing string interpolation. Variable is a helper class that is used to keep track of each variable mentioned in the interpolated string.

The basic use of a SimpleWriter is very (pardon us) simple. An instance is constructed. Then the text for the string to be interpolated is passed to a compile method. This builds an internal representation for the interpolated string that can be used to do one or more evaluate()

or emit() operations. There are methods for discovery. getRep(), which is intended primarily for internal use, can be used to examine the low-level representation of the interpolated string. Think of it as the equivalent of an abstract representation (or intermediate representation) as found in a compiler but much simpler, since the input syntax is very simple compared to a typical language compiler. getVars() and has-Var() enable the discovery of variables that are defined in the interpolated string or determination of whether a particular variable is defined, respectively. The __repr__() method is intended only for printing the information about the SimpleWriter instance. If you print the representation, you'll notice that the output looks somewhat like XML.

SimpleWriter: The Details

Now let's take a look at the SimpleWriter class in greater detail. We will cover the most essential methods only.

First the constructor, __init__(self):

```
1    def __init__(self, emitter=Emitter()):
2        if isinstance(emitter, Emitter):
3          self.emitter = emitter
4        else:
5          self.emitter = Emitter()
6        self.wpPat = re.compile("""
7              <<
8              (?P<var>
9                 [A-Za-z_]
10                [A-Za-z_0-9]*?
11             )
12
13             (%
14             (?P<format>
15                .+?
16             )
17             )?
18             (\|
19             (?P<onfail>
20                .*?
21             )?
22             )?
23            >>
24          """, re.VERBOSE
25          )
26        self.rep = []
27        self.varList = []
```

1   The only parameter expected by the constructor is an `Emitter` instance. `Emitter` is the base class of a small hierarchy of similar classes that collectively implement something called an output strategy. Emitters exist for sending the output to strings, lists, and files.

2–5   This code ensures that a valid emitter has been passed to the constructor. If not, an Emitter instance will be explicitly constructed and maintained in `self.emitter`. `Emitter` (which is covered shortly) directs any output via the `emit()` method to standard output.

6–25   This is the regular expression (`self.wpPat`) used to extract variables from a string passed in a subsequent call to the `compile()` method. Those new to Python might find this verbose; it is actually a feature. Regular expressions tend to get unreadable quickly, and Python allows you to write them in verbose mode, which is indicated by the second parameter, `re.VERBOSE`.

7   This is the beginning of the regular expression (hereafter, regex). Match `<<`.

8–11   This part of the regex matches the identifier (the variable name), which follows the C/Python definition: at least one alphabetic, followed by zero or more alphanumeric. `(?P<var> expr )` is used to denote that the text matched by a regular expression `expr` is to be collected and made available later via a dictionary via the key **var**. (More on this when we discuss the `compile()` method.)

13–17   This part of the regex matches the optional formatting syntax. As long as the percent sign (`%`) is found, any positive number of characters will be consumed until the failure syntax (`|`) or the closer `>>` is encountered. How can you tell that this part of the regex is optional? The entire group has a ? after the parentheses on line 17. As in the previous chunk of regular expression, the text matching this part will be assigned to the key **format** in a dictionary.

18–22   The failure syntax is handled similarly. The pipe symbol (`|`), if present, requires the presence of zero or more characters before the closing `>>`. This text will be available later via the key `onfail` in a dictionary of match information.

23   This matches the closer `>>`.

26   `self.rep` maintains a list of elements in the "compiled" representation of an interpolated string. The compiled representation consists of substrings and `Variable` instances.

27   `self.varList` maintains the names of all variables that are found in the interpolated string. This will be important for discovering the variables that are present in a string.

A few words are in order about Python regular expressions. Perhaps the single greatest difficulty in working with regular expressions (the authors can attest to this problem) is the complexity of writing them: They tend to become congested quickly. With Python's triple-quote syntax for expressing multiline strings, it is possible to define one regular expression that spans many lines. This proves indispensible for comprehension. It is even permitted to put comments in the strings, which are stripped away, if present. (Since we were writing a book, we had better ways to present code via tables and actual paragraphs.)[5]

The "?" operator is used in a couple of different ways in this regular expression. Sometimes it is used to indicate something that is optional, e.g., the parentheses surrounding the format and failover syntax fragments of the regular expression. Sometimes the "?" operator is used to specify that a minimal match should be performed instead of a maximal one. The following is a good example of text that would be matched if we had left out the "?" after the "+" operator in the regular expression above:

`<<X>> <<Y>>`

A maximal[6] method would match ".+" (beginning with X and ending at Y) to consume everything from the first `<<` to the last `>>`. The reason: The dot (".") matches any character, including "<" or ">".

The first SimpleWriter method of interest, beyond the constructor, is the `compile()` method. This method is used to compile the interpolated string into an intermediate representaton (IR) that can subsequently be processed by calls to the `evaluate()` and/or `emit()` methods. The term *compile* might appear to be a misnomer, if you are thinking in terms of what a compiler normally does, but this term

---

5. If you are a student, we encourage you to develop good documentation and commenting skills early. If you are a practicing professional, we probably cannot change your habits, but want to help you become a master Python programmer. Documentation is your friend. Do it!

6. As part of our commitment, we have avoided the use of arcane or elevated language in this book. Some textbooks on compilers refer to the "maximal munch rule" when speaking about maximal matching of a regular expression.

proves quite useful to remind users of the famtlar step that must be performed before any meaningful interpolation can take place. If you look back at the constructor, you'll notice that even the regular expression (re) module makes use of a method named compile() that must be called before you can make meaningful use of a regular expression.

Here is what is going on in code for the compile() method.

```
1    def compile(self, line):
2        self.rep = []
3        self.varList = []
4        pos = 0
5        while 1:
6            matched = self.wpPat.search(line, pos)
7            if not matched:
8                self.rep.append(line[pos:])
9                break
10           var = matched.group('var')
11           self.varList.append(var)
12           textBefore = line[pos:matched.start()]
13           self.rep.append(textBefore)
14           self.rep.append(Variable(matched.groupdict()))
15           pos = matched.end()
```

1   The lone parameter (line) refers to the text containing variables for interpolation.

2–3   The member variables, self.rep and self.varList, are both initialized to empty lists. These variables were initalized in the constructor. Nonetheless, they are reinitialized every time, since compile() always reconstructs the representation from scratch. This design makes it possible to reuse the same SimpleWriter instance to perform multiple interpolations and change the string whenever desired.

4   Start trying to match variables from the beginning of the string. pos will keep track of the last position following the end of a discovered match, initially 0.

5   This is the beginning of the loop to match all occurrences of variables (i.e., things beginning with << and ending with >>). Recall that self.wpPat contains the compiled regular expression to match the variable syntax.

6	Use the regular expression, `self.wpPat`, to match the variable syntax. Here we are trying to match the line of text starting at position `pos`. The `search()` method is used, which offers a great deal of flexibility—as the string need not match exactly at `pos` but may match later or not at all. One of two possible values is returned: a "match object" or None.
7–9	If a match could not be found, we grab the substring all the way from `pos` to the end of the string and save it in the IR (`self.rep`).
10–11	Otherwise, there was a match. We need to extract the information about the match from the match object returned. `matched.group('var')` returns the name of the variable in the interpolated string.
12–13	This collects the text that appeared before the position where the variable was found. Python makes this very easy with its slicing operation. We just take everything from `pos` up to but not including `matched.start()`, which tells the position in the string where the matched text begins. This string is added to the representation.
14	The information about the match is kept in a dictionary. Recall that in the regular expression `self.wpPat`, created in the constructor, we made references to groups named `var`, `format`, and `onfail`. The parts of the regular expression that were matched by the variable are each assigned to names in the dictionary, which is available via the match object's `groupdict()` method.
15	`pos` is set to the end position of the matched text, which is found simply via the `end()` method in the match object. This will allow the next search to be conducted at the top of the loop, beginning at the position immediately following the last matched interpolated string variable.

It is worth stopping for a second just to see how things work, focusing on constructing the instance and invoking the `compile` method. Let's use the Python interpreter to load the SimpleWriter, create an instance of `SimpleWriter` (the class), and see what happens:

```
1    >>> import SimpleWriter
2    >>> sw = SimpleWriter.SimpleWriter()
3    >>> sw.compile('This <<x>> is a test of <<y>>')
4    >>> sw.rep
5    ['This ', <<x>>, ' is a test of ', <<y>>, '']
6    >>> sw.varList
7    ['x', 'y']
8    >>> for part in sw.rep:
9    ...     print part, type(part)
10   This   <type 'string'>
11   <<x>>  <type 'instance'>
12    is a test of   <type 'string'>
13   <<y>>  <type 'instance'>
14    <type 'string'>
15   >>>
```

1–2   Import SimpleWriter module (`SimpleWriter.py`) and create an instance.

3   Here we call SimpleWriter's `compile()` method. Observe that the string being passed contains the interpolation variables `<<x>>` and `<<y>>`.

4–5   `sw.rep` is accessing the intermediate representation of the object `sw` directly. This might seem like a really rotten thing, as most textbooks on object-oriented programming (OOP) tend to discourage direct access to "private" data from within an object. Python does not have private and public access to attributes; we seldom will access object variables, except to show the effect of something in an interpreter session. (You can verify this by noticing the `getRep()` method to return the private variable to a client of SimpleWriter objects.) `sw.rep` is just a list. It contains a mix of strings and `Variable` instances.

6–7   `sw.varList` shows the variables that were extracted from the string. As expected, the variables "x" and "y" appear.

8–15   This loop over the representation, `sw.rep`, demonstrates that the representation consists of a mix of strings and objects (instances). Although everything in the list appears to be a string, you should not be fooled, as what is being shown is actually the string representation of an object. Those familar with Java may have seen the `toString()` method to print the representation of an object. Python has the `__str__()` method, which will result in an object's being converted to string in situations such as this where an object x needs to be printed. When `print` is called, Python invokes `str(x)` to get the string representation of the object. In most of our classes you'll notice the use of `__str__()` to create a printable representation of an object.

Python does a lot with very little code. This makes it particularly suitable for rapid prototyping. You can do most of your coding in interpreter sessions, building up small fragments that do powerful things. Then you can paste your code into the editor and turn it into a module–easily. Debugging is a word that Python programmers seldom find themselves using in day-to-day conversation, since most of the code can be tested interactively and incrementally, leading to modules of classes and functions that just plain work.

Let's continue with a discussion of the remaining functions in the `SimpleWriter` class. Thus far we have only considered the constructor and the `compile()` methods. The constructor is used to construct an object that can do a series of string interpolations, if desired. The `compile()` method allows the user to define a different string to be used for one or more string interpolations. That is where we were before our brief digression into the Python interpreter to see how these methods were actually put to use. Now comes the hard work: doing the actual string interpolation. The rest of the functions are pretty simple and are aimed more at usability than functionality. String interpolation is done by the `evaluate()` method.

```
1     def evaluate(self, evalEnv):
2     myEvalEnv = evalEnv.copy()
3         result = ''
4       for expr in self.rep:
5         if type(expr) == type(''):
6            result = result + expr
7         else:
8            var = expr['var']
9
10           format = expr.get('format', 's')
11           if not format:
12               format = 's'
13
14           if expr['onfail'] != None:
15               onfailValue = expr['onfail']
16           else:
17               onfailValue = str(expr)
18
19           deleteVar = 0
20           if not myEvalEnv.has_key(var):
21               deleteVar = 1
22               myEvalEnv[var] = onfailValue
23
24           pySyntax = '%' '(' + var + ')' + format
25           try:
26               formattedText = pySyntax % myEvalEnv
27           except:
28               pySyntax = '%('+var+')s'
29               try:
30                   formattedText = pySyntax % myEvalEnv
31               except:
32                   convErrorMessage = '<b>Cannot convert ' + var + ' to string.</b>'
33                   formattedText = convErrorMessage
34           result = result + formattedText
35
36           if deleteVar:
37               del(myEvalEnv[var])
38
39     # Hopefully, this results in a GC. The copy should have a 0 RC
40     return result
```

Although this method is lengthy, with the longest code, it still takes only 40+ lines to do something that requires considerably more effort in other programming languages.[7] Let's take a look at the details:

1   evaluate(self, evalEnv) is the interface to perform the actual string interpolation. An incoming dictionary (evalEnv) contains the namespace of variables and values to be substituted when processing variables are encountered in the interpolated string, which has been compiled into an intermediate representation (self.rep).

---

7. We have ported the WriteProcessor components to Java, including the SimpleWriter. The core Java library does not include support for regular expressions and easy-to-use introspective capabilities (although we swear by reflection when programming in Java). The WriteProcessor

2   The namespace is cloned, as this function must be able to change the namespace to support the failover syntax; i.e., when a variable is undefined, the failover value must be inserted into the namespace.

4   For each object (expr) in the representation (self.rep)... Recall that self.rep contains substrings from the string passed to compile() and Variable instances, which is an internal representation that gives all information about the variable: its name, how it is to be formatted, and what value to substitute in case a value was not provided in the evaluation environment (evalEnv). This loop is dedicated to building the result of an interpolation (result).

5–6   If expr is a string, then simply copy this string into the result. Strings found in the representation don't require any special processing, since they represent the literal part of an interpolated string.

7   Otherwise (else) it is assumed to be a variable instance. For all practical purposes, it is just a dictionary and in fact is a class derived directly from the built-in library class UserDict (module UserDict). [The dictionary is the result obtained in the compile() method by calling the groupdict() method on the "match object" returned by re.search().]

8, 10,   expr['var'] gets the name of the interpolation variable.
14   expr['format'] and expr['onfail'] give the format sequence and failover values, respectively.

10–12   If the format string is either None or the empty string, set to 's', meaning '%s' will be used to format it later.

14–17   If the failover syntax was used, set the fail value.

19–22   If the variable found in expr['var'] is not present in the evaluation environment (evalEnv), set the value in the copy of the environment (myEvalEnv).

24   Generate a string that can be used to delegate the actual work to do the interpolation to Python's intrinsic interpolation mechanism, using the dictionary syntax %(var)format.

25–34   Try to perform interpolation of the string that was just constructed (pySyntax), using the local copy of the environment. Only one variable is expected in this string with a particular format. If the interpolation fails, for any reason, try to do the interpolation as a string. If all goes well, concatenate the partial result (formattedText) with the overall result (result) to form a new result.

36–37   Delete the variable (var) from the myEvalEnv if it is marked for deletion. The reason this has to be done is to make sure that a variable is not considered defined if it was not defined coming into this method. This allows multiple occurrences of the same variable (e.g., <<x>> is a <<x>>) in a string to contribute the same value to the overall result.

40   The final steps are to return the complete result of interpolating the string. Note that the temporary dictionary (myEvalEnv) is not freed. This is because this particular variable will go out of scope (it was only defined in this function) and there will be no references remaining to the dictionary, making it an ideal candidate for garbage collection.

Evaluate is, by far, the most involved method in this class. As the code makes use of Python and some of its most advanced features and libraries (regular expressions), we have chosen to give it a significant amount of attention. This method is heavily relied on in the advanced modules, including the WriteProcessor and WebForm classes.

The emit() method is provided to hook the SimpleWriter class into an overall code-generation scheme:

```
1    def emit(self, evalEnv):
2        text = self.evaluate(evalEnv)
3        self.emitter.emit(text)
```

evaluate() computes a result, which can be sent directly to output via a print statement or any form of I/O desired. We will return to a discussion of this function, following a discussion of the emitter strategy, which is a simple design pattern that proves very useful in a number of situations—especially in programming for the Web. For now, a concise explanation is given. An emitter is an object that can send output somewhere. Emitter is a base class that has just a few functions, one of which is the emit() method. This method takes only one parameter, which is a string to be directed to some output stream.[8]

---

8. It is perfectly natural to wonder why this function exists. After all, evaluate() seems to have everything that is needed and a good old print statement will do. Your indulgence is requested. You will see that this seemingly innocent and trite-looking function actually gives us an unprecedented degree of flexibility for doing code generation.

The remaining functions are all simple. Most of them address user-friendliness and exist to make it easy to get certain information out of the class or to print instances for debugging. They represent a very important aspect of programming in any language: The customer does matter. When making a class, it is important to think about the overall experience of using the class. Most of the functionality of this class is contained in the `evaluate()` method. However, if only this method were provided, it would not be much of an improvement over Python's built-in interpolation mechanism. And, as you will see later, these functions prove in one way or another to be highly relevant for building bigger and better things (e.g., the `WriteProcessor` class).

The `getRep()` method exists to get the abstract representation of the interpolated string. As mentioned earlier, this is to be compatible with the way the rest of the free OOP world does things. Python will allow you to access `rep` directly, given an object reference `x` (`x.rep` would give you the same result).[9]

```
1    def getRep(self):
2        return self.rep
```

Like `getRep()`, `getVars()` returns the list of variables.

```
1    def getVars(self):
2        return self.varList
```

The SimpleWriter provides a functionality not found in the built-in interpolation mechanism. You can find out whether a particular variable appears in the string. We use this extensively to support the template processing feature found in the WriteProcessor.

```
1    def hasVar(self, var):
2        return var in self.varList
```

This last function is used to get the string representation of the class. This function (introduced in the first chapter) is often defined in a Python class to allow the object to be printed as a string. If it were not defined, Python would print something generic. The string

---

9. The OOP community is replete with attitude on this subject. In the literature you will find all sorts of arguments for enforced encapsulation of data (information hiding) and the "need" to have accessor/mutator (get/set) methods. We tend to follow this in our own programming, and encourage you to do so whenever possible. However, as our earlier interactive session demonstrated, being able to get the value when developing, testing, and debugging is very helpful. We dismiss religion when enormous productivity gains are the trade-off.

representation we construct is something that "looks like XML." We will not cover this function in detail here, as it is built with features that should now be completely familar to you. However, we will show a session of the SimpleWriter in action, so you can see what happens when attempting to print a SimpleWriter instance.

```
1     def __str__(self):
2        result = '<SimpleWriter>' + "\n"
3        for r in self.rep:
4           if type(r) == type(''):
5              result = result + "  <text>" + r + "</text>\n"
6           else:
7              result = result + "  <var"
8              for attr in r.keys():
9                 if r[attr] != None:
10                   result = result + " " + attr + "=" + '"' + r[attr] + '"'
11              result = result + "/>\n"
12       return result + "</SimpleWriter>"
```

You are strongly encouraged to try this on your own with our code[10] and your Python interpreter. This is an interactive session at the Python interpreter with the classes present in the same directory or available via the PYTHONPATH variable.

```
>>> import SimpleWriter
>>> sw = SimpleWriter.SimpleWriter()
>>> sw.compile('Hello, <<friend|>>. Thank you for purchasing <<book>>.')
>>> friend='Good Customer'
>>> book='Web Programming in Python: Techniques for Integrating Linux,
Apache, and MySQL'
>>> result = sw.evaluate(vars())
>>> print result
Hello, Good Customer. Thank you for purchasing Web Programming in Python:
Techniques for Integrating Linux, Apache, and MySQL.
>>> env = { 'book' : 'the book of love' }
>>> result = sw.evaluate(env)
>>> print result
Hello, . Thank you for purchasing the book of love.
>>> env['person'] = 'Guido van Rossum'
>>> result = sw.evaluate(env)
>>> print result
Hello, . Thank you for purchasing the book of love.
>>> env['friend'] = 'Guido van Rossum'
>>> result = sw.evaluate(env)
>>> print result
Hello, Guido van Rossum. Thank you for purchasing the book of love.
>>> print sw.getVars()
['friend', 'book']
>>> print sw.hasVar('xyz')
```

---

10. This author vividly recalls the words of a great computer science professor: "You type, and you never forget." It was said in broken English but everyone in the class, this author included, knew exactly what he was trying to tell us.

```
0
>>> print sw.hasVar('friend')
1
>>> sw.compile('<<x>> <<y|>> <<z%d>> <<x>> <<y>> <<z>>')
>>> sw.getVars()
['x', 'y', 'z', 'x', 'y', 'z']
>>> sw.hasVar('x')
1
>>> sw.hasVar('z')
1
>>> sw.hasVar('friend')
0
>>> print sw
<SimpleWriter>
  <text></text>
  <var var="x"/>
  <text> </text>
  <var onfail="" var="y"/>
  <text> </text>
  <var format="d" var="z"/>
  <text> </text>
  <var var="x"/>
  <text> </text>
  <var var="y"/>
  <text> </text>
  <var var="z"/>
  <text></text>
</SimpleWriter>
```

Sometimes an example can replace 1,000 words. When we develop useful classes in Python, whenever possible, we try to include a usage session that demonstrates the salient features of the class.[11] There is no substitute for being able to write clear, descriptive documentation and good code. There is also no substitute for showing how the class is used. One of the most famous object-oriented analysis methods is named after the concept of use: use-case analysis. It is a powerful analysis and design method but is equally useful as a documentation and demonstration tool. When writing complex systems, it is utterly necessary to have a clear idea both of how your system will be used and how it will be tested.

Perhaps the most interesting thing in this class came at the end. Here is where you see the result obtained from the __str__() method that was defined earlier. This gives as clear a visual representation as possible. In the future, it will be possible to transform this into HTML

---

11. One of the great lacks of object-oriented programming (and programming language technology) is for designers specifically to address documentation and usage as actual features. Java made some good initial steps with the javadoc tool; something much better is needed. Class browsers and a myriad of man pages are not going to cut it. The answer may come from a low-bandwidth solution: defining a process. Before a class can be published for common use, it must meet certain criteria, and every class should be able to show a coherent example of how it would be used in practice.

using the XML toolkit. Throughout this book we have tried to make every object printable as XML. Although we don't usually take advantage of this, except for debugging, it is not difficult to imagine the day when we might use this output to build a visualization system for running Web applications.

The `Emitter` Strategy Classes

During the discussion of the the `emit()` method in class `SimpleWriter`, we introduced the concept of an emitter, which itself is a class. The concept and implementation of an emitter are very simple and are at the heart of what is needed to do code generation in practice.

Let's first consider code generation. Programming for the Web has always been a story of code generation. The code here is HTML, which is text. Most Web commerce sites require that a great deal of transformation take place on fragments of HTML (or fragments of XML). Partial results (strings) are put together to build larger results (still strings); this culminates in output being sent to your browser. To accommodate this significant need, the ability to generate code using different strategies is imperative. `SimpleWriter` is somewhat of a low-level building block. It is used to perform string interpolation. Most Web development takes place in terms of authored Web pages that represent an interface. This interface must be wired in to actual business logic. Early in the development of `SimpleWriter`, we thought about how to evolve the low-level mechanism into a higher-level one and came to a painful realization: `SimpleWriter` must be able to participate in the code generation scheme. Otherwise, it really isn't much better than Python's built-in mechanism.

Thus a key part of the analysis and design steps was the identification of a role for the `SimpleWriter`. Obviously, it must be responsible for writing output. But how to construct a writer that did not rely upon any mechanism in particular? Python had a lot going for it. However, unlike Java (another language we know and love), Python does not have a sophisticated streams framework. And we were not really prepared to rewrite the Java streams classes.

The emitter framework used by `SimpleWriter` and the `WriteProcessor` has a very simple implementation. The base class, `Emitter`, supports the most common strategy for output, that being to send the text to standard output. Both the base class, `Emitter`, and every subclass must implement the `emit()`, `getResult()`, and `__repr__()` functions. (`ListEmitter`, `StringEmitter`, and

FileEmitter are all available. Only StringEmitter and ListEmitter will be discussed here.)

```
1    class Emitter:
2      def __init__(self):
3        pass
4
5      def emit(self,text):
6        print text,
7
8      def getResult(self):
9        return None
```

The __init__() method is not very interesting but is here for what we believe are very good reasons, grounded in solid design principles. As Emitter is a base class, we defined the __init__() method in the hope that all subclasses would call it explicity—and all of Emitter's direct subclasses do in fact call the Emitter __init__() method explicitly.[12] Should there ever be a need to change the base class and the way it is initialized, it will be easy to identify all of the classes that may need to modify their initialization semantics by modifying their __init__() methods and ensuring that they call the base class' (Emitter's) __init__() method accordingly.

The emit() method for the base class is supposed to send the output directly to standard output. We send the output using Python's built-in print statement. The trailing comma here is not a typographical error. The output is sent without sending a new line sequence.

The getResult() method returns the "result" as is relevant for the Emitter. The Emitter class, clearly, is a stateless emitter. The output is simply passed through to standard output. Most of the subclasses of Emitter are stateful, and they allow different output representations to be built up via a series of emit() calls and then collected later. You will see (later in this chapter, in fact) that such a capability is essential for building Web pages with the WriteProcessor. The ability to emit the output wherever desired will prove indispensible.

Let's take a look at the Emitter family. We will start with the ListEmitter and continue with the StringEmitter, highlighting

---

12. On the author's wish list: programming languages that enforce user-defined initialization. Proper initialization of user-defined classes is at the heart of meaningful OOP. Default initialization is useful (especially in languages like C++, where all sorts of things would go wrong without it) but not without enforcing the definition of at least one constructor. It is impossible to extend a class unless you can properly initialize the superclass's state. In this book, you will seldom see a class without a proper constructor, even if the constructor is performing what appears to be an utterly meaningless or (in this case) no-op (NOP).

the key differences in the process. The `ListEmitter`, as its name suggests, collects the results of a series of `emit()` calls in a list.

```
1    class ListEmitter(Emitter):
2      def __init__(self, initList=[]):
3        if type(initList) == type([]):
4          self.output = initList
5        else:
6          self.output = []
7        Emitter.__init__(self)
8
9      def emit(self,text):
10       self.output.append(text)
11
12     def getList(self):
13       return self.output
14
15     def __repr__(self):
16       rep = ''
17       for text in self.output:
18         rep = rep + text
19       return rep
20     def getResult(self):
21       return self.getList()
```

ListEmitter's `__init__()` method does a little more work than Emitter's `__init__()` method had to do. It is designed to allow a user to specify a list (optionally), which will be used, provided it is actually a Python list. However, if the user did not pass a Python list, an empty list is created and used to initialize the `ListEmitter` instance. Under normal circumstances, we could allow Python to throw an exception when an attempt is made to do something with the list. We opted against this design since the intention of these classes is to be as failproof as possible, working reasonably even when misused. And this works out pretty well, since `getResult()` allows the result to be obtained anyway, in case the client of the `ListEmitter` is surprised to find that the reference that was passed to `ListEmitter` doesn't contain the actual text. Every `Emitter` instance is guaranteed to produce a result appropriate to the specific kind of emitter.

Any `Emitter` subclass can provide its own functions. In the case of `ListEmitter` (and `StringEmitter`), the `getList()` function [(and `getText()` in `StringEmitter`)] allows the data structure being used to be gotten explicitly. In ordinary use, `getText()` is not actually called, since the whole idea of an `Emitter` is to exploit polymorphism to get the result even when the type of `Emitter` is unknown.

As shown, getResult() simply calls getList() on the object itself to return a result from several emit() calls.

StringEmitter is structured along similar lines to the ListEmitter. In fact, we probably use it more often in practice. It defines a getText() method and getResult(), similar to the getList() and getResult() methods of the ListEmitter. It should be pretty straightforward to follow.

```
1    class StringEmitter(Emitter):
2      def __init__(self):
3        self.text = ""
4        Emitter.__init__(self)
5
6      def emit(self, text):
7        self.text = self.text + text
8
9      def getText(self):
10       return self.text
11
12     def __repr__(self):
13       return self.text
14
15     def getResult(self):
16       return self.getText()
```

All of these classes are kept in a module called Emitter. For convenience in instantiation, we provide a factory method, createEmitter(), that will instantiate an emitter with "reasonable defaults" based on the kind of Emitter being chosen.

```
1    def createEmitter(emitter):
2      if emitter in ['Emitter','ListEmitter','StringEmitter']:
3        stmt = 'return %s()' % (emitter)
4        exec stmt
5      else:
6        return Emitter()
```

The emitter framework is very light. It is not intended to replace your I/O (or O) library, although we would very much appreciate a better I/O library for Python. It is deliberately kept simple, because it is being used specifically to manage code generation. We won't go into any detail now but here are two of the applications for the emitters:

ListEmitter is very useful in a database setting. In application servers, there is often a need to issue a series of SQL database calls. The calls themselves can be issued one at a time but this is usually not the way to go, especially when a series of inserts and updates is to be performed and the outcome of one does not affect the outcome of another. By using a `ListEmitter`, a series of SQL statements can be generated as a list. Then the list can be iterated and all calls can be executed as a single transaction (if the underlying database supports it, of course). It can also be quite useful for keeping a journal of the calls that were done for debugging. The applications chapters (see Part III) give examples of this, combined with the `wplLogger` module.

`StringEmitter` is also very useful, primarily when working with HTML or XML generation. It is often the case that temporary results must be obtained. Then the results are substituted into another template, and the code is finally generated. `StringEmitter` and `ListEmitter` keep growing, doing one `emit()` followed by another `emit()`. Finally, the entire result is obtained either as a single string or list, depending on which strategy was chosen.[13]

The WriteProcessor

At last we have arrived at the discussion of the WriteProcessor framework. The WriteProcessor framework is dedicated to automating the process of generating output, which is typically performed by "write" or "print" statements found in programming languages. In many respects, WriteProcessor (the class that implements most of the framework) is a convenience class, as it provides a slightly higher level of abstraction than the SimpleWriter, which (as has been shown in examples) works at the level of individual text strings, and the Emitter framework. WriteProcessor is designed to work one file at a time and ultimately sends its output to standard output. (You are limited to standard output. The Emitter framework that was presented earlier still applies and is available; its use is made transparent for normal use.) This section is organized as follows:

- First, we will introduce the general principles behind the WriteProcessor framework. At the core, WriteProcessor is equivalent to SimpleWriter. Anything SimpleWriter can do, WriteProcessor can do better. The WriteProcessor supports many other capabilities, such as file inclusion, looping rules, and line grouping.

---

13. Java I/O streams provide something very similar (and more sophisticated than what we have built to help our SimpleWriter class, which does not have an equivalent in Java) with their Byte-ArrayOutputStream and StringWriter classes in package java.io. There isn't an equivalent for emitting to a Java Vector instance. Nonetheless, the streams abstraction of Java could easily be extended to support these ideas.

- Second, we will introduce the general structure of the WriteProcessor module. As you observed in the SimpleWriter module, there is often more than one class involved. The WriteProcessor module (`WriteProcessor.py`) consists of several classes, one of which is named WriteProcessor.
- Finally, we will introduce a number of practical applications for the WriteProcessor. We make use of the WriteProcessor extensively for Web (generating HTML and XML), database programming (generating SQL), and other situations (sending mail messages, debugging/logging, etc.)

Principles

We designed the WriteProcessor framework to address a perceived need for the ability to do lightweight text processing to generate HTML.[14] After noticing a number of programs and books on CGI programming[15] (many quite recent) with hand-coded "print" statements, we were surprised to learn that much Web development continues to be done using such primitive techniques. And it is very labor-intensive to maintain codes that embed the HTML code in the business logic (be it CGI or quasi-ASP[16] languages, such as JSP, PHP, etc.)

Directly mixing HTML and business logic is analogous to mixing oil and water. It works effectively only for very simple Web applications. At some point, not separating these concerns results in an unmaintainable mess.

The basic principle of the WriteProcessor was to address the need for a clear separation between HTML and the business logic of the application. In the WWW world, business logic refers to the server side of the equation. Application services require the business logic predominantly to be on the server side. This is not to suggest that the client side isn't important. Scripting languages such as JavaScript, PHP3, etc. can

---

14. Please note that the use of this tool is hardly limited to HTML, working with any text files in which you have a need to do similar processing. The WriteProcessor framework is not intended to replace your C or M4 preprocessors (used mainly for programming language text processing). You are welcome to continue using these tools with or without the WriteProcessor.

15. We will not mention any of these books by name but (suffice it to say) many have a year 2000 publication date.

16. We do not mention companies in this book by name. The one behind Active Server Pages (ASP) is from Redmond, WA. The one behind JSP (Java) is from Mountain View, CA. PHP is the PHP Hypertext Processor. We are not believers in this approach to developing Web applications, but do appreciate why these technologies exist. After all, if the print statement is the vehicle preferred for CGI and Servlet programming, why not just embed code in HTML?

be extremely useful for form validation, visualization of results, and so on. However, there needs to be a clear separation between interface and the business logic. This is the cornerstone of technologies such as XML, which are gaining popularity but slowly, because the same challenge is being presented to the development community–separating the interface from the business logic.[17]

The WriteProcessor class achieves this separation by making it possible to bridge the business logic and the HTML using very simple markup. The markup has been kept deliberately simple in order to rule out even the slightest possibility that business logic that really belongs on the server side does not creep into the HTML.[18] We are firm believers in the server side of a Web application being robust, not just in doing the job, but safeguarding it against attacks from malicious users (an ever-increasing population of Web users). The surest way to safeguard the server side is to avoid shortcuts. It is important to realize that HTTP is a protocol (see Chapter 5). Being a protocol, any application code can talk the protocol and send HTTP requests (most notably, the POST request) to your server code. If your server code has not been carefully written to safeguard against bad input, etc., something bad will inevitably occur. The moral of the story is that the Web browser is just one of an infinite number of clients that can talk HTTP, and relying solely on a client-side scripting language gives you little or no protection on the server side.

Basic Template Processing

At the core, WriteProcessor is the SimpleWriter. The WriteProcessor allows you to mark up HTML with the variable syntax that was defined earlier in the SimpleWriter class. WriteProcessor works by processing the text of an input file one line at a time. If a line of text contains variables, the corresponding values from a supplied dictionary are substituted, using precisely the same syntax and rules found in the SimpleWriter class.

Here is a quick example of a valid WriteProcessor document. It makes use of two variables: "DocumentTitle" and "Person."

---

17. Typical client/server OOP applications make use of the Model-View-Controller design pattern, wherein the model (business logic) and the view (interface) are mediated by a controller. This works pretty well for event-oriented systems but not quite as well for the Web, which enforces more regimented communication structure on the application.

18. For example, many Web applications written in scripting languages, such as JavaScript, assume that validating an input on the client side eliminates the need to validate that same input on the server side when a CGI script (or Servlet) gets called. This is a bomb waiting to go off (most incidents of this go unreported).

```
<title> <<DocumentTitle|No Title>> </title>
<h1> Welcome to <<DocumentTitle|No Title>> </h1>
Hi, <<Person>>. Welcome to <<DocumentTitle>>. This is the WriteProcessor system.
<<hr>>
The End.
```

If "DocumentTitle" was set to "XYZ" and "Person" was set to "George," the following would be obtained:

```
<title> XYZ </title>
<h1> Welcome to XYZ </h1>
Hi, George. Welcome to XYZ. This is the WriteProcessor system.
<<hr>>
The End.
```

Performing substitutions one line at a time itself is quite powerful; however, if this were all that the WriteProcessor class could do, it would be no more powerful than the SimpleWriter class. The WriteProcessor supports a number of other key features that are essential for working with HTML and other situations requiring code generation (XML, SQL).

File Inclusion

The first of these features is file inclusion. Any line of text from the input file can begin with ">filename," which means "include file-name." Unlike the C or M4 preprocessor, includes are processed once and only once for a given inclusion. Let's take a look at how file inclusion works within the WriteProcessor, assuming we have three files: X.html, Y.html, and Z.html.

```
X.html:

I am X.
>Y.html
>Y.html
>Z.html

Y.html:

I am Y.
>Y.html
>Z.html

Z.html:

I am Z.
>Z.html
```

Input from Files or String I/O Objects

This feature allows you to in-line the top-level file, reminiscent of a "here document" in Unix, using the triple-quote syntax found in Python. File inclusion may occur within this string, so you must specify a search path through which included files will be located.

Looping Rules

Looping rules allow a data structure to be iterated implicitly when a given set of variables (matching the data structure) is found on a given line of text (or group of lines). There are only three forms supported:

1. Dictionary looping rules
2. List looping rules
3. List of dictionary looping rules

Dictionaries and lists are the two most commonly used data structures in Python. List of dictionary exists primarily to accommodate result sets from database queries, which can usually be obtained as a list of records (a record set). The record concept is usually mapped to a dictionary where the keys represent the field names and values represent the field values. We will show an example of this after considering the first two cases.

Why are looping rules needed? There are many potential applications. We tend to use them frequently in returning HTML documents to a client on the Web. There are many situations where you can put them to use, so the following isn't an all-inclusive list:

- Selection lists–The examples in this section will show how this is done to motivate the basic looping rules.
- Check box/radio groups
- Tables–We'll show how to quickly render an HTML table.
- SQL processing–Often there is a need to render SQL queries on the fly. We will see that this is also useful to facilitate porting your application from one database to another.

The key significance of the looping rules is that substitutions can be performed easily without the application code having to work directly with HTML (or XML, for that matter). This results in a higher degree of maintainability of application code.

List Looping Rules

Let's consider the basic idea with an example that comes from HTML forms.

When making order forms, it is often necessary to generate selection lists. You usually see selection lists when placing an order on the Internet, for example, to enter your state, country, credit card type, etc.

The WriteProcessor template for a selection list might be something like:

```
<select name="state">
<option value="<<state_code>>" <<state_selected>> >
<<state_detail>> </option>
</select>
```

Here it is desired to take the `<option>` ... `</option>` building block and replicate it for a given set of values.

Many Web sites actually make use of hand-coded selection lists for these common cases, figuring that things will never change. And they may be right. However, things *do* change. In the long run it would make more sense to keep the information for these entities separate from the actual forms in the Web interface and generate them on the fly (or generate them, but cache the results). The problem becomes especially important if you have many forms on your Web site (order, change customer profile, problem report, etc.) that need consistent information.

So let's suppose for the moment that the state information (state code and name) is kept in a file. The data is read into a Python list of tuples that would be constructed by hand as follows:

```
usStates = [ ('AK', 'Alaska', ''), ('AL', 'Alabama', 'SELECTED'), etc. ]
```

Each element of the list is a tuple of identical length (3).

A template was specified above. We want the "option" line referenced to be expanded for each of the different states of the union with the following outcome (to make things interesting, we have made the state of Alabama selected by default):

```
<select name="state">
<option value="AK" > Alaska </option>
<option value="AL" SELECTED > Alabama </option>
etc. (more states would appear similar to the above two lines)
</select>
```

The WriteProcessor can perform this sort of transformation very easily by helping you to map the data to the variable names specified in the template. In the template above, the option line contains "state_code", "state_details", and "state_selected". Coincidentally, the list contains tuples with elements that are in one-to-one correspondence with those names. You can specify a pattern (consisting of variable names) to describe the arrangement of data. The way the pattern is specified depends on the data structure itself. If the data structure is a list of tuples, you just need to mention the variables that are used. It's also permissible to describe the structure with a "picture" of how the fields are arranged.

Let's take a look at an example worked out from beginning to end. Below is a building block for generating a selection list. We will show how to generate two selection lists using the WriteProcessor class in just a bit.

```
<select name="<<opt_name>>">
<option value="<<opt_value>>" <<opt_selected>>> <<opt_details>> </option>
</select>
```

A selection list requires a name to distinguish it from other inputs, including the possibility of other selection lists. Line 1 contains a reference to <<opt_name>>, which will be substituted with a unique name. Line 2 contains variables <<opt_value>>, <<opt_selected>>, and <<opt_details>>. This line will be used to perform substitutions, one at a time, from a list of tuples, where each tuple contains exactly three items (corresponding to the three variables to be substituted). Line 3 contains no variables, so it will be copied with no substitutions taking place.

That is how the template is organized. What are we hoping to produce at the end? Two selection lists: "state" and "country." As order form processing typically requires you to generate these inputs on the fly, we will actually make use of this again later when discussing order processing, where we frequently need dynamically generated inputs of one kind or another. Let's take a look at the output that is to be produced. We show the execution of the program from the command line in Linux:

```
[george@liszt examples]$ python wp_list_rule4a.py
<select name="state">
  <option value="AR"  > Arkansas </option>
  <option value="AK"  > Alaska </option>
  <option value="AZ"  SELECTED> Arizona </option>
  <option value="CA"  > California </option>
  <option value="CT"  > Connecticut </option>
</select>


<select name="country">
  <option value="US"  > United States </option>
  <option value="IN"  SELECTED> India </option>
  <option value="ZB"  > Zimbabwe </option>
  <option value="AR"  > Argentina </option>
  <option value="BR"  > Brazil </option>
</select>
```

Before we dive into the code, a few observations are in order:

- Line 1 in the template has been expanded precisely one time, whereas line 2 has been expanded multiple times. The WriteProcessor framework gives you very fine control over how many times a given line (or group of lines) of text is processed.
- With selection lists in forms, errors are often made. Often a form is rendered according to values that were previously set (or selected). An example of this is a "profile information" form. If a person filled out Illinois as the state of residence, it would be very convenient if Illinois appears as selected if the same person wants to update the information, especially if the person hasn't moved recently. You'll notice that in the "state" and "country" selection lists, the string "SELECTED" appears next to Arizona and India, respectively.
- Finally, the same template is reused to render the two different selection lists. Throughout the book, we'll be making use of a repository of templates for doing these common household tasks. You are invited to use these templates for your own applications (and even to help us expand the collection).

So this has the potential to be fun. Let us now take a look at the code that accomplished this task:

```
1    import string
2    from Path import Path
3
4    from WriteProcessor import WriteProcessor
5    from Emitter import StringEmitter
6
7    states = [
8       ['AR','Arkansas'],
9       ['AK','Alaska'],
10      ['AZ','Arizona'],
11      ['CA','California'],
12      ['CT','Connecticut']
13   ]
14
15   countries = [
16      ['US', 'United States'],
17      ['IN', 'India'],
18      ['ZB', 'Zimbabwe'],
19      ['AR', 'Argentina'],
20      ['BR', 'Brazil']
21   ]
22
23   def CreateSelectList(opt_name, selected, opts):
24     env = { 'opt_name' : opt_name }
25     wp = WriteProcessor('select_list.html', ['.'], env)
26
27     selected_list = ['SELECTED']
28     not_selected_list = ['']
29
30     options = []
31     for opt in opts:
32        if opt[0] in selected or opt[1] in selected:
33           options.append(opt + selected_list)
34        else:
35           options.append(opt + not_selected_list)
36
37     wp.addListLoopingRule(
38         ['opt_value', 'opt_details', 'opt_selected'], options)
39     wp.process()
40
41
42   CreateSelectList('state', ['AZ'], states)
43   CreateSelectList('country', ['IN'], countries)
```

This shows a general procedure for using the WriteProcessor to generate code for selection lists. It could easily be dropped in to your applications; however, the main focus here is to introduce the basic workings of the WriteProcessor. This building block (and others that are useful to HTML) is expanded into a small class library that is covered later in the book.

In the example above the usage is very simple. A Python function is defined, `CreateSelectList()`, with three arguments:

- `opt_name`—The name to be subsituted. We will be using "state" and "country" as shown in lines 42–43.
- `selected`—The list of items to appear as SELECTED. As shown in lines 42–43, "AZ" and "IN" are to appear selected, which is what is expected given the output that was shown above.
- `opts`—A list of lists containing the `opt_value` and `opt_details` values to be substituted. This appears to be in contradiction with what we said; however, a third element will be added to each list to ensure that the looping rule can be applied.

When this function is called, as shown in lines 42–43, a selection list will be generated for the supplied list of states and countries, respectively. Now let us consider the details of the `CreateSelectList()` function, which is where all of the action is:

23   The function definition. We have already described the interface being presented to the user above.

24   An environment is created in which the evaluation will take place. If you find this confusing, go back to the discussion of the SimpleWriter class, where this was explained in detail. This environment must contain variables that are to be substituted in the form. You don't need to include the variables on lines that will be processed with looping rules, as each looping rule is given its own environment (or data structure) in which the line will be evaluated.

27–28   These two lists are maintained as constants that will be used to append "SELECTED" or " " to each of the lists supplied in variable "opts".

30–35   This is best shown by example. The goal is to produce a list of lists, wherein each of the contained lists has a third element that indicates whether or not it is selected.
So `['AZ',  'Arizona']` will result in `['AZ', 'Arizona','SELECTED']`, and `['AL',  'Alabama']` will result in `['AL',  'Alabama','']`.
Although not a strict requirement, we produce a new list (`options`) and leave the supplied list (`opts`) as is. In general, functions should be written so that the side effects are clear. We figure the user probably does not want his or her list to be affected directly and potentially would need the list again.

37   The looping rule is added to the WriteProcessor instance (`wp`). Looping rules are very simple: Specify the names of the variables and they are mapped, positionally, to the elements in the list. When more than one variable is specified (as here), it is assumed that a list of lists was supplied. The usage shown here (a handful of variables) is the most common.

39   Perform the actual processing. What happens here depends on how the output rendering is to be done. WriteProcessor, similar to SimpleWriter, allows you to specify an `Emitter` instance, which by default is constructed for you with standard output as the destination. A subsequent example shows a reworked `CreateSelectList()` that produces a string result.

42–43   Create the "state" and "country" select lists. These two statements cause all of the output that was shown at the beginning of this section.

At this point, the groundwork has been completely established for the basic day-to-day WriteProcessor usage. It should be apparent that the goal has been to take full advantage of Python, and the connection to the list (and other) data structure(s) is by design. As will be shown throughout this book, the WriteProcessor can be used in rather sophisticated ways to build complex Web interfaces and achieve a consistent look and feel on your Web site.

List of Dictionary Looping Rules

The next type of looping rule we consider is the list of dictionary looping rule. (There is also a dictionary looping rule, which is considered as the last case.) This kind of looping rule is very useful for working with result sets, which are commonly returned as the result of a database query. (In a later chapter we will discuss the WPL Record class, which is equivalent to a dictionary and is used extensively in the examples in the second half of this book.)

Let's first consider briefly the general characteristics of a list of dictionaries. Typically, every dictionary has a common key set. There is a set of keys in common for every dictionary item in the list, and the keys usually correspond to a set of WriteProcessor variables to be substituted. Let's take a look at an alternate representation of the list of lists used to represent the "states" that were substituted earlier. Here is the equivalent of the list that is produced by the CreateSelectList() function and assigned to "options" in the previous section's example:

```
1    states = [
2       ['AR','Arkansas',''],
3       ['AK','Alaska',''],
4       ['AZ','Arizona','SELECTED'],
5       ['CA','California',''],
6       ['CT','Connecticut','']
7    ]
```

An equivalent list of dictionaries representation could be constructed as follows:

```
1    states = [
2           {   'opt_value' : 'AR',
3           'opt_detail' : 'Arkansas',
4           'opt_selected' : '' },
5           {   'opt_value' : 'AK',
6           'opt_detail' : 'Alaska',
7           'opt_selected' : '' },
8           {   'opt_value' : 'AZ',
9           'opt_detail' : 'Arizona',
10          'opt_selected' : '' },
11          {   'opt_value' : 'CA',
12          'opt_detail' : 'California',
13          'opt_selected' : '' },
14          {   'opt_value' : 'CT',
15          'opt_detail' : 'Connecticut',
16          'opt_selected' : '' }
17   ]
```

Each of the dictionaries is a record. The keys of the record could be thought of as field names, while the values could be thought of as field values. Before we proceed, it is worth considering why this is a good thing. Lists of lists should be enough for everyone, but as an approach it suffers from comprehension and maintainability problems. In a list, the only name available to access a particular field is an index value (e.g., 0, 1, 2, ...). For example, to find the "opt_value" field in a list of lists representation, say, for the first record in the list, one would reference states[0][0]. Using a list of dictionaries, one can write the (more intuitive) states[0]['opt_value']. As well, over time, the positions of fields can and sometimes do change. With the dictionaries approach it is much easier to make the change, since you know what field is being referenced by an intuitive name. (Clearly, "opt_value" says a lot more than 0.) Lists of lists probably have the edge in terms of efficiency, since the lists could well be frozen as tuples (which you will discover, when reading up on Python internals, have a very efficient implementation, faster than any other Python data structure, except for scalars).

Lists of dictionaries have a special looping rule dedidicated to supporting them directly. Let's take a look at how they work by considering the following code example, adapted from the lists of lists example. In the interest of conciseness, we focus only on the CreateSelectList() function, which prepares a list of dictionaries from a list of lists and then calls the correct "add" method to add the list of dictionaries looping rule, accordingly.

```
1    def CreateSelectList(opt_name, selected, opts):
2        env = { 'opt_name' : opt_name }
3        wp = WriteProcessor('select_list.html', ['.'], env)
4
5        options = []
6        for opt in opts:
7            opt_dict = {}
8            opt_dict['opt_value'] = opt[0]
9            opt_dict['opt_details'] = opt[1]
10           if opt[0] in selected or opt[1] in selected:
11               opt_dict['opt_selected'] = 'SELECTED'
12           else:
13               opt_dict['opt_selected'] = ''
14           options.append(opt_dict)
15       wp.addDictListLoopingRule(options)
16       wp.process()
```

The code here is fundamentally the same as the lists of lists version shown earlier. Here, each list element is a dictionary, which is constructed on the fly to yield a list of dictionaries (options) that has the same general form as the hand-translated version of states shown earlier. This list of dictionaries is passed to the `addDictListLoopingRule()` call. The names of the WriteProcessor variables (`opt_value`, `opt_details`, and `opt_selected`) are omitted, since they are extracted from the first item in options,[19] which happens to have keys corresponding to the needed WriteProcessor variable names.

Lists of dictionaries are the preferred method to use when working with record data. This topic was discussed in Chapter 8, where we showed you how to take the result obtained in a single line of code from a database query and immediately substitute the results into an HTML or XML document.

Dictionary Looping Rules

Yet another kind of looping rule is to construct a dictionary and iterate over the entries of the dictionary by providing a description of how the key and value are packed, as we have shown with the other looping rules.

Consider the `/etc/passwd` file, which maintains the user "`database`" on a Unix system. Each input line has the general structure, where each field is separated by colons:

0. User name
1. `uid`–The user id, an integer
2. `gid`–The group id, an integer
3. Description–Usually the spelled-out user name. The term "description" is used, because you may in fact have users on the system that are not people but represent the name of a particular service (e.g., "`pgsql`" on your Unix system is the "`PostgreSQL`" user, so the database does not have to be run as superuser or "`root`").
4. Home directory–The path to the user's home directory. A home directory can be empty if the account is not intended to support general, interactive login sessions.
5. Shell–The path to the shell, usually `/bin/bash` on Linux systems for all user accounts.

---

19. We have revised the interface to allow you to state the key set explicitly as an additional parameter. This allows the user to pass in a dictionary with more keys than are actually used in the pattern.

Here is a sampling of the `/etc/passwd` file on my home computer.[20]

```
1    root:x:0:0:root:/root:/bin/bash
2    bin:x:1:1:bin:/bin:
3    daemon:x:2:2:daemon:/sbin:
4    adm:x:3:4:adm:/var/adm:
5    lp:x:4:7:lp:/var/spool/lpd:
6    sync:x:5:0:sync:/sbin:/bin/sync
7    shutdown:x:6:0:shutdown:/sbin:/sbin/shutdown
8    halt:x:7:0:halt:/sbin:/sbin/halt
9    mail:x:8:12:mail:/var/spool/mail:
10   news:x:9:13:news:/var/spool/news:
11   uucp:x:10:14:uucp:/var/spool/uucp:
12   operator:x:11:0:operator:/root:
13   games:x:12:100:games:/usr/games:
14   sympa:x:89:89:Sympa Mailing list manager:/home/sympa:/bin/bash
15   gopher:x:13:30:gopher:/usr/lib/gopher-data:
16   ftp:x:14:50:FTP User:/home/ftp:
17   nobody:x:99:99:Nobody:/:
18   xfs:x:100:103:X Font Server:/etc/X11/fs:/bin/false
19   postfix:x:101:233:postfix:/var/spool/postfix:
20   postgres:x:40:234:PostgreSQL Server:/var/lib/pgsql:/bin/bash
21   squid:x:23:235::/var/spool/squid:/dev/null
22   gdm:x:42:237::/home/gdm:/bin/bash
23   mysql:x:102:238:MySQL server:/var/lib/mysql:/bin/bash
24   zope:x:103:239:Zope Server:/var/zope:/bin/bash
25   george:x:504:501:George K. Thiruvathukal:/home/george:/bin/bash
26   gkt:x:504:501:George K. Thiruvathukal:/home/george:/bin/bash
27   nina:x:501:503:Nina Wilfred:/home/nina:/bin/bash
28   pshafae:x:505:501:John Shafaee:/home/pshafae:/bin/bash
```

User "gkt" has "x" in the password field (meaning that `/etc/shadow` is actually consulted to obtain the password), with uid = 504, gid = 501 (the file `/etc/group` contains the meaning of 501, which is not the same as "gkt" but actually stands for "users" on my system), home directory is `/home/george`, and shell is `/bin/bash`. Note that user "postfix" has a home directory `/var/spool/postfix` but no shell (for users on your system that aren't real people).

---

20. With some alterations to the encrypted password field, because we know that some of you hackers out there are just dying to hack into our systems, which we think (wistfully) is pretty secure.

Suppose we wanted to make it possible to view the user account information on the Web. We would probably want the view to be an HTML table, since it would be formatted much more nicely than the current view.

Here is the output we hope to produce, which for brevity's sake will include only the user name, description, and shell fields:

```
1    <title>Demonstration of Dictionary Looping Rule</title>
2
3    <table>
4    <tr> <td>user name</td> <td>description</td> <td>shell</td> </tr>
5
6    <tr> <td>adm</td> <td>adm</td> <td></td> </tr>
7    <tr> <td>bin</td> <td>bin</td> <td></td> </tr>
8    <tr> <td>daemon</td> <td>daemon</td> <td></td> </tr>
9    <tr> <td>ftp</td> <td>FTP User</td> <td></td> </tr>
10   <tr> <td>games</td> <td>games</td> <td></td> </tr>
11   <tr> <td>gdm</td> <td></td> <td>/bin/bash</td> </tr>
12   <tr> <td>george</td> <td>George K. Thiruvathukal</td> <td>/bin/bash</td> </tr>
13   <tr> <td>gkt</td> <td>George K. Thiruvathukal</td> <td>/bin/bash</td> </tr>
14   <tr> <td>gopher</td> <td>gopher</td> <td></td> </tr>
15   <tr> <td>halt</td> <td>halt</td> <td>/sbin/halt</td> </tr>
16   <tr> <td>lp</td> <td>lp</td> <td></td> </tr>
17   <tr> <td>mail</td> <td>mail</td> <td></td> </tr>
18   <tr> <td>mysql</td> <td>MySQL server</td> <td>/bin/bash</td> </tr>
19   <tr> <td>news</td> <td>news</td> <td></td> </tr>
20   <tr> <td>nina</td> <td>Nina Wilfred</td> <td>/bin/bash</td> </tr>
21   <tr> <td>nobody</td> <td>Nobody</td> <td></td> </tr>
22   <tr> <td>operator</td> <td>operator</td> <td></td> </tr>
23   <tr> <td>postfix</td> <td>postfix</td> <td></td> </tr>
24   <tr> <td>postgres</td> <td>PostgreSQL Server</td> <td>/bin/bash</td> </tr>
25   <tr> <td>pshafae</td> <td>John Shafaee</td> <td>/bin/bash</td> </tr>
26   <tr> <td>root</td> <td>root</td> <td>/bin/bash</td> </tr>
27   <tr> <td>shutdown</td> <td>shutdown</td> <td>/sbin/shutdown</td> </tr>
28   <tr> <td>squid</td> <td></td> <td>/dev/null</td> </tr>
29   <tr> <td>sympa</td> <td>Sympa Mailing list manager</td> <td>/bin/bash</td> </tr>
30   <tr> <td>sync</td> <td>sync</td> <td>/bin/sync</td> </tr>
31   <tr> <td>uucp</td> <td>uucp</td> <td></td> </tr>
32   <tr> <td>xfs</td> <td>X Font Server</td> <td>/bin/false</td> </tr>
33   <tr> <td>zope</td> <td>Zope Server</td> <td>/bin/bash</td> </tr>
34   </table>
```

Here is the code to perform this transformation. The explanation of what's going on follows the example:

```
import string
from Path import Path
Path(":", "wp_example3.path")

from WriteProcessor import WriteProcessor

userInfo={}
pwFile = open('/etc/passwd','r')
pwEntries = pwFile.readlines()

for pwEntry in pwEntries:
    pweParts = string.split(pwEntry[0:-1], ":")
    userName = pweParts[0]
    description = pweParts[4]
    shell = pweParts[6]
    userInfo[userName] = (description, shell)

wp = WriteProcessor('wp_example3b.html', ['.'], vars())
wp.addLoopingRule('userName','(description,shell)', userInfo)
wp.process()
```

In this example, the entries of /etc/password are being indexed using a dictionary. The key field of the dictionary is the user name. Each value in the dictionary (associated with a user name) is a 2-tuple containing other fields from /etc/passwd. Here we have just extracted the description and shell fields and packed them into a 2-tuple.

After the WriteProcessor instance has been constructed, addLoopingRule() is called.[21] This looping rule differs from the other two kinds of rules in that you must describe how the key and value fields are packed separately.[22] It will be clear(er) how the descriptions specified to all of these looping rules are used to implic-

---

21. addLoopingRule() is an alias for addDictLoopingRule(), which exists for legacy reasons since the original WriteProcessor supported only this kind of looping rule.

22. The key and value fields need to be specified separately, mainly to break out the key part from the value part. As you'll discover by selecting the code for the DictLoopingRule, we transform what is shown here into (userName, (description, shell)) in dict.items(), where dict refers to userInfo [the supplied dictionary bound to a local name in the DictLoopingRule.evaluate() method].

itly iterate a given line of variables and map everything correctly when we present the details of the looping rules.

Emitters Again

This example shows how you can use `Emitter` instances to drive WriteProcessor code generation to a string:

```python
import string
from Path import Path

from WriteProcessor import WriteProcessor

states = [
  ['AR','Arkansas'],
  ['AK','Alaska'],
  ['AZ','Arizona'],
  ['CA','California'],
  ['CT','Connecticut']
]

countries = [
  ['US', 'United States'],
  ['IN', 'India'],
  ['ZB', 'Zimbabwe'],
  ['AR', 'Argentina'],
  ['BR', 'Brazil']
]

def CreateSelectList(opt_name, selected, opts):
  env = { 'opt_name' : opt_name }

  wp = WriteProcessor('select_list.html', ['.'], env)

  selected_list = ['SELECTED']
  not_selected_list = ['']

  options = []
  for opt in opts:
     if opt[0] in selected or opt[1] in selected:
        options.append(opt + selected_list)
     else:
        options.append(opt + not_selected_list)

  wp.addListLoopingRule( ['opt_value', 'opt_details', 'opt_selected'], options)
  wp.process()

CreateSelectList('state', ['AZ'], states)
CreateSelectList('country', ['IN'], countries)
```

Triple-Quote Syntax to Group Input Lines

A special syntax exists to allow the WriteProcessor to process an entire group of input lines as if it were a single line of input. This syntax resembles Python's triple-quote syntax for multiline character strings. To enable this functionality, add the "triple_quotes" property as shown in the code below when a WriteProcessor instance is created.

```python
import string
from Path import Path

from WriteProcessor import WriteProcessor

states = [
  ['AR','Arkansas'],
  ['AK','Alaska'],
  ['AZ','Arizona'],
  ['CA','California'],
  ['CT','Connecticut']
]

countries = [
  ['US', 'United States'],
  ['IN', 'India'],
  ['ZB', 'Zimbabwe'],
  ['AR', 'Argentina'],
  ['BR', 'Brazil']
]

def CreateSelectList(opt_name, selected, opts):
  env = { 'opt_name' : opt_name }

  wp = WriteProcessor('select_list_tq.html', ['.'], env, triple_quotes=1)

  selected_list = ['SELECTED']
  not_selected_list = ['']

  options = []
  for opt in opts:
      if opt[0] in selected or opt[1] in selected:
         options.append(opt + selected_list)
      else:
         options.append(opt + not_selected_list)

  wp.addListLoopingRule( ['opt_value', 'opt_details', 'opt_selected'], options)
  wp.process()

CreateSelectList('state', ['AZ'], states)
CreateSelectList('country', ['IN'], countries)


<select name="state">
  <option value="AR" >
Arkansas
</option>
<option value="AK" >
Alaska
</option>
<option value="AZ" SELECTED>
```

```
Arizona

<select name="state">

  <option value="AR" >
    Arkansas
  </option>

  <option value="AK" >
    Alaska
  </option>

  <option value="AZ" SELECTED>
    Arizona
  </option>

  <option value="CA" >
    California
  </option>

  <option value="CT" >
    Connecticut
  </option>

</select>

<select name="country">
  <option value="US" >
    United States
  </option>

  <option value="IN" SELECTED>
    India
  </option>

  <option value="ZB" >
    Zimbabwe
  </option>

  <option value="AR" >
    Argentina
  </option>

  <option value="BR" >
    Brazil
  </option>

</select>
```

WriteProcessor Design and Implementation

The WriteProcessor is a fairly involved class. Here the key classes involved in the design and how they interact will be presented, followed by a discussion of the key methods. The basic design of the

WriteProcessor can be understood by taking a look at the constructor, which defines the instance variables shown in Table 9–1.

Table 9–1
WriteProcessor Instance Variables

Attribute	Description
`self.emitter`	Where to send the output generated from a subsequent call to the `process()` method, which performs variable substitution.
`self.searchPath`	A list of directories in which to find any included file. Inclusions can be performed from any input line beginning with ">".
`self.fileName`	The name of the file to be processed. In lieu of specifying a file name, a file handle (`fp`) may be specified at construction time.
`self.fp`	The file handle corresponding to the open file. If a file name was specified at construction time, `fp` is assigned the result of opening `self.fileName` for input.
`self.env`	An environment in which evaluation takes place. Evaluation here means when a SimpleWriter variable is found, against which dictionary the variable bindings will be sought.
`self.stack`	Used to maintain context when file inclusion occurs.
`self.wp`	A SimpleWriter that is used to perform substitutions on each line of input encountered by the WriteProcessor during processing.
`self.loopingRules`	The looping rules are used to substitute values from lists, dictionaries, or list of dictionaries whenever patterns of input variables are found on an input line (see "Looping Rules" on page 468).

The attributes `self.wp` and `self.loopingRules` show that the WriteProcessor collaborates with other classes to get most of its work done. A SimpleWriter object (`self.wp`) is always responsible for actually performing the substitutions of variables against an environment. The looping rules (`self.loopingRules`) are consulted to determine whether a given line of text, which has been determined to have a set of variables (by consulting the SimpleWriter instance), must be evaluated once or via a loop on some data structure.

The looping rules themselves are maintained in a `LoopingRules` object. We opted for a class rather than a simple Python list, first because the list of rules must guarantee uniqueness of a rule with respect to a set of variables, similar to a dictionary. Second, the WriteProcessor instance must be able to consult the list of rules to determine whether a given set of variables actually matches a particular rule. It is possible to rush to judgment about this design decision and suggest the possibility of a data structure (e.g., a dictionary) that guarantees uniqueness and is indexable, since the set of variables for a rule must be unique. This is an interesting possibility; however, it excludes ordering of the rules. One key design goal of the WriteProcessor framework is to support unambiguous semantics: The first rule that matches is the first rule chosen. Any other approach would probably have resulted in user-defined "priority" values, which represent a significantly more complex (and not convincingly more powerful) interface.

This might be an appropriate time to consider what represents a design. Design exists when one is able to conceive an approach to solving a particular problem by identifying the key entities in the system and their interactions, and getting a glimpse of their implementation. This is particularly important in making good software. In the discussion that follows, we have attempted to articulate the design without using obscure language and English that sounds like code. We will adopt the following approach throughout the book when presenting code from the WPL library:

- General design overview and clarifying diagram (if necessary)
- Usage-driven introduction to how the classes work
- High-level presentation of the key classes. We will always present the constructor (which is where we usually define the attributes by convention) and then discuss the key interface methods.
- Detailed walkthrough of essential methods

Class overview   The WriteProcessor class is the only class intended for
export, the class intended for the programmer or the so-called API
(application programming interface). The skeleton of this class is presented below:

```
class WriteProcessor:
    def __init__(self, fileName, searchPath, env, emitter=Emitter(), **props):
    def __repr__(self):
    def addLoopingRule(self, keyPattern, valuePattern, env, sortByKey=1):
    def addListLoopingRule(self, valuePattern, value):
    def addDictListLoopingRule(self, dictList):
    def addRecordLoopingRule(self, dictList):
    def addFileRule(self, fileName, var, function):
    def getEmitter(self):
    def process(self):
    def processFile(self):
    def processFileHandle(self):
    def processList(self, list=[]):
```

The most commonly used methods in this class are __init__()
and process(), which are used to construct the WriteProcessor
instance and do the actual processing of the specified file (fileName) in
a given environment (env).

The add methods collectively support the notion of looping rules
introduced in the earlier section (see "Looping Rules" on page 468).
You have already seen at least four of these methods in action.

The process() method is the method of choice almost all of the
time, since it sends the output directly to standard output–the case most
common in CGI programming, since the output is written to standard
output, which is actually mapped to the outbound socket connection
between the server and the client (browser). The methods
processFile() and processFileHandle() are actually driven by
the process() method, for reasons that were explained in the earlier
design discussion (see "WriteProcessor Design and Implementation" on
page 483). These methods are not intended to be called by application
code directly, since they are "internal" methods. The processList()
can be used in the same manner as process(), where the output is
written line by line to a list instead of to the standard output. This
method is actually deprecated, but has been retained for legacy reasons.
You can direct the output to any of the standard Emitter classes by
passing the "emitter" parameter shown in the constructor. We will
cover the details of the process() method in the next section (after
discussing the essentials of the other important collaborating classes).

The remaining classes in the WriteProcessor module exist to support the looping rules, which are all aimed at making life easy in the

many situations one encounters in programming for the Web with respect to templates, especially in HTML and XML processing.

Looping rules are united by the LoopingRuleAdapter, which is an abstract class. The LoopingRuleAdapter exists with the hope that new looping rules can be added to the framework by taking an existing case and altering it slightly to support the new policy. The skeleton for this class is shown below (i.e., the key interfaces that must be implemented):

```
class LoopingRuleAdapter:
  def __init__(self):
  def preprocess(self):
  def getVarList(self):
  def evaluate(self, wp):
  def getPattern(self, pattern):
```

As always, when we provide an abstract class, we require all subclasses within our jurisdiction to call the superclass's constructor. This is why the abstract class LoopingRuleAdapter has an __init__() method. Although this method is currently empty, this may not always be the case.[23]

We choose the term *pattern* because it is a topic of current interest in the software engineering community. Patterns, after all, are what make other disciplines (the various schools of engineering, science, and medicine) respectable. The computing field has yet to embrace the idea, hence all the "buggy" software and the accompanying perception that it takes more time to develop software with good design principles and documentation. Our experience suggests that it takes more time, effort, and heartache to develop software with a just-in-time methodology, wherein many of the key ideas (documentation, requirements, patterns) are afterthoughts. Thus we will emphasize documentation, design, and patterns throughout the book and show that they can be put into practice.

The LoopingRuleAdapter class addresses tasks that every subclass must do in order for the (new) looping rule to mesh seamlessly into the overall architecture. Every looping rule must:

- __init__()—Provide a constructor that also calls LoopingRuleAdapter's superclass __init__() method
- preprocess(self)—This is explicit preprocessing that must be done immediately after initializing the looping rule class.

---

23. We think of this approach as a way to avoid growing pains later.

This allows initialization to be deferred until the looping rule is about to be used for the first time.

- `getVarList(self)`—A looping rule must always be defined in terms of a list of variables. The list of variables need not be unique, since it will always be converted into a set when placed on the list of looping rules. Similarly, any input line containing a set of variables will also be converted into a set when a match is performed.

- `evaluate(self, wp)`—Evaluate a looping rule using a given WriteProcessor instance (wp). This might appear unusual since the looping rules are maintained by the WriteProcessor, which means a reference to the WriteProcessor itself (`self`) could be maintained in the given `LoopingRuleAdapter` subclass instance. We have chosen our approach as a matter of efficienct use of memory. Since looping rules are used only in connection with a common WriteProcessor, there is really no reason to keep references around that apply only to this particular method.

There are three concrete subclasses of the `LoopingRuleAdapter` class, shown below. Observe that each of these classes religiously follows the pattern by defining all of the required methods.

```
class DictLoopingRule(LoopingRuleAdapter):
  def __init__(self, keyPattern, valuePattern, values, sortByKey=1):
  def preprocess(self):
  def getVarList(self):
  def evaluate(self, wp):
  def __repr__(self):

class ListLoopingRule(LoopingRuleAdapter):
  def __init__(self, valuePattern, values):
  def preprocess(self):
  def evaluate(self, wp):
  def __repr__(self):

class DictListLoopingRule(LoopingRuleAdapter):
  def __init__(self, dictList):
  def preprocess(self):
  def checkStandardDict(self):
  def checkUserDict(self):
  def evaluate(self, wp):
  def __repr__(self):
```

The last of the classes in the WriteProcessor module is the LoopingRuleList class. This class allows the WriteProcessor to maintain a heterogeneous collection of the different kinds of looping rules. Every time one of the WriteProcessor "add" methods is called, one of the three classes shown (DictLoopingRule, DictListLoopingRule, and ListLoopingRule) is constructed and added to a LoopingRuleList instance maintained by the WriteProcessor proper.

```
class LoopingRuleList:
  def __init__(self):
  def match(self, varList):
  def addRule(self, loopingRule):
  def __repr__(self):
```

The following methods are of interest:

addRule()—This method is called by one of the WriteProcessor "add" methods to insert one of the three kinds of looping rules to its list, provided the looping rule is not in conflict with any other existing looping rule.

match()—This method is called both internally and externally. It is used whenever addRule() is called to check whether there is already a rule in the list that matches the variables being used in the looping rule. If there is, a conflict exists. The WriteProcessor also calls this method any time an input line is found having a set of variables. It checks with the LoopingRuleList (this class) instance to determine whether or not a looping rule is to be applied for the current line of text being processed. If so, a looping rule will be returned that can then be used to perform the looping evaluation on the WriteProcessor instance.

That completes the story of the WriteProcessor, a fairly lightweight framework for template processing. Although the code itself, when measured by volume, is fairly concise (thanks also to the world-class Python language), there is a great deal going on in the code itself that we now consider in greater detail.

The devil in the details. This section will give you an understanding of the WriteProcessor code. We will address the following:

- WriteProcessor methods
- The ListLoopingRule class
- The DictListLoopingRule class (fundamental differences from the ListLoopingRule)
- The ListLoopingRule match() method

WriteProcessor Methods

We will begin with a discussion of the WriteProcessor `process()` method, which is the method that (when called) processes a template file in a supplied environment and renders the output using an underlying emitter strategy. Recall that `self.file` (or `self.fp`), `self.env`, and `self.emitter` all refer to the file (file handle), environment, and underlying strategy, respectively. We will not be going through the details of the constructor, so you may wish to take a quick look at the code from the WPL library.[24] Below is the `process()` method, which is a driver to the internal methods that do the work:

```
def process(self):
    if self.fp == None:
        self.processFile()
    else:
        self.processFileHandle()
```

As mentioned earlier, constructing an instance of WriteProcessor is permitted with a filename or a file handle (corresponding to a file that was already opened, usually a `StringIO` instance). If a file handle was specified as the file name, `self.fp` will be set. Otherwise, the file must first be opened by calling `processFile()`, which will call `processFileHandle()` upon succesfully opening the file. Otherwise, `processFileHandle()` is called immediately.

One thing to keep in mind: `processFile()` is called recursively to handle file inclusion (which is done whenever ">" is found at the beginning of a line of text).

The `processFile()` method:

```
1    def processFile(self):
2      for dir in self.searchPath:
3        try:
4          self.fp = open(dir + "/" + self.fileName, 'r')
5        except:
6          continue
7        if self.fp != None: break
8      if self.fp == None:
9        raise "WriteProcessor", "Cannot open: " + str(self.fileName)
10     self.processFileHandle()
```

---

24. This is the first time we will leave it to you to begin studying the code on your own for all of the details. As we get to more complicated cases, we are compelled to present things at a higher level and present details for key methods only. Please make sure you have the book code from http://wpl.sourceforge.net.

Here is a summary of what is going on:

2–7   processFile() has to be sufficiently general to find files that might be included from the very first file (and any subsequently included files). Thus it must look for self.fileName in the search path (self.searchPath contains a list of directories where included files may be found). This means that even the very first file specified at construction time need not be contained in the current working directory and must be found somewhere in the search path. Looking back at the examples, you can see that we were always careful to include "." (the current directory) in the search path.

8–9   Processing fails completely if any file cannot be opened when it is needed; hence the "raise" statement.

10   Assuming all goes well, we can continue processing using processFileHandle().

processFileHandle() is the method that reads the template file one line at a time and directs traffic. This method gets pretty involved and is explained in detail following the code.

```
1    def processFileHandle(self):
2      fileName = self.fileName
3      while 1:
4        line = self.fp.readline()
5        if not line:
6          break
7        if self.triple_quotes:
8          if string.find(line, TRIPLE_QUOTES) == 0:
9            text = ''
10           while 1:
11             line = self.fp.readline()
12             if not line:
13               break
14             if string.find(line,TRIPLE_QUOTES) == 0:
15               break
16             text = text + line
17           line = text
18
19       if line[0] == '>':
20         includedFile = line[1:-1]
21         currentFileState = (self.fileName, self.fp)
22         self.fileName = includedFile
23         self.stack.append(currentFileState)
```

```
24              self.processFile()
25              (self.fileName, self.fp) = self.stack.pop()
26          else:
27              self.wp.compile(line)
28              varList = self.wp.getVars()
29              loopingRule = None
30              if len(varList):
31                  loopingRule = self.loopingRules.match(varList)
32              if loopingRule != None:
33                  loopingRule.evaluate(self.wp)
34              else:
35                  self.wp.emit(self.env)
                    self.fp.close()
```

3–6   While not end of file, do.

7–17   The WriteProcessor supports a feature of allowing triple quotes to be used inside the template file to group a collection of lines. If this feature is enabled and triple quotes are found at the beginning of the line (hence the == 0 test), gobble up the text until a matching triple quote (or end of file) is found. Line 16 demonstrates that the lines of text are concatenated to form a single string (text). Once the end of the block has been found, pretend that a single line of text was found by setting the group of text to the current line of text (line) and fall through to the normal code that processes a line of text.

19–20   If ">" appears at the beginning of the current line of input (even if that line was formed by a triple-quoted block of text), this means a file is being included. The filename must be the only text appearing between the ">" and the end of line, hence the line[1:-1]. line[0] contains the ">" and line[-1] is the end-of-line character, which (unfortunately) is read from the input; this will become (for the moment) the current file of interest (self.fileName)

21–23   Construct a 2-tuple of state information. We will need this in order to resume processing of the current file after completing the recursive processing of the included file. The name of the file currently being processed is stashed in self.fileName; the state information is pushed onto a local stack.

22   Change the current file name.

24–25   Process the included file recursively; when finished, restore the state to the way it was before the call.

26   Otherwise, we are not processing an include; we are processing an ordinary line of input. This is where we finally get to the code that does the processing of the variables in the input and determines whether the substitution is of the "once" variety or requires a looping rule (the "many" variety).

27   Using the SimpleWriter instance (initialized at construction time), `compile()` the line into its internal representation (see "SimpleWriter" on page 443).

28   Extract the list of variables from the line.

29–31   If there are variables on the line, then substitutions must be performed. There are only two types ("once" and "many"). Only if variables were found, find the matching looping rule.

32–33   If a matching rule is found, apply it. Note that the reference to the SimpleWriter is passed to perform this evaluation.

34–35   Otherwise, evaluate the current line of text in the environment supplied at construction time. It is worth noting that the only use of the supplied environment is for lines not matching a particular looping rule. Looping rules each have their own environment (in fact, a whole data structure) dedicated exclusively to evaluating the looping rule.

36   After having visited all lines of text from the current input file, `close()` the current file and exit. This will either return to a context where an include ">" took place or the initial `process()` call, which represents the "port of entry" for most applications of the WriteProcessor.

The `processList()` is a convenient method for generating the output to a list. It is expected that callers of this method will supply a reference to a list object and hold onto it to retrieve the results.

```
def processList(self, list):
  self.emitter = ListEmitter(list)
  self.process()
```

As shown, a `ListEmitter` is constructed to hold the list. All output will be directed to this list and will be available subsequently through the list reference.[25]

---

25. Actually, `self.emitter.getResult()` can also be called to obtain the resultant list.

One might wonder why there are no `processString()` and `processFile()` methods. The `processList()` method is a legacy method that has been retained from the days before WriteProcessor made use of the Emitter framework. Since there are customers out there with existing applications that may use this method, we have chosen to maintain it, with plans to deprecate it at some point. It shows a useful technique for maintaining compatibility.

That is basically all there is to the WriteProcessor. If you removed the looping rules, it might not be all that much more interesting than the SimpleWriter class and Python's built-in string interpolation. The looping rules are where the real meat is found. We conclude with a discussion of how this powerful component of the WriteProcessor works.

List Looping Rules

Let's take a look at the list looping rule (class `ListLoopingRule`). We will go through all of the methods so it is clear how they are constructed, and we will highlight some of the subtleties of the implementation.

Every class must be a subclass of `LoopingRuleAdapter`. We give you some incentive for using it by providing some basic support for handling the patterns, which can be specified either as a string or as a list. When specified as a list, the `getPattern()` method (inherited from the superclass) will translate it into an appropriate string representation.

```
1    class ListLoopingRule(LoopingRuleAdapter):
2      def __init__(self, valuePattern, values):
3        LoopingRuleAdapter.__init__(self)
4        self.valuePattern = valuePattern
5        self.values = values
6        self.variables = []
7        self.preprocess()
```

Constructing the instance is pretty straightforward. Every looping rule has a patterns of variables (here, `valuePattern`) and an underlying data structure (`values`). Care must be taken by the caller not to alter this data structure between construction time and the time the WriteProcessor's `process()` method is called to do the processing of the template. By convention, we simply maintain all of the parameters as instance variables with the same names. The list of variables, `self.variables`, is to be filled in with the names of the variables that were discovered in the pattern (which are ascertained by actually trying to evaluate the string in a "`for`" loop to see whether the data structure matches the packing stated by the caller).

By convention, the constructor always calls an internal method, `preprocess()`, to ensure that the data structure (`values`) can be iterated according to the description provided (`valuePattern`). This process is pretty hairy, because we allow any meaningful tuple expression to be used to define the packing. As shown in the dictionary rule example, the key is just a single string, while the value is a 2-tuple. The key field was described as "`userName`," the value field as "(`description, shell`)."

The preprocess method is shown for class `ListLoopingRule`.

```
1   def preprocess(self):
2     self.valuePattern = self.getPattern(self.valuePattern)
3     testStmt = 'for ' + self.valuePattern + ' in self.values: pass'
4
5     # This code uses metaprogramming to look into the current environment
6     # and find out what variables exist before and after the "exec" statement
7     # is executed below. Thus we need to make sure the namespace does not get
8     # polluted when we call vars(). This is why the next two statements are
9     # defined.
10
11    envBefore = None
12    envNow = None
13
14    # Take a snapshot of the variables in the current environment.
15    envBefore = vars().copy()
16
17    # Now let us check whether the user's pattern is valid. At the same
18    # time, we will determine what variables are actually being used
19    # in the pattern.
20
21    try:
22      exec testStmt
23    except:
24      raise "ListLoopingRule", "Data structure element does not match pattern"
25
26    # Now take a snapshot of the variables after exec.
27    envNow = vars().copy()
28
29    # Compute the SET difference between the new and old environments.
30    for var in envBefore.keys():
31      if envNow.has_key(var): del envNow[var]
32    varSet = BasicSet(envNow.keys())
33    self.variables = varSet.rep
34
35  def evaluate(self, wp):
36    stmt = 'for ' + self.valuePattern + ' in self.values: '
37    stmt = stmt + ' wp.emit(vars())),'
38    exec stmt
```

Summary

Template processing will continue to be an essential part of Web development. Unlike macroprocessors, which impose a great deal of complexity on the developer and are more ideally suited to programming languages such as C, the WriteProcessor class has been designed specifically to facilitate code generation in the Web context: HTML, XML, and SQL are just a few of the languages that work particularly well with this simple yet sophisticated template processing framework.

In the case of HTML, throughout this book we will encounter situations in which there is a need to generate code for key interface elements, including tables, check box lists, selection lists, inputs, etc. And we will be building up fragments of HTML and using the WriteProcessor to drive the code generation. These patterns or fragments can be reused without any needed modifications in your applications to trivially generate code for your forms based on an underlying data structure containing the data.

Go through all of the code examples and try your hand at a couple of your own programs. The WriteProcessor is used extensively, especially to build the applications in Part III of the book, and you will need to master it in order to follow many of the code examples.

10

Form Processing
with WebForm

The WebForm module is one of the core components of the WPL library included with this book. It is used to provide a simpler and more intuitive interface to CGI than found in the current Python CGI module (named cgi). The basic idea of WebForm is to support a more disciplined style of writing CGI scripts, similar to what the Servlets framework provides but with a semipersistent style of operation. We will demonstrate that despite the use of CGI, the framework defined in this chapter and the rest of our book allows you to reap the same (if not more) benefits found in Java Servlets and other Python frameworks such as Zope, with an emphasis on safety and reliability more than on performance.

In this chapter, the focus will be on describing the WebForm approach, explaining its relationship to other WPL components, documenting the WebForm module and related classes proper, and demonstrating its use to write a very simple application (a simple form that does not have any fancy dispatching logic). Although it makes CGI programming easier, WebForm represents a lower level of functionality than typical Web applications require. It is better to think of WebForm as infrastructure, although most programmers familiar with CGI programming in C or the generic libraries shipped with Python (or Perl) will find the WebForm abstraction to be a significant advancement in terms of authoring, comprehending, and maintaining CGI scripts.

Preamble

Hypertext Markup Language is the language used to author Web pages and to present an interface in Web applications. After all, the page remains the interface with the Web. At the time of writing, there are ideas emerging that could revolutionize the notion of a Web page being the interface. Typical Web sites (especially those owned and operated by brick-n-mortar or click-n-mortar companies) employ Java applets and Active/X (and the in-progress .NET initiative) to make "active" client/server-style networked applications. With the exception of JavaScript, the active technologies of Java and Active/X are yet-to-be-proven technologies on the client side and suffer from a number of limitations; e.g., Java is ultraportable and ultracapable, but slow. Browser Java implementations are out of date or broken (sometimes intentionally) in many cases. Active/X and .NET are not yet portable to other platforms such as the Mac and Linux operating systems. As such, the simplicity of the Web interface as found in HTML forms is what you're likely to use to build serious Web applications. As a reader of this book, you have probably already made your choice, but we do care that your application will work with all current browser technologies on the platforms most likely to be used by clients. We impose no limitations on the client whenever possible.

HTML is used to write pages. Increasingly, there are a number of approaches using HTML with embedded code (i.e., the business logic), most bearing the name ?SP (ASP, JSP) but some having different names but the same ideas.[1] If you have already made up your mind to use this approach, you are probably reading the wrong book. We are not advocates of this approach for developing Web sites, especially if you want to maintain them in the long run. We occasionally find ourselves using some JavaScript (when it can help improve client responsiveness), but tend to limit how much we rely upon JavaScript because it tends to impede portability. Nonetheless, JavaScript is excellent when it comes to addressing client-side validation of input, using confirmation dialogs, and generating code dynamically, again when it can improve responsiveness. We prefer JavaScript to the embedding approaches, because the code is a visible part of the document. A strike against embedding code in pages is the "copy and paste" monster, or the "mul-

---

1. PHP[34], PyHP, and others.

tiple maintenance" monster. Suppose you have some code embedded in a page and proceed to copy the page, a normal thing to do when making some "similar looking" pages in HTML. This innocuous act results in an outcome that is unintuitive, and not expected from a software engineering point of view. You now have two copies of the same code in two different pages. If a bug is discovered in the embedded code, it must be fixed and the fix needs to be propagated to all affected files. An interesting rebuttal to this claim might be, "Well, I keep my code organized in functions and libraries, so I won't have the problem." To that we would respond, "We believe you, but have never seen anyone who writes in these embedded languages do it that way."

The ASP and derived languages were created for Web developers and maintainers who are nontechnical and dread even the thought of programming. These languages inhabit the lighter side of programming and tend to cause more harm than good. Typically, powerful linguistic mechanisms for modularization and reuse, such as modules and classes, are missing (despite being fairly trivial enhancements[2]).

So the lowdown is that we reject the notion that HTML and business logic (the code) should be mixed arbitrarily. We think there is strong evidence to support the value of this approach both in software engineering literature and in practice. Client/server applications use the Model-View-Controller design pattern. The XML approach is that HTML should be produced through a sequence of valid transformations. We don't advocate anything as extreme as these approaches; neither works satisfactorily for the Web. The Web is very similar to working with finite state automata (except not quite as elegant from a theoretical perspective). It is theoretically stateless, although state can be maintained through hidden variables and cookies on the client side and persistent session information on the server side. Our approach is to provide as much as possible to make Web development look like regular client/server development, simultaneously recognizing that there are differences and making the process of handling the differences and special cases as elegant as possible by using sound techniques and design patterns.

---

2. But hey, this isn't our framework, so we'll let those who have developed it bring the frameworks up to date with respect to modern software engineering practice.

The Design

The Overall Approach

The idea of WebForm is to provide a basic pattern for processing HTML forms. The basics of CGI were covered in Chapter 7. Basic CGI programming is similar to a remote procedure call: You have a request, an action, and a response. The request is basically typed (GET, POST), has some data (form variables), and possibly has some uploaded file data (a special kind of INPUT variable). The variables are extracted. If there are uploaded files, cookies, etc., these items are extracted as well. Uploaded files are handled specially, since they are processed on demand, whenever the CGI script wants to process them.

In WebForm, variable extraction is the first step. Inputs from a form typically are named uniquely, for example, "username" and "password," but this is not a requirement. There may be many inputs with the same name. A typical application for this is to handle check boxes, which are a tricky case, since a check box input is packed into a request only if the check box was actually selected. If it wasn't selected, no variable is sent.

So how do you handle these? The simplest way is to name all of the check boxes according to the same input. Then you can get all of the values corresponding to particular selected check box items as a single Python list. But what if you also wanted to know what items were not selected? You would have to keep a "mirror" hidden input variable that contains a list of all values present in the check box list. WebForm is still very helpful for managing inputs. In Python's standard "cgi" module, just getting a hold of the inputs is very cumbersome. First, the cgi field storage must be tested, as a dictionary, to see whether the input is defined. Then the singleton versus list cases must be tested separately. In WebForm, a data structure based on dictionary called Directory allows you to organize inputs according to how the application is expecting them. For example, if your Web page does not have duplicate input variable names, you can use the "singleton" option. Otherwise, you can use the "list" or "flattened" options to allow every input to be obtained as a list or flattened. More is said about this later; the idea is to make you aware of the problem.

Once you have the variables, you write the business logic. Not having to worry about how to access the variables means you can focus on the business logic only. (WebForm can even "bind" the variables as if they were attributes of your class, using the Python setattr() intrinsic method. For example, self.username could be used to refer to the username input field.)

Form Inputs Organized As Directories

As mentioned, a feature of WebForm is making it easy to write the business logic by making it possible to view the INPUT variables as entries in a Directory, or as attributes of the instance itself. Let's consider a small fragment of HTML to show some basic principles. Then we will consider a few more complicated examples.

```
<FORM name="myform" action="http://myhost/cgi-bin/myscript.py">
<INPUT name="username" value="">
<INPUT name="password" value="">
</FORM>
```

In this example, there are two inputs, "username" and "password." WebForm can provide access to all of the inputs of a form by making entries in a Directory instance, which is (at the core) a dictionary with the addition of support for hierarchical folders. In most forms, inputs have different names—hence, a particular name appears only once. This means that only a single entry need be made in the dictionary. The interface we provide for the user is via an attribute of WebForm named self.form_vars, which is an instance of class Directory. self.form_vars["username"] and self.form_vars["password"] can be used to obtain the values of these fields.[3]

Thus far, this doesn't seem very different from Python's built-in cgi module and dictionary interfaces. However, consider the following example:

```
<form ...>
<input type="checkbox" name="topping" value="pepperoni">
Pepperoni
</input>
<input type="checkbox" name="topping" value="spinach">
Spinach
</input>
<input type="checkbox" name="topping" value="tomato">
Tomato
</input>
</form>
```

Hey! We live in Chicago, and pizza is an important part of our culture. As it turns out, this is also a good example of when to use inputs with

---

3. We have not yet discussed the notion of default values, which may be specified for the Directory class but not for Python dictionaries. In Python's cgi module, attempting to get an input that is not defined in the form results in a KeyError exception. In WebForm, the policy can be set explicitly by the user (either provide a default value or raise an exception).

the same name. Here we have presented only the part of the form that pertains to toppings, with no emphasis on formatting or appearance.

In Python's `cgi` module, one must go through some contortions to distinguish these inputs from singleton inputs (i.e., the input names that appear only once in the form) with code similar to:

```
if form.has_key("topping"):
   if type(form["topping"]) == type([]):
      toppings = form["topping"]
   else
      toppings = [form["toppping"]]
else:
   toppings = []
```

And yes, this kind of code technically should be executed for every input variable that can occur more than once. (In fact, since it is easy to circumvent a Web page and post requests without going through the browser, your code should always protect against the possibility of outside attacks that could cause it to fail, even if the failure is more or less innocuous. WebForm protects you from such situations.) The selection structure above ensures that `toppings` will be a list, regardless of whether the input appeared 0, 1, or N times (where $N > 1$). In Python's `cgi` module, the case of one time does not result in a list and, instead, results in a single string value.

WebForm allows you to introduce automation into this by setting the `input_naming_policy` configuration parameter. You can specify a number of options:

- `value`—Make an entry for the first occurrence of a found input in the Directory.
- `value_list`—Make a single entry for all occurrences of input in the Directory.
- `subdir_numbered`—Make numbered entries in a subdirectory named after the input. For example, `/topping` would be the Directory name, and the entries would be named with integers, so they can be iterated, beginning from 0. Keep in mind that the numbers simply refer to the number of the occurrence, not its position in a list, etc. Nonetheless, this gives you a great deal of power. Given the `self.form_vars` references, you can do the following to get the inputs:

```
self.form_vars.cd("/topping");
for i in len(self.form_vars.keys()):
   topping = self.form_vars[i]
   ... do something with the topping
```

And if order of the toppings is not important:

```
self.form_vars.cd("/topping")
toppings = self.form_vars.values()
```

This might not seem like a useful thing at first glance. If you take a second look at the interface provided in the standard Python `cgi` module (1.52, 1.6, 2.0), you will have a new appreciation for it.

- `subdir_named`—Named entries in a subdirectory after the input. The entries are named the same as the directory, followed by underscore, followed by the number. In the case of our example, entries are written to `/topping`: `topping_0`, `topping_1`, and `topping_2`, etc. This is for those who might want to make their code more self-documenting, since changing Directory and using subscripts might not have the same readability. (`self.form_vars[0]` doesn't say as much as `self.form_vars["topping_0"]`.)

The Directory provides a powerful interface for being able to manage inputs.[4] And, as shown, the WebForm class introduces a great deal of automation into the entire process, while remaining completely general and extensible. (It would be very easy to add other schemes for organizing the inputs in the directory.) But there does appear to be an interesting omission. What has happened to the ability to organize the inputs having a common name at the top level of the Directory object? Why can't entries such as `topping_0` and so on be written directly at the top level when there are collisions? Consider the following example:

```
<form ...>
<input type="checkbox" name="topping" value="pepperoni">
Pepperoni
</input>
<input type="checkbox" name="topping" value="spinach">
Spinach
</input>
<input type="checkbox" name="topping" value="tomato">
Tomato
</input>
<input type="checkbox" name="topping_0" value="cheese">
Extra Cheese
</input>
</form>
```

---

4. We are sometimes embarassed to write so much about the Directory class, as it is based on an utterly familiar idea. Little did we know that so much mileage could be gotten from such a cheap car!

Here we have introduced a fourth variable to show the dangers of getting too creative with naming. If the entries were not written into a subdirectory for inputs having a common name, a potentially dangerous situation would arise, especially in this case. Here we have introduced `topping_0`, which would result in a top-level Directory collision if the toppings having a common name were written to the top-level directory, using the naming scheme we described for the `subdir_named` option. In fact, the `subdir_numbered` option would be no better, since there would be no way to guarantee the uniqueness of numbered entries without making the overall interface incomprehensible. Using the `subdir_named` option guarantees that no collisions will ever occur in the Directory[5] (at any level).

In summary, the ability to organize inputs into a Directory is a powerful concept of WebForm and is arguably its best feature. But there is a lot more that WebForm can do for you, so don't stop reading. Many programmers go out of their way to avoid naming the inputs the same, despite the fact that doing so can dramatically simplify coding of a script. This feature of HTML forms is actually useful: In the case of check-box lists, it allows you to know what items, if any, were selected and to put all of them in a Python list. This has the advantage of grouping the related check boxes and working with them as a group, instead of having to devise a naming scheme to refer to individual check boxes and map them back to some underlying database record or other data structure.

File Inputs

HTML supports a special kind of `INPUT` known colloquially as a "file upload" input. The use of file upload inputs was covered extensively in "File Input" on page 342 (in Chapter 7). To summarize briefly, a file input looks like this in HTML:

```
<form action="http://192.168.1.1/cgi-bin/submitfile"
    enctype="multipart/form-data"
    method="POST">
<p>
The file: <input type="FILE" name="file" size="20" maxlength="40">
</p>
</form>
```

---

5. This assertion can be proven easily. An exercise about this topic and a proof will be offered in a solutions manual.

When working with file inputs, observe that a file appears to be like any other text input, with a key difference: File inputs work only in the context of the multipart/form-data encoding. If the encoding type is not set accordingly, file inputs will have no effect.

In Python's `cgi` module, file inputs are handled with `FieldStorage` objects. As we mentioned with inputs, the interface is a bit awkward. It is less awkward for working with file objects. In the interest of presenting a uniform interface to WebForm users, we arrange file inputs into a Directory instance, available as `self.file_vars`. Each file input appears in its own Directory and is accessed as a direct subdirectory. In the HTML above, the name of the input is "file," so it will be stored in a Directory named `/file`.

Support for Handling Undefined Variables

A big problem associated with processing forms is the handling of `INPUT` variables that may never be filled in. Consider the following definition of a text `INPUT`:

```
<input type="text" name="username">
```

In HTML it is not required to provide the `VALUE` attribute to indicate a value for the `INPUT`.

Emitter Revisited

Recall the Emitter strategy that was introduced in the discussion of the WriteProcessor. The Emitter concept allows the output to be directed to different destinations. In the case of WebForm processing, the common (and default) case is to direct output to standard output, which is the output file handle associated with the socket connecting the Web server to the client browser. There are times, however, when it is desired to use the WebForm recursively. We will discuss this in Chapter 14.

Cookie Processing

Cookie processing is handled transparently in the WebForm framework. We make use of a third-party package to parse the cookies (which are defined in an RFC), but provide a layer above this that allows cookies to be added and removed.

Encoders

WebForm now has an encoder, which is an application of the strategy pattern to allow alternate encodings, beside text, to be generated.

The Code

Overview of WebForm Class Structure

The WebForm module consists of the WebForm class, which provides the infrastructure for the pattern we have described in the preceding discussion. To be a WebForm, a class simply extends the WebForm base class and provides an implementation of the `process()` method, which is responsible for supplying the business logic.

There are several categories of methods in WebForm, only a small number of which must be mastered to make the most basic CGI scripts:

- **Constructor**–Initialize the WebForm from the CGI form data. The CGI form data is extracted using Python's intrinsic `cgi` module. A number of other features, such as supplying default values for inputs from a properties file, processing WebForm configuration properties (there are a number of them), etc., are performed in the constructor. As we will see, many of the properties give the subclass control over how certain WebForm features work, and always have meaningful default values.
- **Directory-enabled management of input variables, input files, and cookies**–The Directory class (which will be introduced in Chapter 12) allows for sophisticated management of hierarchical dictionaries. Based on configuration properties, the programmer has turnkey control over how the entries are organized in the Directory. The Directory concept can map different inputs having the same name "x" to `x_0`, `x_1`, . . . in the dictionary, or make them accessible as an array of values `x[0]`, `x[1]`, . . ., or as attributes of the class `self.m_x_0`, `self.m_x_1`, . . . or `self.m_x[0]`. This feature of WebForm is utterly indispensible. The Python `cgi` module tries too hard to be a dictionary, and it ends up not being a terribly satisfactory interface for getting the variables, requiring extensive testing of special cases.

- **Content Headers**—Most errors happen when writing Web applications because one forgets to emit the correct "content header." WebForm allows you to emit any content header before any other output is generated. This is made possible because the WebForm intercepts the standard output's file descriptor to defer any output until the content header has been emitted (provided the subclass has not overridden the default behavior).

Template-Driven Code Generation • As every CGI script is responsible for generating a valid MIME document, code generation can be completely automated in the case of `text/html` or `text/plain` encodings. After the `process()` method (which is where the subclass defines the business logic) is run, the `encode()` method is called to drive code generation. Methods are provided to set the name of the file to be used as the template file. It is possible to disable the use of the WriteProcessor, using a configuration parameter at construction time, and to use one's own code-generation method.

The Constructor

There is only one required parameter to the WebForm constructor, which is named `form`. This parameter must correspond to the `cgi.FieldStorage()` that was discussed in Chapter 7. In some respects, WebForm can be thought of as a user-friendly wrapper to the `cgi` module, which is not ideally suited for writing complex CGI programs. WebForm is intended to be a lower-level component and is a key building block for the Slither framework as it pertains to processing form variables and generating code.

The rest of the parameters are Python keyword parameters. Using keyword parameters is the preferred approach to defining a constructor, especially a constructor whose parameters are effectively properties that are set once and used for the duration of the object's lifetime.

Table 10–1 lists the properties that can be set for any WebForm instance. These provide the ability to gain custom control of certain aspects that are normally not provided by the underlying `cgi` module.

Table 10–1
Construction Properties for WebForm

Property	Explanation	Default Value
default_vars	A dictionary containing any default variables. When processing forms that have common inputs, the use of default_variables can ensure that a meaningful default value is supplied.	{}
search_path	Where to find any additional HTML or text files that are included. This is mostly needed for encoding results in a WebForm where a WriteProcessor is used. Of course, any WebForm Encoder can make use of this path to search, if desired.	['.']
content_type	The type of encoding to be performed based on a set of known standard encodings. Presently text/plain, text/html, and text/xml are the only supported encodings for text, and others are supported using the new WebFormEncoder classes.	'text/html'
read_cookies	Read the cookies from the environment. The cookies are read into a SimpleCookie instance, which is an open source cookie package written in Python that stores the cookies in a Python dictionary. Permitted values are 'yes' and 'no' or None (which means 'no').	'yes'
write_cookies	Write the cookies when generating code. The cookies are written as part of the HTTP reply. Permitted values are 'yes' and 'no' or None.	'yes'

Table 10–1
Construction Properties for WebForm (Continued)

Property	Explanation	Default Value
`emit_strategy`	The target for all output. This must be an instance of `Emitter`.	An instance of `Emitter()`. This results in any output being sent to standard output.
`stdout`	Where to redirect output sent to standard output. This must be either `sys.stderr` or a `StringIO` instance.	Output sent to standard output during the call to `process()`, which precedes the call to generate output using `encode()`, is redirected to a `StringIO()` instance. You can also specify your own instance if there is a need to write output while processing. We go out of our way to discourage this so you will focus on business logic and encoding results using a template file. *Note*: Any call, especially `print`, will appear to be ignored. If you need to do logging, see Chapter 11.
`config_dir`	Where to search for a WebForm subclass specific configuration file. This configuration file is read using a Python `ConfigParser`. The configuration file can be used on a per-class basis to set a number of properties that will be used as default values. This is particularly effective for supplying default values for form `INPUT` variables to ensure they are set properly.	`'.'`
`read_config_file`	Whether or not the configuration file should be used.	
`bind options`		

The constructor is where most of the work happens in this class. As this is a fairly lengthy method, it will be presented in blocks of code with commentary:

```
def __init__(self, form, another_web_form=None, **props):
```

Parameters • A WebForm is constructed by using the `cgi` module and getting a reference to `cgi.FieldStorage()` via the form parameter. It is permitted to initialize the WebForm from another WebForm instance as well.

Redirecting Standard Output • A `StringIO` instance is created to intercept any output that is sent to standard output. `StringIO` objects provide a way of sending output to a growable string representation, very similar to a StringWriter in Java or an ostrstream in C++. The reason for intercepting output is that a CGI script should not be writing to standard output before sending the `Content-type` header back to the client.

```
stdout_capture = StringIO.StringIO()
```

Handling Keyword Parameters and Defaults • The default properties are set in dictionary `default_props`. These are values that will be used if the properties are not explicitly set by a customer of WebForm. The key here is to make reasonable settings that (we hope) represent the most common settings. Each of the keys used in this dictionary corresponds to keyword parameters that can be passed to the constructor.

```
1         default_props = {
2             'default_vars' : {},
3             'search_path' : ['.'],
4             'content_type' : 'text/html',
5             'write_content_type' : 'yes',
6             'read_cookies' : 'yes',
7             'write_cookies' : 'yes',
8             'emit_strategy' : Emitter(),
9             'stdout' : stdout_capture,
10            'config_dir' : '.',
11            'read_config_file' : 'yes',
12            'prefix' : 'm_',
13            'encode_target' : None
14        }
```

Checking Keyword Parameters • The code below is used to check the keyword parameters (which come down via the `props` reference).

```
1        self.form = form
2    if another_web_form != None:
3        for prop_name in default_props.keys():
4            prop_value = getattr(another_web_form, prop_name)
5            props[prop_name] = prop_value
6    else:
7        for prop_name in default_props.keys():
8            if not props.has_key(prop_name):
9                props[prop_name] = default_props[prop_name]
```

The constructor for WebForm allows two possibilities: a WebForm is either being initialized for the first time from the underlying `cgi` module or is being initialized from another WebForm. The outcome of this block of code, regardless of which possibility is being considered, is to initialize the dictionary `props`. This dictionary is evaluated (below) to check for valid values, etc.

In lines 2–5 above (where we are initializing from another Web-Form), note the use of `getattr(object, name)` to initialize the `props` dictionary from the attributes (instance variables) of the other WebForm instance. As will be shown shortly, these attributes are set upon validation of all entries in `props`.

In lines 7–9 (where we are initializing a WebForm otherwise), we are setting `props` from `default_props` only if a particular keyword parameter was not used, hence the `not` test on line 8.

Once the dictionary `props` is defined, the next step is to check whether the property has a valid value. If not, we will set a default value.

```
1    for prop_name in default_props.keys():
2        check_method_name = 'check_%s' % prop_name
3        if hasattr(self, check_method_name):
4            check_method = getattr(self, check_method_name)
5            new_value = check_method(props[prop_name], \
6                                      default_props[prop_name])
7            setattr(self, prop_name, new_value)
```

For all keys in `default_props`, we call an internal "check" method to determine whether the property as set is valid. This is done by looking up the internal check method and calling it. This shows Python's excellent support for introspection, which proves ideal for the task. Each check method is expected to be named after the attribute being checked, (e.g., `check_emit_strategy()` is the method that checks whether property `emit_strategy` has been set correctly). Note that once a check has completed, an attribute is set in the instance. For example, after `check_emit_strategy()` is done, `self.emit_strategy` can be used to refer to the value and the entries in `props,` and `default_props` is no longer needed.

Check methods all have the following general form and appear in the WebForm class's source code just beneath the constructor code. For example, `check_content_type()` is defined as follows:

```
def check_content_type(self, current_value, default_value):
    if not current_value in ['text/html', 'text/plain', 'text/plain']:
        return default_value
    return current_value
```

Every check method is a method that checks the current value (`current_value`) of a property and is also given the default value (`default_value`) to which the property will be set if it has been set incorrectly. Here, `current_value` is tested for one of the valid text content encodings. If an invalid value has been passed to the constructor, a default value (`default_value`) is set, which actually comes from the `default_props` table.

Default Form Variables • Once all of the values in `props` have been checked with the appropriate internal check method, the next step is to process the configuration file. The configuration file is read only if the 'read_config_file' keyword parameter was set to "yes".[6]

```
1           if self.read_config_file == 'yes':
2               conf_vars = self.__parse_config_file()
3           else:
4               conf_vars = {}
```

The configuration file is used to supply default values for form variables, which are processed later in the constructor call. Note in lines 2 and 3 that the outcome is always to set `conf_vars`, which is a Python dictionary. The internal method, `__parse_config_file()`, does the actual work, using Python's `ConfigParser`. The format of a config file is the same as expected by the `ConfigParser` class. For example, suppose you had a form with inputs `username` and `password` and wanted to guarantee that these variables are set. Suppose further that the name of your WebForm subclass is `Authenticate`. You could define a configuration file (`Authenticate.conf`) as follows:

---

6. Note here that `self.read_config_file` became initialized as a result of the `props` code just presented. The `setattr()` call was used to set `read_config_file` in `self` after the check was performed.

```
[Authenticate]
username=
password=
```

The outcome of `self.__parse_config_file()` would be to create a dictionary that contains two keys (`username` and `password`) that are both set to the empty string.

We will cover the details of this method after presenting the remaining constructor code. For now, the definition of the outcome should suffice to explain the remaining constructor code. So why do we want default values? There are many reasons:

- The fact that they are listed in a `.conf` file allows them to be clearly identified as having default values, as opposed to when they are listed in the `.py` source code for your business logic.
- It is possible to write much more concise code by having reasonable default assumptions for values. In Python, a dictionary object returns a `KeyError` when one attempts to use a key that is not defined in the dictionary. While we think this is a good policy, it ends up creating work for someone (us). Form inputs are all text, so the approach of a configuration file makes a lot of sense to list the default values.
- The `ConfigParser` makes the processing of defaults a snap.

Cookies • Once the defaults have been processed, the next step is to check for cookies. Cookies are only processed if the keyword parameter `read_cookies` was set to the value "yes."

```
1          self.cookies = []
2          if self.read_cookies == 'yes':
3              cookie = self.__load_cookie()
4              if cookie != None:
5                  self.cookies.append(cookie)
6                  self.startingCookieCount = 1
7              else:
8                  self.startingCookieCount = 0
```

Cookies are maintained in a `SimpleCookie` object, which allows a set of cookies to be accessed with a dictionary-like interface. It is possible there are no cookies in the environment, in which case no `Simple-Cookie` object will be created. The internal method, `__load_cookie()`, handles the details of creating a `SimpleCookie` (if needed) and returns a reference. If a non-null reference is returned, the list `self.cookies` is updated to contain the reference. Consequently, `self.startingCookieCount` is set to 0 or 1 to indicate the number of entries on this list at the beginning.

Building Directories of Form and File Variables • The rest of the constructor code is dedicated to building two directories for the form and file input variables (`self.form_vars` and `self.file_vars`, respectively).

```
1        self.form_vars = Directory({})
2        self.form_vars.update(self.default_vars)
3        self.form_vars.update(conf_vars)
4        self.file_vars = Directory({})
```

As described in Chapter 12, the Directory class is a hierarchical dictionary similar to the Unix/Windows file system. It supports all of the intrinsic dictionary methods (being a subclass of `UserDict`). After an empty Directory is created, the default variables and the other variables read from the configuration file are merged into the directory. Note that after line 4, we still have not processed the form variables (`self.form`). This is achieved in the following line of code:

```
self.__create_directories(form)
```

We will discuss the details of this internal method shortly. The outcome is to place all form and file input variables into the `self.form_vars` and `self.file_vars` Directory objects, respectively.

Et Cetera • Finally, the following code executes at the end of the constructor.

```
self.__encode_count = 0
```

The internal variable, `self.__encode_count`, is used to maintain a private count of the number of times that the `encode()` method has been called to perform code generation since the WebForm was instantiated.

The constructor is the most complex method in the WebForm class. As is often the case in object-oriented programming, when attempting to design an easy interface for users, the setup can get complicated. Since WebForm aims to make it easy for programmers to work with form inputs, cookies, and generating results, there are many tasks to be performed to provide this interface. When a subclass is created for a WebForm (contrasted with the innate support Python provides for CGI programming), the subclass gets everything that it wants or needs. By setting simple properties, a feature can be enabled or disabled with minimum effort.

While discussing the constructor, we alluded to future discussion of the internal methods that do the difficult work. We present the details of implementation in the following sections.

__parse_config_file(self).   This internal method, called only by the constructor, is responsible for reading in the configuration file, if present. The code attempts to read a file that has the same name as the class followed by ".conf". The rest of the work is done by using the ConfigParser interfaces to iterate over all of the variables defined in a section also named after the class. In the interest of clarity, if one creates a subclass of WebForm, say, named Authenticate, the configuration file would be expected to have the name Authenticate.conf and a section [Authenticate]. The actual code appears below:

```
1    formDefaults = {}
2    try:
3        formId = self.__class__.__name__
4        configFile = self.config_dir + '/' + formId + '.conf'
5        confParser = ConfigParser.ConfigParser()
6        confParser.read( configFile )
7        optionList = confParser.options(formId)
8        try:
9            optionList.remove('__name__')
10       except:
11           pass
12       for option in optionList:
13           optionValue = confParser.get(formId, option)
14           formDefaults[option] = optionValue
15       self.config_file_processed = 1
16   except:
17       self.config_file_processed = 0
18   return formDefaults
```

Here is what the code does:

1   `formDefaults` is a dictionary that will be filled in with
          properties defined in the configuration file. We use
          `ConfigParser` to process a list of properties of the form
          `name=value`.

2, 15–17 If for any reason the process of reading the configuration file fails,
          a dictionary will be returned. The constructor has been written
          with the intention of not throwing exceptions, except under the
          worst of circumstances. Not being able to read an optional
          configuration file is an example of a harmless outcome from the
          standpoint of construction, because the intent is to provide default
          values that will be dumped into the Directory object
          `self.form_vars`. Subclasses can test whether the configuration
          file was actually processed and raise an exception, if desired.

3   The name of the configuration file is expected to be the same
          name of the class followed by `.conf`, and `self.config_dir` is
          the value of the keyword parameter `config_dir`. As mentioned
          earlier, this defaults to `"."`   but can be set to an alternate
          location. We do not allow the name of the configuration file to be
          changed, to enforce some degree of consistency between the class
          name and its configuration file. (We do this for much the same
          reason that Java requires a class to be created that has a matching
          filename ending in .java, so this kind of decision is not without
          precedent.)

`__create_directories(self)`..   This internal method, called
only by the constructor, is used to organize the form variables and
uploaded files into directories. Recalling the discussion of the `cgi` module (see Chapter 7, and earlier in this chapter), the interfaces for extracting form and file variables in the `cgi` module are a bit awkward. For
example, suppose you have a variable "username" in your form; you
must either use `form['username'].value` or `form['user-`
`name'][occurrence-number].value`. This is simply not the way
that dictionaries are normally used—the `.value` is used only to cause file
inputs to be read in completely.

We choose to store the variables in a Dictionary object (see "The
Design" on page 500). This proves to be an elegant approach for managing the inputs for the two cases (where an input can occur once or
multiple times for a particular name), freeing you from having to code
complex cases when processing forms.

```
1       def __create_directories(self, form):
2           for var in form.keys():
3               try:
4                   if type(form[var]) == type([]):
5                       form_var = form[var][0]
6                   else:
7                       form_var = form[var]
8
9                   if form_var.filename == None:
10                      self.form_vars[var] = form_var.value
11                  else:
12                      self.file_vars[var] = (form_var.filename, form_var.file)
13                      self.file_vars.create(var)
14                      self.file_vars.cd(var)
15                      self.file_vars['filename'] = form_var.filename
16                      self.file_vars['file'] = form_var.file
17                      self.file_vars.cd('/')
18
19                  if type(form[var]) == type([]):
20                      self.form_vars.create(var)
21                      self.form_vars.cd(var)
22                      self.form_vars[var] = []
23                      varCount = 0
24                      for form_var in form[var]:
25                          if form_var.filename == None:
26                              self.form_vars["%s_%d"%(var,varCount)] = form_var.value
27                              self.form_vars[var].append(form_var.value)
28                              varCount = varCount + 1
29                      self.form_vars.cd('/')
30              except:
31                  raise "WebFormException: %s = %s" % (var, form[var])
```

Here is what is going on:

1   The incoming form is expected to be a reference to `cgi.FieldStorage()`.

2   For all variables defined in the form, including file upload inputs.

4–7   There are actually four cases, due to the possibility of inputs having the same name. If two or more inputs have the same name, they will be grouped as a list in the `cgi.FieldStorage()`. The first form variable is assigned to `form_var`, which is then tested.

9–10   If the filename attribute of `form_var` is `None`, this means that the input is not a file input. The input's name and value pair are saved in `self.form_vars`. *Note*: This is only the first occurrence of the input for `name`. If there were a list, processing would occur later.

11–17   Otherwise, a file input was found. A directory is created at the root level (`"/"`) with a subdirectory named after the input name itself. Two entries are placed in the directory, `filename` and `file`, which allows the user-supplied name and file content to be read later. WebForm actually uses this directory information to supply the file content with an accessor method.

19–29   This code handles the case where more than one input occurs with the same name. When this happens, the inputs are stored in a subdirectory in two ways: as a list entry, and as numbered entries. Suppose you had two inputs named `topping`. After all the code in the loop has executed, you'd have the first variable stored in `"/"` as `topping`. You'd have a directory named `"/topping"` with entries `"topping"` (the list of all inputs named `topping`), `"topping_0"` (the first topping, same value as stored in the root directory `"/"`), and `"opping_1"` (the second topping). This approach allows the case for multiple inputs with the same name to be easily identified and processed through a uniform interface that is as intuitive as the Python dictionary.

Using WebForm

Most of the story in WebForm is about providing a class that has extensive capabilities that can be taken advantage of in any subclass. For the vast majority of Web applications, the WebForm provides a much more convenient interface for processing and dispatching forms and driving code generation than the intrinsic `cgi` module in Python.

Process Method • To take advantage of a WebForm, one creates a subclass of WebForm and includes a `process()` method. As `process()` is an abstract method, the subclass is expected to provide a concrete implementation of this method. This approach should not make an upcall to the superclass method, which throws an exception to indicate the method is "not implemented yet."

In the course of processing (i.e., the `process()` method), a number of calls can be made to a number of methods, in addition to the variables `form_vars` and `file_vars`. The methods are summarized in the following sections. Most of them are accessor/mutator style methods that provide a simple API.

The `process()` method is an abstract method that must be overridden in a subclass. This is where the actual code for processing a form would go. Let's take a look at how a `process()` method would be written to authenticate a user. The HTML for the form (Login.html) might look something like this:

```
1  <form method="POST" action="http://hostname/cgi-bin/Login.py">
2  Login ID <input type="text" name="login_id"> <br>
3  Password <input type="password" name="password"> <br>
4  </form>
```

The processing might look something like this:

```
1  public class Login(WebForm):
2     def __init__(self):
3        ...
4     def process(self):
5        login_id = self.form_vars['login_id']
6        password = self.form_vars['password']
7        if not login_id or not password:
8           self.set_encode_file_name('LoginFailure.html')
9           return
10       if not try_login(login_id, password):
11          self.set_encode_file_name('LoginFailure.html')
12          return
13       self.set_encode_file_name('LoginSuccessful.html')
14
15    def try_login(login_id, password):
16       return 1
```

A few comments:

- This code is much simpler than the equivalent written in the Python cgi module because the code in lines 5–6 does not need to test whether the input is a list or a single value. In Web-Form one can obtain the values of multivalued inputs by retrieving the list of values from the Directory self.form_vars; however, the common case must be easy to code, and WebForm makes the most common case (single input has a single value) as compact as possible.
- The process() method is not supposed to write anything to standard output directly. Any attempt to do so directly results in the calls being intercepted and redirected to a string I/O object. We seldom find a need to do so in practice from a given process() method implementation. Here the calls to self.set_encode_file_name(name) result in eventual calls to generate the final output.
- The try_login(login_id, password) method would check the credentials against a database or flat file. We show the result always being true for concise presentation.

Cookie Processing • The ability to process cookies is transparently provided to any WebForm. Cookies are extracted from the environment and are stored in a `SimpleCookie` instance.[7]

Table 10–2
WebForm Cookie Processing Methods

Method	What It Does
`has_cookies(self)`	This method can be called to determine whether any cookies were found at construction time. `has_cookies()` only returns true when one cookie was found during the construction process.
`get_new_cookie(self)`	This method allocates a new `SimpleCookie` object (discussed earlier) to allow
`match_one_cookie(self, *vars)`	This method returns the first `SimpleCookie` instance that contains all of the vars supplied as extra arguments (vars).
`match_all_cookies(self, *vars)`	This method returns all `SimpleCookie` instances that contain the vars supplied as extra arguments (vars).
`get_cookies(self)`	This method allows all cookies to be retrieved as a list of `SimpleCookie` instances.

Let's consider the `Login` class again. Suppose we want to cache the login credentials in a cookie stored on the client. We could have a different landing page for users who have logged onto the system before. We will call this the `BeenHereBefore` class. It would be structured as follows:

```
1    public class BeenHereBefore(WebForm):
2        def __init__(self):
3            ...
4        def process(self):
5            if self.has_cookies():
6                cookie = self.match_one_cookie('login_id','password')
7                if not cookie:
8                    self.set_encode_file_name('Login.html')
9                    return
10           else:
```

---

7. The `SimpleCookie` class allows one to work with cookies using a Python dictionary. This class also addresses the relevant issue of generating the `Set-Cookie` headers required in the HTTP response. This class was discussed earlier in this chapter.

```
11          self.set_encode_file_name('Login.html')
12          return
13
14      login_id = cookie['login_id']
15      password = cookie['password']
16      if not login_id or not password:
17          self.set_encode_file_name('LoginFailure.html')
18          return
19      if not try_login(login_id, password):
20          self.set_encode_file_name('LoginFailure.html')
21          return
22      self.set_encode_file_name('LoginSuccessful.html')
23
24   def try_login(login_id,password):
25       return 1
```

This code demonstrates the use of the basic cookie interface. Cookie information is obtained by performing a match, based on the expected variables. For example, login_id and password are the variables we want to track. The method self.match_one_cookie() allows any number of arguments to be passed, all of which are expected to be strings corresponding to the names of cookies. The result is either a SimpleCookie instance or None, meaning that the cookie variable names did not appear in any cookie. Observe that login_id and password are obtained from the cookie using the cookie as a Python dictionary.

The Login class requires some modifications to make the cookie processing story complete. (Yes, these two classes can probably be merged, but this solution ends up being cleaner and is easier to understand.) Upon a successful login, a cookie should be set with the credentials. Here is the reworked version that will store the credentials in a cookie for potential use:

```
1   public class Login(WebForm):
2       def __init__(self):
3           ...
4       def process(self):
5           login_id = self.form_vars['login_id']
6           password = self.form_vars['password']
7           if not login_id or not password:
8               self.set_encode_file_name('LoginFailure.html')
9               return
10          if not try_login(login_id, password):
11              self.set_encode_file_name('LoginFailure.html')
12              return
13          cookie = self.get_new_cookie()
14          cookie['login_id'] = login_id
15          cookie['password'] = password
```

```
16        self.set_encode_file_name('LoginSuccessful.html')
17
18    def try_login(login_id,password):
19        return 1
```

Code Generation • How exactly does code generation take place? The answer is a bit involved, since the framework is capable of generating any kind of output, including plain text, XML, and binary data streams (such as Zip.)

In the examples we have considered thus far, calls were made to `self.set_encode_file_name(filename)`. This method can be used to indicate what file is to be run through a WriteProcessor instance and rendered as the output (the next page presented to the user). This is done automatically; any references to WriteProcessor variables within `filename` will be substituted with values from `self.form_vars`.

Here is the general-purpose `encode()` method from class WebForm:

```
1    def encode(self, prepend_text=''):
2        emitter = self.emit_strategy
3        if self.write_cookies == 'yes':
4            for cookie in self.cookies[self.startingCookieCount:]:
5                emitter.emit('cookie' + '\n')
6
7        if self.write_content_type == 'yes':
8            emitter.emit('Content-Type: ' + self.content_type + '\n\n')
9
10       emitter.emit(prepend_text)
11       if self.encode_target != None:
12           wpc = WriteProcessor.WriteProcessor
13           wp = wpc(self.encode_target, self.search_path,
14                    self.form_vars, emitter)
15           wp.process()
16       self.__encode_count = self.__encode_count + 1
17       return emitter.getResult()
```

The `encode()` method is called after the `process()` method. Here is what is being done:

1   The `encode()` method is generally called with some additional text to be emitted. This additional text comes from any stray output that may have been generated during the `process()` method call. Stray output, if written before the header information is written, makes development very difficult. ("Internal server error" is the most common error message!)

2   An emit strategy is an instance of the Emitter or any subclass thereof. The concept of strategies was discussed in Chapter 9. It allows the result of an `encode()` call to be directed to any destination. WebForm processing can actually be nested, which is a capability necessary for building applications.

3–5 If the `write_cookies` keyword parameter was set "yes" when the WebForm was constructed, cookies will be output first. "cookie" results in a number of `Set-Cookie:` lines being written out, as required by the standard.

7–8 If the `write_content_type` keyword was set to "yes," this means that a content header should be written.

10 Any output that is to be prepended will be written as the actual content, only after the cookies and content header (if requested) are written.

11–14 If an `encode_target` was specified and is not `None`, the WriteProcessor will be called to generate the content. The WriteProcessor is initialized with `self.encode_target` (which is expected to be the name of a text file), the `search_path` (where the text file is expected to be), the `form_vars` (variables to be used during template processing), and the `emitter` (where the output should be sent). Note again that the `emitter` could be sending the output to standard output but may also send to `StringEmitter`, `ListEmitter`, or `FileEmitter`.

15   Bump the encode count to indicate the number of times we have encoded. It is permitted to explicitly call this method to cause code generation, and the ability to know how many times (if at all) the method has been called is important in actual practice, which is shown later in Chapter 13.

16   Return the result from the emitter strategy. This allows the results of encode() to be collected and possibly used recursively. A WebForm can be created within a WebForm, where key data structures are shared, to allow nested processing to take place, something we do in Chapter 13.

The encode() method is at the heart of WebForm's power. Any class that is a WebForm essentially does processing (where key processing and business logic typically are found) and code generation. In the Slither Foundation classes, WebForm is used as a base class for the State class, which is an even higher-level interface that frees you from having to use pages to perform state transitions between forms and introduces other objects such as "projects" and "plugins" for operating at a higher level.

Summary

That is basically all there is to WebForm. There are a few methods that we could not cover in depth, but these are reasonably straightforward. For more information, look at the source code for class WebForm, which has been extensively documented. Test cases are also provided.

11

Debugging and Logging Techniques and Tools

Debugging is one of the least discussed topics in CGI texts. This is partially because debugging is an art form. Much like a criminal investigator, the programmer spends most development time tracking down clues that lead to syntactical and logical bugs. CGI applications are especially hard to debug because programming for the Web is very different from programming for a single client. The stateless nature of the Web makes tracking down logical bugs nearly impossible, since there is very little information available about the state of affairs immediately before a crash. Further, all CGI applications are started and terminated by the Web server, creating another layer of abstraction.

Although difficult, debugging Web applications is not impossible. As with other debugging paradigms, there is a finite set of patterns that can be used to find and resolve errors in code and logic. In this chapter, we introduce concepts important to debugging Web applications and present common bug symptoms and remedies. We also introduce logging techniques and tools that can drastically reduce your debugging time and effort. As you will soon see, the same logging techniques can be applied to tracking Web statistics such as user behavior and habits. Such statistics are invaluable for generating marketing strategies or providing customer support.

Python CGI Bugs

Python is an interpreted language. All instructions are converted to byte code and then executed on a stack interpreter. This is different from compiled languages such as C and C++, where the source is compiled into machine code and then executed by the processor. To deal with Python programming bugs and pitfalls effectively, it is imperative to learn the basics of Python's execution model. Independent of Python, there are several key differences between stand-alone client and Web applications. Recognizing these differences will have a profound impact on the amount of time spent tracking and resolving bugs. In the coming sections, we present topics specific to debugging Python CGI applications.

Goodbye Core Dumps, Hello Stack Trace

The interpreter pushes operands onto the stack, executes the instruction, and then pops the stack. In some cases, such as that of function calls, activation records are pushed and popped off the stack until the function call has completed. In the event of an error, Python will dump its stack, referred to as a traceback, to the standard error. Much like a Unix core dump, the traceback lists in order all of the activation records on the stack at the time when the error occurred.

The traceback lists the source file name, line number, and Python instruction of all activation frames on the stack. Figure 11–1 lists the source code of a Python CGI application that has a logical error, and the stack dump caused by the error.

```
[pshafae@vmlinux SimpleStack]$ cat SimpleStack.py

def function_A( arg1 ):
    print "Function A called with argument '%d'."%( arg1 )

def function_B():
    print "Function B called."


if __name__ == '__main__':
    function_A( 'word' )
    function_B()
    function_C()
[pshafae@vmlinux SimpleStack]$ python SimpleStack.py
Traceback (innermost last):
  File "SimpleStack.py", line 10, in ?
    function_A( 'word' )
  File "SimpleStack.py", line 3, in function_A
    print "Function A called with argument '%d'."%( arg1 )
TypeError: illegal argument type for built-in operation
```

Figure 11–1
A Simple Script That Results in a Traceback

The last line of the traceback lists the exception that was raised. As you may recall from earlier chapters, exceptions are objects that can be used to interrupt execution of a Python application. Exceptions can be manually raised using `raise`, and can be handled locally using a `try/except` block. Python has several internal exceptions that are raised by the interpreter when an error is encountered. On the last line of the traceback, we discover that there was an exception of type `TypeError` raised. We must use the traceback to investigate why this exception was raised.

Unlike Java, Python does not have an exception for every type of error that may be encountered. A bare-bones set of generic exceptions is used to flag the errors. In order to pinpoint the problem, you can't rely on the exception type and must "walk up" the traceback, investigating each line printed, starting from the bottom. Walking up the traceback produced by our `SimpleStack` example, we notice that the instruction that lead to the `TypeError` was encountered on line 3 of the file `SimpleStack.py`. The offending instruction is also printed, immediately following its location information. This does not provide any clues as to why a `TypeError` was raised since the argument, `arg1`, being passed to the interpolated string can contain any value and be of any type. Walking further up the traceback, we find that the instruction executed just before the one leading to the `TypeError` is a function call having the string `"word"` as an argument. So now we know why the `TypeError` occurred: We attempted to print a string using an integer format identifier.

By walking up the traceback, you are essentially rewinding through the source code executed by the interpreter. Each line of the dump provides additional clues about the state of affairs leading to the exception. This is especially useful since many logical errors, like the one in `SimpleStack`, are encountered only at runtime, where the values of variables play an important role in identifying the problem. Another important feature of the traceback is its text format. Unlike core dumps, which are binary, you can read the traceback without any additional debugging tools, decreasing the time spent debugging. Later we will take advantage of this feature by accessing the traceback via the `traceback` module and logging specific pieces of information regarding a system crash.

You can also use exceptions strategically as debugging break points. In the next section, you will discover that exceptions raised in Python CGI applications are written to the Web server's error logs. The Linux command `tail` allows you to view the last few lines of a file.

Using `tail` with the `-f` option, however, keeps the file open and continuously prints any new changes made to the file. Using `tail -f` on the Web server's error log allows you to monitor exceptions as they are raised. Then you can raise exceptions at various points in your CGI application to inspect `state` and catch logical bugs.

Dealing with Big Brother: The Web Server

One of the perks of client-side programming is having total control over the execution of the application. During development, the programmer can start an application, trace the execution of each instruction, and analyze the direct output of the program every step of the way. Web programming does not provide the same luxuries. A CGI application is started by the Web server, executes as a forked child of the server, and has its standard input, output, and error streams redirected. This difference in programming environments requires different testing and debugging strategies when developing applications.

The most important piece of information with regard to the Web server is knowing how it redirects the forked CGI application's standard streams. With this information, you will be able to trace the execution and output of your Python CGI application.

There are three standard streams: input, output, and error. In client programming, by default the standard input stream is set to read data from the keyboard, and both the standard output and error streams are set to direct all output to the terminal. In Web programming, each of the streams is redirected to fit the HTTP model. The standard input stream is used to pass HTTP `POST` data to the CGI application. As you may recall from Chapter 5, when an HTML form is filled out, the data from the input field is packed as a list of parameter/value pairs. Upon executing the CGI application, the Web server will write this information to the forked child's standard input stream. The CGI application will then read and parse this information to process the form.

All data written by the CGI application to the standard output stream (via the `print` or `stdout.write()`) is redirected to the TCP/IP network pipe associated with the HTTP call. This gives the CGI application total control over the communication with the browser. As a consequence, your CGI application must follow the HTTP protocol when sending data back to the browser. As part of the protocol, the CGI application must first send back a response header that describes the data that follows. Unlike client-side programming, you cannot simply print `state` information, such as variable values, as the program is executing. Later, we discuss strategies for wrapping the standard output stream so that it can be used to output debugging information to the browser safely.

The standard error stream is redirected to the Web server's error log. By default, Apache creates a file called `error_log` to log all errors encountered with HTTP requests. Entries include reports of missing images and HTML files as well as any data written to the standard error stream by a CGI application. The `error_log` is the first place to look when you encounter errors at startup or during the execution of your CGI application. You may safely log entries to this file by writing data to the standard error stream using `stderr.write()`. Many programmers use this strategy in place of `print` statements to output `state` information as the CGI application is running. Although this strategy is effective when debugging, it is not convenient. In some cases, many users may be accessing the Web server, and your logged `state` information is interleaved with other error reports.

Another difference between client and CGI applications is the handling of execution errors. By default, Apache will execute all CGI applications as the user `nobody`. This means that all the files associated with the CGI application must be readable and executable by the `nobody` user. If they are not, the Web server will not be able to execute the program and report execution permission errors.

Unlike a client application, the CGI application plays an intricate role in completing a network request, and any execution errors encountered must be handled gracefully. Upon detection of an execution error, Apache will log the error and return to the user a static HTML page indicating that a general error was encountered. Unlike with client applications, Apache will not print the specifics of the internal error to the browser: This would compromise system security by reporting information about the CGI application's vulnerabilities.

Snapshot of the Error without Any State Information

The fact that HTTP is a single-transaction, stateless protocol also affects how CGI applications are debugged. When developing client-side applications, you have total control over the application's actions. Throughout execution, you can interact with the program, analyze `state` information, or even restart the application. In the Web model, CGI applications are reinitiated by HTTP requests. They execute to completion, and in turn complete the HTTP request by sending back a response. Since HTTP is a single-transaction protocol, once the request is made, the user cannot interact any further with the CGI application.

Once the CGI application has completed the request, it terminates. All of the variables and objects created during execution are lost and cannot be used in subsequent requests. This aspect of HTTP has a profound effect on the implementation and debugging of CGI applications: The programmer is responsible for the preservation of any state information that is needed between requests. One strategy is to store values in hidden FORM input fields. This not only compromises internal information, but is difficult to work with when there are many state variables that must be preserved. Another strategy is to store the state information on the server using Python's object serialization framework. In this strategy, all of the state information is written out to the server's disk and then associated with the request via a unique session cookie or URL parameter. No internal state information is passed to the browser, and since most Python object can be serialized to disk, saving large quantities of state variables is relatively painless.

The most effective strategy for debugging CGI applications is the manual logging of state information across HTTP requests. This can be broken down into three smaller tasks: uniquely identifying a user; associating the user with actions performed by the CGI application; and writing important state and action descriptions to disk. The first task ensures that all messages written to disk can be traced to a browser invocation. This is especially important if you are part of a programming team that shares a single log file for the top-level application messages. The second task associates a unique user session to actions performed on the server side by the CGI application. This typically is facilitated by storing a randomly generated session key as a browser cookie or as a URL parameter that is passed to your CGI application on each request. The third task is the storage of important application activity to disk. During development, you may use any number of logging statements to track the state of variables. Since statements can be traced to individual Web requests, you can trace the CGI's activity relative to your actions.

Logging server activities makes the debugging of CGI applications similar to that of developing client applications. You can use the logs freely to trace your application from start to finish. You will see the value of this strategy almost immediately. In a later section, we formalize the three tasks involved in logging CGI activity into a formal logging library. The library will manage the tasks involved in setting up and managing logs.

Usual Suspects: Resolving Common Python CGI Errors

There are several CGI programming pitfalls so common in development, and we have documented them here. All of the pitfalls meet one or more of the following criteria: Resulting error reports are ambiguous and hard to follow, a very common occurrence; or it is difficult to pinpoint the source of the problem. By learning the symptoms, you can save time that is usually wasted on solving recurring errors.

Overoptimized Browsers: Problems with Caches

The design focus of Web browser developers has always been the end user. Over time, browsers have become increasingly more intelligent and optimized. One of the key optimization features is the use of a Web page cache. Almost all browsers will store a copy of a visited Web page on the local disk in what is referred to as a cache. When the user attempts to access a recently visited page, the browser will check for a local copy of the Web document in the cache. If it exists, it will render the local copy to the screen. In some cases, the browser may perform an HTTP HEAD operation to ensure that the document has not been modified since it was last cached. By using the local copy, the browser will not have to pay the heavy cost of re-downloading the document. This is especially important for users who connect to the Internet via a low-bandwidth modem.

Caching can cause many hours of frustration when developing Web applications. In an effort to optimize network calls, by default the browser will cache all Web pages visited. In some cases, this may include Web pages that are dynamically generated by CGI applications. As a result, you may modify your Python CGI application and then attempt to review the changes in the browser, but find that the expected code changes did not take effect. Most browsers will provide the option to clear both the disk and memory cache. You can also configure the browser to use a more conservative caching policy.

At the time of writing, both Netscape and Internet Explorer provide facilities to cache not only Web pages but also the HTTP POST requests for forms. As a result, previously entered form values are posted to a CGI form. You may encounter unexpected results as a consequence of this time-saving feature. It is best to turn off all such features when debugging and testing your CGI application.

Premature End of Script Error and Friends

The most frequently encountered errors are script execution errors reported by Apache. Apache reports these errors to the `error_log` file and, by default, presents the user an HTML page indicating that an internal error has occurred. These errors indicate that Apache could not *successfully* execute the requested application.

Emphasis is placed on the word successfully, because there is no concrete way for Apache to determine if a Python CGI application executed correctly. Remember that typically all CGI applications are executed as forked child processes of Apache. After execution, Apache redirects the forked child's streams and then awaits its termination so that the HTTP transaction can be completed by closing the TCP/IP connection. Apache does not use the exit value of the CGI script to determine if the script properly executed, for a number for reasons. First, the exit value of a script can have an arbitrary value depending on the developer, the development environment, and system errors. Second, the HTTP protocol requires that the server's response be posted in two parts: response header followed by a response body. Apache cannot use the exit value to determine if the script's response followed the HTTP protocol specifications.

So what criterion does Apache use to determine successful execution of a CGI script? The answer is simple: Apache inspects the data written to the script's standard output stream to determine if a proper HTTP response has been formed (see Chapter 5 for more information on HTTP). Apache assumes that if a script was able to construct a well-formed server response, the script must have run successfully. This is a good assumption, because any errors that arise in attempting to execute the CGI script would not, in many cases, result in a properly constructed HTTP response. If Apache did not inspect the CGI application's response, any errors during execution would be sent to the user's browser. This could threaten security, as a seasoned hacker can use the error message to advantage. For this reason, all standard output from CGI applications is (loosely) inspected by Apache before being sent to the browser.

If the first few lines of the response do not form an appropriate HTTP response, Apache prints an error message to the error log indicating that a premature end of script header was encountered. Figure 11–2 depicts a sample error log entry for such an error. Since successful execution is indicated by the response type, after the appropriate response header has been written, there is no way for Apache to deter-

```
[Sun Dec 31 03:11:25 2000] [error] [client 192.168.96.1] Premature end
of script headers: /home/httpd/cgi-bin/wplBook/test.py
```

Figure 11–2
Sample Premature Script Header `error_log` entry

mine if additional errors were encountered. We will manipulate a simple Python CGI script called `test.py` to show how Apache reacts to various errors encountered in the script. Reading these case studies will help you learn to use Apache's error messages to pinpoint the source of errors in your applications.

Let's first attempt to execute `test.py` using a bad path to the Python interpreter. Figure 11–3 has the source code for `test.py` along with the `error_log` entry that results from the bad Python interpreter path. Line 1 of the source code incorrectly references `/usr/local` as the complete path to the Python interpreter. Attempting to execute this script results in an internal server error because the Python interpreter could not be loaded to execute the script. As a result, lines 5 and 6, which form the appropriate HTTP response header, could not be emitted to the standard output stream, causing Apache to determine that an error occurred during the execution. Also of importance is the lack of additional Python-specific errors, indicating that the script never even started. By carefully inspecting the `error_log` entries, it is possible to determine at which point an error was encountered. Script initialization errors are most common when a Python CGI application is developed on one system and transported to another system for final release.

On the second attempt, we will fix the bad path to the interpreter, but create a deliberate syntax error on line 5. Figure 11–4 depicts the modified script, with all modifications in bold text, followed by the

```
1    #!/usr/local
2
3    if __name__ == '__main__':
4
5        print "Content-type: text/html"
6        print
7
8        print "<h1>Congratulations!</h1>Python test.py executed successfully!"
```

```
[Sun Dec 31 04:22:07 2000] [error] [client 192.168.96.1] Premature end of script
headers: /home/httpd/cgi-bin/wplBook/test.py
```

Figure 11–3
`test.py` with Bad Path to Python Interpreter

```
1    #!/usr/local/python/bin/python
2
3    if __name__ == '__main__':
4
5        prin "Content-type: text/html"
6        print
7
8        print "<h1>Congratulations!</h1>Python test.py executed successfully!

File "/home/httpd/cgi-bin/wplBook/test.py", line 5
    prin "Content-type: text/html"
                                  ^
SyntaxError: invalid syntax
[Sun Dec 31 04:34:29 2000] [error] [client 192.168.96.1] Premature end of script
headers: /home/httpd/cgi-bin/wplBook/test.py
```

Figure 11–4
test.py with a Deliberate Syntax Error Prior to Printing Response Headers

resulting Apache error_log entry. This time the interpreter started, but encountered a syntax error before the script could execute. As a result, a premature end-of-script headers entry is written to the error_log and the default internal server error page is presented to the user. We are sure that the interpreter at least started, since just prior to the premature end-of-script headers entry, there is a Python stack trace. Note that Apache did not catch or interpret the exception. The stack trace was written by the Python interpreter to the standard error stream of the process, resulting in the error_log entry.[1]

It is easy to find the source of this error in test.py, because there are only eight lines in the script and a single path of initiation and termination. It is much more difficult to pinpoint the source of this error in a larger application that has multiple points of entry and termination. With large applications, you must trace the execution of the script by progressively logging statements.

The most common reasons behind this scenario are generally syntax errors and attempts to import missing or nonavailable modules. If you are importing any nonstandard Python modules (this includes third-party modules and any others that you have created for your own use), you must make sure that the path to the module source is set in the PYTHONPATH environment variable (see Chapter 12 on how the wplPath module can be used to remedy this problem) and that all module directories and files have appropriate permission settings.

In our last attempt, we will cause a deliberate logical error after printing the appropriate response header. As before, Figure 11–5 lists

---

1. See earlier section on Apache stream redirection.

the modified source along with the resulting error_log entry. Upon execution, the user will see an HTML page containing the text "Congratulations! Python test.py executed successfully!" In this case, the exception for the logical error was encountered after the response headers were printed, so no internal error is encountered by Apache and all of the output of the script is sent to the requesting browser. The Python interpreter does write the exception to the processes' standard error stream, which results in the error_log entry. It should now be clear that Apache uses the response header to determine if the script successfully executed. It is the programmer's responsibility to consistently monitor the error_log for any Python exceptions.

Why did we make a logical error as opposed to a syntax error in the last incarnation of test.py? Python first compiles all source code into byte code before execution begins. A syntax error would have been caught and an exception would have been raised before the script ever executed, making this last example very much like the former.

From the user's point of view this last version of test.py ran successfully, but as you can see, there were additional instructions that did not execute because of the logical error. As in the previous example, it is easy to catch this error in a script that only contains 11 lines of code and very simple business logic; this is not the case in more complicated applications. You must log the script's activity and closely monitor the error_log file to ensure that the script is performing the expected operations.

```
1    #!/usr/local/python/bin/python
2
3    if __name__ == '__main__':
4
5        print "Content-type: text/html"
6        print
7
8        print "<h1>Congratulations!</h1>Python test.py executed successfully!"
9
10       print "This line will cause an error because strings \
11               can't be printed using integer field descriptors: %d"%( "Boo!" )

Traceback (innermost last):
  File "/home/httpd/cgi-bin/wplBook/test.py", line 10, in ?
    print "This line will cause an error because strings \
TypeError: illegal argument type for built-in operation
```

Figure 11–5
test.py with Logical Error

The premature script headers error is by far the trickiest to debug. Other Apache errors are not so ambiguous and can easily be discovered and resolved. Table 11–1 lists some other common Apache errors along with the source, of the problems and possible solutions. Refer to the Apache documentation for more authoritative information.

Beside interpreting the meaning of the Apache `error_log` entry in resolving internal server errors, you can attempt to execute the CGI script manually in a shell. This is not a reliable strategy, as your script may not experience the same errors until some or all of the form variables have

Table 11–1
Apache error_log Entries Specific to CGI Errors

`error_log` **Entry**	**Cause**	**Solution**
Python can't open file: `'/home/httpd/cgi-bin/wplBook/test.py'` Premature end of script headers: `/home/httpd/cgi-bin/wplBook/test.py`	Python interpreter could not read the requested script file.	This is usually caused by inappropriate read permissions set for the script file. Remember, the Apache server, by default, executes all CGI scripts as the system user `nobody`.
File permissions deny server execution: `/home/httpd/cgi-bin/wplBook/test.py`	Apache did not have execution permission for the requested script.	Check file execution permissions to make sure that the user `nobody` can execute the script.
Malformed header from script: `Bad header=<some text>: /home/httpd/cgi-bin/wplBook/test.py`	Script did not print appropriate response header; some other text was encountered.	Look for the value of `<some text>` in your source code and make sure that an appropriate response header is being printed before the indicated string.

been accessed. However, this strategy is effective for instances when there is an import error or a resource access error in the script.

Before we end this section, it is important to note that there are rare instances when you may encounter premature end of script headers as a result of an ambiguous error. This scenario is most popular on Apache servers that are compiled with `suexec` support. The `suexec` directive allows Apache to change users from `nobody` to a specified user account before executing the CGI application. As a result, the CGI applications will retain the permissions of the specified user. This is especially useful in shared hosting environments where hundreds of domains are managed by a single Apache installation. You must make sure to follow the tight file permission restrictions set by `suexec` or your script will not be allowed to execute. If you encounter a premature end of script header error on an Apache server that has `suexec` support, you should be sure to consult the `error.cgi` file in addition to `error_log` for additional `suexec` errors.

Another source of ambiguous premature end of script headers error is sudden and fatal interpreter crashes. Since Python allows users to extend the language through C-extensions, a nonstable module may cause serious execution errors that result in the core dump of the interpreter. If you have exhausted all of your resources when debugging, make sure that the interpreter has not crashed or created a core dump file.

Lights Are On, but No One Is Home: Browser Hangs

The hardest bugs to catch are those that leave the faintest trail of clues. In some instances the only clue that you have to go by is a browser that hangs for long periods. No errors are ever reported to the Apache `error_log`. At first it may appear as if there is a serious problem with the Apache Web Server or the browser. Closer inspection will reveal that the error is actually caused by two possible issues: a script that is blocked waiting for another resource or a poorly authored recursive algorithm.

The classic case is attempting to connect to a MySQL server using incorrect host and port information. The MySQL Python module will hang indefinitely for a server that does not exist at the specified network address. The only tried-and-true strategy for catching this bug is to log debugging statements so that you can trace the execution of the script. A failed log write statement will flag the point at which the script hung. Another popular resource that provides similar results is the SMTP server. The server may be busy or may have encountered an offending e-mail address causing a lengthy wait for a connection time-out.

Runaway recursive algorithms are another reason for browser hangs. Many search and graph algorithms depend on recursion. Recursive algorithms are error-prone, as it is relatively easy to create an infinite cycle. Fortunately, the interpreter eventually will raise an exception. The best strategy for catching such errors is to include debugging log entries in the algorithm and trace the execution of the application through the log file.

Poorly designed multithreaded Python applications can also cause similar results during deadlock. Deadlock occurs when threads block on a mutex lock that will never be freed up. As an example, one thread may enter a critical section, code that is shared by more than one thread, and terminate prematurely. The critical section will remain locked and all other threads will block for an indefinite period of time. These are among the hardest bugs to catch since they not only leave very few clues, but they are rare and difficult to reproduce.

Python-Specific CGI Errors

Programming Python is relatively easy. Attempting to build the same CGI applications in a language such as C requires considerably more effort. This does not mean that Python lacks programming pitfalls. Furthermore, working in the Web environment makes catching and resolving pitfalls much more difficult. Here are several of the most common Python pitfalls.

Incorrect Code Indentation • Python code structure is defined by indentation rules. Code blocks are organized based on the number of spaces that each line is indented from the left. Python allows users to use both spaces and tabs when writing scripts. Using a mixture of tabs and spaces, however, leads to problems. First, both spaces and tabs are clear characters. You can't easily determine what grouping of tabs and spaces are used when viewing Python source code. Second, not all text editors are created equal. The popular `vi` editor, by default, will use the tab character, while `Emacs` and `XEmacs` translate tabs to a predefined number of spaces. In most cases, the code will appear properly formatted when viewed by both editors.

An incorrect mixture of tabs and spaces may cause a syntax error to occur. Emphasis is placed on the unlikelihood of this occurrence since in many cases an incorrect mixture of tabs and spaces leads to business logic errors that are far more difficult to catch. In pre-1.6 releases of Python, the interpreter raised a syntax error when misplaced tabs were encountered. Not only is it difficult to catch the misplaced tab character, but the fact that a syntax error is raised confuses programmers of all degrees of expertise. In version 1.6 and later, an `IndentationError` is raised to identify inconsistent spacing.

The modified exception remedies only half of the problem. As a developer you still need to find the incorrectly used tab character. There are several strategies for solving this problem. First, there are many freely available utility scripts that will comb through Python source code and convert all tabs to a set number of spaces. You can even write a simple Python application to perform this task. Second, choose your editor carefully. Most of the source code presented in this book was authored using `Emacs` and `XEmacs`. Both editors provide LISP macro-utilities specific to writing Python source code. Among the features available are proper code indentation and syntax highlighting. The new `vi` editor, based on the `vim` engine, also provides similar utilities. If you are using a combination of editors, make sure that you are consistent with your use of tabs and spaces.

Abstaining from the use of tabs is probably the best solution. Almost all popular editors allow you to configure the Tab key to emit spaces, as opposed to the tab character. As long as you are using only one spacing system, you should have no difficulty finding and resolving spacing issues.

Import Errors • Python applications can be organized into modules. A module identifies a namespace. Typically algorithms, services, and frameworks are organized into one or more modules forming a library of Python code that can be easily distributed and reused. In order to use a module, you must import it into your application's namespace using the `import` statement. Table 11–2 lists the various ways that a module can be imported.

Table 11–2
Using `Import`

Code Example	Result
`import string`	Imports the module named `string` into the current namespace. All of the resources defined in `string.py` can now be accessed using the fully qualified name of the resource such as `string.lower()`. This is the safest form of import because the resources defined in `string` are collectively imported.
`import string as MyString`	Imports the `string` module into the current namespace under a different alias. To access the resources defined in `string`, you must now use the fully qualified alias name such as `MyString.lower()`. This is only available in version 2.0 or higher of Python.
`from string import lower`	Imports a single resource (in this case, a function named `lower()`) from the `string` module into the current module. You can now use `lower` as if it were defined locally. This may be dangerous if you have already defined a function with a matching name.
`from string import *`	Imports all resources defined in the `string` module into the local namespace. This is very dangerous, as the possibility of name collision is high.

Modules are not without problems, the most common being name collisions. Be very careful when importing a resource from another module. If you have a locally defined resource with the same name, you will witness inconsistent results during runtime. The classic example is importing all resources in `sys`. The `sys` module defines many resources that are common to all Python programs. Some programmers attempt to take a shortcut by ubiquitously importing all resources in `sys`. Since the resource names in `sys` are so general, such as `argv`, the chances of having a name collision are high.

Another common mistake when working with modules in CGI applications centers on availability issues. Module names are directly mapped to file names where the module source code lives. For example, the resources in the module `string` are defined in the source file `string.py`. To use a module, Python must be able to find the respective file. Python uses the environment variable `PYTHONPATH` to search for modules. If the module lives outside the standard Python library path, the interpreter will not be able to find the module and an `ImportError` exception is raised. This problem commonly occurs when working with third-party modules such as those specified in this book.

In the CGI model, setting environment variables is not a convenient task, especially if it has to be done for each application that you author. Luckily, we have created the `wplPath` module. The full design and implementation details of `wplPath` are available in Chapter 12. `wplPath` allows you to specify in a local file any number of search paths. You simply import `wplPath` into your script to make the paths available to the interpreter.

Once the appropriate module path is defined, you must ensure that the interpreter has the appropriate permissions to access the module files. When writing CGI applications, it is easy to forget that Apache, by default, will execute the code as user `nobody`. Therefore, all the source files associated with the modules that you import must be accessible by the `nobody` user. The easiest strategy for solving this problem is to make all nonstandard Python CGI source code owned by the user `nobody`. This usually makes development difficult—sometimes impossible—since you must be able to change into user `nobody` to access the files. Another strategy is to use the `nobody` group for all nonstandard Python files and allow group read/execute permissions to nonstandard. By far the best solution is the use of the `suexec` Apache directive. This allows Apache to access and run code as a user other than `nobody`. Please refer to the Apache documentation for more information on `suexec`.

At all costs, avoid setting world read/execute permissions for your Python source code. This opens up many security holes, and can lead to problems when the code is distributed or transferred to another server for final release. A good programming practice is to use a single directory, under the `cgi-bin` Apache document root, to contain all third-party Python modules that you intend to use in your CGI applications. This centralizes the modules and simplifies management and maintenance tasks.

Working with Stale Byte Code • Python compiles all source code into an optimized byte code before execution. The byte code is saved in a binary file that has a `.pyc` extension. Upon execution, the interpreter will search for the presence of a matching byte code file. If one exists, the interpreter will check the modification date of the source code against the creation date of the byte code to determine if a recompilation is needed. There are situations in which Python relies on stale byte code to execute an application. This leads to unexpected results. Since the only clues available are unexpected results, it may take some time to discover the real source of the problem.

A change in system time is one factor that can lead to the use of stale byte code. To best illustrate the problem, we will run through a quick programming scenario. Let's assume that you author several Python scripts on one system, which we will label as system A. After several hours of development, you decide to move the code to a test server, which we will label as system B. Let's also assume that the clock on system B is slower than that of system A. When the scripts are moved onto system B and edited, the modification date and time will be older than those of the byte code files that were created on system A. During execution, the interpreter will favor the older byte code files, as they appear to be more current than the script we just edited, leading to unexpected behavior.

You can solve this problem during development by deleting all byte code before the application is executed. You should not rely on byte code; when transporting an application from one system to another or when packing code for distribution or version control, make sure to exclude all byte code files from the distribution. If you do not want to release the source, then freeze your application.

File ownership and permission can also lead to the use of stale byte code. This is especially prevalent in CGI programming, where changing file ownership and permissions is a common task. Once again, we will use a scenario to illustrate the problem. Let's assume that you create a series of Python scripts. After some development, you decide to tighten access to the source code by disabling group and other read permissions using the following Linux command: `chmod -R 700 *.py`. Next, you make minor changes to the source, but notice that they do not appear to have taken effect. The oversight is in the use of `*.py`. By default, the Apache server will execute all CGI scripts as the user `nobody`. By changing the read permission on the source code to include only the original user, you have in effect locked the interpreter out from accessing the source. The interpreter may default to using the available byte code file, which still has the appropriate read/execute permissions. A similar situation may arise when changing file ownership.

As in the first scenario, the best solution is to remove all byte code files before executing the application. With no byte code to default to, the interpreter will raise an exception that identifies the problem, leading to immediate resolution.

Overprotection • A popular programming practice is to use an all-encompassing `try/except` block to catch errors. This looks especially appealing when programming CGI applications that rely on user-supplied values. Consider, for instance, a Web-based calculator. The Python CGI script must convert the user's input into numerical types such as integer and float to carry out the calculation. If the user supplies an offending numerical value, such as a string of alphabetic characters, Python will raise a `TypeError` exception when you attempt to convert the string into a numerical type. This exception would be silently caught.

A general `try/except` block can add hours to development time by absorbing critical exceptions. Figure 11–6 lists a validation function that is part of a larger CGI application, which uses a large `try/except` block. We have also deliberately created a syntax error on line 10 to highlight the problem of using general exception-handling routines. When the function is invoked, unexpected results are obtained, regardless of the value of the supplied parameter, because the `SyntaxError` exception is absorbed by the general except clause. It is nearly impossible to trace the problem to the syntax error because we do not log the stack trace that results from handling the exception.

```
1    def validateMonth( month ):
2    """Returns the original value of month
3      if the value is within the appropriate
4      range; otherwise 0."""
5
6      try:
7        if month > 12 or month < 1:
8            return 0
9        else:
10            return mont
11      except:
12        return 0
```

Figure 11–6
Source Code Using General Exception-Handling Routine

Avoid using general exception-handling routines when possible. However, if the need arises, be sure to log the occurrence of the exception in the handling routine. It is good programming practice to log the occurrence of all exceptions, regardless of type. In the log, you should include an identified statement that can later be used to locate the problem and the stack trace for the exception. In the next section, we develop a logging utility that will handle many of these tasks for you.

Logging

We have identified logging as one of the key strategies for debugging CGI applications. Logs can be used to track important state information throughout CGI invocation. You can use this information to trace the execution of your application. Another benefit of logging is capturing valuable information about user activity. Strategically placed log statements can be used to obtain usage statistics. Capturing this type of information in larger, enterprise-grade CGI applications results in invaluable data that can be used by marketing and executive personnel to focus sales efforts. The same information can also be used to tune and optimize application activity.

In this section we identify various logging strategies and present the design and implementation of a Python module for creating and managing logs. It is highly recommended that you begin using this module in all of your CGI applications. At first glance, logging may appear to be time-consuming, but you will see an immediate improvement in the amount of time spent debugging errors. Also, note that the practice of using logs will improve your general coding skills as well as the legibility of your source code.

Writing Activity to the Standard Streams: `stdout` and `stderr`

The simplest way to log activity in a CGI application is to write entries to the standard streams. There are two standard streams suitable for logging: stdout and stderr. They provide the simplest solution because the streams are available to all CGI applications at no additional overhead, require no initialization or management, and are available regardless of the operating system platform. These advantages are nullified by many disadvantages. Each standard stream plays a unique and important role in the view of CGI programming. We will start by discussing the challenges involved with writing activity reports to the standard output stream.

You can print data to stdout by using the print command or directly calling the stream's write() method. As you may recall, all data written to stdout is considered part of the server response and is sent back to the browser. In the HTTP model, the server response must be organized into a response header followed by the message body. This implies that an appropriate response header must be formed and printed before the first activity is written. This sounds like an easy goal to meet, but practice proves differently. The most effective strategy is to wrap the stdout.write() method with a function that uses a global Boolean to track the number of times the function has been called (similarly, the wrapper can be a class method using a member variable as a Boolean). On the first invocation, the appropriate response header is formed and emitted, followed by the first activity report. All successive reports are written without any alteration or preparation.

Writing to stdout works for reporting debugging messages during development, but it cannot be used in the final release of the application. Similarly, you cannot write valuable statistical or user activity information to stdout. This is not to say that writing error messages to stdout during development is discouraged. In Chapter 10 we presented the WebForm programming framework, which redirects Python exceptions written to the standard error stream to stdout. This simplifies development by centralizing application output and error messages on the browser. The developer can turn this feature off when the application is released.

Writing to stderr is a lot less complicated. As you have seen, all data written to stderr are redirected to Apache's error_log file. Since the entries are written to a server-side file, this makes stderr a good choice for logging debugging and activity reports. Unlike stdout, there is no overhead required to ensure that a proper response has been formed. In addition, the error_log file is managed by Apache, alleviating all file creation and management tasks.

The primary disadvantage to using stderr is the lack of control over the data written to the log. Apache uses the error_log file to report any error encountered with any requested operation. As a result, the error_log file typically is cluttered with many entries that are irrelevant to your Python debugging efforts. This not only makes it difficult to search for valuable information, but complicates gathering usage statistics and other such information. The difficulties of using error_log are heightened in an environment where a single Apache installation is shared by several developers.

Another disadvantage to using `stderr` is lack of control over the file name, file size, and record format. Yes, one of the advantages of writing to `stderr` is also considered a disadvantage. The lack of control makes archiving logs very difficult. By default, Apache does not rotate the `error_log` and the file is allowed to grow without any limitations. Each entry written to the `error_log` follows the Apache log entry format; Apache entries are accompanied with a date and time stamp, while CGI output is written without any manipulation or formatting. The missing date and time stamp makes locating the most current error message difficult and error-prone.

Working with Raw Text Files

We just explored the challenges of logging to the standard output and error streams. This leads to our next logging option: writing to a locally created text file. Using a local text file combines all of the benefits of writing to `stderr` with complete control over the creation and management of the log file. The strategy is very simple. Upon initialization, your application creates or opens an existing text file. During execution, the file handle is made available to all functions and objects. The programmer can use the file handle to log any debugging or statistical report. The file is closed once the application terminates.

As with the `stderr` stream, there is no overhead in making sure that the log entry follows the appropriate HTTP response format. Similarly, all entries are written to a single, infinitely growing file without any manipulation. A benefit over using `stderr` is that only entries specific to the script are reported. There is no need to fish through a series of non-relevant entries in search of a Python exception or the value of a particular variable. In addition, the file can easily be archived and analyzed.

The first time that you attempt to practice this strategy, you will discover that there are numerous details which were not included in the description. For starters, when working with files there is no guarantee that the file is accessible. Any number of I/O errors may result, disabling reports being written to the file. Next, in each application where you use a log file, you must implement a `wrapper` function to provide a date and time stamp as well as manage the rotation of the log file over time. The `wplLogger` addresses both of these issues.

Writing and Managing Logs: `wpl.logger.Logger`

Although the text file strategy is a great improvement over writing to standard streams, there are many repetitive routines that can be organized into a central module for reuse. This is the goal of the LogWriter class.

Design Philosophy • Throughout this chapter we have concentrated on the deficiencies of available logging strategies. The solution, as mentioned earlier, is the use of a logging utility. In designing a logger, we not only aimed to address the needs of a debugging utility, but included several features that allow you to extend the logger and use it for gathering production statistics.

At the highest level, the logger is organized into two abstractions: a logger and one or more log strategies. The logger publishes an interface that applications can use to write entries to the log. The log strategy provides a standard interface to any number of data collection schemes such as files, mailers, and standard streams. There is one caveat: The logger must be instantiated with at least a file name, implying that at a minimum the logger will always write entries to a file. Rather than relying on a log file strategy, all of the details of writing to the file are managed within the logger. This does not mean that you cannot have additional file loggers, as we will explore shortly.

The logger is a simple abstraction that is made increasingly more complicated by comfort features and goodies. Figure 11–7 depicts the various functional components of the logger.

The Application Programming Interface (API) is used to log entries and set customization options. There are four different interface methods that can be used to make a log entry. The details of these are discussed later, but it is important to note that they all result in a single call to a private `Logger` method. This design decision allows for any number of interface methods to be created without ever compromising the low-level details of generating the log entry.

There are also a number of interface methods that are used to safely set logging options. Although Python does not honor private object attributes in the true sense of object-oriented programming, we still prefer to wrap customization attributes with interface methods to protect the user from accidentally introducing otherwise avoidable runtime errors and exceptions.

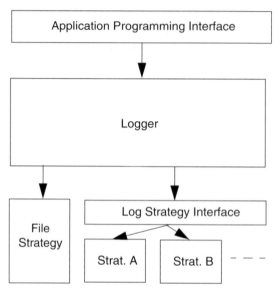

Figure 11–7
Functional Parts of the Logger

The logger plays an important role as the negotiator between the API and the low-level logging strategies. Since all log entry requests must pass through this component, it serves as a suitable location for filtering and tagging entries. We take advantage of this design pattern to support categorization of log entries and auto-gathering of log entry details. Categories can be used to differentiate between types of entries. By default, the logger provides three standard categories: debug, warning, and error. Using the appropriate API, you can generate messages that are used for debugging, or to indicate that an error has occurred or a warning was raised. The logger simply tags the log entry message with a specified category label.

At first glance categories appear to be rather useless. However, the logger also provides a mechanism for specifying a list of categories that are to be logged. This allows you to sprinkle your code with any number of debugging entries that can be turned off when the application is released for production use. If a particular category is turned off, the logger will simply ignore the entry creation request. All of the API calls that you use in your code for that particular category can permanently remain in the code. Unlike in the past, you do not need to delete them only to add them again when a new bug is discovered. This saves a lot of time both when the application is released and when additional bugs are found post-release.

The logger also provides the option of automatically generating and recording entry details. The logger can use the interpreter stack to identify the file name, line number, and function call leading to a log entry call. When this option is activated, the logger uses various utilities from the `wpl.trace.Trace` module to identify where the call is being made from. Since the logger intercepts all messages, it can perform this operation before the entry is recorded.

Autogeneration of log entry details proves useful when debugging larger applications. When your application approaches 5,000 to 10,000 lines of code, it becomes difficult to easily trace through an operation. Logging debugging entries will help you capture the state of variables, but may also mislead you if you do not take care to make each message unique. As an example, if you were watching the value of a variable called `count` with a logging message that emits the message "`count = %s`"`%(count)`, you will quickly discover that the log messages are useless unless you can trace the entry to the logging statement. The auto detail generation does just that.

The auto detail generation is also able to discover occurrences of exceptions. If an exception has occurred and you create a log entry, the logger will automatically concatenate the traceback to the log message, saving you one extra step. You can then use the traceback to quickly identify the bug. This feature is most useful when developing large Web applications; the more information available, the easier it is to identify and patch bugs.

Below the logger are the low-level interfaces for committing an entry either to the log file or to any number of additional logging strategies. The logger relies on several internal methods for managing and working with the log file. These methods handle the creation of the log file, rolling over the log file daily, and committing entries. The rollover feature provides a clever scheme for limiting the amount of data written to a single log file. A beneficial consequence of this scheme is auto archiving of logs.

The rollover strategy cannot be customized. Daily rollovers are adequate for almost all applications. Each time a new log message is to be committed, the low-level file strategy checks to see if the log needs to be rolled over. If so, the log is rolled over, the old log is closed, and the message is written to the new log. To accommodate this, the logger uses a base log file name and then generates actual log file names based on the system date and time. At midnight, the logs are automatically rolled over.

The low-level file strategy is also thread safe. Prior to committing a log entry to the file, the log file is locked, minimizing data corruption that may result in a race condition. This does not provide protection for additional log strategies. Thread safety is assumed to be the responsibility of the designer and implementor of additional logging strategies.

The logger communicates with additional logging strategies through a common interface. Communication is unilateral, with the logger instructing a strategy to commit an entry. The logger does not handle errors that may result from the call to the strategy interface. All additional logging strategies must extend from a common interface class before they can be used by the logger. The interface ensures that the implementor meets the minimum requirements for communicating with the logger.

The additional strategies must first be instantiated by the user before being accessed by the logger. This simplifies the logger code and does not impose additional constraints on how the strategy is instantiated or initialized. Since more than one strategy can be used, the user must place each strategy instance in a dictionary. The dictionary is then passed to the logger's constructor. Later, when a log entry is being made, the user can reference one or more strategies to be used for that entry. The strategies are referenced by the key used to associate the strategy instance in the dictionary.

The per-entry granularity of strategy usage proves paramount when your application must handle unexpected or fatal errors in a special manner. You can use a general `try/except` block to safeguard against unforeseen errors, such as those resulting from offending user input. In most cases it would be beneficial for the application to send an e-mail to the developer indicating that an unforeseen error (almost always fatal) has occurred. The entry that logs the occurrence of the error (located in the `except` block) can be used to specify a mail strategy. This causes the logger to send an e-mail for just this entry; all other logging calls simply commit entries to the file. Without this type of control, you would have to handle these types of situations manually.

As you have seen, the design of the logger adequately addresses all of the issues raised in the earlier parts of this chapter. Furthermore, the logger provides some key features that make debugging applications a breeze, such as support for filtering based on entry category and autogeneration of entry details and tracebacks. In the next section, we will explore how this design is implemented in Python.

Implementation • The implementation of the logger provides an excellent display of how Python's rich syntax can be used cleverly to express the design patterns and strategies introduced in the previous section. The main logger is implemented as a self-contained class in the `Logger.py` file. Two additional files are available to support strategy extensions. In the following we present the main methods and member variables of the logger classes along with a detailed explanation of each.

```python
1    class LogWriter:
2
3        def __init__(self, base_log_file_name, ** options ):
4            """ Initializes the logger. Relies on the setOptions()
5                method for transforming keyword arguments into
6                preferences. Also, attempts to load the main log
7                file and inspects additional strategies for
8                proper initialization."""
9
10       def setCategoryList( self, cat_list ):
11           """Set reference to category list."""
12
13       def resetCategoryList( self ):
14           """Clear the category list."""
15
16       def setOptions( self, ** options ):
17           """ Method used to set various custom
18               options supported by the logger. """
19
20       def extendContext( self, extension ):
21           """ Lets users add more values to the end of the
22               context field. """
23
24       def getMessageCache( self ):
25           return string.join( self.__msg_cache, '' )
26
27       def writeError(self, message, strat_list=[] ):
28           self.__write( self.__context, ERROR, message, strat_list )
29           pass
30
31       def writeWarning(self, message, strat_list=[]):
32           """Similar to writeError() for Warnings."""
33
```

Figure 11–8
Logger.py

```
34      def writeDebug( self, message, strat_list=[] ):
35          """Similar to writeError() for Debug messages."""
36
37      def writeEntry( self,
38                      message, category='no category', strat_list=[] ):
39          """Used to write custom messages."""
40
41      def __write( self, context, category, message, strat_list=[] ):
42          """ Base method for writing a log entry to
43              all log strategies. """
44
45          # log only specified categories
46          if category not in self.__category_list and \
47             ALL not in self.__category_list:
48             return
49
50          # load the file
51          self.__load_log()
52
53          # if we could not load the file, exit silently
54          if self.__log_file == None:
55             sys.stderr.write( "\nERROR: Null log file \
56                               descriptor; no log entry written." )
57             return
58
59          # log details if user desires
60          if self.__log_details == 1:
61             message = string.strip( message )
62
63             details = "(logged in %s on line %s)"%( \
64                          getSourceFileName(2), getLineNumber(2) )
65
66             tb = ""
67             if traceBack() != "(no exceptions)":
68                tb = "(traceback)\n%s"%( traceBack() )
69
70             message = "%s\n%s\n%s"%( details, message, tb )
71
72          try:
73             # first log to the log file
74             self.__file_lock( 'lock' )
75             self.__write_to_file( context, category, message )
76             self.__file_lock( 'un-lock' )
```

Figure 11–8
Logger.py (Continued)

```
77
78                # write all available strategies
79                for strat in self.__strategy_dict.keys():
80                    if strat in strat_list or 'all' in strat_list:
81                        self.__strategy_dict[ strat ].write_entry( \
82                            context=context, \
83                            category=category, message=message )
84                    else:
85                        pass
86
87            except:
88                sys.stderr.write( "\nERROR: Could not write to one or \
89                                    more strategies.\n" )
90                sys.stderr.write( "\nMESSAGE:\n%s\n"%( message ) )
91                sys.stderr.write( "\nTRACEBACK:\n%s\n"%( traceBack() ) )
92                self.__file_lock( 'un-lock' )
93
94        pass
95
96    def __file_lock( self, operation ):
97        """ Attempt to lock or unlock the main log file."""
98
99    def __load_log( self ):
100        """ Loads a specified log file, rotates logs,
101            and sets the today link to the currently
102            loaded log. """
103
104        # load the log file if the log file name is none
105        # or if the file name has changed
106        if self.__log_file == None or \
107            self.__generate_file_name() == 1:
108            try:
109                self.__log_file = open( self.__log_file_name, 'a' )
110
111                # if link exists remove it
112                if os.path.islink( os.path.join( self.__path, \
113                                    TODAY_S_LINK ) ):
114                    # DEBUG
115                    #print "removing link."
116                    os.unlink( os.path.join( self.__path, \
117                        TODAY_S_LINK ) )
118
119                # set a softlink 'today' to point to the current log
120                os.symlink( self.__log_file_name , os.path.join( \
121                        self.__path, TODAY_S_LINK ) )
```

Figure 11–8
Logger.py (Continued)

```
122            except:
123                sys.stderr.write( "\nERROR: LogWriter could not \
124                                create log file name '%s'."%( \
125                                self.__log_file_name ) )
126                sys.stderr.write( "\nTRACE BACK:\n%s."%( \
127                                            traceBack() ) )
128                self.__log_file = None
129        else:
130            pass
131
132
133    def __generate_file_name( self ):
134        """ Generates a log file name based on the
135            specified base name and the current local time.
136            Returns a 1 or 0 to indicate if the file name
137            has changed since last call. """
138
139    def __write_to_file( self, context, category, message ):
140        """ Internal method for writing to the log file.
141            We always, regardless of preferences, log to a log
142            file; that's why this is included here as opposed to
143            being handled as a strategy. This method also handles
144            formatting the message to exclude white spaces, pretty
145            print multi-lined entries and add date/time stamps."""
146
```

Figure 11–8
Logger.py (Continued)

The Logger.py file can be found under the wp1.logger package hierarchy. In an attempt to conserve valuable text space, we have removed most of the in-line comments and the test application found in the original Logger.py file

All of the code for the logger is implemented in the LogWriter class, for two important reasons. Classes allow the programmer to provide public methods for interacting with an object. These methods form an API, which is one of the design components of the logger. Second, classes can contain both internal attributes and methods for encapsulating and hiding various low-level details, which is also a design requirement of the logger. The LogWriter class then uses public methods to serve the API and private attributes and methods to implement the logger component as well as the low-level text strategy. The following text provides more details of the code presented in Figure 11–8.

3   This is the LogWriter constructor. Notice that a base log file name is required. The logger, regardless of usage intentions, will always write entries to a log file. The base file name can contain both a path and filename, but a filename is required. Later, the logger will attempt to create a file at the provided path. Care must be taken to ensure that the user has the appropriate permissions to create the specified file. The constructor also uses a keyword variable argument list for additional functionality. This allows us to extend the logger easily without fear of breaking existing code relying on the logger interface.

One of the design requirements for additional logging strategies was the use of a common low-level interface between the logger and the various log strategies. We use the isinstance() function to verify that the additional logging strategies are an instance (subclasses) of the LogStrategy interface class. If so, we allow the user to access the strategy; otherwise, it is silently discarded.

Also of importance is the data structure used. The user must pass down a dictionary containing keyed instances of additional log strategies. Dictionaries are perfect data structures for binding names to a strategy instance. The public API allows the user to access various strategies based on the dictionary names.

20   All CGI applications adhere to the stateless nature of the HTTP protocol. As a result, a logger object is created each time that the parent CGI application is invoked. Sometimes it is helpful to view a list of entries that were generated in a single CGI invocation. The context allows us to do just that by optionally tagging each entry with a context number. The number is the machine time recorded when the logger was instantiated. This same number is used for all entries written during the life of the logger instance, allowing you to easily identify entries belonging to a single run.

Notice that the context is broken into two separate private attributes. This is done to allow the user to specify additional context identifiers, such as the name of the class that is currently executing. Each additional extension is separated by a period, following OOP conventions of specifying a hierarchy. This rule makes the period character reserved, and as a result, all periods used in extensions are first converted to underscores before being added to the context.

27–39   Public methods for creating new log entries. There are four separate methods that call the same internal function. Based on our design discussion, this is the interface between the API and the logger component. There is one API method for each of the three standard categories WARNING, ERROR, and DEBUG. The fourth API method, writeEntry, allows for optional use of custom categories. Notice how we take advantage of OOP practices to provide a convenient set of API for the user. We can easily add to the API in case we later decide to extend the core category list. This pattern also makes internal improvements transparent to the user.

41   Internal method for processing all entries and committing them to low-level log strategies. This method is the workhorse of the logger. It represents the logger component of our design. There are three required parameters: context, category, and message. The context is set on behalf of the user by each of the API methods. In case we change our policy on the context, we will not have to modify the __write method. The category and message values are passed down directly from the values that the user supplied the API. Optionally, the user may have specified a list of categories that are to be emitted.

46–48   Validate the current log category against the log category list. This logic lets us mask which messages are emitted and which ones are discarded. If the category is not in a specified list and the internal category list does not have the __all__ keyword, the message is discarded by simply returning from the __write function.

51–57   Attempt to load the log file. A load is performed only when the log file needs to be rolled over. We will go into the details of how that works below. If the file could not be loaded, we emit an error to the standard error stream, but do not raise an exception as done in the constructor. This ensures that logging problems due to system changes do not break an application that is in production.

60–70   Optionally generate and add details regarding the current entry. The design discussion indicated that the logger component can be instructed to obtain the file name and line number that resulted in the current API call. We take advantage of the wpl.trace.Trace utilities to comb through the current execution frame for the API call details. Notice that in both getLineNumber() and getSourceFileName() methods, we set the step value to 2. This instructs the methods to obtain details from the third entry in the stack. In other words, skip over the current call and the call made by the API to __write, but return details of the code that made the call to the API method. We also check for available traceback due to an exception. Entry details are added to the front of the message and any available traceback is appended to the end. Later you will see an example of how details appear in the log file.

74–76   Attempt to lock the log file, write the entry, and unlock the file. The log file
           strategy is always used and is therefore separate from the call to the additional
           logging strategies. We perform a file lock to prevent race conditions from
           corrupting the log file. This activity is performed inside a `try/except` block to
           catch and safely handle any low-level I/O errors. In the event of an error, an error
           message along with the user's log entry are emitted to the standard error stream.

79–85   Iterate over additional strategies and emit the context, category, and message. In
           the design discussion, we referred to a common low-level interface used by the
           logger component to propagate messages down to the low-level logger strategies.
           All logger strategies are required to overload the `write_entry()` method. Here
           we call this method for each strategy that the user has specified in the
           `strat_list` provided by the API.

99–130   Loads the log file for writing. This method is invoked both in the constructor and
           in the `__write()` method. We check to see if the log file needs to be opened
           based on two conditions: No log file is currently open or the log file name has
           changed since the last call. The first clause applies to calls made by the
           constructor. The second clause is used for rolling logs over just prior to
           committing a new entry. The `__generate_file_name()` method will return 1
           if the file has changed names, indicating that a rollover has occurred. We then
           proceed to load the file. We also attempt to create a soft link to the new file. Since
           logs are rotated daily, the link can be used to refer to the current or "today's"
           log, another convenience feature of the logger.

133   Generate a file name using a supplied base file name and the current date. This
           internal method is invoked by the constructor and the `__load_file()` method.
           In the latter call, it performs a rollover of the file if necessary. In each invocation,
           we generate a new log file name and compare it to the current log file name. If it is
           different, then the log file has been rolled over and we return a 1 to the calling
           method. This coding strategy saves you from having to track date information
           using internal class attributes and additional logic. Since the same logic is used
           each time to generate the log file name, we simply have to flag instances when the
           generated file name differs from the one that we are currently using.

139   Assembles entries and commits them to the log file. Here we assemble the
           context, category, and message into a formal log entry that contains a date and
           time stamp. We also take care to indent multilined messages. Indentation makes
           reading the log file easier and allows us to parse the log file during data-mining
           operations.

           Now we will discuss the details of the `LogStrategy` class. This is
           an interface class that must be extended in order to create additional
           custom log strategies. The `LogStrategy` class is implemented in the
           `LogStrategy.py` file, listed in Figure 11–9.

```
1    # Standard imports
2    import time
3
4
5    class LogStrategy:
6        """
7        Base class for all logging strategies. Lists
8        all of the public interfaces that must be implemented
9        and provides access to commonly used routines.
10        """
11
12       def __init__( self ):
13           raise Exception( "LogStrategy is an interface and cannot be
             instantiated." )
14
15       def write_entry( self, ** data ):
16           raise Exception( "write_entry(...) is a required interface and
             must be defined in the subclass." )
17
18       def getTimeASCII( self ):
19           return time.asctime( time.localtime( time.time() ))
20
21       def getTimeSeconds( self ):
22           return time.time()
```

Figure 11–9
LogStrategy.py

The LogStrategy class is very simple. It is used solely as a means of ensuring that all logger extensions adhere to the same interface. The guarantee is made by checking two separate criteria. First, all strategy objects passed to the LogWriter constructor must be instances of LogStrategy. All classes of the subclass LogStrategy will be considered instances of the class and will therefore have met the first criterion.

Second, the base write_entry() method is set to raise an exception if invoked. Python, unlike Java, does not have real support for interface classes. All Python classes can be instantiated and utilized. By raising an exception, we have created a pseudo-interface class. The class can still be instantiated and used to pass the first check, but will fail since an exception is raised every time the LogWriter class invokes the base write_entry() method. This ensures that the interface is properly overloaded by the subclass.

Two additional methods are provided for conveniently accessing the current date and time. These methods, along with any other commonly used routines, are available to all strategies in the subclass LogStrategy.

This wraps up the discussion of implementation details. In the next section, we will go over how the logger is created and used in your CGI applications.

Using the LogWriter • Included with the LogWriter is a test routine that serves both as an example of how the logger is used and as a way of testing the core functionality of the logger. In this section, we will go over the basics of creating a new logger and using the API to tailor functionality and create new log entries.

First you must import the `WriteLog` class from the `wpl.logger.Logger` module into your current module.[2] Next, you must instantiate a new logger instance as follows:

```
wpll = LogWriter( "TestLog" )
```

The `LogWriter` constructor requires that you specify a string containing the base file name to be used. The string can contain both absolute and relative paths to an existing or a new file. We could have created the same log file in the `/home/pshafae` directory with the following call:

```
wpll = LogWriter( "/home/pshafae/TestLog" )
```

The resulting log file will start with the base file name concatenated to a string containing the current date and a `log` extension. The above call would result in a file with a name similar to `TestLog.02-18-2001.log`. Additionally, if you are using the logger class on a UNIX-based system, a new soft link called `today.log` is created which references the current log. This convenient feature takes out a few steps when attempting to read today's logs (most useful during development).

The constructor also takes a number of optional parameters. Table 11–3 lists a brief description of each option. The following code segment sets all of the options available. Since the constructor uses a keyword argument list, you must make sure to specify the option name and its value.

---

2. This simple operation can be made complicated depending on how you have set your PYTHONPATH environment variable. See the Python manual and Chapter 12 for more details.

```
my_strat_dict = {}
my_strat_dict[ 'stderr' ] = StderrStrategy()
wpll = LogWriter( "TestLog", log_details=0, log_context=1,
strat_dict=my_strat_dict )
```

Table 11-3
LogWriter Constructor Option

log_details	Boolean value set to either 1 or 0, used to turn on autogeneration of log entry details and traceback stamps. By default, this is turned off.
log_context	Boolean value set to either 1 or 0, used to turn off emitting of log context. By default, this feature is turned on.
strat_dict	A dictionary containing instances of additional logger strategies. Additional strategies must be instances of the LogStrategy class.

Once you have a LogWriter instance, you are ready to create log entries. There are four methods for creating entries. The most general is writeEntry(), as shown by the following:

```
wpll.writeEntry( "Simple log message with no category or strat. list." )
```

The log entry as a result of the above would be something similar to:

```
Sun Feb 18 09:05:51 2001 [[context:982508751.73]] [[category:no
category]] > Simple log message with no category or strat. list.
```

Optionally, the writeEntry() method will accept a category and a list of strategy names to be used in logging the entry. You can take advantage of the list of strategy names to direct the current (and only the current) log entry to a specific strategy other than the log file. For example, when logging details of an exception, you may choose to emit the message to the standard error stream.[3] You may also choose to select a custom category for the message. Earlier, we did not specify a category, and as a result the logger recorded no category in the category field. The following call to writeEntry() performs both of these tasks:

```
wpll.writeEntry( "Logging to stderr strategy.", "MyCategory",
strat_list=[ 'stderr' ] )
```

---

3. This is the common case in CGI programming, as all data written to the standard error stream is logged by the Apache Web Server.

Notice that the list of strategy names corresponds to the key we used when storing an instance of `StderrStrategy` in the `strat_dict` dictionary. LogWriter will ignore all invalid strategy names. Also, note that the second argument to the API call is the category name. Shortly we will demonstrate how additional API methods can be used to filter out certain entries based on their categories. The other three API methods for creating entries are `writeDebug()`, `writeWarning()`, and `writeError()`. They have the same profile and functionality as `writEntry()`, but do not provide a means of specifying custom categories. Instead, they supply DEBUG, WARNING, and ERROR, respectively, as the entry category. These methods shorten the length of the method call for standard entry categories and make your code more legible.

Using the `setCategoryList()`, you can specify a list of category names that are to be emitted. The specified list will be used for all entries written until the application is terminated or another call is made to `setCategoryList()` or `resetCategoryList()`. You can use the `resetCategoryList()` method to instruct the logger to log all messages. The following instructs the logger to emit only entries belonging to the ERROR, WARNING, and "MyCategory" categories:

```
wpll.setCategoryList( [ DEBUG, ERROR, "MyCategory"] )
```

Take note that both DEBUG and ERROR are constants imported from the `Logger` module. The use of this method is most useful when you are releasing your application for production use. You can simply specify to log all categories except for DEBUG. However, this requires that you take advantage of categories while developing your application. At first this appears to be a waste of time, but the more it becomes a habit, the more time it saves in maintaining and extending your application.

You can change various logging options using `setOptions()`. You should refer to release logs for a listing of exactly which options can be set via this method. At the time of writing, `setOptions()` handled `log_detail` and `log_context`. The method takes keyword arguments and is used as follows:

```
wpll.setOptions( log_details = 1 )
```

All entries following the call to setOptions() will be affected; nothing will happen to previous entries. Here is an example of a log entry after turning on the log_details options:

```
Sun Feb 18 09:10:42 2001 [[context:982509042.935]] [[category:DEBUG]] >
    (logged in Logger.py on line 337)
    An exception just occurred.
    (traceback)
        File "Logger.py", line 335, in test_func
        raise Exception( "Error! Raised a test exception." )
    Exception: Error! Raised a test exception.
```

Notice that prior to the message "An exception just occurred," there are details regarding the location of the log entry method call between parentheses. Also, notice that following the log entry there is a traceback. This indicates that an exception was raised recently and is being handled. If no exception had occurred, no traceback information would have been provided.

You can also modify the context using extendContext(). The API will take a string argument and append it to the end of the base context, separating the two with a period. The base context is always set by the logger, and is used to group entries generated by a particular instance of the logger. If your extension string contains periods, they are automatically converted to underscores. This feature is most useful when used in larger applications to track which module committed the entry.

Your application can terminate without any additional overhead. The logger will automatically close the log file. All references to additional log strategies will be set to None and resources will be freed.

Creating Log Strategies • In this section, we will explore the details of creating StderrStrategy, a custom log strategy for emitting messages to the standard error stream. Writing to the standard error stream is a good practice when developing CGI applications.

All messages written to stderr are logged by Apache in the error_log file. However, Apache does not time-stamp error_log entries, and the Python sys.stderr.write() method does not add new lines to the messages written. This results in clumping of messages without any indication of when the message was created. We will attempt to resolve these shortcomings in StderrStrategy.

The StderrStrategy class is implemented in StderrStrategy.py. The complete source code is listed in Figure 11–10. We begin by importing the sys module so that we can access

the stderr file handle. Next, on line 5, we import the LogStrategy
class. Pay close attention to line 7; here we subclass LogStrategy to
meet the first of two criteria for writing additional logging strategies. The
LogWriter class will now be able to recognize StderrStrategy as
an instance of the LogStrategy interface class.

On line 9, we define an empty constructor. StderrStrategy is
very simple and does not require constructor parameters or any
attribute initialization. You may need to use the constructor when
developing more complicated logging strategies such as an e-mail
strategy. Always keep in mind that you pass an instance of a strategy to
LogWriter; the LogWriter does not instantiate the strategy for you.
This allows you be free in how you implement your constructor and
instantiate the strategy.

On line 12, we override the LogStrategy interface method. This
meets the second and final criterion of giving a new definition to the
write_entry() method. Notice that the methods **must** take a
keyword argument list. Any deviation from this model will result in
errors. On lines 13 to 15, we store the values of the parameters set by

```
1    # Standard imports
2    import sys
3
4    # Non-standard imports
5    from LogStrategy import LogStrategy
6
7    class StderrStrategy( LogStrategy ):
8
9        def __init__( self):
10           pass
11
12       def write_entry( self, ** data ):
13           context = data.get( 'context', '' )
14           category = data.get( 'category', '' )
15           message = data.get( 'message' )
16
17           # time stamp
18           time_stamp = self.getTimeASCII()
19
20           entry = """\n%s [%s] : %s\n"""%( time_stamp, \
21                                            category, \
22                                            message )
23
24           sys.stderr.write( entry )
```

Figure 11–10
StderrStrategy.py

LogWriter to local variables for convenience. As of the time of writing, LogWriter invoked the write_entry() method with values for the context, category, and message. Future versions and extensions may provide additional values.

The rest of the method attempts to make logging to the standard error stream convenient and useful. Note that on line 18 we take advantage of a LogStrategy method for obtaining a local date and time string. At the end of the method, we commit the constructed log entry to the standard error string file handle by invoking the write() method.

Using the same formula, you can create extravagant and complicated strategies that can be used to send e-mails on fatal errors. The possibilities are endless.

Summary

Logging and debugging are essential and time-consuming tasks that are part of every programming project. Unfortunately, this topic is rarely discussed in programming texts. In this chapter, we provided present techniques for hunting down CGI bugs as well as reviewed common errors and programming pitfalls. We would like to stress that the most effective strategy for debugging CGI applications is logging. The more information you log, the more evidence you have in tracking and killing bugs.

We also explored the design, implementation, use, and extension of the Logger module. In its current form, the module not only meets the basic requirements of a logger, but also provides several key features that make debugging and production data collection a breeze.

However, by no means do we believe that the logger has all of the features needed to meet all possible projects. We hope that you begin by utilizing the module in your everyday development. The more you use it, the more you will realize the benefits of collecting debugging and statistical information from your code. Once you have joined the ranks of other believers, we hope that you help extend the functionality of this module either through suggestions or direct implementation. It is this fluid nature of open-source programming that makes good applications into great applications.

Miscellaneous Utility Modules and Classes

This chapter describes a number of miscellaneous utility classes that we have developed that do not fall under any particular chapter.

Path

The Path module is designed to automate the construction of the Python path (`sys.path` or `PYTHONPATH`), which is used to locate modules that are being imported. When working with CGI and Python, getting the Python path correct is a bit of a nuisance. The application needs to do one of two things: Set the environment variable PYTHON-PATH before the script begins running; or set `sys.path` on the fly from within the Python script.

Neither of these options is terribly attractive. Setting environment variables usually has to be done externally to the script. There are several ways to get the environment variable set prior to invoking the interpreter. The most common are to set a global variable within `/etc/profile` (usually requiring **root** permission on Linux) or to set the variables in the profile for the user id under which the interpreter (and hence the CGI script) is being run. Both of these are fine, but tend to make long-term deployment of the application dependent on things that may not be consistent on the systems where the application will ultimately be deployed. The other approach is to modify `sys.path` directly within the application. This also has problems, since the application loses transparency with respect to file systems, etc., because it is now dependent on specific directories being present.

The Path class was developed to allow the best of both worlds, and it does so in a very concise package. The sys.path variable is far preferable to working with environment variables, since it represents a form of dynamic configuration and is totally centered on the application's ability to find the modules it needs. Using something like the profile is useful for keeping the actual list of directories to be searched in a file. The paths to the various module directories need not be hard-coded into the application itself. Thus the Path class is essentially a convenience class that allows your script to be dynamically configured with an appropriate path for locating modules, but it does so from a configuration file.

By default, the configuration file is stored in the directory where the top-level scripts in your application are located. It is named .pythonpathrc (in keeping with Unix tradition, the file name begins with "." and ends in "rc", indicating that its a "dot-python-path-rc" file). As well and by default, the directories may be separated by ":" or listed on separate lines. The contents of .pythonpathrc are read in their entirety and used to set the path using sys.path.append(dir), where dir is the directory being added to the path.

The class Path is a class that can be directly instantiated by the user. There is usually no need to keep an instance of class Path for long, since its only mission in life is to update sys.path.[1] So the module itself, when imported *in its entirety* (i.e., when "import Path" is used), will automatically create an instance and try to read entries from .pythonpathrc, assuming that ":" or newlines (or a combination) are used to separate the list of directories.

The structure of the Path module is shown below:

```
1    class Path:
2      def __init__(self, sep=":", rcFile=".pythonpathrc"):
3
4      def addDir(self,dir):
5
6      def __repr__(self):
7        return 'Path: '+`sys.path`
8
9    Path()
```

The class itself is very simple. It has a constructor (the __init__() method), which allows you to specify a separator and the

---

1. Having said that, we chose to make it a class for that one weird application that may come along that needs to add directories to the search path on the fly. This might be the case if you're writing an application that generates Python code and then needs to be able to load it from a particular directory.

name of the configuration file. Most of the time, you won't want to change this.[2] Our approach is to make things as configurable as possible; the addDir() method allows you to add more directories after the instance has been constructed. (This interface is not generally needed, since most applications know the list of directories up front, but has been left here for completeness.) Observe that the last line creates an instance. If you import the module as a whole instead of merely importing Path, you'll automatically have your path constructed using the defaults, assuming the .pythonpathrc is actually present. The __repr__() method is added to allow you to print the path directly, in keeping with the tradition that every class should have a method to make instances printable in a meaningful string representation.

Let's take a look at how the __init__() and addDir() methods are implemented, first considering the __init__() method:

```
1    def __init__(self, sep=":", rcFile=".pythonpathrc"):
2        try:
3            fp = open(rcFile,'r')
4            dirs = fp.readlines()
5        except:
6            dirs = []
7        for dirs in dirs:
8            dirList = string.split(dirs[0:-1],sep)
9            for dir in dirList:
10               if not dir in sys.path:
11                   sys.path.append(dir)
```

The "rc file" is opened for input and read in its entirety on lines 3–4. Configuration files are typically short, so reading the entire file at once is a good idea from a performance perspective. If the file cannot be opened for any reason, dirs is set to an empty list. This might seem error-prone, but it is precisely the way the shell in Unix works. If the profile cannot be read or does not exist, it is ignored and no message is printed. This code has been written to guarantee successful execution no matter what hapens. Once the file has been read, the list of all input lines is processed, one at a time. Each line is split using the delimiter (sep). Each of the directories (dir) is added to the path, provided the directory is not already in the path.

So why have an object for this if the intention is to "throw it away" anyway? Clearly, the constructor is simply updating sys.path and

---

2. We decided to leave open the possibility that all of our code would work properly with Windows, which has the obnoxious "drive letter" file system that uses ":" and requires you to consider a different delimiter for separating directories.

then the object is (technically) no longer needed. There is the possibility you will want to update the path again later, and having an object reference handy for doing so gives you that ability. And that is why there is an `addDir()` method, which allows you to add a directory to the Python path afterward:

```
1    def addDir(self,dir):
2        if not dir in sys.path:
3            sys.path.append(dir)
```

The body of this method is essentially the work being done by the loop over all directories in the constructor.

Directory

Scoped Dictionaries for Python

The Directory class is an implementation of a scoped namespace. Scoped namespaces have a wide variety of applications in compilers, document processing (XML), and CGI programming (where we'll be making use of it the most). Let's consider how scoped namespaces are typically used. Initially, there are no scopes. That is because no entries have been made in the symbol table yet. As processing is done, scopes are created. In the case of a compiler, a scope is seen when encountering a function definition, a nested block of statements, etc. Why do you need scopes here? Because duplicate symbol definitions can and do occur, and you need scopes to unambiguously determine the meaning of a symbol. For example, the variable "x" in a function could refer to a definition in the body of a function (or nested block), the parameter list, a global variable, or an external variable (at least in processing the C language). Similarly, in XML processing, scopes are useful. You might want to be able to find an XML element quickly starting from the top or inside of another element.

We use the Directory class in the `wpl.wf.WebForm` class that appears in Chapter 13 and use it to keep track of the form variables. We also use the class in our portal framework for our persistent storage framework. As different scripts want the ability to save information between invocations, it's imperative that a segmented namespace be used to prevent collisions while making it possibile to go from one script to another seamlessly. There are many situations in which directories are useful.

The directory concept is one that is familar to most computer users. It lends itself naturally to the scoped namespace, and can be conveniently wired into Python using the `UserDict` class. This is particularly advantageous to the programmer, because the scoping mechanism can be used as if it were a built-in Python dictionary, using all of its familiar operations. The magic of the dictionary class, however, comes from its ability to preserve all of the dictionary interfaces while allowing arbitrary movement between namespaces (up, down, and across) with operations as familiar as the easiest Unix directory commands.

So the question arises: How does it really work? First and foremost, the goal is to give the programmer the impression that he or she is working with a single dictionary, although the dictionary has potentially many nested directories. This is made possible by keeping track of a current dictionary. Through this dictionary, entries can be made as if it were the only dictionary in existence. (This is not altogether different from how the Unix or Windows shell works.) There is a notion of a current directory (or folder) into which files and directories may be created. In Unix, you can "cd" from one folder to another, merely by knowing the path to the folder. Once you get there, you can "ls" the contents of the folder. In Python terms, you would be able to iterate the `keys()` and `values()`. The directory class, based on the current scope, returns different values for `keys()` and `values()`, depending on what is found. These functions return only the values that were inserted—not subdirectories. This makes it easy to consider only the entries that are present in the namespace by virtue of regular "set item" usage.

Let's take a look at how a scoped namespace works. Figure 12–1 shows the directory concept.

A directory is represented as a rectangle with rounded corners. When a rectangle is contained within a rectangle, the nested rectangle is a subdirectory. The outermost directory is called the "root" directory and is referred to as "/". There are several directories present: /, /A, /B, /C, /C/A, and /C/B. The notation used here indicates the absolute path to a particular directory. Within each directory, there are a number of entries, which represent the familiar concept of associations found in Python's dictionary class, where a key is mapped to a value. Although we have only shown string keys associated with integers, any kind of data can be stored, including Python lists, dictionaries, and other objects.

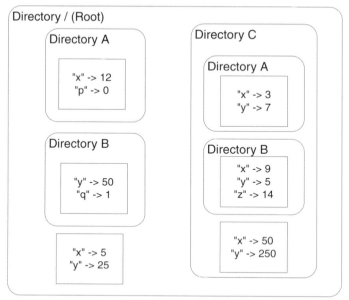

Figure 12–1
Directory concept

The Directory class is thus equivalent to a dictionary at some level. It is designed, however, to support features not found in the dictionary, including:

- Path creation, manipulation, and traversal
- "Scoped" lookups from the inside to the outside
- Other operations
- Find and apply operations

First, let's consider the need for path functionality. A path is a way of referring to a directory. It's simply a character string in which the directories are separated by "/". Path specifications are absolute in this version of the Directory class, so you must always begin a path with "/". An advanced version supports relative path specifications using "." and ".." but does add complexity and really doesn't prove to be necessary for most of our applications. When working with a Directory, there is a notion of a current path. The current path allows you to indicate the directory where any dictionary operation takes place first. For example, if the current path were /A and you inserted an entry into the Directory using Python's subscripting syntax, it would only affect the dictionary associated with /A. Looking up values is also done in /A, but "/" is also considered.

The scoping principle refers to how a value is found. To understand the scoping principle, consider the notion of the current path, which can be thought of as the "You are here" symbol that you find on a typical map at a shopping mall or in a train station. Let's consider a current directory, using the figure again, /A. In directory /A, two keys are present, "x" and "p", containing values 12 and 0, respectively. The scoping principle allows you to see what is within your current view (/A) and what is within the chain of directories leading all the way out to the root ("/") directory. As /A is a subdirectory of "/", we get "x" and "p" from "/A" and "y" from "/". Table 12–1 shows how the scoping principle works by showing what variables are visible from within a particular directory that is set as the current directory.

Table 12–1
Entries Visible at Various Scope Levels

Directory	View
/	"x" -> 5, "y" -> 25
/A	"x" -> 12, "p" -> 0 "y" in "/"; "x" in "/" is obscured (but available)
/B	"y" -> 50, "q" -> 1 "x" in "/"; "y" in "/" is obscured (but available)
/C	"x" -> 50, "y" -> 250 "x" and "y" in "/" are obscured (but available)
/C/A	"x" -> 3, "y" -> 7 "x" and "y" in "/C" and "/" are obscured (but available)
/C/B	"x" -> 9, "y" -> 5, "z" -> 14 "x" and "y" in "/C" are obscured (but available)

The concept of a scope comes up routinely in programming. Every language has scoping rules that define how a variable's declaration (or definition) is found, based on where the program is presently executing. Compilers maintain something very similar to a directory, called a symbol table, that is used specifically to look up the meanings of variables, based on the current scope. We needed something similar for a number of our programming modules, and thus decided to take a classic idea and add a few twists to make the ultimate data structure. (The class is one of just a few we'll present in this book that are useful to general programming, not just Web applications.)

Design and Implementation

The Directory class as found in the WPL modules has a fairly straight-forward design. In a typical directory found in a file system, there are only two kinds of entries to be found:

- files
- directories (so-called subdirectories)

Our design is similar. There are also two kinds of entries. Of course, our class is not intended for use as a true file system. The dictionary of Python is a general-purpose object container, and our Directory class is a specialization of Python's dictionary. (In fact, Directory is a subclass of `UserDict`.) We merely specialize the dictionary concept to introduce hierarchy.

To support this notion, we introduce two classes to support subdirectories:

- `PathRef`: Used to refer to a given subdirectory. A `PathRef` instance is created for each subdirectory contained in a given directory. This allows the Directory class to distinguish between subdirectories and other entries placed in the Directory instance.
- `PathElement`: Used to hold the content of a given subdirectory. A `PathElement` is nothing more than a container for a nested dictionary into which subdirectory entries (and their sub-directories) will be deposited.

The directory concept as we define it is somewhat different from the same notion found in file systems. In our scheme, it is entirely possible for a subdirectory and an entry that is not a subdirectory to have the same name. This is because subdirectories are actually names that are shrink-wrapped in a `PathRef` instance. Furthermore, any other entry in a directory may or may not be a string. This is an innate property of Python's dictionary: Anything can be a key. We happen to be taking advantage of this, in fact, by using `PathRef` instances to reach a subdirectory.

We'll now go over the implementation briefly. The Directory class is a significant class in terms of number of methods, so this discussion will be focused on essentials. The discussion here should give you enough detail to fully understand the details not presented here.

Let's first take a look at the `PathRef` class, which is used by the Directory class to refer to a subdirectory (a `PathElement` instance):

```
class PathRef:
    def __init__(self, name):
        self.name = name

    def __hash__(self):
        return hash(self.name)

    def __cmp__(self, other):
        if isinstance(other, PathRef):
            return cmp(self.name, other.name)
        else:
            return 1
```

We have excised some methods that are not essential, such as those for printing and/or obtaining the representation of the class. The PathRef is nothing more than a wrapper for the subdirectory name. The __hash__() method defined here results in any instance of PathRef having the same hash value as the name of the subdirectory (self.name) when used in a collection, such as a dictionary. This can present a problem if another entry is deposited into such a collection, hence the presence of the __cmp__(self, other) function. This is used to perform a comparison in the event two objects in the collection have the same hash value. __cmp__() is supposed to return 0 when two objects are equal, less than 0 for less than, and greater than 0 for greater than. The code here will return greater than (1) if this object (self) is compared to anything other than a PathRef instance. Otherwise, comparison is performed between this object's name and the other object's name instance variable. For a discussion of these hooking functions [such as __hash__() and __cmp__()] and the built-in function cmp(), see Chapter 3, where many examples are provided.

The PathElement class is presented below:

```
class PathElement:
    def __init__(self, name, data):
        self.name = name
        self.data = data
```

PathElement instances are used to hold the content of a subdirectory. The content is just stored in a regular Python dictionary. In a strict sense, we did not need to create a separate class for this and could have just kept a Python dictionary associated with a PathRef. This decision more than likely stems from our obsession with using classes in the event that we want to change some aspect of the implementation later.

For now, it is truly just a wrapper class to hold the subdirectory data and not much more.

The Directory class itself is a subclass of the Python `UserDict` class with specialization to support subdirectories and the lexical scoping concept described in the preceding discussion. Let's take a look at the constructor, which gives some insight into the overall implementation.

```
def __init__(self, init_data={}, default_get=None):
    UserDict.__init__(self, init_data)
    self.top_path = '/'
    self.top_data = self.data
    self.current_path = self.top_path
    self.default_get = default_get
    self.stack = []
    self.pe_cache = {}
```

Table 12–2 summarizes the key attributes of the Directory class.

Table 12–2
Directory Instance Attributes

Attribute	Description
top_path	The top-level (root) directory name.
top_data	The top-level (root) directory's dictionary. The parameter init_data allows the root directory to be populated initially with the content of any Python dictionary.
current_path	The current working directory. Initially, the current working directory is the root-level directory "/".
default_get	The value to be returned if an attempt to get an undefined entry name from the directory occurs. By default, this is set to None.
stack	A stack of directory changes. This is used to maintain directory changes that are made using the pushd() interface.
pe_cache	A cache of PathElement instances. This is used to speed the lookups of subdirectories. At present, all subdirectories are cached for fast lookups.

Creating a Directory: A View of the Implementation

By far the method that provides the most insight into the implementation of the Directory class is the method create(self, path), which creates a directory. The value of this path can be either an absolute or relative path (e.g., /usr/bin or usr/bin, respectively). Here is the create() method code:

```
1        def create(self, path):
2            path_elements = self.__compute_path_list(path)
3            data = self.top_data
4            for dir in path_elements:
5                pe = self.__getPathRef(dir)
6                if not data.has_key(pe):
7                    data[pe] = PathElement(dir,{})
8                data = data[pe].data
9            return data
```

This code is very short but does a lot; it is summarized in the following line-by-line account:

2   This computes the canonical path from *path*. path_elements is set to a list of path components (all strings) to be taken relative to the root directory. We will not present the details of the internal routine __compute_path_list(); however, this routine is smart enough to handle an absolute or relative path specification.

3   Start at the top-level directory (self.top_data, which is the root directory) to do the creation.

4   Now, list all of the path components in the canonical path.

5–7   See if the subdirectory exists. This is done by getting the PathElement instance associated with that subdirectory. If the directory does not exist, create a PathElement for this directory with an empty Python dictionary to hold the directory's entries.

8   After line 7, it is assured that a subdirectory exists, so we now need to "enter" this directory to create any further subdirectories that need to be created.

It is clear that the create() function has been designed for the convenience of users. (We are in this category, having used the Directory class extensively in the Slither class library for developing Web applications.) As an example, suppose the directory /usr/local/bin were to be created in a Directory instance. The value of path_elements would be ['usr','local','bin']. Now, if subdirectory 'usr' did not exist in directory '/', it would be created. Then 'local' would be created in 'usr' (if it did not exist), ultimately leading to the same behavior for 'bin'. By default, the mkdir() command in Unix (and Windows) does not support the same functionality if any subdirectory in the list path_elements does not exist. The other aspect of create() that differs from its counterpart in the Unix/Windows world is what happens when the directory already exists. In the case of create(), nothing will happen. Whenever a directory is created that already exists, a reference to the subdirectory is returned and the existing directories are left as is. This overall user-centric approach results in a great deal of convenience and eliminates the need for users to test whether a directory exists before attempting to create it.

The remainder of the methods in the Directory class, despite supporting a multitude of different functions, all are coded somewhat similarly to the create() method. The available interfaces are discussed in the next section.

Interface Methods

The Directory class contains many functions that resemble many of the file utilities found in the Linux (Unix) operating system. Table 12–3 lists all of the methods provided to users of the Directory class and their purpose.

Table 12–3
Key Directory (User Interface) Methods

Method	What It Does
def cd(self, path=None)	Change the current working directory (in the Directory data structure) to *path*. If *path* is None, set the current working directory to the root directory (/).
def clear_all(self)	Clear the entire Directory. This is equivalent to clear() in an ordinary Python dictionary. Any subdirectories and entries in the Directory are destroyed.

Table 12–3
Key Directory (User Interface) Methods (Continued)

Method	What It Does
`def clear(self)`	Clear the entries of the Directory. Note that this differs from `clear_all()` as any subdirectories are preserved. Only the entries themselves are deleted.
`def copy_dir(self, path1, path2, **props)`	Copy one subdirectory represented by *path1* to another subdirectory represented by *path2*. If *path2* does not exist, it will be created. *path1* must exist or an exception will be thrown to indicate the path was not found.
`ef create(self, path)`	Create a path *path*=/x1/x2/.../xN or x1/x2/.../xN. If any of x1...xN do not exist, each of the missing subdirectories will be created up to and including xN. This emulates the functionality of `mkdir -p` in Unix. A reference to the dictionary for this path is returned.
`def dirs(self)`	Return a list of all subdirectories relative to the current working directory.

`def find(self, key, **props)`	Similar to the Unix `find` command, search for an entry according to additional attributes specified in `props`. These attributes include:
	`type = dirs | keys`
	`result = tuple_list | dictionary`

`def get_dir(self, path)`	Get an entry from a subdirectory without having to change directory. The value of *path* contains at least one directory and one entry and is of the form `prefix/entry`. `prefix` and is an absolute or relative path to a subdirectory.
`def getpwd(self)`	Return the current directory as a canonical path /x1/x2/.../xN. This can be used to change directory later, if the current working directory is subsequently changed.

Table 12–3
Key Directory (User Interface) Methods (Continued)

Method	What It Does
`def get(self, key, failobj=None)`	Similar to the regular `get()` method on a Python dictionary. If *key* cannot be found, the value *failobj* is returned.
`def has_key(self, key)`	Similiar to the `has_key()` dictionary method. If an entry *key* is present, true is returned and otherwise false. Note that `has_key()` returns false in the case where there is a subdirectory having *key* as a name. Only non-directory entries named *key* return true.
`def import_list(self, content)`	A convenience method that allows you to import `content`, where `content` represents a list of fully qualified entry names and values. An example of this method is shown in the source code.
`def items(self)`	Similar to the built-in Python `dictionary` method. This returns the items in the dictionary corresponding to the current working directory.
`def keys(self)`	Similar to the built-in Python `dictionary` method. This returns the keys in the dictionary corresponding to the current working directory.
`def popd(self)`	Change the current working directory to the directory atop the stack of directories, which was modified by a previous `pushd()` call. Then pop the directory stack. If for some reason no `pushd()` call has been made prior to a `popd()` call, the current directory will be set to the root directory.
`def pushd(self, path)`	Push the current working directory on a local stack and change directory to `path`.

Table 12–3
Key Directory (User Interface) Methods (Continued)

Method	What It Does
`def scoped_get_list(self, key, **props`	Based on the current directory, return a list of all entries associated with `key` by considering the current directory's dictionary and the dictionaries in all parent directories.
`def scoped_get(self, key)`	Starting in the current directory, search the parent and all of its ancestors for `key`. If not found, return `None`.
`def set_dir(self, path, value)`	Similar to `get_dir()`, set the dictionary entry in `path=directory/entry` to `value`.
`def values(self)`	Similar to the built-in Python `dictionary` method, get the values of the dictionary corresponding to the current working directory.
`def walk_bfs(self, "/", max_depth=None)`	A breadth-first search (BFS) walker for the Directory.
`def walk_dfs(self, walk_obj, anchor="/", max_depth=None)`	A depth-first search (DFS) walker for the Dictionary.
`def walk(self, **props)`	A general walker for the Directory. This method is actually used by both `walk_bfs()` and `walk_dfs()`.

The next section provides a glimpse of how to actually use the Directory class and its methods.

Using the Directory Class

Let's now take a look at how the Directory class is used. The source code for the Directory class itself contains a number of integrated "test" functions that demonstrate how it is used. We will illustrate the Directory class by considering categories of functions and showing how they are used interactively.

Construction

We begin by importing the Directory class and constructing an instance of it.

```
Python 2.1 (#1, Apr 24 2001, 16:10:35)
[GCC 2.95.3 19991030 (prerelease)] on linux2
Type "copyright", "credits" or "license" for more information.
>>> from wpl.directory.Directory import Directory
>>> d = Directory()
>>> print d.toString("/")
{
  # directory /
}
```

The Directory class includes a method toString() that can be used to do a "directory listing" to observe the current contents of the directory. As this directory was just created, it contains nothing. The "# directory /" line of output is a comment to indicate that this is the content of the root directory.

Creating a Directory

Now let us create a few directories to demonstrate the create() method that was presented in the design discussion.

```
>>> d.create("/x")
{}
>>> d.create("/y")
{}
>>> d.create("z")
{}
>>> print d.toString("/")
{
  # directory /
  {
    # directory /z
  }
  {
    # directory /x
  }
  {
    # directory /y
  }
}
```

We now have a total of three subdirectories. The first two creations are done using an absolute path. That is, a path is specified relative to the root directory named "x" and "y". The third creation is taken relative to the current directory. By default, the root directory is the current directory until changed somehow (more on that shortly).

As mentioned in the design discussion, `create()` can also be used to create any arbitrary path of directories:

```
>>> d.create("/usr/local/bin")
{}
>>> d.create("/usr/local/lib")
{}
>>> d.create("/usr/local/include")
{}
>>> print d.toString("/")
{
  # directory /
  {
    # directory /usr
    {
      # directory /usr/local
      {
        # directory /usr/local/lib
      }
      {
        # directory /usr/local/include
      }
      {
        # directory /usr/local/bin
      }
    }
  }
  {
    # directory /z
  }
  {
    # directory /x
  }
  {
    # directory /y
  }
}
```

Observe that when creating directories where the parent directory does not exist, the `create()` method automatically creates any "parent" directories.

In the directory hierarchy we have created thus far, there are no entries. We now turn to a discussion of this functionality.

Adding or Getting Entries to or from a Directory

To add entries to a directory, there are two basic methods provided. These are:

- Change directory and use the intrinsic subscripting capability of Python's dictionary.
- Use the set_dir() method.

We will demonstrate both methods. Let's use the first method to add some entries to "/x" and then display the directory:

```
>>> d.getpwd()
'/'
>>> d.cd("x")
>>> d.getpwd()
'/x'
>>> d['x1'] = 5
>>> d['x2'] = 100
>>> print d.toString("/x")
  {
    # directory /x
    'x1' : 5
    'x2' : 100
  }
```

We first check what the current directory is by using the getpwd() method. Then we change directory to "x" (using a relative path to the current working directory). Then the entries x1 and x2 are created in the directory. Observe that Python's standard method of accessing an entry has been used but is cleverly able to keep the entries in the correct directory (/x) as shown by the toString() method call.

Another method is to use the set_dir() method, in which a full path to the entry (of the form directory/entry) is specified.

```
>>> d.set_dir("/y/y1", "y1 is here")
>>> print d.toString("/y")
  {
    # directory /y
    'y1' : 'y1 is here'
  }
```

This sets an entry y1 in directory /y to the value "y1 is here".

Once entries have been placed in a given directory, the get_dir() method can be used to access the entries. This works as follows:

```
>>> d.get_dir("x/x1")
5
>>> d.get_dir("/x/x1")
5
>>> d.get_dir("/y/x1")
Traceback (most recent call last):
  File "<stdin>", line 1, in ?
  File "/home/apache/cgi-bin/wpl/directory/Directory.py",
      line 770, in get_dir
    return dict[entry]
KeyError: x1
```

Here we demonstrate that an absolute or a relative path to an entry can be used to get an entry from any given directory. As is the case with Python's standard dictionary, an attempt to get a nonexistent entry results in a KeyError exception. The key x1 is listed as the offending key, because the directory /y does not contain this key.

Changing Directory

The cd() method is used to change the current working directory.

```
>>> d.cd("/y")
('/', {PathRef "usr": PathElement "usr" w/1 Entries, PathRef "z":
PathElement "z" w/0 Entries, PathRef "x": PathElement "x" w/2 Entries,
PathRef "y": PathElement "y" w/1 Entries})
```

Upon changing the working directory, a tuple is returned that contains the name of the directory you just left and the content. You'll be able to read more about this in the Directory source code itself. In this example, we just left the root directory.

Pushing/Popping Directories

The pushd() and popd() interfaces come from Unix. They are used to maintain a stack of directories that have been visited recently. This can be useful if the working directory needs to be changed temporarily and returned to upon completion of any changes.

```
>>> d.getpwd()
'/y'
>>> d.pushd("/x")
>>> d.getpwd()
'/x'
>>> d.popd()
('/y', {'y1': 'y1 is here'})
>>> d.getpwd()
```

Here we are in directory /y initially, and then we change directory using pushd("/x"). This results in the directory being set to /x (as shown). After the call to popd(), the directory is changed back to /x. If a popd() call is made without having done a pushd() call earlier, the current working directory is set to the root directory. An exception is not thrown.

Importing

Sometimes when working with a lot of entries, it is desired to be able to create an entire directory structure quickly. This is achieved using the import_list() method:

```
>>> d = Directory()
>>> d.import_list([ ('/','a','5'),
...                 ('/a','a',10),
...                 ('/b','a','15'),
...                 ('/a/c','a','1000') ])
>>>
>>> print d.toString("/")
{
  # directory /
  'a' : '5'
  {
    # directory /b
    'a' : '15'
  }
  {
    # directory /a
    'a' : 10
    {
      # directory /a/c
      'a' : '1000'
    }
  }
}
```

This results in an entire hierarchy of directories and entries being created. The format of each entry in the list being imported is a Python tuple (*directory*, *entry*, *value*).

Scoped Access

The motivating factor for creating this class in the first place was to have a data structure that could be used for creating symbol tables (something compilers typically have to do). In a symbol table, it is often necessary to find a binding that has been made in an outer scope. We've already described the scope concept at the very beginning of the Directory class discussion, and now focus on demonstrating how it can be used.

Based on the example in the preceding section. We will now add a subdirectory to /b, called b_inner:

```
>>> d.create("/b/b_inner")
{}
>>> print d.toString("/")
{
  # directory /
  'a' : '5'
  {
    # directory /b
    'a' : '15'
    {
      # directory /b/b_inner
    }
  }
  {
    # directory /a
    'a' : 10
    {
      # directory /a/c
      'a' : '1000'
    }
  }
}
```

The concept of scoping allows the entries from the enclosing (or parent) directories to be seen when the current working directory is the subdirectory. Let's change the directory to /b/b_inner and see how the scoping concept is put into practice:

```
>>> d.cd("/b/b_inner")
>>> d.scoped_get("a")
'15'
```

This results in the value 15 being fetched from the outer directory /b.

For most uses, the scoped_get() method is all that is required, especially when only the value of the entry is needed. It is also possible to find out where the variable is defined. A special method, scoped_get_list() can be used for this purpose:

```
>>> d.scoped_get_list("a")
{'/b': 15}
```

This method gets a list or dictionary of all places where the entry "a" was found, beginning with the current scope. By default, this method returns a Python dictionary of all places. Here the directory /b is where the entry "a" was found with a value of 15. To see why you might need this, suppose the directory /b/b_inner were to take on a new entry "a" with value "George." Here is the dictionary that would be returned when calling the `scoped_get_list()` method from directory /b/b_inner:

```
{'/b/b_inner': 'George', '/b': 15}
```

This should give you a pretty good idea of how the Directory class works. Clearly, it is not possible to show everything here. For more examples of these and the other methods, please visit the source code for the Directory class and take a look at the many built-in tests. These provide much insight into the many available functions and their potential uses.

Trace

The Trace module is a collection of functions that facilitate interactions with the Python interpreter stack. You may be wondering why you would ever want to interact with the interpreter. As you may recall, Python application errors are always accompanied with a dump of the interpreter stack. This dump is referred to as a traceback, as it is obtained by tracing backward through the stack of instructions that were executed just prior to the crash. The traceback provides a wealth of information for debugging an application. Interacting with the interpreter stack allows you to mine for information if your application suddenly crashes.

Facilities for interacting with the interpreter are most valuable when building Web applications. Unlike with console-based applications, you cannot simply send the results of the traceback to the console and hope that your limited set of users will report the bug. The Web is open to an unimaginable number of users. An unexpected crash, due either to programming errors or to bad or malicious user input, can cause problems of varying degrees, from loss of business to unveiling of holes and vulnerabilities.

One strategy is to use a generic `except` clause with every `try`/`except` block to capture unexpected errors. For example, Figure 12–2 depicts the use of a generic `except` clause in a simple function that executes an SQL statement using a connection to the MySQL database.

```
def get_customer_info ( db, customer_id ):

...
    try:
        ...
        db.execute( """ SELECT * FROM Customer WHERE id = '%s'"""%( customer_id ) )

        result = db.getRecords()

    except DBWarning, detail:
        # handle db warning
    except:
        # handle any other exception
```

Figure 12–2

In this case, the user could provide an offending value for customer_id, causing MySQL to raise a DBError. Our oversight in checking the value of customer_id is protected by the generic except clause. However, there is one problem: In handling the generic except clause, you are responsible for capturing and analyzing the state of the stack. In Web programing, you will almost always want to log the fact that an exception was caught by the generic except clause and then display the traceback. These two pieces of information make debugging your application painless.

Before we discuss how you can use the Trace module functions to obtain and report the traceback, it is important to discuss how the interpreter handles exceptions. When an exception is raised, the interpreter sets three internal parameters: exc_type, exc_value, and exc_traceback. These values can be obtained as a tuple by invoking the system.exc_info() function. The first two values, exc_type and exc_value, refer to the exception raised. An exception will always have a type. Standard exceptions all refer to a subclass, called the Exception class, but this is not a requirement. Python allows you to raise any object as the object of the exception. The value of an exception plays an important role in selecting an appropriate handler.

Exceptions can optionally have a value. The value component is used to provide more detailed information as to the cause of the exception. For example, in Figure 12–2, if a DBWarning exception is raised by the DBFactory class, we can use the information stored in the value field to detect the MySQL error. Finally, the traceback value references a traceback object. This is *not* a string representation of the stack, but an object that encapsulates references to stack frames. Avoid directly using or referencing the traceback. Take special care when assigning the traceback value to a local variable, as this can cause a circular reference to occur in the interpreter.

Once these values are set, the interpreter attempts to find an appropriate handler for the exception. The interpreter searches for handlers that match the type of the exception raised, starting in the current stack. If no handler is found on the stack level, the exception is "bubbled" upward through the stack until the interpreter reaches the end of the stack. If no appropriate handler is found, the interpreter writes a dump of the traceback to the standard error stream and terminates.

If a suitable handler is discovered, Python attempts to execute the handler code and resets the exc_type, exc_value, and exc_traceback values. The exception code is not available outside of the exception handler code. Therefore, you must log the exception type, value, and traceback in the exception handler section of your code.

The traceback module is available as part of the standard Python module library. The functions in traceback are geared mainly toward developing Python debuggers. An example: The **print_tb** (traceback[, limit[, file]]) function commits the traceback to a file object. This is most useful when you want to write the traceback to one of the standard streams or to an open file descriptor. If you want to obtain the traceback as a string, one option is to use the StringIO class to commit the traceback to a file like a string object. Conversely, you can use the traceBack() function available in our Trace module. The traceBack() module provides an efficient option for retrieving the traceback as a string. The function relies only on the sys module for tapping into the interpreter to obtain the information about an exception. Figure 12–3 lists the traceBack() algorithm.

In traceBack(), first we check that an exception was raised by examining the value of the exc_info() function. Then we attempt to create a printable string representation of the traceback. The task of converting a list to a string is common when working with the Python stack, as most of the traceback module functions return values as lists of tuples. Notice that we do not concatenate any string with the plus '+' operator. Each time that you concatenate strings, the interpreter has to create a new string object; a more efficient mechanism is the string.join() function. The traceBack() function returns the traceback string as it would appear in the Python interactive interpreter. The traceBack() function is heavily used in all other components introduced in this book. We suggest that you investigate how the traceBack() function can be used to help debug your Web applications.

```
.def traceBack():

    if sys.exc_info()[0] != None:
        exc_type = string.join( string.split( str(sys.exc_info()[0]), '.' )[1:] )
        return "%s%s: %s\n"%( list_to_string( traceback.format_tb(
sys.exc_info()[2] ) ) , exc_type, sys.exc_info()[1] )

    else:
        return "(no exceptions)"

def list_to_string( l ):
    """Internal function for converting
        a list of string values into a single string. """

    return string.join ( l )
```

Figure 12–3
traceBack() Listing

The standard Python traceback module also allows you to review the stack during normal operation. This is most useful when you need to verify the origin of a certain function call or to log the line number, function name, and filename where a call's source code resides. Unfortunately, the available functions are too terse for everyday use. As with the traceBack() function, we have developed higher-level functions for easy extraction of stack information. Figure 12–4 lists the functions available for extracting stack information.

The get_stack_tuple() function uses the traceback.extract_stack() module to retrieve the raw stack data as a tuple of values. The tuple is organized as four values related to a particular function call: filename, line number, function name, and instruction. The key function of get_stack_tuple() is the safe retrieval of a particular stack step. Each function call is placed onto the stack. You can selectively retrieve a stack step to determine where a call originated or what the predecessor of a particular function call was. You can inadvertently create an exception if you attempt to obtain a step level that exceeds the stack's length. Thus, calling get_stack_tuple() provides a safe way to obtain information for a particular step.

The other functions listed, getFunctionName(), getInstruction(), getLineNumber(), and getSourceFileName(), are wrappers used to extract the appropriate value from the tuple returned by the traceback.extract_stack(). Using these methods eliminates the need to remember the position number of the values in the tuple. Take note of the adjustment made to

```
def getSourceFileName( steps=0 ):
    steps = steps + 3
    return get_stack_tuple( steps )[0]

def getLineNumber( steps=0 ):
    steps = steps + 3
    return get_stack_tuple( steps )[1]

def getInstruction( steps=0 ):
    steps = steps + 3
    return get_stack_tuple( steps )[3]

def getFunctionName( steps=0 ):
    steps = steps + 3
    func_name = get_stack_tuple( steps )[2]

    if func_name == '?':
        func_name = '__main__'

    return func_name

def get_stack_tuple( steps ):
    stack_tuple = traceback.extract_stack()
    if steps > len( stack_tuple ) or steps < 0:
        steps = 0

    steps = -1 * steps
    return stack_tuple[steps]
```

Figure 12–4
Listing of Additional Functions in `wpl.trace.Trace` for Extracting Stack Information

the step value. This is done to compensate for the calls to these functions and any other additional function calls made locally. In each wrapper, we need to compensate for the call to the wrapper itself, the call to `get_stack_trace()`, and finally, the call to `traceback.extract_stack()`. This compensation is made by adding 3 to the requested stack step. This allows the user to specify a stack step level relative to where the call to one of the Trace functions is made.

We use these functions in the Logger module to report additional information about where the log statement was initiated. This provides invaluable information if you unintentionally used the same log statement in several areas. We also use this function to restrict access to specific class methods. Say we want to restrict the `run()` method so that it is invoked only by the `process()` method of the Driver class. By reviewing the result of the `getFunctionName()` function, we can determine whether or not to proceed with the execution of the `run()` method.

Although the Trace functions appear light, they save many lines of repeated code in your main applications.

KeyGen

Random key generation is one of the most common tasks performed in all programming paradigms. One attractive property of random numbers is their lack of pattern. We have a very difficult time remembering (or guessing) the value of randomly generated series of numbers. This point is further supported by the important role that random numbers play in cryptography libraries and applications. Many cryptography schemes rely on a long sequence of unique characters at some point in the generation of keys and ciphers. Guessing the value of a randomly generated key has proven to be a fairly effective yet simple security measure.

Another attractive property of random numbers is their randomness. Perfectly random numbers have a very low probability of being duplicated. We commonly take advantage of this property to uniquely select or group items. For example, think of your everyday transaction tracking number. Many systems use a random number to generate a unique tracking number that can be used to identify a single transaction. The value of random numbers is realized in systems where the number of transactions is in the millions.

Random numbers can also be used to generate random strings. At some point, all character strings are converted to a series of binary encoding. This allows us to use the mapping between numbers and characters to generate random sequences. If we were to take advantage of the full ASCII character set, there would be 254 characters to choose from for each member of the random sequence. However, much of the ASCII table consists of nonprintable and cryptic characters, which makes it difficult for users to type or reference them.

In this text we rely on random sequences in a multitude of settings. The `wpl.logger` module uses random keys to tag and track contexts. Log contexts play an important role when you log messages and events in nonpersistent CGI applications. The CGI life cycle begins with an HTTP request and ends once the request has been fulfilled. The context mechanism in `wpl.logger` enables you to identify uniquely a single CGI life cycle. The logger creates a random sequence at instantiation. Each message that is logged can have this random sequence appended to it, tagging each entry as a member of a randomly named group of entries.

We also use random sequences to manage sessions. In Chapter 13, we introduce a Python-based portal development framework called Slither. One of the key features of Slither is persistent session management. The framework automatically serializes and saves the state of select variables and data structures between user invocations. Each session is assigned a unique, randomly generated session key which is stored on the user's browser as a cookie. The key is also used in the filename of the saved persistent data. Each time that a Web request is made, the framework matches the session key to a session file and restores the serialized data. From the programmer's point of view, programming Slither applications is not much different from programming a persistent client-side program. Select variables retain their values without any additional overhead.

The KeyGen library provides several Python functions for generating random sequences and keys. Before we present these functions, it is important to note that KeyGen functions build random sequences out of the alphanumeric series of characters, which is a small subset of the ASCII character set:

```
good_chars = string.digits + string.lowercase[:26] + string.uppercase[:26]
```

The module variable `good_chars` is a Python list that encompasses three separate lists defined in the string module: numbers, lowercase letters, and uppercase letters (notice that we join the lowercase and uppercase letter lists.) In some Python distributions, the alphabet lists will also contain accented characters suited for authoring strings in languages other than English. We have decided to exclude these characters since they are not part of the standard 101-key keyboard, making it difficult for users to type and reference them.

Figure 12–5 is a listing of the `generate_key()` function. This function generates a string of random characters. It takes two optional parameters: `length` and `char_set`. The `length` option is an integer that describes the total number of random characters in the string sequence. By default, there is a sequence of 10 characters created. The second option, `char_set`, is a string that selects the set of characters used in generating the sequence. In some situations, you will want a sequence of only random numbers or characters. By default, all of the characters included in the `good_chars` list will be used to generate the sequence.

```
1    def generate_key( length=10, char_set='all' ):
2        if char_set == 'digits':
3            char_list = string.digits
4        elif char_set == 'letters':
5            char_list = string.lowercase[:26] + string.uppercase[:26]
6        else:
7            char_list = good_chars
8
9        char_list_limit = len( char_list ) - 1
10
11       key = ''
12       i = 0
13       while i < length:
14           key = string.join( [ key , char_list[ whrandom.randint( 0, char_list_limit ) ] ], '' )
15           i = i + 1
16
17       return key
```

Figure 12–5
Listing of generate_key function

As you might have guessed, sequence generation is done in the while loop (lines 13–15 of Figure 12–5). We take advantage of the string.join() method to iteratively concatenate the next random characters. The next character to be added is determined by generating a random integer and using it to select a single character from the selected list. The standard Python module, whrandom, provides the randint() function, which takes two integer values that specify an upper and lower limit on the resulting integer. We take advantage of this feature by setting the boundaries to fit perfectly the limits of the selected list. As an example, when the string.digits list is used, we set the lower limit to 0, corresponding to the index of the first member of the list, and the upper limit to len(string.digit) - 1, for the index of the last item in the list. We must subtract 1 from the length, as all Python list indexing begins at 0. This process is continued until the desired string length is obtained.

This simple algorithm is sufficient for most tasks. You may want to modify the algorithm slightly to improve readability of the generated sequence. For example, often people will mistake the uppercase letter O with the number 0 and the lowercase letter 'l' with the number '1'. The simplest solution is to avoid the use of all letters and digits that create confusion. Here is an improvement:

```
while i < length:
    rand_char = whrandom.randint( 0, char_list_limit )
    if rand_char not in [ 'l', 'O', '1', '0', 1, 0 ]:
        key = string.join( [ key , rand_char ], '' )
        i = i + 1
```

Randomly generated sequences are perfect for tagging and tracking user sessions. A sequence can be assigned to a session at the point of user authentication and used from that point on to track properties, data, and state parameters associated with the session. Simply using a random sequence sometimes leads to undesired results. For example, in a shopping portal you will want to store every persistent session object created. These objects can provide a wealth of information regarding user habits and the effectiveness of your portal. Depending on the length of the generated sequence, as more sequences are generated, the chance of generating matching sequences increases.

One solution is to further qualify a sequence with a date stamp. The KeyGen library provides the generate_dated_key() function that generates dated sequences of random characters. Figure 12–6 lists the source code for generate_dated_key(). We take advantage of the generate_key() function for generating the actual sequence, which is concatenated with a string containing the current date and/or time. This function clearly demonstrates the value of code reuse.

The generate_dated_key() function takes four optional parameters. Two of the parameters, length and char_set, are passed directly to generate_key() to control the length of the sequence and select the list of characters. The format_string parameter specifies how the date and time stamp should appear. The Python time module provides the strftime() function that uses this format string to generate date and time strings. The Python documentation on the time module lists all of the different format specifiers that can be used in the format_string. By default, the function will use date-only strings that have the format mm-dd-yyyy. The delim parameter is used to set the string used in concatenating the date string with the generated sequence. By default, we use a period, which results in dated sequences like 10-23-2001.s876454kjh.

```
def generate_dated_key( format_string="%m-%d-%Y", length=10,
                        char_set='all', delim="." ):
    return string.join(
           [ time.strftime(format_string, time.localtime(time.time()) ),
             generate_key(length=length, char_set=char_set)
           ], delim )
```

Figure 12–6
Listing of generate_dated_key()

Generated keys also help identify collections based on the date of creation. Using our session management example, dated session keys provide a very simple method of identifying all sessions created on a particular day, or a single session created on a specified date. As with `generate_key()`, you may wish to extend or modify `generate_dated_key()` for more customized control. As an example, you may wish to specify a time stamp as opposed to using the current system date and time. Both `generate_key()` and `generate_dated_key()` provide good starting points for any application-specific changes.

Summary

This chapter covers a number of useful classes that are used later in the book, in particular, to support the Slither application development framework. To some extent, the term "*miscellaneous*" is a misnomer, as there is the connotation that the classes might not be important. The classes presented here are indispensible and are by no means optional or superfluous. We'll be making extensive use of them later in the book, so you might find yourself revisiting this chapter, especially when studying the application source code on your own.

Part 3

APPLICATIONS

The rest of this book is dedicated to actual working applications. We discuss our application development framework, Slither, which is used to develop Web applications in Python. Slither shares some features with the Java Servlets™ framework; however, Slither goes beyond what is provided in Servlets by addressing the complexities of transitioning between business logic states, code generation issues (using the WPL foundation), and managing session information. Our work on Slither demonstrates that it is possible to write elegant and comprehensible applications that are based on CGI, without the sloppiness of the CGI model.

Two representative applications are presented to demonstrate the power of Slither and the numerous technologies presented in the book (Python, Linux, MySQL, and some others). These applications include a text collaboration system (SlyWiki) and a shopping portal (Slither Shopping). The applications are developed entirely using Slither and require no add-on modules within the Apache Web Server. Source code is provided so that the code can be downloaded, minimally configured, and installed within minutes.

13

The Slither Application Development Framework

The Web is becoming increasingly more sophisticated and interactive. In 1995, we were dazzled by sophisticated HTML pages used in a variety of different activities, from selling goods to describing abstract ideas, theories, and scientific findings. It wasn't too long before the masses began craving more interaction, a craving that static HTML pages would never be able to satisfy. To meet the demand, Web developers began adding small server-side CGI applications to their Web sites. CGIs introduced bidirectional exchange of information. Users could now search specific topics, register for products, and personalize sites.

Over time, CGIs came to be used in more creative settings, giving birth to the Web portal. Portals allow Web developers to provide personalized service to each and every Web user. Web portals like MyYahoo! provide an alternative to the local operating system's graphical interface. Users of MyYahoo! can store files, retrieve e-mail, read personalized news and magazines, create small Web sites, and much more. The allure of MyYahoo! is its connection to the Web's most important feature: worldwide availability. All of the files that are stored in MyYahoo! can be retrieved from anywhere on the planet where there is an Internet connection.

The portal concept has even greater implications for the business world. What if whole office applications were made available on the company Web site? This is the future of computing! As personal Internet connections and wireless technology become more prevalent and powerful, companies will invest more in making their applications available from the Web. The Application Service Provider (ASP) concept has taken the Web by storm and is becoming the de facto standard mode of serving business applications to employees. ASPs are complicated business portals that attempt to provide a powerful Web-based solution with the same look and feel of client-side applications. Such applications can be accessed anywhere, never need to be installed or upgraded by the end user, and provide a steady stream of income for service providers.

Whether your interests are in serving personalized dynamic information such as MyYahoo! or building business ASPs, you are fundamentally having to build a portal. We will begin by discussing portals in detail, highlighting the facilities they provide and the role they play in your design of the Web application. Then we will survey various popular portal development platforms in use by industry leaders, and their pros and cons. Finally, we will introduce Slither, a Python-based portal development framework.

Slither is a culmination of concepts and components described in earlier chapters. It attempts to meet all of the requirements of an easy-to-use, light yet powerful portal development platform, without the extra overhead that is prevalent in competing platforms. After reading about and using Slither, you will see how easy it really is to design, implement, and deploy Web portals.

Facilities and Features Common to All Portal Frameworks

We have discussed how Python can be used to build CGI applications. Python CGI applications are not that different from regular Python shell scripts: Both have a main point of execution, use environment variables and command-line parameters, can read from the input stream and write to the standard out and error stream, and take advantage of the full Python module library. So what differentiates a Python CGI script from a Python shell script? Surprisingly, not much. The main difference is in how the scripts work with user-supplied data. When a user fills out a Web form, the data are sent to the CGI script's standard input stream in an encoded format, which is quite different from shell scripts that allow the user to interactively supply data.

Python provides the cgi module, which can be used to parse the encoded format and retrieve the Web form data as a set of parameter/ value bindings. This works quite well for simple CGI scripts that perform relatively simple tasks. For example, you may wish to ask your user's opinion on an issue. You would create a simple survey form that references a Python CGI script that obtains the form data, formats it a particular way, and then sends the results to your e-mail box. You can take the script a step further by having it add the data to a MySQL database.

At this point, you may be thinking, "Wow, it would really be cool if I could make the contents of the survey results available on the Web." So you decide to build yet another simple CGI script (separate from the one that handles the survey form) that opens a connection to the same MySQL database, retrieves and formats the survey entries, and sends the resulting table to the Web.

After a while you decide that you really don't want everyone to see the survey results, and would like to restrict access to only a small set of users. Even this task can easily be accommodated with Apache's access directives. You can direct Apache to request a username and password from users accessing the survey result rendering script.

This should show that the Python `cgi` module goes a long way to allow you to create an interactive and rather sophisticated Web site. It should also demonstrate that, as the requirements of the CGI applications evolve, it becomes increasingly more difficult to accommodate the changes in an efficient and maintainable manner. For example, you may decide to extend the survey to act more like a private discussion forum. Now you will have to create additional scripts that allow you to search through the entries, nest entries, edit entries, etc. Since HTTP is stateless, you find that in each script you are forced to repeat the same steps prior to executing the core business logic for which the script is responsible. The repeated tasks range from opening database connections to validating and authenticating sessions. Furthermore, the repeated tasks are very similar regardless of the CGI script's purpose or functionality.

This leads to the simple definition of a portal development framework: a development platform that factors out repeated tasks and provides centralized access to common facilities. As we saw with the survey example, a portal evolves from two main ingredients: ever-increasing functionality and more personalized user facilities.

A good portal development framework eliminates repetitious code used to authenticate users and manage sessions. The task would be done transparently, allowing the developer to concentrate on the business logic served by the portal. The portal development framework also provides simple access to various external facilities such as connections to databases and LDAP trees. The developer provides the minimum configuration needed to open the connections, and the portal framework ensures that the connection is available for all business logic code. Finally, the portal development framework provides tools for working with HTML. As with client-side applications, the user interacts with the portal via HTML pages. The developer will need tools for easily obtaining data from forms and reporting the results of the business logic. The following sections explore each of these points in greater detail. We will refer to them as we explore currently available portal development platforms, as well as our own platform called Slither.

Factoring Out Repeated Programming Tasks

The success of a portal development framework can be measured by the quantity of repetitious code that has been factored out of the development of the portal business logic.

There are many tasks that are repeated in every portal. We have described session management as one such piece of logic that is required in almost all portals. A session identifies the state of the portal for a single user. For example, in MyYahoo!, your session captures all of the preferences that you have set, which may drastically differ from another user's. Sessions allow the developer to build applications that are stateful on top of a stateless protocol such as HTTP. The client and server have no knowledge of the previous HTTP transaction; the developer must save this information for each user per transaction.

There are two primary strategies for capturing state. First, state information can be stored as hidden input fields within the HTML doc being returned to the browser. On the next transactions, the CGI application would read the hidden input fields to restore the state of the portal. (This strategy does not scale well in larger portals, where the amount of state information saved is in hundreds of variables.)

Alternatively, the server can store the state in a file or a database and use a hashing scheme to associate the saved state with the user. Usually the hashing scheme relies on cookies for storing the hash key on the user's browser. In each HTTP transaction, the browser sends the cookie to the portal application, which then looks up and loads the associated saved state. Since the hash key is all that is required to load the state, the developer may use a combination of the two schemes to store the session key as a hidden input field. This is usually preferred over the use of cookies, since there are no limitations on how the key is sent to the user.[1]

---

1. Cookies are sent to the server based on the domain name and directory values set by the server application in a previous call. Cookies may also have an expiration date, which can lead to problems.

In either case, the developer will need to perform a series of routines before and after each HTTP transaction in order to save state. This makes session management a perfect portal logic to factor out. The portal development framework would provide a default strategy for saving state. The strategy is applied between each transaction. From the developer's point of view, the state of the application is magically saved and restored. This makes developing CGI applications very similar to client-side programming.

Another commonly used portal logic is user authentication, which authenticates a user based on a supplied username, password, or certificate against a matching record stored on the server. The authenticated user is then granted access to selected portal features and operations. In most cases, the authenticated user is granted access to some personal information that the server has retained from a previous session, such as credit card and bank account numbers. Most people associate user authentication with session management; although you almost always use sessions to track authenticated users, they are two distinct tasks.

There are many different strategies available for authenticating users. The UNIX operating system relies on a simple flat file scheme that lists valid usernames and passwords. A more sophisticated system utilizes a relational database for storing user profiles. The user profile may include a username and password that can be used to access the system (for example, a shopping portal would store the username and password of a customer as a database record that is referenced each time that user makes a purchase online). Although using databases works quite nicely for most authentication schemes, it does not scale well in large company intranets. Relational database records are seldom general-purpose, usually difficult to maintain and access, and fairly resource-intensive when used only for user authentication.

In large institutions, a much more scalable solution is the use of directories such as LDAP. Directories are hierarchical databases that organize data in a tree structure. As with a company phone directory, at the top of the directory there may be a listing of headquarters around the world. Under each, there may be a listing of one or more departments. Under each department there may be a listing of various staff members, and so on. Each user profile in the directory can contain a username and password attribute. All software systems, including the company's Web-based intranet, can authenticate the user based on this attribute, eliminating the need to have multiple username and password combinations for each system. Directories are designed mainly for this purpose and are optimized for fast and efficient read access. What's more, directories can be easily replicated and synchronized, providing a highly scalable solution.

Portal applications authenticate users in two separate phases. The first time that the user accesses the portal, a username and password combination typically is requested to authenticate the user against a server-side record (this process is referred to as logging in). The user is then provided with the main portal interface. In a traditional client-side application, the user's authenticated state would be kept in memory. Subsequent actions would be permitted, since we know that the user would not be able to access the private user interface without first logging in. Unfortunately, since HTTP is a stateless protocol, we cannot guarantee that the user cannot access a private interface without first logging in. To help illustrate this, suppose that a portal user first logs in to the system, then visits a private interface. A user who adds the URL of the private interface to a personal bookmark list can later access the same URL without first logging in.

This leads to the second phase of portal authentication: authenticating each request against a valid session. After the user has successfully logged in, we must store in the session a special key or flag that indicates that the user has provided valid credentials. Before performing each subsequent request, we must check that the user has logged in. If the user has not logged in or the session has expired, the portal should not allow the user to access the private interface, and instead should direct the user to the main login page. All authentication information is stored on the server, making it difficult for the user to manipulate URLs or Web forms to gain unauthorized access to the private pages.

A portal development framework should provide facilities for authenticating users against any of the popular strategies. The framework should also factor out the task of authenticating the session for each request and updating session access times.[2]

Accessing Server-Side Facilities

Developers are increasingly using HTML to build interactive Web-based applications. Unlike client-side applications, HTML does not provide sophisticated graphical widgets such as menus, panes, and windows. However, form tags can be used to provide the same look and

---

2. Some systems automatically log users out if a specified amount of time has passed since the user's last request. This precaution makes it difficult for unauthorized users to access the portal from an abandoned browser window or cached HTML pages.

feel. As is the case in all trade-offs, the loss in graphical sophistication is compensated for by ease of development and scalability.

The most important feature of HTML is that it can be used to build interfaces to server-side facilities, allowing users worldwide access to resources. A typical shopping portal uses a database connection to display information on retail items. When a customer makes a purchase, the portal must charge the customer's account using a credit card charging system. Once a successful charge has been made, the portal will have to access a packaging and shipping interface for scheduling the delivery of the purchased items. As you can see, the portal serves an interface to these server-side facilities. The same paradigm can be applied to an intranet portal that company employees use as an interface to access e-mail, accounting information, etc. The portal development framework should provide access to any number of server-side facilities.

One of the most important server-side facilities is the database. Almost all relational databases provide a persistent database managing server. The developer would use a client API to access the database manager from anywhere on the network. The client API allows the developer to connect to the server (typically with a username and password) and execute SQL queries. In a CGI application, this connection must be made each time that you plan to access the database.

The implication of this is that the same DB connection code must be repeated in each CGI application. This clearly does not scale. Imagine if the access information (username or password) were to be changed. Now you would have to hunt down each instance of the connection code and make sure it is using the updated values. As another example, you may wish to change the database system you are using from MySQL to PostgreSQL. Once again, you will need to locate all DB connection code and make repeated revisions. These are just two popular examples, and there are many that arise as your portal becomes more sophisticated. A simple solution would be to wrap the connection call in a parameterless function that you access each time that you need to use the database. Now you have a central location for making updates, but this strategy will not easily scale in portals where multiple connections are needed to a variety of databases, or if you plan to update the function's interface.

The most elegant and scalable solution relies on a centralized scheme for initializing access to the facility and a transparent scheme for making the access globally available to all portal business logic code. The portal framework views server-side facilities as resources. Each resource is accessed via a handle. Much as with a file handle, the developer will need to initialize the resource handle. In the case of the database, the developer will need to create the database connection. This task is performed in a single block of code prior to executing any business logic.

Once the resource has been initialized, the requested business logic is executed. The business logic code can take advantage of the previously initialized resources by accessing the globally available resource handle. The business logic code is blind to any resource initialization changes. Another important aspect of this design is that the business logic code can rely on the availability of a proper connection, since initialization is performed prior to the business logic code execution. All initialization errors can be handled globally, removing the need to check for errors each time you access the resource. This design also allows you to add any number of additional resources without having to change previously used interfaces: You simply initialize the resource and it is available to all existing and future business logic.

There are several different implementations of this design. Later in this chapter, we present a variety of portal development frameworks and review how they access server-side facilities. All portal business logic use server-side resources in some way, making access to these facilities a critical component of the portal development framework.

Structured Processing of Business Logic

One of the core functionalities of a portal development framework is to map Web requests encoded in URLs to the execution of business logic. As you saw in Chapters 5 and 7, servicing HTTP requests requires parsing input data, performing a specified business logic, and returning a well-formed response. Although these steps appear to be simple, they can actually become quite complex as your portal expands in size and functionality.

To illustrate the issues at hand, we will explore all of the steps involved in handling a single HTTP request. Let's imagine that we are building a Web-based activity logger. One of the operations of the logger is searching for a particular record based on one of several criteria. The user fills out the Web form with a specific search criteria and presses Submit. The browser encodes the form data in the POST format (See Chapter 5 for more information on POST) and makes an HTTP call to the server. The server takes the information and invokes a specified CGI application.

The application must now parse the encoded form data from the standard input stream. Luckily Python provides the `cgi` module, which extracts the parameter/value pairs from the standard input stream and stores them as a dictionary-like object called `FieldStorage`. Although this is an improvement on manually parsing the encoding, it is still a rather complicated and difficult means for working with form input. For example, the following depicts how you would use `FieldStorage` objects to work with a simple text form field:

```
if fs.has_key('data'):data=fs['data'].value
```

You must check that the field exists before attempting to work with it. As you may recall, all fields that are left empty in the form are *not* included in the data set passed to the script. So if the user left this field blank, the `CGI` application would have no knowledge of such a field even existing. If the form fields were stored as true Python dictionaries (or a class that implemented all of the `UserDict` methods), we could have simply performed the following operation:

```
data = form_vars.get( 'data', None)
```

This eliminates the need to check fields before using them. In Chapter 10, we introduced the WebForm class, which provides a more comprehensive and elegant solution to this problem.

Next, the search application must use the input fields to perform the search. In complex searches, this may require loading and invoking other objects, methods, and functions. The branching can become so complex that it may actually be easier to map URLs to specific search scripts as opposed to a single search application. This design results in code repetition, which greatly limits scalability and makes maintenance a difficult task. A more elegant and scalable solution is to create a general-purpose application that uses additional URL-encoded data to invoke a particular method or function. This allows each function to take advantage of universally available routines, as well as performing a customized task.

Once the search has been completed, the results must be formatted and returned to the browser. HTTP dictates that the results must be formatted as shown in Figure 13–1.

The response is usually written directly to the standard output stream. The problem arises when there are multiple functions that write out results. Since we must emit the content type declaration only once,

```
Content-type: <<specific MIME type describing returned data; usually
text/html>>
<<blank line>>
<<data being sent to the browser>>
```

Figure 13–1
HTTP results

how do we coordinate printing? What happens when the routine selected to print the `Content-type` declaration is not always the first routine that prints results? A Boolean flag may be used to track if the `Content-type` has been emitted. This works well in small CGI applications that are relatively simple, but still has problems. For example, each time you want to print to the standard output stream, you will need to check the flag to make sure there is no need to emit the `Content-type`.

Another solution is to put all of the output stream in designated functions that are dedicated to formatting parameters into final results that are printed. This, too, has its shortcomings. For instance, what if part of the data has been written and an error is encountered? You now invoke the error routine, which now emits data to the browser without having any knowledge of where the data will appear.

The more scalable and reliable solution is to use a specific object for storing all data to be sent back to the user's browser. In Chapter 10, we discussed how WebForm performs this task. Basically, the developer writes to the Emitter object all data that needs to be sent to the browser. The most fantastic thing about WebForm and other similar portal facilities is the object-oriented view of the resulting document. You can use templates to describe the general appearance of the resulting document and include special tags that are replaced with dynamic data before being sent to the browser. Since there is only one route to the standard output stream, we can easily guarantee that the `Content-type` will only be emitted once.

In addition, this design makes emitting additional server response header parameters very easy. For example, you may wish to set cookies in your applications. Once again, you must make sure the cookie declarations are emitted before the `Content-type`. Having a centralized and object-oriented view of the resulting document makes this task trivial. We simply schedule any number of cookies to be set and let the document object worry about the formatting of the result.

The portal development platform plays a critical role as the foundation of your Web portal. As we have shown, it handles parsing and mapping requests to individual objects, methods, and functions; provides a much-improved, more efficient, and fail-safe facility for working with form data; and provides facilities for coordinating the proper formatting of results. Together, these features allow the developer to concentrate on the design and implementation of the portal's business logic. The portal development framework gives a predictable structure to how each request is handled. More sophisticated portal development platforms provide a skeleton-like structure that lists all of the basic features and functionality of a basic portal, with clearly identified sections for adding new business logic.

Working with Dynamic Content

All Web applications must at some point return a result to the user. In general, all formatted output is printed to the standard output stream. As discussed in the previous section, coordinating the proper format of the resulting document is not a trivial task. Even more cumbersome is formatting results in a specific order or position in the resulting document. Since HTML is line-oriented, the format and location of content is determined by the specific format tag and the order in which that tag appears relative to the rest of the document.

In larger portal applications, each aspect of the interface may be managed by a complex and completely separate business logic routine. Traditionally, the developer is responsible for making sure that all resulting values are printed in the appropriate order so that the resulting document follows a specific layout. Not only is this a very difficult task, but it makes the design of the portal more rigid, less scalable, and very difficult to maintain. The fundamental problem is that the design of business logic code is now dictated by HTML formatting rules.

The same problem arises when developing client-side applications. Over time, developers have subscribed to the model-view-controller design pattern to break the tie between the business logic and the view of the results. This same pattern can be applied to portals. The portal development platform provides facilities for working with HTML in an object- oriented way.

The implementation of this design varies from one portal framework to another. In general though, the strategy is to use a partially constructed HTML file as a template. Within the HTML document, you include special tags that are replaced with data when the portal is executed. Some portal platforms even allow you to include business logic code right in the HTML template file. Although this is convenient, it takes the problem to the opposite extreme, making it very difficult to change the general look and feel of the results. Ideally, the developer binds data to the special tags and lets the portal development framework handle proper formatting and display of the page.

More sophisticated portal development platforms provide additional tools for dealing with common tasks such as printing the contents of a list or a list of dictionaries. For example, the result of all DB queries is usually a list of records. You typically need to print the results in an HTML table. The portal facilities would allow you to specify how a single row of the table would appear, and then use this as a subtemplate for printing the result list. In Chapter 9, we presented the WriteProcessor utility that can be used to perform such tasks.

Currently Available Frameworks

There are many portal development platforms to choose from. Each has a set of advantages and disadvantages. In this section we will discuss the design of several popular platforms, and attempt to identify how the framework addresses each of the general Web portal criteria listed in the previous section.

PHP

PHP is a server-side scripting language geared toward developing dynamic server pages. The PHP process is fairly simple. You first create all of your HTML pages as they would appear. This includes forms and sample form results. Then, the HTML file is updated to include the PHP directives. PHP directives are HTML-like tags that have the following syntax:

```
<?php [php code] ?>
```

The [php code] block is replaced with PHP code. PHP's syntax can be described as a cross between basic shell directives and Perl. PHP is remarkably powerful, as it provides support for basic data types as well as objects. You also have access to the common operators and control flow structures. PHP also allows you to organize code into functions. There are a number of powerful functions included in the standard library. These functions are the real reason for PHP's popularity. The functions cover a wide range of logic from accessing DB connections to connecting to CVS repositories and parsing XML documents. The standard function library, combined with embedded HTML code, provides a very fast means for developing Web portals.

PHP does provide a number of functions to manage sessions. You can add any number of data to the session register. This data structure is serialized and maintained between HTTP requests. You can also take advantage of cookie-handling functions to propagate the session ID out to the user. Since this is not a default task, it adds overhead to the development of your portal. You will have to create a number of PHP functions that are invoked at the start of your form-processing logic to authenticate a session based on the cookies sent by the user or the session ID found in the form or the URL.

PHP's rapid development philosophy does have its disadvantages. The biggest disadvantage is the connection between PHP scripts and HTML pages. The business logic code used to process a form is typically disjointed from the code that renders the form. Also, since HTML code can be embedded within the PHP source, it becomes difficult to update the appearance of the entire site without disrupting the business logic. This paradigm breaks with the classical model-view-controller design pattern, and is hence plagued with difficulties in maintaining the code and expanding it to perform additional tasks.

PHP does not provide a structured foundation for handling requests. All of the requests are directed to a PHP script that can take advantage of code written in other PHP scripts. This makes planning and organizing a large Web portal development project difficult. Furthermore, scalability and code reuse become larger issues as the PHP-based site grows in complexity.

Since PHP is a scripting language, it is yet another language that you will need to learn in order to develop a portal. Although this is not a big issue, it does prevent you from reusing any Python source code that you developed for other projects. You are also missing out on the cornucopia of Python modules that have been contributed by developers from around the world. There are far more Python libraries than there are PHP functions. Both Python and PHP provide a means to extend the language to access C-based algorithms and routines.

In short, Python provides all of the features of PHP, plus a lot more. In the last section of this chapter, we introduce Slither, a Python-based portal development framework. Slither allows you to take advantage of Python's power to develop complex Web portals that are scalable, maintainable, and efficient.

Active Server Pages (ASP)

Active Server Pages (ASP) is a Microsoft-based, server-side scripting language intended for building dynamic Web pages. ASP, like PHP, allows you to embed HTML within your application. Your ASP directives are set off by special tags, as shown by the following:

```
<% [ASP code] %>
```

Unlike PHP, ASP allows the developer to select a primary scripting language for developing the portal. Some of the possible choices are VisualBasic, Perl, and Python. This is a very powerful concept: It allows you to write code in the scripting language that you are most comfortable with while taking advantage of the ASP portal development platform.

ASP-based sites follow a similar design philosophy to PHP-based sites. Each form or dynamic content link is associated with one ASP source file. The ASP files are processed by the Microsoft Internet Information Server (IIS) upon request; the results are sent to the user. There is very weak coupling between the code that renders the forms and the code that processes them. This makes it difficult to reuse ASP code or to extend and scale a portal to meet more complex demands. To overcome this shortcoming, most developers build a set of core objects in other languages such as VisualBasic and C++, and access them from their ASP pages. This technique is also used to access and utilize many server-side facilities such as DB connections.

The power of ASP lies in the object model. There are six objects provided by the ASP framework for developing a portal:

1. Application
2. ObjectContext
3. Request
4. Response
5. Server
6. Session

Without going into too much detail, it is helpful to understand the resources provided by each of these objects. The Application object contains a global view of the entire ASP site. All of the ASP pages associated with a particular installation share an Application object. The ObjectContext object is used to interact with the Microsoft Transaction Server. The Request and Response objects are used to obtain form data and render pages, respectively. Both objects provide a set of methods to facilitate operations. The Server object provides access to the IIS server constants and routines. You can use this in your portal to manipulate how the IIS server behaves. Finally, the Session object contains ASP data associated with a user session. This object persists on the server and is available upon each HTTP request. Since ASP runs under IIS, all of the application's objects persist between invocations. As a result, ASP applications have a fast response time.

If poorly designed, ASP applications are difficult to scale and maintain. Combining HTML with code makes the business logic more rigid and less apt to change. Another consequence is difficulty in updating the appearance of the site. In order to update the look and feel of your site, you will have to update all of the HTML fragments, which may break ASP code. Most large portal projects use ASP to serve server-side objects. Microsoft provides many server-side components and additions that allow companies to build e-commerce sites with almost no effort. As with anything, there is a cost. The Microsoft solution is usually expensive and not very customizable.

Another problem with ASP is portability. Currently, the full ASP API is supported only by the IIS server running on MS Windows. There are Linux-based libraries, such as ChillieSoft, that allow you to run very simple ASP pages using the Apache Web Server, but functionality is limited by the fact that most of the external facilities are not available.

The ASP model is well suited for developers who intend to use off-the-shelf components to build generic Web portals. The best use of ASP is in building an e-commerce site that follows the basic shopping cart paradigm. The solution will be expensive and hard to efficiently scale and maintain, but will require very little development time. Since you are reading this book, it is logical to assume that you have decided to stay away from the Microsoft solution. We encourage you to read on to discover how Slither can be used to build portals that are much more flexible and maintainable. The best aspect of using Slither is the cost: It's free.

ColdFusion

ColdFusion is a server-side scripting language for building portals. Much like PHP and ASP, ColdFusion advocates embedding HTML within the source document. ColdFusion directives are set off by Cold-

Fusion Markup Language (CFML) tags, which are a derivative of XML. The following is a sample CFML directive:

```
<CFQUERY NAME="MyAddress" DATASOURCE="MyAddressBook">
SELECT * FROM AddressTable
</CFQUERY>
```

These directives are stored in .cfm files on the server. The files are accessed from the Web via a URL that points to the ColdFusion server housing the file. Upon receiving the request, the ColdFusion server reads the .cfm file, processes the directives, and returns to the user a dynamically generated HTML page. All of the CFML tags are processed by the server and, as a result, are never visible to the user.

ColdFusion started out as a Web-to-database gateway. A Web developer could write relatively complex applications using very simple directives that access and work with existing database connections. In the example above, the CFML directives execute an SQL query against a database identified by MyAddressBook. The important feature here is that no database connection or initialization is ever performed. The DATASOURCE attribute refers to a Microsoft Windows Data Source Name (DSN), which in turn refers to a database profile. The DSN is all that is needed to access a particular database.

ColdFusion applications are typically organized like ASP and PHP applications. A .cfm file may contain code that prints a form that is processed by another .cfm file, which contains the partial HTML used to create the form result. When a .cfm file is processed as a result of a form submission, all of the parameters of the form are bound to the application as local variables. This is a convenient feature, as it allows the developer easy access to form data, but it also creates a dependency between the form and the business logic that processes the form content. As with ASP and PHP, this model can become difficult to manage and maintain as the portal increases in size and functionality.

Over time, ColdFusion was upgraded to include additional features such as session management and hooks to more server-side resources. The session management framework provides the developer with a persistent namespace where data can be saved between invocations. ColdFusion manages loading the namespace using either a cookie or a URL-based strategy of mapping users to session data. There is no standard facility for authenticating users. Developers seeking to build sites with complex access control must provide all of the logic needed to authenticate the user. Although this logic is not entirely throw-away, there are several complications in sharing code between ColdFusion projects. As a result, the developer must either abstract authentication out of the project or build very generic authentication modules that can be easily used between portals.

Access to server-side resources depends on ColdFusion support for the particular resource. The framework provides several hooks and functions for accessing many popular server-side resources, such as the local file system and LDAP trees. Less popular resources typically require special handling. Although this is typically not a big issue, it limits the freedom that the developer has when building a complex portal.

ColdFusion provides several key features required to build a Web portal. Unfortunately, much like ASP and PHP, ColdFusion applications may become difficult to maintain and scale as the portal becomes ever more complex. Changing the look and feel of the site may pose a problem, since the business logic is tightly coupled with the rendering and view logic (HTML). ColdFusion also requires that the developer learn yet another markup language just for building Web applications. Learning a new language is always a good skill, if the language provides unique features and enhanced semantics that are not available elsewhere. Based on our survey, ColdFusion does not provide any features that are radically different from those available in competing frameworks.

Java Servlets and JSP

Java has become a very popular language for developing server-side applications and components. The language provides a robust set of packages for developing a range of applications, from servers to client-side graphical user interfaces. As a result, many developers continue to build a strong set of server-side components. The JavaServlet and JSP framework together provide Java developers an avenue for building Web applications that can seamlessly take advantage of both Java and Java-based components.

JavaServlets are like persistent CGI applications. All servlets are accessed via a servlet runner. There are both commercial and freely available servlet runners. One of the most popular commercial servlet runner is WebSphere by IBM. WebSphere is a servlet runner at its core, but provides access to many robust, commercial resources such as facilities for working with XML documents and access to powerful databases such as DB2 and Oracle. Some of the more popular free and open-source servlet runners are Sun's ServletRunner, mod_jserv for Apache, and Tomcat/Jakarta by the Apache group.

As with all Java applications, your servlet will need to be compiled and loaded into JVM by the servlet runner. Unlike PHP, ASP, and ColdFusion, the servlet is typically loaded once when the servlet runner boots or the first time it is accessed. The servlet runner maps the request URI to a servlet zone, which is conceptually a single project. The developer must extend a servlet class and override one or more of the base methods in order to process the data obtained from the Web request. The two methods that are almost always overloaded are:

1. `doPost()`
2. `doGet()`

As you might have guessed, they map to the two most frequently used HTTP methods. When a POST request is obtained, the servlet runner will invoke the `doPost()` method of the referenced servlet. At this point, the servlet processes the request. The servlet can now communicate with the user via two key objects: Request and Response. These objects are initialized by the servlet runner and are passed in to the `doGet()` or `doPost()` methods.

The Request object provides an interface to all of the data sent to the servlet runner by the browser. This includes request headers, form data, cookies, and any other data available from the HTTP or HTTPS request. Each form field and form data is available through a series of method calls on the Request object. For example, to get the value of an input text field called "first_name", you would perform the following operation:

```
String first_name = request.getParamter( "first_name" )
```

The Response object provides a buffered interface to the servlet runner's standard output stream. Since Response object implements Java's buffered writer interface, the user simply calls the `write()` method and passes in the content to be sent to the browser. The Response object can also be passed around the servlet so that any component of the application can communicate with the user.

The servlet framework also provides access to a relatively powerful session management system. As in other frameworks, the session management system allows the developer to select from a URL or a cookie-based scheme of tracking users. The session can be used to store data in between invocations. However, the servlet management system is truly user-aware. A user must first join a session. This typically happens when a user first accesses the servlet. Once joined, the session can have an optional expiration date and time. After this time has expired, the user's session data is no longer considered valid.

Along with session management, servlets also provide an authentication and access control framework. The security API allows the developer to create a series of roles that the user can belong to. Changing the access rights of a role will affect all users who subscribe to the role profile. Another benefit of the security framework is that it allows the developer to customize both the default authentication and access control.

Servlets also support request filtering and dispatching. Filtering allows the developer to write reusable modules that sit between the Web request and the servlet. The filter can then be used to condition the data before it is processed by the servlet. This allows the developer to perform a series of preprocessing operations before any code executes. Dispatching enables a servlet to load another servlet. This feature is critical for building maintainable and scalable applications, as it allows the developer to connect and reuse various pieces of business logic to process requests.

Unlike ASP, PHP, and ColdFusion, servlets are not embedded in HTML files. So how do servlets work with dynamic content? There are many Java packages for processing HTML forms. As an example, the WriteProcessor framework introduced in Chapter 9 has been ported to Java and can be used to render dynamic content. Another option is the use of JavaServerPages (JSP). The JSP model allows the developer to mix Java and HTML in a single file, which is processed and then rendered to the screen.

Java servlets meet and exceed all of the key requirements of a portal development framework that we identified in earlier sections. This makes servlets one of the best and most powerful Web portal development frameworks. We have ported many of the same features to Slither. The main benefit of Slither is the use of Python for developing business logic. This is especially important if you are developing a portal independent of any server-side components that may have been authored in Java.

Zope

Zope began as two separate projects aiming to solve problems in dynamic content management. Zope views a Web site as a collection of objects. These objects are published to an object database and accessed by the user via the Web. Content managers and Web administrators can create any number of these objects using graphical user interfaces. The greatest feature is that the actual HTML pages are typically not edited to include new content, and they serve as templates for creating the general look and feel of the Web site. Zope's dynamic content management is best suited for time-critical information sites such as `chicagotribune.com` and `cnn.com`.

Zope consists of two distinct components: the Z Object Database (ZODB) and the Z server. These are connected via the Zope core. The Z Server is a persistent, stand-alone object, Web, and FTP server. The most important function of the Z server is mapping Web URLs to published objects. Users can then access these objects with their browsers. The ZODB is used to store and maintain Zope objects. The Zope core loads and stores objects in the ZODB between Web requests. The combination of the Z Server and ZODB results in a fast, powerful, object-oriented Web development platform.

Zope is built entirely on top of C and Python. As a result, Zope can be used to create, publish, and maintain any Python-based object. Objects can be as simple as content wrappers or as complicated as contained business logic rules used to create a Web portal. Zope objects inherit basic functionality from the ZClass. The Zope core acts as an Object Resource Broker (ORB) by storing the objects in the ZODB and making them available based on URL requests from the Z Server. The ZClass adds an object into an object hierarchy, which is mapped to the application namespace. This allows the developer to access any object using the Zope Acquisition framework. When you attempt to access a particular object, Acquisition will search the object hierarchy for a matching object. This is a powerful feature, as it allows the developer to organize business logic based on functionality. Any number of these objects can be accessed when processing a single request.

Although Zope was designed mainly for dynamic content management, it can be extended to develop powerful Web applications. The Zope core supports the concept of Zope Products. Zope Products basically extend the Zope core to perform customized operations. You can create any number of objects that contain Web portal business logic. These objects are published and accessed via the Z server, ZODB, and the Zope core, but the portal's functionality and logic dispatching are performed by the Zope Product.

The Zope request life cycle is similar to that of Java servlets. Requests are mapped to REQUEST and RESPONSE objects which maintain all of the data communicated between Zope and the browser. For example, when processing a Web form, the ZServer will parse the request, load the appropriate object, and invoke the requested method. The method is typically passed two parameters: REQUEST and RESPONSE. The developer can access form data through the REQUEST object. Conversely, all results are written to the RESPONSE object. The RESPONSE object can also be used to set cookies and any other server-response parameters.

Since Zope is a persistent framework, it can easily support session management. There are a number of session management objects that can be used to manage user data between HTTP requests. Unlike Java, Zope does not provide the developer with a session object. When developing a Web portal, the developer can easily support user-to-session mapping by first using a cookie or URL-based strategy to uniquely identify users. Once identified, a dictionary can be created to maintain the user's data. This dictionary can be made to persist during the life of the Zope server. A more robust strategy would require that the user data be pickled from time to time so that sessions can be recovered after restarting Zope.

Zope does provide a rather complex access control framework. This was created to help the content manager restrict access to certain content. Over time, the access control mechanism has been extended so that it can be used to restrict access to any Zope object.

The Zope core provides access to many server-side resources. Most importantly, Zope supports RDBMS integration, which allows the developer to access Oracle, Sybase, MySQL, and many other database servers. Since Zope is Python-based, most server-side resources and components can be accessed via third-party modules or C/C++ extensions. Zope developers have also taken the extra step of distributing general Zope components that can be used to interoperate with resources.

Zope also provides a powerful framework for rendering dynamic content to the browser. The Dynamic Text Markup Language (DTML) is very much like JSP. It allows the developer to create HTML-based templates that contain XML-based tags that reference Zope objects. The template provides the basic look and feel of the portal, while the DTML tags allow the developer to render the value of an object attribute or a function call. Similar to the WriteProcessor, there are various control flow tags that allow for conditional texts and loops over Python data structures. Another advantage of DTML is interoperability with Web-based Distributed Authoring and Versioning (WEB DAV), which allows all of the DTML files to be safely accessed by Web designers to perform a face-lift on the portal.

Overall, Zope provides a powerful platform for developing Web applications. However, since Zope was originally targeted toward dynamic content management using GUIs, some of the internals of Zope are not easy to understand and typically require a large learning curve on the part of the developer. Zope does a lot to hide the complicated process of serving and maintaining objects in a database. As a result, the user typically experiences unexpected side effects that may require some effort in tracking down and resolving. Zope is also not as developer-friendly as Java servlets; most of the effort has been put into object resource management and access. The developer can certainly take advantage of the available resources and API, but at the cost of attaining an intimate and in-depth understanding of how Zope works.

The framework introduced in the next section, Slither, supports several Zope features such as hierarchical object organization and support for loading and accessing additional objects when processing a request. Slither was designed strictly for developing Web portals, and is considerably easier to use to develop Web applications.

Slither: A Python-Based Portal Development Platform

As you saw in the previous section, there are already several well-developed and fully functional portal development platforms to choose from. So why bother to create another? Portals typically grow without any warning or limitation. As the number of users increases, more functionality will be demanded. Your portal will need to scale with these demands smoothly, in the absence of a major rewrite.

Each portal development framework is like a tool in the toolbox: You must pick the appropriate tool for the task at hand. Slither is designed to be the perfect tool for developing portals authored in Python with emphasis on developing complex business logic routines.

In the first section of this chapter, we listed several major features common to all portals. Slither was designed to support all of the basic tasks expected of a portal development platform. As you will see shortly, many commonly performed routines have been factored out of the developer's day-to-day task. There is support for general session management and basic flat file and database authentication. Slither also provides a plug-in interface that can be used to initialize and access server-side resources such as database connections. Slither also provides an exception-handling interface that allows the developer to bind customized error handlers to specific exceptions.

Slither uses extra path information from the request URL to locate and load business logic code. This feature has two very important and powerful side effects. First, it forces the developer to organize business logic code in a maintainable file directory structure. Second, all business logic code exists under some directory, allowing the developer to perform global operations, such as restricting access to a group of business logic code, based on the directory that the user is attempting to access. Slither is built on top of WebForm and therefore provides the same elegant solutions to working with form data and formatting results.

As you review the design of Slither in this chapter and begin writing your own Slither portals in the next chapter, you will see that this is a light yet powerful platform that caters to the Web developer. It is very much a developer-centric framework as opposed to competing platforms, which are more accurately categorized as Web-centric frameworks.

Bird's-Eye View of Slither

The best way to learn a new programming framework is to discuss at a high level the various components and how they work in handling requests. In following sections, we will visit each component of the framework and discuss its design in much greater detail. We concentrate on Slither internals in this chapter. Please skip to Chapter 14 for a discussion on how you program with Slither.

Figure 13–2 depicts all of the main Slither components and how they relate to one another. Slither is organized into two major components: the Driver and one or more projects. The Driver is responsible for dispatching requests to the appropriate project. Each project must first be registered in the Driver project registration table. The Driver consults this table during each request to locate a matching project module and class. The Driver then proceeds to load the project module and hands off further execution to the project. All results bound for the browser are returned to the Driver after the project has completed executing. The results are then printed to the standard output stream, resources are freed up, and the Driver terminates. All errors that result from project execution are eventually caught and logged by the Driver. This ensures that important project errors are not lost or made available to the Web user.

Each project is further broken down into two main components: the Project and one or more State classes. The Project class is a base

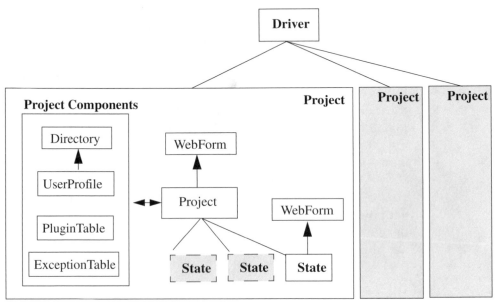

Figure 13–2
Overview of Slither Component Organization

class used to create a portal. The role of the Project class is to map the extra path information in the URL to a specific State class and dispatch execution to that State. Project extends WebForm and therefore inherits all of the power and functionality of the WebForm class. Project also supports several methods that are invoked either prior to or after a State has been dispatched. Developers can use these methods to override commonly performed routines, such as authentication and session management, or to initialize server resources and bind error handlers.

In addition, there are two methods, preprocess and postprocess, that are invoked just prior to execution of a State and right before terminating the Project, respectively. These methods provide the developer with a designated location for performing global checks, such as authenticating requests, and actions before any State code has executed.

The Project class contains a run() method that is invoked by the Driver. This method drives the execution of the project's business logic. First, all of the preprocess Project methods are invoked. Next, the specified State code is executed. Based on the result of the State code, one of several actions is taken, including loading and executing another State code. Eventually the method terminates by invoking all of the post-processing methods and returning the resulting page to the Driver. The code execution of State classes is governed by the actions performed in the `run()` method.

Project relies on several modules for managing user sessions, project resources, and State exceptions. The UserProfile module provides classes that store session variables. Since UserProfile extends the Directory class, it provides a hierarchical namespace for storing variables. The PluginTable module is used to load and bind resources; once a resource has been bound, it is transparently available to all State objects. Finally, the ExceptionTable module provides a set of classes for binding specific exception handlers to Python exceptions. This is a powerful utility that allows the developer not only to take full advantage of Python exceptions, but also to recover from them in a flexible and elegant manner.

The State class is a base class for the portal business logic code. It extends WebForm and therefore provides all of the same facilities. However, the WebForm instance of State is initialized from that of the Project class. This ensures that all form fields and cookies propagate down to the State class. There are three methods that the user can override: `init()`, `render()`, and `process()`. The `init()` method is invoked after the class has been instantiated. As you will see later, this ensures that the State class has access to all variables and resources at initialization. The `render()` and `process()` methods can be invoked from the URL and are used either to render a page or process the results of a form from a rendered page. This aspect of the State class is quite complex and will be discussed in more detail in the following section.

The State class has access to several Project data members, most important of which are UserProfile and `page_vars`. The portal business logic code can store and retrieve any Python data type in UserProfile. The stored values will persist between requests, giving the developer the feel of programming a stateful application. The `page_vars` data member is a dictionary that contains dynamic variable bindings referenced in the main project template. The developer can use this data member to manipulate the dynamic content presented to the user. Although `page_vars` is simple in structure, it can be quite powerful for formatting results. We will explore the use of `page_vars` in Chapter 14.

Now we will discuss how the components work in handling requests. We will also provide a brief summary of each component's design and implementation. All Slither components are light and simple in design, but don't let this fool you: They are quite powerful. Their simplicity only makes them more tempting. We highly recommend that you look over the implementation of each component to have an understanding of how Slither works and how it can be used or extended to fit any portal development project.

Design Philosophy

In this section we will present how Slither handles requests. We begin by tracing the sequence of steps taken by Slither to handle a single Web request: the request life cycle.

Driver • The Driver uses the request URL to locate and dispatch projects. Figure 13–3 lists a sample Slither URL. There are three key components:

- Reference to the install directory of Slither and the `Driver.py` script
- First component of the extra path: `MyProject`
- Remaining extra path components: `aDir/aState.render`

All Slither URLs must reference the installed Driver code because dispatching begins here. The Driver will parse the extra path component into two subcomponents: project name and state path. The project name is the first extra path component. In Figure 13–3 this is `MyProject`. The remaining extra path information is stored but ignored by the Driver.

Once the URL has been parsed, the Driver attempts to locate and load an appropriate project. All projects must be registered with the Driver by being added to the registration table. The registration table is a simple Python dictionary that binds a project URL name to a project profile dictionary. Figure 13–4 is a sample registration table stored in a file called `MyConfModule.py`.[3] The most important item in this file is the declaration of a dictionary called `project`. You *must* name the

---

```
http://www.mydomain.com/cgi-bin/slither/Driver.py/MyProject/aDir/aState.render
```

Figure 13–3
Sample Slither URL

---

3. This file can have any name. The only requirement is that you set the `CONFIG_MODULE` constant in the `DriverConf.py` file.

```
TestProject = {
    'webroot':'/usr/local/apache/cgi-bin/slither_projects/TestProject',
    'project_module':'MyProjectModule',
    'project_class':'MyProjectClass',
}

projects = {
    'MyProject' : TestProject,
}
```

Figure 13–4
Sample Project Registration Table

dictionary as it appears here, since Driver will attempt to import this dictionary from the module. The `project` dictionary is used as the project registration table. Notice that `project` maps the key `MyProject` to a project profile dictionary named `TestProject`. To access `TestProject`, you would specify `MyProject` as the first component in the extra path. This design allows you to rename project files and directories without ever having to change previously defined links.[4]

The project profile dictionary contains a set of parameters used to locate the project source code, the main project module, and the project class name. In Figure 13–4 the `webroot` binding describes the physical location of the project source code. The `project_module` and `project_class` bindings are used to identify the module that contains the class which extends the Project class. The `project_class` binding is optional, and when omitted the Driver will look for a class that has the same name as the specified `project_module`. These bindings are the minimum required to register a project.

If an appropriate project is not found, the Driver will display an error page similar to the famous Apache 404 error page. This error page can be edited to display any desired message, which is especially useful when the code is released for production use. The less information that is given to the user, the more secure your system will generally be.

---

4. Throughout Slither we use actual Python source code for all configuration parameters. This allows us to create elaborate configuration routines without the hassle of having to parse and evaluate the results. For example, the Driver registration table is a dictionary of dictionaries. We could have created our own proprietary configuration language, but it would be limited at best and would bloat the code. The disadvantage of using Python source for configuration is portability. It would be difficult to port Slither to another language such as Java, because there isn't a one-to-one correspondence between data types and data structures. This is a cost that we are willing to pay, since we don't plan to port this application in the near future.

Once a matching project profile is found, the Driver will attempt to load the project by invoking the internal __load_project() method. Loading begins with changing the current working directory to the specified project webroot. This is done for two reasons: First, we validate that the specific directory exists; second, it avoids having to develop a complex Python path managing scheme to ensure that all modules are properly specified in the path. By changing the current working directory, the project module and class can be loaded without any changes to the path.

Next, we import the module and attempt to instantiate the specified project class. We then check that the instantiated class extends the Project class. Finally, we call the project's init() method. This is used to initialize the project by passing down all of the project profile bindings and any arguments specified after the extra path component of the URL in an ISINDEX-type encoding (see Chapter 5 for more details).

The __load_project method returns a tuple containing a dictionary and a string message. The dictionary contains a reference to the instantiated project class. If there were complications in loading and instantiating the project, the first value of the tuple is set to None and the string message is updated to reflect the errors encountered. If the project was successfully loaded, the Driver will dispatch the project class by invoking the run() method.

The Driver logs all activities to a log file. You can choose to turn off the debugging messages in order to save disk space and make the logs more legible. The Driver also attempts to handle all errors gracefully. For example, the Driver invokes the project's run method within a try catch block to ensure that all exceptions are caught and handled appropriately. This feature also makes debugging applications in Slither very easy. The Driver will even provide suggestions in resolving common errors.

Project • The Project class is a base class for defining a portal. Figure 13–5 lists the skeletal structure of Project. The methods are organized into three groups:

1. Public interface methods that are overridden to customize functionality
2. Utility methods used to work with extra path components and State classes
3. Internal methods used to consolidate frequently accessed logic

```
class Project( WebForm ):

    #----------------- Project initialization method ---------------

    def init_project( self, ** options ):

    #----------------- Public Interface Methods ---------------

    def init( self ):

    def render( self ):

    def preprocess( self ):

    def postprocess( self ):

    def load_plugins( self ):

    def load_exceptions( self ):

    def session( self, operation, user_profile=None ):

    #-------------------- Utility Methods -------------------

    def add_var( self, var, value ):

    def add_vars( self, env ):

    def setTemplate( self, template_file_name ):

    def load_state_module( self, load_path ):

    def parse_state_path( self, state_path ):

    #-------------------- Main Process Method --------------------

    def run( self, emitter ):

    #-------------------- Internal methods --------------------

    def __cookie_strategy( self, operation, user_profile=None ):

    def __load_state( self, state_profile ):
```

Figure 13–5
Skeleton of the Project Class

Each method plays an important role in the execution of the project. Rather than presenting each method sequentially, we will defer detailed explanations of each method until they are referenced in the project's main processing loop.

The main processing loop of Project is defined by the `run()` method. Once Project has been initialized, the Driver invokes the `run()` method and awaits the method's termination. The `run()` method contains three separate phases: preprocessing, state execution, and postprocessing. The preprocessing and postprocessing phases are performed exactly once. The state processing phase is inside a loop and may be performed several times.

Here are all of the activities that are performed at each phase of the `run()` method's execution.

- Preprocessing
  - bind Emitter object supplied by Driver to the base WebForm class
  - invoke `session()`
  - invoke `load_exceptions()`
  - invoke `load_plugins()`
  - invoke `preprocess()`
  - invoke `parse_state()` and identify the state to be loaded
- State Execution
  - load the specified State class
  - change current working directory to that of the loaded State class
  - invoke either `render()` or `process()` State method
  - handle any state errors and evaluate results
- Postprocessing
  - change the current working directory to the project directory
  - invoke `postprocess()`
  - invoke `session()`
  - return to the Driver

The first action in the preprocessing phase is binding the Emitter object supplied by the Driver to the base WebForm class. In Chapter 10 we discussed how WebForm uses an Emitter object to manage output bound for the browser. Next, we invoke the `session()` method with the string parameter `"load"` in order to restore the session state. By default, the Project `session()` method invokes an internal method called `__cookie_strategy()`. This method will locate a session cookie and attempt to load a previously pickled[5] UserProfile object associated with the session. If the object is not found, a new UserProfile object is created and returned.

The developer may choose to override the `session()` method to implement a different session management strategy. The `session()` method is invoked with an action parameter and an optional UserProfile object reference. The action parameter is set either to `load` or `save`. When the action is set to `load`, the value of the UserProfile object reference is expected to be `None`. In the case of `save`, the value of the UserProfile reference is set to the current UserProfile state object. This is an out-of-the-box routine for session management that can easily be customized to suit any special programming needs.

Next, the `load_plugin()` and `load_exceptions()` methods are invoked. By default, these methods do not perform any operations. They simply provide a designated location for initializing and binding resources and exception handlers. Both features require that the developer use the PluginTable and ExceptionTable API, respectively. These methods are not really required; they only exist to help the developer organize and consolidate code. As a side effect, the developer can make certain resource initialization decisions based on the URL request. For example, you can include conditional statements that load a DB connection only when a certain State or group of States is to be loaded.

At the end of the preprocess phase, we invoke the `preprocess()` method. By default, no actions are taken in this method. The developer may overload this method to perform general tasks that apply to the entire portal. As an example, you may decide to restrict access to a group of States that are under the `Admin` directory. The developer can easily implement this feature by adding conditional logic in the `preprocess()` method to validate access. The following is a pseudo-code of the logic required:

```
if state_path contains /Admin:

    if user not logged in:
        direct user to the login page
    else:
        grant access
else:
    don't do anything
```

---

5. *Pickling* is Python's terminology for object serialization. Basically, it is a means for saving an object to a file so that it can be restored at some later time. This works perfectly with Web applications, since it provides a convenient means of saving state between HTTP requests. See the Python documentation on the `cPickle` and `pickle` libraries for more details.

The preprocess() method provides a powerful design strategy for performing global tasks. Combining this with the directory structure of States, the developer can make very specific or general policies.

The last action performed in the preprocess phase is parsing out the State call path from the remainder of the extra path information. As you may recall, everything after the first path component of the extra path data is considered part of the State call path. The State call path is a relative path to a specific State module. The call path is further broken down to a path, State name, and one of two method names: render() or process(). The parse_state() method performs this task and stores the results in a dictionary that will serve as the state profile (similar to the project profile dictionary used by the Driver). The parse_state() method is used throughout the code to extract various components from the extra path.

The state execution phase is marked by the start and end of a while loop. At a high level, the loop performs three basic tasks:

1. Loads a State module.
2. Dispatches the State logic by invoking one of two methods: render() or process().
3. Evaluates the results of the State execution and performs further processing if necessary.

The task of loading a State module is very similar to the logic used by the Driver when loading a Project module. First, the State path and module name are extracted. Next, an attempt is made to instantiate the State module. Finally, the instantiated State module is initialized with various Project data members, the most important of which are the plug-in resources, WebForm data members, and the UserProfile object. The specifics of the State module initialization and bindings are discussed in the following section.

After successfully loading the State module, we change the current working directory to that of the module's and invoke either the render() or the process() method. Changing the current working directory avoids having to modify the Python path to include the State module path, and allows the State module to load file resources relative to its path. The method invoked is determined in the extra path information by the string that is concatenated with the State name using a period. For example, the following URL results in the render method being called:

```
http://www.somedomain.com/cgi-bin/slither/Driver.py/MyProject/aDir/State.render
```

If the method name is omitted, we default to loading the render() method. This is a sound assumption, since the render method of a State module is expected to generate an HTML page to display to the user. This is the safest policy for handling poorly referenced method names, short of displaying an error page.

After the appropriate method is invoked, we proceed to process the results. There are several different outcomes based on the method invoked and the results returned by the method. Figure 13–6 displays all of the different outcomes that may result. At first, this seems like a very complicated system. Upon closer examination, you will discover that the logic is designed to accommodate two different form-processing strategies: free-form and pipelined. Free-form processing occurs when a particular form is first rendered and then processed. This is the most common design strategy in portal development, and why the State class has both a render() and a process() method.

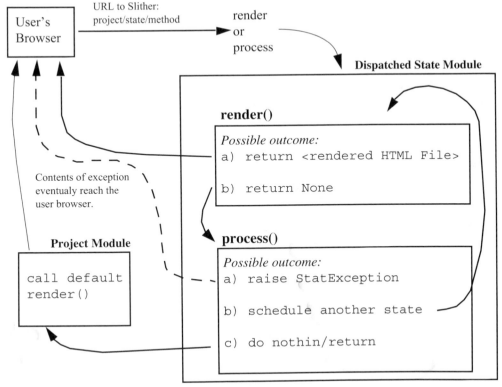

Figure 13–6
All Possible Paths for a State Transition

In Figure 13–7 we see that in the first step of free-form processing, the render() method of a State is called, and the return value is obtained. Since the user must first fill out the newly rendered form, we terminate the loop processing, perform the postprocessing phase, and return the page to the user. Once the user selects the Submit button, we load the same State again, but this time invoke the process method.[6] When the process method completes, there are two possible outcomes: Another State has been scheduled and further processing is needed, or there is nothing else to do. In the former case, we proceed to the top of the execution loop and begin dispatching the scheduled State. In the latter case, we invoke the Project's render() method and generate a default HTML page that is sent to the user.

You may be wondering why we don't send the output of the process() method to the user. Doing so would break the design strategy of separating form rendering from form processing. We always display a default page when all processing has been done and no HTML has been generated. This is in tune with how most portals are designed. As an example, think of the common shopping portal. There

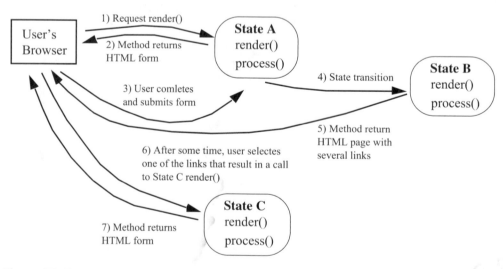

Figure 13–7
Free-form State Transition

---

6. The state name is determined by the value of the form's ACTION field. When the page was rendered, we set the ACTION attribute to reference the same State URL, except that this URL references the process() method, as opposed to the render() method.

are a number of actions that you can perform, but at the end of each you typically are returned to the storefront. In this situation, the storefront is the default page rendered. This pattern is prominent in nearly all portals because, logically, there needs to be at least one point of entry into the portal.

The state execution logic also supports a pipeline execution strategy. As the name implies, pipeline processing is linear and typically results in several selected stages running in sequential order. The best examples of Web-based pipeline processing strategy are order forms, whereby you must go through several HTML forms to obtain a product or service. Each form is one step of a larger process. There does not need to be a one-to-one correspondence between HTML forms and steps. Typically there are several steps that do not result in any HTML and are used only to execute some additional business logic code.

Figure 13–8 illustrates the steps involved in a sample pipelined strategy with a single pure business logic stage between two forms. First, we invoke the render() method of a State. This results in the generation of an HTML page. You can consider this step number one of our two-step pipelined order form. After the user completes the form and presses the Submit button, we execute the process() method of the State. Since this is a pipeline, we already know which State needs to be

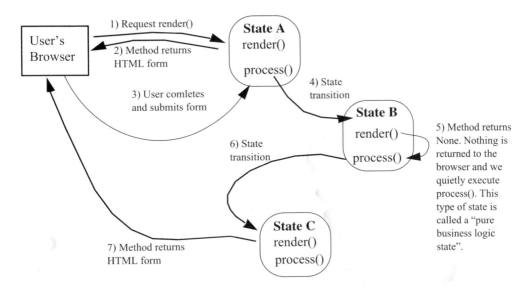

Figure 13–8
Pipelined State Transition

executed next, and just before the `process()` method completes, the next State is scheduled for execution.

In our example, the next State is a pure business logic state. There are no HTML pages generated and rendered in this State. Instead, we perform additional processing on the data obtained in the previous State. The user is not aware that this State exists or that it is being executed before the next HTML page is rendered. All pure business logic States return `None` in their `render()` method. Since no HTML page is returned, the Project `run()` method continues processing and invokes the State's `process()` method. This programming pattern gives us the desired result of having a pure business logic State. Once again, before `process()` terminates, we schedule the next State in the pipeline, which in our example obtains more information from the user by rendering another HTML form. Any number of pure business logic States can be executed sequentially using the same pattern.

There are several variations on the pipelined strategy that provide you more control over how your portal processes information and interacts with the user. One variation is a semi-pure business logic State. A semi-pure business logic State contains logic in the `render()` method that controls whether the State renders an HTML page or not. For example, in a shopping portal you typically force the user to log in before completing a transaction. However, once the user has logged in, you do not wish to depict the login page. The State that handles this process can include logic in the `render()` method that verifies if the user has already logged in, and if so, no login page is rendered nor processed; we simply skip to the next State.

You can also use this pattern to conditionally load States based on the user's prior selections. In complicated order forms, the ability to conditionally display States allows the developer an avenue for translating the decision tree into a sequence of steps.

Another variation to the pipelined state is scripted pipelines. A scripted pipeline uses a master script file to determine the next State in the pipeline. In this paradigm, the scheduling logic uses a central script file[7] to look up and schedule the next State to be loaded, as opposed to directly loading a named State. This pattern allows the developer to cre-

---

7. In most cases, the script file is a Python source file containing a list or a dictionary structure that defines the sequence of States to be executed.

ate a number of State objects that can be rearranged and reused in creating a variety of pipelines. As an example, you may decide to do business in China and would like to retarget your order form to obtain orders in Chinese. Beside translating the HTML, there may be a number of changes in business logic based on how commerce is performed in China. You may be able to reuse most of the original order form States, but may be forced to create several new variations. Using the scripted pipeline pattern, you can create a new pipeline using previously created States along with new States targeted at Chinese commerce.

After the state execution phase, the `run()` method executes the third and last phase, postprocessing. The activities performed in postprocessing mirror those performed in the preprocessing phase. First, we change the current working directory back to the Project's directory so that all remaining code has access to the appropriate files. Next, the Project's `postprocesss()` method is invoked. Similar to the `preprocess()` method, you can override `postprocess()` to perform a series of checks or tasks before returning results to the user. By default, `postprocess()` does not perform any actions.

Finally, we invoke the Project's `session()` method with the operation parameter set to `save` and the `user_profile` parameter set to reference the UserProfile object associated with the user's session. By default, `session()` will pickle and save the UserProfile object to disk so that it can be restored and used later. To track the user's session, the `session()` method will by default set a cookie that contains the user's session ID. As you may recall from our discussion of the preprocess phase, the `session()` method will use this cookie to load the user's session in later transactions.

The Project `run()` method terminates by setting up the WebForm environment so that an HTML page can be rendered. During the state execution phase, the method variable `state_output` is used to store the rendered HTML page. This method is added to WebForm's environment dictionary by invoking the `add_var()` method. (You may recall that Project extends WebForm. WebForm is discussed in greater detail in Chapter 10.) When the `run()` method terminates, the Driver will invoke the Project's `encode()` method that is inherited from WebForm. The `encode()` method will process the selected HTML template and return a rendered HTML page. To view the results of your stage, simply include a reference to the `state_output` variable in your template. You can place this anywhere. Here is an example of a minimalist template that renders the State output in a table cell:

```
<html>
<body>
<table border="1">
<tr><td>
<<state_output>>
</td></tr>
</table>
</body>
</html>
```

Your project can utilize a number of templates. You can use the `setTemplate()` method to change the template file at any time. You will usually want to include conditional code in the Project's `postprocess()` method to select and set the appropriate template. Project also sets a group of debugging variables that you can reference in your template. The `base_project_url` variable contains the entire URL required to access the Project's default `render()` method. You can use this to build more complicated URLs that access a specific State. For example, you may wish to provide a link that is displayed on all pages which, when invoked, will allow the user to fill out a survey form that is e-mailed to you. This can be a link to a stand-alone State and can be formed using `base_project_url` as shown by the following:

```
<a href="<<base_project_url>>/survey.render" >Click here to fill out survey</a>
```

The rendered link will look similar to the following:

```
<a href="http://somedomain.com/cgi-bin/slither/Driver.py/MyProject/
survey.render">Click here to fill out the survery</a>
```

Beside `base_project_url`, you may also access the value of the `log_cache` variable. This contains all of the log entries written to disk for the last transaction. Viewing this data in the HTML template cuts down on the number of terminals that you use during development to view the log file, and eliminates the need to select and identify all of the log entries written during the last HTTP transaction.

The Project class is the most complicated class by far in the Slither framework. This is because it contains all of the logic required to load and execute States. However, relative to competing frameworks, the

Project class is quite simple. It is lean yet powerful. Also, since part of the project code exists as an extension of the Project class, you are free to take advantage of the Project and WebForm API to extend the Project class in any way that best suits your programming project.

State • As we have seen, the business logic for a Slither project is contained in a class that extends the State class. The State class forms the foundation for your project's business logic. After creating the Project class, you will need to create one or more classes that extend State. As described in the previous section, the Project class uses the extra path information from the request URL to dispatch (load and execute) a specific State class.

The State classes for a project live under the project's directory. For example, the project `MyTestProject` may live on your server's file system in `/home/user/slither_projects/MyTestProject`. All of `MyTestProject's` State classes would need to be saved in `/home/user/slither_projects/MyTestProject` or in a subdirectory of this path. Since State classes cannot be saved outside of this path, the project path is referred to as the base path. The State call path is always given relative to the base path. For example, the call path for a State class that lives in `/home/user/slither_projects/MyTestProject/aDir/aStateClass.py` would simply be `/aDir/aStateClass.py`. The State call path is used in the Slither URL to reference a specific State class to load. It is also used to schedule a State transition, as described later.

Understanding the structure of the State class is central to programming with Slither. The State class extends WebForm much like the Project class. As a result, the State class provides all of the interfaces and member variables available in WebForm. In Chapter 10, we discussed how WebForm plays a key role as a foundation for CGI applications. It provides facilities for working with form variables, cookies, and HTML templates. As you may recall, the Project class also extends WebForm. Since the Project class dispatches State classes, the State's WebForm class is initialized by the Project class to reference the same core data structures. As a result, the business logic code in your State class has the same view of the CGI environment as the Project class. You can use the WebForm API in your State class to set cookies and mime types transparently.

The Project class provides, via WebForm, an HTML template to use to render the results generated. The HTML template file in the State class is unique to your State class and is used to render the results generated by the State class. This architecture allows you to use the

Project's template file to set the general look and feel of your portal and the State's template file to generate and render dynamic information such as tables, lists, etc.

You can use the `set_encode_file_name()` method to change the State's template file. The template file can reference any State variable that is added to the template parser using the `add_var( variable_name, variable )` method. WebForm uses the WriteProcess for dynamic content generation. As a result, you can refer to your variables in the template file by using the `<<>>` notation. You can also take advantage of looping rules and other WriteProcessor features. For more information on this, refer to Chapter 9.

Beside the initialization of the parent WebForm class, the State class also inherits several data structures from Project. The four main data structures that are critical to programming with Slither are `argv`, `user_profile`, `page_vars`, and `project_profile`. These data structures are bound to the State class as member variables and can be accessed using the `self` identifier. `Argv` is simply a list of parameters that were passed to Slither in an `ISINDEX` query.[8] The `user_profile` data structure is an instance of the UserProfile class. This class maintains the state information for a particular session, and is described in more detail below.

The `page_vars` data structure is a Python dictionary that will be used by the Project class to render the final page. This is a deceivingly simple data structure. It is used heavily in controlling the entire view of the portal. For example, your portal may have one or menu pads. The rendering of the menu is consistent between HTTP requests, but the menu pad is not in an HTML frame. You can bind a variable in `page_vars` that contains the rendered menu. The rendering can be done by another state or by a stand-alone function that you have created. Then you can reference the variable in the main template (the Project's template) in order to render the menu in a designated location. You can also use `page_vars` to manipulate exiting bindings, such as headers and footers. In general, `page_vars` is an abstract view of your canvas. We will show how `page_vars` can be used in Chapter 14.

The `project_profile` data structure is also a simple Python dictionary that is used to store various Project attributes and values. As you will see in Chapter 14, each project is configured through variables

---

8. For more information on these types of queries, please review Chapter 5.

defined in a file called `ProjectConf.py`. These bindings range from project path information and basic operation options to user-defined values and complex Python data structures and objects. These values are passed down to each state via `project_profile`. This provides the developer a channel to pass down configuration information to a particular state.

Thus far, we have concentrated on the details of how the Project class instantiates a State class and discussed some of the facilities and data structures that connect the State class to the Project class. We will now explore the State class' interface.

There are three methods that you must override once you have subclassed State: `init()`, `render()`, and `process()`. The `init()` method is invoked *after* the State class is instantiated. It is absolutely critical that you do not create the traditional `__init__()` class constructor. If you do, make sure to avoid any Slither-specific calls. The `__init__()` method of a class is invoked during class instantiation. As a result, many of the data members and facilities provided by the State class have not yet been initialized and made available. Instead, you should override the `init()` method and treat this as the class constructor. This method is invoked after the State class has been successfully instantiated and all Slither resources have been properly initialized.

The `render()` and `process()` methods are the only two methods that the Project class will invoke. The State call path portion of the URL is used to select one of these methods. For example, the following URL will result in the invocation of the `process()` method:

`http://www.somedomain.com/cgi-bin/slither/Driver.py/MyProject/aDir/aStateClass.process`

By default, the `render()` method is invoked. Once again, it is very important to recognize that Slither will only invoke the `render()` or the `process()` methods of a State class. You cannot call any other methods via the URL.

You may be wondering why there are two different methods, or why Slither restricts access to any other custom-named method. The `render()` and `process()` methods trace their origins to the two common steps that must be performed to process a single HTTP form. In the first step, the form must be displayed for the user to complete. The `render()` method is intended to be used for this purpose. All strategies begin with the invocation of the `render()` method. If the `render()` method returns a value, the Project class ends execution and renders this value to the screen. Otherwise, the Project class will move forward and attempt to invoke the process() method. The render() method is central to identifying the form-rendering step as a critical part of form processing, and its presence as one of only two methods invoked by Slither makes it easy to trace the portals execution and forces the developer to organize logically the portal code.

The process() method is traditionally invoked after calling render(). The form rendered as a result of calling render() usually references the same State's process() method. The process() method is used to contain the business logic needed to process the form. There are three possible outcomes:

1. Another State class may be scheduled. In this case, the render() method of the scheduled State is invoked and we begin processing the new State.
2. A StateException may be raised. The value of the exception, if one exists, is delivered to the user. Otherwise, we invoke the Project's render() method.
3. The method exits normally. Since there is nothing else to do, the Project's render() method is invoked to display the default page. The process() method fulfills the second and last step of processing an HTML form.

We could have easily allowed the developer to invoke any method defined in the State class, and in some platforms, such as Zope, this is the preferred strategy. The Slither model is a lot simpler; there are only two possible methods that can be called from the outside. Furthermore, their names help guide the order in which they are called. Since the Slither model is based on the steps required to process a form, it is much easier for the developer to design and implement a large portal site that is very easy to maintain and expand. The State is the smallest unit of business logic; there is no need to add methods to existing classes in order to process additional forms. You simply create a new State class that handles the tasks of the new form. You can just as easily create classes that perform a common business logic routine used by other States. After writing your first Slither application, you will see exactly how easy it is to develop portals in this paradigm.

You may be wondering how the State class got its name. The State class derives its name from its similarities to states in a finite-state machine. Each State class contains business logic that, when executed, determines the state of the project. Much like a finite-state system, the business logic in one State class can perform a state transition to another State class. State transitions are accomplished through scheduling. The State class provides the following methods for scheduling a state transition:

```
def scheduleState( call_path )
def getNextCallPath()
def anotherStateScheduled()
```

The `scheduleState( call_path )` method takes a state call path as a parameter. Once the State completes execution, control is returned to the Project class. If another State has been scheduled, the Project class will use the state call path to dispatch the scheduled State. The `getNextCallPath()` method is used primarily by the Project class to obtain the scheduled call path. It can also be called within your State's business logic to determine if an appropriate State has been scheduled. The `anotherStateScheduled()` method returns a 1 or a 0 to indicate whether a State has been scheduled.

The State class is the second most important class in Slither. It links your business logic to the Project, and it is the smallest unit of work. To master Slither, you must first master the State class and the role it plays in developing a portal. In Chapter 14, you will have the opportunity to experiment with the State class as you write your first Slither portal.

UserProfile • The UserPorfile object is used to maintain state variables between HTTP calls. As discussed earlier, the Project session logic provides a default cookie-based session management scheme that is responsible for loading and saving UserProfile objects to disk. This ensures that all data placed in UserProfile will remain there for the life of the session. From the developer's point of view, the UserProfile object provides a very simple and powerful scheme for storing important Python variables that are available to all State code until it is removed. This gives the developer the illusion of developing in an environment similar to client-side applications, where state is maintained at all times.

UserProfile inherits from the `wpl.directory.Directory` all of the functionality and features of a hierarchical data structure. In Chapter 12, we discussed how the `Directory` API can be used to create a virtual directory, change to the directory, and store a value. We take advantage of the hierarchical properties of `Directory` to allow the UserProfile object to provide a scoped namespace for storing state information.

The namespace hierarchy of UserProfile mimics the directory structure used to organize the State code. As an example, your project may contain two subdirectories, `Admin` and `Shop`. Under each of these, there may be any number of State objects or even other subdirectories. When you attempt to access `<project doc root>/Admin/SomeState.render`, the Project dispatch logic would transparently change to the `/Admin/SomeState` virtual directory in UserProfile prior to loading and dispatching the `SomeState` state. In `SomeState`, the developer continues to save state information without any concern or regard for the current working UserProfile virtual directory. This results in a transparent strategy for avoiding variable name clashes between States, which becomes more of an issue as the portal increases in complexity.

Another benevolent side effect of using a hierarchical namespace is ease of maintenance. The developer may decide to reset all state information for the `/Admin/Search` State. This can easily be accomplished by deleting all data under the `/Admin/Search` virtual directory in the UserProfile object. If we did not have a hierarchical namespace, we would have to locate and individually remove State data that is set by the `/Admin/Search` State.

Beside inherited `Directory` features, the UserProfile object also provides a few additional interfaces for dealing with session management. At instantiation, the UserProfile object will generate a dated random session key, called a session ID. This can be retrieved or overriden when performing session management operations.

PluginTable and ExceptionTable • The PluginTable and Exception-Table objects are used within the Project object to manage server-side resources and error-handler bindings, respectively. All of the server-side resources that you want available in the State code needs to be registered with the PluginTable object. First, the resource is initialized. Next, the reference to the initialized resource is added to PluginTable. Finally, the system will automatically bind all of the resource references to the State object that is dispatched. The developer simply uses the resource in the State code as if it were initialized as a local data member. For example, you may wish to use a DB connection when processing a particular form. You would override the Project's `load_plugin()` method and include code that initializes the DB connection and add the connection object to the PluginTable under the resource name "db". You would then proceed to access the DB connection in the State code by working with "`self.db`". From the development point of view, the resource initialization is centralized and automatically bound to any State that is dispatched.

Unlike the PluginTable, the ExceptionTable is used only by the Project `run()` method to look up an error-handler reference when an exception is raised in the code. This concept is modeled after signal handling in C. You can create an ExceptionHandler object and register it to a particular exception. When that exception is raised, the Project's `run()` method will load the handler and invoke the `handleException()` method. This provides a powerful scheme for catching particular exceptions and handling them in a specific manner. As an example, imagine that during processing of a State code an unexpected exception was raised in the DB module. The exception would bubble up and result in the loading of a bound exception handler. The developer can now recover by attempting to track all of the changes that did not take place which could have put the DB or the entire operation in an inconsistent state.

You may be wondering why these objects exist when we could have simply used a Python dictionary to do the job. The simple answer is scalability. Both of these objects hide the underlying implementation. The developer works with these objects via their interface. If in the future we extend the capabilities of either object, existing code will not have to be changed.

Another benefit of this design decision is the ability to perform more sophisticated operations on an otherwise simple data structure. For example, in the ExceptionHandler table, we include the logic necessary to reliably compare a bound exception name with one that was reported from the system. Typically, when a general exception is raised, Python will refer to the general exception with the fully qualified name, such as `slither_exceptions.GeneralException`. The developer should not have to create multiple handler bindings for all possible combinations that the exception name may be reported as. Instead, we use the exception's common name to bind a handler, and we use a smart conversion routine that will extract this name from the system information to look up the appropriate handler.

Over time, these objects will be upgraded to perform even more sophisticated tasks. In the case of the PluginTable, it is not too far-fetched to extend the object so that certain resource connections are kept persistent between calls.

Summary

The Internet has become a complicated world of highly sophisticated applications and services. Many of the popular Web sites take advantage of the latest tools to create elaborate and highly personalized Web portals. Portals allow developers to target services to a select number of users. Many popular shopping sites use portals to store user account information on the Web, making the shopping experience more convenient. Other sites like mp3.com and travelocity.com use portals to track user preferences and target sales.

In this chapter, we reviewed the core qualities of a Web portal as well as a number of popular portal development platforms. In the review of portal development platforms, we concentrated on the programming strategy employed and the main advantages and disadvantages.

In the second half of the chapter, we introduced the internals of a new portal development platform called Slither. We were able to describe the inner workings of the entire platform in just a few pages. Slither was developed for two important reasons. First, the platform serves all of the best qualities prevalent in competing frameworks, with minimal shortcomings. Second, we wanted to prove that much of the hype surrounding competing frameworks is just that–hype. Over time, marketing slogans and campaigns have transformed the relatively simple concept of portal development into a complex activity. Look past the hype and you will see that a framework as simple as Slither gives you all that you need to develop a sophisticated portal.

14

Slither Applications

In the preceding chapter we introduced Slither, a Python-based CGI portal development framework. We focused on Slither's component organization and execution philosophy. In this chapter, we will explore the basics of writing Slither portals and Web applications.

The information in this chapter is presented in the form of a hands-on tutorial. We use a variety of portal projects as case studies and walk you through all of the steps involved in developing a Web portal. Each case study has been specially selected to depict a different feature or programming technique unique to Slither. Since portals are more than a collection of scripts, we will also present all of the preplanning required before each of the case studies is implemented. Each case study covers three areas: requirements and use cases, design, and implementation details. We hope that this will help illustrate the most important aspect of any development project: preparation and planning. You should attempt to follow similar (but more strict) software engineering guidelines when you are ready to build your own Slither portal.

We recommend that you follow each case study and attempt to reproduce the same results. You will be surprised to discover that each of the applications presented here took only one day to design and implement. This chapter should not be used as a user manual to Slither, and as such, we assume that you have already installed the Slither and wpl libraries on your system. Please refer to the documentation supplied with the latest distribution for details on installing and developing with Slither.

Your First Application: the NumberGame

Traditionally, all tutorials begin by presenting the famous "Hello World!" application. "Hello World!" has become a symbol of the simplest application for presenting the core of a programming language or framework. Slither's "Hello World" application is the NumberGame. The NumberGame has a basic set of requirements and can be written in less than 20 minutes. As a result, it is perfectly suited for presenting all of the steps involved in writing your first Slither application. We will also take this opportunity to present the various configuration files that you must edit before running the NumberGame for the first time. These edits must be performed for all future Slither applications.

Requirements and Use Cases

The NumberGame is a simple Web application that allows the user an unlimited number of guesses for finding the value of a secret integer. The game begins by presenting to the user an introductory paragraph followed by a simple set of instructions to follow when playing the game.

The objective of the game is very simple. The application randomly selects a number that the user must guess. The number is an integer that is within a configurable range. The user is given an unlimited number of chances to guess the correct number. The user also has the ability to restart the game at any time. Restarting results in new random numbers being selected.

The application must keep track of the number of unsuccessful guesses that the user has made. Furthermore, to help the user reach the target number, the application should provide clues after each guess to guide the user. For example, if the secret number is 55 and the user selects 35, then the application should indicate that the secret number is of a higher value.

Design

Based on the requirements and use cases presented, we can now lay out the design of the NumberGame. The game will be composed of several Slither components. You may wish to refer to Chapter 13 for a clear definition of each component and how it is used in Slither.

Figure 14–1 provides a basic Slither state diagram of how the NumberGame works. The game begins when the user accesses the NumberGame project component, which we refer to as the Main Game Info state. Based on the requirements, the default page that the user is taken to is the

Info page. We will want to code this state as a Slither Project. As you may recall, Slither Project provides a `render()` method, which is loaded by default when there are errors or when no specific State object is referenced. We want to override this method so that it prints the Number-Game's info page, as well as a link to start the game.

When the user has selected to start a new game, the Main Game Info page will select a new random number and then perform a state transition to the Guess Number state. The Guess Number state performs two functions:

1. It depicts a form for the user to submit a guess.
2. It checks the user's guess against the secret number and tracks the number of unsuccessful guesses. Each time that the user makes an incorrect guess, the Guess Number form is depicted, along with some clues.

We will want to make GuessNumber a Slither State component. We will want to overload the `render()` method to depict the Guess-Number form along with any error messages. The `process()` method will be overloaded to check the guess against the secret number and either depict an error message or perform a state transition to the Congratulations state.

The Congratulations state is very simple. It depicts a congratulations notice to indicate that the user has guessed the appropriate number. Optionally, we can display the count of bad guesses. There are no

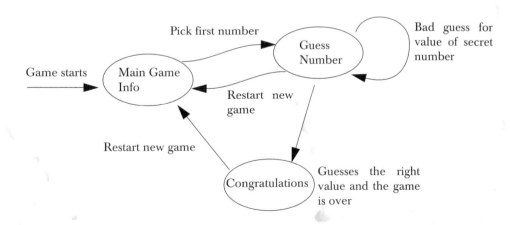

Figure 14–1
NumberGame State Design

forms depicted and, as a result, the state does not process any information. The rendered page will provide a link to the Main Game Info
state. We have two choices when coding the Congratulations state.
Since the State `process()` method cannot explicitly render an HTML
page, we will have to create a new State object and overload the `ren-`
`der()` method. The rendered page will include a link to the Main
Game Info state so that the user can play the game again.

We could have coded the NumberGame with only two states. This
would require that the Congratulations State be eliminated and instead
we raise a `StateException` in the `process()` method of the Guess
Number State. The content of the `StateException` raised could
include the congratulations message. Although functional, this design
goes against the Slither philosophy. The `StateException` is reserved
for instances when the State has experienced a processing error and will
want to display an error message. In most instances, the error message
will be the form rendered by the `render()` method with some additional error messages. In the NumberGame, when the user has guessed
the correct number, we did not encounter an error. Instead, we experienced a state transition. The user is no longer in the guessing state and
has now reached the end of the game.

It is critical that you follow these subtle design rules when working
with Slither. Although such operations are permitted, they can create
problems in the future. The design that we have come up with will
allow us to expand the game easily in the future to include more functionality.

Before we begin implementing this design, we need to discuss our
strategy for storing the secret number, restarting the game, and tracking
the user's progress. As you may recall, Slither provides by default a
cookie-based session management system. We can take advantage of
the session by storing a game's secret number and the user's guesses in
the UserProfile object. We are guaranteed that the appropriate session is
loaded each time that the user submits a new guess or selects to restart
the game.

Each time that the user selects to start a game, a new random integer will be selected and stored in the UserProfile object. The valid range
of numbers will be defined in the project's configuration file. We will
also store a count of the number of bad guesses that the user has made.
This value is increased by one with each bad guess, and reset to zero
when a new game is started.

Implementation

We will now convert the design into a working implementation. The first step is to create a new NumberGame project and register it with the local Slither installation. You will want to pay close attention to these steps, as they are required for creating and registering any Slither project. Next, we will create two State files, one for the GuessNumber state and another for the Congratulations state. Finally, we will need to create several HTML templates that contain the information the application will render to the user's brower.

First Project Configuration Details • It is recommended that each Slither project be stored in its own directory. Directories help organize a project by centralizing all of the code and configuration files. Our NumberGame implementation will live in /home/pshafae/www/ cgi-bin/slither_projects/NumberGame. From this point on, we will refer to this directory as NG_HOME.

The first step is to create a new project module containing the new project class. Since the project module and class follow some foundational guidelines, the best approach would be to copy all of the code included in the TestProject directory that is bundled with the Slither package. Looking at the contents of the TestProject directory, you will discover a file named MyProjectModule.py. You will want to rename this file to the desired project name, which in our case is NumberGame. The final result is a new module called NumberGame.py.

You will need to make a few basic changes to the project class defined in NumberGame.py. You will want to rename the project class from MyProjectClass to NumberGame. We are naming the project module and class the same thing to ease configuration tasks. You are free to name them anything you like. In just a bit you will see how these names are used when binding the project to the Slither Driver.

These are all the main changes needed to get the basic core of your project up and running. Before testing our setup, we need to configure the new project and register it with the core Slither system. The first task involves modifying a special file called ProjectConf.py. This file is included in the TestProject directory and should be copied into the $NG_HOME/NumberGame. The file name must be preserved, as it defines a module that some of the core Slither files attempt to import. The ProjectConf module is used mainly to communicate project-specific configuration information to the core Slither components.

In the example `ProjectConf.py`, you will need to modify the DOCROOT variable to point to the current working directory of your NumberGame, which we refer to as $NG_HOME/NumberGame. The DOCROOT refers to where all of the files generated by Slither for the NumberGame should be written. A closer inspection of the other variables reveals that the DOCROOT is used as a reference for all other file and directory-related settings. For example, the LOG_FILE_NAME variable has the following syntax:

```
SESSION_DIR = '%s/session'%( DOCROOT )
LOG_DIR     = '%s/logs'%( DOCROOT )
LOG_FILE_NAME = '%s/TestProject'%( LOG_DIR )
```

This setup allows us to define the value of LOG_FILE_NAME relative to some directory called LOG_DIR, which is located relative to the DOCROOT. This strategy makes relocating your code a snap; simply update DOCROOT and everything will work magically. Another benefit of creating values relative to DOCROOT is ease of file permission management. You simply make sure that Apache has the appropriate permissions to read and write to all of the files and directories below the DOCROOT directory. Keep in mind that this does not safeguard your system from being compromised; you still need to follow the Apache guidelines for making sure that the appropriate permissions and ownership rights are set for all of your files.

Since we are creating an entirely new project, you will want to modify all other instances of TestProject with the new name Number-Game. The two other variables in `ProjectConf` that play an important role in the execution of the NumberGame are HTML_SEARCH_PATH and LOCAL_PROPS. HTML_SEARCH_PATH is a list of strings that identify directories that Slither should search through when looking for HTML templates. For now, you will want to make sure that the list includes the $NG_HOME/NumberGame and the period ".". The period "." identifies the current working directory at the time of execution, which will in most cases be $NG_HOME/NumberGame. When Slither changes directories to load one of the two states, the period will instruct Slither to look in that directory as well.

The LOCL_PROPS variable is a Python dictionary that defines a few key values. The three main values that must be defined are "log_file_name", "encode_target", and "search_path". The values of "log_file_name" and "search_path" were defined by LOG_FILE_NAME and HTML_SEARCH_PATH. You can simply plug those in as the values to those keys. All that Slither will look for are the values to the keys in LOCAL_PROPS. We created the additional values to simplify the conf file. Can you imagine how complicated it would be to define the value of "log_file_name" in-line, relative to some log directory which is itself relative to DOCROOT? The same thing goes for "search_path". "encode_target" defines the main template file to use for **all** generated output. From the TestProject installation, the value is set to "BasicTemplate.html". This file actually exists, and can be used to get the ball rolling. In general, though, you will want to create a custom template file.

You can also create any number of additional key/value pairs in LOCAL_PROPS. These will be made available to the NumberGame project and state modules. This allows you to define any number of project-specific configuration parameters that can be used during execution. In the NumberGame, we can specify the low and high integer values that are to be used as boundaries for the randomly selected number, or you can set the maximum number of guesses that a user can make. In your project file, reference self.project_profile, which is a dictionary that contains all of the values defined in LOCAL_PROPS.

We are now ready to register the NumberGame with the Slither Driver. First change to the Slither directory. We assume here that you have followed the instructions included with Slither for installing, configuring, and testing Slither on your system. (If you have not yet installed the core Slither files, you will want to do so now.) In the Slither directory you will find a file named DriverConf.py. As part of the installation steps, you modified this file to list installation-specific parameters.

One parameter of great importance is CONFIG_MODULE. The preset value is MyConfModule, which corresponds to another file in the Slither directory called MyConfModule.py. Now that we know where all of the project bindings exist, we will want to close DriverConf.py and open MyConfModule.py. By the way, feel free to change the value of CONFIG_MODULE, but make sure that the new value references a module containing the same layout and structure as the included MyConfModule.py file.

MyConfModule contains two different dictionaries, named projects and TestProject. It is very important that you do not rename the projects dictionary. Much like LOCAL_PROPS, the core Slither components expect this dictionary to exist during execution. You will, however, want to rename and modify the TestProject dictionary to reflect values corresponding to the NumberGame installation. There are three keys that you will need to define: "webroot", "project_module", and "project_class". The value of "webroot" should reflect where the NumberGame project files live, which is the same as $NG_HOME/NumberGame. The "project_module" and "project_class" keys should reflect the name of the project module and the class that extend the Project class. Since we renamed both MyProjectModule and MyProjectClass to NumberGame, we can safely set both of these values to "NumberGame", which would instruct Slither to look for a file called NumberGame.py that contains a class-extending Project called NumberGame.

Last, you will want to bind the new dictionary to the project dictionary. The key used to perform the binding is also the key used to load the project from the URL. This allows you to specify any name to be used in the URL to load the NumberGame. You will want to take advantage of this feature if you have multiple versions of a project, but do not want to modify any previously defined URLs. The final version of our MyConfModul.py looks like this:

```
NumberGame = {
    'webroot' : '/home/apache/cgi-bin/slither_projects/NumberGame',
    'project_module' : 'NumberGame',
    'project_class' : 'NumberGame',
}
projects = {
    'NumberGame' : NumberGame
}
```

We are now ready to load the basic shell of the NumberGame. By loading the URL "http://www.mydomain.com/cgi-bin/slither/Driver.py/NumberGame" we are greeted with the contents of the BasicTemplate.html file and the words "Default render page called." You will need to modify the URL to reflect the proper host name and port of the Apache server serving your Slither and NumberGame installation.

If you do not see the same page, then an error has occurred. The specific error message is usually sent to the browser and can be used to remedy the problem. If no decipherable error message appears, look through the Slither log files for specific error messages. Refer to the documentation provided with Slither for possible errors and solutions.

Implementing the Project and State Modules • Now we are ready to create the NumberGame logic. The project file contains a `render()` method that is called by default on errors or when a user accesses the project's URL without specifying a state name. As part of the requirements, the NumberGame should display some introductory notes about the game and provide a link that can be used to start playing. First we need to define our two main states, GuessNumber and Congratulations. Once these states have been implemented, we will modify `BasicTemplate.html` to reflect the appropriate "start game" URL.

Let's start by defining GuessNumber. You will want to copy `state1.py` and use it as a template for defining GuessNumber. From our discussion of Slither in Chapter 13, you should already be familiar with the structure of `state1.py`. First, we will rename the class from `state1` to `GuessNumber`. Next, we will implement the `render()` and `process()` methods to fit the design described in the previous section.

The final `render()` method is listed in Figure 14–2. It is very short. In our design we indicated that the GuessNumber state would perform two key operations:

1. Guess a new random number if this is a new game.
2. Display a form that allows the user to guess a number and check the guess.

The first criterion is met by the code on lines 2 and 3. Here we use the reference to the UserProfile object[1] to see if we have already

```
def render( self ):
        if not self.user_profile.has_key('random_number'):
            self.user_profile['random_number'] = random.randint(1,100)
        fv = self.form_vars
        fv.update(self.user_profile)
        self.set_encode_file_name('PickNumber.html')
        return self.encode()
```

Figure 14–2
Final State Output

---

1. As you may recall, UserProfile is a wpl `Directory` class that is associated with a session. The value of `self.user_profile` is determined based on a cookie set on the user's browser. As a result, you can safely use `self.user_profile` to store any number of persistent data values. The values are guaranteed to be made available to your application on each HTTP request.

selected a random number for the user to guess. If a value exists, this indicates that a game is already in progress; nothing further is done. If no value has been set, we create a new random number and store it.

Notice also that we hard-coded the random number range to be between 1 and 100. These values could have been set in the project configuration file. The rest of the `render()` method simply sets the name of the HTML page that needs to be rendered. The HTML page `"PickNumber.html"` describes a very simple form that lets the user guess a number. Figure 14–3 lists the contents of `PickNumber.html`. We then call the WebForm `encode()` method and return the final rendering of the `PickNumber.html` file.[2]

Now we need to define the `process()` method. The process method is invoked when the user submits a guess. We must check the guess against the value of the stored random number. If the guess is correct, the user is transitioned to the Congratulations state. Otherwise, the user is returned to the GuessNumber state and we display the same guess number form. On a bad guess, we will display a simple error message that indicates whether the guess was too high or too low.

```
<form action="<<base_project_url>>/PickNumber.process">>

<b>Please enter a number from 1 to 100</b>
<br>
<input type="text" name="number" value=""> <br>
<input type="submit" name="go" value="Guess">
<br>
<i><<what_to_do|>></i>
</form>
```

Figure 14–3
Listing of `PickNumber.html`

Figure 14–4 lists our implementation of the `process()` method. Amazingly, the `process()` method is not that much longer than the `render()` method, which was pretty short to begin with. To clear up any confusion, on lines 2 and 3 we create local references for `self.user_profile` and `self.form_vars` purely as a convenience measure. On line 5 we retrieve the value of the secret random number.

---

2. As you may recall from Chapter 10, the `encode()` method takes a template HTML and substitutes dynamic tags with the appropriate values. The result is a fully rendered HTML page that can be displayed to the user.

Then we attempt to retrieve the value of the user's guess from the WebForm `form_vars`. This section is wrapped in a `try/except` block in case the user entered a non-integer in the guess form. In the event that this happens, on lines 9 and 10 we define an error message and raise a `StageProcessException`. When a `StageProcessException` is raised in the `process()` method, Slither will stop processing the request and return the value of the exception to the user. By setting the exception value to the return value of `self.render()`, we are essentially stopping the processing of the current guess, and displaying to the user the guess form page with an error message. Notice that we set a variable named `"what_to_do"` in `self.user_profile`. This value corresponds to a dynamic tag set in the `PickNumber.html` template, which only displays when a nonempty string value has been set. In the render method, the `fv.update( self.user_profile )` call copies the `"what_to_do"` variable along with all other values into `form_vars`, so that they can be used when processing the dynamic contents of the template.

```
1    def process( self ):
2            up = self.user_profile
3            fv = self.form_vars
4
5            random_number = up['random_number']
6            try:
7                number = int(fv['number'])
8            except:
9                up['what_to_do'] = 'Illegal Value Encountered; only a numeric value is permitted!'
10               raise StageProcessException(self.render())
11
12           if number == random_number:
13               self.scheduleState( "/NumberGame/Congratulations.render" )
14           else:
15
16               if (number < random_number):
17                   up['what_to_do'] = 'Your guess was too low. Try higher!'
18               else:
19                   up['what_to_do'] = 'Your guess was too high. Try lower.'
20
21               raise StageProcessException(self.render())
```

Figure 14–4
Implementation of the `process()` method.

Once we have retrieved the user's guess, we check to see if the guess was correct. If so, on line 13, we perform a state transition to the Congratulations state. Notice that the path used is relative to the project name

NumberGame. This implies that you can jump to any state in the NumberGame. Refer to Chapter 13 for details of how state transitions work.

If an incorrect guess was made, on lines 16–21 we use the "what_to_do" variable to provide hints to the user and then send the user back to the guess number form. This process continues until the user guesses the correct value of the secret number. There are many additional features that can be added to this state. For example, you may wish to track all of the numbers that a user has guessed and then warn the user who guessed the same number more than once.

Now we must implement the Congratulations state. As with GuessNumber, make a copy of state1.py as a starting point. Rename the file to Congratualtions.py and the class to Congratulations. Based on our design, Congratulations performs two main tasks:

1. Displays a page indicating that the user has won.
2. Resets the random number so that a new game can be started.

Figure 14–5 lists all of the code for both the render() and process() methods. The render() method encodes the contents of the Congratulations.html template and clears the UserProfile directory used to store the random number. This will make the game restart the next time that we invoke the GuessNumber state. The process() method does not do anything, since there are no new forms rendered. The Congratulations.html template lists a link that can be used to restart the game, thus completing all of the requirements set for this project.

```
1    def process( self ):
2            return "Nothing to Return"
3
4    def render( self ):
5            self.user_profile.clear()
6            self.set_encode_file_name('Congratulations.html')
7            self.user_profile.pushd('/NumberGame/PickNumber')
8            self.user_profile.clear_all()
9            self.user_profile.popd()
10           return self.encode()
```

Figure 14–5
Render() and process() methods.

Now we can create the URLs needed for the "start game" link. The link can be considered as having two distinct parts: the main URL for accessing the project, and the specific state to call. Since the game starts by accessing the GuessNumber state, we want to build a link with a URL that points to the `GuessNumber.render()` method. The following piece of HTML code will do just that when placed in an HTML template file that is rendered by Slither.

```
<<base_project_url>>/GuessNumber.render
```

The dynamic variable `<<base_project_url>>` will be replaced by Slither, with the base URL used to access the Number-Game project file. If you saved your states in a different subdirectory of the NumberGame project, you will have to include that information here as well. For example, if the GuessNumber state was saved in `$NG_HOME/states/GuessNumber.py`, the URL would be modified as follows:

```
<<base_project_url>>/states/GuessNumber.render
```

We will modify `BasicTemplate.html` and `Congratulations.html` to include this link. And that's it.

NumberGame Summary

You have completed all of the design goals of the basic Number-Game application with almost no code. Slither takes care of most of the dispatching tasks, allowing you to focus on what is important: the business logic that accomplishes the program's goals. Furthermore, the Slither design makes creating states a very natural thing. In the NumberGame example, there was a one-to-one correspondence between the logical states and the physical Slither states.

SlyWiki: A Capability-Based Text Collaboration System

A *wiki* is a simple yet powerful collaborative text-authoring system. The seminal ideas were pioneered by one of the great thinkers in object-oriented computing, Ward Cunningham (also known for HyperCard and CRC cards).

The essence of a wiki system is simplicity. *Wiki* is a Hawaiian word, which means *quick*. Since Ward first introduced the idea of a wiki, a number of so-called wiki clones have popped up all over the Net and are gaining use for requirements and design discussions, especially in software development teams. Wikis are particularly useful for capturing domain knowledge and documenting the design of software as it is being developed, as well as for improving team communication.

There are a number of ingredients of a wiki system:

- Very simple markup—The idea is that content can be authored using more or less plain text with simple markup. HTML is not generally considered simple markup, so wiki systems typically do not employ it for authoring pages.
- Ubiquitous editing—Anyone should be able to revise a page, assuming the person has something "reasonable" to contribute. Revisions of any kind are permitted.
- Anarchic—There is no notion of control or management. In many respects, a wiki system is self-healing, as it is more or less community-based.
- Not WYSIWYG—When creating pages, there is no WYSIWYG: The way the page is written may not be how it is rendered.

In short, a wiki system is very much aligned with the phrase coined by Mies van der Rohe, "Less is more." We agree with most of the goals of the wiki design and have observed in particular that the emphasis on very simple markup and no WYSIWYG leads to vast improvements in productivity when it comes to content authoring. We do not agree with the goal of anyone being able to edit at any time. Instead, we prefer a model in which users can join the system freely and be given whatever capabilities the owner of the wiki wishes to extend. This model is very similar to Internet Relay Chat (IRC), where there is a concept called first mover. The first mover is the one who creates a conference and benevolently allows others to join, subject to access controls.

Functional Requirements

SlyWiki was designed in the context of the wiki way with the intention of enabling a large number of capabilities. The system remains under development, with new features being added; however, care has been extended to ensure that new capabilities can be added to the system. This is because clear requirements were established:

- Must clearly separate the page-processing model from the various non-page-processing functions of the system.
- Must support a **proper access control** model that is capability-based. As new features (capabilities) become available, it must be trivial for an access control check to be added by the developer of the new feature.

- **Guest access** must be possible. It must be possible to provide any desired level of guest access by a site administrator. This allows the possibility of using the wiki in an anarchic fashion while making it possible for a workgroup to rest assured that their pages will not be hacked.
- **Simple navigation**. Most wiki systems suffer from very limited navigation capabilities. Users should be able to make pages that show up on the navigation (at the left, top, bottom, or all of the above). It should also be possible to generate a tree of the site relative to a particular page. (A BFS-style search can accomplish this idea quite conveniently.)
- **Concurrency control** is a serious issue in an environment where anyone can edit a page at any time. For a wiki system to be taken seriously in a commercial environment, it must not get confused by concurrent edits. Users must be informed when edits can cause conflicts. The system should do adequate book-keeping and journaling to ensure that no change is lost and fails to be recoverable.

We should point out that we have plans for this software. Stay tuned to our Web site (which is based on our wiki) for information about our latest work.

Design and Implementation

SlyWiki consists of many modules. The following is an essential set for understanding the design and implementation as a whole:

- Database
- Query Processing
- Processing-Page Markup
- The General Interface
- Creating Pages
- Showing Pages
- Authentication
- Access Control

We cover enough of the system so you can see the general ingredients that make up a Slither project in a nutshell and how to integrate the interface (HTML) with your back-end code. It is not possible to cover every module and line of code in the space allowed; however, in discussing the most significant functions of the system (page management, authentication, and access control), a reasonable amount of detail is presented so that understanding the remaining uncovered modules and making your own Slither application should be achievable.

This discussion includes both design and implementation. We advocate always doing these activities separately when it comes to real-world projects; however, we have forgone this formality for your benefit. We urge you to consider mapping out the requirements and design space in sufficient detail and to combine these activities with prototyping to refine the requirements before implementing the entire system. Slither itself encourages good software engineering by forcing you to think in terms of classes and modules, but will not prevent you from writing bad code.

Now we present the actual design and implementation details. Download the latest code from the book Web site in order to fully appreciate and understand this discussion.

Database • SlyWiki maintains all of its pages in a database. The tables are shown as SQL create statements. We describe each of these tables beneath its SQL create statement:

```
CREATE TABLE wiki_names (
  id int(11) NOT NULL auto_increment,
  name varchar(80),
  PRIMARY KEY (id)
);
```

wiki_names is a table that keeps track of all of the wiki names being used in the system. In the database, unique integers are used as keys in most (if not all) of the tables. As described in Chapter 8 on databases, auto_increment is used in MySQL to number uniquely the entries in this table upon insert. Wiki names must be unique within the wiki system. The actual code for creating and editing pages ensures that no duplicates ever occur in the database.

```
CREATE TABLE wiki_page_content (
  id int(11) NOT NULL auto_increment,
  wiki_id int(11) NOT NULL,
  user_id int(11) NOT NULL,
  page_text longtext DEFAULT '' NOT NULL,
  PRIMARY KEY (id)
);
```

The actual content for wiki pages is maintained in the wiki_page_content table. Each wiki page inserted is given a unique identifier. It just so happens (at the moment) that every entry in wiki_names will have a corresponding entry in wiki_page_content. This may not always be the case; some wiki names may ultimately point to something else, such as an uploaded file. The wiki_id field is used to index the wiki_names entry; user_id refers to the user id who last modified the page; page_text contains the actual text for the wiki page. One of the reasons we separated the content into a separate table from the names is the limited support some databases have for processing large fields (called text or blobs) efficiently. When we want to know what pages are in the wiki system (e.g., to generate the navigation list of pages), we don't need to know the actual content of the pages—just the names. The largetext type, introduced in Chapter 8, allows the page text to be very large, meaning for all practical purposes that there is no practical limit to how much text can appear in a page. (There is probably only so much text a person can tolerate entering in an HTML <TEXT-AREA> region, however!)

```
CREATE TABLE capabilities (
   id int(11) NOT NULL auto_increment,
   capability text DEFAULT '' NOT NULL,
   standard int(11) DEFAULT '0' NOT NULL,
   PRIMARY KEY (id)
);
```

The capabilities table is used to maintain the list of features for which a user can potentially be given access. In the current system, this is the list of capabilities:

```
mysql> select * from capabilities;
+----+--------------+----------+
| id | capability   | standard |
+----+--------------+----------+
|  1 | CreatePage   |        0 |
|  2 | EditPage     |        0 |
|  3 | WikiIndex    |        1 |
|  4 | ShowWikiPage |        1 |
|  5 | AddUser      |        0 |
|  6 | EditUser     |        0 |
+----+--------------+----------+
6 rows in set (0.00 sec)
```

There is one capability for each function within the system. For example, the CreatePage capability is associated with the corresponding code, CreatePage.py. This allows for practically automated testing of access control. The `standard` field is used to make life easy for site administrators. When creating a new user, it is desirable to have a reasonable set of default capabilities enabled for that user. In SlyWiki, the default is to allow WikiIndex (show a listing of all pages) and Show-Wikipage (show the content of a page). This is what it means for the site to be read-only. A key aspect of our approach to access control is that it is totally configurable. When creating the initial database, the site administrator can set any standard permissions desired. This allows those who are accustomed to an anarchic setup (where anyone can do whatever he or she wants) to enable any default capabilities arbitrarily.

```
CREATE TABLE user (
  id int(11) NOT NULL auto_increment,
  username text DEFAULT '' NOT NULL,
  password text DEFAULT '' NOT NULL,
  capabilities text DEFAULT '' NOT NULL,
  PRIMARY KEY (id)
);
```

The user table maintains the type of information one would expect for a user: username and password should be obvious. The field, `capabilities`, requires some explanation. This field contains a comma-separated listing of capabilities that are enabled or `"*"`, which matches all capabilities. This is where the relational model can be seen to break down. Good relational design suggests that fields cannot (and should not) be multivalued. This is too bad. Ideally, I could have any number of capabilities in an array of integers that could then be iterated and validated. Unfortunately, this is not a standard SQL feature, let alone a MySQL feature. In any event, the approach we have adopted works quite elegantly (and is simply coded, as well). It is possible for this field to get corrupted, since the database itself does not check this field for whether it contains valid data or not.

Database Queries • All database queries are maintained in a module called `DbQueries.py`. The alternative to this approach is for the different modules to issue SQL queries directly to the database. We adopted this approach to make it easy to modify (add, edit, or update) queries that need to be performed by the various functions of the wiki system without having to chase down (and modify) multiple files.

Let's take a look at part of the `DbQueries` module. This module contains a class, `Query`, which encapsulates a reference to an existing database connection, `db`, which is an instance of the DataAccess class described in Chapter 8. (DataAccess configures a connection to a data provider from a configuration file that specifies the host, port, type of database, and database name to be connected.)

```
class Query:
    def __init__(self, db):
        self.db = db

    # users queries

    # wiki_names queries

    def createWikiName(self, wiki_name):
        wiki_name = self.db.clean(wiki_name)
        query = "insert into wiki_names values (null, '%s')"
        query = query % wiki_name
        self.db.execute(query)
        return self.db.getDb().insert_id()

    def findWikiName(self, wiki_name):
        wiki_name = self.db.clean(wiki_name)
        query = "select * from wiki_names where name='%s'"
        query = query % wiki_name
        self.db.execute(query)
        return len(self.db.getRecords())

    def getWikiNameId(self, wiki_name):
        wiki_name = self.db.clean(wiki_name)
        query = "select * from wiki_names where name='%s'"
        query = query % wiki_name
        self.db.execute(query)
        return self.db.getRecords()[0]

    def createWikiPageContent(self, user_id, wiki_name_id, wiki_text):
        wiki_text = self.db.clean(wiki_text)
        query = "insert into wiki_page_content values (null, %d, %d, '%s')"
        query = query % (wiki_name_id, user_id, wiki_text)
        self.db.execute(query)
        return self.db.getDb().insert_id()
```

The methods of the Query class are nothing more than appropriately named methods that describe what the query itself is doing. This technique, which we call UDM (universal data model), is used to encapsulate SQL statements in a more procedural interface such that it is clear what the query depends upon in order to complete successfully. For example, createWikiPageContent(self, user_id, wiki_name_id, wiki_text) is a method that makes a new entry in the wiki_page_content table. It is expected that user_id, wiki_name_id, and wiki_text are all passed down in order for this query to be performed successfully.[3] These values are substituted into an SQL template, which is executed through self.db, which references the database. Upon completion of the query, a new row has been created and its unique key value (the value placed in the `id` field of the `wiki_page_content` table) is returned via the `insert_id()` method.

A number of methods return record sets, which were also presented in Chapter 8. The data access framework provides support for lists of Record instances. After a query is executed, `self.db.getRecords()` returns a list of results. In most of our methods that "get" something from the database, you'll often see one of two statements:

1. `return self.db.getRecords()[0]`—This will return the first result from a list of results. We do no error checking most of the time, since we seldom call a method when we are expecting a result unless we know there is a result to be found. Besides, exception handling is used whenever there is a possibility of zero results being returned.

2. `return self.db.getRecords()`—This will return all results that were selected from the database. If there are no results, the DataAccess framework guarantees that an empty list will be returned.

Table 14–1 shows a naming convention that is roughly followed when coding queries for inclusion in the `DbQueries` module.

Table 14–1
Conventions Used in the `DbQueries` Table

Prefix	Explanation
create	Used to make a new entry in a table
get	Used to get one entry from a table
getAll	Used to get all entries in a table
delete	Used to remove entries from a table

---

3. This is effectively a contract. If we need to change the database query, e.g., when adding information to the table or perhaps changing the query altogether, we are protected by having the query in a method. This is why many database vendors tout the benefits of stored procedures. We are not big believers in the stored procedure methodology but are big believers in the design by contract principle. Things tend not to break when procedural abstraction is used effectively—and this is one situation where it pays off, more so than anywhere else in our software.

Table 14–1
Conventions Used in the DbQueries Table (Continued)

Prefix	Explanation
find	Used to determine whether an entry exists in a table; usually returns a count which can also be used in a Boolean context

The decision to centralize the queries in a single module does not always make life easier. One typically thinks of the query spontaneously while coding, only to be forced to visit another file to actually create the query. This is certainly not so difficult when you are working in an IDE, but for an old vi hacker such as the author, it tends to require moving (slowly) from one file to another. Nevertheless, this technique has the enormous benefit of being self-documenting and makes the code much easier to follow in the modules that are interacting with the database.

Preprocessing • Slither provides a great deal of support for minimizing the amount of coding one has to do by supporting a concept called preprocessing. Here we are not talking about the same concept as a preprocessor as found in the C language. The Slither notion of preprocessing allows some work to be done before dispatching a given state. This can be useful, for example, for doing user authentication, URI rewriting, or any appropriate function that literally needs *always* to be done. Most Web frameworks are deficient in this regard, which is why you see so many Web applications that put all of the code in one module or in which the same code gets duplicated across many modules.

The SlyWikiModule.py file contains various functions that can be overridden in Slither. Only the preprocess() method has been overridden as follows:

```
1   def preprocess( self ):up
2       up = self.user_profile
3       up.create( "/Wiki/Login" )
4       try:
5           visited_pages = up.get_dir("/Wiki/Login/visited_pages")
6       except:
7           up.set_dir("/Wiki/Login/visited_pages",[])
8       psp = self.project_profile['project_state_path']
9       top_dir = self.parse_state_path(psp)['path']
10      state_path = self.project_profile['project_state_path']
11      if string.find(state_path, "/Wiki/Login.") >= 0:
12          return
```

```
13          up.cd( "/Wiki/Login" )
14          if not up.has_key('username'):
15             self.project_profile[ 'project_state_path' ] = \
16                "/Wiki/Login.render"
17             up.set_dir("/Wiki/Login/state_path", state_path)
18          else:
19             try:
20                username = up["username"]
21                password = up["password"]
22                capabilities = up["capabilities"]
23             except:
24                self.project_profile[ 'project_state_path' ] = \
25                   "/Wiki/Login.render"
26                up.set_dir("/Wiki/Login/state_path", state_path)
27          if state_path == '' or state_path == '/Wiki':
28             self.project_profile[ 'project_state_path' ] = \
29                "/Wiki/Login.render"
```

Here is what the preprocessing code does, by groups of related lines:

2   self.user_profile is the persistent dictionary containing the state information for the current session. We make up an alias for the purpose of concise presentation.

3   As the profile is a directory, we are able to use it like a symbol table. The login information and capabilities are kept in subdirectory "/Wiki/Login". Recall that the create() method in the Directory class is parsed as "create if directory does not exist."

4–7   An entry is also maintained for "visited pages" since the user logged in. This list is maintained in the "/Wiki/Login" directory data structure as well.

8   self.project_profile["project_state_path"] is the URI. The parse_state_path method call here splits the URI into its components. The path component gives the path to the top level of the project. (This returns http://hostname/SlyWiki/Wiki.)

10   state_path refers to the extra path components after the base path returned in line 8. It is called the state path because it refers to the name of the state to be invoked next.

| 11–12 | To enter the `/Wiki/Login` state, bypass the rest of the preprocessing code. The purpose of the preprocessing code is to ensure that someone has logged on to the system before any other function can be attempted. |

| 13 | We now change directory to the `"/Wiki/Login"`. This is so we can check for certain entries that must be present for successful authentication and subsequent ACL checking. |

| 14–17 | Not finding `"username"` means that no successful login has taken place previously. This forces the scheduling of the `"/Wiki/Login"` state. In line 17, we stash the current value of `"state_path"`, which will allow whatever function the user wanted to perform to be dispatched upon successful login. This is very similar to a push-down automation, which is used to save context in a particular state for subsequent use in another state. |

| 20–22, 23–26 | Try to assign `username`, `password`, and `capabilities`. These should all be defined if `username` was defined, but this is a final check to ensure the authentication information is not corrupted. Is this secure? Yes, because `self.user_profile` is kept only on the server side (and could even be encrypted). Keeping this information persistent eliminates the need to perform authentication repeatedly; however, the persistence of information is subject to a session timeout, if sessions have been configured to timeout upon inactivity. On any exception, lines 23–26 cause a login to be rescheduled. |

| 27–29 | This last block of code forces a re-login if any attempt is made to access a URI that contains path components that do not map to a valid Slither project name. |

Before we proceed to a discussion of how pages are created, edited, and viewed in the SlyWiki system, we need to say a bit about how pages are written and processed.

Processing page markup. Wiki systems all feature a text-processing engine. This engine takes what is often called "dirt simple" or "structured" markup and translates it into HTML. We decided to borrow an existing renderer from one of the open-source systems, named Moin-Moin, that has done a particularly decent job of parsing the structured text and making it possible to generate HTML, XML, and even plain text. We will introduce the MoinMoin code as we make use of it. Here we comment briefly on the type of markup that can be inserted into a page and how it is rendered. This is summarized in Table 14–2.

Table 14–2
Selected Markup Available in MoinMoin Wiki Parser

Markup	Description and Example

`= Heading1 =`
`== Heading 2 ==`
`=== Heading 3 ===`
	Headings; the number of "=" determines the level of the heading
	`= Heading = ` is mapped to `<h1>heading</h1>`

`Blank Lines`	`<p>`
`WikiName`	`<a href="url to show page">WikiName</a>` `<a href="url to edit page">[edit]</a>`
`"text"`	italics
`'''text'''`	bold
`{{{text}}}`	fixed text, text inside `{{{` and `}}}` taken verbatim

`{{{`
`text`
`}}}`
	fixed text, text is taken verbatim; newlines, etc. are also preserved

`http://text`	Translated into `<a href="text">text</a>`
`[http://text1 text2]`	Translated into `<a href="text1">text2</a>`

The MoinMoin structured markup supports many features. The idea here is to provide a glimpse of how pages are written. The idea of the structured text approach (contrasted with HTML and XML) is to make it very easy for someone to learn to write a page and to spend very little time thinking about how the page will look. The structured markup supports many additional features, including simple table creation, list generation, and the ability to hook into a page-processing macro. For more details on the full language supported, you can visit our site or the MoinMoin home page at `http://moin.sourceforge.net`.

Interface and a hint of implementation. Before we delve into the code, it will be helpful to get an idea of what the interface looks like and understand how what you "see" in the interface ties to implementation. Figure 14–6 shows what the user first sees upon login.

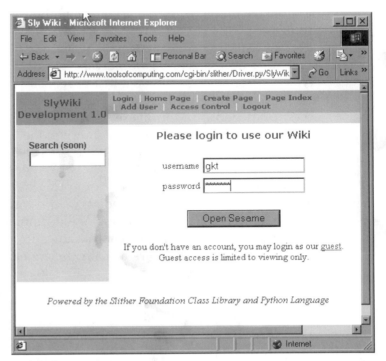

Figure 14–6
The Login Screen

The interface is shown exactly as it appears when the user types the top-level URL to reach the SlyWiki system, which is `http://`*hostname*`/cgi-bin/slither/Driver.py/SlyWiki`. The interface style was constructed using an authoring tool to obtain the general appearance; however, what you see here is dynamically built up from (mostly) simple HTML fragments. This is shown in Figure 14–7.

The file `WikiTemplate.html` contains the part of the interface that was authored with DreamWeaver. The HTML for this interface was then hacked by the author to include placeholders for dynamically generated content. In the figure, these placeholders for dynamically inserted content are labelled `<<quick_links>>` and `<<state_output>>`. The output shown in this screen was generated from the state named `"/Wiki/Login"` and then substituted into `WikiTemplate.html` with the help of the WriteProcessor. As control flows from one state to another, this area will change. Similarly, some of the states dynamically generate navigational output, depending on whether it is appropriate. Nothing should be visible until the user has performed a proper login. Thus you see nothing on the left-hand side of this figure.

Now let's take a look at what happens upon login, shown in Figure 14–8. After a successful login, the very first page in the wiki is shown. (Typical wiki systems provide a first page, called FrontPage in our system, that can be edited as any other page can be edited, subject to access restrictions.) In this figure, you can see that the output is generated into the two regions that were shown in the login figure (Figure 14–3). The state "/Wiki/ShowWikiPage" is scheduled after a successful login to show the home page for the wiki system. The output of this state is substituted for <<state_output>>. The output appearing where the <<quick_links>> points to in Figure 14–7 is generated by a call to ShowWikiPage's superclass, WikiCommon, which is contained in WikiCommon.py. The two circles shown in Figure 14–8 for "Pages Visited" and "Quick List" are actually generated from templates from the WikiCommon class.

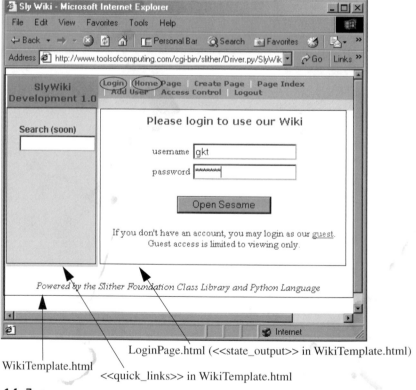

LoginPage.html (<<state_output>> in WikiTemplate.html)

WikiTemplate.html

<<quick_links>> in WikiTemplate.html

Figure 14–7
Under the Hood

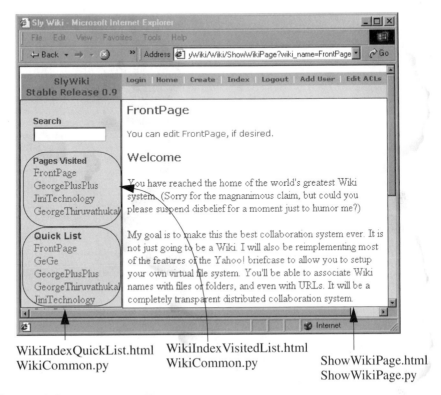

WikiIndexQuickList.html   WikiIndexVisitedList.html
WikiCommon.py   WikiCommon.py
                                                    ShowWikiPage.html
                                                    ShowWikiPage.py

Figure 14–8
After Login

In any event, all of the remaining code in the system works in a similar way. When the state runs, it can generate whatever output it wants. This output will be substituted into the top-level site template in place of the write processor variable <<state_output>>. Any state that wants to perform some common activities, such as including some navigational elements, makes an upcall to the superclass, WikiCommon, which exposes a method named common() that does the actual work of generating the output that appears and is ultimately substituted for the WriteProcessor variable <<quick_links>>.

The key to understanding a Slither example is recognizing that it works in a compositional fashion: Any time something needs to be done, it can be built recursively. Unlike ASP and JSP, the WriteProcessor functions of Slither allow results to be built up arbitrarily from small and focused pieces. This leads to concise code that is easy to understand. When code generation must be performed, a given state can be coded with the assumption of working in isolation, because it need not be concerned with how the interface as a whole is working. The same is not true of the multitude of Web programming "frameworks" available on the commercial market today.

We'll now take a look at the implementation of the various functions pertaining only to creating, editing, and viewing pages. For each of the features we discuss, the following will be shown:

- Snapshot of the Interface
- Relevant HTML snippet
- Code for the responsible states

`CreatePage.`   The primary purpose of a wiki system is to allow users to author and edit page content. The page content is written using the dirt-simple markup that was shown in Table 14–2. The interface presented is fairly straightforward: the name of the page to be created and the text for the page. The screen shot is shown in Figure 14–9.

We have already described in some detail how elements of an interface get built up with what is effectively a compositional

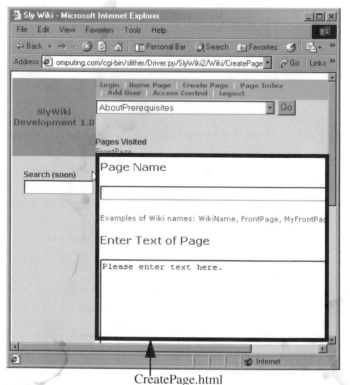

Figure 14–9
The Create Page Form

approach. The topmost level of this interface consists of a template named `SlyWikiTempate.html`, which was authored with DreamWeaver. This template contains WriteProcessor variables, one of which is named `<<state_output>>`. The `CreatePage` feature of the SlyWiki system is mapped to a state path `/Wiki/CreatePage` (these are the trailing components of the URI). Slither automatically provides support for this, as the path is taken relative to the project's base directory. The code for `CreatePage` is actually contained in a file named `CreatePage.py`. The template file used by this state (just for presenting the interface part shown here) is `CreatePage.html`. Every aspect of this SlyWiki system is coded consistently, using the conventions described here.

HTML   The HTML code contained in `CreatePage.html` is shown below. This code has been presented in an abbreviated form. The only significant thing omitted is the JavaScript code that has been inserted to perform validation of the input field for the wiki page name.

```
<!-- Shortened version for book presentation. -->
<script language="JavaScript" >

function validate_wiki_name() {
    wiki_name = document.create_page.wiki_name.value

    // Returns true if "wiki_name" is a proper Wiki name.
    // Returns false otherwise.
}

</script>

<form name="create_page" onSubmit="return validate_wiki_name();"
action="<<base_project_url>>/Wiki/CreatePage.process">

<table width="100%" cellpadding=0 cellspacing=0 border=0>
<tr>
<td>
<h2 class="V16">Page Name</h2>
<input onChange="return validate_wiki_name();"  type="text"
name="wiki_name" value="" size=75>
<p class="V10">
Examples of Wiki names: WikiName, FrontPage, MyFrontPage, FrontPage2000
</p>

<h2 class="V16">Enter Text of Page</h2>
<textarea name="wiki_text" rows=25 columns=75 wrap="virtual" size=75
style="width:100%">
Please enter text here.
</textarea>
```

```
<input type="button" name="submit" value="Submit" onClick="return
validate_wiki_name();">
</td>
</tr>
</table>
</form>
```

A few words about this HTML are in order. The HTML placed in this file is only the HTML that is relevant to the part of the interface that was enclosed in a thick rectangle. This file is used in the render() method of the CreatePage class and is taken verbatim and substituted by the WriteProcessor into the top-level site template. Life will not always be this simple. As shown in the discussion of EditPage shortly, it is often necessary to perform some substitutions or other processing before rendering the page.

State code.   The code responsible for rendering the interface and subsequently processing it is shown below. The details of this code are presented below the code.

```
1     class CreatePage( WikiCommon ):
2
3         def render( self ):
4             profile = self.user_profile
5             form_vars = self.form_vars
6             if not AccessControl.checkAccess(profile, "CreatePage"):
7                 self.set_encode_file_name("CreatePageAccessDenied.html")
8                 return self.encode()
9             self.common()
10            form_vars.update(profile)
11            self.set_encode_file_name('CreatePage.html')
12            return self.encode()
13
14        def process( self ):
15            profile = self.user_profile
16            form_vars = self.form_vars
17            if not AccessControl.checkAccess(profile, "CreatePage"):
18                raise StageProcessException(self.render())
19
20            self.query = getQuery(self.db)
21            if not self.validate():
22                raise StageProcessException(self.render())
23
24            wiki_name = profile['wiki_name'] = form_vars['wiki_name']
25            wiki_text = profile['wiki_text'] = form_vars['wiki_text']
26
27            if self.query.findWikiName(wiki_name):
28                profile['page_exists'] = 'Page already exists.'
29                raise StageProcessException(self.render())
30
31            wiki_name_id = self.query.createWikiName(wiki_name)
32            user_id = profile.get_dir("/Wiki/Login/user_id")
33            wiki_page_id = self.query.createWikiPageContent(user_id, wiki_name_id, wiki_text)
34            self.scheduleState( "/Wiki/ShowWikiPage.render" )
```

`CreatePage` 1	Every class being dispatched by Slither must be named for the file in which it is contained. In this case, `CreatePage` is contained in `CreatePage.py`. The class itself must be a subclass of `State` (directly or indirectly).
`render()` 6–8	The `render()` method is responsible for generating the interface to the `CreatePage` feature of the SlyWiki system. Check whether the user has access. This is part of the `AccessControl` module, which is discussed later. Similar code is presented in all remaining modules that pertain to pages.
9	Make an upcall to the `common()` method, which exists for the purpose of generating code for common parts of the interface, such as the navigation of pages on the left-hand side and any other features that we want generated for every page in the future.
10	`form_vars.update(profile)`. Get used to it. This is an idiom that allows the variables in the current state-specific profile directory (i.e., variables that persist across invocations) to be copied to the `form_vars` directory. When you want to substitute variables into the template file, it is necessary to perform this call. `CreatePage.html` does not contain any variables, but may in the future. By always coding a state the same way, we eliminate the possibility of bugs.
11–12	This idiom is also going to seem like a broken record. Basically, set the template file and actually generate the code. This result will ultimately become part of the larger result.
`process()` 17–18	The `process()` method is responsible for handling the submission of the form to create the page. As in `render()`, `AccessControl` is checked. Why both in `render()` and in `process()`? Here, we want it to be in both places. In some cases, we may want to `render()`, regardless of whether the user has access to the actual function of the system, but only prevent `process()` from taking place. Our approach to access control is to provide something very general that can be easily checked by the module responsible for a particular feature. The `StageProcessException(self.render())` pattern allows the page for the state to be rendered again. (We often use this to render an input form with suggested corrections and/or other status messages inserted.)

21–22   Internal validation method. This code is not shown here but checks
               whether the input variables are valid. This will return false only if
               someone tried to maliciously post a request to our code without
               using the Web pages that were rendered. It is important to guard
               against such things, which is why we perform validation both with
               JavaScript and in the server-side code.

24–25   Get the input fields, `wiki_name` and `wiki_text`. Save these
               variables to the persistent state information for the current session.
               This is where you finally get to see how the claims about persistent
               servers being so much better than CGI are not true when it comes
               to variables. These variables are stored in a session directory named
               `"/Wiki/CreatePage"`. (*Note:* The use of the term *directory* does
               not mean that a directory is created in a file system. Directory is a
               data structure, described in the miscellaneous modules chapter,
               Chapter 12.)

27–29   Check whether `wiki_name` is already in the table of
               `wiki_names`. A given name may appear only once. If the name is
               already in the table, the page for this state will be re-rendered to
               create another page.

31   If the name is unique, add it to the database. The id for this new
               wiki name is captured as `wiki_name_id`.

32   Find out who is logged in and performing this operation by looking
               at the persistent session directory and extracting from the
               `"/Wiki/Login"` state directory. We know it is completely safe to
               go to this directory because without login, no function of the system
               can be accessed.

33   Now add the page content itself to the database. It was a tough
               decision, but the page names and content are separated because in a
               general sense we wanted to leave open the possibility of wiki names
               referring to something other than a page in the future (e.g., an
               uploaded file, etc.)

34   Schedule `"/Wiki/ShowWikiPage"` to execute next. After Slither
               processes a state (using the `process()` method), it is useful to
               schedule a state that will actually display something. It could be a
               general "success" state or anything desired. In most wiki systems, it
               is customary after creating or editing a page to show the page. That
               is what is done here. The page to be shown will be obtained by the
               state itself from the persistent state information.

Showing pages.   Showing pages is integral to the success of a wiki system. It is used in many different contexts:

- After creating a page
- From the list of available pages
- After editing a page

Showing pages requires a call to the page parser and formatter. We have actually integrated the existing parser/formatter from the MoinMoin system. The work required to do this is somewhat beyond the scope of this discussion.

The interface for showing pages is shown in Figure 14–10.

As described in the discussion of creating pages, our efforts will be focused on describing the part shown in the rectangle, which is based on the `ShowWikiPage.html` template.

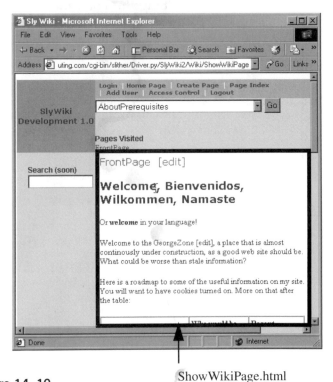

ShowWikiPage.html

Figure 14–10
The ShowWikiPage Output Screen

HTML

```
1    <table width="100%" cellpadding=0 cellspacing=0 border=0>
2    <tr>
3    <td>
4    <b><h2 class="V16"><<wiki_name|>></h2></b>
5    <p class="V12">
6    You can
7    <a class="lnlink" href="<<base_project_url>>/Wiki/EditPage.render?wiki_name=<<wi
8    ki_name|>>">
9    edit <<wiki_name|>></a>, if desired.
10   </p>
11   <p class="V12">
12   <<wiki_text|>>
13   </p>
14   </td>
15   </tr>
16   </table>
```

State code. In describing the code for the ShowWikiPage state, we will focus only on the render() method. There is no form associated with this state requiring processing; hence there is no process() method.

```
1    def render( self ):
2        if not AccessControl.checkAccess(self.user_profile, "ShowWikiPage"):
3            self.set_encode_file_name("ShowWikiPageAccessDenied.html")
4            return self.encode()
5
6        self.common()
7        wiki_name = self.form_vars['wiki_name']
8        if wiki_name == None:
9          wiki_name = self.user_profile.get_dir('/Wiki/EditPage/wiki_name')
10
11       if wiki_name == None:
12           self.set_encode_file_name('ShowWikiPageError.html')
13           return self.encode()
14
15       wiki_text = self.form_vars['wiki_text'] = \
16           self.generatePage(wiki_name)
17       self.set_encode_file_name('ShowWikiPage.html')
18       return self.encode()
```

<table>
<tbody>
<tr><td>2–6</td><td>Similar code has been covered before; see <code>CreatePage</code> discussion, page 672.</td></tr>
<tr><td>7–9</td><td>If the <code>wiki_name</code> has not been specified, we check whether it has been set as a result of a previous edit or create operation. Entries are made in the <code>/Wiki/EditPage</code> state directory when a page is either created or edited.</td></tr>
<tr><td>11–13</td><td>If we get here and <code>wiki_name</code> is <code>None</code>, this means the page is truly not defined. We must report an error. This error message will be substituted in the <code>ShowWikiPageError.html</code> template file.</td></tr>
<tr><td>15–18</td><td>Call the <code>generatePage()</code> routine to generate the HTML. We'll go into this method shortly. This is where a page gets turned from structured page markup into HTML. We then embed this result in the <code>ShowWikiPage.html</code> template.</td></tr>
</tbody>
</table>

This method relies on another internal method, `generatePage()`, which is responsible for passing the page text as last modified in `CreatePage` or `EditPage` and using the MoinMoin parser to format the page as HTML.

```
1    def generatePage(self, wiki_name):
2        wiki_html_formatter = Formatter()
3        results = getQuery(self.db).getWikiPageContent(wiki_name)
4
5
6        if results:
7            login_dir = "/Wiki/Login/visited_pages"
8            visited_pages = self.user_profile.get_dir(login_dir)
9            if wiki_name not in visited_pages:
10               visited_pages.append(wiki_name)
11           wiki_text = results[0].page_text
12           wiki_text = string.replace(wiki_text, '\015\012', '\n')
13           formatted_output = StringIO.StringIO()
14           Parser(wiki_text).format(wiki_html_formatter, None, \
15                                    formatted_output)
16           formattedHtmlPage = formatted_output.getvalue()
17           f = StringIO.StringIO(formattedHtmlPage)
18           se = StringEmitter()
19           wp = WriteProcessor(f, ['.'], self.form_vars, se)
20           wp.process()
21           return se.getResult()
22       else:
```

```
23          se = StringEmitter()
24          self.form_vars['wiki_name'] = wiki_name
25          wp = WriteProcessor('ShowWikiPageCreate.html', \
26                              ['.'], self.form_vars, se)
27          wp.process()
28          return se.getResult()
```

2   Formatter is a class from the MoinMoin system. This class is used to apply HTML formatting from within the Wiki page parser (Parser class, also part of MoinMoin).

3   Fetch the page content from the database. This is handled by the DbQueries module.

6–21   This is the code of interest. If the page we are trying to render actually exists in the database, the code here is executed.

7–10   This code keeps track of all visited sessions since the user logged in. The /Wiki/Login directory is used to maintain the list of visited pages.

12   This converts carriage return/line feed combination into a proper newline. This is necessary to perform proper I/O on the string.

13   StringIO is Python's way of performing I/O on a string. This class implements all of the interfaces normally required for performing I/O. The output of the formatter will be written to this string (and we will use it toward the end).

14–15   This creates an instance of the MoinMoin page parser. This parser handles the structured markup.

16   At this point, we have the output of the MoinMoin parser captured in the StringIO object. This output must be processed to perform final substitutions.

17–21   Perform final substitutions (self.form_vars is used as the evaluation environment for these substitutions) and render the page for final substitution into the top-level template.

22–28   If the page did not exist, render the form to ask the user to create the page. In a wiki system, it is considered good form to request that nonexistent pages are created rather than reported as "undefined links."

Other functions.   This discussion has focused on the states related to page creation and viewing. There are a number of other functions in the system: editing pages (very similar to create), viewing the page index, accessing control functions, file uploading/downloading, etc. It should be relatively easy to understand these modules after having seen the detailed walkthrough of the modules presented thus far.

Login.   The `Login` state is essential for understanding how the user gets authenticated and bound to a set of capabilities. It is also essential for understanding how some common navigational items (such as the visited pages) and other important persistent information are maintained. We have already seen a number of states where entries are pulled from the `/Wiki/Login` state directory. Now we'll provide a glimpse of how these values got placed in this directory in the first place. Here is the `process()` method for the `Login` class.

```
1    def process( self ):
2        profile = self.user_profile
3        form_vars = self.form_vars
4        self.query = getQuery(self.db)
5        if not self.validate():
6            raise StageProcessException(self.render())
7
8        username = form_vars["username"]
9        password = form_vars["password"]
10
11       user_info = self.query.lookupUser(username)
12
13       if not len(user_info):
14           profile["login_error"] = "no such user '%s'" % username
15           raise StageProcessException(self.render())
16       elif user_info[0].password != password:
17           profile["login_error"] = "bad password '%s'" % username
18           raise StageProcessException(self.render())
19       else:
20           profile["login_error"] = None
21           del(profile["login_error"])
22
23       profile["username"] = user_info[0].username
24       profile["password"] = user_info[0].password
25       profile["capabilities"] = string.split(user_info[0].capabilities,",")
26       self.user_profile.set_dir("/Wiki/EditPage/wiki_name","FrontPage")
27       self.scheduleState("/Wiki/ShowWikiPage")
```

Much of this code should make sense based on our coverage of earlier modules. In particular, the code in lines 2–21 is dedicated to processing the form inputs (username, password) and checking against the information in the database. If any error occurs during this process, an appropriate error message is assigned to "login_error" and the page is re-rendered. Upon success (lines 23–25), entries are written into the profile. The username, password, and the capabilities in split form are saved into the profile. It may not be apparent from earlier examples–anything can go into the profile, including arbitrary Python list/dictionary data structures and other objects. When the AccessControl module is asked to check a capability, it will obtain the list from the /Wiki/Login directory (which is the current directory when the Login state executes) and perform a simple test for set membership. Upon successful login, we set the name of the page to be displayed (by making an entry in /Wiki/EditPage, line 26) and then schedule the ShowWikiPage state for execution. (Recall from our earlier discussion that the ShowWikiPage looks for pages to be shown by first checking whether the page name appears as an input variable. If not, it checks for whether an entry exists in the /Wiki/EditPage directory.)

The AccessControl Module • The Access Control framework of the wiki system is fairly straightforward. Earlier in this section, we described the capabilities table, which maintains the list of capabilities. The capabilities themselves are useless unless they happen to be used in a user record. Let's take a look at some user records from our current tables:

```
+----------+------------------------------------------------------+
| username | capabilities                                         |
+----------+------------------------------------------------------+
| gkt      | *                                                    |
| guest    | WikiIndex,ShowWikiPage                                |
| pshafaee | *                                                    |
| nina     | CreatePage,EditPage,WikiIndex,ShowWikiPage           |
+----------+------------------------------------------------------+
```

Here you can see that the capabilities are either listed in a comma-separated value format or "*". The "*" is the match-all operator in our capability framework, which means that the users having that capability are gods who rule the universe. These capabilities are loaded at login time and kept in the /Wiki/Login state directory for all access control checks, which are the responsibility of the individual modules.

How does the access control code work? Actually, it is remarkably simple. Let's take a look.

```
1    def checkAccess(user_profile, capability):
2        try:
3            capabilities = user_profile.get_dir("/Wiki/Login/capabilities")
4        except:
5            return 0
6
7        if capabilities[0] == '*':
8            return 1
9
10       return capability in capabilities
```

This method is very straightforward. Given a `user_profile` and a capability to be checked, return 1 if access can be granted, 0 if access is to be denied. The code does the following:

3	Obtains the capabilities that the user actually has from the `/Wiki/Login` directory. We have already covered how this information actually gets loaded into the state directory.
5	If for any reason this information is not found, the fallback position is to return 0, meaning access is unconditionally denied. This could only happen if there were a bug in the login code, which is highly unlikely.
7–8	If the match-all capability has been found, access is unconditionally granted.
10	Finally, once the obvious cases have been considered, check whether the capability is in the list of capabilities. This is Python at its best. You simply do a set membership test on the list of capabilities to determine whether the user has the capability.

SlyWiki Summary

The SlyWiki system is available from our Web site. At the time of writing, many features are being added, with the goal of developing a general-purpose (free) collaboration and file exchange facility. You will want to check our site to learn of the latest updates to the code, and you are invited to join us in adding new features, which are discussed on our Web site (which, incidentally, is written entirely using the SlyWiki system itself) and through user request for comments, which we call enhancement proposals in the spirit of the Python Enhancement Process developed by Guido van Rossum and the core Python language development team.

SlyShopping: Selling with Slither

The NumberGame and SlyWiki have each displayed how easy it is to write powerful applications with Slither. In this section, we will see how Slither can be used to develop a customized e-commerce solution called SlyShopping. SlyShopping is a Web-based shopping cart that will be used to sell books to customers around the world. As in the previous use cases, first we will gather requirements, then develop a design and implementation based on the Slither framework. Since by now you are familiar with how Slither works and with the basics of creating Slither projects, we will limit the implementation discussions to include the key points not covered earlier. We recommend that you look over the source code in order to gain additional practice in using Slither.

Requirements

SlyShopping will be modeled after popular shopping cart systems such as Miva Merchant and OpenMarket. SlyShopping will be based on the concept of an Internet store. The store has three main components. First, there is the storefront. This is where customers are presented with all of the products that are on sale and are given the opportunity to view a detailed description of any specific item. Items may be as complicated or as simple as you like. Since SlyShopping is meant to be a simple implementation of a shopping cart, we will limit the complexity of our items to include a price, brief description, availability indicator, and an optional picture.

The second store component is shoppers. Shoppers must be able to enter the storefront, view the products, and make a purchase. Since our store is on the Internet, our shoppers will need to be presented with an easy-to-use listing of all the products. In this version, we will not categorize the items and we will assume that the user will not need to search for a product in the store. Each shopper will need a basket to store items in while touring the store. We will need to provide the user a view of the basket and some minimal editing options, such as removing an item or reading the description of an item.

As in any other store, the shopper does not need an account to view the store products. However, before a transaction can be completed, the shopper must log in to an existing account. If this is the shopper's first time at the store, the shopper should be presented with an option to open up a new account. After the account has been created, the shopper is greeted with the login. After successfully logging in, shoppers can view their subtotal and any additional fees related to the purchase. In our example, we will exclude tax and shipping charges. Furthermore, we will not provide any facilities for charging the shopper's credit card.

Once a transaction has taken place, the customer is considered to be logged in. The customer's basket is emptied and reset for additional purchase. However, when the customer completes the second round of purchases, the system should recognize that the customer is still logged in and the customer is directed to the checkout page. Customers are considered logged out when they terminate their browser sessions.

The third component in the store will be the administrator's account. All stores have a manager who adds products to the store and periodically updates product descriptions, prices, and availability. Sly-Shopping will need to provide a secured login for the shop manager. Once logged in, the manager can perform any number of administrative operations, such as viewing customer transactions and editing product offerings. The manager should have the option of logging out. Once logged out, the manager will need to log back in before performing any additional administrative actions. Unlike the customer, we do not want to force the manager to close all browser sessions in order to log out of administrative mode.

With these three components we have the skeleton of a basic Internet shopping cart. All of the off-the-shelf solutions are based on these foundational requirements. They have been extended to support more elaborate shop management options, such as providing discounts and sales, better product categorization and departmentalization, and support for credit card processing and basic accounting utilities. These features can easily be added to SlyShopping. They were excluded from our requirements list to simplify the use case. Extend SlyShopping in any way that you please.

Design and Implementation

All requirements can be implemented in four to five hours of programming.

Database Setup • All of SlyShopping's data will be warehoused in a MySQL database called shop. We will need to develop a schema that best describes our data. In Chapter 8 and in the SlyWiki example, we explored some of the basics of relational database design. Thus, we only present the most important details of the SlyShopping schema here, so that we can concentrate on additional Slither features not covered previously. Figure 14–11 depicts all of the relational tables used by Sly-Shopping. The `product` table is used to list all of the products that our store maintains. Some of the fields, such as `id` and `product_id`, will only be displayed to the store manager. The `id` field name is used as the primary key. We use this field in other tables when referring to a specific product. The `product_id` is a unique `id` set by the store manager for internal product tracking. Its value may change, making this field a bad candidate for a primary key.

```
mysql> show tables ;
+-----------------+
| Tables in shop  |
+-----------------+
| AdminUser       |
| Customer        |
| Product         |
| Transaction     |
+-----------------+

mysql> desc AdminUser;
+----------+-------------+------+-----+---------+----------------+
| Field    | Type        | Null | Key | Default | Extra          |
+----------+-------------+------+-----+---------+----------------+
| id       | int(11)     |      | PRI | 0       | auto_increment |
| username | varchar(25) | YES  |     | NULL    |                |
| password | varchar(25) | YES  |     | NULL    |                |
+----------+-------------+------+-----+---------+----------------+

mysql> desc Customer ;
+-------------+--------------+------+-----+---------+----------------+
| Field       | Type         | Null | Key | Default | Extra          |
+-------------+--------------+------+-----+---------+----------------+
| id          | int(11)      |      | PRI | 0       | auto_increment |
| first_name  | varchar(50)  | YES  |     | NULL    |                |
| last_name   | varchar(50)  | YES  |     | NULL    |                |
| street1     | varchar(100) | YES  |     | NULL    |                |
| street2     | varchar(100) | YES  |     | NULL    |                |
| city        | varchar(100) | YES  |     | NULL    |                |
| state       | varchar(100) | YES  |     | NULL    |                |
| country     | varchar(100) | YES  |     | NULL    |                |
| zip         | varchar(25)  | YES  |     | NULL    |                |
| username    | varchar(50)  | YES  |     | NULL    |                |
| password    | varchar(50)  | YES  |     | NULL    |                |
| cc_number   | varchar(20)  | YES  |     | NULL    |                |
| cc_exp_month| char(2)      | YES  |     | NULL    |                |
| cc_exp_year | varchar(4)   | YES  |     | NULL    |                |
+-------------+--------------+------+-----+---------+----------------+

mysql> desc Product ;
+-------------+--------------+------+-----+---------+----------------+
| Field       | Type         | Null | Key | Default | Extra          |
+-------------+--------------+------+-----+---------+----------------+
| id          | int(11)      |      | PRI | 0       | auto_increment |
| product_id  | varchar(25)  |      | UNI |         |                |
| name        | varchar(25)  | YES  |     | NULL    |                |
| description | text         | YES  |     | NULL    |                |
| price       | float(10,2)  | YES  |     | NULL    |                |
| in_stock    | tinyint(4)   | YES  |     | NULL    |                |
| img_link    | text         | YES  |     | NULL    |                |
+-------------+--------------+------+-----+---------+----------------+

mysql> desc Transaction ;
+---------------+-------------+------+-----+---------+----------------+
| Field         | Type        | Null | Key | Default | Extra          |
+---------------+-------------+------+-----+---------+----------------+
| id            | int(11)     |      | PRI | 0       | auto_increment |
| date_and_time | datetime    | YES  |     | NULL    |                |
| customer_id   | int(11)     | YES  |     | NULL    |                |
| product_id    | varchar(50) | YES  |     | NULL    |                |
| quantity      | int(11)     | YES  |     | NULL    |                |
| total         | float(10,2) | YES  |     | NULL    |                |
+---------------+-------------+------+-----+---------+----------------+
```

Figure 14–11
SlyShopping Database Schema

The `Customer` table is used to store customer contact and account information. We also store the customer's login information here, which is used when the customer chooses to complete the transaction. If the username supplied by the customer at the time of checkout does not exist in this table, we assume that the customer does not have an account with our store. As a result, the username is expected to be unique.

The username is a good candidate primary key. However, if the username is selected as the primary key, the user cannot change the username in the future; doing so would lead to select, update, and delete anomalies. For example, if the username changes, all transaction entries that reference the username will no longer have a valid meaning. We will use the auto-incremented integer field as the primary key. This allows us to make changes to all other fields without suffering any consequences.

Another interesting point about the `Customer` table is the storage of the contact information. What would we have to do if we decided to store a separate billing address? In the current schema design, we would need to add additional `billing_street`, `billing_city`, `billing_state`, `billing_zip`, and `billing_country` fields. We are adding rows as columns; although the meanings of the new fields are different from those storing the contact address, the type of data stored in the field is the same. The better solution would be to create another table used only to store contact information. In addition to the contact fields, we would add a `customer_id` field to associate a record with a customer, and a `type` field to provide meaning to the data (i.e., indicate if the record corresponds to billing, contact, or shipping information). Since having additional tables indirectly implies additional business logic code for managing the data, we have decided to include the contact information and user account information in a single table to simplify implementation details.

The `Transaction` table is used to track customer transactions. The data in this table are essentially read-only, as they describe actions that a customer has taken. The `AdminUser` table is used to manage account information for the administrative users. Many medium- to large-size shops typically have multiple managers, each with varying degrees of access to store administration privileges. By storing administrator accounts in a table apart from customer accounts, we can easily expand SlyShopping in the future to include access control information for store managers. In this version, we will assume that there is only one store manager. Furthermore, we will have to enter the manager's login information using the MySQL monitor application, since by default all the tables are empty.

All of the SQL code required to create these tables is included with the SlyShopping source. The details are covered in Chapter 8.

Slither States • SlyShopping will be developed as a single Slither project with multiple states. Based on the requirements, there will be two separate sets of interfaces, the storefront and store administration. Slither provides several features that make access control and user session management a breeze, allowing us easily to support both types of interfaces in a single project. In the discussion that follows, we assume that you have already set up a basic project site for SlyShopping and have made all of the necessary configuration changes needed to access the default render page.

Figure 14–12 depicts the logical states required to fulfill all of our requirements. The states related to the storefront are separated from those used to manage the store. Although both sets of states are implemented in a single Slither project, we will consider them separately; there are no logical connections, indicating very little if any code-sharing between the states.

Based on the number of connections to and from the Product List state, we can safely choose this state as the default state that the user is directed to. The render() method of the project class will need to be modified to display the product list. Doing so will allow us to default to this page after each state execution. Figure 14–13 lists all of the code required to accomplish this task.

In Chapter 13 we explored how Slither automatically dispatches states based on the URL. Here we take advantage of the same machinery to manually execute a state's render() method and retrieve the resulting product list page. This avoids having to copy and paste the render method logic of the Product List state into the SlyShopping project render() method, allowing us to reuse the same code. You may be wondering why on line 7 we are changing the UserProfile directory. When the Product List state is executed, it expects that the UserProfile will be in the appropriate directory. This task is automatically performed by the dispatcher and we will need to do the same thing if we expect to have the same results when executing the state code. On line 8 we return the rendered result of the Product List state.

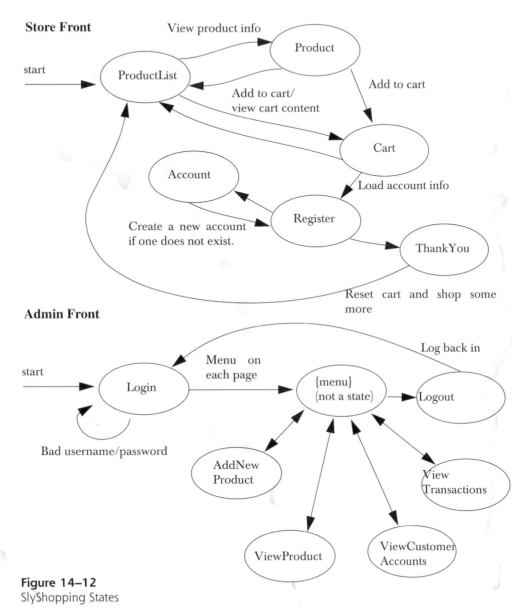

Store Front

View product info

start → ProductList

Product

Add to cart/
view cart content

Add to cart

Cart

Load account info

Account

Create a new account
if one does not exist.

Register

ThankYou

Admin Front

Reset cart and shop some
more

Log back in

start → Login

Menu on
each page

{menu}
(not a state)

Logout

Bad username/password

AddNew
Product

View
Transactions

ViewProduct

ViewCustomer
Accounts

Figure 14–12
SlyShopping States

Alternatively, we could have included all of the code used to render the product list page in the project render() method, but this would greatly limit how we access and use the product list. The product list could be rendered only by causing the project to display the default render() method. Beside listing the products, we would like to provide

```
1    def render( self ):
2
3         # load the product list module
4         prod_list_mod_profile = self.load_state_module( "/Store/ProductList.render"
)
5
6         # change to the appropriate dir
7         change_cwd( prod_list_mod_profile['full_path'] )
8
9         return prod_list_mod_profile['state'].render()
```

Figure 14–13
Project's render() Method

links that will allow us to add the product to the user's cart, view detailed product descriptions, and direct the shopper to the checkout page. In the traditional Slither design, we would create a state and use the render() method to display the product list and use the process() method to perform actions on a specific product. Listing products and performing operations is a self-contained task that is better implemented as a state.

Since SlyShopping uses MySQL to store data, we will need to overload the project's load_plugins() method to initialize and add a MySQL connection to the plug-in list. Figure 14–14 lists all of the code required to use the wpl.DBFactory utility to create and maintain a DB connection.

On line 7 we create the connection and on line 8 we add the connection to the plugins table. Later, when implementing the logical states, we can take advantage of this connection as if it were a member variable. We also take this opportunity to create and bind a wpl.Logger instance. We can use the Logger to log actions taken by the states. This is useful both for debugging purposes and gathering usage information.

```
1    def load_plugins( self ):
2         # create and add logger plugin
3         logger = LogWriter( self.project_profile['state_log_file_name'], log_details = 0 )
4         self.plugin_table.addPlugin( 'logger', logger )
5
6         # create a DB connection
7         db = getNewMySQLDataAccess( self.project_profile[ 'db_conf' ] )
8         self.plugin_table.addPlugin( 'db', db )
```

Figure 14–14
Project's load_plugin() Method

SlyShopping Logical State Design

As identified earlier, the most popular state in the storefront is the Product List state. Figure 14–16 lists the Product List code. On lines 4 and 5 we set the default HTML page to render for this state. The file `ProductList.html` (Figure 14–15) contains a number of WriteProcessor looping rules that are used to list the data retrieved from the database. Pay close attention to lines 16 and 21. Here we are generating dynamic links to access other states. The links include parameters for passing in a product ID. When implementing the `Product` state, we will look for this parameter and use it in rendering the detailed product description page. On line 21, we pass in both the product ID and an operation parameter with the hard-coded value `add`. As you will see, the `Cart` state performs a number of operations and, since the operations are slightly different from one another, we use the `operations` parameter to tailor what the state should do with the product ID that is passed in. In the product list view, the desired action is to add the product to the

```
1       <center><b>The Store</b></center>
2       <p>
3       <table border="1">
4
5         <tr>
6           <td><i><b>Product ID</b></i></td>
7           <td><i><b>Product Name</b></i></td>
8           <td><i><b>Price</b></i></td>
9           <td><i><b>Description</b></i></td>
10          <td><i><b>Image</b></i></td>
11          <td><i><b>Add to Cart</b></i></td>
12        </tr>
13
14      """
15        <tr>
16          <td><a href="<<base_project_url>>/Store/Product.render?id=<<id>>"><<product_id>></a></td>
17          <td><<name>></td>
18          <td><<price>></td>
19          <td><<description>></td>
20          <td><<img_link>></td>
21          <td><a href="<<base_project_url>>/Store/Cart.process?operation=add&id=<<id>>" >add</a></td>
22        </tr>
23      """
24
25      </table>
26
27      <p>
28      <center><a href="<<base_project_url>>/Store/Cart.render">View Shopping Cart</a></center>
```

Figure 14–15
SlyShopping `ProductList.html`

cart; hence, the operation parameter is hardwired to take the value add. (See Figure 14–16.)

Looking at Figure 14–16, the bulk of the work performed by the Product List state is on lines 12–14, where we retrieve a list of rows from the Product table. A majority of the states follow the same pattern of retrieving db information in the render() method and using the process() method to perform some operation on a selected row. This is fitting with most e-commerce applications. Such applications are gateways to the data stored on server-side databases. The Web application performs very little processing on the data supplied. Instead, a bulk of the application is centered around validating user input, directing the user to the correct state, and submitting and retrieving data from the database.

```
1    class ProductList( State ):
2
3        def init( self ):
4            self.prod_file = './ProductList.html'
5            self.set_encode_file_name( self.prod_file )
6
7        def process( self ):
8            raise StageProcessException( self.render() )
9
10       def render( self ):
11
12           self.db.execute( """
13           SELECT id, name, product_id, description, img_link, price
14           FROM Product """ )
15
16           result = self.db.getRecords()
17
18           # add items to the record to be looped over
19           for rec in result:
20               rec[ 'base_project_url' ] = self.form_vars[ 'base_project_url' ]
21
22               rec[ 'price' ] = "$ %s"%( string.strip( "%8.2f"%( rec['price'] ) ) )
23
24           emitter = StringEmitter()
25           writer = WriteProcessor( self.prod_file, self.search_path, self.form_vars, emitter, triple_quotes="YNumberGame" )
26
27           writer.addDictListLoopingRule( result, ['product_id', 'id', 'name', \
28                                          'price', 'description', 'img_link', 'base_project_url' ] )
29
30           writer.process()
31           return emitter.getResult()
```

Figure 14–16
SlyShopping ProductList state

The Product and Cart states follow the same implementation details, so they are not included here. The Register state, however, has a slightly different implementation. Based on our requirements, the customer must log in to an existing account before completing a transaction. Once logged in, the user can check out any number of times without having to log in again. As a result, the Register state sometimes reroutes the shopper to an account login or account creation state if the shopper has not yet logged in. Figure 14–17 is a listing of the Register state. To meet these requirements, the render() method (lines 13–17) has been set up to check if the user has already logged in by looking for a valid customer ID that is stored in the shopper's session object. If a valid ID is not found, the state renders the account login form. Otherwise, we don't do anything and move right on to the process() method.

The process() method once again checks for a valid customer ID. If one exists, then there is no need to authenticate the shopper. The absence of a valid customer ID indicates that the shopper reached the process() method as a result of filling out the account login form. We then authenticate the username and password against the database. Any number of errors may be encountered during authentication, such as an invalid username or password. In each case, we set an error message and raise a StageProcessException, which causes Slither to stop processing and redisplay the account login page with a detailed description of the error encountered. On successful login, we set the valid customer ID in the shopper's session object so that the shopper can silently avoid the login process the next time the Register state is accessed.

You should have a good understanding of how the storefront is implemented. Now we will concentrate on the details of the store administration states. In both the storefront and the administration states, the bulk of the business logic is centered around retrieving and storing data in the database. However, the administration states differ in two respects. First, all of the administration states are considered protected and should only be allowed access by users who have logged in as store managers. Second, we would like to display a navigation menu that will help the administrator select an operation. We will explore a subset of the administration states to depict our strategy for dealing with these two differences.

One of the most useful features of Slither is its mapping of the extra path component of the URL to a project state on the server. This feature allows a developer to organize states into any number of subdirectories relative to the project directory. More important, this feature

```
1     class Register( State ):
2
3         def init( self ):
4             self.set_encode_file_name( './Register.html' )
5
6         def process( self ):
7             username = self.form_vars.get( 'username', '' )
8             password = self.form_vars.get( 'password', '' )
9
10            customer_id = self.user_profile.get( 'customer_id', 0 )
11
12            if customer_id < 1:
13                # check for login and password
14                if self.form_vars.get( 'username', '' ) == '' or\
15                    self.form_vars.get( 'password', '' ) == '':
16                    self.logger.writeWarning( "Customer failed to login \
17            with username '%s' and password '%s'."%( self.form_vars.get( 'username', '' ), \
18                                                    self.form_vars.get( 'password', '' )
19                                                        )
20                                            )
21                    self.add_var( "error_msg", "Invalid username or password.")
22                    raise StageProcessException( self.render() )
23
24                # auth. agains the DB
25                self.db.execute( """
26                SELECT *
27                FROM Customer
28                WHERE username = '%s' AND password = '%s'"""%( self.db.clean( username ), \
29                                                    self.db.clean( password )
30                                                        )
31                    )
32
33
34                result = self.db.getRecords()
35                if len( result ) > 0:
36                    self.user_profile['customer_id'] = int(result[0]['id'] )
37                    self.logger.writeEntry( "Customer '%s' logged into the sys-
tem."%(self.form_vars['username'] ) )
38                else:
39                    self.logger.writeWarning( "Customer failed to login with \
40                    username '%s' and password '%s'."%( self.form_vars.get( 'username', '' ), \
41                                                    self.form_vars.get( 'password', '' )
42                                                        )
43                                            )
44        self.add_var( "error_msg", "Username or password did not match database records." )
45                    raise StageProcessException( self.render() )
46
47            # schedule the showing of the main admin page
48            self.scheduleState( "/Store/ThankYou.render" )
49
```

Figure 14–17
SlyShopping Register state

```
50        def render( self ):
51            customer_id = self.user_profile.get( 'customer_id', 0 )
52
53            if customer_id < 1:
54                # display the login form
55                return self.encode()
56            else:
57                pass
```

Figure 14–17
(Continued)

allows a developer to treat states in a particular subdirectory as logically grouped. In other words, Slither allows the developer to perform high-level branching based on the subdirectory that houses the state the user is attempting to access. We rely on this feature when implementing the access control logic required to protect access to the administrative operations.

Our strategy is simple: If we group all of the administration states in a single subdirectory, we can check the user's access rights each time that the user attempts to access a resource in the subdirectory. The alternative would be to include access control checks at the start of each `render()` and `process()` method for each store administration state. The ability to work with grouped states provides a great deal of power to the developer and drastically reduces the number of lines of code required to implement any access control system. In SlyShopping, we group states in a single subdirectory, but this is not a limitation. You can create any number of additional subdirectories for fine-grained organization of states. Similar to an LDAP schema, you can add logic to govern which manager has access to which subdirectories. Slither uses a fundamental file system concept to provide a foundation for building complex and highly customizable access control systems.

After storing all of the administration states in the `Admin` subdirectory, we overload the project's `preprocess()` method to include the access logic. The `preprocess()` method is invoked before any state is dispatched. This provides us with an opportunity to validate the state being accessed against the user's access rights. We can then decide to let the user continue and eventually access the state, or redirect the user to a login page. Figure 14–18 lists the `preprocess()` code that performs this operation.

On line 6, we use basic string operations to inspect the URL's extra path value for the `'/Admin'` string. If such a string exists, then we are sure the user is attempting to access a state that is stored in this

```
1     def preprocess( self ):
2
3                # check if user is attempting to access admin page
4                top_dir = self.parse_state_path( self.project_profile[ 'project_state_path' ]
) ['path']
5
6                if top_dir == '/Admin' and \
7                  string.find( self.project_profile[ 'project_state_path' ], '/Admin/Login.' )
== -1: # we want to allow these Admin request
8                     # if so, make sure user has logged in
9                     self.user_profile.create( "/Admin/Login" )
10                    self.user_profile.cd( "/Admin/Login" )
11
12                    if self.user_profile.get( 'login_id' , 0 ) <= 0:
13                         # invalid user
14                         self.project_profile[ 'project_state_path' ] = "/Admin/Login.render"
15                         self.logger.writeWarning( "User does not have a valid session; sending
user to the login page." )
16                    else:
17                         self.logger.writeDebug( "Valid session discovered.")
18                else:
19                    # this is not a protected state; allow access as before
20                    pass
```

Figure 14–18
Project's preprocess() method

subdirectory, and since this subdirectory is protected, we must make sure that the user has adequate access rights. If such a string cannot be found, the user is attempting to access a non-protected state and we continue to the state dispatch phase. By searching for '/Admin', we are implicitly blocking access to all states as well as subdirectories relative to the Admin directory. This feature is handy, since we can add any number of additional directories and states under Admin and we are guaranteed protection.

On line 12, we check the user's session object for a valid manager login. Much like customer account authentication, the presence of a valid login ID in the session profile indicates that the user has successfully logged in. One interesting scenario occurs when a user attempts to access an administration state without the proper access right. In this case, the desired outcome is to direct the user to the administration login page. On line 14, we do just that by rewriting the URL that the user is attempting to access to point to the store administration login page.

As you might expect, the Login state implementation is very similar to the shopper account authentication performed by the Register state. We request from the user a username and password combination that is verified against the database records. The `Logout` state is quite interesting. Since our authentication test is limited to checking for a valid login ID in the session object, all we have to do is clear the set login ID; that's all the `Logout` state does.

Now we will explore the implementation of a menu bar. When a manager logs in, he or she is greeted by a menu bar that lists all of the administrative options that SlyShopping supports. Figure 14–19 depicts a screen capture of this interface. In the Slither design philosophy, each state has a single `render()` method that is invoked to paint the page, which makes it difficult to render a certain interface component on a number of pages. One strategy would be to include the code needed to render that component in each state. This limits our flexibility in the future, because a small change in the component will require repeated changes in multiple states. The preferred solution is always to render the menu when the user is logged in as an administrator.

Slither provides several implementation options for rendering the administration menu. The first option is to use the `page_vars` dictionary. The `page_vars` dictionary stores a set of bindings that are used

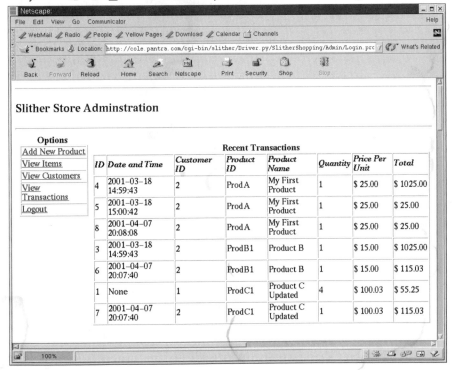

Figure 14–19
Screen Capture of a Sample Admin Page

by WebForm to render the final template. As a result, you can create a function that is responsible for rendering just the menu and then bind the results to a name in the `page_vars` dictionary. The binding can happen in the project's `preprocess()` method, which is invoked just before Slither renders the final page and after the last state has been executed. We would bind the variable only if the user is logged in as a manager. This option is best suited for rendering menus that include dynamic links. For instance, the SlyWiki system uses `page_vars` to render the quick list. The list is consistently changing, requiring it to be rendered each time.

The second option is to statically embed the menu in the main template. All Slither projects include a base template used to render the results of executing a state. By including our menu in this template file, we are guaranteed that it will display on every page. Since we want the menu to display only when the user is logged in as an administrator, we will need to select the appropriate base template based on the user's access level. In each of the administration states, we invoke the project's `set_main_template()` method to change the base template. We could have made this method call in the project file, but we wanted to depict how this could be done at the state level.

This concludes our discussion of SlyShopping. You are encouraged to walk carefully through all of the code and explore how the concepts can be applied to your own project. We have attempted to display some of the major features of Slither, as well as various strategies for programming a Slither project. The take-home message is that Slither has all of the features required to build a portal site, without any of the programming complications.

Summary

In this chapter, we have shown three examples that tie together most of the programming ideas presented in this book. We have used the Slither foundation classes to develop the NumberGame (a very simple application to show the key aspects involved in building a typical Slither application) and two moderately complex applications, SlyWiki (a collaborative text-processing application) and SlitherShopping (a shopping portal application). These applications provide ample evidence that Slither can compete with the "big iron" frameworks to develop serious Web applications without the complexity. We encourage you to download these applications and try them out for yourself.

Setting Up Apache and Secure Sockets Layer

Security is the one aspect of doing business on the Web that is likely to consume many resources, even to get it up and running. This appendix covers how to get a secure Web server installation performed using the Apache Web Server and `mod_ssl`, an Apache module that effectively adds the secure capabilities to AWS.

Configuring Secure HTTP

Getting this working will test your patience. There are technical and nontechnical issues that amount to what are typically unanticipated challenges, and it is advisable to get a fully working nonsecure[1] setup in place before exploring this option with any seriousness.

HTTP is a protocol based on TCP/IP using socket connections. Secure HTTP (HTTPS hereafter) is a protocol based on TCP/IP using *secure* socket connections. The idea of secure sockets is that the communication between a browser and the server will take place over an encrypted channel.

In order for SSL communication to work, the browser and the server must use some form of public key encryption. This requires an exchange of keys to take place. Encryption happens on both sides of the equation. The browser encrypts requests, and the server encrypts responses.

---

1. We prefer the term *nonsecure* to *insecure*. Using the term *insecure* gives the impression that the Web server has feelings and is struggling with self-confidence.

Certificates and Certificate Authorities

A certificate is needed if you have any intentions to use your configured Web server for any serious Web commerce application. Certificate generation is supported under Unix with the OpenSSL toolkit; this toolkit can be easily downloaded and installed. What exactly is a certificate? A certificate is a standard way of encoding your public (and private) key for secure communication. Certificates are used in a number of contexts (the Web being just one).

Anyone can generate a certificate. This presents a bit of a problem when it comes to the issue of trust. If you and another user (Bob) can generate a certificate, it is possible for both of you to generate the same certificate. While the odds are low that you and Bob will ever know that you have generated the same certificate (key information), it is entirely possible that a malicious user (or a benevolent hacker) could generate the same certificate and be able to crack what appeared to be a secure communication channel. The recognition of this fact led the browser purveyors to push for certificate authorities, which are trusted companies that can digitally sign a certificate that will be considered trustworthy to the major browsers.

This sets the stage for understanding what to do after getting secure Apache configured. For the purposes of development and/or just tinkering around, it suffices to generate a self-signed certificate (a process that is automated by the latest Apache and mod_ssl Makefile). When you are about to go commercial, it is imperative that you invest in a certificate from one of the certificate authorities. While we are not generally in the business of endorsing particular companies (as we really think all of this stuff should be free), we personally own a certificate from Thawte, which is a company owned and operated by VeriSign.[2]

What Will You Need?

In order to set up Apache with SSL support, you will need to download code from http://www.modssl.org. Secure HTTP is supported in Apache using extension modules. (Apache provides a complete API for extending Apache with new features.) Thus both the Apache Web Server source code and mod_ssl source code will be required in order to build a secure version of Apache. Releases of mod_ssl are tied to releases of

---

2. Thawte specializes in support for the Apache Web Server. Their pricing is reasonable. They even provide support and online documentation to help with setup issues; however, you probably will not need this much after reading our discussion.

Apache, so it is necessary to ensure that the version of `mod_ssl` you have downloaded matches the version of Apache you have downloaded.

Upon unpacking the `mod_ssl` source code, you will learn of other details that at first will lead you to believe that the process is going to be time-consuming and cumbersome. The installation instructions mention that you will have to download a number of other packages, which are all mentioned when we get around to actually configuring the Apache and `mod_ssl` combination. This list of packages more often than not does *not* apply to Linux users but to other Unix platforms (e.g., Solaris) where open-source packages must typically be installed from scratch. Users of RedHat, Mandrake, and Debian are likely to find the needed packages installed in the latest distributions.[3]

In any event, you should not be discouraged by having to install the mentioned packages. It is simply a matter of going to the site, downloading the package, configuring (using the default configuration options in most cases), and installing, as we have shown many times throughout the text.

Building Secure HTTP

The build process for the combination of Apache and `mod_ssl` is a bit unusual compared to how most open-source or GPL packages are typically built. The configuration is done in the `mod_ssl` directory. The build and install are conducted from the Apache directory. There are a number of reasons for this:

- The `mod_ssl` configuration process actually works by making a number of patches to the Apache source code.
- After the patches are made, the Apache configuration script is run. Thus when configuring `mod_ssl`, it is necessary to also configure Apache with any desired initial options. Everything we have shown earlier with Apache is still relevant (and highly necessary) to get the secure Web server configured.
- After everything is configured, the Apache source directory is now configured with the extra code to support the SSL functionality. This is why the build must be performed from the Apache directory and not the `mod_ssl` directory.

It all seems a bit awkward the first time one does this, which is why we have taken the trouble to assure you that (despite its awkwardness) it

---

3. The OpenSSL package is increasingly becoming available as the export laws of the U.S. cease to be annoying.

can all be done without losing one's mind in the process. The Apache
2.0 effort seems to be working toward the ultimate goal of integrating all
these efforts, such as mod_ssl, but appears to be some time away from
achieving this result. We recommend using the combination of Apache
1.x and mod_ssl for the foreseeable future.

In this example, we assume you have unpacked the code to a
hypothetical build directory (subdirectory named "build" in your
home directory) with the following packages:

```
apache_1.3.19
mm-0.9
openssl-0.9.4
modssl-2.8.2+1.3.19
rsaref-2.0
(and whatever)
```

To configure the secure Web server, the following must be done in the
modssl-2.8.2+1.3.19 directory:

```
./configure --with-mm=../mm-0.9 \
  --with-apache=../apache_1.3.19 \
  --with-ssl=../openssl-0.9.4 \
  --prefix$HOME/apache \
    --htdocsdir=$HOME/web/htdocs \
    --cgidir=$HOME/web/cgi-bin --iconsdir=$HOME/web/icons \
    --with-port=8080 --server-uid=george --server-gid=george
```

The options specific to the mod_ssl configuration are shown in
boldface. We have also added all of the options to build the secure
server to work similarly to the configuration we performed earlier for
the nonsecure Apache installation.

After completing the configuration, it is a matter of going to the
Apache source code directory (here apache_1.3.19) and doing the
build by running the make command. This will start the compilation of
many files as before, and should eventually result in the secure version
of Apache Web Server being built.

At this point, it is not okay to run make install. You must
now go through the process of certfication, which involves generating a server key and certificate that can be used to test your installation. We discuss how to do this and the process for getting a signed
certificate in the next section.

Certification

Certificate generation is best done with the `openssl` command. This command can be found in the `openssl-0.9.4 build` directory, which was required to do the Apache + `mod_ssl build` in the preceding section.

This discussion will center on how to get Apache + `mod_ssl` configured to work with a certificate that is ultimately signed by a company called Thawte Consulting (a VeriSign company).[4]

The process of acquiring a certificate involves a number of steps:

1. Acquiring a domain name
2. Key Generation
3. Generating a "CSR" or "Certificate Signing Request"
4. Generating a Temporary "Self-Signed" Certificate
5. Configuring the Temporary "Self-Signed" Certificate
6. Waiting
7. Configuring the Signed Certificate from Thawte

Acquiring a Domain Name

This has become a relatively painless process in recent years. Network Solutions is probably the most famous service, having been the original registrar for the Internet. We will assume that you are able to acquire a domain name.

Key Generation

Now you need to use `openssl` to generate a server key. It is important to note beforehand that this key must be kept private. If someone other than you or a trusted member of your organization gets hold of this key, it is possible (and likely) that the security of your site can be compromised easily.

```
$ openssl genrsa -des3 -rand file1:file2:...:file5 -out
www.virtualhost.com.key 1024
```

This generates an RSA key using DES3 encryption. The `-rand` option indicates that the following files are to be used to seed the random number generator. You can choose any five files but should ensure they are sufficiently "large" (where large is anything over 1 MB in size.) The `-out` should be followed by the domain name acquired in the pre-

---

4. We use Thawte Consulting and have been pleased with both their product and service; however, we make no guarantees that their products and services will meet your requirements. Please see http://www.thawte.com for more details.

ceding section. This file, strictly speaking, need not be named exactly the same as your domain name; however, by naming it this way you have some assurance of being able to remember the name later. The last parameter, `1024`, indicates the number of bits to use for the key length.

Let's take a look at how the key is generated for **my_new_domain.com**:

```
[gkt@www BookOpenSSL]$ openssl genrsa -des3 -rand /bin/ls:/bin/cat
-out www.my_new_domain.com.key 1024
56564 semi-random bytes loaded
Generating RSA private key, 1024 bit long modulus
...............++++++
..................++++++
e is 65537 (0x10001)
Enter PEM pass phrase: xyzpdq
Verifying password - Enter PEM pass phrase: xyzpdq
```

Once this is done, you can verify that there is a certificate using the **cat** command:

```
$ cat www.my_new_domain.com.key
-----BEGIN RSA PRIVATE KEY-----
Proc-Type: 4,ENCRYPTED
DEK-Info: DES-EDE3-CBC,E58DFA36DC066C31

pFriKLNkamzh/k1sD4X4Cnfz6GZAdhWAy+4embKHMsfntMZaHTg2VcqophtoJqsQ
cu0sZCkbTX74EwY3PRrhh0GkuAMRhvxs1LRFkFiU+cWjnE7QJ5PSrslYgo7cdh12
OVDDy+J3zSBpxskhFJjRD5r9TEMWro40YBsE0F0FG7yyEIHhMLu/VWylMxNogOyG
GH7FWSRPvAo98rtdlY7IgJH7YhPy7Z5BQMbVxzZ5IN0tDom4pK+UxM0YGWx07EQE
1jJHZcC5ArIR0ma+kQxMBqFNS55t8p8yGgZHetaBsEm0GdP0VbKNEOUxIki9qXSg
R/6U9L46LqWi2/GaRa41l4f6gK5bg8HXAbdkKrWBLiMvdK2+gwJz18pPgtJ6egO2
jKAp4Ff7jms5mOgLb2Q5V3IhwRMpcQ7fJUOSoluXhklEVXPDRvu+jf5jZQhpR4mc
dnKiowfHL3zEI9vljQoegy+qM47MGjAGoRdMMREVPBcci6fzuBalgUMnD5wuufxV
f1nUe2oen+HyMMGD8kGHJdigBKDdV/JzR3TAqA1PwEhDQcEwoJ33vwTULvJTx8mI
N0JrTEl5mmqJUFlxPTkp4Q9Afb9LzA9nR/CzMzJ3VdYcVwU5k8C/lxKWOpenTje1
mbc+HMLq8gYhk+Ci/uk2SidqPsnSx5v98Mz9cBw5u0/Wi0ThVOqvZ6yzx1swgXhe
HD2Fd049jtuUIm099/Tseht3eyzAA/oHuHFTUXO7s0Zx3OyBN/BOy8eLXi1j9J/Y
Kb7OFaiWCdaM6Hd9Al/uyr7nttWiIkeLwL50JqlffT6dMaL6e0y9Pw==
-----END RSA PRIVATE KEY-----
```

Generating a CSR Request

Once you have generated a key, the next step is to generate a CSR request. The CSR request, similar to the key, is generated with the `openssl` command using the `req` subcommand:

```
$ openssl req -new -key www.virtualhost.com.key \
  -out www.virtualhost.com.csr
```

This is, of course, all typed on one line. We have shown it on two lines for the purpose of formatting. The "\" is how you can type a single command using multiple physical input lines in all Unix shells. A few words are in order about this command. First and foremost, the key generated in the previous step must be specified using the -key option. This is what formally ties your server's private key to the request. The -new indicates the request is a "new" one and -out the file is needed to contain the request. It is this file that will be sent to the Certificate Authority for signing and to issue your server certificate.

The following shows what happens when you run this command for your own domain name:

```
[gkt@www BookOpenSSL]$ openssl req -new -key www.my_new_domain.com.key
-out www.my_new_domain.csr
Using configuration from /usr/local/ssl/openssl.cnf
Enter PEM pass phrase:
You are about to be asked to enter information that will be
incorporated
into your certificate request.
What you are about to enter is what is called a Distinguished Name or a
DN.
There are quite a few fields but you can leave some blank
For some fields there will be a default value,
If you enter '.', the field will be left blank.
-----
Country Name (2 letter code) [AU]:US
State or Province Name (full name) [Some-State]:Illinois
Locality Name (eg, city) []:Chicago
Organization Name (eg, company) [Internet Widgits Pty Ltd]:The Ultimate
Gadget Company
Organizational Unit Name (eg, section) []:
Common Name (eg, YOUR name) []:George K. Thiruvathukal
Email Address []:gkt@toolsofcomputing.com

Please enter the following 'extra' attributes
to be sent with your certificate request
A challenge password []:
An optional company name []:
```

We have indicated in bold the text that is being typed by you. When making a request, you are prompted for a number of things. You should take special care to ensure the information being typed is meaningful and is not just random noise. The extra attributes should be left empty

as we have done here. Again, you can verify that this step was successful by displaying the resulting file:

```
[gkt@www BookOpenSSL]$ cat www.my_new_domain.csr
-----BEGIN CERTIFICATE REQUEST-----
MIIB5DCCAU0CAQAwgaMxCzAJBgNVBAYTAlVTMREwDwYDVQQIEwhJbGxpbm9pczEQ
MA4GA1UEBxMHQ2hpY2FnbzEkMCIGA1UEChMbVGhlIFVsdGltYXRlIEdhZGdldCBD
b21wYW55MSAwHgYDVQQDExdHZW9yZ2UgSy4gVGhpcnV2YXRodWthbDEnMCUGCSqG
SIb3DQEJARYYZ2t0QHRvb2xzb2Zjb21wdXRpbmcuY29tMIGfMA0GCSqGSIb3DQEB
AQUAA4GNADCBiQKBgQC5kh23e9SpWu2y+uct9Ql0UGSuiEJBalUZzDqQvAREirZb
hmso243LgLVefhvKj3oVz2fo67NTlMPwgPMdEvt9PsVyULWt2RNGlFAADa6PvjYU
7LUiVgk5rqTTwTRQRDsub8jRnOg+taHGACKBW1htkl93E12nbG/kR07KtZ0I0QID
AQABoAAwDQYJKoZIhvcNAQEEBQADgYEAPZt09d3Arlj6EHM4aiRQ/mmF6nKoN4dU
nZYisiyQ3ZxYd6FD7hE/k544AoScWa0esAgvax2ZpuLp2OoCBnyrSjcvm9GnlhJ7
If56eK0MwXq6JBpJD/P+oDetpOUVhVYLU5m1yArfKcLhK+Ji8kTXgZWAjyZGVX4V
TJT9nEFI+OO=
-----END CERTIFICATE REQUEST-----
```

Assuming that all has gone well, the `.csr` file will contain text similar
to the above. The opening and closing stanzas indicate that the content
is in fact a certificate request.

This request must be sent to Thawte (or to whatever certificate
authority you decide to use). If you decide to go with some company
other than Thawte, take care to check their rules for CSR generation, as
there may be slight differences from what we have shown here.

▸ **TIP:**

You now have a CSR. This file is important and is the only file you need to send
to the certificate authority (Thawte). The CA may also ask you to supply other
documentation as part of the certification process, but will not ask you for your
private key or anything else pertaining to the private key, such as your
password.

Self-Signed Certificates

The notion of a self-signed certificate is what allows you to get a
"secure" site up until the CA is able to issue your certificate formally.
The process can sometimes take a few days. A self-signed certficate
allows you to get started but should not be relied upon for anything that
requires near bulletproof security. To generate the certificate, the
`openssl` command is again used:

```
$ openssl x509 -req -days 90 -in www.my_new_domain.com.csr \
-signkey www.my_new_domain.com.key -out www.my_new_domain.com.crt
```

This generates a certificate that is good for 90 days. You must supply the `.csr` and `.key` files that were generated in the preceding sections.

This results in a certificate (`www.my_new_domain.crt`) that can be used by the Apache and `mod_ssl` combination.

Completing the Apache Installation and Configuration

At long last it is now possible to complete the installation of the `mod_ssl`-enabled Apache configuration. From the Apache build directory, go ahead and install:

```
$ make install
```

This will install the binaries for the Apache Web Server just as we did earlier in the book when installing Apache without SSL support. If you are prompted for any information about certificates, just go ahead and fill out the requested information. We will be installing our own self-signed certificate at the end. (Some of the releases of Apache automatically perform the steps of temporary certificate generation. We do it separately to avoid confusion.)

Once the binaries are installed, the final step is to edit the Apache configuration file, which is `$HOME/apache/conf/httpd.conf`, and to ensure that the `.key` and `.crt` files are being used. This is done by setting the `SSLCertificateFile` and `SSLCertificateKeyFile` properties to the absolute path where the files you generated are located. We suggest that you create a directory `$HOME/apache/certs` and place the `.crt` and `.key` files there. We further suggest that you make this directory unreadable to other users on the system (`chmod 700 $HOME/apache/certs`). Then set the variables. On my system, `$HOME` expands to `/home/gkt`, so I would do the following:

```
SSLCertificateFile /home/gkt/apache/certs www.my_new_domain.com.crt
SSLCertificateKeyFile /home/gkt/apache/certs/www.my_new_domain.com.key
```

Starting the Secure Server

Assuming you have done everything correctly, you can now start the server:

```
$ $HOME/apache/bin/apachectl start_ssl
```

Then you can test everything, using your Web browser to connect to `https://www.my_new_domain.com` or `http://my_new_domain.com`.

Waiting for and Installing the Signed Certificate

As mentioned, you may have to wait for several days to receive the server certificate from the certificate authority. Once it arrives (usually by downloading from the Web), you must copy the certificate into a file (which could be named the same as the self-signed certificate) and then copy this file into the `$HOME/apache/certs` directory that was created in the preceding section. Choosing the same name will allow you to avoid making further changes to the configuration file. In order for the new certificate to be used, you must restart the Apache server using `apachectl restart`.

Here we do not show you the signed certificate because, after all, the only one we have to show you is our server certificate. Were we to let you see that, it is likely that we would be hacked soon. Hopefully, this terse summary is sufficient to convince you of the importance of keeping your signed certificate and key private.

Happy hacking!

Appendix B

Modules and Packages

Writing large programs can be a problem. One aspect of the problem is just the quantity of code that must be written. Being able to reuse code is a great help, but a problem with top-down design is that it is not directed at reusability. Each section of code you write, you write in a particular context, with particular inputs and outputs. It is natural that each piece of code is specialized, and that makes it harder to reuse elsewhere later.

However, the quantity of code to be written is not the largest problem. The problem is writing correct, maintainable code. In fact, part of the problem is even getting the code completed. Programs can exceed the capacity of one person to implement, even the capacity of one person to understand.

One important way to manage the complexity of software systems is *modularity*–breaking the system down into smallish, meaningful, coherent chunks. These chunks have an interface, preferably small, through which the rest of the system interacts with them. They hide the details of their implementation from the rest of the system.

In this chapter, we study Python's modules, one way of grouping code to hide details from the outside. We look at how to import modules, how to access the names they declare, and how to organize them into packages.

▌ **Principles of modular programming**

- A system should be composed of modules. A module is a self-contained collection of related code.
- A module should be devoted to one kind of thing; it should have a single theme, you might say. That means, among other things, that if you need to look something up, you know where to look.
- A module should provide *encapsulation*. A module has an interface to the outside world. It makes certain functions, variables, and data definitions visible. Users of the module should need to know only the interface, not the details of how the module is implemented. Conversely, a module should hide the details of its implementation from the outside. There may be some functions and variables and data structures that only the code in the module uses. These should be hidden from the users of the module.
- Modules should be used for *information hiding*. Although some people use it as a synonym for encapsulation, information hiding originally meant hiding major design decisions inside modules. Information hiding allows the design decisions to be reconsidered without having to change the rest of the program. You might want to change a data structure or an algorithm. You might want to do a first implementation that is simple to debug, but change it later if it's too inefficient. If you hide a major design decision in the implementation in a module, you should be able to change the decision without having to change any other part of your program.
- Modules in a system should form *layers*. Each layer of a system provides facilities that can be used by the layers above it. This concept has become important in operating systems, where it is sometimes said that each layer of the system provides a "virtual machine" for the layer above to run on. The code for each level is written using the facilities provided by the lower levels.

Importing Modules

The syntax of module imports is shown in Table B-1. When you tell Python to import a module, M,

```
import M
```

you will get a reference to a module object in variable `M`. `M` is also the name of the module that Python tries to find. Python first tries to look up module `M` in memory, in case it has already been loaded. If Python finds the module in memory, Python assigns the module object to the identifier `M` in the current scope. If the module is not already in memory, Python tries to find it in the search path, as we will describe shortly. The module name `M` corresponds to a file with a name `M.pyc` (for already compiled modules) and `M.py` (for source code). If there are files with both names `M.pyc` and `M.py`, Python will use whichever has the more recent modification time. If `M.py` is more recent, Python will recompile it and store the compiled version in `M.pyc` to use the next time. There could also be a file `M.pyo` for an optimized, compiled version, the result of using the `-O` option on the Python command line.

When a module is loaded, its code is executed with its own global name space. The code assigns values to names in this name space. At the end of initialization, the name space becomes the attributes of the module object, a dictionary available through the module object's special `__dict__` attribute.

You can import any number of modules in one `import` statement, listing the module names separated with commas. For example:

```
import sys, os, math
```

Importing Names from Modules

Once you have imported module `M`, you can refer to variables, classes, and functions in it with qualified names, such as `M.x`. If you wish to refer to them without qualification, you could make assignments to local variables, for example, `x=M.x` or you can import the names directly, using the `from-import` statement:

```
from M import x
```

In this case, the identifier `M` is not assigned a value, but module `M` is loaded if it has not been already and `x` is assigned the value of `x` within `M`. You can import more than one name at a time:

```
from M import x, y, z
```

If you wish to import all the names defined in a module, you can use '`*`' for the import list:

```
from M import *
```

Actually, this only imports all those names defined in the module except for those beginning with an underscore. Those names are considered private. Importation of all names is fine for some modules, but other modules have a larger number of names, and a great many of them are for specialized purposes only. Importing them all would fill up the local namespace with a large number of names, and it would increase the risk that some of these names might collide with names being used for other purposes. You could be using some of the names yourself, or perhaps worse, the same name could be used in different modules.

Filling up a namespace with a large number of unused names is called "namespace pollution." Namespace pollution is made even worse by the fact that if you import a module that itself imports * from a third module, you get all the names from the third module.

Avoiding Namespace Pollution

There are a number of techniques for avoiding namespace pollution, or cluttering up your namespace with a large number of names with the attendant risks of mistaken and inconsistent uses.

One way is to avoid using the `from modname import *` statement except in special cases. You may also need to refer to modules by different names than their own. The name of one module may be a name of a function or class you need to use frequently in another module, or it may be a very intuitive name for a variable or function in your module. You need to import the module, but assign it to a variable with a different name. You can do this with the `as` clause:

```
import modname as varname
```

This imports the module with the name `modname`, but assigns the module object to `varname`. You can also use the as phrase in the `from-import` statement; for example:

```
from M import x as y, y as z
```

to rename the objects being imported from a module.

In version 2.1 of Python, a feature was added to modules that allows you to restrict the names that another module can import from them with `from ... import *`. Assign a list of names to attribute `__all__` and only those names can be imported with a *; for example:

```
__all__ = ["PureSet","emptySet"]
```

Reloading Modules

When you are debugging a module, M, interactively, you repeatedly need to make changes in the module and try it again. The problem is that you cannot just change the module's source file and import it again with the `import` statement, `import M`.

The import statement will first look for module M in memory; finding it there, it will assign the module object to the variable M. You need to force Python to reload the module from disk by calling the `reload()` function. Calling `reload(M)` has Python reload the module corresponding to the module object. The reload is done in place, overwriting attributes of the same module object. Since all the places in your program where you have imported the module will have references to the same module object, the reload will work retroactively for all of them. You do not have to reload other modules that import the module you have changed; their references to the module are fine.

However, there are some problems with reloading modules. Although the module object is the same, the objects contained in the module are not. When you execute:

```
import M
from M import f
```

you get a reference to the `f` contained in the module at the instant the `from-import` statement is executed. Suppose `f` is a function, and you change its code in the module source and reload the module:

```
reload(M)
```

If you call

```
M.f()
```

you will get the new function definition, but if you call

```
f()
```

you get the old one. The `from M import f` assignment to `f` is not re-executed. One way around this is to reload not only the module you've changed, but all the modules that import names from it. If you've changed module M and module N that imports a name from M, you need to reload them in order:

```
reload(M)
reload(N)
```

Another alternative, of course, especially during program debugging, would be to import the module only as a whole, not import names from it.

Another problem with reloading is that it does not clear out the dictionary of attributes in the module object it is reloading. If you remove a function or class definition from the module source code, it will still be present in the module object after reloading. This is likely to be confusing: "I thought I got rid of that."

Search Paths

When Python searches for modules, it looks in each directory in a search path in order. You can find the search path in a list in the `sys` module, `sys.path`. The elements of the list are strings that are paths to directories in the computer's file system. This list is initialized either in an installation-dependent manner or from the environment variable `$PYTHONPATH`. The first element of the list, `sys.path[0]`, is the directory containing the script that invoked the Python interpreter. If there was no script, for example, because Python is being executed interactively, `sys.path[0]` is the empty string, and it tells Python to search the current directory first. Since Python searches the directories in the path in order, it will look for a module in the directory containing the script or in the current directory first. However, certain built-in modules are not on the search path; for example, there is no module `sys` in any of the directories listed in `sys.path`.

Python does a case-sensitive import. It looks for a module whose name exactly matches the identifier being imported. Some operating systems have case-insensitive file systems, so hedgehog.py, Hedgehog.py, HedgeHog.py and HEDGEHOG.py are indistinguishable. If you wish to use a case-insensitive import, set the `PYTHONCASEOK` environment variable before starting the Python interpreter.

No matter what order you use to search for modules, there is a potential problem with name collisions. If you have a module with the same name as a system module, you will hide the system module. This may not seem to be a problem, but it is when another standard Python module tries to access the module you have hidden; it will get yours instead. It is another example of namespace pollution—not of the names being used within your program, but of names in the space of modules. Packages provide a way to get around this module namespace pollution.

Table B–1
Import statement syntax

`import mod1, mod2 ,...`
 	
`import mod1 as name1,`
`    mod2 as name2,...`
 	
`from mod import ident1,`
`    ident2, ...`
 	
`from mod import ident1 as`
`name1, ident2 as name2, ...`
 	
`from mod import *`
 	
`from __future__ import facility`
	The import statement allows you to load and initialize a module (if it hasn't already been loaded).
	`import m` imports module m and assigns the variable m a reference to the module object. You can then get at a variable or other member x in m as `m.x`.
	`import m as n` imports m but assigns it to variable n.
	`from m import x` imports module m, but doesn't assign the module to a variable. Instead, it assigns the module's attribute x to variable x. With `as y`, it assigns the value of the attribute to variable y.
	`from m import *` imports m and assigns all its attributes to variables with their same names. The module names can be qualified:
	`ident1.ident2....,`
	indicating importing from a package.
	The `from __future__ import` does not import a module. It allows access to a new feature of Python that is available but not standard yet. It must come before any statements that can generate executable code, since it may influence code generation. Examples:
	`import math`
	
	`import math as mathfns`
	
	`from math import sin`
	
	`from math import sin as sine`
	
	`from math import *`
	
	`from __future__ import nested_scopes`

Packages

Packages try to get around the problem of module namespace pollution by creating hierarchical names for modules, of the form:

```
packagename.subpackage1.subpackage2.....modulename
```

When you import a hierarchical name that your program has not seen before, Python searches for the module roughly the same way as it searches for a simple module. Python searches the `sys.path` list, looking for a subdirectory with the name `packagename`. Within that directory, it looks for a subdirectory with name `subpackage1`, and so on, until it finds the file `modulename`. There are, however, a number of complications.

A first consideration is what the naming conventions should be for packages. One suggestion is to use Internet domain names of the companies and organizations that are the sources of the packages. For example, the company Tools of Computing LLC (of which the author is a principal) has a domain `toolsofcomputing.org` to distribute its open source, publicly licensed software. The software available in this book might be in several packages:

- `toolsofcomputing_org.adt`, for the abstract data types;
- `toolsofcomputing_org.threads`, for the threading modules;
- `toolsofcomputing_org.tcllk`, for the parsing modules; and
- `toolsofcomputing_org.PPPexamples`, for Python programming pattern examples.

After you import a module from a package, using, for example,

```
import toolsofcomputing_org.adt.Set
```

you can refer to class `Set` in module `Set` as `toolsofcomputing_org.adt.Set.Set`. What do you get if you just refer to `toolsofcomputing_org`? You get a module object. Internally, a package becomes a module: Following a path through packages and subpackages simply involves fetching attributes from module objects.

If `toolsofcomputing_org` is not already loaded, the subdirectory `toolsofcomputing_org` must be found on the search path, a module object created for it, subdirectory `adt` found in it, and a module created for that. A Python file (`Set.py`, `Set.pyc` or `Set.pyo`) must be found in `adt`, a module must be created for the Python file, and that module must be initialized. Indeed, as module objects `toolsofcomputing_org`, and `toolsofcomputing_org.adt` are created, they are initialized as well. Their attributes can be more sub-modules: whatever attributes their initialization code creates. Their initialization code is found in files `__init__.py` within their directories. Indeed, a directory without an `__init__.py` file will not be recognized as a package.

The command `import toolsofcomputing_org.adt` does not automatically import all the modules in directory `toolsofcomputing_org/adt` and in its subpackages; however, you can have the `__init__.py` files import modules and subpackages themselves. For example, the file `toolsofcomputing_org/adt/__init__.py` could contain

```
import Set
import PureSet
import prioque
import prioqueunique
import rational
import DEQueue
```

which would make those modules available as `toolsofcomputing_org.adt.Set`, and soon The downside is that they would all always be loaded, whether they are needed or not.

Notice that when we are importing another module in the same package directory, we can simply use its name. We do not have to write an entire path to it.

Consider trying to import all the modules in a package with the '`*`' option:

```
from toolsofcomputing_org.adt import *
```

The '`*`' option with package imports is problematic. Because Python is case-sensitive, but not all operating systems are, Python cannot be certain of knowing what internal names to use for the Python code files in a package directory. You can get around this by making the package initialization code define a variable `__all__`. Upon encountering a '`*`' option on an import list, Python will import all the modules whose names are in the `__all__` list of the source package's module object. Since the package's module object is created and initialized before Python tries to import these contained names, its `__all__` attribute

will have already been assigned a value. For example, the file
`toolsofcomputing_org.adt.__init__.py` could contain:

```
__all__=["Set","PureSet","prioque","prioqueunique",
    "rational","DEQueue"]
```

which would make the `from-import` statement equivalent to

```
from toolsofcomputing_org.adt import Set,PureSet,prioque,
    prioqueunique,rational,DEQueue
```

Example Stack Module

Suppose we need a stack, or a LIFO data structure. We can push things on the top of the stack. We can pop them off the top. We can look at the top element. In a language with static or dynamic arrays, we might allocate an array to hold the elements and keep an integer index of the top element. In Python, however, we keep the stack in a list and change the size of the list as we push and pop. This module has functions to treat a list as a stack. Function `new()` will create a new, empty stack. It is not needed if we know that a stack is really just a list. Function `push(stk, v)` pushes value `v` on the top of the stack `stk`. Function `pop(stk)` pops the top value off the stack `stk` and returns it. Function `top(stk)` returns the top value on stack `stk` without removing it. Function `isempty(stk)` returns `true` if stack `stk` is empty, and returns `false` otherwise.

Here is a test of the module:

```
>>> import stack1
>>> s=stack1.new()
>>> s
[]
>>> stack1.push(s,1)
>>> stack1.push(s,2)
>>> stack1.push(s,3)
>>> s
[1, 2, 3]
>>> len(s)
3
>>> stack1.pop(s)
3
>>> stack1.top(s)
2
>>> stack1.isempty(s)
```

```
0
>>> stack1.pop(s)
2
>>> stack1.pop(s)
1
>>> stack1.isempty(s)
1
```

Now look at the code in Figure B–1. Function push(skt,s) calls list's append() method, stk.append(v), which increases the length of stk by one and puts the value v at the end (i.e., the rightmost, or highest, position).

```
def new():
    return []
def push(stk,v):
    stk.append(v)
def pop(stk):
    tmp=stk[-1]
    del stk[-1]
    return tmp
def top(stk):
    return stk[-1]
def isempty(stk):
    return len(stk)==0
```

Figure B–1
Stack operations (stack1.py).

Function pop(stk) saves a copy of the last element in stk, removes that element, and returns it. It shows two things of interest:

1. Negative subscripts–You can use negative subscripts to access elements relative to the right end of the list. For indices, i, in the range 1 to len(x), x[-i] is the same as x[len(x)-i].
2. The del statement–You use the del statement to delete things. In this case, the statement del stk[-1] deletes the last element of stk.

The implementation of pop() was designed to show negative subscripts and the del statement. Actually, lists have their own pop() operation that does just what we want.

Critique of Modules

Let us consider how well Python's modules suit our needs when writing modular programs. We want a module to provide a separate scope for declarations. We should be able to declare variables and functions in the module without the names colliding with those declared elsewhere. Python handles this well: Each module is in a separate file. When Python imports it, Python creates a separate scope and executes the code for the module within that scope. This satisfies another desire: We want a module to execute some initialization code to set up its data structures.

We want the ability to import the names from another module to access the variables and function there. This is handled in Python by the `import` and `from-import` statements.

We want the ability to restrict the visibility of some names declared in the module so that they can be seen only by code inside the module. That is, we want encapsulation. Python doesn't provide this completely. All names in a module are visible, although those beginning with an underscore are not as visible; they will not be imported from a module with a `from name import *` statement.

Wrap-Up

With modules, we particularly have to worry about namespace pollution, the appearance of a multitude of confusing and potentially conflicting names. Some namespace pollution is internal to a Python program. Some is external to the program, within the search path that Python uses when hunting for modules being imported. Some forms of the import statement help to combat internal namespace pollution. To help combat external pollution, we can use Python packages. Packages are kept in directory hierarchies on the module search path and are translated into trees of modules when loaded. They allow us to partition the names into subspaces where they will not conflict.

Exercises

B.1. Try to write two modules that import names from each other; for example, module A contains a `from B import X` statement and module B contains a `from A import Y` statement. What happens? Use function `dir(M)` to get a list of the names defined in module M.

B.2. Critique the design of packages in Python.

B.3. Critique the `from name import *` statement in Python.

Bibliography

It has been a collective goal among all of us to write a book that covers just about everything you would need to know to develop Web applications using Python on the Linux platform with the help of other open-source software such as MySQL and our own programming libraries. You may have a need for more information. We have organized useful tutorial and reference information by category for further study, including material that we just find to be useful from an intellectual point of view. We recommend that you own or borrow these, and read them!

Python

In general, the documentation at http://www.python.org is an excellent starting point for those who know programming well and want to learn Python. You can find documentation for Python, its tools, its built-in modules, and its various activities at this site. Here are some other references:

1. Lutz, M. and Ascher, D., *Learning Python*, O'Reilly and Associates
2. van Rossum, G. and Drake, Jr., F. L., Python Tutorial, http://www.python.org

Linux

Linux is not completely for beginners yet, although there are some companies that are shipping versions of Linux that are aimed at the Linux "newbie" market. We particularly like Red Hat (http://www.redhat.com) and Mandrake (http://www.mandrake.com) and think these two versions of Linux are most appropriate for the hard-core user and novice user, respectively. We have also tested everything in this book on these platforms.

The best online source of information is http://www.linux.org, which among other things is the home of the Linux Documentation Project. Here are some other references that we have found particularly useful:

1. Kofler, M., *Linux: Installation, Configuration, and Use*, Addison-Wesley
2. Sobell, M., *A Practical Guide to Linux*, Addison-Wesley
3. Welsh, M., Kalle, M., and Kaufman, L., *Running Linux*, 3rd ed., O'Reilly and Associates

Networking

Doing anything on the Internet requires at some point that you have a complete understanding of what is going on and the bigger picture. We are particularly fond of Andrew Tanenbaum, who is one of the best computer science writers of all time. We have also been greatly influenced and touched by the works of W. Richard Stevens. Their books belong in everyone's library.

1. Tanenbaum, A.S., *Computer Networks*, 3rd ed., Prentice Hall PTR
2. Kurose, J. and Ross, K.W., *Computer Networking: A Top-Down Approach Featuring the Internet*, Addison-Wesley
3. Hunt, C., *TCP/IP Network Administration*, O'Reilly and Associates
4. Stevens, W.R., *TCP/IP Illustrated, Volume 1: The Protocols*, Addison-Wesley
5. Stevens, W.R., *UNIX Network Programming, Volume 1: Networking APIs–Sockets and XTI*, Addison-Wesley
6. Stevens, W.R., *Advanced Programming in the UNIX™ Environment*, Addison-Wesley
7. Albitz, P. and Liu, C., *DNS and Bind*, 4th ed. O'Reilly and Associates

HTML

There are almost more HTML books than profitable Web sites. Here is our lone recommendation:

1. Graham, I.S., *HTML Sourcebook*, 3rd ed., John Wiley and Sons
This author has written several books on HTML and has new offerings on XHTML.

Apache Web Server

We almost did not make a recommendation in this category. There have been few good books written on Apache. Even the Web site documentation leaves much to be desired. The following book has many favorable reviews on Amazon.com:

1. Wainwright, P., *Professional Apache*, Wrox Press

MySQL

The home of MySQL, http://www.mysql.com, is an excellent source of information and has a pretty good reference manual on their implementation of SQL. There are a couple of good books available:

1. DuBois, P., and Widenius, M., *MySQL*, New Riders
2. Yarger, R.J., Reese, G., and King, T., *MySQL and mSQL*, O'Reilly and Associates

Other Web Frameworks

1. Hunter, J., *Java Servlet Programming*, O'Reilly and Associates
2. Hall, M., *Core Servlets and Java Server Pages*, Prentice Hall PTR

INDEX